Iran

the Bradt Travel Guide

Maria Oleynik

edition
6

www.bradtguides.com

Bradt Travel Guides Ltd, UK
The Globe Pequot Press Inc, USA

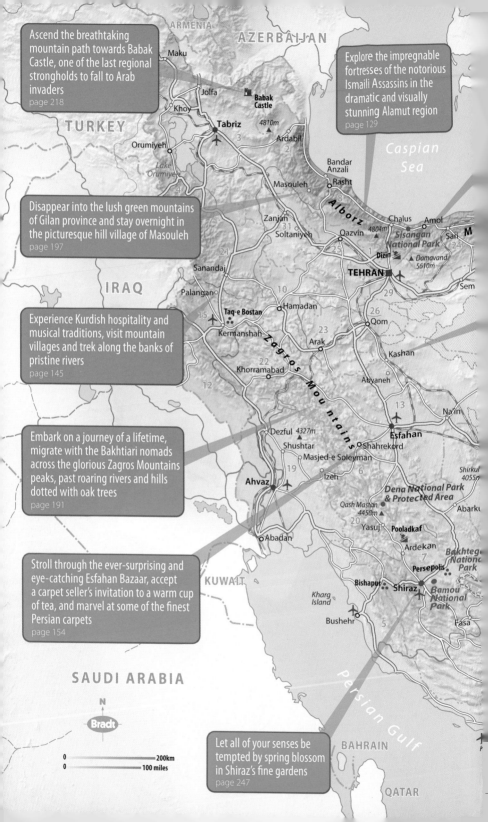

Ascend the breathtaking mountain path towards Babak Castle, one of the last regional strongholds to fall to Arab invaders
page 218

Explore the impregnable fortresses of the notorious Ismaili Assassins in the dramatic and visually stunning Alamut region
page 129

Disappear into the lush green mountains of Gilan province and stay overnight in the picturesque hill village of Masouleh
page 197

Experience Kurdish hospitality and musical traditions, visit mountain villages and trek along the banks of pristine rivers
page 145

Embark on a journey of a lifetime, migrate with the Bakhtiari nomads across the glorious Zagros Mountains peaks, past roaring rivers and hills dotted with oak trees
page 191

Stroll through the ever-surprising and eye-catching Esfahan Bazaar, accept a carpet seller's invitation to a warm cup of tea, and marvel at some of the finest Persian carpets
page 154

Let all of your senses be tempted by spring blossom in Shiraz's fine gardens
page 247

ARMENIA
AZERBAIJAN
Maku
Jolfa
Babak Castle
Khoy
TURKEY
Tabriz
4810m
Ardabil
Orumiyeh
Lake Orumiyeh
Caspian Sea
Bandar Anzali
Rasht
Masouleh
Alborz
Chalus
Amol
Zanjan
4804m
Sisangan National Park
Sari
M
Soltaniyeh
Qazvin
Dizin
Damavand 5610m
IRAQ
Sanandaj
TEHRAN
Palangan
Sem
Taq-e Bostan
Hamadan
Kermanshah
Arak
Qom
Khorramabad
Kashan
Abyaneh
Na'in
Dezful
4327m
Esfahan
Shahrekord
Shushtar
Shirkuf 4055m
Masjed-e Soleyman
Izeh
Dena National Park & Protected Area
Ahvaz
Abarku
Qash Mastan 4450m
Yasuj
Pooladkaf
Bakhteg National Park
Abadan
Ardekan
KUWAIT
Persepolis
Bishapur
Shiraz
Bamou National Park
Kharg Island
Fasa
Bushehr
Persian Gulf
SAUDI ARABIA
BAHRAIN
Bradt
QATAR
0   200km
0   100 miles

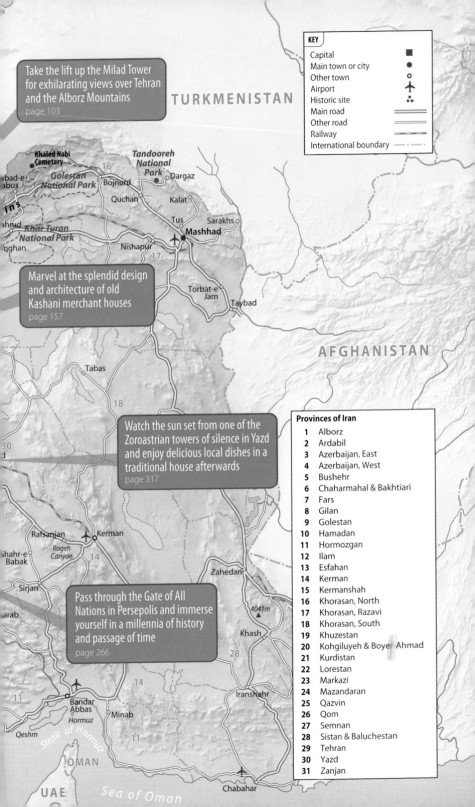

Take the lift up the Milad Tower for exhilarating views over Tehran and the Alborz Mountains
page 103

Marvel at the splendid design and architecture of old Kashani merchant houses
page 157

Watch the sun set from one of the Zoroastrian towers of silence in Yazd and enjoy delicious local dishes in a traditional house afterwards
page 317

Pass through the Gate of All Nations in Persepolis and immerse yourself in a millennia of history and passage of time
page 266

TURKMENISTAN

AFGHANISTAN

OMAN

UAE

Sea of Oman

KEY

Capital	■
Main town or city	●
Other town	○
Airport	✈
Historic site	∴
Main road	
Other road	
Railway	
International boundary	

Khaled Nabi Cemetery
Golestan National Park
Bojnurd
Quchan
Dargaz
Kalat
Tus
Mashhad
Sarakhs
Nishapur
Torbat-e Jam
Taybad
Tandooreh National Park
Khar Turan National Park
Tabas

Rafsanjan
Kerman
Rageh Canyon
shahr-e Babak
Sirjan
Zahedan
Khash
Iranshahr
Minab
Bandar Abbas
Hormuz
Qeshm
Strait of Hormuz
Chabahar

Provinces of Iran

1   Alborz
2   Ardabil
3   Azerbaijan, East
4   Azerbaijan, West
5   Bushehr
6   Chaharmahal & Bakhtiari
7   Fars
8   Gilan
9   Golestan
10 Hamadan
11 Hormozgan
12 Ilam
13 Esfahan
14 Kerman
15 Kermanshah
16 Khorasan, North
17 Khorasan, Razavi
18 Khorasan, South
19 Khuzestan
20 Kohgiluyeh & Boyer-Ahmad
21 Kurdistan
22 Lorestan
23 Markazi
24 Mazandaran
25 Qazvin
26 Qom
27 Semnan
28 Sistan & Baluchestan
29 Tehran
30 Yazd
31 Zanjan

Iran
Don't miss...

Esfahan
The regal dome of
the Sheikh Lotfallah
Mosque in Esfahan rises
in homage of Iranian
craftsmanship
(SS) page 179

Tehran
The Azadi Monument, clad
in white marble, has been
a symbol of Tehran since
its completion in 1971
(MO) page 108

Shiraz

The mausoleum of 13th-century poet, Saadi, whose powerful verses were quoted by President Obama during his 2009 address to Iran

(AT/S) page 249

Persepolis

The zenith of the Achaemenid Empire, Persepolis is simply magnificent in both scale and beauty

(s/S) page 263

Ilam Dam

The Ilam Dam Lake is one of the numerous freshwater reservoirs scattered across Iran, creating picturesque scenery for visitors to admire

(MO) page 150

Iran in colour

top The Se-o-se Pol bridge over Zayandeh River in Esfahan was built in 1603 and remains the central landmark of the former Safavid capital (MO) page 184

above left An evening stroll along Chahar Bagh Street in Esfahan takes you past the delicately decorated, arched porticos of Madrasa Chahar Bagh (MO) page 184

above right The Hamam Soltan Amir Ahmad in Kashan is one of the few examples of historic bathhouses that the wealthy spent time in, scrubbing away their worries of the day (A/S) page 157

below The Amir Chaqmaq complex has a magnificent façade and is the unrivalled centrepiece of a leisurely walk through Yazd (J/D) page 315

above left The Timcheh Amin al-Dowleh in the historic bazaar of Kashan is the most beautiful and atmospheric example of a storage section for expensive goods in a bazaar in Iran (MO) page 154

above right The masjed-e jame in the UNESCO-listed historic city of Yazd is one of the most glorious examples of Islamic architecture in Iran (SS) page 314

below The tiny mountain village of Masouleh in Gilan, a popular natural retreat from the buzz of the city, is famous for its local arts and crafts (MO) page 197

AUTHORS

Maria Oleynik MLitt, who has updated the fourth, fifth and sixth editions, is a freelance translator fluent in ten languages, including Persian and Arabic. She has studied in Yemen, Lebanon and Egypt, and was hired to translate a biography of a Libyan politician from Arabic, while based in Tripoli, Libya. She has also studied Persian at the University of Esfahan and the Dekhoda Institute in the University of Tehran. She has a profound interest in and knowledge of the Middle East, and calls Iran her home. In 2019 she finally decided to settle there permanently and has started studying for a degree in Persian literature at the University of Shiraz.

Caravan is gone, you are asleep,
And the desert is ahead,
When are you leaving? Whom you ask the direction?
What are you going to do?
What would be your destiny?

Hafez

PREVIOUS AUTHORS

Patricia Baker PhD was the author of the first two editions of this guide but died in 2008. Prior to her death she was working with Jennifer Wearden on cataloguing 19th-century Iranian textiles in the Victoria and Albert Museum, London. The resulting book was published in October 2010.

Patricia was an independent lecturer and researcher specialising in Islamic art, who spent a decade teaching the history of ceramics and glass to undergraduates. She first visited Iran in 1971 and subsequently went back numerous times. Her interests were primarily Islamic glass and especially Islamic court dress, on which, along with aspects of Zoroastrian costume, she wrote for various academic journals; her monograph *Islamic Textiles* was published by the British Museum Press in 1995 and *Islam and the Religious Arts* by Continuum in 2004.

Hilary Smith MPhil, who took over the update of the third edition, is an independent lecturer and guide with wide-ranging interests focusing particularly on the cultural history of central Asia and the Indian subcontinent. She first visited Iran in 1976 and has been returning regularly ever since.

IRAN ONLINE

For additional online content, articles, photos and more on Iran, why not visit **w** bradtguides.com/iran?

PUBLISHER'S FOREWORD — *Hilary Bradt*

In 1996 I was invited to visit Iran, which was just starting to open up to tourism. I accepted with some hesitation, having been thoroughly brainwashed by the media's portrayal of a dangerous, restrictive and intolerant country. But I loved the place from the moment I stepped off the plane, dressed in my headscarf and long *rupush*. Far from being restrictive, it left me feeling freer to explore the markets and other places on my own than almost anywhere else I've been. Since I looked just like the Iranian women around me, there were no stares, and no hassle. And the sights! The great ruins of Persepolis and Bishapur, and the cities of Esfahan and Shiraz, all left an indelible impression. Iran continues to be in the news for the wrong reasons, but those who visit despite the media coverage will find the people as warm-hearted, and the landscape and ruins as impressive as on my visit. You owe it to this troubled country to see for yourself.

Sixth edition published February 2020
First published 2001
Bradt Travel Guides Ltd
31a High Street, Chesham, Buckinghamshire, HP5 1BW, England
www.bradtguides.com
Print edition published in the USA by The Globe Pequot Press Inc,
PO Box 480, Guilford, Connecticut 06437-0480

Text copyright © 2020 Bradt Travel Guides Ltd
Maps copyright © 2020 Bradt Travel Guides Ltd; includes map data © OpenStreetMap contributors
Photographs copyright © 2020 Individual photographers (see below)
Project Manager: Heather Haynes
Cover research: Marta Bescos

ISBN: 978 1 78477 577 3

British Library Cataloguing in Publication Data
A catalogue record for this book is available from the British Library

Photographs Adam Balogh (AB); Dreamstime.com: Javarman (J/D); Medhi Eshraghi (ME); istockphoto. com: mazzzur (m/i); Petri Lyytikäinen (PL); Maria Oleynik (MO); Andrew Prior (AP); Shutterstock.com: aaabbbccc (a/S), Leonid Andronov (LA/S), Enselme Arthur (EA/S), Artography (A/S), Massimiliano Lamagna (ML/S), Alexander Mazurkeyich (AM/S), angela meier (aM/S), Borna Mirahmadian (BM/S), M Khebra (MK/S), Michal Knitl (MI/S), steba (s/S), Aleksandar Todorovic (AT/S), Alireza Vafa (AV/S); SuperStock (SS)
Front cover Nasir Al-Mulk Mosque in Shiraz (m/i)
Back cover Howraman is one of the most spectacular mountain villages in Iranian Kurdistan (MO); twice a year Bakhtiari nomads cross the Zagros Mountains. By 2019, Yasna (pictured) had already made this journey three times (MO)
Title page Masjed-e jame in the UNESCO-listed historic city of Yazd (SS); Persian warrior guarding the Achaemenid kings in Persepolis (s/S); Zagros Mountain rivers present hazardous obstacles for Bakhtiari nomads (MO)

Maps David McCutcheon FBCart.S and Daniella Levin; relief map base by Nick Rowland FRGS

Typeset by D & N Publishing, Baydon, Wiltshire and Ian Spick, Bradt Travel Guides Ltd
Production managed by Jellyfish Print Solutions; printed in India
Digital conversion by www.dataworks.co.in

Acknowledgements

Patricia Baker PhD was the author of the first two editions of this guide. After her death in 2008, her friend Hilary Smith took over the update of the third edition. The fourth, fifth and sixth editions have been updated by Maria Oleynik.

Iran is simply striking. It is the most beautiful country in the world, frozen in time and yet ever changing. I am grateful to all my Iranian friends, my fantastic teachers from Dekhoda Institute and the Iranians that I have had the pleasure to speak to on my travels for sharing their lives and thoughts and encouraging me to learn more. Travel guides mentioned in this edition are some of the most knowledgeable and I am certain that their help and advice will make any traveller's journey pleasant and delightful. As for me personally, Iran is the country of my heart and I have tried my best to bring this across to help the traveller navigate on their journey across Iran, open their hearts and minds and be moved by the friendliness of the people and the beauty of this extraordinary land.

Preparing this sixth edition has been a special personal experience for me and, relying on the advice of my closest friends here, I have tried to find and select the most authentic and special places that resonate with what I believe represent and reflect the true Iran.

This work comes from my heart and is dedicated to all the Iranians living in Iran, for their resilience, patience, gentleness, humility and finesse, and for preserving and taking care of this country's identity, traditions and history.

Maria Oleynik

AUTHOR'S STORY

Before coming to Iran for the first time in 2013 I decided for myself, quite by chance in some way, that Iran was the missing link in my understanding of the Middle East and perhaps even more. I felt convinced it was the real, pure and only Orient to discover. I had prior to that spent a lot of time in the region learning Arabic, but still felt that something was missing.

The first trip to Iran was a two-month Persian-language course with the University of Esfahan and it did not leave me disappointed. Here I felt that I had finally found so many answers, including to the questions of my own cultural belonging, and so many things suddenly fell into place. Iran has become my compass and my home.

Maria Oleynik

Contents

KEY TO SYMBOLS

—··—··—	International boundary	■	Shopping/mall
═══	Main road	⊠	Post office
═══	Other road	⌂	Hotel
======	Track (4x4 etc)	✖	Restaurant
▬▬▬	Railway	†	Cathedral/church
✈	Airport	Ϛ	Mosque
⛌	Bus station etc	♦	Minaret
⛟	Car hire/taxi	🏛	Tomb/mausoleum
M	Metro station	❀	Gardens
ஃ	Bike stand/rental	◉	Cave/rock shelter
🛈	Tourist information	★	Rock relief
Ⓔ	Embassy/consulate	○	Spring/hot spring
♨	Museum/art gallery	∴	Archaeological site
🏛	Historic/important building	●	Other place of interest
🏰	Historic castle/fortification	✵	Stadium
▮	Statue/monument		Urban park
⊞	Hospital		Urban market/bazaar
✚C	Islamic Red Crescent		National park
$	Bank		Salt lake
€	Currency exchange		Desert

vi

Introduction

Mention to relatives and friends that you are going to Iran, and the chances are that they will stare, swallow and, hesitantly if not incredulously, ask 'Iran? Are you sure?' Getting confused, they might ask 'Isn't Iraq dangerous to travel to at the moment?' Reading the latest news about Iran, you may well feel they have a point, but the reality could not be more different. And although a lot of foreign nationals can now avail themselves of a simplified electronic visa, British citizens do still require a visa in advance. Your first contact with Iranian consulate staff could easily make you feel that officialdom (but not necessarily any official) is conspiring against your visiting Iran and learning first hand something about the country, its history and its culture, past and present. Filling in a visa application form seems nothing short of a spy-movie security check. Why do they want to know where and who I am meeting in Iran? Is there really no easier way that will save everyone concerned time, energy and good humour? Just play along and dress accordingly. Women are strongly advised to cover their hair and lower torso when entering the embassy grounds, although there's no official instruction to do so. Remember, this is part of the cultural etiquette that you should already be familiar with. Be patient and persevere and the rewards will be worth all the angst.

Iran is one of those countries where issues concerning religion and the modern world confront you at all turns and compel you to consider your own stance. It is impossible to return from even a short visit and not feel that, while seeing magnificent historic architecture and evidence of ancient civilisations, you have also been witnessing history in the making. Make a point of visiting one of the Iranian tea houses and cafés to observe the ingenuous youth embody all the dilemmas and contrasts of this complex society and rest assured, your dogmas will be shaken.

Yet some people will say that, having travelled and stayed in Iran before the Islamic Revolution, they have no wish to return to see it now. We cannot agree. The experience is invaluable, and you will come back with a better-informed opinion – perhaps changed, perhaps confirmed, but at least based on evidence seen at first hand.

Of course, there have been changes since the early days of the revolution when officialdom frowned on all music save for martial tunes and religious songs. Western instruments such as pianos may now be purchased, and Iranian 'rap' is broadcast on the airwaves. Besides, Iranians appreciate good cinema and national movies openly talk about un-Islamic issues that, living abroad, you would think could never be possible in the Islamic Republic of Iran. There are also increasingly more bicycle-rental shops renting bicycles to women and ingenious Iranian tour guides offering short- or long-distance bicycle trips. Only a tiny fraction of what you read about Iran is true and people here are more liberal than some of the most arduous liberals in Europe. Changes are subtle, but not less dramatic for that reason. The 'Down with USA' graffiti outside Taleqani metro station in Tehran is now gone, replaced with a colourful display of Iranian handicrafts.

But not all changes are occasioned by official policy. It is true that women now tend to wear more black *chadors* (although Shirazi women beg to be different, claiming the title of the most liberal in the country) often due to family pressure, and black or dark blue *manteaux* on the streets of Tehran, instead of the pastel coats seen earlier, but it is also true that more women are now working for the government (where black is the standard uniform) and that Tehran's increasing pollution was persuading many to wear darker colours to reduce washing and dry-cleaning bills. Besides, you will be amazed to find out how many girls are attending universities (where the chador is next to mandatory). When in Esfahan, and with some free time on your hands, drop into the extensive University of Esfahan campus and be smitten by the friendly chatty chador-clad aspiring scholars.

And while the appalling, senseless driving of many private car-owners is certainly a problem, foreign visitors to Iran are pleasantly surprised at the general cleanliness of the streets, and the care and upkeep of the central reservations and the roundabouts, resplendent with park benches, tea houses and children's swings, as if they're rewards for risking life and limb against oncoming cars. And thanks to the Iranian obsession with picnics, the country is awash with green roadside or inner-city picnic areas.

As a foreign visitor, you will be struck by the friendliness, warmth and genuine curiosity of the locals throughout Iran. In other countries it is sometimes difficult for individuals within a tour group to talk with anyone other than the guide, the driver, or the hotel and shop staff, and some argue that to experience fully a country and a people, you must be an independent traveller. In Iran this is not the case. Indeed, it could be argued that in Iran, forces conspire against the independent traveller, especially those who don't know the language. Everything takes so much longer to sort out, and indeed the visitor is so dependent on Iranians helping that the term 'independent traveller' is almost a misnomer. Group travel, even in small groups, can and does open doors in more senses than one – it cuts down endless queuing and waiting for buses and the like.

No Iranian is deterred by numbers; guides and lecturers are often interrupted in their 'spiel' by a crowd asking if the group is German or American, how long are they staying, will they come for tea, how many children do they have, do they like Iran and have they visited the breathtaking Persepolis or have they tasted a *fesenjan* dish, etc. Yes, Iranians know their country and its history well and will happily share what they can with you.

That said, the exceptional safety, increasing numbers of comfortable authentic accommodation options and endless number of historic, natural and simply interesting places to visit in Iran has meant that more travellers come here on their own. There are also many independent and upbeat local guides in Iran and their assistance is recommended.

What else can we say? Of course there are downsides to Iran, as to everywhere, but go now, while it is still authentic and untouched by mass tourism and so special, only yours to discover.

HOW TO USE THIS GUIDE

AUTHOR'S FAVOURITES Finding genuinely characterful accommodation or that unmissable off-the-beaten-track café can be difficult, so the author has chosen a few of her favourite places throughout the country to point you in the right direction. These 'author's favourites' are marked with a ✳.

PRICE CODES Throughout this guide we have used price codes to indicate the cost of those places to stay and eat listed in the guide. For a key to these price codes, see page 66 for accommodation and page 66 for restaurants and cafés.

MAPS
Keys and symbols Maps include alphabetical keys covering the locations of those places to stay, eat or drink that are featured in the book. Note that regional maps may not show all hotels and restaurants in the area: other establishments may be located in towns shown on the map.

Grids and grid references Several maps use gridlines to allow easy location of sites. Map grid references are listed in square brackets after the name of the place or sight of interest in the text, with page number followed by grid number, eg: [342 C3].

On occasion, hotels or restaurants that are not listed in the guide (but which might serve as alternative options if required or serve as useful landmarks to aid navigation) are also included on the maps; these are marked with accommodation 🏠 or restaurant ✕ symbols.

Alleyways Although the towns and cities of Iran have lots of alleyways, the scale of the maps in this book does not allow for these to be shown. Therefore, only the main and secondary roads are featured.

WEBSITES Although all third-party websites were working at the time of researching the book, some may cease to function during this edition's lifetime. If a website doesn't work, you might want to check back at another time as they often function intermittently. Alternatively, you can let us know of any issues by emailing info@bradtguides.com. (See also the box on page 2.)

Part One

GENERAL INFORMATION

IRAN AT A GLANCE

Location Asia; land borders with Iraq, Turkey, Armenia, Azerbaijan, Turkmenistan, Afghanistan and Pakistan

Area 1,648,195km², three times the size of France

Climate Most regions: long, hot summers; short, sharp winters. Marked contrasts in northwest, east and central desert regions.

Population Over 83 million (2019); more than 70% living in cities and towns.

Government A theocracy with a Supreme Leader, an Assembly of (Theological) Experts, a Council of Guardians and elected Parliament and President

Capital Tehran (population over 12 million)

Other major cities Mashhad (population over 2 million), Esfahan, Shiraz, Tabriz, Ahvaz (over 1.5 million each), Qom (1.2 million) and Hamadan (1 million)

Language Farsi (an Indo-Aryan language) alongside dialects of Turkish, Arabic and Kurdish

Alphabet Based on the Arabic script, reading from right to left

Religion Predominantly Shi'a Muslims, with some Sunnis; also Christians, Jews and Zoroastrians

Currency Rial IRR (10 rials = 1 tuman)

Exchange rate US$1 = 124,000 rials; £1 = 150,000 rials; €1 = 135,000 rials (November 2019)

International telephone code +98

Time GMT +3.5

Weights and measures Metric

Electricity 220 Volts, 50Hz

National flag Three horizontal stripes of green, white and red with repeated legend 'Allah Akbar' ('God is great') around the edge and the red emblem of Iran on the white stripe

National anthems 'Sourud-e Jomhuri Islami Iran' (Song of the Islamic Republic of Iran); 'Sourud-e Iran' (Song of Iran); 'Ey Iran' (unofficial, but much-loved anthem)

Public holidays Fixed holidays: 11 February, 20 March and the week following (Nou Rouz), 1 April, 4 and 5 June. Also numerous Muslim holidays dated to the lunar calendar, which means these fall approximately 11 days earlier each Gregorian year.

NOTE

As we go to press, there is no internet available within Iran. This is due to the contemporary political situation in the country, and may have changed by the time you read this.

IRAN ONLINE

For additional online content, articles, photos and more on Iran, why not visit **w** bradtguides.com/iran?

1

Background Information

GEOGRAPHY AND CLIMATE

It is difficult to convey the reality of a land mass of 1,650,000km², but Iran, with its 31 provinces, is three times the size of France, or the size of the United Kingdom, France, Spain, Italy and Switzerland combined. The Zagros Mountains in the west form a natural barrier with Iraq, and to the north are the Caucasian republics and those of central Asia, all of which were once within the territory of the former Soviet Union. To the north the Caspian Sea also marks Iran's sea border with Russia and Kazakhstan. To the east are Afghanistan and Pakistan, while the Persian Gulf and the Sea of Oman mark Iran's southern limits. It is a land of great contrasts, physically and climatically, as mountain ranges push up the mostly desert plateau of the centre. Apart from the green Zagros chain in the west, there are the snowy crags of the Alborz range in the north, the Makran Mountains in the south and the westernmost extension of the Hindu Kush, which force up the landscape of Iran's eastern provinces.

This geological 'upturned bowl' effect means that towns on the same latitude but on either side of the same mountain range receive very different amounts of rainfall: Dezful (western Zagros, 143m altitude) gets approximately 358mm a year whereas Esfahan (eastern Zagros, 1,570m altitude) receives a mere 108mm. Much less rain falls in the Great Desert basin, where some areas are pretty much unable to support any life at all. Generally speaking, regions south of latitude 34°N get rain mainly during January, while those north of this receive most rainfall during the spring, especially April. An exception is the Caspian region, where the heaviest month for rain is October.

Few in the West are likely to associate snow with their mental image of Iran, yet about two-thirds of the Islamic Republic's land mass usually endures heavy winter snowfalls (January–February) because of the average high altitude throughout the country. More than three-quarters of its territory is located above 1,000m. Tabriz (1,349m) in the northwest has about 30 days of snow a year, about ten days more than Arak (1,753m) to the east, whereas Esfahan, at a higher altitude, gets about seven days and Yazd (1,230m) about half this. Of course, areas of very high altitude, such as 5,610m-high Mount Damavand (known as the roof of Iran) and especially its northeast face, Takht-e Soleyman in the Alborz range, and Sabalan (4,500m) near Ardabil in Iranian Azerbaijan, have perennial snow as well as glaciers. Indeed, many Tehranis escape the smog and pressure of life within the overcrowded capital by flocking to the ski runs that drape the mountains, within a few hours' drive of the city.

There are three if not four distinct climates in Iran: most regions have the continental climate of long, hot summers and short, sharp winters. In the northwest, the Iranian province of Azerbaijan shares a similar climate to that of Switzerland,

3

and further east, along the south shore of the Caspian, it is as humid as the south, but without those gruesome higher temperatures. In August 2015 the town of Bandar Mahshahr in southern Iran recorded a 'heat index' of 74°C, the second highest ever registered.

NATURAL HISTORY AND CONSERVATION

FAUNA Despite the enormous area of the country, only around 10% of the landscape is officially protected by designation as national parks or reserves, and there is little supervision of hunting even among these regions; sadly, the government ministry concerned is massively underfunded and understaffed. Since the revolution the total area of the reserves has doubled, although most of the 25 national parks and more than 100 reserves and protected areas are strewn with rubbish and under constant encroachment from illegal (and at times legal) construction and resource extraction nibbling at their borders.

Ironically, it was at Ramsar on the Caspian coast in 1971 that the Ramsar Convention was signed by many of the planet's nations, formalising the protection of wetlands worldwide for the survival of both indigenous and migrating **birds**. Although little in practice has been done in recent years to keep up Iranian obligations to the treaty they helped organise, nearly 500 species of bird have been recorded within the borders of the country, and many species are easily observed from the road when driving across Iran. Serious birders should consider packing a copy of *Birds of the Middle East* by Christenson, Porter and Schiermacker-Hansen. The desert regions south and southeast of Tehran are home to bustards, coursers, sandgrouse and ground jays, while in the steppes the long-legged buzzard, Eurasian kestrel, and various species of roller and bee-eaters can be seen. As you would expect, birds preferring colder temperatures, such as the golden eagle, bearded vulture, alpine swift, wallcreeper and snow finch, frequent the mountain ranges, while in the forests and woodlands of Iranian Azerbaijan there are woodpigeons, green woodpeckers, shrikes, nightingales and thrushes. In this region Lake Orumiyeh, the largest body of water in Iran, was made a bird reserve in 1967. In the 1970s 186 bird species and a breeding colony of over 20,000 pairs of wintering greater flamingos has been recorded here, but with the shrinking of the lake in recent years bird populations have plummeted. A little further south, the seasonal marsh of Talab-e Aqgul, some 90km south of Hamadan and 20km south of Malayer, is a favourite migration stage for Siberian and Scandinavian wetland birds for some four or five months. The lush wetlands of the southern Caspian shore are wintering grounds for pelicans, Siberian cranes, herons, gulls, spoonbills and cormorants. Caspian seals and otters may very rarely be seen there, but even this tiny vestigial population is under threat from urban development, overfishing and industrial pollution related to oil and gas extraction further north and out in the Caspian. As temperatures drop, so the herons and pelicans, along with plovers, ospreys and oystercatchers, make their way south towards the Persian Gulf, where the mangroves and palm forests are home to oriental Afro-tropical birds, such as the palm dove and Indian roller.

As for **mammals**, the mountains and forests of the north have many types of deer, such as red, roe and fallow deer, as well as the Mesopotamian deer, and predators such as wolves and foxes, but hunting (totally unlicensed) has taken a very heavy toll. The red Caspian deer, which inhabits the lush forests of northern Iran, is now a protected species. It used to fall prey to the shah's hunting endeavours while now the Persian leopard is its only threat. Wild boar in northern Iran are on the increase, partially due to the cultural Islamic tradition of avoiding these animals and also because there are fewer threats for them than before. There are also a few-dozen Persian brown bears remaining in the Alborz Mountains area, but their numbers are decreasing due to illegal logging. A few small brown bears (*Ursus arctos syriacus*) can also still be found in the Zagros region. Wild sheep and goats were once common in the northeast of Alborz and north of Shiraz, with wild boar further east and Pazan ibexes in the Bisotun area, but few survive. Native of the Zagros Mountains, the wild mountain ancestor of the domesticated goat (*Capra hircus*), often represented on ancient ceramic vessels (eg: Susa), can still be frequently spotted. It seems likely that snow leopards, which once inhabited the area east of Mashhad, and certainly the Mazandaran tigers are now extinct, as is the lion, last seen in 1942. There are few details about the cheetah population, officially estimated at fewer than 50 in number in 2019. Despite the official Asian Cheetah Conservation Project, their probable fate seems as desolate as the deserts they recently roamed. The hotter central and southern provinces of Iran are home to jackals and mongooses, who haunt the ruins of both Persepolis, where they are understandably nervy, and the Sasanid site of Firuzabad, where bolder mongooses fed from the hand on the remnants of the author's chicken picnic lunch. Date and palm squirrels, gerbils and jerboas also scurry in these regions. Camels, signifier of any desert worthy of the name, are usually dromedary rather than the shaggy twin-humped Bactrians of eastern central Asia. Several areas are known for bat caves: Shapur's cave near Bishapur for *Rhinolophus euryale* and *Miniopterus schreibersi*; the village of Ahmad Mahmoudi, southwest of Shiraz, for *R. hardwickei* and *Rousettus aegyptiacus*; and the northern shores of Lake Parishan (formerly Famur) nearby for *Pipistrellus kuhli*. Perhaps the most curious (and unlikely) animals to be found within the borders of Iran are the small population of 250 to 300 mugger crocodiles (*Crocodylus palustris,* locally known as *Gando*) that lurk in Bahu Kalat River and the surrounding waterways of desert Sistan province, the far southeastern tip of the country. Crocodiles were historically widely spread across Asia and the muggers of Iran are a vestigial population of a subspecies still to be found hunting in the Ganges and Indus. Iranian crocs also carry their full set of teeth and the last fatal attack was in 2003, when a 12-year-old boy was taken and eaten while swimming in Bahu Kalat River on a hot afternoon. The government has organised an official protection programme for the species, and despite the very real risk of injury to local communities it seems to have stabilised the population of crocodiles thanks to somewhat surprising local support.

Pollution of the Caspian Sea during the dying years of the Soviet Union and current illegal netting (much of it controlled by mafia groups from Russia and Azerbaijan) has had a severe effect on Iranian **fisheries**, but sturgeon are still breeding – just. Salmon-trout, chub and carp are found in mountain streams, while warm-water sea fish abound off the southern coast of Iran.

FLORA The best time to see the natural flora of Iran, some 6,000 recorded species, is around April and early May when the mountains and steppes are once more carpeted with new grass, fruit-tree blossom and masses of wild flowers, now that the high price of imported artificial fertilisers and pesticides has led to a decrease in extensive use. Wild irises and poppies can be seen almost everywhere, but *Iris barnumae* is found only in the Azerbaijan region and *Iris spurgia* in the Caspian wetlands. Of the 80 species of tulip, 12 are recorded in Iran, the most widespread being *Tulipa biflora*. Especially striking is *Tulipa clusiana* with its red and white petals and the yellow *Tulipa urmiensis,* found, as its name suggests, north of Lake

Orumiyeh. The saffron crocus (*Crocus sativus*), one of the eight Iranian species, is mainly found in eastern Iran and the so-called autumn crocus, although it has six stamens rather than the three of crocuses, is well represented, including the *Colchicum persicum* of central Iran, which flowers from March to April.

The city of Shiraz is justly proud of its sweet-smelling roses, which are used in the local production of rose jam, syrup and rosewater perfume. And, of course, most people know of the Shiraz grape. Most of Iran's vineyards were ripped up during the early years of the Islamic Revolution but there has been extensive replanting in the last decade, albeit not for wine production.

WATER Water has always been a perennial concern in Iran, especially after 13th-century Mongol conquests destroyed dams and irrigation channels; indeed, parts of Khorasan, Sistan and Baluchestan provinces have never recovered their populations. The ingenious engineering of *qanat* (underground water channels), whereby water was tapped from the aquifer level on the mountainsides and guided down to the cultivated fields, has largely fallen into complete disuse now that new irrigation systems are being installed. However, the lines of *qanat* inspection holes, looking like disintegrating termite hills, still mark the landscape, especially in the Yazd region. According to the official statistics in 1998 there were 32,164 *qanats* across the country. The oldest *qanat*, which still supplies 40,000 people with water, is 45km long and is located in Gonabad, Razavi Khorasan province. The longest (88km) is Zarch *qanat* in Yazd and its first well is 180m deep, while the Moon *qanat* in Ardestan runs on two levels. Tehran originally relied on a system of 36 *qanats*, some of which were built 250 years ago. Then it was sufficient to meet the water needs of a population of 1.5 million people.

Features of Iranian towns are the roadside water channels (*jub*), which are permanently or daily flooded with water. These serve to lower the temperature as well as move rubbish, but can also trap unwary car drivers attempting to squeeze into parking spaces.

Iran suffers from scarce water resources and has only one perennial river, Karun in Khuzestan. All other rivers are seasonal and depend on the rainfall. While the winter in 2019 was unusually long with generous snow and rainfall, in particular in Khuzestan, shortage of water, not apparent to the unaccustomed eye, remains a significant problem, as attested by numerous billboards and government campaigns aimed at increasing awareness. Drinking water is, however, available free of charge from water dispensers in mosques and at most metro stations in Tehran and other major cities.

HISTORY

A note on dates: as in India and China, official circles in the Iranian Republic prefer the designation BCE (before the Common Era) and CE (Common Era) rather than the Western/Christian abbreviations, BC and AD; this will be the system used here. Where the Muslim lunar year – as recorded in a building inscription – falls between two solar years (eg: the Muslim Hijra year 1347 ran from 20 July 1928 to 8 July 1929), only the latter year is noted. Less frequent references to the Muslim Hijra year that start counting from the day of the Prophet Mohammad's 'Hijra' (migration) to Medina in 622CE, are denoted as 'AH' (anno hegirae).

Archaeological excavations have revealed a Neolithic period in Iran from around 7000BCE, with early cereal and animal domestication occurring in the fertile valleys of the Zagros Mountains. Evidence of copper smelting, pottery making and textile production have been found, along with evidence of the potter's wheel, dating from around 3500BCE. The sites of Tel-e Iblis and Tappeh Yahya, east of Kerman, have provided artefacts and clear signs of settlement dating from the so-called Proto-Elamite period, 3200–2800BCE, known for high artistry and the system of writing to record commodity transactions. The recently excavated (and sadly looted) site of Jiroft has produced exquisite and extraordinary ceramics, as well as evidence of an indigenous writing system unrelated to either cuneiform or Indus Valley script, dating to the end of the 3rd millennium BCE.

The archaeological survey conducted in the 1970s and published relatively recently, revealed that the region between Susa and Malyan is rich in surface finds from the 4th millennium BCE. Trading contacts with the Sumerians of Mesopotamia (now Iraq) increased as the Elamite centres of Susa and Haft Tappeh were established. It is worth noting, however, that the turmoil following the 1979 revolution and subsequent Iran–Iraq War (1980–88) made it exceptionally difficult to carry out archaeological digs and research. It would be safe to assume that a lot has yet to be revealed, in particular in the provinces of Khuzestan and Lorestan.

For today's visitor, the most important visual evidence of Elamite civilisation is the site of Choga Zanbil, where the remains of a stepped-pyramid temple dominate the landscape, and bear more than a passing resemblance to the great ziggurats of southern Iraq. Political interference by Mesopotamians into Elamite territory and vice versa repeatedly led to armed confrontation, and in c2006BCE an Elamite army captured the last king of Ur, exiling him to Anshan (modern Malyan in central Fars), which was the capital of Cyrus the Great just as he set out to conquer the world. Despite stray finds across the central plateau and the stunning material from Jiroft, it is clear that the Elamites never controlled all of Iran.

In the northwest of the country, below the Caucasus, archaeological finds from Haftvan and Dinkh Tappeh, near Lake Orumiyeh, reveal that people living here also traded with Mesopotamia, and there was significant technical innovation, with very fine zoomorphic ceramic vessels such as those found in the Hasanlu excavations dating from c1350BCE. Extensive and repeated military campaigns by the martial Assyrian kings throughout the 9th, 8th and 7th centuries BCE spelt the subjugation, if not the end, of most settlements specialising in horse breeding, which were clustered in the high, green valleys of the Zagros Mountains, and communities squatting on the eastern flank of the Zagros were repeatedly devastated.

Little is known of eastern Iran during this time, but by the 8th century BCE, two tribal groupings appear in the west of the country from out of the historical murk: the Medes (from the region of Media, in the north of the Zagros) and the Persians (from Pars, the region around Shiraz), which were first mentioned in written sources in 836BCE, namely in the Black Obelisk of the Assyrian king Shalmaneser III. Median tribes, who were polygamists, first settled in the area between Hamadan and Kermanshah, and were the first to revolt against the Assyrian rule in Upper Asia.

We know about these tribes from the tribute lists of vainglorious Assyrian kings. Both groups spoke an Indo-European language, alien to the dwellers of the Mesopotamian plain and Elam alike, and were linked to one another by ties of marriage, culture and a great love of horses and celebratory, drunken feasting. Initially, the Medes were most successful in pushing back against Assyria, and in alliance with Babylon and the southern Persians they successfully scorched the Assyrian capital of Nineveh in bitter house-to-house fighting in 612BCE. The political convulsions emanating from the overthrow of Assyria elevated Media to the rank of ancient superpower. However, rather than accept Median rule, a

Persian aristocrat known to Western sources as Cyrus II (the Great), defeated the Median king – who also happened to be his maternal grandfather – and pushed the boundaries of his fledgling kingdom to include the rich Elamite cities south of the Zagros, and out on the alluvial plains. This marked the bloody beginnings of the glorious Achaemenid dynasty and the first world empire.

THE ACHAEMENIDS (550–330BCE) From these somewhat ignominious beginnings in the high mountain valleys of southwestern Iran, the Achaemenid Empire stretched west into the Balkans and eastwards perhaps as far as the Tian Shan Mountains (today's Chinese frontier), all controlled from a northern summer capital at Hamadan (former capital of the Medes and the Ecbatana of Alexander the Great); a winter capital at the old Elamite city of Susa, in the south; Pasargadae, the wind-blasted launch site of the Persian imperial mission; and later a grand ceremonial capital at Persepolis ('City of the Persians' in Greek).

Cyrus II spectacularly captured Lydian Anatolia and its famed King Croesus during a series of daring military campaigns traditionally dated to 547BCE. (The exact date has, however, remained a point of contention and is disputed among historians coming up with various interpretations of the events.) Cyrus then took Babylon, where he was officially invested as king, and Syria in 540/539BCE, earning in the process a particular reputation for both justice and religious tolerance in allowing the Jews to return from Babylonian exile, paying for the construction of a new temple in Jerusalem and returning Babylonian divine images to their traditional shrines. In recognition of his deeds, Cyrus II's name is mentioned in the Bible on 23 occasions. The famous Cyrus Cylinder discovered in 1879 and on display in the British Museum is believed by some to be the world's first charter of the rights of nations. Central Asia was the great conqueror's next goal and before meeting his end there, he introduced agriculture in those regions and laid down the fortress foundations of Samarkand.

A pragmatic ruler, Cyrus the Great did not impose cultural or religious practices upon the subjects of the empire, taking the title of the 'king of kings'. His death is traditionally dated to c529BCE and, according to Herodotus at least, he was killed in a battle defending his kingdom from the nomads of Iranian origin attacking from the east. Xenophon, however, recorded that he had died of natural causes. Such a setback should have seen the foundations of Cyrus II's great imperial venture crumble. With the death of his son Cambyses II, the ruler of Babylon under Cyrus the Great, four years later and following a successful conquest of Egypt, this was the time when the nascent Achaemenid state – a huge and unprecedented collection of noble ancient cities and kingdoms paying homage to what was effectively a jumped-up mountain bandit king – should have ended as a merely curious footnote in the dusty recess of Near Eastern history. Unfortunately for those subject peoples hoping to wriggle free from beneath the elegantly turned boot of the Persian Great King, an equally brilliant – if surprisingly distant – relative of Cyrus II was then proclaimed King: Darius I ('the Great'). His extraordinary triumphs over enemy and birthright alike are recorded at the site of Bisotun (page 142). Darius I inherited both the military genius and ambitions of his distant grandsire, and his own campaigns extended Achaemenid control into Ethiopia from Egypt, Afghanistan and India, and west into Europe along the Danube and into Greece. During Darius's reign he had, in fact, 're-founded' the Achaemenid Empire that could have broken apart during the tumultuous years after the unexpected death of Cyrus's son. The empire was at its highest point, not only in terms of its geographical expansion, but also internal tax and administrative reforms. Cambyses II succeeded his father to the throne, but his rule was followed by numerous revolts, as recorded on the Bisotun rock relief. Unlike Cyrus II, however, Darius the Great (d486BCE) clearly understood that the business of empire requires able administrators as much as fierce warriors, and continued the tradition instituted by Cyrus of governing local affairs with a light and deft touch. An able administrator, he divided the empire into 20 *satrapies* (provinces), each governed by a *satrap* (governor) and a military commander, who would be independent of the *satrap*. Darius simultaneously undertook a massive road- and canal-building programme (including the precursor to the Suez Canal) in order to bind together tightly his newly forged, disparate dominion. He also began the construction of a great ceremonial palace complex at Persepolis as a grand showcase for his imperial splendour (page 263). Darius did not force the numerous peoples subject to him to convert to Zoroastrian beliefs, preserving Cyrus's tradition, and his rule is still associated with unusually far-sighted tolerance and economic prosperity. An empire-wide banking system, uniform weights and standard measures were instituted, and a powerful navy was established to repress piracy and encourage trade.

Even under Darius, Persian military momentum occasionally stalled (most famously at Salamis and Platea), and under his successors, in particular Darius III at the Battle of Gaugamela in 331BCE, the famously even-handed administration of Persian *satrapies* began to ossify, leading to corruption and rebellion. Alexander the Great timed his invasion well, and in a series of incredible campaigns from 334–326BCE subjugated the once-mighty Achaemenid Empire, which at the time stretched across the Asian and European land mass, from Greece to India. Although he survived only seven years after his capture of Persepolis in 330BCE, Alexander has passed into Iranian history with a somewhat mixed image: a great king and warrior, responsible for building a wall (page 205), protecting truly civilised people (Iranians) from the savage Barbarians of the central Asian steppe, but also the great destroyer of Persian might and power, and the burner of Persepolis, that symbol of supposed eternal Achaemenid and Iranian glory.

Under the Achaemenid dynasty, Persians ruled over an empire extending over 8,000,000km² from present-day Libya in the west towards Pakistan in the east, with Greece and Saudi Arabia marking its northern and southern borders respectively. Modern historians claim that during this period about 44% of the world's total population (50 million people) lived in the Persian Empire.

Archaeological interest during the 1960s and 1970s concentrated on sites associated with Achaemenid history, even more so when the late shah Mohammad Reza proclaimed that his reign was a direct extension of 'uninterrupted Iranian rule' established by Cyrus II (politely ignoring Alexander and his successors, among a panoply of other monarchs). The shah even introduced a short-lived dating system to embody this idea, for example 21 March 1976 was re-dated as New Year's Day 2535. Massive restoration projects and new excavations were undertaken at Persepolis, Pasargadae, Susa, Naqsh-e Rostam and Bisotun in time for the 2,500th anniversary celebrations of this rule in 1971.

THE SELEUCIDS (323–c240BCE) Alexander's sudden death stunned his men; he had seemed invincible. His military generals and governors strove to retain control over the conquered territories, with Seleucus Nicator (Seleucus I) grabbing the bulk of Iranian lands in the chaos and civil wars of the Macedonians that followed Alexander's death, and subsequently ruling from Ctesiphon, south of today's Baghdad. Greek cities and temples were established, Greek replaced Aramaic as the official language of the empire, but from around 310BCE an Iranian-speaking people, the Parthians, pushed south from the region of today's Turkmenistan and re-established a Persian-speaking kingdom. The Seleucids withdrew from their eastern provinces in order to defend the rich lands west of the Euphrates, and a series of Greek-speaking breakaway successor states briefly flourished in the mountains of modern-day Afghanistan and Pakistan. With Seleucid abandonment, the conventional frontier between East and West came to be located very definitely west, not east, of the Zagros Mountains. An exhausted Seleucid dynasty finally succumbed to Roman martial prowess after the Battle of Magnesia in 180BCE.

The Seleucids left little to posterity. Having relied on bronze as the main material, most of the Seleucid items produced during that period were melted by subsequent rulers.

THE PARTHIANS (c238BCE–224CE) The early history of this family (also known as the Arsacids) and its founder Arsaces (Arshak or Ashk) is shrouded in mystery, but we know that as the Seleucids withdrew, the power vacuum was filled by the Parni, a tribe moving down from the central Asian steppes in c238BCE. Preoccupied with defending Syria, the Seleucids failed to challenge Arsaces of Parni, and in 210BCE he was recognised as a powerful vassal ruler in Parthia in the northeast and the southern Caspian regions; the southwest provinces remained largely under the control of the Elymais (c147BCE–c225CE) who paid annual tribute to the Parthian shahs. This regional power group who, unlike the Seleucids and Achaemenids, had retained their feudal system of governance, is known from its coinage and a few Aramaic inscriptions, and perhaps represent the last remnants of the earlier non-Indo European-speaking Elamite people.

Most information about the Parthians comes from Roman historical records; any other sources are otherwise scarce. The Parthian shah Mithridates I (c171–139BCE) campaigned against the Seleucids, winning control of Media by 148BCE, but in the east Scythian tribes were causing serious problems, a threat implicitly recognised in the location of the first Parthian capital, Nisa (now in Turkmenistan). As internal security was established, so trade along the Silk Road flourished, carrying Chinese silk westwards in payment for glass, jade and the 'blood-sweating' horses of Ferghana, central Asia. By 113BCE Mithridates II (c124–87BCE) had moved into eastern Syria and the Caucasus against Rome, but family squabbles after his death stopped further advances. Rome moved into action, only to have half its forces slain and a further 25% captured. Nevertheless, continuing family feuds prevented the Parthian command from taking advantage. An uneasy truce dramatically ended with the invasion of Mesopotamia by the Roman emperor Trajan in 114CE. His death three years later, as foretold by the oracle at Baalbek, Lebanon, prompted Hadrian to accept the Euphrates as the frontier, but peace was in name only. Major campaigning recommenced in 195, with the Parthians losing most of Mesopotamia but inflicting a massive defeat on the Roman army in 217. However, there was an internal challenger to Parthian domination, the emergent Persian family of Sasan, based at the city of Istakhr, sited near the ruins of Achaemenid Persepolis and within view of the great Achaemenid royal necropolis at Naqsh-e Rostam. In April 224, at the battle near Golpayegan, Parthian rule was finally brought to an end by the Sasanids.

The Parthian dynasty lasted 474 years and was the longest in Iranian history, but remarkably little of its civilisation and culture is visible to the visitor in Iran; you will need to journey to Hatra in Iraq, Nisa in Turkmenistan or Palmyra in Syria. Apart from the striking bronze Shami statue (page 287) there are only a few eroded low-reliefs and fragmentary archaeological finds. Later Sasanid occupation of the major Parthian settlements of Damghan, Rey, Hamadan and Ctesiphon destroyed the architecture, and until recently officialdom had other archaeological priorities. However, the military skill of the Parthians has been recorded throughout Europe and the East, with depictions of the famed Parthian shot (which gave us the 'parting shot' expression), in which the warrior on horseback turns back in the saddle, drawing his bow. Parthian mobile warfare became particularly acclaimed after the defeat of the superior Roman army in the Battle of Carrhae in 53BCE.

Renowned also were the Parthian trousers, dismissed by the Roman military as 'effeminate' garb, but carefully portrayed in all their finery by 2nd- and 3rd-century sculptors of Palmyra (Syria) and Hatra (Iraq). As with the Achaemenids, the Parthians were Zoroastrian (page 34) and established a firm association between the priesthood and kingship by constructing 'coronation' fire temples and developing the cult or temple fire.

THE SASANIDS (224–658CE) Persian tradition holds that Sasan, who gave his name to the dynasty, was high priest at the Zoroastrian shrine of Anahita, at Istakhr (page 271). Claiming family ties to the Achaemenids, one of Sasan's descendants, Ardashir I (d255), then in control of the Shiraz and Kerman regions as a vassal ruler, defeated the last Parthian shah, Artabanus V (page 282), and established a dynasty that ruled Iran for over 400 years and included the entirety of Parthian territories, with the exception of Armenia. The main Sasanid sites of Bishapur, Firuzabad and Taq-e Bostan reveal little of the efficient administration, which included town planning, irrigation systems and a system of schools, colleges and hospitals. But the exploits of the Sasanid kings are recorded in the famous Persian epic poem, the *Shahnameh* (see box, page 349), combining both magic and part-remembered history, which later inspired many Iranian artists and re-established Persian as a language of culture and art during Islamic rule in the late 10th and early 11th centuries CE. The Sasanid dynasty instituted an imperial formulation of Zoroastrian scripture, complicated somewhat by Alexander the Great's destruction of the Achaemenid royal archives. However, this new orthodoxy, so at odds with the religious pluralism of Cyrus and Darius I, was accompanied by the hearty persecution of existing Buddhist, Jewish, Manichaean and Christian communities in Iran; such intolerance helped to sow the seeds of their own later destruction. It was, however, under Sasanid rule that the Quran was first translated into Farsi.

Political and military rivalry with Rome, and later Byzantium, continued throughout the first half of the 1st millennium CE. Sasanid armies headed west from their capital, Ctesiphon, almost reaching the walls of Constantinople (Istanbul) and regularly occupying the Roman provinces of Syria and Egypt and sacking their wealthy cities. Sasanid victories over Rome were recorded in huge rock carvings (as at Bishapur), but constant military campaigning exhausted both empires, which levied ever-increasing taxes to finance their interminable wars. As they fought their pointless battles and mounted their fruitless sieges, both empires utterly exhausted their wealthiest and most fertile provinces.

ISLAM AND THE ARAB CONQUESTS The Western perception of the spread of Islam is largely based on 19th-century opinion: fanatical Muslims eager to attain paradise by dying in battles against the 'infidel'. However, this fails to explain the staggering speed of the territorial conquests after the death of the Prophet Mohammad in 632 in Arabia: averaging 16–19km a day, Syria was taken in 636, Egypt in 641 and Mesopotamia in 648. One answer is to be found in the centuries of religious intolerance vigorously pursued by both the Byzantine and Sasanid empires, a gradual ossifying of social mobility within the Sasanid world, and heavy taxes levied on their subject peoples by both regimes. By contrast, the Muslims offered freedom of religious practice to the 'People of the Book' (eg: Jews and Christians), social equality, in the eyes of God, to those who converted, and lower taxes.

The bulk of the Sasanid army was defeated in 637 in modern-day Iraq, with the conclusive battle fought at Nahavand near Hamadan in 642. The last Sasanid shah, Yazdegerd III, was finally tracked down and killed in 651, but it was some 350 years before the cursive Persian Pahlavi script was totally abandoned for the Arabic script. The administration of the Islamic Empire, which in its heyday stretched from Spain/Portugal and north Africa in the west to the Great Wall of China in the east, was run first from Syria, and later from Iraq (Baghdad) under the Abbasid caliphate (749–1258).

Iran was not a unified country throughout this period and various local dynasties were ruling over its territory from their respective bases. The first local dynasty was the Tahirid (821–873) in Khorasan, which was eventually replaced by the Saffarids governing over Khorasan and southern Iran.

The Samanids (892–999) based in eastern Iran were the first authentic Iranian dynasty and have greatly contributed to the emergence of Iranian Islamic art. The Buyyids were ruling western Iran during approximately the same time and the Ghaznavids with their base in Ghazni, modern-day Afghanistan, were the last separate dynasty to rule over fragmented Iran before the Mongol invasion.

Islamic history is tortuously complicated, with territorial boundaries changing in almost every campaign season; today's borders were fixed only during the early part of the 20th century with the demise of the Ottoman Empire. When the opportunity arose, warlords throughout the empire took advantage of weak caliphs, paying only the merest lip service to whoever occupied the throne of Baghdad. This meant that from 800CE various families were in effective control of certain parts of Iran, the most important in this context being the Seljuk dynasty. Despite such fragmentation, this early medieval period (750–1200) was a time of flourishing trade and commerce with Europe and the east, and of great scientific and technological advance in most fields.

THE SELJUKS (1038–c1220)

From around 800, numerous Turkic-speaking tribes spread into the Islamic regions from central Asia, mostly to act as mercenaries, or *ghulams*. One of these was the Seljuk clan (also spelt Saljuq), who entered the service of the Khwarizm shah, ruler of the area of modern Turkmenistan, during the 1020s. Quickly tiring of taking orders issued by the Khwariszm shah from the comfort of his grand capital at Konya Urgench on the banks of the famed Oxus River (present-day Amu Daria), the family turned the tables and by 1043 had seized firm control of Nishapur and the eastern provinces. Seljuk authority spread south and westwards, with governance of the regions shared among the family. The Seljuk sultans gained a reputation for being firm but just rulers of Sunni Islam, and great patrons of the arts and sciences, constructing mosques and tomb towers, colleges and caravanserais. Exciting artistic and technological developments in architecture, ceramics, metalwork and textiles took place, influencing work for centuries after. Trade and commerce also flourished; it looked as if peace, territorial unity and continuity had finally arrived. The invading roughnecks of the 12th century, the Crusaders, were a mere irritation in the Seljuks' western provinces. More problematic were the so-called Assassins (see box, page 131) of the Ismaili Shi'a, who murdered political and military leaders, and, even more dangerous, the advancing Mongol armies.

THE MONGOLS (c1220–c1340) The first Mongol invasion in 1218 virtually destroyed Seljuk authority. Although modern Mongolian commentators promote Genghis Khan as a statesman and military hero, contemporary 13th-century Persian and Arabic chroniclers portrayed him and his men as an utterly destructive force, perhaps even sent by God as divine retribution for mankind's many crimes. Even if accounts were slightly exaggerated, many historic cities were most definitely razed to the ground and the country's water irrigation system destroyed, with only southern Iran escaping relatively unscathed. The unfortunate inhabitants of cities such as Nishapur and Rey, however, would have seen their entire world consumed by fire and destruction, great cities entirely depopulated and the countryside emptied of people. The second Mongol invasion of the 1250s under Genghis Khan's grandson, Hulagu, ended Abbasid authority in Baghdad in an equally cataclysmic fashion, with the great libraries of the city (including the famous House of Wisdom) burned and its population alternately butchered or sold into slavery. Hulagu even managed to eradicate the Ismaili Assassin threat, a feat that was beyond the powers of even the mighty Seljuks, by besieging their mountain-peak castles, which had been thought impregnable. And yet, in time, even the Mongols – who came to be known as the Ilkhanids within Iran (which timewise corresponds to their conversion from nomads to settled people) – were seduced by the culture and sophistication of the Persian-speaking world, which they had almost destroyed. They converted to Islam and an exquisite monument survives as evidence of their pious patronage: the Mausoleum of Oljeitu at Soltaniyeh (page 236). Commerce and trade recovered too, as noted by Marco Polo, although the other Mongol legacy, the Black Death, endured for centuries.

Nevertheless, Iran experienced political fragmentation: a commander in the Mongol army, Mubariz al-Din Mohammad, seized control over central Iran (Esfahan, Yazd and later Kerman), but his newly established Muzaffarid dynasty was short-lived (1314–93). A small Sunni madrasa in Esfahan has remained as a testimony to its brief rule and artistic quality and craftsmanship of the Muzaffarids (page 175). In northern Iraq and Azerbaijan, a Mongol tribe, the Jalayrids, took control (1336) but yielded authority to the house of Timur Leng in the closing years of the 14th century.

THE TIMURIDS (1375–c1415 IN WESTERN IRAN; UNTIL c1500 IN EASTERN IRAN)

National hero of the Republic of Uzbekistan, Amir Temur or Timur Leng (Tamerlane), was nonetheless one of history's tireless warriors with bloodstained hands. Claiming direct descent from Genghis Khan, this Turkic chief dreamt of re-establishing the Mongol Empire. Ruling from Samarkand, he led annual campaigns into Syria, Anatolia, India (sacking Delhi in 1399), Russia (up to the gates of Moscow) and even China, before his death in 1405. Family squabbles resulted in territorial fragmentation but by 1420 his son Shah Rukh (d1447) controlled most of the Iranian provinces from his Herat capital, and it is in eastern Iran, around Mashhad, where much Timurid architecture, with its distinctive ceramic-tiled exteriors and 'ribbed' vaulting, still survives.

In western Iran power had passed in the late 14th century to two Shi'a tribal confederations, the Aq Qoyunlu and the Qara Qoyunlu (White and Black sheep, respectively). The heartland of Aq Qoyunlu authority was in today's eastern Turkey, and by 1470 it had taken control of the Qara Qoyunlu's Azerbaijani and Iraqi territory. Expansion continued into southern Iran and eastwards, which explains the Aq Qoyunlu buildings in Esfahan. However, a resounding defeat in 1473 against the Ottomans meant that it was only a matter of time before a new political force, the Safavid family, took centre stage.

THE SAFAVIDS (1501–1736) The Safavids ruled Persia longer than any other dynasty after the Arab conquest. Safavid court historians were so successful in manufacturing their ancestral links that little is certain about the family's actual origins. The story goes that a famous Sufi sheikh, Safi al-Din (d1334), was a popular Sunni mystic and teacher at Ardabil, on the western Caspian shores, and as the two Qoyunlu confederations battled for supremacy and the Ottomans attacked, people looked to this Turkish-speaking 'guru' for spiritual and political leadership. During the 15th century his followers, among whom was one of the sheikh's descendants Ismail, future Shah Ismail I and founder of the Safavid dynasty, became known for their commitment to Shi'a Islam (page 33) and so the lines of future dynastic rivalry were drawn: the Sunni Ottoman sultanate and the emerging Shi'a Safavid dynasty. In 1502 Shi'a Islam was declared the state religion and from then onwards it has started becoming closely associated with Iranian nationalism.

The Muslim pilgrimage centres of Mecca and Medina passed into Ottoman authority, so in their place the Safavid shahs promoted the Shi'a shrines of Karbala, Mashhad and Ardabil, after proclaiming Ithna 'Ashari Shi'ism as the state religion. Sultan and shah fought constantly for control of the Zagros Mountain regions and their populations, while Uzbek tribes carried out damaging raids in the northeast, and the Afghans attacked from the east. The Safavids had nonetheless successfully reunited all Iranian lands and made the lion holding a sword in its hand and carrying the sun on its back the official insignia of their empire.

It was during the Safavid rule that political relations were established for the first time between Iran and Europe and despite the turmoil, European traders could now freely marvel at the magnificence and wealth of the Safavid court in Esfahan, which became the empire's capital under Shah Abbas I (the Great) (1571–1629). They were seduced – as are so many of today's visitors – by stunning turquoise domes, fine palaces, elegant bridges and lush tree-lined streets, watered by sweet-water fountains, and the soaring tiled portals first seen in Timurid constructions, while fine textiles and carpets attracted hundreds of merchant adventurers vying for trading privileges awarded by the shah.

It was under the Safavids that Iranian faïence tile art has taken the form we know today. Tiles were used to decorate the new buildings of the Safavid capital Esfahan and by then this art found its way to carpet weaving, making Esfahan and Kashan two major carpet production centres. Safavid Iran had also become the centre of flourishing Shi'a legal, theological and philosophical literature, a substantial part of which was Sufi inspired. The clergy started gaining more power, eventually taking on the role of the guardians of Shi'a purity, and accepting the shah as the embodiment of these religious ideals.

In 1636, the Safavids also succeeded in signing a treaty with the Ottoman Empire establishing the borders between the two states that essentially remained in effect until the 19th century.

THE AFSHARIDS (1736–c1750) The Sunni population of Afghanistan increasingly questioned Safavid authority and found a leader in Mirwais, a former Safavid governor. Attacks began in earnest in 1722, with many Iranian towns falling to the Afghan rebels until Nader Qoli, a Safavid general and military genius from eastern Iran, took control. By 1727 Nader Qoli had recaptured territory seized by the Afghans and been rewarded with governorships that amounted to the complete control of all of Iran except Azerbaijan, Esfahan and the southwest. Before him, only the Seljuks, Mongols and the Safavids had managed to achieve the same level of control. All other dynasties had power installed only over specific areas, which often resulted in disagreements inside their power houses as well as with other families simultaneously ruling over other parts of the Iranian plateau.

Three years later Nader Qoli forced the Ottoman army out of Hamadan, Azerbaijan and the Caucasus and in 1735 with the Treaty of Rasht he had successfully driven the Russians out of Iran. Tired of installing Safavid puppet rulers, Nader Qoli took the crown and title with the dynastic name of Afshari in 1736, and proclaimed Sunni Islam as the state religion from his Mashhad capital. Extensive campaigning continued, including into Dagestan (modern-day Russia), Iraq and India, exhausting the Iranian people and an economy already disrupted by Afghan incursions, famine and plague. Nader Shah, as he was now known, was assassinated in 1747, and once again Iran's territorial unity was divided among various regional warlords.

THE ZAND FAMILY (1750–94) Zand rulers, especially the founder, Karim Khan Zand (d1779), believed to be of Kurdish descent, never assumed the title 'shah', always claiming that they acted in the capacity of regent (*vakil*) for the Safavids only. An army officer of the last Safavid shah, Karim Khan assumed control of southern Iran in the chaotic years following Nader Shah's assassination and the reintroduction of Shi'ism. After his death the usual family disputes broke out. Despite the reassertion of authority by the able Lotf Ali Khan Zand, the chaos enabled the muscular Qajar family, powerful in the northern provinces, to extend their dominion southwards. Agha Mohammad Qajar captured Lotf Ali Khan in the city of Kerman and executed him (and a large number of the unfortunate locals for good measure) in 1794. It was the end of Zand rule, which was noted for its justice and moderation, particularly in Shiraz, the former Zand capital, which retains charming examples of Zand architecture (page 250).

THE QAJAR DYNASTY (c1794–1925) The Turkoman Qajar family from the Caspian region had fought as vassals and retainers for the Safavid dynasty on the battlefield so, as Safavid authority imploded, the Qajar family seized authority in Azerbaijan, grabbed Esfahan from the Zands and moved into the eastern Iranian provinces, again re-establishing Shi'a Islam. The man in charge was Agha Mohammad, whose renowned brutality was partly attributed to his forced castration by an Afsharid shah. His petty sadism proved too much even for his courtiers, who contrived his murder in 1797. Establishing Tehran as the capital, his nephew and successor Fath (pronounced *Fat'h*) Ali Shah (d1834) showed considerable political savvy, unusual for his family, and managed to survive the interventionist policies and expansionist ambitions of Napoleonic France, Victorian Britain in India, and Tsarist Russia, while fighting off Ottoman campaigns in the Zagros range and Afghan incursions in the east. It was no easy task: the Treaty of Golestan (1813), signed with the mediation of the British ambassador in Tehran, resulted in Iran losing most of its Caucasian lands to Russia and giving Russia an exclusive right to keep a fleet in the Caspian Sea, while the Treaty of Turkomanchay (1828) reaffirmed Russian permanent control over the Caucasus, this time also including Nakhichevan and Yerevan, and imposed on Iran a massive war indemnity, bankrupting the state. In the 1857 Treaty of Paris, the Qajars gave the British control of the strategically important city of Herat.

As with contemporary Ottoman sultans, the Qajars reorganised their army and administration and considered a comprehensive modernisation project along European lines as the solution to most of their problems. To the Qajar shahs, such reforms presupposed the centralisation of power in royal hands, but many of their disgruntled subjects argued that genuine modernisation should lead to democratic constitutional rule, entirely free from foreign interference. Russia and Britain had in the meantime repeatedly tried to divide Iran and, with the signing of the Anglo-Russian Treaty, Britain had secured its supremacy in Afghanistan and presence in the Sistan area (currently Sistan and Baluchestan) en route to India, allowing for some degree of non-interference of other foreign powers in Iran's internal affairs.

The discontent among Iranians with the Qajar rule grew, exacerbated by the government's failure to create a national army and a unified tax system. Inspired by the ideas of the Russian Revolution and socialist movements in Azerbaijan, the unrest culminated in the 1906 Constitutional Revolution. Shortly before his death in 1907, Shah Muzaffar al-Din was forced (when Shi'a theologians withdrew support) to agree to a constitution on Belgian lines, limiting the power of the shah by *majles* but his successor and son Mohammad Ali Shah was understandably hostile.

Iran did not formally participate in World War I, but in 1914 Turkey occupied Khoy, Orumiyeh and Tabriz, while Russia counterattacked and in 1915 seized Tabriz, Hamadan and Kermanshah. The southern cities of Mekran, Kerman, Shiraz and Yazd were under British control and the shah's power was practically fictive. Following the Bolshevik Revolution, the Russians had fully withdrawn their forces from Iran and had in 1918 returned all the Tsarist monopolies in the country (including shipping on Lake Urmia and the Lianozovo fishing concession on the Caspian Sea) while nationalist forces seized Esfahan and then Tehran, deposing the new shah in favour of his son, a minor.

A Cossack brigade commander called Reza Khan quickly cemented his authority over the country, engineering a coup d'état in 1921 and becoming prime minister in 1923. Two years later the National Assembly declared the formal end of Qajar rule. Calls for a republic on the lines of the newly established Kemalist Turkey gathered strength and – concerned that this would inevitably mean increased secularism and a decrease in their authority, wealth and influence – Iranian theologians pressed Reza Khan to take the throne and make himself shah.

THE PAHLAVI DYNASTY (1925–79) Reza Shah adopted 'Pahlavi' as the dynastic name, we are told, because it was a popular title for an unbeatable warrior, a champion wrestler (see box, page 172), and readopted the language and cursive script of pre-Islamic Iran. Whatever your personal views of Reza Shah's rule – his tomb in Rey was quickly destroyed in the early days of the Islamic Revolution – like Kemal Ataturk in Turkey he successfully managed to save Iran from being totally absorbed by one or other of the Great Powers; other leaders were not so successful. Much of his reform programme was aimed at welding Iran into one nation (compulsory school teaching in Farsi, dress reform, etc) while establishing a national system of schools and hospitals, and constructing roads and railways (by the start of the Pahlavi rule only two all-weather roads existed in the whole country – a fairly stunning indictment of Qajar governance). The new shah also, with assistance from Sweden, established the police force and gendarmerie. When Reza Shah was ousted by Britain and the Soviet Union in 1941 – because of concern for his pro-German leanings – in favour of his son, Mohammad Reza, Iran was a very different nation from when he had assumed control. It should be noted that Reza Shah's personal finances had also undergone a great change, mysteriously increasing from 1 million rials in 1930 to 680 million rials (then £7 million sterling) in 1941.

After World War II, British influence at court paled as the USA increasingly exerted its authority, while Soviet military withdrawal from the Tabriz region meant pressure from that quarter lessened too. An understandable concern over foreign control of Iran occupied the chatter in the middle-class salons, newspaper columns and tea houses of the bazaar alike. The popularly elected (if somewhat mercurial) Prime Minister Mohammad Mossadeq (1951–53) nationalised Iran's oil industry in the early 1950s. Infamously, with support from the British, who had enjoyed concessions and unquestionable control over Iranian oil, and Mohammad Reza Shah himself, the CIA instituted a counter-coup, 'Operation Ajax', in 1953, organised chiefly by Kermit Roosevelt, a grandson of the former US president Teddy Roosevelt and a senior CIA operative. This returned the shah to power and led to the removal of Mossadeq, an action which would haunt American–Iranian relations for many decades. These events also brought with them previously unseen anti-Western feelings amid Iranians. After the coup d'état the shah's rule became absolute; political parties were banned and censorship installed. In 2009, former foreign secretary Jack Straw publicly commented on Britain's part in toppling Mossadeq, which he described as one of many outside 'interferences' in Iranian affairs in the last century. In 2000 President Bill Clinton and Secretary of State Madeleine Albright publicly acknowledged the US role in the 1953 coup.

Various reform programmes were introduced by the reinstalled shah, including the so-called White Revolution, primarily designed to reassign land ownership from the clergy and local wealthy landlords to the peasantry. Lauded by many contemporary Western commentators as a savvy political move to counter communist influence, more recent appraisals argue that it was actually disastrous, increasing hardship for farmers and creating a deep resentment among an increasingly hostile clergy, while safeguarding the riches of the wealthy and connected at the imperial court.

In 1967, Mohammad Reza Shah crowned himself as 'King of Kings', the title used for the first time by the Achaemenid rulers of Iran, and became increasingly autocratic and remote. Political parties were banned, save for the one which he controlled, and parliament (*majles*) merely rubber-stamped all royal decisions. Leading theologians, including a certain Ayatollah Ruhollah Khomeini (see box, page 22), were deported or jailed, and many Iranians with left-wing or centrist leanings either fled the country or risked imprisonment. Press, radio and television were all heavily censored and even in book publishing all texts had to be approved or be shown to have pre-publication orders for a minimum of 3,000 copies, in an attempt to prevent the dissemination of political tracts. The reputation of Mohammad Reza's secret police, the SAVAK, was fearsome. Meanwhile, revenue from oil was pouring into the country, only to flow out again to pay for a massive armaments programme. The gap between rich and poor yawned, while middle-class dissatisfaction at soaring inflation and extensive corruption increased. The West, chaperoned by the United States, however, being deeply apprehensive of Soviet territorial ambitions, continued its almost unquestioning support of the shah's rule. Somewhat blinded by such encouragement, the shah engaged in senseless exhibitionism. Perhaps the ultimate fin de siècle follies were the costly celebrations marking the so-called 2,500th anniversary of 'uninterrupted Persian rule' in 1971. In the decade preceding the Revolution, Iran, and in particular Tehran, in the early 1970s had become a thriving centre for thousands of expats, brought by the Iranian government to work on numerous projects. Thanks to the increasing oil prices, the government's spending seemed infinite, but it did not in fact go where it was needed most. By 1976 there was almost no public support for the shah: soldiers and government employees were bussed into events to provide 'spontaneous' cheering for royal motorcades and celebrations. The following year, government funding for religious institutions and the 'clergy' was substantially cut. As serious unrest grew, those who could do so left Iran, or sent their children abroad. During a state visit to the US in November 1977 the Iranian royal family was met with tear gas and demonstrations. The same year at the New Year's Eve dinner in Tehran, Jimmy

1

Carter toasted Mohammad Reza, crediting 'the great leadership of the shah' for tranforming Iran to 'an island of stability in one of the more troubled areas of the world'. Martial law was imposed in the autumn of 1978 but public demonstrations continued, despite hundreds being killed in hails of bullets.

A vicious cycle of funerals, followed by demonstrations, followed by the shooting of demonstrators, engulfed all of Iran's major cities. Telephone lines were cut off and the only connection was that to Paris, where Khomeini was in exile. In the closing years of Mohammad Reza's rule, Muslim theologians throughout Iran refused to hold the Friday service, as a sign of their disapproval of the regime on religious grounds. Instead, smuggled tape cassettes of the speeches of Ayatollah Khomeini and other banned theologians passed from hand to hand.

Mohammad Reza finally fled the country on 16 January 1979, dying in exile in Egypt in 1980.

THE ISLAMIC REPUBLIC With the shah now gone, Khomeini returned from his French exile to ecstatic popular acclaim in February 1979 and quickly set about undermining support for a democratic government, overturning a millennium of Shi'a theological tradition and instead establishing an administration based on Shi'a Islamic law. He dismissed Shapur Bakhtiar, the last prime minister under the shah, and his offers to form a unity government, and appointed his own prime minister Mehdi Bazargan. A referendum was held on 30–31 March 1979, when 98.2% of the population voted for the new Islamic Republic and 1 April was pronounced as the National Day. The name of the country was officially changed from Iran to the Islamic Republic of Iran. Based on the results of the referendum, the supreme power went to the clergy while civil and political power was allocated to the president, *majles* and prime minister. The first general election in May 1980, following a selective round-up of potential political opponents to the new regime, confirmed Khomeini's new grip on the levers of power. Many women supported the revolution in the hope that the new Islamic system would bring them dignity and respect previously taken away with the forced modernisation of the Pahlavi monarchy. The cultural revolution that followed saw increasing attacks against communists and liberals, including women or anyone believed to oppose the new clergy. By the mid 1980s, around 3 million people reportedly left Iran.

The Iranian Revolution has acquired a prophetic and powerful significance across the region. Praised by many as the successful victory against Western hegemony, it has been an inspiration for various regional revolutionary groups, to the unease of many local and foreign players in the Middle East.

By the end of the Iran–Iraq War in 1998, many young Iranian men had been killed (perhaps as many as 1 million), martyrdom had become formally enshrined within the Islamic Republic's definition of what it meant to be a good Iranian, and without a fully developed welfare system in place, martyrs' wives and families suffered further distress. Although barely understood in the West, the utter futility of the Iran–Iraq War (1980–88), and its needless extension due to the stubborn pride of Khomeini, who insisted on prolonging the war, had a similar impact on the Iranian culture and psyche as World War I did in the UK or France: no community was left untouched by death, a generation of young men was left crippled and scarred by war wounds, and widows and orphans became commonplace in Iran's streets.

During this difficult time, a full reorganisation of the legal system, administration and taxation was undertaken; Iran was to become a theocracy. Just as the shah had brooked no opposition in his last years, so the new regime was determined

THE IRAN–IRAQ WAR 1980–88

On 17 September 1980, the President of Iraq raised territorial claims to the Khuzestan area south of the Arvand River (known to Arabs as Shatt al-Arab). Believing that he had full American support, Saddam Hussein of Iraq invaded four months later, claiming the oil-rich and partly Arabic-speaking region of southwest Iran, and justifying his action on the grounds of 'liberating' the Arabs of Khuzestan from the 'tyranny of the Persian'. Iranian forces quickly regained lost territory (with boys as young as 13 tragically walking into landmines to clear the path for their comrades), but the war continued with grotesque losses on both sides, and hellish rocket attacks on most of western Iran's major cities. Iraq openly used chemical weapons against Iranians and many people have sustained irreparable damage, both physical and psychological.

Pictures and paintings of the fighters and ordinary men fallen during this war, known in Iran as the Holy Defence, still decorate buildings and streets across Iranian cities, towns and villages; every city and village has a 'Shohada Square', honouring the 'martyrs' fallen during the Iran–Iraq War.

Khomeini utilised the chaos of war to crack down on potential domestic political opponents. As many as 30,000 Iranian leftists, communists, trade unionists, university students, high school pupils, intellectuals and others who disagreed with Khomeini's vision for the country following the revolution were rounded up, imprisoned after short show trials, if any, or tortured and shot. The 'internal security' apparatus of the shah's feared secret police, the SAVAK, including the infamous Evin prison, was reactivated with a vengeance against the very people who had fought so hard to remove the shah. A ceasefire was finally agreed between Iraq and Iran in 1988, although an official peace agreement remained unsigned until a Shi'a-dominated government took power in Iraq following the US-led invasion that removed Saddam Hussein from power.

to forestall any restoration of the monarchy. Theologians and officials moved to eradicate every element of *gharbzadegi* ('Westoxification') from Iran.

The prolonged detention of American embassy staff in Tehran from 4 November 1979 for 444 days, and the Western conviction that the Islamic Revolutionary government was deeply involved in the training and funding of certain hard-line politico-military organisations elsewhere, resulted in a total breakdown of diplomatic relations between Iran and the West, exacerbated by the Salman Rushdie (*The Satanic Verses*) issue, Iran's backing of Hezbollah, the suicide bombing of a US Marines barracks in Beirut in 1982, and the shooting down of an IranAir passenger jet, killing 250, by the US cruiser, USS *Vincennes*.

Ayatollah Khomeini died in June 1989, and since then there have been changes, some with official blessing, some merely tolerated. For the visitor, perhaps this is most apparent in the changed appearance of Khomeini in paintings. In the first years of the revolution he was shown as a glowering, prophetic figure with black beard, furrowed brow and heavy eyebrows, but increasingly now a benign, avuncular image with soft white beard and a slight smile is portrayed. His tomb is a monstrous carbuncle that grows larger every year, lit up like a Las Vegas casino and for the most part politely ignored by Iranian travellers driving to the Imam Khomeini International Airport from Tehran.

THE ISLAMIC REPUBLIC: FROM THE 1990S UNTIL THE PRESENT The decade that followed the establishment of the Islamic Republic was the adjustment period of coming to terms and getting used to the new realities, both internationally and within Iran. In 1997, Mohammad Khatami, a reformer and liberal member of the Shi'a clergy, was with overwhelming support elected president and the wind of hope ensued. The burden of sanctions was slightly relaxed and economic reforms, albeit modest, meant Khatami's undisputed re-election in 2001.

Things, however, took a very different turn following the election in 2005 of a conservative and populist candidate Mahmoud Ahmadinejad. Backed by many from rural areas, historically overlooked by government reforms, the new president set about increasing social payments to the poor and reversing the relatively moderate stance in international politics, which resonated well with some of the more conservative members in society.

Mahmoud Ahmadinejad was eligible to stand again and win the 'stolen' 2009 election. Focusing his campaign on rural Iran and small towns, he enjoyed unquestionable support from the Revolutionary Guard. Far from being the overwhelming victory of 62.6% claimed by the regime, however, it soon emerged that the result was highly contested and led to the most serious civic disturbances seen in the country since popular movements overthrew the shah and established the Islamic Republic in 1979. The Green Movement, often presented in the West as the Green Revolution, emerged in response and took the form of a social movement against corruption in the government. Its main objective was to purify and improve the Islamic Republic; no claims for its overthrow were made. Demonstrations continued throughout 2009 and many young and vocal opponents of the more oppressive aspects of the Islamic Republic's security apparatus were rounded up, arrested and imprisoned after show trials, or no trial at all. Rumours in Iran have it that Mir Hossein Mousavi, the main opposition candidate who officially received 33.8% of the vote, was notified that he had won immediately after the election. Both Mousavi and Mehdi Karroubi, a former speaker of the parliament and another reformist candidate, are still being held under house arrest in Tehran at the time of going to print. Ayatollah Khamenei publicly backed Ahmadinejad's election win despite the strength of the protests, and this shredded any pretence or illusion of impartiality on the part of the supreme leader. Despite many Shi'a theologians and Iranian politicians having traditionally written off Khamenei as a 'broken reed' or mere compromise candidate among bigger political beasts, he has actually shown himself a true master of the political sphere, outmanoeuvring long-standing political rivals such as former president Rafsanjani – even having Rafsanjani's sons and daughter, who publicly backed Mousavi, arrested and imprisoned in 2012 – and now stands truly supreme in the realm of Iranian domestic politics. Khamenei's/Ahmadinejad's government predictably blamed foreign countries and media for fuelling the protests and in 2011 a (presumably) orchestrated attack on the British embassy in Tehran resulted in both countries withdrawing their ambassadors and closing down direct diplomatic relations. Khamenei, an adept strategist, does not hesitate to oppose and openly criticise Iran's incumbent president, Hassan Rouhani, in particular when it comes to the latter's negotiation of the 2015 nuclear deal.

On 14 June 2013, Iranians elected Hassan Rouhani as the new president of the Islamic Republic. The only cleric in the contest, Rouhani received 50.7% of the vote, and united support from centrist and reformist politicians, including Rafsanjani and Khatami. One of Rouhani's challenges has since been the pressure from the conservative-minded members of the Parliament (*majles*), which he has managed to resist. Despite the unrest across the Middle East and the dissatisfaction of

Iranians with their own government, the 2013 presidential elections ran smoothly and without confrontation, albeit not without a little political wrangling (Rafsanjani was disqualified from running in the elections by the Council of Guardians).

Rouhani, Iran's chief nuclear negotiator in 2003, is an open supporter of rapprochement with the West. At his first press conference as president, he called for 'serious and substantive' negotiations on Iran's nuclear programme, while asserting Iran's right to civil nuclear energy. Rouhani's efforts in tandem with those of Iran's Minister for Foreign Affairs and current chief nuclear negotiator Mohammad Javad Zarif have borne fruit. Rouhani is credited as the chief architect of the nuclear agreement (also known as the Joint Comprehensive Plan of Action for limitations on Iranian nuclear development) signed in summer 2015 (see box, page 26).

In May 2017, on the promise of a better social and economic situation, Rouhani was re-elected president. Despite a noticeable boom to tourism and upbeat political rhetoric, the nuclear deal has not brought any significant improvement to the lives of Iranians. Most sanctions remain in place and the economy is not growing as expected. Conservative elements in the Iranian Parliament took advantage of the momentum to try and unsuccessfully impeach Rouhani after the mass protests across Iranian cities in December 2017. In response to this and in an attempt to bring about changes, the Iranian president replaced the head of the central bank. By then, however, the US position towards Iran has taken on a new and much more aggressive tone, precluding any possibility for improvement of the situation.

GOVERNMENT AND POLITICS

THE SUPREME LEADER AND THE PRESIDENT Under the current constitution, Iran is governed by a *faqih* or Supreme (spiritual) Leader in line with Khomeini's theory outlined in his book *Hokumat-e Islami: Velayat-e Faqih* (*Islamic Government: Regency of the Jurist*), until the re-emergence of the 12th imam, or Mahdi (page 33). This Supreme Leader is chosen for life by the Assembly of (Theological) Experts, whose members have been elected for a seven-year term once their candidacy has been approved by the Leader and the Council of Guardians of the Constitution. Ayatollah Khomeini, it was widely acknowledged, clearly had been one person capable of filling this office, and certainly possessed the faculties of a most pious and able theologian, but such unanimity was not immediately accorded to his successor, Ayatollah Ali Khamenei.

The important Council of Guardians is headed by the Supreme Leader who selects six voting members, while a similar number is selected by the Supreme Judicial Council and approved by parliament (*majles*). Currently clerics make up under 10% of the *majles*. As Iran is a theocracy, all are from the *ulama* ('clergy', theologians-cum-jurists) and, under current legal interpretation, no woman can 'join' the *ulama*. This council undertakes to safeguard and uphold the Islamic state, the constitution, and approve all parliamentary dealings, decisions and resolutions. An Expediency Council of 25 members has been established to 'negotiate' between the *majles* and the Council of Guardians, consisting of the Guardians, the president, the head of the judiciary and the parliamentary speaker.

The president of the republic is directly elected by all resident Iranians over the age of 16 for a four-year term, but stands for office only with the approval of the Council of Guardians. After two successive terms in office he cannot offer himself for a third term.

On taking office, a president may appoint 24 cabinet ministers who have to be confirmed in office by the *majles*; following constitutional amendments

1

1902 Birth of Ruhollah Khomeini. By 1944 he was a Qom madrasa teacher, proposing active 'Muslim' involvement in politics, and supported *velayet-e faqih* (government control by Islamic law), later the cornerstone concept behind the Islamic Revolution.

1962 Khomeini opposed the new government ruling revoking requirement of swearing-in on the Quran by any newly elected local and provincial officials, arguing that this would allow Bahais open participation in politics.

January 1963 Joined with other theologians against the shah's White Revolution, saying it increased the shah's power and American influence in Iran.

March 1963 Paratroopers attacked Khomeini's college in Qom, causing fatalities.

June 1963 (Ashura) Khomeini described the shah's government as 'fundamentally opposed to Iran'. His arrest was followed by demonstrations during which many protestors were killed (the 15th day of Khordad).

August 1963 Released; re-arrested and held October 1963–May 1964.

October 1964 Khomeini condemned as 'high treason' the new legal status protecting American personnel in Iran. Arrested and exiled first to Turkey, and then to Najaf, Iraq, for 14 years. His lectures, publicly criticising the shah, were published in 1970.

December 1970 Demonstrations were held in Khomeini's name by Tehran University students, and by Qom students in 1975.

during Rafsanjani's presidency, the office of prime minister was abandoned, but constitutional amendments stripping the office of president of its powers have been under discussion since then. Perhaps surprisingly, following his contested 2009 victory, Ahmadinejad proclaimed himself the carrier of a 'popular mandate' and has proven to be the most publicly vocal critic of the Supreme Leader; unsurprisingly, many of Ahmadinejad's closest advisors have since been arrested on corruption charges and accusations of 'witchcraft' have even been laid at the door of his chief of staff.

The *majles* currently has 290 directly elected members serving a four-year term, and for the last few parliaments there have been several women MPs. In the 2016 *majles* elections female candidates secured a record number of seats – a total of 17, eight more than previously. According to guaranteed representation, the Zoroastrian community is represented by one MP, so is the Jewish population, while Iranian Christians numbering around 100,000 have four seats in parliament. There are no well-defined, established political parties as in the West, but candidates known for their individual leanings and factions are the dominant vehicles for political expression and personal ambition.

The speaker of the *majles* has an important and influential position. On 29 May 2016, winning over his moderate opponent Mohammad Reza Aref, Ali Ardashir Larijani was re-elected (with 61% of votes) to hold the speaker's seat for the third

October 1977 Sudden death of Khomeini's eldest son led to Tehran demonstrations, accusing SAVAK of involvement.

January 1978 Mass protest in Qom following scurrilous Tehran press attack on Khomeini; many killed. Forty days later (customary funeral commemoration) a demonstration was held in Tabriz, and 40 days after that there were similar protests in 55 cities across Iran.

8 September 1978 Around 300 protesters killed and thousands hurt by the shah's forces in Tehran during the largest anti-government demonstration at Jaleh Square (now Shohada Square), which became known as the 'Bloody Friday'.

October 1978 Khomeini moved to France after the shah demanded his expulsion from Najaf. On Khomeini's orders crippling strikes, including by Iranian oil workers, began. Within one week, oil production fell from 5.8 to 1.1 million barrels per day. Soldiers were guarding oilfields, shops closed and cars disappeared from the streets that now seemed to be a warzone.

December 1978 (Moharram) Iranian theologians and students demonstrated against the curfew. On the ninth day, 1 million demonstrators collected in Shahyad/Azadi Square, near the airport; the next day (Ashura) 2 million protesters demanded the abolition of the monarchy.

16 January 1979 The shah left Iran.

1 February 1979 Following pressure from Khomeini's supporters, Prime Minister Shapur Bakhtiar opened Mehrabad Airport to allow Khomeini to return from exile.

time in a row since 2008. Although a conservative politician, Larijani supports President Rouhani's politics and the nuclear agreement.

With all the promising developments it is nonetheless important to bear in mind the political influence of the Revolutionary Guard in the parliament, which has in turn had a definite impact on policy-making, confirming that the power centre in Iranian politics is an axis of Khamenei, combined with the Revolutionary Guard, whose economic strength and influence has grown to rival its military and political control over the levers of power.

The next parliamentary elections in Iran are scheduled to take place in February 2020 and based on the current political and economic situation within Iran and internationally, conservatives may well take the majority of the seats. But, there again, the surprise factor can never be underestimated.

WESTERN PERCEPTIONS OF REVOLUTIONARY IRAN Anyone visiting Iran for the first time should remember that in the 1970s the Western media was largely uncritical of the shah's regime. The praise lavished on the shah and his immediate family in publications was occasioned more by official stipulation than reasoned investigation. The widespread notion, still found today in the West, that the late shah had established an active Western-style democracy in Iran before he was ousted, is unfounded: his rule was autocratic. Image stills from those days that appear so liberal and familiar to anyone in the West, were in fact showing only a limited picture of the reality of Iranian daily life before the revolution.

Many new visitors to Iran presume that all Iranian theologians speak with one voice, but there have been numerous outspoken declarations among the *ulama*, not always finding favour with the authorities. Many senior clerics feel that having established an Islamic state to its satisfaction, the *ulama* should withdraw from active political life and resume its former pastoral responsibilities; presently the official view is that active involvement in politics should continue. The evolving relationship between Islam, Iran and the modern world is avidly discussed and the passion these debates arouse should not be underestimated.

Parliamentary debates are just as highly charged. There are essentially two main positions: the 'conservative' wing which holds that the quickest route to achieve a (spiritual) well-being nationally is by a uniform path; that a woman's role is primarily associated with the family and the home; and that the fortunes of the poor will be improved by spiritual care and government subsidies, with the awarding of franchise allocation in the market. Support for this view is generally found among the rural communities and *bazaaris* (merchants). The 'liberal' wing prefers another vision of society, one relating the spiritual ideal to the individual and the material world, arguing for the individual to progress along the spiritual path at his/her own pace; recognising the importance of investments in major projects to revitalise the economy and to create new jobs for the ever-increasing population; and working towards reintroducing Iran to the international community and creating greater opportunities for women (even within the *ulama*). Such ideas find favour among the increasingly urbanised population and in particular with the voters of Tehran, Shiraz, Esfahan, women and among the young (many having benefited from the educational campaigns of the Islamic Revolution), as seen in the mass demonstrations across the country during 2009, which were met with a swift and brutal reaction from police and militia, and in turn filmed by the outraged population.

Western women may feel an understandable hostility towards the Iranian regime, and in particular to its treatment of women. This is largely based on a (mis) understanding of the situation in pre-revolutionary Iran – and a personal reaction to the official stipulation requiring head coverings for all women in Iran (see box, page 84). However, while the last shah of Iran was educated in the West and held Iranian doors open to Western values and foreigners – there were reportedly around 50,000 Americans and quite a significant number of Israelis living in Iran by 1979 – his social reforms at home proved inadequate. Approximately 68% of the population was still illiterate and many of these were women. Fathers from poorer and more conservative backgrounds were afraid to send their daughters to mixed schools. In the 1970s, opportunities for Iranian women were virtually confined to the upper socio-economic classes, and indeed 'grassroots' and 'religious' women's groups played a very important role in bringing about the Islamic Revolution. In post-revolutionary Iran, on the other hand, where classes are segregated and the hijab is mandatory, there has been an increase in literacy rates among girls. This, nonetheless, creates a dichotomy – over half of the Iranian population is female and well educated, but yet marginalised.

For Iranian youth overall, opportunities are hard to come by. Over 65% of the population is under 30 years old and these young people require education and training and later employment to the tune of 800,000 new jobs every year. According to official figures, youth unemployment stands at around 30%, and many in work have to moonlight in order to cope with continually rising inflation and prices. In the late 1970s less than 50% of those aged between six and 24 were literate; today, despite a doubling of the population, Iran has a literacy rate that rivals that of Western nations at around 98%, and university student numbers have increased tenfold. Places available to study for qualifications in professions such as medicine and law are increasingly dominated by women, and this has in the past alarmed the conservative faction within the regime: in 2012 a proposal was put before parliament to restrict the numbers of women studying at the more prestigious institutions. To the disgust of many Iranians, over 30 universities put the restrictions in place for the 2012/13 academic year. This did not bring the desired result. At present over 60% of university students are female and it is becoming common for some girls to study for PhDs or apply for another degree in order to avoid being forced into marriage and to maintain some level of independence. The government stance may be explained in part by the fact that many Iranians postpone marriage to later in life and have fewer children.

DIPLOMATIC RELATIONS From the American perspective, the Islamic Republic and its position in the region is the direct threat to the 1980 Carter doctrine allowing the US to directly intervene in the Middle East. The purpose of the crippling economic sanctions and the international isolation of Iran is therefore, as it has been publicly acknowledged by US authorities, to bring about the change of government and limit Iranian influence in the region.

The official US D'Amato trade embargo, briefly relaxed during the Khatami presidency, has nonetheless remained in place, reportedly owing to fear of Iran's nuclear programme. Diplomatic relations soured after 9/11 despite public demonstrations in the streets of Tehran, Esfahan and Shiraz in support of the victims and official condemnation from Khamenei and Khatami of the Al Qaida attacks, and particularly following the second, stolen 'Green' re-election of Iranian president Mahmoud Ahmadinejad in 2009 and the regime's concurrent hardening stance regarding Israel and nuclear research.

From 2016 Iran has cut off its diplomatic ties with Saudi Arabia following the execution of a prominent Shi'a cleric Nimr al-Nimr and the ransacking of the Saudi embassy in Tehran, which President Rouhani publicly disapproved of. Following the death of 450 Iranian pilgrims in the 2015 Mecca stampede (a total of 2,300 people died), the two countries failed to agree on mutually acceptable safety provisions and Iranian pilgrims could not travel on the hajj in 2016. The situation has since improved, but hajj remains a sensitive political leverage in the relations between the two countries.

Despite the promising January 2016 prisoner exchange between the United States and Iran, a significant improvement in US–Iran relations seems unlikely. Back in 2003, leading up to and during the coalition action in Iraq, the Bush administration described Iran as part of the 'axis of evil', which in some way to this day defines the general Western perceptions of Iran and its regime. Furthermore, on 20 April 2016 the United States Supreme Court ruled that the Central Bank of Iran must pay to American victims of terrorist attacks (*sic* Iranian support for Hezbollah who were behind the 1983 attack at the US marine compound in Beirut) almost US$2 billion, to be taken from the Iranian accounts frozen in American banks. Iran has in return filed a complaint with the International Court of Justice against the United States for the confiscation and theft of the US$2 billion. The case is still pending.

The hope and the lifting of some economic and financial sanctions and the improvement in diplomatic relations following the signing on 14 July 2015 of the nuclear agreement with the P5+1 group of powers (USA, China, Russia, UK,

France plus Germany), has alas dissipated with Donald Trump taking office as US president in 2017.

Diplomatic relations have been equally unstable with other Western countries. In the 1990s a German businessman was detained in Iran, and in the early 2000s a female Iranian-born Canadian photojournalist arrested for photographing the Tehran Evin jail, died in custody, while her police interrogator was acquitted of her murder in June 2004. In 2012 Canada severed its relations with Iran, having accused the Islamic Republic of supplying weapons to Syria, and closed its embassy in Tehran. Despite the wary nature of the British–Iranian relations, the UK embassy reopened in 2015 and there is a bilateral dialogue between the two countries.

The isolation of Iran by Western powers has in the meantime meant Iran's rapprochement with potential regional allies. In 2019, Pakistani prime minister Imran Khan made his first official trip to Iran, and the relatively stabilising situation in Syria, although with Bashar al-Assad's rule significantly weakened, gives a certain

NUCLEAR AGREEMENT OF 2015

The Nuclear Agreement (also known as the Joint Comprehensive Plan of Action for limitations on Iranian nuclear development or *barjam* in Persian) signed in summer 2015 between Iran and six member countries of the UN Security Council – United States, United Kingdom, Russia, Germany, France, and China – has meant the annulment of seven UN resolutions against Iran as well as lifting of many of the sanctions that have been crippling the Iranian economy for over 30 years.

Iranian oil could be sold freely, US$100 billion of Iranian money frozen in banks abroad was released and the UN arms embargo was lifted. Iran has in return undertaken to allow the UN to carry out inspections of Iranian nuclear, including military, facilities. The agreement also imposed restrictions on the sale of atomic energy to Iran for peaceful purposes for a period of ten years starting from 2015.

On 8 May 2018 the United States unilaterally withdrew from the Nuclear Agreement, having accused Iran of failing to comply with its conditions, despite the International Atomic Energy Agency (IAEA) repeatedly assuring the international community to the contrary. Harsher sanctions were imposed, prompting Iranian currency to plummet, the economy to stagnate, and the language of war replacing that of diplomacy. The inflation rate in Iran in 2019 increased to 37.6% from 10.2% in mid 2018. In 2017, shortly after the Nuclear Deal had come into effect, the rate stood at 9.8%, for the first time in single digits in 26 years. After the signing of the Agreement, more than 15 countries had confirmed their involvement in investment projects in Iran, but most of these have since been stopped indefinitely. In 2019, the trade between Iran and the EU fell by more than 76%. Only 14 of the 114 Airbus planes purchased by Iran in 2016 have actually been delivered with the fate of the rest pending.

In response, Iran announced its partial withdrawal from the Agreement and, in July 2019, the Iranian government declared that it would no longer hold within the established uranium enrichment limits, namely over 3% (20–80% enrichment is required for military purposes). The remaining signatory parties have since cautiously reiterated their existing commitments and are awaiting further developments.

boost to Iran's authority in the region. Members of the Russia–Syria–Iran–Iraq coalition actively seeking to counterbalance Western policy in the war-torn Syrian Republic, and joint declarations between Iran and Iraq about strategic co-operation also provide a certain degree of support to the Iranian government.

Tehran also has close relations with the Shi'a groups in Yemen, which have been counterattacking Saudi attempts to control its southern neighbour and the Shi'a-dominated Iraqi government. Iranian agents and units of the Revolutionary Guard move freely within these states, much to US and Saudi displeasure.

ECONOMY

PRIOR TO THE REVOLUTION OF 1979 For centuries Iran's economy and trade were based on textiles and carpets, in processed or raw yarn, dyes and mordants, but by the end of the 18th century foreign mass-produced fabrics were flooding the home market (watch out for Chinese silk in your Persian carpet). The economy collapsed. In the 19th century under foreign pressure, the Qajar administration sold off trading concessions in tobacco, sugar, railway construction and telegraph installation to non-Iranians; even carpet production was largely foreign owned. By the early 20th century the exploration and exploitation of Iran's oil reserves were in foreign hands, prompting nationalisation in the 1950s and a political crisis. The shah's White Revolution of 1961–63 (reassigning agricultural land rights) resulted in more power passing to the shah and tens of thousands of peasants barely able to survive. The oil boom and heady prices for petroleum products in the 1970s, especially following the Yom Kippur War in 1973, had nonetheless brought great wealth into the country, but rampant inflation too. The shah reasserted Iran's position and his leading role in OPEC (Organization of the Petroleum Exporting Countries) brought higher returns on oil sales for the country. A lot of money, however, was being spent on the military.

AFTER THE REVOLUTION OF 1979 With the establishment of the Islamic Republic all foreign and private industries were nationalised, and work on international projects (like the Tehran metro or the Bushehr power plant) was abandoned as foreign consortia withdrew. The new administration faced a brain drain, while heavy losses in the Iran–Iraq War resulted in a further scarcity in skills and expertise. During the war itself, the Khomeini regime was forced to send imprisoned 'shah' pilots to fight the Iraqis. The three-year closure of universities and colleges during Iran's 'Cultural Revolution' in the 1980s meant fewer still were qualified to fill the vacuum. The post-revolutionary government had also set out to spend large amounts of government earnings on the oppressed and disinherited members of society (*mostazafin*) through the newly established foundations and institutions. Even today Iran can be described as a welfare state on the basis of the assistance the state provides to the poor.

The economic reforms set in motion by President Rafsanjani in the 1990s and continued subsequently under Khatami have brought in a siege economy dominated by industrial conglomerates with links to the Revolutionary Guard and Basij militia, senior government figures and powerful members of the clergy. The US trade embargo and other economic sanctions, drop in world oil prices, production difficulties and a steep decline in tourist numbers (far below the half-million visitors per annum in the mid 1970s) have created additional problems. Fearing yet more assets leaving the country, the government even banned the export of Iranian carpets for some years (see box, page 180). The two-term Rafsanjani presidency was marked by a massive surge in imports, very lucrative business for the right-wing *bazaari* classes, and little else. Few of Rafsanjani's large-scale projects, which numbered in the tens of thousands, were completed, other than a massive and successful programme of road upgrading and railway construction. Unfortunately, two major projects in health and sewage provision, supported by the EU, were turned down by the World Bank, yielding to American pressure. Khatami's eight years in office saw low oil prices, around US$10 a barrel, so his decisions on the allocation of the national budget were somewhat constrained, though during his presidency, Iran enjoyed a period of delegated authority.

Despite the instability and vulnerable nature of the Iranian economy with an inflation rate in 2018 of over 27%, the country is essentially self-sustaining. Approximately 82% of food products are manufactured nationally and only 4% of pharmaceuticals are imported.

In 2019, as the Islamic Republic celebrated its 40th anniversary, the economic situation in Iran seems more volatile than ever and it becomes increasingly difficult to make predictions. Back in 2013 when Rouhani was elected for his first term, the exchange rate was 30,000 rials to US$1, but in the summer of 2018 it reached 80,000 rials while with the political situation in the autumn of 2019 it stood at 124,000 rials to US$1. Since 2018 prices have been soaring and car prices have tripled, making it almost impossible for an average citizen to buy an Iranian-made Khodro. The corruption and stagnation which so infuriated Iranians during the shah's unyielding rule in the 1970s is back with a vengeance and many of the grand houses of northern Tehran seized from figures close to the royal court are now occupied by 'Revolutionary Princes' and their families.

On 5 November 2018 the United States Treasury reinstated all the sanctions that had previously been lifted following the signing in 2015 of the Nuclear Deal. The international companies Total, Peugeot, Renault, Siemens, Daimler and Volkswagen speedily left Iran and the Society for Worldwide Interbank Financial Telecommunications (SWIFT), which provides necessary codes for processing international banking transactions, blocked access for Iranian banks. Despite its promises, the European Union has yet to establish the SPV (special-purpose vehicle) mechanism allowing European companies to trade with Iran notwithstanding the American sanctions. In spring 2019, Hassan Rouhani suggested that the current economic situation in Iran could become more difficult than the situation during the Iran–Iraq War of 1980–88.

Iran has since been disputing the sanctions through the International Court of Justice. Until now other than a formal reprimand of the US, no concrete actions have followed. The United States have in the meantime been trying to hold Iran responsible for the 9/11 attacks, but in 2019 a Luxembourg court ruled against a group of 9/11 victims seeking US$1.6 billion in Iranian assets. However, since 1979 the US has succeeded in blocking the start of negotiations between Iran and the World Trade Organization (WTO).

OIL Oil still forms the main government income (67%) and there continues to be substantial investment in the energy sector (Iran has the world's largest-proven natural gas reserves and the fourth-largest oil reserves) to improve economic forecasts. The first attempts to drill for oil in Iran were made in the last decade of the 19th century by Dutch merchant Albert Hotz near Dalaki in Bushehr province.

Fifty years ago the shah spent huge sums importing arms and weapons, which then sat rusting in military stores, and into sending students abroad to further their education. For the past few years money has been poured into the nuclear energy programme, defence and development of religious, architectural, educational and administrative structures. Funds have also been sent abroad to Hezbollah in Lebanon and Syria, and Hamas in Gaza, to the fury of many Iranians and the United States. Little has been done to revitalise or restructure the oil industry, partly as a result of sanctions against the Islamic Republic, and because the Iranian government's own economic forecasting unit has predicted that Iran will be a petroleum product importing nation by 2020 owing to a lack of refining capacity and skilled personnel. The situation has slightly improved since the signing of the 2015 Nuclear Deal, as internal production of oil in Iran in 2016 increased by approximately 12%, compared with the four years preceding that. Since 2018, Iran has effectively become unable to sell anything other than oil, and following the US administration's stance and determination to punish anyone willing to buy it, the growth in the Iranian oil sector is at the most uncertain level it has ever been. China, India and South Korea are the main buyers of Iranian oil but in spring 2019, the United States decided not to extend the earlier exemption on the purchase of Iranian oil granted to eight countries (China, Greece, India, Italy, Japan, South Korea, Taiwan and Turkey), while Iran has in response promised to close the Persian Gulf.

There are a number of **free-trade zones** operating in Iran, including the Persian Gulf islands of Kish and Qeshm, and the port of Chabahar, along with a few special economic zones which function in a similar fashion and are primarily dominated by the economic organs of the Revolutionary Guard and the conservative faction. Both types of zone did permit unlimited foreign involvement, including bank operations, a free-market exchange, removal of import restrictions and 20 years of tax exemption, but have been effectively closed to Western involvement with the tightening of sanctions. Instead, Chinese and, to a lesser degree, Indian companies have been taking up the economic slack in an attempt to secure Iran's oil at favourable discounts. In 1992 some restrictions concerning foreign shareholding in Iran-based companies were lifted, but a certain official ambivalence remains; rather than amending or revoking laws, it is more usual to turn a blind eye to circumvention. Iranian companies have established offices in Dubai in an attempt to bypass both bureaucratic difficulties and economic sanctions and, in 2012 some 300,000 Iranians were resident in the Emirates. According to Dubai's own customs and excise department, trade between the two dropped in 2011 but was still measured at a whopping US$12 billion. Agriculture struggles on with a lack of machinery, limited irrigation systems and a poor infrastructure of cold-storage units and refrigerated trucks. The drop in the value of the rial has meant that purchasing new equipment is out of the question for the majority of local producers and manufacturers. Although visitors to Esfahan's central *maydan* (square) will see most of the shops occupied and trading, poor earnings and high unemployment still affect the bazaars of Yazd and Kerman. The major employer, as in the 1960s and 1970s, continues to be the government, despite a revolutionary pledge to reduce such staffing drastically.

After the tightening of sanctions and political attempts by the US to isolate Iran, including the anti-Iranian conference in Warsaw in 2019, Iran has been trying to increase its trade with other countries. China remains Iran's major trading partner, followed by Iraq. The trade with its neighbour to the West increased by 45% in 2018 and Iraq can possibly overtake China in terms of volume. The same year the trade with Russia and Pakistan increased by 30% and 58% respectively. India is now paying for Iranian oil in rupees and there are talks for Iran to join in 2021 the free-trade zone with the Eurasian Economic Union. There are also plans for

THE CASPIAN SEA DECLARATION OF 2018

On 12 August 2018, after more than 20 years of negotiations, Azerbaijan, Iran, Kazakhstan, Russia and Turkmenistan have finally signed a Convention regulating the status of the Caspian Sea.

The delay is partially due to the ongoing dispute over the rights to the ground under the sea, to which the UN Convention on the Law of the Sea of 10 December 1982 does not apply due to the Caspian's unclear status – sea or lake? Tehran and Moscow have from the start insisted on sharing the sea equally, meaning 20% of the sea shelf to be assigned to each country, while the other three partners preferred to divide the shelf based on the 'modified median line', thus leaving Iran with only 13–14%.

The 2018 Convention makes it easier to build pipes, clearing the way for Turkmenistan (with the world's fourth-largest gas reserves) to export gas to Europe via Azerbaijan.

The Convention pays special attention to the ecology of the Caspian Sea and the security, whereby none of the signatory countries may allow a third party to operate a military base in the region (in reaction to Kazakhstan's openness to allow a US military base in Aktau).

Iran to become the central point of the International North–South Transport Corridor (INSTC), the north–south trade route from Russia to India which is expected to cover 7,200km. Despite challenges to the agricultural sector and the heavy floods that in 2019 killed 20 people, injured 94 and destroyed huge areas of agricultural lands in the north of the country, Iran plays a key role in a number of areas. The country produces 90% of the world's **saffron**, the most expensive spice on earth (US$2,600/1kg in 2019), and most of it is exported. Harvested manually by removing the three red stigmas from the saffron crocus flower, 170,000 flowers are needed to produce one pound of saffron. Iran's earnings are, however, relatively low, as the exported goods have to be rebranded to be sold on the free market. In 2018 saffron export increased by 40% compared to 2017. Iran is also the world's fourth-largest producer of **figs**, supplies 98% of the world's **barberries** and exports more than 90% of its **pistachios**. Iran also supplies more than half of the **steel** in the Middle East and according to the World Steel Association (WSA) it is the world's tenth-largest steel producer. Zob-e Ahan, located approximately 40km southwest of Esfahan, is the main steel factory in Iran.

There have also been a number of renewable energy projects, such as solar energy plants in Tabriz and Hamadan as well as Tarom Wind in Qazvin province which have been completed in the past few years to improve Iran's self-sustainability.

PEOPLE

Caught in a Tehran traffic jam, your thoughts inevitably turn to Iran's population. In 1979, the year of the revolution, the population of Iran stood at 35 million. The 1992 census determined that it totalled just under 60 million, with a density of 35 people per square kilometre. Official statistics for 2016 suggested the population was 79.9 million people, up from slightly over 75 million in 2011. Approximately 40% of the population are between 15 and 34 years of age. Currently, over 75% live in the major cities: Tehran, the capital, with more than 12 million residents, Mashhad (over 2 million), Esfahan, Shiraz and Ahvaz (over 1.5 million each), Tabriz and

Hamadan perhaps slightly less, with more people each year moving from rural areas to find work. During Rafsanjani's presidency (1989–97), 400,000 jobs were created in one year; now 800,000 new jobs are needed each year just to keep pace with the growing population. Iran has also experienced something known as the 'Japanese curse': despite semi-apocalyptic predictions of the country's population hitting 110 or 120 million by 2015, Iran has in fact experienced one of the most dramatic declines in birth rate ever recorded. Whereas in the 1970s a typical rural family had five children, now that Iranians are mostly urbanised there are rarely more than two children per family. This is undoubtedly a product of improved education for women and increased access to state-run birth-control programmes. These are now being slashed, and in July 2012 the government announced financial incentives for women to have more babies, with Khamenei publicly endorsing the changes. Whether they will have the desired effect remains to be seen; economics is perhaps of greater importance. Ask any Iranian why they would not consider having more children, and the answer will be 'it is too expensive'.

Much has been made of Iran's **nomads**. Apart from anthropological studies, most publications could be classed as romantic fiction, extolling the 'freedom' of seasonal wanderings (which are actually finely orchestrated migrations). For decades official concern over epidemics, child education, drug and arms smuggling, national security and taxation led to village-settlement programmes, while the 1960s' White Revolution caused serious problems of overgrazing and water rights for the nomads. It has meant that from making up 25% of the population in 1900, nomad-pastoralist numbers fell to 6% in the 1970s. However, if you happen to be travelling in the Shiraz region during late April or mid/late October, you are still very likely to see one or more extended Qashqai family groups, perhaps numbering as many as 75, accompanied by hundreds of sheep and goats, moving to fresh pastures. Traditional tents are now often fitted with televisions and the traditional horse and donkey replaced by utility vehicle or 4×4, but nomadic people are still very much a part of modern Iran's landscape, even if their political and economic influence has waned even further since Freya Stark and Robert Byron penned their elegies during the 1930s.

LANGUAGE

Only about 50% of Iranians speak Farsi (Persian) – the official language of Iran – as their mother tongue, though nearly everyone can understand and read it. In the south and southwest, Arabic is spoken, while Azeri (the Turkic language of Azerbaijan) along with Gilaki and Taleshi are common in the north and northwest. Around 16 million Iranians are ethnically Azeri and have family connections in Azerbaijan. Armenian is present in the Caucasian foothills and in Esfahan; a small ethnic Georgian community outside Esfahan still uses a form of Georgian spoken in the Caucasus over 500 years ago. Kurdish, including Sorani and Kurmanji dialects, is spoken in the western Zagros and Khorasan. Bakhtiari and Baluchi dialects are used in the southeast. There are further numerous and less-frequently spoken dialects, for instance Zargari in Qazvin province. The recent influx of Afghan refugees has seen an increase in Pashto and Dari. In the 1930s Reza Shah Pahlavi tried to 'purify' Farsi of Turkish and Arabic words along the lines of the Académie Française, but the Islamic Revolution has led to an increased emphasis on Arabic, the language of the Quran.

In addition to the various ethnic groups originally from Iran, a little more than 2% of the total population are foreign nationals. Afghanis make up more than half of the total number of foreigners living in Iran, while Iraqis come second.

Farsi is an Indo-Aryan language so there are some similarities in words (eg: *madar* for mother) and grammar with certain European languages. Arabic has had the major impact on the modern Persian vocabulary, but a number of French words have also found their way into Farsi. After the Arab Muslim conquests of the 7th century, the Pahlavi script, which was based on Aramaic script, for Farsi was abandoned and the one now used is based on Arabic (reading from right to left), with additional letter forms for specific Farsi consonants, such as *p*, *g* and *ch*, so the alphabet consists of 32 letters. Words are not capitalised and each letter has three written shapes, depending on its location within the word, just as certain European handwritten lower and upper letters (eg: *o, e*) have when joined to other letters. Unfortunately, there is no one accepted transliteration system to render Farsi into the Roman (eg: English) alphabet, so the city of Esfahan may be shown as Espahan, Isfahan, Ispahan, etc, and Qom as Qomm, Qom or even Ghom (the exact pronunciation of 'q' in Persian is 'gh', except for the Quran). Major road signs are usually given both in Farsi and in the Roman alphabet; distances are also shown in both numeric forms, both reading left to right. In this book, the most common or simplest rendering is given, for example Quran rather than Qur'an or Koran, but at times the transliteration found in publications or on maps will also be included. Following usual transliteration convention, the glottal stop in Farsi is indicated by the symbol ' (eg: as in Shi'a). This so-called glottal stop reflects the position of the letter 'eyn', which in Persian, unlike Arabic, is pronounced as an ordinary vowel. 'Hamzeh', a letter in the Arabic alphabet, in Persian represents merely a sound and does not have any exact phonetic reference. Generally speaking Persian 'hamzeh' has the same value as Arabic 'eyn' and can both indicate a glottal stop or is not pronounced at all. It is most common in words of Arabic origin.

Apart from Arabic (for Quranic studies), the other foreign language taught in schools is English, but some older city dwellers may know French or German.

LINGUISTIC POINTERS

These few linguistic points might help make your journey around Iran easier – *bandar* means 'port', so any city name that starts with 'bandar' (eg: Bandar Anzali) refers to its seaside location; *maydan* means 'square' (eg: Maydan-e Imam); *shahid* stands for 'martyr' (referring to fighters who died in the Iran–Iraq War); *rud* means 'river' and any city name that starts with 'rud' (eg: Rudbar) should in theory be located by a river; *gonbad* means 'dome', but is essentially used to designate dome-shaped towers (eg: Gonbad-e Qabus); *abad* stands for 'residence' or 'abode' (eg: Najafabad). *Tang* means 'gorge' and is often used in place names with rock reliefs. *Robat* (eg: Robat-e Sefid), which frequently appears in town names, means the same as caravanserai, which suggests that the location in question had once had a caravanserai on the Silk Road.

And, most importantly, 'q' in Persian is pronounced as 'gh', which explains occasional double signage (eg: Qom/Ghom).

Another linguistic curiosity has taken root. Arabs do not have the 'p' and 'v' sounds in their language, but have started giving new sounds to Persian names, such as Gonbad-e Qabus (from Qavus) or Fars (from Pars), etc. This partially explains the myriad alternative spellings of Persian words.

For names, the spelling of Mohammed is most common in Arab countries, while Mohammad, which is used in this guide, is most frequent in Iran.

Travelling independently around Iran (with the exception of Tehran) without a modicum of Farsi is an adventure, but made easy thanks to the good nature of Iranians, especially younger people eager to practise English – often the result of expensive private language lessons – which means that in the larger urban centres someone nearby will be able to converse with you. However, apart from major sites and museums, road signs and the occasional tourist menu, *very* little information is given in any language other than Farsi. (See also page 31.)

RELIGION

The state religion of Iran is the Shi'a Ithna 'Ashari branch of Islam (Twelver Shi'a), whose members constitute approximately 90% of the more than 98% of Muslims in the country; Sunnis account for only 8% of this total. The remaining 2% of the population consists of non-Muslims, but estimates of numbers vary. Only three small minority religious groups are protected and accorded seats in the parliament: Jews, Christians and Zoroastrians. Article 12 of the constitution recognises and protects the rights of all religious minorities in Iran (Zoroastrian, Christian and Jews) with the exception of the Bahais. There are also other smaller religious denominations, such as Manichaeans, but their numbers are so small that they barely constitute communities.

ISLAM According to Muslim belief, Allah, the one uncreated God, has revealed the message of salvation three times. The first time, believers mistakenly assumed the revelation was meant only for them, the chosen people (eg: the Jewish community), so it was revealed again through the Prophet Isa (Jesus), but his followers (Christians) erred in believing that Isa was the son of the creator God – an impossibility given that there is but one God. So it was revealed a third and final time as the Quran, through the Prophet Mohammad (d632CE), the last of God's prophets ('the seal'). Thus there are references in the Quran to several biblical episodes, as well as shared beliefs, such as the Day of Judgement, the concept of paradise and hell, free will, the continuing battle between good and evil, and the messianic promise.

There are two main branches of Islam, Sunnism and Shi'ism, the latter being further subdivided. The Shi'a (from Shi'at Ali or Party of Ali) do not recognise the three caliphs (from *khalifa*, meaning 'deputy') who assumed control in 632–656 after Mohammad's death, believing that the Prophet had transferred all spiritual and temporal authority to his cousin and son-in-law, Ali, and his descendants through his wife Fatima, Mohammad's daughter. For the Shi'a the prophetic tradition has continued through divinely guided, sacred and infallible leaders (imams) who hold the key to the hidden meaning of the Quran – continued, that is, according to one section of the Shi'a community, until the seventh generation when Imam Ismail went into concealment; in time he will reappear to prepare the community for the Day of Judgement. His followers are known as the Ismailis (or Sevener Shi'a), whose temporal leader today is the Agha Khan. But other Shi'a (later known as the Ithna 'Ashari, which means literally 'Twelvers') believe that another descendant was chosen as the seventh imam and that this line continued for another five generations before the (12th) imam disappeared (or was 'occluded' in theological parlance) in 940, to reappear in due time as the 'Mahdi' (the Guided One; the Hidden Imam, Lord of Time, etc). This branch of Shi'ism is also known as Imamiyya and has since the 16th century been predominant in Iran. Shi'a Islam had nonetheless remained largely unknown until the establishment of the Safavid dynasty in 1501 and 1502 when it became the official religion of Iran. Shi'ism had been perceived as an undesired sect in Islam. Unlike Sunni, in Shi'a there are only three mandatory prayer times – morning, midday and evening. In the 1980s some Iranians wondered if Ayatollah Khomeini was indeed the reappeared 12th imam; the overthrow of the Pahlavi regime and founding of the Islamic state seemed nothing short of miraculous.

The Sunnis, in contrast, believe that the prophetic mission ended with Mohammad's death and so reject the idea that Ali and his family were divinely guided. Accordingly, they accept the validity of the first three caliphs and other rulers who followed, holding that they are acting in accordance with the *sunna* (example) of the Prophet.

At the outset, the unique and sole source of law, faith and tradition in Islam was the Quran, supplemented later by the Hadith (sayings of the Prophet Mohammad concerning his daily practices). Shi'a Muslims have later added to it traditions of the Imams, and Iranians, impressed by Shi'ism, have further infused it with their own interpretations and beliefs. Shi'a Islam, however, became Iran's majority sect and state religion only in the 16th century.

ZOROASTRIANISM This faith is often described as the earliest formulated religious philosophy in the world to have survived to the present day. Recent linguistic analysis of the Zoroastrian scriptures, collectively known as Avesta, and Gatha hymns, composed by Zarathustra and preserved by his community, indicates that the message preached by Zarathustra (or Zoroaster as he was known to the ancient Greeks), was promulgated in the Irano-central Asian region in c1400BCE, if not earlier. While it is impossible to establish his life timeframe with certainty, it is suggested that Zarathustra had lived between 1700 and 1500BCE. The three wise Magi were in fact Zoroastrian priests, the main religion at the time of Jesus in the Parthian Empire. The ancient origins of the faith go back to the ancestors of the modern-day Iranians and Indians, who then inhabited steppes east of the Volga River and were devout pastoralists. Water would give life to the steppe and fire warmth in cold nights and winters and enable cooking of meat. Fire was indeed so sacred that following death, bodies were laid on a barren place to be devoured by scavengers, as opposed to burning them. In other words, fire could not be used for polluting matter. Bones would then be collected and buried.

The message of Zarathustra, both priest and prophet, pre-dated Judaism, Christianity and Islam, and is centred on the uncreated God, Ahura Mazda, creator of all things, as well as concepts of paradise and hell, on a messianic promise, the struggle between good and evil in which good would ultimately triumph, and, most revolutionary of all in the ancient world, free will for all mankind. In addition to Ahura Mazda ('Lord Wisdom' in Avestan) Zoroastrians believe in two other principal gods: (Ahura) Varuna, the god of the oath and the lord of the waters; and (Ahura) Mithra, the God of the Covenant and the Lord of Fire (see box, page 232), which personified Truth and Loyalty respectively. The gods were ethical by nature. Zoroastrians believed the world was created in seven stages, thus the special significance of the number seven in Iranian culture. The Zoroastrian moral code is based on three tenets: good thoughts, good words and good deeds. It is a faith with strong emphasis on justice as whether you go to paradise or hell after life is determined on your deeds throughout life. Zarathustra was the first to talk about the concepts of heaven and hell, resurrection, last judgement and the unity of the body and soul. According to his doctrine, each individual is responsible for the fate of his soul, judged on the sum of his thoughts, words and deeds.

The Achaemenids were the first imperial rulers of Iran to establish Zoroastrianism as a regally patronised cult, if not a formal state religion (page 33), and it remained dominant following reorganisation under the Sasanid dynasty until the spread of Islam in the mid 7th century CE. The status of the Zoroastrian community in Islamic law was not as clearly defined as it was for Jews and Christians, and in the 9th and again in the late 17th/early 18th centuries official state persecution caused many Zoroastrian families to flee to northern India, where they became known as the Parsi.

In 19th-century Qajar Iran, thanks to British and Indian involvement, Zoroastrians enjoyed greater freedom and openly endorsed the monarchy. In 1979 the community suddenly announced its support for the Islamic Revolution. Today there are just over 25,000 Zoroastrians living in Iran, with constitutionally enshrined parliamentary representation, and the community is concentrated in Tehran and Yazd. The difficulty is that Zoroastrians do not accept converts, which makes it difficult for their numbers to increase. There are nonetheless thriving Iranian Zoroastrian populations in England, the USA, Canada and Australia as well as India (particularly Mumbai), where there are approximately 69,000 followers.

JUDAISM Jewish presence in Iran dates back to the Assyrian exile in 722BCE. The religious tolerance shown by Cyrus the Great, the Achaemenid ruler (d529BCE), to the Jewish people is remembered on two counts: first, after conquering Babylon he permitted the Jews to return to Jerusalem from Mesopotamian exile; and second, he actively assisted and paid for the rebuilding of the temple there. All this earned him the right to be the only non-Jew mentioned in the Old Testament.

There were at least two Jewish consorts of Iranian kings. The first of these is the biblical Esther, wife of Ahasuerus, as the name is given in the Book of Esther. Esther may be equated with Xerxes I, and her story is depicted in the 3rd-century CE synagogue murals from Dura Europos in the National Museum in Damascus. She is said to be buried in Hamadan. Alternatively, the tomb found there could be that of the second Jewish consort, of the Sasanid shah Yazdegerd I (d420CE). Later Sasanid rule saw persecution of both Jews and Christians, but generally speaking the Jewish community was protected in early Islam because of its Quranic legal status of the People of the Book and international trading connections. Conversions during this time were mainly voluntary in order to avoid paying taxes.

Life became much harder later, especially after the Safavid declaration of Iran as a Shi'a state and forced conversions, especially under the rule of Shah Abbas I (1571–1629) followed. There was some respite under the Qajar dynasty; but not prolonged. Pogroms, especially in Mashhad in 1839, led the community to ask for British protection and many fled to Herat (Afghanistan), only to be forcibly repatriated in 1856. When opportunities arose, many travelled northwards into central Asia and west into Ottoman lands.

Iranian Jews (referred to as *kalimi*) were never forced to leave Iran after the creation of Israel in 1948. Many of them saw their identity as inseparable to that of Iran and have preferred to stay despite active Zionist repatriation propaganda. In 1969 Israel officially stopped trying to bring Iranian Jews to the Promised Land. In 1951 the Mossadeq government cut diplomatic ties with Israel and closed the Iranian consulate in Jerusalem. In the decade before the Iranian Revolution about 80% of Jewish Iranians were members of the affluent middle class and of those who left after 1979, only 30% moved to Israel, while the remainder emigrated to California and still fewer to Europe.

At the start of the 20th century there were approximately 100,000 Jews in Iran and in 1979 there were 20 Jewish schools operating across the country, but the current figures suggest that there are no more than 25,000 Jews left, mainly in Tehran and Esfahan, and the numbers are decreasing. In Hamadan, for example, at present there are only five Jewish families left, numbering 15 people. The BBC has reported ten Jewish families present in Yazd, most of whom are related. In Shiraz and Esfahan, however, Jewish communities are more numerous and openly practising, although *kippahs* are only worn indoors. It is assumed by the conservative faction within the Iranian government that many have strong Zionist sympathies, and there have been arrests under suspicion or charges of espionage. In the last few years foreign visitors have been occasionally advised by their own governments not to visit Jewish sites, cemeteries or synagogues, but you are unlikely to encounter any problems from the local people. The only difficulty might be in locating the synagogues (*kanisa*), gaining access to some sites and finding the man with the key (eg: the Jewish cemetery in Pirbakram outside Esfahan). There is a strong distinction between how Jews and Israelis are viewed in Iran and many Iranians would generally be eager to inform you that whatever the official policy to Israel may be, it should not reflect upon the extraordinary hospitality you will experience from ordinary Iranians.

CHRISTIANITY A certain John of Persis attended the 325CE Council of Nicaea when numerous Christian communities in Mesopotamia, the Caucasus and elsewhere were under Sasanid authority. The reign of Shapur II (d397CE) brought severe persecution during which perhaps 35,000 Christians were killed, but in 424 the Iranian Church was still recognised as largely independent. The official break from Byzantium and the Orthodox Church came in 431, when Patriarch Nestor, a Persian by birth, was accused of denying the concept of Christ born Incarnate, thereby rejecting the title of Theotokos ('Mother of God') for Mary. His followers, later known as Nestorian Christians (now the Assyrian Church), fled for safety into Sasanid lands, only to find that unrest in the Caucasus had provoked Shah Yazdegerd II (439–57) to order the forced conversion of Armenian Christians (the Gregorian Church) to Zoroastrianism. Despite such persecution few Christians assisted the Byzantine war effort against the Sasanid regime because Byzantium rejected the theological validity of the Eastern Churches, forbidding their rituals and liturgies. When Muslim Arabs entered Iran in the late 7th century and offered religious freedom and lower taxes, they were welcomed and indeed those promises were kept for many years. However, later waves of persecution, particularly under Timurid rule, dramatically reduced the Christian community. Matters improved again under the Safavid regime (1502–1735) as the shahs were mindful of both European trade and Armenian Christian and Jewish expertise in silk trading, along with their international mercantile links. A Capuchin Monastery was established in Esfahan in the mid 17th century.

The great influence wielded by the French, British and Russian ambassadors at the 19th-century Qajar court also ensured a measure of protection for the Christians of Iran, and in 1898 a large number of Nestorians in the Orumiyeh region were received into the Russian Orthodox Church. Between 1925 and 1950 the Christian, in particular Armenian community, enjoyed a period of stability and growth. Before the Islamic Revolution there were approximately 30,000 Assyrians and Chaldeans, but these numbers have since halved. Chaldean, whose patriarchal seat is in Baghdad, mainly live in Ahvaz in Khuzestan province. The Anglican Church was formally declared dysfunctional in 1981.

Today there are around 117,000 Christians in Iran, mainly of the Armenian Church, recognising the Yerevan Patriarch and generally living in Tehran, Esfahan and Shiraz. As a legacy of 19th-century foreign missionary work, there are Presbyterian, Anglican, Lutheran and Catholic congregations, especially in the capital. Immediately following the Islamic Revolution, the then Iranian Anglican bishop and his wife (but not their son) survived assassination, and Anglican schools and hospitals were closed. Later the Persian Bible Society in Tehran also closed and all its files confiscated. Other than in Esfahan and eastern Azerbaijan (with the exception of Orumiyeh) – where churches are usually open to visitors – and Tehran, it can sometimes be difficult to get access to churches without prior arrangement.

BAHAISM Iran will always be connected with the Bahai movement, which is estimated to have 6 million followers worldwide, but for many the term 'persecution' is too gentle a word to describe the situation in Iran. Before the revolution there were approximately 150,000–300,000 Bahais living in Iran. At present, there are officially no longer any Bahais residing in the Islamic Republic, although many do live there in secret, operating a clandestine system of worship and education – famously, the Bahais run an online university (Bahai Institute for Higher Education), with lectures either recorded or provided live by sympathetic scholars worldwide. The Bahai faith affirms the ultimate unity of all the great religious leaders (Zoroaster, Jesus, Mohammad, the Judaic prophets, Siddhartha Gautama (the Buddha) and Krishna) as historic manifestations of The Word, saying 'the earth is but one country and humanity its citizens'.

The story of this reformist and revivalist Islamic movement, which was part of the Twelve Shi'a Islam tradition, known as Babaism until the 1860s, begins in the 1840s when a charismatic theologian, Seyyed Ali Mohammad Shirazi, won over many followers by his piety, saying that he was the intermediary or the gate (*bab*, a traditional term for a person acting on behalf of an imam) opening the way for the imminent return of the Hidden (12th) imam. His later proclamation in 1848 that he himself was the imam led to his imprisonment and execution in Tabriz in 1850, after some 3,000 of his followers were killed. Further persecution followed after a Bahai assassination attempt on Nasir al-Din Shah failed, and many Bahais fled to Iraq and Syria and onward to South America, Turkey and Europe. One of the most prominent leaders of the movement was Mirza Hossein Ali Nuri (1817–92), known as Bahaullah, meaning 'the glory of God'. A follower of the Bab, whom he had not met, he was exiled to Baghdad, where he gathered extensive support following the split from his half-brother Mirza Yahya (Subh-e Azal) and appointed by the Bab himself as the leader of the movement. Bahaullah left in 1863 for Constantinople and eventually settled in 1868 in Acre in Palestine. Bahaullah pronounced the split with the original faith known as Babism and renamed it Bahaism, after himself.

His followers have since become known as Bahais, while those who remained loyal to his brother were known as Azali. Bahaullah died in 1892 in the place called Bahji (Palestine), which has since been considered the *qibla* for the followers of the faith.

Bahais believe that the divine revelation did not end with Mohammad, but with the Bab, and their religious aspiration is the establishment of the unity of the world, and that Bahaullah was the divine manifestation to help humanity achieve this. The books that Bahaullah left behind constitute the divine revelation literature of the adherents to this belief.

Following the death of Abd Al-Baha, Bahaullah's eldest son, the absolute authority on the interpretation of his father's books, the centre of the faith has moved to Haifa. The funeral was attended by important dignitaries, including the British High Commissioner. After Abd Al-Baha's death the authority was passed on to Shoghi Effendi and finally to the Universal House of Justice, which is the headquarters of Bahaism established in 1963 in Haifa, present-day Israel. To many Muslims, especially to the leaders of the Islamic Revolution, this smacked of strong Zionist involvement, which they used as an excuse to persecute Bahais back home.

Following the 1979 revolution, thousands of Bahais were rounded up, arrested and executed, the Bab's house in Shiraz was destroyed, Bahai cemeteries were desecrated, and all endowments, properties and personal records were confiscated. At present the largest Bahai community resides in India, in particular in New Delhi.

EDUCATION

Schooling for both boys and girls is compulsory from the age of seven years to 15, but only in nursery schools are both sexes taught in the same class. Mixed schools also exist in smaller villages, where pupil numbers do not justify segregation in the classroom. In larger cities there are also mixed summer learning centres, but these are privately run. Literacy rates, so woefully low in the 1970s, have dramatically improved and a much greater part of the curriculum is now given over to Arabic/Quranic studies, with a few hours per week assigned to English teaching in most secondary schools. With a high youth population and few job opportunities there is a tremendous demand for university education, although many places remain reserved for children of Iran–Iraqi veterans ('Families of the Martyrs'), whatever their pass marks in the national examinations; the leaving certificate examination in Iran is known as *konkur*. Introduced in 1982, it is highly competitive. The number of both state-run and private universities has mushroomed. The private Islamic Azad University was established in 1983 and has campuses in the areas where previously no university education was available.

Attempts to introduce segregated instruction at this level during the 1980s were not successful, but students sit according to gender. Many of the protestors demonstrating against the stealing of the 'Green Election' in 2009 were university students of both genders. A considerable number of Iranians believe that recent government efforts to curtail the number of women enrolling in higher education are an attempt to punish 'upstart girls', many of them from traditionally pious and conservative families, who were especially outraged by the hypocrisy shown by the government.

Iran leads the world in the field of theological studies at university level along with Saudi Arabia, with student numbers increasing over 500% since the 1970s. The main centres are Qom and Mashhad, where the basic seven-year course (eg: secondary level) includes Arabic grammar, rhetoric and literature, plus studies of the Quran, the Hadith (sayings of the Prophet Mohammad) and Islamic law. Students can then follow another eight years' study and qualify as a *mujtahid* (interpreter of theological law). The teaching method is by convention, instruction and rhetoric, rather than being discursive, hypothetical and analytical.

ARTS AND CULTURE

If there is something that Iranians have over the centuries remained true to, it is their deep-rooted refined culture and the idea of longing for past glory, arts and poetry. The country's rich artistic tradition, going back centuries, takes on various forms, both in music and theatre. **Naqqali** (نقالی) dramatic storytelling, known as the forefather of traditional Iranian theatre, involves a traditional story being narrated by a *naqqal*, who can be either a woman or a man, simultaneously acting all the story's characters out in front of the public. Performances are usually accompanied by traditional music. After the publication of the Ferdowsi's *Shahnameh*, this masterpiece has become the most popular theme in *naqqali* performances. A specific form of *naqqali* is known as *pardehkhani* (reading a screen). Originating in Safavid Iran, it entails explaining and describing to the audience what is portrayed on the screen.

Opera and **theatre,** as these are known in the West, were introduced to Iran after World War II. Roudaki Hall (currently known as Vahdat Hall) (page 101) inaugurated in Tehran on 25 October 1967 and modelled on the Vienna Opera, became the pride and joy of the last shah. It had an extensive repertoire of Iranian traditional performances as well as classic ballet and opera. Rudolf Nureyev, British ballerina Margot Fonteyn and Iranian prima ballerina Haydeh Changizian danced on its main stage. Women with a headscarf and men without a tie were not allowed in. Closed after the revolution, it reopened in the 1990s, but under the name of Vahdat Hall, and offers a rich programme of events.

The **Iranian National Ballet Company**, in existence between 1958 and 1979, was based in the Roudaki Hall. Les Ballets Persans was established abroad in 2002 by Nima Kiann as a continuation of the disbanded ballet company and currently performs in collaboration with various international theatre companies outside Iran, working closely with the National Ballet of Kyrgyzstan.

As for classic Iranian **music**, Mohammad-Reza Shajarian stands as the grandest and most outstanding singer, probably of all time; his son Homayoun successfully follows in his father's footsteps. Iranian national and ethnic musical instruments are too many to name and a visit to the **Tehran Music Museum** (page 107) is highly recommended.

Since the arrival of Islam, **calligraphy** has become one of most recognisable and distinctive art forms in Iran. It is not just the message of the Quran, not only the book, but the writing itself that has acquired a divine meaning. According to the Prophet's sayings, a calligrapher who succeeds in beautifully writing down God's words (the Quran) will be a dweller of Paradise. On the basis of the *Kufic* original Arabic font, Iranian masters in the 14th century devised an Iranian font called *Nastaliq* and subsequently *Nastaliq shekasteh* used for most of the calligraphy works today. As a souvenir, consider bringing home an Iranian miniature painting bearing a line or two of classic poetry written in fine *Nastaliq*.

According to one of Iran's greatest literary sons, Mohammad Ali Jamalzadeh, Iran in the 20th century lagged behind other countries in terms of literary works. This has not, however, quenched Iranians' love of **poetry**. Mentioning Hafez (page 248) is a great conversation icebreaker in Iran. Be prepared to hear your driver recite a few verses and even talk about the meaning between the lines. Some have even suggested that Iranian culture is as hard to comprehend as it is to find the true meaning of any Persian poetry. This has a lot to do with the language itself. While Arabic predominates over Persian in religious matters, day-to-day interactions are clearly inspired by Persian, which is a softly spoken language, stressing the importance of humility in speech. You are unlikely, for example, to hear people shout or speak loudly in Persian. Along the lines of French *vous*, Persian places a strong emphasis on the use of formal vocabulary and, unless the person you are talking to is a child, you must always use the polite *shoma* form. Otherwise, you risk causing offence.

2

Practical Information

WHEN TO VISIT

Visits to the south coast of Iran (eg: Bandar Abbas) are best made in the winter months of December, January and February when humidity and heat levels are at their lowest, while spring (March to mid-May) and autumn (mid-September and October) are the best times to travel around central and northern Iran. The summer months of June through to early September are best avoided as the temperature can be in the high 40s (°C), although it is a dry heat except on the south coast. It is also advisable to avoid visiting northeastern Sistan and Baluchestan province (Zabol and Zahedan) in the summer, as it is the windy season. That said, while winter outdoor temperatures are cool, indoor temperatures (including on trains and buses) tend to be hot as Iranians prefer the warm comfort of blasting heat. So, carrying around a light long-sleeved shirt is a good idea.

Take the numerous public holidays (page 70) into account if your visit is connected with business and/or your time is limited. Try to avoid Ramadan, the first ten days of Moharram (the sacred month) and the first week of the Nou Rouz celebrations, when staffing in offices and government departments will be minimal and all forms of long-distance transport and hotels will be extremely busy and expensive. However, during Nou Rouz and throughout the high-season summer months, most historical sites and buildings have extended opening hours (until 20.00 or 23.00 for gardens).

HIGHLIGHTS

- Masouleh, Qaleh Rudkhan and the mountains of Gilan province, overnighting in a cosy ecolodge amid orange groves and tea plantations (page 195)
- Shopping in Esfahan Bazaar (page 180)
- The mountain path to Babak Castle (page 218)
- Nomadic migration (*kuch*) across the glorious Zagros Mountains with Bakhtiari nomads (see box, page 191)
- Tehran's Milad Tower for exhilarating views and an evening meal in one of Tehran's best restaurants (page 103)
- Iranian Kurdistan with its spectacular mountain villages and serpentine roads (page 145)
- Spring flower blossom in Shirazi gardens (page 249)
- The Gate of All Nations in ancient Persepolis (page 266)
- The architecture of Kashan's old merchant houses (page 157)
- Experiencing sunset at one of the Zoroastrian 'towers of silence' in Yazd (page 317)

SUGGESTED ITINERARIES

The following itineraries presuppose all arrangements have been made in advance, or that a taxi or car will be used. If local bus transport is used, extra time will be needed to organise tickets, and journey times will be longer.

EIGHT TO TEN DAYS Two days' sightseeing and savouring Persian cuisine in Tehran; flight to Esfahan for at least three full days' city sightseeing; drive to Yazd for one night and a day of sightseeing; then to Shiraz for three nights (if coming by car, a stop in Abarkuh is suggested), including a full day in and around Persepolis, and another day in Bishapur or Firuzabad; flight home from Shiraz.

TEN TO 15 DAYS
Option 1 As above, with the addition of two more nights in Yazd to explore nearby mud villages and two nights in Kerman (or one in Kerman, the other exploring Mahan and surrounds), and, if possible, overnighting in Kashan as the first destination after leaving Tehran and heading south.

Option 2 Before visiting Esfahan and Shiraz, travel to Ardabil from Tehran, stopping for a few hours in Rasht and overnighting in one of the ecolodges at the mountain foothills (or conversely fly from Tehran to Tabriz); one night in Tabriz for city sightseeing and a day trip to Maku (Black Church) and Jolfa; travel south to stay in the Kurdish village of Dowlab outside Sanandaj; then to Qazvin for overnight or to Tehran for Esfahan; then Shiraz.

The shrines of Qom, south of Tehran, and of Mashhad in the northeast will be important visits for any Muslim and will certainly give a wealth of information to any other curious traveller. There are also splendid historic buildings in the vicinity of Mashhad, but these are not located in 'clusters' as in Esfahan and Shiraz. Iranians enjoy visiting the coast and forests of the southern Caspian shores and wonderful beaches of the Persian Gulf (especially Kish and Qeshm islands).

TOURIST INFORMATION

Theoretically, but not always in practice, every major city in Iran has a tourist information office. Your hotel or any of the local guides mentioned in this book will happily provide you with any information you are looking for. Official road and city maps are available from well-stocked street kiosks, at airports, hotel bookshops or any bookstore. In different cities you can purchase local maps that identify the approximate locations of petrol stations and tourist inns as well as incorporating new roads. However, the best Iranian-made maps are produced by **Gita Shenasi** (w gitashenasi.com), widely distributed in Iran, and from **Stanfords** (w stanfords. co.uk), where other maps more reliably written in English and Farsi with distances and highway numbers are also available.

The British **Foreign and Commonwealth Office** (FCO) issues travel advice (w gov. uk/foreign-travel-advice/iran). Here you will find the latest general and specific area advice as well as information about consular assistance to British citizens in Iran.

TOUR OPERATORS

If telephoning from outside Iran, omit the first 0 from the regional code or mobile number. There are no 'official' published telephone directories for Iran, not even for Tehran, and no equivalent of *Yellow Pages*. Tour operators in Iran can arrange for trips and site visits, but do not always have the most accurate long-distance bus/train timetables. Bus/train tickets are best purchased at bus terminals or sales offices in the cities.

GENERAL
UK
Magic Carpet Travel 11 The Poplars, Ascot, Berks SL5 9HZ; +44 (0)1344 622832; w magic-carpet-travel.com. Escorted group tours & tailor-made itineraries. They also deal with the visa procedure for independent travellers for about £120.

Oasis Overland Blandford Rd, Coombe Bissett, Salisbury SP5 4LN; +44 (0)1963 363400; w oasisoverland.co.uk; see ad, page 88. Adventurous overland journeys through central Asia.

Persian Voyages 71–5 Shelton St, Covent Garden, London WC2H 9HQ; 07803 098650; w persianvoyages.com; see ad, page 88. Offers a number of itineraries or tailor-made solutions; also assists with visa procurement.

Regent Holidays 6th Floor, Colston Tower, Colston St, Bristol BS1 4XE; +44 (0)20 3588 2971; w regentholidays.co.uk; see ad, inside front cover. A well-established tour operator which includes Iran among its worldwide holiday destinations.

Wild Frontiers Adventure Travel 78 Glentham Rd, London SW13 9JJ; +44 (0)20 8741 7390; w wildfrontierstravel.com. Founded in 2002, offers a wide range of both group & tailor-made private tours across Iran & the Middle East.

Australia
Adventure Associates PO Box 246, Blackheath NSW 2785; +61 (0)2 6355 2022; w adventureassociates.com. Accompanied small-group tours to destinations around the world, inc to Iran.

Iran
Dream Persia Unit 21, 2nd Floor, Mehr Bldg, Atlasi Sq, Yazd; +98 (0)35 38271888; m +98 (0)935 9357123; w dreampersia.com; see ad, 3rd colour section. A new tour operator specialising in cultural tours offering visitors to Iran an opportunity to experience finer aspects of local culture & traditions.

Gapa Tour [99 G4] 8 Motahhari St, Tehran; m +98 (0)912 5850450; w gapatour.com; see ad, page 88. A local tour operator since 2002, offering a variety of tour packages, inc those themed on religion & women-only groups.

Iran Persia Tour Masjed-e Jame St, Yazd; +98 (0)35 36227828; m +98 (0)913 3514460; w iranpersiatour.com; see ad, inside back cover. Based in Yazd & run by very experienced Iranian guides, offers a variety of tours around Iran.

Iranian Tours 3 Eskan Shopping Centre, Mirdamad, Tehran; +98 (0)21 85318558; UK office: +44 (0)20 7193 6437; w iraniantours.com. With representatives both in Iran & the UK, Iranian Tours offers 6 classic tours, as well as customised options.

Nomad Tours 11 Mobara Alley, Khayyam St, Grand Bazaar, Tehran; m +98 (0)912 5220511; w nomad.tours. One of Iran's best tour operators specialising in nomad migration (*kuch*) tours to Zagros Mountains & promoting sustainable tourism. Group numbers are limited, ensuring a personal experience. Eco-friendly & adventure tours last up to 7 days & follow Iranian nomads along their spring or autumn migratory routes.

Pasargad Tours 145 Africa St, Tehran 19156; +98 (0)21 22058833; e info@pasargad-tours.com; w pasargad-tours.com. All tours are accompanied by a national guide, if required.

Pazira Travel Mollasadra Av, Beside Alley 8, 2nd Floor, Shiraz; +98 (0)71 36474204; e info@uppersia.com; w uppersia.com; see ad, 1st colour section. Trading as Uppersia, this operator offers tours to suit a variety of budgets and interests, & day tours out of 20 towns & cities throughout Iran.

Safarestan Iran 12 Bimeh Alleh, Villa St, Tehran; m +98 936 3636173; w sitotravel.com; see ad, 3rd colour section. A recommended & customer-friendly tour operator, offering a wide range of tours, inc classic Persian sites, desert & mountain hiking.

Thunder Tour & Travel 488 North Jamalzadeh, Dr Fatemi St, Tehran; +98 (0)21 66936435; w thundertour.com. With many years of experience, offers itineraries inc trekking & boating tours; can also arrange hotel/air/train/car rental reservations, as well as customise their package for individual travellers.

Trip to Persia Karim Khan Zand Bd, Shiraz; +98 (0)71 32301316; w triptopersia.com; see ad, 3rd colour section. Offers tour packages varying from 4 to 21 days, cooking & nature tours, as well as day trips out of Shiraz, Tehran, Esfahan, Yazd, Ahvaz & Kerman. Also provides visa assistance, hotel reservation & transportation across Iran.

SPECIAL INTEREST
UK
Martin Randall Travel Voysey Hse, Barley Mow Passage, London W4 4GF; ✆+44 (0)20 8742 3355; w martinrandall.com. Offers lecturer-led itineraries of the major sites.

Steppes Travel 51 Castle St, Cirencester, Glos GL7 1QD; ✆+44 (0)1285 601783; (✆US toll free) +1 855 203 7885; w steppestravel.co.uk. Offers tailor-made & expert-led group tours to Iran, inc combined tours to Iran & the Caucasus region.

USA
GeoEx 1008 General Kennedy St, PO Box 29902, San Francisco, CA, 94129-0902; ✆+1 415 922 0448; within the US +1 888 570 7108; w geoex. com. Has been running tours to Iran since 1993 & currently offers cultural 'customisable' Essential Iran, Persia & the Silk Road by Train as well as Treasures of Persia tours.

MIR Corporation Suite 210, 85 South Washington St, Seattle, WA 98104; ✆+1 800 424 7289; w mircorp.com. The USA's Russia & central Asia expert offers exceptional tours of Iran, inc multi-country trips & Silk Road tours, but also one-off art, dance & cultural tours. Iran can be combined with neighbouring republics, inc Uzbekistan. Highly recommended.

World Affairs Council of Philadelphia (Educational organisation) 1 South Broad St, Suite 2M, Philadelphia, PA 19107; ✆+1 215 561 4700; w wacphila.org. WACP organises a number of tours per year, having resumed their services to Iran in 2014.

Iran
Adventure Iran 688 Najar Kala, Imam Khomeini Bd, Lavasan, Tehran; ✆+98 (0)21 26566026; m +98 (0)938 1168502; w adventureiran.com; see ad, 3rd colour section. Specialist & highly recommended tour operator if active tourism is what you are after. Offering a wide range of tours, inc long-distance mountain & desert trekking as well as a very special cycling route from the Persian Gulf to the Caspian coast, desert safaris & skiing. They also arrange for all the necessary equipment & insurance.

Iran Mountain Zone PO Box 15875–3816, Tehran; ✆+98 (0)21 88208087, +98 (0)26 44724053; w mountainzone.ir. Runs field trips for the Mountaineering Federation in Tehran, & will organise hill walking & trekking for foreign visitors (min 4 people). The best time for the wild flowers is in spring. The office can arrange bike rental for mountain biking. Men can wear shorts for this, either knee- or mid-thigh length, but for all trips (except skiing) women must wear full-length trousers (or skirt) & long-sleeved, knee-length shirt or tunic, with the obligatory scarf. Skiing can also be organised. The office will deal with the visa paperwork for the visit, & reserve any hotel accommodation in Tehran, etc. The managing director answers email enquiries promptly & Tehran friends recommend the office.

Kassa Tours 27 Naghdi Alley, Shariati St, Tehran 15637; ✆+98 (0)21 77510463–4; e info@ kassatours.com; w kassatours.com. Organises a variety of adventure tours, inc trekking & skiing, as well as more extreme wall climbing & heli-ski. Run by a group of professional & highly experienced nature enthusiasts.

TIME DIFFERENCE

Iran time is GMT + 3 hours 30 minutes (eg: 12 noon GMT is 15.30 in Iran). Since 2007, daylight saving has been in operation from late March to late September though this may change, given the post-1979 governments' on-and-off practice of observing it. One time zone operates throughout the country. To catch BBC or other Western news, tune in on the half-hour.

RED TAPE

Almost four years after its closure following the attack on 29 November 2011, the British embassy in Tehran officially reopened in August 2015 with the Iranian embassy in London following suit the same month. Both embassies operate normally and issue visas to the UK and Iran respectively.

VISAS All nationalities except Israelis are allowed to apply for a visa. Anyone domiciled in the USA should approach the **Iranian Interests Section of the Embassy of Pakistan** (1250 23rd St NW, Suite #200, Washington, DC, 20037; ☏ +1 202 965 4990; w daftar.org) or the nearest Pakistani consulate or the **Iranian Mission at the United Nations** (622 3rd Av, 34th Floor, New York, NY 10017; ☏ +1 212 687 2020; e iran@un.int). Those resident elsewhere, including US passport holders, should contact the Iranian embassy or consulate in their country of residence for information regarding their embassy's opening times, methods of payment and exact visa application details. Although the procedure for British and US passport holders is complex (for instance, US citizens are not allowed to travel independently and must come to Iran as part of a group or a pre-arranged tour), other nationalities, including those from Germany, the Netherlands, Scandinavia and Italy, have fewer problems in this respect. Women without headscarves will generally be allowed on to Iranian embassy grounds; however, it is advisable and strongly recommended that you do wear a headscarf as it makes a good impression.

If you are going on an **organised tour** you will be able to get a tourist visa by contacting a travel agent or independent tour guide in Iran directly, who will effectively issue an 'invitation' (or rather confirmation of your tour with them) into the country. You can alternatively contact your local tour operator and arrange the trip through them. Confirmation of your trip printed on official paper or a scanned copy from the agent in Iran will be sufficient for the embassy. You should then apply for a visa electronically via the Islamic Republic of Iran Ministry of Foreign Affairs website (w evisa.mfa.ir/en) and once a confirmation with an authorisation code has been issued and emailed to you, you can then bring it with your passport to the local consulate; a visa is usually issued within a few days. Payment for the travel agent's service varies, but is usually around US$30–50, and it is made to the travel agent on arrival in Iran.

Despite the legalese, **individual travellers** not in possession of any pre-booked trip should not encounter any problems applying for a tourist visa. Visa applications must first be made via the Islamic Republic of Iran Ministry of Foreign Affairs website (w evisa.mfa.ir/en) and then follow the procedure as described above. You may need to explain to the embassy staff your travel arrangements and whereabouts throughout your stay in Iran. This should normally be sufficient, unless requested otherwise. In this case you might have no other choice but to pay a fee to a travel agent to obtain a reference number/authorisation code from the Ministry of Foreign Affairs in Tehran on your behalf. You can then present the official letter with this reference number to the nearest embassy of Iran. Most tour operators quoted in this guide can help to obtain the code. US citizens are required to have such a code before applying to the Pakistani embassy for a visa. Please note that generally single travellers are more likely to arouse suspicion and reasons for questioning. It is always best to go to the embassy in person and clarify your application should any additional information be required.

Please note that visas are no longer affixed into the passport and the Ministry of Foreign Affairs e-visa confirmation page will be stamped instead on arrival to Iran. You would thus need to print it out before travelling and keep it until departure. It will be exit-stamped by the Iranian authorities and it will effectively be the only paper evidence of your visit to Iran.

Since 2016 it has also been possible to obtain a 30-day **tourist visa on arrival** in the following international airports in Iran – Esfahan, Mashhad, Shiraz, Tehran

Imam Khomeini, Tehran Mehrabad and Tabriz. Note that visa applications on arrival are not automatic and payment in euros is preferred. US, UK and Canadian passport holders are not eligible for this option and are required to apply in advance through the embassy.

A number of travellers try to avoid the red tape by applying for a visa through the Iranian embassy in Istanbul. However, do note that there is no guarantee here either. There was a case of a British traveller who had applied for a visa through the Iranian embassy in Istanbul, where she was informed the embassy had reportedly lost her documents, whereby she was forced to prolong her stay in Turkey following submission of a new visa application. On a different occasion, a Dutch tourist travelled to Istanbul where she was directed to Erzurum 1,220km away. She was then informed that the Iranian embassy in Ankara (877km of backtracking) had sole issuing authorisation in Turkey; there she was told processing would take more than four weeks after the surrender of her passport. In brief, apply through the closest embassy or consulate first!

For the actual visa application, you will need a completed visa form with two photographs, the passport (valid for six months from date of departure), letter or printout from a travel agent with a reference code and a fee. The fee varies depending on where the application is submitted and what nationality the applicant is, but in the UK the fee is £170 which should also be submitted to your nearest Iranian consulate. The embassy of Iran in London will also take the applicant's fingerprints, which is not a common practice in Iranian embassies elsewhere. Overall, while a visa may take a day to obtain for some nationalities, UK, US and Canadian citizens are advised to start the application procedure at least a couple of months before the planned trip.

For **business travellers** wishing to stay in Iran for more than 72 hours, their Iranian business contact needs to prepare an invitation letter filling in the correct forms available from the Visa and Passport Office of the Foreign Ministry of Iran, after which the visa procedure outlined above will start. Only when the reference number has been received will the embassy staff accept the visa application form, photographs and passport. It sounds horrendously complicated but it isn't (unless you hit a cluster of national and religious holidays), though a few extra grey hairs are guaranteed. With other Iranian consulates, this system is not necessarily in operation. In Holland, for example, applicants may write to the consulate requesting a visa without an 'invitation', though apparently less than 50% of such unsupported applications are successful.

For stays of less than 72 hours, the Iranian business contact still has to apply to the ministry for approval and a reference number, but the traveller then picks up the relevant 72-hour visa on arrival (not available to UK, US and Canadian passport holders) at Imam Khomeini International Airport, Tehran. Remember to take a photocopy of the relevant visa notification for the airline check-in desk, to show that your entry has been approved.

Female applicants are not required to wear a headscarf for their visa photographs when applying from abroad, but it may be a good idea to do so nonetheless. Visa validity is determined by the duration of your stay, but visas are usually valid for one month after entry. A request for a multiple-entry visa has to be submitted by the sponsor in the 'invitation', not by the applicant at the consulate, and is currently only available in the business category.

For the duration of your stay in Iran, you remain the 'invited guest' of the person, company, or institution who/which initiated the procedure. In other words, that sponsor bears total responsibility for your well-being and good behaviour and will bear the brunt of any repercussions.

For a **visa extension or amendment**, go to the local Immigration and Passport Office, in Persian *edare-ye gozarnameh va etba' hariji*) with two photographs (with headscarf for women), a copy of your passport, your actual passport and the original and copy of the electronic visa page. The fee is approximately 400,000 rials (around US$4), but varies depending on the office (for instance it is more expensive in Bandar Abbas than in Yazd) and is payable to the nearest Bank Melli branch. It usually takes three days to get the extension. However, in urgent cases and in smaller towns (for example Yazd) you should be able to get it on the same day.

There is a **visa waiver system** (also applicable to US citizens travelling from the United Arab Emirates (UAE)) in operation for Kish Island (page 297), but it is valid only for Kish Island and lasts 14 days; while there, however, visitors can apply for a normal tourist visa to the rest of Iran.

Please note that an Iranian visa in your passport may cause difficulties if you intend to travel to the US. In January 2016, as part of its anti-terrorism law, the US government introduced a new visa requirement for dual-nationals of Iran, Iraq, Syria and Sudan, or anyone who has travelled to those countries in the last five years. In these cases, visa waiver no longer applies and when travelling to the US, the applicant will have to follow new rules when applying for a visa.

As for travellers to Iran with an **Israeli stamp** in their passports, applicants may now only be issued an Iranian visa one year after their visit to Israel and Palestine.

Note: Any woman, whatever her nationality, will be refused actual entry into Iran if her dress does not conform to acceptable standards (see box, page 84). This 'suitable' dress and a headscarf must be donned before approaching the border or disembarking from a flight and retained until leaving Iran. If travelling by an IranAir international flight to Iran, women must check in wearing or showing a headscarf, which can then be removed until entering the boarding lounge; in other words, the IranAir flight is considered Iranian territory.

EMBASSIES, CONSULATES AND MISSIONS

EMBASSIES OF IRAN ABROAD

Ⓔ **Belgium** Embassy of Islamic Republic of Iran, Av de Tervueren 415, Woluwe-Saint-Pierre; ☏ +32 0272 54095; e consular@iranembassy.be

Ⓔ **France** Embassy of Islamic Republic of Iran, 4 Av d'Iena, Paris 75016; ☏ +33 1 40 69 79 00; e ambassadeur@amb-iran.fr

Ⓔ **Germany** Embassy of Islamic Republic of Iran, Podbielskiallee 67, PO Box 10439, 14195 Berlin; ☏ +49 3084 3530; e info@iranbotschaft.de. There are also consulates in Frankfurt, Hamburg & Munich.

Ⓔ **Ireland** Embassy of Islamic Republic of Iran, 72 Mount Merrion Av, Blackrock, Co Dublin; ☏ +353 1 288 0252, +353 1 288 2967, +353 1 288 5881; e iremb@indigo.ie

Ⓔ **Italy** Embassy of Islamic Republic of Iran, Via Nomentana 361, 00162 Rome; ☏ +39 06 8632 8485, +39 06 8632 8487

Ⓔ **Turkey** Embassy of Islamic Republic of Iran, Tahran Cad 10, Kavaklidere, Ankara; ☏ +90 312 4682820-21; e iranemb.ank@mfa.gov.ir

Ⓔ **UK** Embassy of Islamic Republic of Iran, 50 Kensington Court, London W8 5DB; ☏ +44 20 7937 5225; e lon.visa@mfa.gov.ir

Ⓔ **UN** Iranian Mission to the United Nations, 622 3rd Av, New York, NY 10017, USA; ☏ +1 212 687 2020; e iran@un.int

FOREIGN EMBASSIES IN IRAN

Ⓔ **Germany** 324 Ferdowsi St, Tehran, PO Box 11365–179; w teheran.diplo.de

Ⓔ **Sweden** 27 Nastaran St, Boostan St, Tehran; ☏ +98 21 23712200; e ambassaden.teheran@gov.se

Ⓔ **Switzerland** (Foreign interests section) 39 Shahid Mousavi (Golestan 5th), Pasdaran St, Tehran; ☏ +98 21 22542178; e tie.vertretung@eda.admin.ch

Ⓔ **UK** 198 Ferdowsi St, Tehran, PO Box 11316–91144; ☏ +98 21 64052000

BY AIR The main international airport in Iran is Tehran's **Imam Khomeini International Airport (IKA)** (w ikac.ir), but foreigners with valid visas can also enter/exit Iran by way of various Persian Gulf states (eg: Dubai to Shiraz, Dubai to Bandar Abbas, Oman to Kish). Sometimes officials check your baggage receipt against the tag on your luggage. (For transport from Imam Khomeini International Airport into the centre and other parts of the country, see page 92.)

There are at present no direct flights from American or Canadian airports and most direct flights from European cities have been cancelled following the US unilateral withdrawal from the Nuclear Deal in 2018. The only European carriers flying direct are **Austrian Airlines** (w austrian.com) and **Lufthansa** (w lufthansa. com). **Turkish Airlines** (w thy.com) has the most extensive flight network in Iran and flies regularly via Istanbul to a number of cities in Iran, including Esfahan, Mashhad, Shiraz and Tabriz. Consider Turkish Airlines when flying into Tehran and out of Shiraz, or vice versa. **Pegasus Airlines** (w flypgs.com), the Turkish low-cost carrier, flies to Tehran via Istanbul with regular flights from/to Europe. **Aeroflot** (w aeroflot.com) has good connections with European cities to catch its daily evening Moscow–Tehran flight, which takes only 3 hours. Iranian carrier **Mahan Air** (w mahan.aero) has six weekly flights between Moscow's Vnukovo and Imam Khomeini International Airport and also flies twice weekly to Barcelona. **Azerbaijan Airlines** (w azal.az) has daily 1-hour-long flights from Baku to Tehran with numerous connections to European cities from Baku. **Ukraine International Airlines** (w flyuia.com) can also be a reasonable connection for the London–Kiev–Tehran route. There are five flights per week from Muscat with **Oman Air** (w omanair.com) and two to three weekly services from Dubai with UAE low-cost carrier **Flydubai** (w flydubai.com). All the flight carrier options listed here, when booked in advance, cost around or under £400 for an economy-class return fare.

BY ROAD There are three border crossings from Turkey (see box, page 229); from Armenia (via Nourdouz; ⏰ 24hrs); from the Republic of Azerbaijan (via Astara; ⏰ until 18.00); from Turkmenistan (via Ashgabad Sarakhs or Lotfabad); and from Pakistan at Mirjaveh. Some maps indicate an international border crossing at Pishin, but this is incorrect, as this crossing does not have immigration police on site and you will not be let through even with a valid Pakistani visa. There are numerous border crossings to Iraq, including to Iraqi Kurdistan at Bashmaq.

BY TRAIN Provided you can obtain a visa (page 45) there is a daily train, the Trans-Asia Express, from Ankara to Tehran (24hrs). The Man in Seat Sixty One (w seat61. com/Iran.htm) provides up-to-date information on timetables, booking, prices and train facilities.

BY SEA Iran can be accessed by sea from Dubai to Bandar Lengeh (12hrs), from Kuwait to Khorramshahr (10hrs) and from Sharjah to Bandar Abbas (12hrs). Ferries are operated by Valfajr Shipping (w valfajr.ir) with normally two departures per week. Contact one of the company's offices to make a reservation.

HEALTH *with Dr Felicity Nicholson*

BEFORE YOU GO It is advisable to be up to date with all primary immunisations including **tetanus**, **diphtheria** and **polio** – an all-in-one vaccine (Revaxis) lasts for ten years. There is no risk of yellow fever, but a yellow fever certificate is required from all travellers over nine months of age arriving in Iran from a country with a risk of yellow fever and for travellers who have transited for more than 12 hours through an airport of a country with a risk of yellow fever. Since July 2016, all yellow fever vaccination certificates, regardless of when they were issued, are 'for the life of the person vaccinated'. Some travellers (those on repeated trips, longer-stay trips or trips to more remote regions where sanitation and food hygiene are likely to be poor) would be wise to be protected against hepatitis A and **typhoid**. Hepatitis A vaccine (eg: Havrix Monodose or Avaxim) comprises two injections given about a year apart. The course costs about £100, but may be available on the NHS; it protects for 25 years and can be administered even close to the time of departure.

Hepatitis B vaccination should be considered for longer trips (two months or more) or for those working with children or in situations where contact with blood is likely. Three injections are needed for the best protection and can be given over a three-week period if time is short for those aged 16 or over. Longer schedules give more sustained protection and are therefore preferred if time allows. Hepatitis A vaccine can also be given as a combination with hepatitis B as 'Twinrix', though two doses are needed at least seven days apart to be effective for the hepatitis A component, and three doses are needed for the hepatitis B. For children aged 15 or younger, Ambirix can be used to protect against hepatitis A and B in one injection, with a booster after six months or longer which needs to be taken before the 16th birthday.

The newer injectable typhoid vaccines (eg: Typhim Vi) last for three years and are about 85% effective. Oral capsules (Vivotif) may also be available for those aged six and over. The effects of three capsules over five days lasts for approximately three years but may be less effective than the injectable forms as their efficacy depends on how well they are absorbed.

Vaccinations for **rabies** are advised for everyone, but are especially important for travellers visiting more remote areas, especially if they will be more than 24 hours away from medical help and definitely if working with animals. For more information, see page 50.

Visit your doctor or a recognised travel clinic (page 50) around eight weeks before you leave.

As on any trip a small medical kit is useful. Consider some or all of the following:

- A good drying antiseptic, eg: iodine or potassium permanganate (don't take antiseptic cream)
- A few small dressings (Band-Aids)
- Suncream
- Insect repellent; anti-malarial tablets; impregnated bednet or permethrin spray
- Paracetamol or ibuprofen
- Antifungal cream (eg: Canesten)
- Azithromycin or norfloxacin, for severe diarrhoea
- Tinidazole for giardia or amoebic dysentery
- Antibiotic eye drops, for sore, 'gritty', stuck-together eyes (conjunctivitis)
- A pair of fine-pointed tweezers (to remove hairy caterpillar hairs, thorns, splinters, etc)
- Alcohol-based hand rub or bar of soap in plastic box
- Condoms or femidoms
- For more remote travellers consider taking a travel thermometer

Should you need any assistance when in Iran, do not hesitate to contact any local pharmacy. These are numerous and usually well stocked.

Travel clinics and health information A full list of current travel clinic websites worldwide is available on w istm.org. For other journey preparation information, consult w travelhealthpro.org.uk (UK) or w wwwnc.cdc.gov/travel/ (US). Information about various medications may be found on w netdoctor.co.uk/travel. All advice found online should be used in conjunction with expert advice received prior to or during travel.

IN IRAN In the major cities, it will be said that the water is safe for cleaning teeth as it is heavily chlorinated (neighbouring Afghanistan suffers cholera outbreaks). However, it is always safer to use bottled water both for drinking and for cleaning your teeth.

Opportunities to strip off and sunbathe are obviously severely limited in the Islamic Republic, but the force of the Iranian sun is powerful and there is comparatively little shade so avoid excessive exertion during midday hours and wear a sunhat. Women should wear theirs over a scarf. Clothing in natural fibres is most comfortable for the hotter months but evening temperatures can drop suddenly, especially in the hills, so take a light sweater too.

Take the usual precautions when walking across rough and stony ground, and through shrubbery and vegetation, against snakes, scorpions, etc. If you are entering a ruined building from broad sunlight, make a noise so that any snakes retreat.

Malaria There is a low risk of malaria from March to November in the rural southeastern provinces of Iran. It is also in the north in Ardabil on the border of Azerbaijan and near the border of Turkmenistan in Khorasan. For most travellers, malaria tablets are not recommended and insect bite prevention is advised. However, a minority of travellers will be advised to take tablets if they are travelling to risk areas. This would include longer-term travellers visiting friends and relatives, the immune suppressed, those aged 70 or over, pregnant women or those who have complex medical conditions. The recommended prophylaxis is proguanil and chloroquine, but you should take advice as the tablets may not be suitable for you. To minimise the risk of nausea, try taking the tablets in the evening with food and wash down with plenty of fluids. It is imperative to complete the prescribed course unless you have been advised by someone suitably qualified to stop.

Insect repellents and cover-up clothing can help ward off voracious mosquitoes. These should be used both day and night when mosquitoes are around. Products containing around 50–55% DEET are considered effective and are safe for use in pregnancy and on children from two months upwards. For those who prefer a more natural approach then repellents containing p-menthane 3,8 diol, also known as lemon eucalyptus, can be used instead but is considered equivalent to 15% DEET and must be applied every 1 to 2 hours. Mosquito coils and the like can be purchased everywhere. Regarding other insects, avoid flea-pit hotels and very cheap local buses; saving a few dollars can result in great discomfort.

Rabies Iran is classified as a high-risk rabies country. Few dogs in Iran are kept as pets, so they are not domesticated in the same way as in Europe or North America. In particular, avoid sheepdogs as they are trained to see off unwelcome guests. Stand still and if necessary, make as if you are throwing a stone in their direction,

It is dehydration that makes you feel awful during a bout of diarrhoea and the most important part of treatment is drinking lots of clear fluids. Sachets of oral rehydration salts give the perfect biochemical mix to replace all that is pouring out of your bottom but other recipes taste nicer. Any dilute mixture of sugar and salt in water will do you good: try Coke or orange squash with a three-finger pinch of salt added to each glass (if you are salt-depleted you won't taste the salt). Otherwise make a solution of a four-finger scoop of sugar with a three-finger pinch of salt in a 500ml glass. Or add eight level teaspoons of sugar (18g) and one level teaspoon of salt (3g) to one litre (five cups) of safe water. A squeeze of lemon or orange juice improves the taste and adds potassium, which is also lost in diarrhoea. Drink two large glasses after every bowel action, and more if you are thirsty. These solutions are still absorbed well if you are vomiting, but you will need to sip it rather than drink it down. If you are not eating, you need to drink three litres a day plus whatever is pouring into the toilet. If you feel like eating, take a bland, high carbohydrate diet. Heavy greasy foods will probably give you cramps.

If the diarrhoea is bad, or you are passing blood or slime, or you have a fever, you will probably need antibiotics in addition to fluid replacement. A dose of norfloxacin or ciprofloxacin repeated twice a day until better may be appropriate (if you are planning to take an antibiotic with you, note that both norfloxacin and azithromycin are available only on prescription in the UK). If the diarrhoea is greasy and bulky and is accompanied by sulphurous (eggy) burps, one likely cause is giardia. This is best treated with tinidazole (four × 500mg in one dose, repeated seven days later if symptoms persist).

shouting angrily. If you intend to spend a long time travelling or are staying in rural areas, consider having a course of rabies shots before departure. Ideally three doses of vaccine should be given over about 21 days, although shorter courses over a week are now available but require an extra booster after a year. Rabies is passed on to humans through a bite, scratch or simply a lick on skin from any warm-blooded mammal. You must always assume any animal is rabid, and seek medical help as soon as possible. Meanwhile, scrub the wound with soap under a running tap or while pouring water from a jug for a good 15 minutes. Then pour on a strong iodine or alcohol solution. This helps stop the rabies virus entering the body and will guard against wound infections, including tetanus. If you think you have been exposed to rabies then seek medical help as soon as possible to obtain the relevant post-exposure prophylaxis. Those who have not been immunised will probably need a blood product called Rabies Immunoglobulin (RIG) injected around the wound and four doses of rabies vaccine given over 21 days. RIG is expensive (around US$800) and is very hard to come by – another reason why pre-exposure vaccination should be encouraged as if you have had the full pre-exposure course you will not need RIG and most people should only need two further doses of vaccine given three days apart following the exposure. And remember that, if you do contract rabies, mortality is 100% and death from rabies is probably one of the worst ways to go.

Ticks Tick-borne relapsing fever caused by infection with spirochaetes of the genus *Borrelia* is endemic in Iran. Infections typically occur during the summer months in rural and mountainous areas in both the north and the south of the country. Tick-borne relapsing fever is a febrile disease, but it is treatable with antibiotics. To avoid this unpleasant disease, it is wise when walking in forested areas to cover up by wearing trousers tucked into socks and boots, and consider wearing a hat if there are overhanging branches. Always check for ticks at the end of any walk and follow the advice below.

Ideally ticks should be removed as soon as possible because leaving them on the body increases the chance of infection. They should be removed with special tick tweezers that can be bought in good travel shops. Failing that, you can use your fingernails: grasp the tick as close to your body as possible and pull steadily and firmly away at right angles to your skin. The tick will then come away complete, as long as you do not jerk or twist. If possible, douse the wound with alcohol (any spirit will do), soap and water, or iodine. Irritants (eg: Olbas oil) or lit cigarettes should not

LONG-HAUL FLIGHTS, CLOTS AND DVT

Any prolonged immobility including travel by land or air can result in deep vein thrombosis (DVT) with the risk of embolus to the lungs. Certain factors can increase the risk and these include:

- Previous clot or close relative with a history
- People over 40 (increased risk over 80 years)
- Recent major operation or varicose veins surgery
- Cancer
- Heart disease
- Obesity
- Pregnancy
- Hormone therapy
- Heavy smokers
- Severe varicose veins
- Being over 1.83m (6ft) or under 1.52m (5ft)

A DVT causes painful swelling and redness of the calf or sometimes the thigh. It is only dangerous if a clot travels to the lungs (pulmonary embolus). Symptoms of a pulmonary embolus – which commonly start three to ten days after a long flight – include chest pain, shortness of breath, and sometimes coughing up small amounts of blood. Anyone who thinks that they might have a DVT needs to see a doctor immediately.

PREVENTION OF DVT
- Wear loose comfortable clothing
- Do anti-DVT exercises and move around when possible
- Drink plenty of fluids during the flight
- Avoid taking sleeping pills unless you are able to lie flat
- Avoid excessive tea, coffee and alcohol
- Consider wearing flight socks or support stockings, widely available from pharmacies

If you think you are at an increased risk of a clot, ask your doctor if it is safe to travel.

be used since they can cause the ticks to regurgitate and therefore increase the risk of disease. It is best to get a companion to check you for ticks; if you are travelling with small children, remember to check their heads, and particularly behind the ears. Spreading redness around the bite and/or fever and/or aching joints after a tick bite imply that you have an infection that requires antibiotic treatment, so seek medical advice.

Travellers' diarrhoea Travelling in Iran carries a fairly high risk of getting a dose of travellers' diarrhoea; perhaps half of all visitors will suffer and the newer you are to exotic travel, the more likely you will be to suffer. By taking precautions against travellers' diarrhoea you will also avoid typhoid, paratyphoid, cholera, hepatitis, dysentery, worms, etc. Travellers' diarrhoea and the other faecal-oral diseases come from getting other people's faeces in your mouth. This most often happens from cooks not washing their hands after a trip to the toilet, but even if the restaurant cook does not understand basic hygiene you will be safe if your food has been properly cooked and arrives piping hot. The most important prevention strategy is to wash your hands before eating anything. The maxim to remind you what you can safely eat is:

PEEL IT, BOIL IT, COOK IT OR FORGET IT.

This means that fruit you have washed and peeled yourself, and hot foods, should be safe but raw foods, cold cooked foods, salads, fruit salads which have been prepared by others, ice cream and ice are all risky, and foods kept lukewarm in hotel buffets are often dangerous. That said, plenty of travellers and expatriates enjoy fruit and vegetables, so do keep a sense of perspective: food served in a fairly decent hotel in a large town or a place regularly frequented by expatriates is likely to be safe. If you are struck, see box, page 51 for treatment.

Medical facilities and pharmacies Every major hotel in the main Iranian cities has doctors or paramedics on call; otherwise, any business contact or friend, or your embassy, will recommend a doctor or dentist. Note that few dentists operate during the 28 days of Ramadan. The hospitals are good, as we (and great numbers of Azerbaijanis and Omanis flocking to Iran for medical services) can attest, but somewhat basic by Western standards and few medical staff have had any opportunity to study in the West. The Iranian authorities give international 24-hour medical emergency services every assistance, but American citizens should be aware that the current US embargo could be problematic as payments cannot be made by credit card.

Even small towns have well-stocked pharmacies as Iranians vie with the Lebanese as the world's worst hypochondriacs. That said, take adequate supplies of any prescribed drug you need, or at least full details, so the best equivalent can be traced, because most Western brands are not available.

SAFETY

CRIME Any crime carries severe penalties in the Islamic Republic. It is likely that the greatest danger you will face (other than crossing the road – see page 54) is having your wallet, purse or camera snatched. Keep photocopies of the most important pages (including the visa if possible) of your passport and tickets, and spare passport photos separately, and don't flash money or expensive camera equipment ostentatiously. The British Foreign and Commonwealth Office has warned that bogus policemen have approached some visiting foreigners, advising that in such circumstances you should insist on seeing an identity card and inform the restaurant, shop or hotel of the incident. Remember that no Iranian policeman has the right to take or retain your passport unless you are in a police station (see opposite).

Iran is very safe for **women travellers**. Harassment is minimal; especially if you wear the *manteau*, decently cover your hair and lower part of the torso. Be aware, however, that in some areas or city districts (eg: southern Tehran around Imam Khomeini Square), it is very unusual for a single woman to walk unescorted in public at night. It is best to avoid being alone in the evening in particular in the old town in Yazd, or Ahvaz and Khuzestan generally. If you do feel, however, that you are being harassed, you are strongly encouraged to bring this to the attention of other people present, in particular men (eg: a bus driver). Such behaviour is looked down upon by other members of society. By expressing your indignation publicly, you will be doing other female travellers, and yourself, a great favour. Keep in mind that harassment often happens simply because it is perceived as acceptable.

TERRORISM Although 2018 saw two terrorist attacks perpetrated in Iran, in September against a military parade in Ahvaz, killing 25 people, and in December killing two policemen and injuring 40 people, risk of terrorism in Iran is minimal and remains within the boundaries of Sistan and Baluchestan province, where the military are the main targets.

ROAD SAFETY The road safety record in Iran is poor. The number of deaths, however, seems to be slowly decreasing from the peak of 27,759 in 2005 to 15,932 in 2018. New road restrictions that have been put in place, eg: trucks are banned from the Tehran–Qom motorway, although not always observed, do appear to have had a positive effect. Iranian-made cars are mostly manufactured without air bags or anti-locking brake systems. This is slowly changing under pressure to comply with increasingly rigorous international and Iranian road safety standards. Leaving aside the nightmare of Tehran traffic, which guarantees road rage and stomach ulcers, be aware that Iranian lorry and coach drivers work very long hours and that few private vehicles have reflectors or working lights. Drivers often disregard every rule in the book. Traffic does not necessarily stop at a red light, nor wait until green before setting off, with the exception perhaps of Kish and Qeshm. Regard zebra crossings as merely road surface decorations. Pedestrians take their life into their own hands crossing the road and the sight of their terror-stricken faces forms the chief entertainment for motorists. If a driver flashes his/her lights it does *not* mean it is safe to cross; your presence is being acknowledged, but not necessarily your continued existence on this earth. On the other hand, having started to cross, do not turn tail or break into a run; both actions constitute a personal challenge to the driver to continue the pursuit.

PERSONAL CONDUCT Be aware that it is easy to break an important social convention without realising it and this can affect your safety. For instance, smoking of 'hubble-bubble' waterpipes (*qalian*) in public has in the past been banned on the grounds that it promoted 'licentious behaviour'. Men can, however, smoke in public and in some cafés or restaurants that allow it, but it may be more difficult for women, as traditional tea houses would not serve *qalian* to women or mixed groups. Ask in advance if *qalian* is what you are after.

If you are confronted with officialdom, do not lose your temper, shout or threaten. Be polite and apologetic if not abject. Women: forget all feminist scruples and cry. Always insist on seeing someone who speaks English (any other Western language will be difficult).

POLICE Various police forces in Iran operate under a central control. The traffic or road police wear white caps and have white cars with a blue stripe while the security police have bright green uniforms with a dark green cap, and white cars with a dark green stripe; some security police wear 'combat fatigues'. The rank is shown by the stars or pips on the shoulder (officers) and by stripes on the sleeve (non-commissioned officers).

EMERGENCY NUMBERS	
Emergency	115
Fire brigade	125
Police	110
Red Crescent	112

GAY AND LESBIAN TRAVELLERS Homosexuality is forbidden, illegal and carries harsh penalties in Iran.

NOTES FOR TRAVELLERS WITH DISABILITIES   *Lieke Scheewe*

Planning an accessible trip to Iran may be challenging, as the required information is not easy to come by. Nevertheless, the ancient beauty of this unique country can very well be enjoyed by anyone, with or without a disability. Since the establishment of the Ministry of Social Welfare in the 1970s, public services for people with disabilities have improved, and many disability organisations are active to achieve general inclusion.

PLANNING AND BOOKING There are, to my knowledge, no travel agencies that run specialised trips to Iran for travellers with disabilities. Yet, many travel agencies will listen to your needs and try to create a suitable itinerary. However, the easiest way may be to find local operators through the internet and plan your trip directly with them, as they will also be available for you after arrival.

GETTING THERE AND AWAY At the international airports in Tehran you can expect good assistance and a narrow aisle chair to help you embark and disembark. Lifts and car parks for travellers with disabilities are also common.

VISITING PLACES Tehran is a modern city with many parks and museums where you will find relatively few obstacles to getting around with a wheelchair. To visit the ancient archaeological sites you will often find stairs and rough terrain, but also friendly Iranians to give you a hand.

ACCOMMODATION Finding accessible accommodation is not easy. In general, only top-of-the-range hotels will be largely 'obstacle-free', for example Abbasi Hotel in Esfahan (page 166).

TRAVEL INSURANCE Most insurance companies will cater for travellers with disabilities, but it is essential that they are made aware of your disability. Examples of specialised companies that cover pre-existing medical conditions are Free Spirit (\ 0845 230 5000; w freespirittravelinsurance.com) and Age UK (\ 0800 389 4852; w ageuk.org.uk), who have no upper age limit.

WHAT TO TAKE

Backpacks are no longer identified with amoral behaviour and increasingly more young Iranians use backpacks themselves. Alternatively, a **case or bag** may be easier to manage if travelling on an organised tour. Luggage has to be securely locked for intercity bus trips and internal flights, and padlocks are readily available. A **torch** is useful for exploring ruined buildings, etc, and because street lighting is erratic. The water is heavily chlorinated and very hard; a **moisturising cream** may sound effeminate but is a godsend, as is **lip salve**. Extra body lotion may also be handy, as water in Iran often has a drying effect on the skin. As Muslim law stipulates washing under running water, bath and basin **plugs** are not usually provided. For the same reason, **toilet paper** is usually found only in the better hotels and restaurants (to be deposited in waste-paper bins, as Iranian soil pipes have small diameters); you may not fancy using the toilet's cold-water douche. Feminine **sanitary products** are expensive and difficult to obtain outside urban centres. Take an electrical **plug adaptor**; the voltage is usually 220V and the plug is the two-pin rounded variety as found in France (though at least one Tehran hotel has been refurbished with three-pin square British-style plugs). **Camera** batteries and extra memory for digital cameras are easy to find in big cities such as Tehran and Esfahan but slide (diapositive) films and some lithium batteries for 'conventional' cameras are difficult to obtain. Don't forget **sunglasses** and extra supplies of **prescribed medication**. Make sure to bring **good shoes** with anti-slip soles, as many street surfaces are tiled and slippery.

Where possible, in *Part Two* of this guide we have given Quranic references for building inscriptions (we like knowing what the calligraphy says), so if you share this interest pack a paperback translation of the **Quran**, with chapter/verse notation.

As you will meet friendliness and kindness throughout Iran, why not take some local **souvenirs or fridge magnets** from home to give as small mementos? They give pleasure to adults and children alike.

Finally, with regard to **clothes**, it really depends on the season and the area in Iran you are travelling to. For mountainous areas, such as eastern Azerbaijan or Tehran in winter, you will need warm clothes suitable for continental European winters and preferably waterproofs if you decide to go hiking. Also, bring a warm hat and a pair of gloves. For the Persian Gulf region and Khuzestan, lighter, preferably linen, clothes and a pair of flip-flops will be sufficient all year round. Central areas, such as Esfahan and Shiraz, are hot in summer and cool in winter, and spring is easily the best season to travel here. Generally speaking, it is important to bring with you good ventilated **hiking shoes**, one jumper and a light jacket for travelling on the bus or sleeping in the desert. It gets a little more complicated for female travellers who must ensure that whatever clothes they wear, the lower part of their torso is covered at all times. See page 83 for advice on more specific **dress codes**.

EXPORT AND IMPORT RESTRICTIONS

The export of **gold** over 150g in weight, antiques (interpreted as items over 50 years old) and certain electrical goods is technically forbidden. Some export restrictions remain on **carpets and rugs**, largely relating to the place of production, size (totalling a maximum of 12m²) and value. There are no special restrictions on the export of modern or contemporary artworks. If in doubt, contact Art Tour in Tehran (see box, page 109). If you are with a travel company, the Iranian guide will advise; otherwise it is best to have a friend or colleague accompany you to the

Bottle of water, 1.5 litre	25,000 rials
Bottle of ZamZam lemonade	35,000 rials
Single local bus ride without changing	15000 rials
Single metro ticket	15,000 rials
'Bavaria'/'Baltika' beer (non-alcoholic)	70,000 rials
16GB camera card	750,000 rials
Cinema ticket	150,000 rials
'Pizza' Iranian style	250,000–500,000 rials
Double hamburger	150,000–500,000 rials
Carton of Winston cigarettes	140,000 rials
Cup of 'Nescafé' (instant coffee)	50,000 rials
Cup of brewed coffee	100,000–250,000 rials
Cup of tea in Hotel Abbasi	150,000 rials
Cup of tea at petrol stations	10,000 rials
A litre of diesel (car)	6,000 rials
A litre of petrol (car)	30,000 rials

airport so that, if the customs officials object, you can hand the offending article to your friend and try another time. The duty-free section on departure from Tehran's Imam Khomeini International Airport sells such items as art or history books published in Iran, CDs, Iranian caviar and American cigarettes; all purchases are priced in both US dollars and rials.

Concerning imports into Iran, the usual restrictions on narcotics, weapons and pornographic material such as videos, DVDs, tapes and books, etc, apply; leave any lurid dust jackets at home. No **alcohol** may be imported into the Islamic Republic of Iran, even for private use; if supplies are found in your baggage, you, your companions and your sponsor will suffer. Do note that all luggage is scanned at the baggage reclaim section before you exit to the arrivals hall.

If importing your **car** temporarily, you will need a current international driving licence, a *carnet de passage*, car registration, third-party insurance (valid for Iran), a nationality badge, a red warning triangle and spare parts. When you leave the country again, Iranian customs officials will not believe any story of theft or vehicle write-off unless you have proof. They will assume you have sold it and fine you accordingly.

MONEY

Notes are printed in denominations (rials) of 1,000,000, 500,000, 100,000, 50,000, 20,000, 10,000, 5,000, 2,000 and 1,000, and coins 1,000, 500, 250, 100 and 50. You may sometimes get sweets or chewing gum in return if shops do not have the exact change. Although the rial is the stated currency, Iranians refer to tuman (eg: 10,000 rials), thus something priced as 100,000 rials is generally spoken of as costing 10 tumans or 10,000 tumans, so do clarify before agreeing to purchase. For small purchases such as fruit, nuts and so on a basic recognition of Farsi numerical symbols is useful (page 362).

WHAT TO CARRY Short-stay visitors will find it much easier to take quantities of US dollars, pounds or euros in **cash**, preferably in large denominations. It may be difficult to exchange small amounts like $10 or £5. Memories of the large-scale forgery of dollar bills in ex-Soviet territories in the early 1990s still linger, so post-1996 bills are essential. **Travellers' cheques** cannot be exchanged or used for any direct payments and are thus best avoided. Carrying a few extra copies of your passport, including pages with the Iranian visa, is also a good idea.

CHANGING MONEY There are two foreign currency exchange rates: the official and the 'free market' one, and the former, quoted in banks and the press (including local English-language newspapers), is about one-third of the free-market value. It drops during Nou Rouz holiday season when Iranians plunge into excessive spending. You can exchange money (but only in large denominations; US$10 or US$20 banknotes are less likely to be accepted) in an exchange shop (*sarrafi*) or any of the numerous gold shops; Iranians save their money buying large quantities of gold and coins. Between April and summer 2018 when the Iranian rial lost almost 50% of its value, the government imposed restrictions on the sale and purchase of currency, although some exceptions were made for tourists. 'Free market' exchange kiosks are available on the main streets of major cities and near tourist attractions. Please note that the only 'free market' exchange kiosk in Tehran's Imam Khomeini International Airport is on the first floor at the departures area. Do not attempt to exchange foreign currency with illegal street traders. Flights and accommodation purchased through an Iranian travel agent must be paid for in rials. Hotel bills may sometimes be settled in foreign currency, preferably US dollars or euros.

BUDGETING

The following is a rough approximation of a daily budget for a single independent traveller – who has not prepaid for any domestic travel and hotel/meal arrangements – intending to visit one important and one minor tourist site each day. Note that stays, meals and visits in tourist centres such as Tehran, Esfahan and Shiraz will be more expensive than those in other less-visited towns.

In March 2013 the Iranian government reintroduced a double-pricing system, whereby foreign tourists pay higher admission rates to museums and historic sites. The average ticket price at present stands at 500,000 rials but prices are most likely to increase from 2020 onwards. Accommodation prices are also usually higher for foreign tourists. Do ask for a discount during the low season.

Hotel overnight	US$15–20
Three meals	US$5–10
Transport (eg: intercity bus or half-day taxi)	US$5–10
Site/museum charges	US$5
Other (eg: coffee, soft drinks, laundry, photocopy)	US$5
Total	**US$35–50**

GETTING AROUND

On all forms of public transport that are not pre-segregated already, and excluding planes, men will probably be asked to change their seats to avoid sitting next to female strangers.

When travelling around, a copy of the Iranian solar calendar might come in handy and save a lot of time when planning your travel (page 71). The calendar can also be downloaded as a phone app (Persian Calendar app by Ali Shooshtarian). Note that transport costs given are approximate.

CITY TRANSPORT Tickets (10,000 rials for a single direct journey) for **public buses** are purchased before boarding, at kiosks and/or shops nearby. Transport cards are also widely available and recommended if staying in a specific city (eg: Esfahan) for an extended period of time. Single ride fare reduces in this case by around 15%. Alternatively, passengers pay the driver when getting off. Female travellers must leave through the back door and then come up to the front and pay the fare (note that on some buses in Tehran, the front section of the bus is reserved for women). On some occasions, however, when the bus is not full and there is no barrier separation, it is acceptable to come up to the driver through the bus without having to get off. If travelling with a companion of the opposite sex, agree beforehand on a meeting place as you may well get separated in the crush. In the metro, however, it is acceptable for female and male travellers to travel together in the cars assigned to male passengers. Please note that unlike Europe, intercity bus and train stations are located on the outskirts of the city and will always require a taxi to town. Keep an eye on your wallet/purse on buses and trains. Although not a regular occurrence, pickpocketing may happen.

Private taxis are hailed from the roadside, and it's best to use the locally registered ones with a taxi sign. As the driver swerves towards you, yell out your destination; if he brakes or nods, he's willing to go that way. Before the journey, ask colleagues or hotel staff the approximate cost of the journey and get written or verbal directions, unless the ride is to a notable landmark; taxi drivers do not undergo the same rigorous tests as, say, London cabbies. Outside Tehran, consider hiring a taxi for a day or half

2

a day, especially in Ahvaz, Esfahan, Mashhad or Shiraz, as it is the cheapest and most convenient form of transport offering freedom of routes and stops. The cheapest taxi service is the state-run fixed-rate *azhans*, which hotel personnel can arrange for you. Getting a private taxi in the street is called *darbast* (which in Persian means 'door closed' to other passengers). **Shared taxis** (official ones are green or yellow) are called *savari* and these operate on pre-established routes, usually driving in straight lines. The procedure for hailing the taxi is the same: a driver will swerve towards you or honk his horn and you shout out the destination. If he nods, it is usually a shared service and more passengers will be collected en route. A short *savari* ride along Vali Asr Street in Tehran, for example, costs around 20,000 rials. Taxi *khatti* (fixed-route shared taxi) depart from special terminals (eg: Tajrish Square) and, once full, head to a specific destination within the city or outskirts.

The **Snapp** taxi service phone app is a version of Uber and operates in most cities. Rates are usually one-third of a taxi hailed in the street or ordered from *azhans*. The app requires some time to learn and get used to and it is in Persian only so you might need initial assistance from a local to download it, but once you get the hang of it, a great deal of money can be saved if using taxis on daily basis. Like with standard taxis, the Snapp fare depends on the traffic. Be prepared to pay double during rush hour or to drive very cheaply around Tehran on Ashura holy day when everything is closed and everyone is out of town.

On some intercity routes yellow *savari* taxis (or *savari dowlati* meaning 'government' service) are more common (eg: Tehran–Qazvin or Kerman–Jiroft). These usually leave from a separate terminal or square on the outskirts of the city of departure. A *savari* fare is approximately 50% more expensive than the corresponding bus ticket, whereby a front seat usually costs up to 20–30% more. *Savari* fare covers individual traveller insurance and tickets are name-issued. Please note that *savari* drivers often transport private packages and make deliveries along the way. There are also private cars at *savari* terminals competing for passengers and promising to leave immediately, but these are not recommended. Tickets on such routes are purchased from an official kiosk, if such is available, or to the assistant who usually woos passengers and helps the driver fill up the car.

INTERCITY ROAD TRANSPORT There are a number of transport companies offering similar routes, albeit at different times, and sometimes more original departures (eg: the morning departure from Esfahan to Kermanshah is only serviced by Adl). The largest companies are Hamsafar, Iran Peyma and Adl. Although competing, there is no real price difference on the same routes. There are usually two types of **bus** service: VIP and *ma'mouli*. The price difference is negligible but the level of comfort isn't, so treat yourself. If VIP is not available it is acceptable to pay for two seats for some leg room. The VIP bus service includes small snack packs, tea and fresh water. The 895km drive from Shiraz to Tehran by 'deluxe' Volvo costs up to 970,000 rials. Seats are numbered and assigned according to gender or family groups. Tickets can be purchased up to a week in advance or on the same day from the bus station or bus company's city office, with three or four departures an hour on the busiest routes. During Ramadan and Nou Rouz, reservations must be made well in advance. When buying bus tickets, avoid tourist agencies specialising in tours. These usually charge a commission of up to 100,000 rials for their service and may not always have complete bus schedules. It is best to purchase tickets at Iranian bus/train/air ticket sales offices in town or at the bus/train terminals. Online purchases are more economical, so do not hesitate to ask hotel personnel to make a booking for you.

The **bus terminal** (with toilets near the *namazkhaneh* or prayer room – where you are welcome to rest in case of a long wait; *namazkhaneh* are, however, closed at 07.00, even at major stations) is generally located on the outskirts of town but large cities have more than one, so check which terminal your bus leaves from. Short stops are made every 5 or 6 hours (ensure you know the departure time), but it's best to take some food/drink with you. In case of an overnight journey with a departure time after 17.00, buses stop at a local restaurant for dinner at around 21.00. Daytime long-distance buses also stop for lunch at around 13.00. As in pre-revolutionary times, all public vehicles have to register at the police control points entering and leaving city limits, so carry your passport in your hand luggage in case it is required. The only time, however, when your passport might be inspected is in Kerman, and Sistan and Baluchestan province owing to rigorous anti-drug smuggling checks. All items going into the baggage holds should be padlocked. Note that bus stations in Iran do not have luggage-storage facilities.

When travelling to distant places around and in between relatively close towns (eg: Hamadan and Kermanshah), there are usually **minibuses** (often called *mahalli*, meaning 'local'), but such journeys take longer.

BY RAIL There are a number of overnight services, including Tehran–Ahvaz, Tehran–Mashhad, Tehran–Tabriz, Tehran–Esfahan–Kerman and Esfahan–Yazd–Tehran–Mashhad, as well as frequent short-distance journeys, eg: Tehran–Qazvin or Tehran–Semnan. As with intercity buses, the price difference between first and second class on long journeys is minimal but the standard of comfort is significant. Train tickets are usually sold out well in advance. Below is an indicative (not daily) train departure timetable and price list (summer 2019):

From	To	Departure	Price (rials)
Tehran	Ahvaz	14.05; 15.20; 16.45; 18.40	606,000–1,300,000
	Bandar Abbas	12.15; 13.15	900,000–1,135,000
	Esfahan	22.45	458,000
	Mashhad	00.25; 00.52; 06.00; 07.40; 08.00; 13.55; 14.35; 16.05; 18.05; 19.20; 19.35; 20.35; 21.15; 21.50; 22.45; 23.05; 23.45	476,000–1,410,000
	Semnan	00.25; 05.10; 06.00; 07.45; 08.00; 13.55; 15.00	116,000–265,000
	Shiraz	16.10; 18.05	890,000–1,289,000
	Tabriz	19.20; 20.15	478,000–730,000
	Yazd	11.25; 12.15; 13.15; 15.50; 19.55; 22.10	386,000–844,000
	Zahedan	11.25	870,000

The train service isn't fast, but it is comfortable. Tickets are sold at travel agencies or train stations. There are two types of train: the state **Iran Rail** (w raja.ir) and private services, which means there is a variety of trains and services on most routes. Major train stations, unlike bus stations, have luggage storage areas.

BY AIR Internal air travel is reasonably priced and, as well as the national flag carrier, **IranAir**, **Iran Aseman Airlines**, **Mahan Air**, **Kish Air** and **Iran Airtour** operate a number of services across the country and internationally. IranAir allows a 50% discount on one internal flight if your international flight was with them. A one-way ticket from Tehran to Shiraz costs 3,600,000–4,700,000 rials, and from Tehran to Yazd 2,700,000–5,700,000 rials. You can book tickets online, but a knowledge of Persian is required. So it is best to ask a friend to help or use a local travel agent.

To purchase a domestic flight ticket in Iran, you will need to book in advance, take your passport and pay in rials. It is easy to purchase tickets once in Iran, but organising this in advance from home takes time and patience so, unless you have time to waste, consider booking in advance through a tour operator such as Magic Carpet Travel (page 43) or an agent such as Thunder Tour & Travel (page 43). The agent will keep the booking active and will also confirm and reconfirm your ticket at the local IranAir office. Your Iranian tour guide can also book flights for you.

Allow plenty of time to get to the airport (particularly in Tehran where traffic is frequently gridlocked) and to check in. On entry to any airport terminal building there is a security check: men with all their baggage go through one door, and 'sisters' with theirs through another. At the check-in desk abandon any idea of polite queuing; block all-comers and use elbows forcibly. You may be required to show your passport on passing to the next security check – again arranged according to gender – leading to the departure lounge.

An airport porter will expect at least 20,000 rials per case to/from the baggage hall and car or taxi, and more if he is required to 'negotiate' with the authorities on your behalf. Rates at train stations are similar, but usually (eg: Tehran) also include a fixed 50,000 rial fee payable to the station authorities. Porters are then paid on top of this amount.

Some of the aircraft used on domestic **IranAir** (w iranair.com) flights are nearing the end of their serviceable life, especially those purchased from ex-Soviet republics whose service history cannot be guaranteed. The last major crashes were in July 2009; both involved Russian-made planes and the first killed 168, the second 17. The state, however, seems to be monitoring the condition of the internal airlines' air fleet. In April 2013 Iranian Saha Air was forced to stop operating as the last airline in the world still using Boeing 707 planes more than 36 years old. Of the newly purchased Airbus fleet, only 14 made it to Iran; the remaining 100 were blocked by US sanctions. Note that no alcohol is permitted on board flights, and that women should dress suitably (see box, page 84).

BY PRIVATE CAR New rental car service **Navaran** (\021 44666294; w navaran. com) has made it very easy to rent a vehicle and drop it off in another city. With its head office on Kish Island, the company has the largest fleet of cars in Iran with offices in all international airports in the country and a 24/7 support service.

It is possible to rent a car in Iran. **Europcar** (w europcar.ir) has three offices in Tehran – Imam Khomeini International Airport (\021 51007539, 55678243), Mehrabad Airport (m 0901 8380361; e mehrabad@europcar.ir) and Tehran's northern suburb of Shahrak-e Gharb [90 B3] (2 11th Alley, Falamak St; \021 88366615), Esfahan (\031 32208683; e isfahan@europcar.ir), Shiraz, Mashhad and Bandar Abbas. Payment can be made with Visa or MasterCard. They can also arrange for an English-speaking driver, if so desired and for car drop-off in a different city. A car can be rented for a minimum of 24 hours at a daily maximum of 250km; an extra per-kilometre charge applies for distances above this limit. Daily car rental costs start at 2,000,000 rials (rental for 3–6 days) and there is also an additional charge for a car drop-off in a different city. Alternatively, a **private taxi** can be hired for a day or longer through a hotel or directly from the taxi driver or *azhans*. Note that the charge for the return leg of a journey is always half the one-way rate (eg: 100,000 rials to the destination and 50,000 rials to return, plus waiting time).

Cheap diesel used to be rationed in Iran, but not anymore. A litre of petrol costs 10,000 rials and it is available at all fuel stations. A lot of Iranian cars drive on gas and if your *savari* taxi stops for 'regassing' you will probably be asked to leave the vehicle for safety reasons.

Even with experience of other chaotic cities, we would not choose to drive in Iranian cities, especially Tehran. Iranians have a habit of driving in between two lanes. That said, the roads are well engineered with very few pot-holes, and with good road signs (in both Farsi and the Roman alphabets). Fuel stations, however, might be hard to find in more faraway regions of the country. Motor spares, especially for foreign-made and rarer cars, are difficult to find (the US embargo again) even in the main urban centres. In Tehran, your best bet would be the area around Amir Kabir Street, the mechanics' market of the capital. Fuel station toilets are usually acceptable, but more preferable are *namazkhaneh* (prayer room) washrooms.

When driving, it is compulsory to wear seat belts, although many drivers and front-seat passengers don't. Speed limits are in operation, at least in theory: up to 95km/h on motorways, and 85km/h at night; country roads 85km/h day and 75km/h night. Some roads with particularly dangerous curves have lower limits: for example, the speed limit on some sections of the Kermanshah–Abadan road is 40km/h. There are also speed cameras in operation on selected road sections. Motorcycle riders are expected to wear helmets but, as you will notice, very few do.

Most motorways in Iran are toll-free, but there are some stretches of road where you are required to pay (20,000–40,000 rials for a private vehicle), for example the motorway between Tehran and Qazvin, Qazvin and Zanjan or Tehran to Kashan. The toll for crossing the bridge over Urmia Lake en route from Orumiyeh to Tabriz is 55,000 rials for a private vehicle. Several towns operate commercial vehicle and/ or bus drive zones, and police seem to operate on a fine-incentive system. Driving at night is extremely hazardous (page 54) and is to be avoided. If you break down, display the obligatory red warning triangle some distance behind the car, and ask passing vehicles to summon police, garage assistance or both.

As the driver, do not even think of leaving the scene of any accident before police agree to your departing. Any incident involving a person will probably mean imprisonment until the matter is investigated, especially if it resulted in a fatality; considerable financial compensation will have to be deposited for possible payment to the victim's family *before* any release can be contemplated. If your car is badly damaged, obtain an official report (especially necessary for the frontier customs if you have temporarily imported it; page 57).

The emergency police number is 110. Traffic police have white caps, and their cars are white with a dark blue stripe.

One small note regarding street names: since the revolution many street names have been changed predominantly in honour of *shahid* (martyrs who died in the Iran–Iraq War) and religious figures. Keep an eye and ear open, as what you hear might not be on the map: the pre- and post-revolution names may be used interchangeably (eg: most Tehranis will direct you to Adan Street, which is in fact called (Shahid) Azodi Street).

ACCOMMODATION

There are various types of accommodation across the country and major Iranian cities are awash with hotels. Iranians themselves travel a great deal within Iran and over the past few years a number of historic houses have been converted into very pleasant traditional hotels or ecolodges (known in Persian as *bumgardi*). In a number of cities there are also Tourist Inns offering suitable, average-priced, rooms.

Distances (in km) between major Iranian cities:

	Ahvaz	Bandar Abbas	Esfahan	Hamadan	Kerman	Shiraz	Tabriz	Tehran
Ahvaz	Ahvaz							
Bandar Abbas	1,130	Bandar Abbas						
Esfahan	518	970	Esfahan					
Hamadan	585	1,471	473	Hamadan				
Kerman	1,098	495	557	1,204	Kerman			
Shiraz	540	581	483	959	551	Shiraz		
Tabriz	1,144	1,847	908	545	1,517	1,397	Tabriz	
Tehran	820	1,314	447	319	985	926	623	Tehran
Yazd	779	696	323	761	366	451	1,150	621

Remember that since no travellers' cheques or credit cards are accepted for payment of bills (eg: rooms, meals) by hotels or restaurants, individual travellers making their own arrangements must carry with them enough Iranian currency.

Hotel rates in Iran are seasonal and prices vary significantly:

Low season	**High season (up to 50% extra)**
January	Second half of March
February	April
First 15 days of March	May
June	First 15 days in August
July	Second half of September
End of August	
First 15 days in September	
November	
December	

Refer to sections in this book on individual towns for recommended hotels but note that the prices relate to 2019 and all include breakfast, unless mentioned otherwise. Foreign nationals are allowed to share the same room irrespective of their marriage status.

The *bumgardis* (or 'ecolodges') have over the past few years sprung up in cities, towns and villages across Iran and offer traditional, authentic and a very affordable way (€10–20 pp) to experience the country. Quality and comfort differ substantially and accommodation ranges from very basic to traditionally and finely decorated with taste and attention to local traditions and culture. A *bumgardi* usually implies a traditional house of five to ten rooms grouped around an inner courtyard with a small pool (*khowz* in Persian) and often a few fruit trees. Roll-up mattresses (*lahaf toshak* in Persian) are usually used for sleeping, and toilet and shower facilities are typically separate, which should be borne in mind when travelling in Iran during the winter months. Although rooms are very well heated (including with *korsi,* a traditional Persian low table heater), a quick trip to the toilet in a mountain ecolodge in winter may require getting fully dressed. That said, staying in *bumgardi* is not only a terrific way to experience genuine Iranian hospitality and taste local food (all food served is homemade), but offers an opportunity to take part in various arts and cultural activities organised by *bumgardi* and visit exceptional places off the tourist path. Recommended *bumgardis* are marked with a ✳ sign. Particularly recommended is the 'Mehmoun' (m +98 (0)902 2004210; w mehmoun.com; see ad, 3rd colour section) association of four *bumgardis* in four different locations in Iran – Howzak House in Esfahan, Javaheri in Buien-Miyandasht, Nartitee in Taft and Maymandmoon in Meymand.

The **mosafirkhanehs** (literally 'traveller's place') or **mehmanpazirs** (Iranian hostels) catering for Iranian nationals also accept foreign tourists, but remember little English is spoken and facilities are usually very basic; toilets are more likely to be of the squat variety and unlikely to be en suite. Single female travellers should also bear in mind that most *mosafirkhaneh* guests are male. Check the room and think whether saving a few dollars is really worth it (though you could always have a scrub-down next day in the local *hamam* or bathhouse; a real cultural experience – see box, page 323). Tourist Inns (*hotel jahangardi*) run by the Iran Touring & Tourism Investment Company (ITTIC) offer more than adequate accommodation, usually with private facilities and there tends to be an inn in most Iranian cities. The quality of inn accommodation and the cultural experience on offer, especially compared with *bumgardis* or traditional hotels is average, but it does the job if nothing better is available.

Then there are **standard** and **traditional hotels**. Traditional hotels are usually slightly more modern and sometimes even very luxurious versions of *bumgardi* (eg: Manouchehri House in Kashan), offering three- to five-star accommodation with excellent facilities and en-suite rooms. Smaller traditional hotels are often family-run and are recommended over standard hotels. Most 'two-star' (very basic) hotels will have rooms with private (mainly squat-style) facilities. Prices are fixed according to demand rather than a regulated system linked with an internationally recognised hotel 'star' rating. In Iran there are also a number of local four- to five-star hotel chains (eg: Homa, Parsian, etc) offering good accommodation and in addition there are some exclusive hotels in converted caravanserai, not to be missed (eg: Hotel Abbasi in Esfahan or Robat-e Zayn al-Din south of Yazd).

In the rooms there will be a symbol (an arrow, a picture of the Ka'ba in Mecca, etc) indicating the *qibla* direction for prayer, a prayer mat, a *mohr*, small clay tablet for Shi'a prayer prostrations and a Quran. If plastic mules or sandals are provided in the room, these should be used for the bathroom and left by its door. High-end hotels usually have swimming pools and sauna with separate gender timings, unless the only swimming pool is outdoors, in which case it is for men only.

Not all hotels offer single rooms, but single travellers can expect to get a 30% discount for a double room. While most hotels advertise their rates in rials, some hotels use double pricing (US$ for foreign tourists; rials for Iranians). You can nonetheless choose to pay in rials. Hotel staff will calculate the amount due based on the applicable exchange rate. No youth hostels affiliated to Hostelling International are available in Iran, but a few **hostels** (eg: Heritage Hostel in Tehran) welcoming foreign travellers and married and female locals have now taken over the backpacker travel niche. While **camping** or staying in a stationary vehicle overnight will arouse suspicion or at least curiosity, camping in the vicinity of Iranian campers is acceptable. For staying in the **desert**, there are various camps in the dunes with basic facilities in situ. There are a few such desert camps around Yazd (page 318) or near Varzaneh, where Mohammad Ebrahimi (page 162) can assist in arranging an overnight stay.

EATING AND DRINKING

If accepting an invitation to visit a family home, it is usual to take a small present (page 82).

In local restaurants and cafés, the portions are quite large and it is acceptable to ask for a doggy bag. All you need to say in this case is *meesheh yek zarf bedaheed ke gazaa ra meekham bebaram* ('Could you please bring me a bag to take food home?'). Restaurants in larger hotels serve Western dishes. All the meat served is halal (slaughtered according to Muslim law; eg: without pre-stunning); pork products are not available except to Armenian Christian families resident in Esfahan (check Ararat supermarket for some imports from Armenia), so all sausages, salami and mortadella are made from beef or lamb. You can also come across pork sausages from Armenia or Russia on sale in supermarkets along the Caspian Sea coastal motorway. Forks and spoons, but not knives, form the usual table cutlery and, as in other Muslim countries, the right hand is used for taking bread, etc. Drinks are normally served with the food and you will have to wait until the meal is ready, unless you ask for it to be brought in advance. Food is normally served quickly, especially in traditional restaurants.

In town and village restaurants, women or mixed company will be directed to the 'family' area, whereas men without female companions will sit in a male-only section. In modern cafés men and women tend to sit according to relationship. In a private house in villages, you may eat at floor level rather than at a table, so prepare for aching leg muscles. The kitchen is considered the women's domain so men should not enter unless invited.

Managing to pay for a restaurant meal with Iranian friends is a major problem. The habit of 'going Dutch' is simply not an Iranian convention, and if you are a woman, the problem is compounded. It may sound like a freeloader's paradise but of course it is not. One possible answer is to talk to a sympathetic waiter to ensure that you get the bill, and have extra cash in case other friends or relatives join your table.

There are enormous difficulties finding a café or restaurant open during the daylight hours of Ramadan (page 70), when it is very important not to be seen in public smoking, drinking or eating.

DRINKS All alcohol is banned in Iran although the Christian communities, in Esfahan for example, are allowed wine strictly for communion use. However, Iran's famous vineyards are now being recultivated after most were uprooted in revolutionary zeal; the grapes are for eating, and for the production of grape juice, syrups and vinegar. Iranian (non-alcoholic) beer is drinkable at best, though Delster is just about palatable if well chilled. A very passable non-alcoholic 'lager' is Bavaria, now imported from Dubai or Russian non-alcoholic Baltika.

Local Iranian Zam Zam producer makes cola and Fanta-like carbonated soft drinks, but they tend to sweetness, and the fruit juices, either freshly pressed or in cartons, are more thirst quenching; try pomegranate juice (*ab anar*), cantaloupe melon (*ab talebi*) juice, and carrot juice with a scoop of ice cream (*ab havich bastani*) from fruit-juice shops, which is most delicious. The refreshing, pressed-lime sodas of pre-revolutionary Iran are slowly making a comeback and are sold in the streets (where you get it cheaper if drinking on the spot and returning the bottle) or local eateries. Another refreshing drink, *dough* (yoghurt and water, like Turkish *ayran* or Indian *lassi*), is available. A summer favourite in Iran is *khak-e shir*, a refreshing drink made with *sisymbrium irio*, a herb in the *Brassica* genus.

Tea is consumed continually. In larger cities there are now numerous cafés serving good coffee.

FOOD Iranian cuisine is one of the world's finest, an intriguing mixture of sweet and sour that owes nothing to the Chinese version. Savouring of the regional varieties is a fantastic feature of travelling in Iran. The first impression of a hungry traveller would certainly be that food choices are limited to kebabs and sandwiches, but this is certainly incorrect. Meals in restaurants are served and consumed with the speed of light, no Mediterranean-style nonchalant dinners here, but traditional food in local restaurants is an experience to look forward to.

The first rule to remember is that the balance between hot and cold foods is the essential part of Persian cuisine and you will need to know what foods can be combined and which have to be consumed separately. There is a whole science about what to eat or not to eat together in order not to upset your stomach and you will be surprised; it actually works. For example, rice and vegetables are considered cold and can thus be eaten with meat and high-fat foods, which are considered hot. It is not, however, recommended to drink *dough* and eat fish with *mast* (yoghurt) at the same time, as these are all cold foods. If in doubt, ask your waiter; in Iran everyone knows about these basic rules. Also remember that *dough* is generally believed to lower blood pressure, and a slice of lemon, or a spoon of freshly squeezed lemon or *narenji* will help your digestion after the meal.

Iranian *khoresht* – stewed dishes of meat and fruit – may sound uninspiring but wait until you've tried chicken in pomegranate and walnut sauce (*fesenjan*), lamb with morello cherries or apricots, beef or lamb with spinach and prunes (*aloo*) and chicken and *zereshk* (barberries), etc. The old-time favourite is *gormeh sabzi*, lamb or beef stew prepared with various herbs and beans. Delicious. Also try *abgoosht* (literally water-meat, a filling stew with meat and potatoes), or *dizzi* stew served in a jug-like container with a pestle and commonly available even at bus station restaurants. This is a concoction of slowly simmered pulses, meat and vegetables. *Abdoughkhiar* is a cold *dough*-based soup with cucumber: absolutely delicious and a must-try on a hot summer day. It is a vegetarian dish and so is *keshk-e bademjan*, a

2

RESTAURANT AND CAFÉ PRICE CODES

RESTAURANT PRICE CODES Prices indicate the average price of a main course for one person.

$$$	700,000 rials+
$$	300,000–700,000 rials
$	up to 300,000 rials

CAFÉ PRICE CODES Prices indicate the average price of a warm drink.

$$$	200,000 rials+
$$	100,000–200,000 rials
$	up to 100,000 rials

grilled aubergine dish eaten as a thick dip with fresh bread and is an all-time classic. *Keshk* is one of the Iranian specialities. Containing 75% protein, its benefits cannot be overestimated. A similar dish, *halim-e bademjan*, aubergine mashed with lentils and meat, is common for lunch. Saffron (in particular from Mashhad) itself is a very common ingredient that you will even taste in chicken kebab and rice.

There is also a great variety of regional dishes. A typically Caspian vegetarian dish *mirza qhasemi* of fried aubergine with a lot of garlic and butter, has since made its way into most traditional restaurants around Iran. In Azeri-populated areas *jegar* (liver) or *dureh* (intestines) kebab is common and very tasty. Tabriz is famous for *kofteh tabrizi*, a large meat ball with a plum inside. A Yazdian speciality is *ash-e shooli* or vegetable soup. When in Esfahan, try *beryani*, boiled lamb minced and fried with onion and spices or Esfahani favourite *khoresht-e mast*, sweet yoghurt stew. Mashhad is the home of *shishkik* lamb ribs (usually the most expensive dish on the menu) and *panirak* (also known as *kurg*) is a Qeshmian delicacy of palm date inner core. Milky in colour it is a little bitter to taste. There is also the classic winter dish *kalleh pacheh* (sheep's head soup) served in traditional *kalleh pazi* eateries.

White rice and bread are the staple foods. Much of the rice consumed in Iran is imported from India; it is cheaper than local produce. Authentic traditional and slightly more expensive restaurants will, however, serve local rice. Gilan rice is one of the best: a little mushy, but all the tastier. A delicious change is rice with butter slowly steamed until a crunchy, caramelised layer is formed. In Iran this is called *taqdiq* and is usually served on top of the plate of rice or separately. The time-honoured way of serving a number of dishes beside the main course, namely Iranian salads, servings of fresh mint leaves, etc, is called *sofreh* and traditional restaurants are then often called s*ofrehknaneh*, meaning a 'house of sofreh'. The Iranian equivalent of British fish and chips, or American hamburger and French fries, is *chelo-kebab*, a skewer of grilled lamb, served with plain rice. There is also Iranian coleslaw, which is often available in restaurants in place of salad or in addition, and is called *salad-e kalam* (cabbage salad). A local version of Lebanese *tabouleh* is called *salad-e shirazi* and is equally delicious while Olivier mashed potato salad served with a generous portion of bread will not leave you disappointed. *Zorat-e mekziki* (Mexican corn) is the all-time favourite snack on sale practically everywhere in the major cities.

And of course, there's the originally Shirazi sweet delight of *falludeh* ice (there are also regional Kerman and Yazd varieties), a sorbet with wispy 'noodle'-like strands, served with lime juice and ice cream. One of the joys of visiting Iran is eating *falludeh*, sipping tea or smoking a pipe in the attractive surroundings of a historic tea house. *Gooshfil* deep fried and *poolaki* caramelised sugar sweets are also widely popular.

During Ramadan, most restaurants serve special dinners for ending the day's fast, known as *iftar*. These are usually buffet-style or consist of a set of small dishes and start with sweet starters, such as figs, baklava and watermelon.

Meals Traditional breakfast includes bread, a white *feta*-like cheese with green herbs, *mast* yoghurt and tea taken without milk. Coffee, also taken without milk, is imported and thus is not widely available outside cafés and luxury hotels, where a wider breakfast menu is also served. Fried eggs (*nimru*) are also common and cost approximately 80,000 rials. Another typical breakfast dish is *halim-e gandom*, wheat porridge boiled and mashed with meat (usually beef). *Adasi* lentil mix is also commonly served in local eateries.

There are four main types of bread: *lavash* is a thin, flat white bread, best when very fresh as otherwise it looks and tastes like a bathmat; *sangak* is made from brown flour, and is thicker and oval in shape (but check for any stones that have become embedded during the milling/baking process); *taftun* (most common in Sistan and Baluchestan province) is crispy and round; and lastly, there's *barbari*, a deep oval white loaf with a crispy crust. A rough price for breakfast in a four-star hotel would be up to 400,000 rials, or half this in a two- or three-star hotel.

Lunch, taken around midday, is generally a rice and meat dish, often *chello-kebab*, served with a dish of either green herbs, or cucumber, spring onions and tomatoes and usually with a sweetened yoghurt dressing, often luridly coloured like some American-style bottled dressings. In a good tourist restaurant, the main dish at lunch will cost around 500,000 rials; fish is more expensive.

Dinner, eaten after 20.00, is generally at least three courses, consisting of thick barley or lentil soup, perhaps an appetiser, then a meat or fish dish with rice and a side salad, before finishing with seasonal fruit. Expect to pay 400,000 rials, though in smart Tehrani locales it can be double that or more. Few Iranians will take hot tea after eating chilled melon, and for most foreign visitors drinking iced or chilled water just after eating watermelon is a guaranteed stomach-churning combination. Thick black coffee akin to Turkish or Arab coffee, served in a small cup and always without milk, is occasionally available. As sugar is added during its making, specify the amount of sugar required as you order: *sa'adeh* (without sugar) or *kam shekar* (with a little sugar).

There is generally no tipping in Iran but most upmarket places in Tehran would add a compulsory service charge to the bill plus 9% VAT.

PUBLIC HOLIDAYS

Iran uses both the **solar calendar** and the **lunar calendar**. Lunar holiday dates vary, changing by about 11 days each year, as the lunar calendar has 11 days or so fewer than in the solar year, and is linked to the sighting of the new moon. Gregorian calendar dates mean very little to an average Iranian.

Gregorian calendar	Solar calendar	Lunar calendar (Hijra)
25 December 2020	05 Dey 1399	10 Jumada al-Awwal 1442
25 December 2021	04 Dey 1400	21 Jumada al-Awwal 1443
25 December 2022	04 Dey 1401	01 Jumada al-Akhira 1444

The Iranian solar calendar consists of 365 days and starts on 21 March, the first day of spring. The first six months of the year have 31 days each, the following five 30 days and the last month is 29 days long. Developed by the extraordinary poet and mathematician Omar Khayyam, the calendar was adopted in 1925 by Reza Shah as part of his nationalism project and is exceptionally accurate.

The lunar calendar (also known as Hijra) is used for religious Islamic holidays, while holidays such as Revolution Day and Nou Rouz will always fall on the same days of the solar calendar (although Nou Rouz, celebrated on the exact moment of the vernal equinox, sometimes starts on 20 March rather than the next day).

Iran has national holidays (NH) and religious holidays (RH) (feast or mourning ceremonies). On mourning occasions all sites will be closed. To try and make things more accessible we have provided Gregorian calendar dates in which some of these occur (both according to the lunar and solar calendars) on page 70. Low-key and extremely decorous behaviour during religious holidays is strongly recommended.

2020	2021	2022	Description
29 Jan	17 Jan	07 Jan	Martyrdom of Fatima (NH), the Prophet Mohammad's daughter, who according to the Shi'a belief died while trying to save her husband Imam Ali
11 Feb	11 Feb	11 Feb	Revolution Day (NH)
20 Mar	20 Mar	20 Mar	Nou Rouz – Iranian New Year holiday (NH)
02 Apr	02 Apr	02 Apr	Sizdah bedar/Nature Date (NH)
09 Apr	29 Mar	19 Mar	Imam al-Mahdi's birthday (RH)
23 Apr	12 Apr	02 Apr	Ramadan (Muslim month of fasting) (RH) begins
14 May	03 May	23 Apr	Martyrdom of first imam Ali (RH). Sites are closed.
24 May	13 May	03 May	Eid al-Fitr (RH) – the last day of Ramadan when Muslims celebrate the end of fasting and thank Allah for his help with their month-long act of self-discipline
17 Jul	06 Jul	27 May	Martyrdom of sixth imam Sadegh (RH). Sites are closed.
31 Jul	20 Jul	10 Jul	Eid al-Adha (in Iran called Eid al-Qorban) – Festival of Sacrifice marking the day after Arafat (RH). The Day of Arafat is the most important day in the hajj ritual. This is a four-day holiday.
08 Aug	28 Jul	18 Jul	Religious feast Eid al-Ghadir (RH) commemorating the occasion when the Prophet Mohammad designated his cousin Ali as the first imam
20 Aug	10 Aug	30 Jul	Al-Hijra – Islamic New Year (RH). Marks the migration of the Prophet Mohammad and his followers from Mecca to Medina.
28 Aug	18 Aug	07 Aug	Tasua – mourning holiday for martyrdom of third imam Hossein (RH). Sites are closed.
29 Aug	19 Aug	08 Aug	Ashura – Islamic holy day observed on the 10th of the Islamic month of Moharram (RH). Shi'a Muslims regard it as a major festival marking the martyrdom of the Prophet's grandson, Hossein.
08 Oct	28 Sep	17 Sep	Mourning bank holiday for Arbaeen of Imam Hossein (RH). Sites are closed.
17 Oct	07 Oct	26 Sep	Martyrdom of eighth imam Reza (RH). Sites are closed.
03 Nov	24 Oct	13 Oct	Milad al-Nabi (Birthday of the Prophet Mohammad). (NB: if Sunni Muslims mark this event, they do so some five days earlier but many of them regard its celebration as a religious innovation.) Birthday of sixth imam Sadeq (RH).
21 Dec	21 Dec	22 Dec	Shab-e Yalda (winter solstice) is considered an inauspicious time, so many people stay at home or pass the time with friends. Yalda – Syriac word for origin, meaning birth – rebirth of the sun on the morning following the longest night of the year.

Organising travel, accommodation and any business appointments during lengthy holidays such as Nou Rouz will require much planning and repeated confirmation to keep the bookings active. The situation is similar during Ramadan. It will be difficult during the daylight hours of the 28 days of the Muslim holy month to find restaurants and tea houses open except in four- and five-star hotels, and few dentists will accept patients (to avoid giving mouthwashes). Fasting inevitably means tempers are shorter, and little work is achieved. Try to avoid such times.

Nou Rouz is essentially a family holiday and unless arrangements have been made to spend it with Iranian friends and family, travel, in particular to Esfahan and Shiraz, can prove problematic as these two cities are the main destinations during the holiday season. Tehran, on the other hand, is best visited during this period. The Iranian capital is effectively vacated by its residents, making it hassle- and traffic-free to move around and about.

SOLAR Holidays of the solar calendar are deep-rooted in Persian culture and some have been celebrated for thousands of years. Iranians have a special affinity to the ancient Persian traditions and successfully combine solar calendar holidays (although some are essentially pagan) with religious Muslim celebrations.

Nou Rouz (meaning *new day*) is a very special celebration of life and spring. Calculated in accordance with the solar calendar, it is originally a Zoroastrian festival, and an established part of Iranian life. In 2010 it was even added to the UNESCO List of the Intangible Cultural Heritage of Humanity. It is a time for wearing new clothes and giving gifts, so if visiting or staying with friends it would be wise to get a supply of new banknotes for the children of friends, janitors, cleaning staff, etc. It is a tradition to celebrate Nou Rouz in a clean house and two weeks prior major cleaning of windows and the entire house begins. The same rule applies to hotels. Smaller hotels even close entirely in preparation for the busy holiday season. The first week is usually observed with family visits following a strict, unstated protocol. During Nou Rouz many offices, especially government departments, will be minimally staffed and keep erratic and shorter hours. The official state holiday closure is, however, only for four days, but most people are off for two weeks. There is a total closedown of services on the first day, and thereafter, reduced services, which slowly improve as the days go by. On *sizdah bedar* or the Nature Day that falls on 2 April and is the 13th day of the Nou Rouz holiday, transport is limited to very basic in major cities and to *savari* taxis and evening bus services. This is the day when Iranians occupy every inch of land to picnic and spend time with family and friends in the open air and take *sabzeh* (sprouts) from *haft-sin* out of their houses back into the open, usually transported on the top of vehicles.

The most characteristic feature of Nou Rouz is a *haft-sin* (meaning 'seven 's' in reference to the first letter in the name of the seven items displayed) table arrangement on display both in private houses and in public throughout the entire holiday season. Goldfish, symbolising happy life, go on sale everywhere a couple of weeks prior to this.

LUNAR All of these are Muslim holy days; the shorter lunar calendar means the holiday date advances approximately 11 days each year. Under the Pahlavi regime most of these were officially ignored but they are now observed; some are specifically Shi'a in character. Such holidays can mean office (including Iranian consulates abroad), bank and shop closures.

Arbaeen-e Hosseini The 40th day after Hossein's death.

Eid al-Fitr An important three-day feast marking the end of Ramadan with gifts given. Full-day closure on the first day.

Eid al-Ghadir Khom Held on the 18th day of Dhu al-Hijjah. The day the Prophet Mohammad appointed Ali as his successor.

Eid al-Qorban (Also known as Eid al-Adha) This feast marks the end of the pilgrimage season; sheep are sacrificed in the Muslim month of Dhu al-Hijjah.

Imam Hassan's martyrdom and Prophet Mohammad's death Held on the 28th day of the Muslim month of Safar.

Imam Sadeqh's martyrdom Held annually on the 25th day of the Muslim month of Shaval.

Moharram A full 28 days commemorating the tragic death of the third imam, Hossein. Radio and television programmes will be subdued during the first ten days, and women wear more sombre clothing. Locals, however, enjoy the celebrations and charity food known as *nazri* is served to people and mourners in the streets for free. Moharram commemorations often feature public scenes of emotional self-flagellation.

Ramadan Ramadan (pronounced *ramazan* in Persian) occurs 28 days from the sighting of the new moon. During this time, all Muslims with very few exceptions must refrain from drinking, eating and smoking during daylight hours. Even non-Muslims must not be seen in public doing any of these things; the consequences will be very serious. No weddings are held in this month.

Ruz-e Qatl-e Ali Imam Ali's martyrdom, 21st day of Ramadan.

Tasua and Ashura On the ninth and tenth day of Moharram respectively, marking the eve and actual day of Hossein's death with performances of the *taziyeh* (passion play) retelling the Karbala story (see box, opposite). On the ninth day in Yazd and Abyaneh, for instance, processions of athletic young men carrying the giant wooden *nakhl* (a large structure shaped like a palm leaf) are avidly watched by girls. Attend plays or procession *only* if invited and accompanied by friends, and leave your camera behind.

OTHER PUBLIC HOLIDAYS In addition, government offices and institutions, and some shops, will be closed on the following days:

Birthday of the 12th imam Held annually on the 15th day of the Muslim month of Sha'ban.

Imam Reza's birthday On the 11th day of the Muslim month of Dhu al-Qa'da. The city of Mashhad is especially busy.

Imam Sadeq and Prophet Mohammad's birthday On the 17th day of the Muslim month of Rabi al-Awwal; but note that Sunnis celebrate the Prophet's birthday on a different date. Sadeq (also spelt al-Sadeq) was the sixth iman and the last recognised as such by all Shi'a groups.

SHOPPING

Shopping hours are generally 09.00–13.00 and 16.00–20.00 (later in the summer); shops are usually closed on Fridays until around 17.00. During Nou Rouz, Ramadan and Moharram, expect shorter opening hours, especially in the bazaars.

For daily supplies, small **corner shops** sell everything, but check the expiry dates. In the large cities there are a few **supermarkets**. Refah, for example, has branches all across Iran, and the Cambo chain is most frequent in smaller towns. Upscale shopping malls in larger cities, in particular Tehran, also have their own exclusive supermarkets with foreign and local goods. Prices, especially of luxury and electrical goods, can range widely depending on whether the supplier is a small-scale importer or a franchise operator for a government-registered charity (page 85); certain cheaper items (eg: motor car spares) may be counterfeit. For **books** in English, there are plenty of stores in larger cities (see individual chapters).

The **bazaars** of Iran have well-earned reputations both as rabbit warrens and for haggling. Very few (eg: Tabriz and Zanjan) are located within a defined block; most (eg: Esfahan) have developed over the centuries to no predetermined plan. The medieval system which facilitated market inspection for weights and measures, pricing and quality, by gathering like trades in sectors (eg: coppersmiths in one quarter, goldsmiths in another, booksellers elsewhere) has been largely retained, so it is a matter of finding the correct section. Never presume you will easily find it or the actual shop again, so take the trader's business card and next time ask directions. Almost all traders have electronic calculators that facilitate bargaining for foreigners. Check whether rials or tumans are being quoted (page 57). The best souvenir bazaars are in Esfahan and Shiraz. Iranians usually shop in the smaller-scale shopping centres, called *passages* or go to a predefined street. In Esfahan, for example, children's toys and prams are sold on Abdulrazzaq Street and lamps and lights on Ferdowsi Street.

If you loathe haggling then the **Iranian Cultural Heritage, Handicrafts and Tourism Organisation** (ICHHTO) shops are strongly recommended. Prices are fixed in rials/tumans, but do check what exchange rate is being used, as it can be extremely disadvantageous. A visit to an ICHHTO at least gives an idea of local prices, and Iranians often frequent these centres too.

THE TRAGEDY OF KARBALA

Hossein, the younger son of Ali and Fatima, was born in Medina (in today's Saudi Arabia) in 626CE. On the death of the (Umayyad) caliph Muawiya in 680, recognised as the leader of all Muslims by the Sunni community, Hossein was 'invited' by the Medina governor to take an oath of allegiance to his successor, Yazid. Aware of imminent danger, Hossein, advised by Medina citizens to avoid taking this oath, left the city for Mecca and then Kufa in Iraq. Pursued by the Umayyad army, he told his supporters, numbering 72 excluding women and children, to leave him to his fate but they refused to desert him. The Umayyad forces poisoned the waterholes en route and Hossein's relative, Abbas Abu'l Fazl, volunteered to find drinkable water, losing both hands in the process. The small force reached Karbala on the second day of Moharram and again Hossein ordered his men to flee. They refused and battle commenced. Hossein, the third imam, and all 72 supporters were killed on 10 Moharram 61AH (680CE).

Iran has a well-established and efficient national cashless payment system. It is so good that some cafés or restaurants will not have cash to give back the change. Iranians are now paying with cards for the smallest of purchases and carrying a variety of notes in your wallet will be handy.

The **gold** (18 carat unless specified otherwise) and **silver** prices are published in newspapers every day, so the jeweller will weigh the piece and add something for the workmanship. The gold is of a high quality but often set with paste and semi-precious stones. It is unlikely that you can find a bargain without active participation by an Iranian friend, as gold is the established hedge against inflation. What Iran does have, however, is the world's best **turquoise**, widely available across the country, but of course best from Nishapur.

We cannot stress enough how useful, comfortable and cheap women's *manteaux* are (page 84). There is a universal size, though the length may need adjusting. The price is about 600,000 rials or upwards depending on the quality of fabric, colour, trimmings, seasonal weight, etc. In recent years there have appeared increasingly more shops selling exclusive and finely designed *manteaux*. These can be quite dear, but well worth the money, as the design and quality are excellent.

Carpets, miniature paintings, printed cottons, marquetry work (eg: picture and mirror frames, pen and cigarette boxes) and leather goods are popular purchases, but consider too a pair of cotton *giveh* (slippers), *gaz* (nougat), pistachio nuts and dried apricots or limes, spices like saffron or *sumak* (*Rhus coriaria*), or pomegranate juice to make *fesenjan* at home. As will be noted in the relevant sections, some towns are famous for certain products, for instance the rose water of Kashan and the sweetmeats or *termeh* cloth of Yazd. Esfahan is known for its block-printed cottons; the price range reflects the fabric quality, the number of blocks and dye/mordant baths involved; salted cool water is recommended for the first washing. Good-quality Kerman embroideries (on scarlet wool fabric) and Rasht patchwork are now difficult to find; look and compare. Miniature paintings are produced by college-trained artists in traditional styles; the finer the detail, the higher the price. Painting on 'bone' is always more expensive as tourists seem to prefer such work. Forget about acquiring an antique example of classical Persian painting. Firstly, export authorisation will be needed, and secondly there is a lively market in buying antique paper, washing it and painting on top.

As for handmade **carpets**, as distinct from machine-made, there are essentially two types and two pattern compositions. In both, look for secure fringes, good firm weft-edges and selvages or cords (clumsy oversewing can hide cut edges). *Ghelims* are plain weaves without any pile knotting, involving less yarn and production time and cost less. The quality can range from the very fine (used as throws, or drapes) to thick and hard-wearing. Complex and fine pattern detail means extra weaving time, which will be reflected in the price. *Ghelims* with long weave-slits in the pattern are more prone to future wear and tear. The second type incorporates pile-knots over the whole or part of the surface, which involves more work and yarn, so these carpets attract higher prices than *ghelims*. The official ban on exporting pile carpets was lifted a few years ago, but on your departure customs officials may ask to see your carpet, and the receipt (see box, page 180).

There are two essential pattern compositions: one is based on classical 'court' designs characterised by curvilinear motifs carried on arabesque scrollwork, and the other on 'tribal' patterns which have a more angular, geometrical appearance. The variations in patterns are infinite, as are their prices, quality and indeed the number of books about carpets. Always remember that so-called vegetable dyes and countless hours of work cannot transform a bad design into a work of art. You are more likely to get a bargain (though not necessarily 'authentic' Persian production) at home rather than from Esfahan, whose carpet dealers are notorious among Iranians.

With expensive purchases such as carpets (see box, page 180), avoid going into a carpet shop with a group to buy and don't be hassled into deciding within 30 minutes. If you do buy, it is safe to get rugs sent home (probably routed through Italy or Germany), and if you pay by credit card the billing will probably travel the same route (the US embargo again), and you'll have to the cover the card fee.

CULTURE AND ENTERTAINMENT

Social life in Iran tends to be firmly family orientated; 'friends' are usually members of the family.

In the first years of the Islamic Revolution, most of the theatres, the Tehran Opera House, cinemas and, of course, discos and nightclubs were closed, as it was considered that such entertainment was morally reprehensible, tainted by 'Westoxification'. But in recent years Iranian **theatre**, and especially **film**, with directors like Kiarostami, Ibrahimifar, Mehrjui, Bahmalbar, Farhadi et al, have blossomed. Films such as *Children of Heaven*, *The White Balloon*, *Taste of Cherry* and *A Separation* have all been nominated for or won prizes abroad. Subjects range from women in Islamic society, modern life and religious devotion, to themes such as the Iran–Iraq War and child abuse. The **Iranian International Film Festival** – the Fajr Film Festival (**w** fajrfilmfestival.com) – takes place annually in Tehran, usually in late January to early February to coincide with the anniversary of the Islamic Revolution. During this time, there are also important music and theatre festivals, which take place around Tehran.

During the Pahlavi era (1926–79) the traditional annual *taziyeh* or 'passion play' (comparable to the Oberammergau passion play) performed during Moharram (page 72) was officially banned. In his travel diaries from 1778, as the sole returnee from the Danish Royal voyage to Arabia Felix (Yemen), visiting Kharg Island, Carsten Niebuhr described a ceremony that was greatly similar to the modern *taziyeh*, where processions would last over nine days and conclude on the tenth day. Today most towns organise a performance that retells the tragedy of Ali's son, Hossein, and his family in their final hours at Karbala. Casual foreign visitors are not appreciated on these occasions, so attend only if specifically invited by a close Iranian friend. This advice also applies to the Moharram processions.

In the early years of the revolution only martial music, recitations and chanting of religious works were allowed but shortly before Ayatollah Khomeini's death it was announced that the sale and purchase of musical instruments was permitted. **Musical performances** now take place (with certain provisos), and since August 1999 the import of 'Western' instruments, such as pianos, has been allowed. In 2000, *The Phantom of the Opera* could be heard on the tannoy system in an Esfahani five-star hotel and music with a Latin American beat was being transmitted on radio and television. However, official disapproval of American and Western rock, reggae, etc, remains. Recordings (at times clandestine) of favourite émigré Iranian singers and musicians, along with upbeat Indian pop, can be bought in shops in major cities, and there is a growing home industry promoting young singers who sound like the émigré stars. In the mid 1990s it was not permitted for men to listen to female singers (passions would be inflamed) so it was usual practice, while driving, to change CDs when driving up to and departing from road checkpoints. Classical Persian music, however, is available without restrictions. Recordings of Mohammad Reza Shajarian are highly recommended. And over the past few years increasing numbers of street musicians are busking in cities around Iran (for instance outside the Azadi cinema in Tehran.

CRAFT Iran has a long tradition of art and craft, dating back centuries and even thousands of years. Persian **carpet making** is easily its most long-standing craft and dates back to the Achaemenid Empire (550–330bce), reaching its peak under the Safavid dynasty, with encouragement from Shah Abbas I. **Persian miniature paintings**, popular since the 13th century, with wonderful painted representations from the *Shahnameh* epic or the classic *gol-o morgh* (flower and bird) motif, can be seen as museum exhibits and souvenirs, while beautifully decorated **wooden items** such as pen boxes (*qalamdan*), or backgammon boards are simply exquisite.

SPORT Sports in Iran are strictly gender-segregated so public attendance is limited to male spectators, except where segregated seating (rarely found) has been installed. In 2006 President Ahmadinejad tried, alas unsuccessfully, to change the rules that banned women from watching football matches, but it was only in October 2019, under pressure from FIFA, that women were for the first time in 40 years allowed in. That day Iran beat Cambodia 14:0 in its 2022 World Cup qualifier.

When it comes to sports facilities, you will be pleasantly surprised to see a wide range of exercise equipment installed in parks all around the country and most parks also have bicycle-rental shops. At present you will also notice a few women hill walking (especially in northern Tehran) and there are, of course, sports training grounds and gyms for women in large cities, but access to facilities beyond that is quite limited. Indeed, medical concern has been voiced over women's health, and ex-president Rafsanjani's daughter, Faizeh, was a prominent campaigner in the late 1990s for greater access to facilities for women.

A major problem for women in sports has been the absence of a 'proper' sports dress design which is acceptable in all quarters, and which would allow the televising of women's team events and full participation in international events abroad. In September 2005 Tehran hosted the fourth Women's Islamic Games, which included participants in at least two disciplines from Britain, the first non-Muslim state to compete. At the 2008 Beijing Olympics, Iran's team included about 15 women all kitted out in headscarf and *manteaux* for the opening ceremony but clothed in more regular sports attire with headscarf for competition. More recently an Iranian woman who refused to remove her headscarf in an international karate competition and was excluded from the *tatami* mat as a consequence, was awarded a new car by the president in a public ceremony. However, the strict dress code is not acceptable in all quarters and does exclude female athletes from various competitions. In 2011, for example, the Iranian women's football team was banned from playing against Jordan in the London 2012 Olympics qualifier match. FIFA had previously banned the wearing of hijab, but allowed it again in 2014.

In 2017 Iranian female motocross rider Behnaz Shafiei organised Iran's first all-female race and continues training in her native country. Iranian women also perform well at world chess championships. Sara Sadat Khademalshariyeh took second place at the 2018 World Rapid Chess Championship.

Iranian men are sports mad, especially for **football** – as seen in the 1998 World Cup – **volleyball** and **basketball**. The Iranian national football team has the reputation of being one of the strongest in Asia. Tehran's national Azadi stadium is the 13th largest in the world by capacity and has been voted as the most intimidating in Asia for visiting teams because of the noise from spectators. Iranians also excel at wrestling, winning medals at major world championships, including five medals at the Olympic Games in Rio in 2016. Wrestling has been practised in Iran since antiquity, and it is also accessible to the majority of Iranian men, unlike skiing, for instance. If you have the opportunity, visit a local *zurkhaneh* (see box, page 172) to see the rigorous calisthenic routines the wrestlers perform. Many *zurkhaneh*s were

MUSEUMS AND TOURIST SITES

The double pricing policy, reintroduced in March 2013, has effectively been made obsolete by the drastic drop in 2018 and 2019 in the value of the Iranian currency. While the 500,000 rials entry ticket for foreigners to UNESCO-listed sites back in 2014 was worth approximately US$6, when going to print it was approximately US$4. With the exception of some smaller museums expect to pay up to 500,000 rials at each site.

closed by the late shah to curb the spread of anti-royalist propaganda, but have now reopened; even the most intellectual Iranian males know all the vocal audience responses for the sessions. Running in marathons is open for everyone, both male and female, and various races are held around the country at different times. Ultra Train Mount Damavand (w utmdamavand.com) partly organised by Adventure Iran (page 44) is particularly scenic.

Camel riding has its supporters, especially in the south, while in the north and west **shooting** and **horseriding** are popular.

The London 2012 Olympics saw two female Iranian athletes compete in shooting and one Iranian woman took part in the 1996, 2000 and 2012 Olympics archery competitions. Once a year in early June there is a women's horse race near Khorramabad.

Tehran has **tennis** clubs and an 18-hole **golf** course, but this is mainly reserved for middle- and upper-class Iranians. So is **skiing**, popular in Tehran, Shiraz, Hamadan and in Northern Azerbaijan province from January to the end of March, snow allowing (see box, page 121) and at weekends, particularly Thursday and Friday.

Mountain climbing is both exciting and popular. You can do it almost anywhere in Iran. The usual safety rules apply: wear suitable clothing for any unexpected weather conditions and always tell people of your route, estimated arrival and return times. It is wise to obtain official permits, and the tour company **Kassa** (e info@ kassaco.com) (page 44), which organises trips for the Mountain Federation of Iran, is very helpful. Useful information is available on the website w mountainzone.ir. Perhaps more popular among young Iranians (as it offers rare 'boy-meeting-girl' opportunities) is *kuh navardi* or **hill walking** in the mountains, especially along the paths of Darband, Tochal, Kolakchal and Jamshidieyh Park, north of Tehran, which are dotted with rudimentary tea houses ideal for short breaks. Again, Kassa or Adventure Iran can assist with routes and maps.

As for **swimming**, there are certain segregated pools or designated times/days for male or female use. At the seaside, women sit on the shore in a certain area and enter the water fully clothed, including the headscarf; foreign women are also expected to swim fully clothed, with the exception of specially segregated beaches on Kish Island, for example. Bathing shorts, but not thongs, are permitted for men on public or male-only beaches. **Scuba diving** is possible off Kish Island, where there is a good beach open to tourists, with showers, toilets and a (dry!) bar – swimsuits are permitted, but take your passport. There are **sailing** and **waterskiing** facilities on the public beaches of the Caspian Sea and in the Persian Gulf.

BOARD GAMES All 'gambling' is prohibited under Islamic law. Cards and dice-playing for money are also theoretically banned, but backgammon and chess are allowed and you can find sets to play at cafés in Tehran and Shiraz, but less frequently so in Esfahan. The revolutionary proscription on the sale and purchase of chess sets was lifted in 1989, and now chess competitions take place. Iranians are in fact famous for their chess skills. In February 2016, 19-year-old Sara Sadat Khademalshariyeh took second prize at the FIDE (World Chess Federation) Women's Grand Prix Championship held in Tehran. Esfahan Bazaar around Maydan-e Imam has a wonderful variety of lacquered and beautifully painted backgammon and chess boards to bring home as a souvenir.

HAMAMS Particularly if you are staying in very modest hotels, think of visiting a *hamam* (public bath); those still in operation are open to men only. There are some exceptions (eg: in Varzaneh or near Tajrish Bazaar in Tehran) where local *hamams* might have opening times for women as well. Always go before, not after, eating a meal. You will emerge squeaky clean and scoured to one surviving millimetre of skin. The desk person will organise your session after you decide whether to have a massage or shampoo as well as the 'bath' (somewhat of a misnomer because hot and cold water are sloshed over you). 'Plunge pools' are available only if the *hamam* is in a special spa area. Your clothing and valuables can be secured under lock and key, but never undress to the point of nudity. Towels, bath wraps, soap and shampoo can be provided at a small extra charge, as can tea and coffee.

MEDIA AND COMMUNICATIONS

POST Postage is inexpensive: to send a postcard to anywhere in the world will cost approximately 100,000 rials; the service takes about a week. Postboxes are yellow and are located near to post offices, where stamps are obtained, or in the vicinity of tourist areas. There are very few postboxes anywhere else. Letters or parcels that require weighing involve a visit to the post office, and many good hotels will undertake this kind of service on the traveller's behalf.

TELEVISION AND RADIO Iranian television has more than 18 channels: the first two are general; the third one was initially intended for younger audiences, but is similar in content to the first two. The fourth channel is dedicated to poetry and science, the fifth is all about Tehran news, the sixth is news only, the seventh broadcasts educational programmes, while the eighth is the Quran channel. A few channels are dedicated to film; one to health and one to sports. The 15th channel is PressTV, broadcasting news in English.

Until recently, Iranian television films were increasingly based on historical themes, or recalled the heroic sufferings of the Iraqi conflict. The pace was never more than slow and there was always an unambiguous moral to the plot. TV series and movies now focus more on social and family issues and many Western 'morally acceptable' films are freely broadcast on national television. Satellite dishes were banned in 1995 as the authorities feared unsuitable programmes were being received (reportedly the American *Baywatch* series, with its silicone-endowed females, was very popular), but now with the internet, there is no longer a need to have a satellite dish installed. Depending on the geographic location in Iran, Turkish, Azerbaijani or Arab channels can be received.

Regarding radio, tune into BBC Radio World Service/VOA on the half-hour for news broadcasts. Many people watch the VOA Farsi channel on the Hot Bird satellite and the BBC has an excellent television service (w bbc.co.uk/persian/).

NEWSPAPERS AND BOOKS Three newspapers, under direct or indirect government control, are printed in English: *Kayhan International* (w kayhan.ir/en), *Tehran Times* (w tehrantimes.com) and *Iran Daily* (w iran-daily.com). There has been a marked change in content and criticism since the elections in February 2000, when there was full coverage of the notorious vote-counting muddle, offering a wide diversity of views. A crackdown in press coverage ensued and another followed in 2004, after public disquiet over the disqualification of some 2,000 parliamentary candidates from standing for election. Over 20 newspapers and magazines have been closed by the Council of Guardians and the standard of reporting now verges on the innocuous. Parliamentary requests for an official investigation into press closures have been rejected by the Supreme Leader as being against Islamic law. That said, there are dozens of newspapers in Iran and although the content is written and presented in a certain format, not all of it is unbiasedly pro-government.

Nowadays, there is a variety of English-language books, including learning materials, novels and history, on sale in major cities across Iran. Bestsellers published abroad are quickly translated into Persian and although Iranian-published English translations of such important Persian poets as Omar Khayyam, Hafez and Saadi are generally poor, these are widely available and recommended as introductory literature to the country.

TELEPHONE AND INTERNET These days most travellers have a **mobile telephone** but as roaming charges are high, you may prefer to buy a local SIM card, either Irancell or Hamrah Aval, with the latter offering better coverage in mountainous areas, for example. Irancell now offers a tourist SIM card for one month with 1.5–5GB coverage (w irancell.ir; 300,000–580,000 rials). If calling a mobile number within Iran, use all 11 digits. That said, if you are staying in Iran longer than a month, your actual phone device would have to be registered, otherwise it will be blocked from being used with any SIM card, including the one from back home. Only holders of residency permits in Iran can register their device purchased abroad.

The **internet** is widely available, though be aware that some sites may be blocked and the connection may not be very fast. In addition, some Iranian websites do not open when checked from abroad. Hotels generally have Wi-Fi and in most towns and cities it will be reasonably easy to find cheap internet access. Do note that Facebook and Telegram (a Russian-developed messaging service) are officially blocked, but the young and creative have their ways around it. You can access it by downloading a VPN shield for your phone. (See also the box on page 2.)

For communication, around 20 million Iranians, including businesses and teenagers, use the Telegram messaging service. WhatsApp is less frequent, but is growing in popularity as it is unfiltered. Instagram is also very popular, with some local businesses opting for it instead of creating their own individual websites.

Telephone numbers Iranian **landline** numbers have 11 digits and always start with a 0 (eg: 021 66727026 for Ferdowsi Grand Hotel in Tehran). The first three digits denote the city or province code (eg: 021 for Tehran). If dialling a landline number from a landline within the same city or province, omit the first three digits (landline). Otherwise, from a mobile phone or nationally, the number has to be dialled in full. There are some special shortened numbers (eg: 75426 for Hestooran Restaurant in Tehran) and these have to be dialled as they are. **Mobile** numbers also have 11 digits, but the first four stand for the network provider and always start with 09 (eg: 0937 9652371 for Howzak House in Esfahan). When dialling a mobile number from a landline or another mobile number within Iran, all 11 digits have to be dialled. When dialling from abroad, add 0098 and omit the 0 in both the landline and the mobile number (eg: 0098 21 66727026 for Ferdowsi Grand Hotel in Tehran).

One of the perks of being a businessman involved in overseas work is that glowing feeling that someone else is paying for the travel and accommodation. Even better when the destination is unusual and redolent of the mysteries of faraway lands. Iran will not disappoint the attentive traveller: it has a rich history and cultural traditions. Above all, it is very different from Europe and America. Scratch beneath the surface of modernity and you will find a world of cultural nuance, literary allusion and a history to match any, involving the sweeps of empire and transition.

There are several issues of business culture in Iran to rapidly absorb. In general, overseas business travellers may talk of prevarication as an artform in the Middle East but it will mostly come down to doing the homework about what the client requires and whether there are funds in hand. Business in Iran is booming and contracts are being placed all the time so somewhere the prevarication is replaced by action. The savvy will be able to spot the drift of an opportunity by asking firm questions and getting their Iranian counterparts to follow agendas and sign minutes of meetings. Politeness and warm greetings are no substitute for serious and contested negotiations. As a measure of development of the business, the strength of the discussions – as opposed to mere civility – will tell the businessman he is on the right track.

Iranians are practised negotiators from birth. Children will be seen haggling over prices in the corner grocery store. Negotiation is a national sport that most Iranians love. It is a highly entertaining form of conversational jousting with (often) considerable humour. Just listening to two Iranians twist and turn to gain the upper hand in settling a price is a delight. So the overseas businessman brought up on fixed prices and glacial, or simply bored, stares from shop assistants is an innocent waiting to arrive.

BUSINESS

The working week is theoretically around 40 hours long, with annual leave of about 30 days per annum. Most government offices are open 08.00 to 14.00 Saturday to Wednesday and 08.00 until noon on Thursday, with other offices, workshops, bazaars, etc, generally having longer working days; bazaars close between 13.00 and 16.00.

There is a confusing multiplicity of public holidays (page 70) when offices, government departments and bazaars are shut. If visiting Iran for business, do allow at least three times the number of days you think necessary to see people – even if appointments have been confirmed. To cope with inflation and low wages, many Iranians may have more than one job, which usually involves crossing town and meeting the inevitable traffic jam, so appointments are often subject to long delays or last-minute cancellations.

OPENING TIMES

Opening times in Iran are seasonal and vary from sector to sector. Banks, for example, are usually open from 09.00 until 13.00, Sunday to Thursday. Major tourist sites are open from around 10.00 until 18.00 in autumn and winter, and from 09.00 or even 08.00 until 20.00 in spring and summer. In the summer, Persian gardens stay open until 22.00, but sites may sometimes be closed for unofficial holidays (eg: Cyrus Day always falling on 29 October).

The overseas businessman must prepare for this sport. Practise a sour or disappointed look at the first mention of a discount. Work at this in front of the mirror. Until tears roll down your cheeks looking at your reflection, you have not practised enough. Even with this new skill you will need resilience, patience and determination.

The business traveller should be aware that the Iranian authorities take a dim view of foreign travellers wandering off to remote and possibly sensitive spots such as border regions. Stick to the beaten path of tourism; it is not overly patronised, contains plenty of interest and means you avoid coming under suspicion.

Other helpful hints (purely random) would be:

- Always look both ways before crossing a one-way street
- Do not believe zebra crossings are there for the pedestrian to cross unharmed
- Do not blow your nose in public
- However inappropriate for the weather, wear a collar and tie as far as possible, because it fits the Iranian idea of a foreign male businessman
- Men should not try to shake the hand of a woman
- Be careful where you take photographs (page 26)

Most of all I would recommend that the businessman should expect to be surprised. We all get jaded travelling around the world from one concrete and glass bunker to another; Iran will definitely not be like that. Try the local food; go beyond the delicious kebabs and fruit juices and revel in the difference. This guide outlines so many fascinating places to see around Iran and hopefully the business traveller can be encouraged to experience some of them.

Shops, but not shopping centres or malls, are closed from around 13.00 until 16.00, then reopen until 20.00. Restaurants are usually open for lunch from noon until 16.00 and for dinner from 18.00 until 23.00. In larger cities and tourist areas restaurants and eateries are open throughout the day daily. Bazaars are also open Saturday to Thursday, with some reopening in the evenings.

CULTURAL ETIQUETTE

Just to repeat: no eating, drinking or smoking in public during daylight hours of the 28 days of Ramadan (page 70). The repercussions otherwise may be very serious. You'd also do well to abide by the following:

SHOES Entry into a 'working' religious building or into a private home entails removing shoes at the edge of the carpet, rug or floor covering in order to prevent street filth being brought in. Feet (especially women's) should ideally be covered with socks or nylons which should be put on discreetly beforehand – it has been argued that women's bare toes may drive men to thoughts of sexual fantasy. It is, however, common to wear sandals in the summer and thus enter a house with bare feet once invited. Shoes are removed just at the transition of pavement or earth to floor covering. *Not* before. *Not* after. By all means untie or slacken shoes before, but remove shoes/sandals only at the transition point and likewise on leaving, when you slip on your shoes; they can be fastened up later at leisure. Ignoring this convention causes great disquiet and disgust, perhaps akin in Western society to excavating your nasal passages in public and examining the contents minutely before consumption.

If visiting a family house (removing your shoes in the entrance hall) and using the bathroom or toilet, slip on the sandals placed near the bathroom door and return them when re-emerging. Such footwear is not worn elsewhere in the house.

TOILETS The toilet won't necessarily have toilet paper, but if you take some with you, this and any other used sanitary product should be jettisoned into the waste-paper bin as the small waste pipes become easily blocked. This often explains the shaky nature of the actual WC in some hotels, as these are often unscrewed and untied to clean up blockages.

TRANSPORT In taxis, long-distance buses and so on passengers sit according to gender or family. On city buses, men go to the front, women to the back section (although on some routes in Tehran it is the other way round). Some buses have separation barriers in between and, if you are travelling with a companion, agree where to meet before you are separated! That said, this rule is not strictly adhered to, in particular in major cities, as long as the bus is not busy and there is no actual physical contact between the male and female passengers. In the **metro**, the first and the last few cars are for women only. It is not uncommon outside rush hour, however, to see male and female passengers travelling together in the cars reserved for men.

CONTRABAND All forms of pornography are banned, and of course the definition of 'pornography' never lies with the owner. All publications by Salman Rushdie are banned, along with all alcohol (page 57) and drugs. The authorities are very determined to stamp down on the growing drug problem (Iran has the highest addiction rate in the world), so lorries, intercity buses, etc, are often searched; penalties are severe. As in China, homosexuality 'does not occur' in Iran and such behaviour is forbidden and illegal, carrying harsh penalties. Men often hold hands and embrace each other, but this is a sign of friendship and has no sexual connotations. In contrast, 'lady-boys' or men who have clearly had a sex change may cross your path, especially in major cities, as gender change is permitted in the Islamic Republic and applicants even receive subsidies to 'correct' their being trapped in the 'wrong body'.

INTERACTING WITH PEOPLE Apart from close family relatives (eg: husband/wife, parent/children, brother/sister), it is not done for a Muslim to touch the opposite sex except in an emergency or danger. Thus if an Iranian ignores an outstretched hand, this is not rudeness: strictly speaking, handshaking between the sexes is not acceptable. In post-Ahmadinejad Iran, however, increasingly more young and liberal Iranians shake hands and hold hands with the opposite sex or even kiss on the cheek. That said, we nonetheless recommend that visitors to Iran refrain from overtly liberal behaviour, unless their Iranian counterpart indicates that it is acceptable. Remember that a German businessman was detained for years on the grounds of 'having knowledge' (British Foreign and Commonwealth Office biblical coyness!) of an unrelated, unmarried Iranian woman. If asked out by a member of the opposite sex, you should enquire who else will be coming.

When visiting Iranian friends or a family, it is customary to take flowers, sweetmeats or chocolates, etc, and, if possible, wrap them. To show you are more important than any gift, your host will probably place it unopened to one side but the gesture has been really appreciated. By all means praise the house, the food and hospitality offered but never a household item (eg: dish, glass) unless you are sure it is nailed to the floor or otherwise permanently fixed, or you could be deeply embarrassed having to accept it as a gift (and having therefore to part with a prized possession when the visit is reciprocated).

At a family meal, even your third refusal to eat or drink more will not be accepted, but persevere. This rule of etiquette is known as **ta'arof** in Persian, which effectively implies that it is common sense to say 'no' for the first time and second time and even third time, even to something you badly want. Strictly speaking, when in the desert and thirsty the first answer to an offer of a bottle of chilled water should still be 'no'.

Ta'arof extends to even the most straightforward interactions. Asking to confirm the fare at the end of the taxi ride, the driver will most likely reply *qabel-e nadare*, meaning that it was so little that it was not even worth mentioning in your presence. Politely say *merci* and hand over the amount, saying *befarmaeed* (there you are/ please)! Insist if the driver perseveres. At the end, after a couple of smiles and words exchanged, you will both feel to have shown sufficient respect towards each other and concluded a transaction to the satisfaction of both parties.

As in visiting any Muslim household, foreign women should expect to be closeted with the women, although on some occasions they may be treated as 'honorary men' for the visit. Similarly, foreign men might not see the women of the household during their stay. It is also customary for female visitors to leave their hijab on indoors as well, unless the female host suggests it is acceptable to take it off and perhaps does it herself.

For any appointment, arrive on time but with little expectation that others will do the same; often business appointments or meetings will be cancelled with little or no notice.

Iranians are knowledgeable and intensely proud of their country, its history and cultural heritage, and rightly so. They often make very amusing and critical jokes about themselves, their society and public personalities, but can be quickly hurt or insulted by any jokes or denigration expressed by a foreigner. Just be an appreciative audience, not a commentator.

Owing to hunger and tiredness, even the sweetest-tempered Iranians tend to be irritable during Ramadan (page 72).

If you wish to compliment someone on a child, a new baby, a new possession, etc, it will really be appreciated if you precede or supplement your compliment with the phrase *mashallah*, which asks for Allah's blessing, so thwarting evil.

If in need of help or assistance, it is best to approach a person of the same gender, unless you wish to complain about harassment. Here only another man can rightly put the culprit in his place. As previously mentioned, single women should avoid walking unescorted in dimly lit public areas at night; it will be assumed they are prostitutes. However, it is acceptable, especially during mild summer evenings, for women to walk alone in northern parts of Tehran or busy public areas, such as Naqsh-e Jahan Square in Esfahan. It is always important to exercise situational judgement; be cautious, but not excessively so thus precluding yourself from enjoying the evening and the trip.

DRESS
Men Before 1997 full-length shirtsleeves were required but now elbow-length is deemed acceptable. Garish colours and vivid Hawaiian shirts should be avoided.

Shorts, even knee length, are not acceptable, except for mountain biking. Ties are not widely worn by Iranian men; during the first years of the Islamic Revolution some believed that the *kravat* was a hallmark of anti-revolution intellectuals, similar to how the Red Guard in 1970s China viewed spectacles. Designer stubble is still in fashion (formerly the mark of a revolutionary), but most Iranian men visit a barber every other day or so for a shave; it is cheap (US$3 including tip) and very relaxing, we are told.

Women Spring 2007 saw the first 'fashion' show in a hotel, with the state saying it was 'happy' (undefined) as long as the garments and colours were modest. The dress code is simple and inexpensive, but to ignore or flout it is guaranteed to upset people, even if this is not expressed in words, and Iranian women clearly and warmly appreciate foreign women making the effort. The scarf, to be worn all the time except in the privacy of the hotel bedroom, should be at least 1m² so that the nape of the neck and the ears are concealed; long cotton ones may be best with the ends over the shoulders. A nun-like coif is not needed; Iranian women will soon warn you if too much hair is showing. At holy sites in Qom and Mashhad, women will also be reminded to cover their hair fully.

As for the actual dress, the essential requirement is to conceal distracting feminine bumps and curves and any bare skin save hands and face. Equally, refrain from wearing see-through clothes and low cleavages. Forget the semi-circular chador, which takes years of practice to wear successfully, especially when carrying bags, cameras and packages. (It is, however, required in some shrines such as Shah Cheragh in Shiraz, and the Qom and Mashhad precincts, but may be hired or borrowed.) Instead, wear the loose-fitting *manteau* (or *rupush*), a full-length, long-sleeved 'coat' made of lightweight cotton, poplin, etc, for summer, and thicker fabrics for winter. *Manteaux* can be purchased easily for US$10; many visitors buy several to use as evening coats back home. If you are on an organised tour though, beware, as it is not always possible to buy a *manteau* immediately on arrival and it may be advisable to search out an 'overall' before leaving home, perhaps from a shop supplying uniforms; alternatively Indian-style dress of *shalvar kameez*, basically baggy trousers and tunic, is acceptable. If you are saving every penny, a knee- or lower thigh-length, long-sleeved, loose tunic works, but only if worn with an ankle-length skirt or loose trousers underneath. The *manteau*, however, is so much cooler and more comfortable in high temperatures. The fabric should be opaque, of course, and plain or discreetly patterned. Other than

MANDATORY HEADSCARF

Mandatory headscarf, called *rusari* in Persian, often causes discomfort and conflicting feelings among many female visitors to Iran. It was initially banned in 1936 by Reza Shah, prompting 8 January 1936 to be known as the Emancipation Day. Chador, which is the full-length from head to toe typically black garment, was subsequently banned within three weeks. First, women were not allowed covered in Tehran's outer districts, then on the main streets and finally in the heart of the city, including the bazaar. The same applied to Esfahan and Shiraz. In the early 1980s, however, after the Islamic Revolution, this has been reversed and although the new generation of Iranians has redefined what it means to cover your hair, the wearing of a headscarf remains mandatory in all public areas in Iran.

during Moharram (page 72), when more muted colours are generally worn, pastel colours such as rose pink, powder blue, beige and old gold are popular. White (a mourning colour), and emerald green (recognised as the Prophet's colour) are best avoided. As for the headscarf (*rusari*) or hijab (its more formal version), when you arrive in Iran, make sure you have one in your hand luggage so you can put it on before leaving the plane. When in Iran you may also like to purchase *maghnae*, a tighter official form of hijab worn by schoolgirls, female university students and any female in an official capacity. It is easy to wear and hassle-free. No need to fix your hair and you can blend in better. Despite the end of the Ahmadinejad administration, the wearing of the hijab is strictly enforced. In 2016, as a showcase for their power, the authorities arrested a number of Iranian models posing on the internet without hijab for 'promoting Western promiscuity'.

Women are advised to refrain from **smoking** in public; it is considered vulgar with all sorts of negative connotations attached.

TIPPING As a general rule you are not expected to tip in restaurants, especially not in local ones. In others there is a compulsory service charge (up to 15%). Hotel porters will be satisfied with 10,000 rials for each bag or case, while airport porters will expect 10,000 rials and more if you want help through customs. For toilet attendants, 5,000–10,000 rials is usually the fixed price. Mosque and tomb guardians unlocking doors, etc, should be given upwards of 20,000 rials, depending on their help. As for taxi drivers, if you have negotiated the price already (eg: a half-day trip), he will hope this does not include a tip; if he has been extra helpful, why not add 10% extra? If you are using the Snapp taxi service, a little tip will always be welcome as their rates are the lowest across the market. For an Iranian tour guide, so much depends on the time, effort and work he or she puts into the job, but think of at least US$3 a day from each person if it's a large group, or US$8 a day each if travelling by yourself or with one or two friends; the driver might be given about a third less, but again much depends on whether he has been particularly helpful.

Remember that wages are low and inflation high, and the benefit system for the mentally ill, disabled and elderly is not as generous in Iran as it is in the West.

TRAVELLING POSITIVELY

The concept of 'charity' differs in each culture, and both Iranian officials and individuals will be affronted by any action they see as patronising and interventionist. On all streets, there are metal blue and yellow charity-box stands, often decorated with a rose or tulip symbol, placed by the kerb. If you wish, you can contribute money. These boxes are usually for the Imam Khomeini Relief Foundation (**Emdad**) for orphans and the poor; its administrators are responsible to the Supreme Leader. An important series of charitable trusts is **Bonyad** (one of which is the Organisation for the Oppressed and Disabled of the Islamic Revolution), which administers most of the Iranian property and holdings of the late shah's Pahlavi Foundation charity, and of former high-ranking courtiers (thus a number of tourist hotels are run by Bonyads). Said to be the franchise holder of Mercedes, BMW, Volkswagen and Toyota, the full scale and financial value of Bonyad's assets is not known as there is no legal requirement to make its annual accounts public; its head answers only to the Supreme Leader and over 40,000 people are in its direct employment.

There is also the *vaqf*, or religious endowment, for mosques and other religious buildings. Since early Islamic times, individuals and businesses have

Frances Harrison, former BBC Tehran correspondent 2004–07

It's the traffic that hits you first in Tehran. I was amazed that even the British Foreign Office travel advisory warns visitors that they may have trouble with the style of driving. Huge six-lane highways, named after ayatollahs who would otherwise have long been forgotten, teem with pollution-spewing, Hillman Hunter taxis interspersed with Mercedes and 4×4 jeeps and the odd pick-up truck with a bleating sheep being transported for slaughter. Late at night Iranians play real-life speed cars – inspired by computer games – chasing strangers on the highway. You can't live in Tehran without experiencing a few car accidents – sometimes all on one day. Friday lunchtime, when everyone goes out for kebabs because it's the weekend, is one of the most dangerous times because the roads are a little less clogged with commuters going to work and so drivers can go faster. I've seen several dead bodies and appalling pile-ups in Tehran – even a man writhing in pain after his foot was run over by a woman driver.

Statistics for road accidents in Iran are horrific and exceed death rates for major earthquakes. Most Iranians will think nothing about driving at speed the wrong way down a one-way road or reversing down a main thoroughfare if they've missed a turning. Once you get used to the style it's very hard to adjust to driving in somewhere like London again. It's frustratingly sedate.

Transport aside, it's pretty safe if you're not involved in politics. When I first arrived and went out shopping I stood in a queue for ice cream for my son and was amazed to find the man in front of me insisted on buying the ice cream for him. He was a total stranger but realised we were foreigners and wanted to be friendly. Personal hospitality is deep-rooted even though the revolution has led to officials being staggeringly rude at times. Clerks will hardly look up from their TV screens or ledgers and often throw the relevant bit of paper at you without

assigned property and/or rents over to a building to pay for its upkeep, repairs and equipment. Thus a popular monument might be awash with funds but another falling into terminal decline. For instance, the person heading the *vaqf* administration for the Shrine of Imam Reza, Mashhad, is responsible for donations and also for investment in all associated economic activities such as manufacturing, farming, housing projects and food-processing plants. It is one of the most influential and wealthy institutions and, as with the Bonyad, its head reports to the Supreme Leader and there is no legal requirement for the publication of annual accounts.

From talking to people in Iran and asking them about 'travelling positively', the reaction is always the same: tell your friends and family how much you enjoyed your visit to Iran. So the greatest gift to them will be in disseminating accurate information rather than hyperbole about the current situation in Iran, arguing for and promoting a better understanding. And, of course, redistributing some of your hard-earned money in the bazaars of Iran will improve the lot of everyone.

It is at present not easy to locate a specific charity in Iran. You can either give something directly to a person in the street or ask your hotel for advice. In Shiraz, however, contact Peyman Soodmand (page 242) who can help not only with information about the charity in khanqah Ahmadi, providing food and care for the homeless in the city, but will make sure that whatever you would like to contribute reaches those in need.

even making eye contact. But the most intimidating woman in a black chador at a security check post will melt when she realises you are a foreigner and especially if she finds you speak a few words of Farsi. Even demonstrators shouting 'death to England' will find it hard to be really rude and unpleasant to an individual Englishman or woman.

There are many pleasures in living in Tehran: the snow-capped Alborz Mountains on a sunny spring day with the mountain water running down the open drain channels (known as *jubs*) on either side of the roads, or whole families barbecuing elaborate meals for picnics in parks and even on spare strips of grass alongside motorways.

Iranian food helps the quality of life. On the way to my house there was a small corner shop selling pomegranate juice – freshly squeezed as you wait and decanted into used plastic water bottles. Few know Iran produces its own brand of mozzarella cheese, and sour cream and chives crisps that would rival anything you'd find in a giant Western supermarket. Getting away from global consumerism isn't entirely possible in Iran but there is no McDonald's – just an Islamified burger joint, Mac Marshallahs. There are traditional restaurants in the foothills of the mountains – retreats from the summer heat where you can lounge on carpet-covered beds while drinking mint-flavoured yoghurt and nibbling on fresh herbs, goat's cheese and hot flat bread. Afterwards it's traditional Persian ice cream – something you can't find anywhere else in the world – sticky, chewy and served sandwiched between wafers. Even 18th-century European travellers to Persia commented on how obsessed the locals were with talking about their cuisine. I have sat at dinners where 80% of the conversation has been about the food – the process of cooking, the quality of the raw materials, the price of ingredients and so on. The other 20% is about how awful their journey was to get there.

UPDATES WEBSITE

You can post your comments and recommendations, and read feedback and updates from other readers online at w bradtupdates.com/iran.

Part Two

THE GUIDE

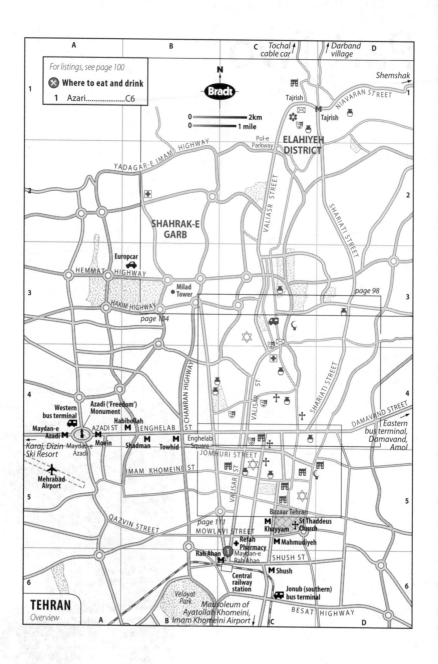

3

Tehran and the Road South

TEHRAN تهران *Telephone code 021*

Looking at the sprawl of modern Tehran spreading up north into the Alborz foothills and to the east absorbing the town of Karaj, the capital of Alborz province, it is difficult to believe that before 1795, when it became the Qajar capital, it was an insignificant village of approximately 15,000 residents, 'possess[ing] nothing, not even a single building, worthy of notice' (Thomas Herbert, 1627). Then, there were unimpeded views of Mount Damavand (5,610m) and the Alborz. By 1850 the city's population had escalated to around 90,000, more than a fourfold rise in 50 years, enjoying its improved water supply, extended bazaars and newly built caravanserais (see box, page 165). In late 1867, inspired by the urban planning in St Petersburg and the work of Haussmann in Paris, Naser al-Din Shah ordered the French military engineer General Buhler to tear down the city walls, fill in the defensive ditch to form thoroughfares wide enough for European-style carriages, extend the walls of the Arg (citadel) and double the number of gates to 12 (all of which have since been destroyed). By 1920, the population was estimated at 210,000 and it then quadrupled again by 1946. Since then the figures have soared: a conservative estimate in 1992 was over 6.5 million in the immediate centre with half again in the outlying suburbs. Currently the population of Tehran is over 12 million, which is approximately one-seventh of the country's total figure. While population growth in Iran from 2006 until 2011 had only been around 1.3%, the general urbanisation rate has now passed 70%, which may suggest further growth of the capital as more people from the villages are moving here in search of employment. Tehran now accounts for more than half of the country's economic activity and the inner areas of the city are home to around 50 colleges and universities, making it the most dynamic student city in the country.

Today, with the number of private cars almost doubling since 1985, low-lying smog usually hides the mountains 2 hours after sunrise. A weather phenomenon known as 'inversion', which happens when a thick layer of smog is trapped over the city by colder weather from the surrounding mountains, is also regular here. In 2014, out of 365 days, 12 were considered to be unhealthy for everyone and 148 unhealthy for individuals with respiratory health problems. No wonder the citizens of Tehran escape when they can to the hills and the Caspian region to breathe fresher air. The gravity of the problem has nonetheless been acknowledged and since 2016 numerous campaigns and billboards inside the metro encourage commuters to use the underground transport network and refrain from driving cars. Pollution, however, is not the only challenge to living in Tehran. The city is located in a seismic zone and as recently as December 2017 experienced a 5.2-magnitude earthquake, forcing people to sleep outside for fear of returning to their homes.

Many tourists shun Tehran and proceed directly to the historical south, but the Iranian capital is a wonderfully diverse and vast city with a vibrant café culture, the best art scene in the country and pleasant parks scattered around the city perimeter. If visiting Tehran before and around Nou Rouz, you will be pleasantly surprised by light traffic, fresh air and flower blossom aromas at the city's largest Mahallati flower market, selling more than 5 million flowers every day.

While its southern parts (around Golestan Palace) offer, or rather conceal from the general view, a vast range of historic monuments, upper affluent northern Tehran (Alborz foothills) is the place for an evening stroll or weekend mountain hiking (Tochal). It is easier to get around if you think of Tehran as one never-ending Valiasr Street and everything else springing from it, like branches from a tree. When flagging down a taxi, make sure to give the driver not the house number, but the Valiasr Street intersection.

GETTING THERE AND AWAY

By air Tehran is usually the first stop on any visit to Iran. Despite the distant perceptions of Iran, its capital is located at a surprisingly short flying distance from major European capitals and Istanbul. That said, most European airlines, including **British Airways** and **Air France/KLM** all cancelled their services to Iran in September 2018 following the withdrawal of the US from the Nuclear Agreement. **Austrian Airlines** still operates its daily flights from Vienna to Tehran, but has cancelled services to Esfahan and Shiraz. **Lufthansa** also still flies to Tehran, but prices with European carriers to Iran are notoriously high. **Azerbaijan Airlines**, **Aeroflot**, **Pegasus Airlines** and **Turkish Airlines** have daily flights to Tehran from their respective hubs. In February 2016 **Mahan Air** began direct regular flights from Moscow and St Petersburg, which is convenient if travelling from Scandinavia. Tehran is also well serviced by regional routes from Ukraine and Georgia. See page 48 for airline websites.

Imam Khomeini International Airport (IKA) (now also called Imam Khomeini Airport City (w ikac.ir)) [map, page 124] is located some 30km south of Tehran on the road to Qom. A joint venture with Austrian and Turkish companies, it was completed at a cost of US$330 million, but shortly after the airport's opening in 2004 it was forced to close by a section of the Iranian army, concerned about such an important national symbol being under a foreign, namely Turkish and Austrian, 'authority'. This airport now services all international and some internal flights and can be reached by **metro** (alas irregular) from the city centre (40mins) or by **taxi**. A new terminal is currently being built, but no opening date has yet been set.

From the airport, a private taxi, usually green or yellow, into the city centre costs approximately 1,100,000 rials; there are no 'shared' taxis on this route. *Never* accept lifts in 'unofficial' private taxis without a taxi sign. From the airport you can also order a taxi to other parts of the country. A taxi to Esfahan, for example, 421km away, costs around 7,000,000 rials.

Mehrabad International Airport (THR) [90 A5], 12km west of the city, formerly the only airport serving Tehran, is used essentially for internal flights. Mehrabad serves 20 Iranian centres (see individual cities in this guide); some international flights also depart from here during the final month of the Islamic calendar (page 70) when the annual pilgrimage of the hajj takes place. Mehrabad International Airport is accessible by **metro**, **bus** or **taxi** and costs approximately 400,000 rials from the city centre or 1,100,000 rials from Imam Khomeini International Airport.

By train The railway station is located at Railway Square [90 C6] (maydan-e rah ahan) and it is usually the final stop of the buses running along Valiasr Street. The ticket office is not in the station but in a building to the right. Allow at least 1 hour before train departure time. For details on intercity trains, see page 61.

By bus Tehran has four main bus terminals servicing arrivals from various Iranian cities: Southern (Jonub) [90 C6] for buses from Kashan and some from Mashhad (departures from this terminal often do not leave on time, as cheaper bus companies based here tend to wait for as long as possible for more passengers to fill up the seats); Western (Azadi) [90 A4] for Hamadan and Zanjan; Beyhaghi (Argentine) [98 D2] for Mashhad and Tabriz; and Eastern (Damavand Street) [90 D4] for Damavand and other routes. There is also a smaller Tehranpars terminal [99 G6] with services to Mazandaran province. All of the bus stations are conveniently accessible by Bus Rapid Transit (BRT) buses.

GETTING AROUND
By bus Women normally go to the back and men to the front of the bus, but on some routes in Tehran this arrangement is reversed. It is worth mentioning, however, that buses are quite efficient in Iran and are by far the most preferred mode of transport for women, who deem them safer than taxis.

Buses operate throughout the city and although timetables are not readily available, there is often less than a couple of minutes' waiting time between departures. Bus stops, in particular along Valiasr Street, are clearly marked and numerous. Otherwise, you can ask a passer-by for the nearest stop. Day services are frequent, but in the evenings (some buses do not run after 21.30) and on Fridays these are more sporadic. Always buy a ticket (15,000 rials) either at the kiosk or from the driver himself, paying at the end of the journey. Female travellers may need to exit the bus and then come up to the driver at the front to pay for the ticket.

Ten efficient BRT routes service the city 24 hours a day from north to south (along Valiasr Street from Tajrish Square [105 E2] to the railway station [90 C6]) and from west to east (Azadi Square to Tehranpars bus terminal). Buses run with 5- to 10-minute intervals. BRT bus stops are usually fenced off and can be accessed by scanning your transport card at the ticket reader machine, manned by a BRT official. Please note that tickets on these routes cannot be purchased from the bus driver or BRT official and you will need to buy a transport card in advance (see below). Some major stops (eg: Enghelab) have ticket sale kiosks, but this is more an exception than the rule.

By metro (w metro.tehran.ir) The metro project in Tehran was developed before the revolution, but was postponed owing to the Iran–Iraq War. The first line, built by the ZRJC Chinese Railway, eventually opened in 2000. The underground system currently has seven different lines, each colour coded. Many new stations are under construction and the maps inside the trains do not often reflect the actual situation. The total length is more than 174km and parts of the system run above ground and parts underground. Used by 2 million people daily, it is a reliable form of transport, albeit crowded during peak times. Owing to the increasing air pollution in Tehran, the authorities have over the past few years been encouraging people to travel by metro, as attested by numerous posters and campaigns in the trains and at stations.

A new **transport card**, a small key ring called *ezpay*, can be purchased for 70,000 rials and charged with any amount desired. It saves time on buying individual metro (12,000 rials) or bus tickets, it's easy to use (by placing it on the fare scanner) and very convenient. Trains run from 05.46 until 22.46 every 4 to 10 minutes depending on the time of day. Rush hour, best avoided, is from 06.00 to 09.00 and from 14.00 to 17.00. Metro carriages are gender-segregated, although this is not strictly enforced. Metro travel is safe and efficient, and signs are written in both Persian and clear English.

By road Travelling by **taxi** in Tehran is easy and inexpensive. Taxis operating on specific routes depart from designated points (eg: Tajrish Square, Sanat Square, etc) and cover vast expanses of this immense megapolis. A shared taxi (*savari*) costs 20,000 rials and private hire (*darbast*) depends on the destination, but an average fare is 300,000 rials. Ordering a taxi via mobile, the **Snapp** app is always cheaper and a small tip will be appreciated by the driver. Do remember that Tehran is not a pedestrian-friendly city and a short *savari* ride up Valiasr Street may save a great deal of energy. Please note that according to Tehran traffic rules, restrictions apply to vehicles (both private and taxis) up until 17.00, depending on the even or odd number of the car registration plate. This is of importance when coming by taxi from outside Tehran into the city centre, as the driver might have to leave you at the street where restrictions apply. If it happens the driver himself will most likely help you fetch a 'connection' taxi from the drop-off point.

It is also possible to **rent a car** in Iran and there are a few options in Tehran for those who are fearless and feel compelled to take this chance. A newly established **Navaran** Rental Company (w navaran.com) is fairly priced and has 100,000 vehicles to choose from. **Europcar** (w europcar.ir) has three offices in Tehran – Imam Khomeini International Airport [map, page 124] (\ 51007539, 55678243), Mehrabad Airport (m 0901 8380361) and Tehran's northern suburb of Shahrak-e Gharb (2, 11th Alley, Falamak St; \ 88366615).

TOUR GUIDE For cultural and nature tours in Tehran and around, contact the English-speaking guide Houman Najafi (m 0912 2023017; e houman.najafi@gmail.com). For art and gallery tours, see box, page 109.

The **Free Walking Tour** ✴ (m 0935 8914604 (Ehsan); 0912 2262778 (Mersa); e info@persianwalk.com; w persianwalk.com) is an enjoyable initiative run by friendly Mersa and Ehsan, who are happy to acquaint visitors with Tehran. Daily walking tours start at the entrance to Golestan Palace. Specialised walking tours in northern Tehran, including an evening walking tour in Tajrish and tasting tours at the bazaar, are highly recommended. Tipping is welcome.

 WHERE TO STAY The Tehran International Fair (w iranfair.com), usually held in the last week of September or the first week of October, means all hotels in Tehran are busy and often room charges are increased during this period. In addition to the hotels and hostels mentioned below, there are numerous **mid-range** and **budget** *mehmanpazirs* along Amir Kabir Street and South Sadi Street. Toilets, however, are mainly squat style and not always en suite. Do note that while during the day the area is a bustling car-parts market, it is not the place to walk around after dark, especially for single female travellers.

Luxury

Homa Hotel [104 D6] (172 rooms) 51 Khoddami St; \ 43941–43969; w homahotels. com. One of the most luxurious hotels in Iran with indoor swimming pool & impressive décor. The cherry of the Homa Hotel Chain, it is also its most expensive option. Rooms are spacious & bright & staff are courteous with a pleasant manner. **$$$$**

Laleh [98 A5] (380 rooms) Fatemi St; \ 88965021–9; e info@lalehhotel.com. This is the most central 5-star hotel (& a favourite with Western correspondents reporting the early days

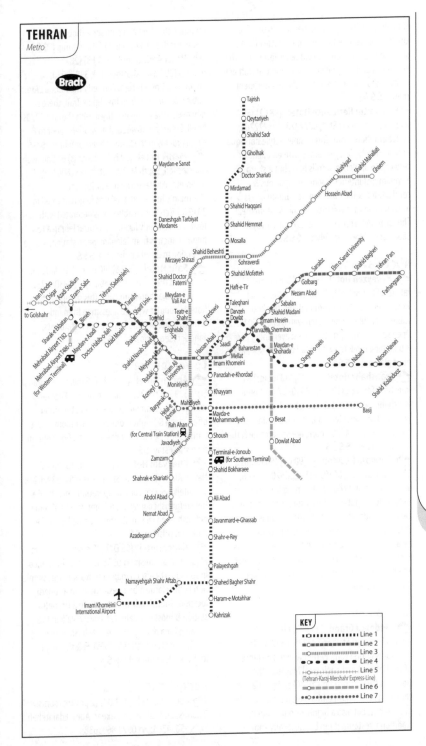

TEHRAN
Metro

Bradt

Tajrish
Qeytariyeh
Shahid Sadr
Gholhak
Doctor Shariati
Mirdamad
Shahid Haqqani
Shahid Hemmat
Mosalla
Shahid Beheshti
Sohraverdi
Shahid Mofatteh
Haft-e-Tir
Taleghani
Darvazeh Dowlat

Maydan-e Sanat
Daneshgah Tarbiyat Modarres
Mirzaye Shirazi
Shahid Doctor Fatemi
Meydan-e Vali Asr
Teatr-e Shahr
Ferdowsi

Nushyad
Shahid Mahallati
Ghaem
Hossein Abad
Saratsz
Elm.o.Sanat Univeristy
Shahid Bagheri
Tehran Pars
Farhangsara
Golbarg
Nezam Abad
Sabalan
Shahid Madani
Imam Hosein
Darvazeh Shermiran
Maydan-e Shohada

Iran Khodro
Chigar
Azadi Stadium
Eram-e Sabz
Tehran (Sadeghieh)
Tarasht
Sharif Univ.
to Golshahr
Sharak-e Ebotam
Bimeh
Mehrabad Airport T1&2
Mehrabad Airport T4&6
(for Western Terminal)
Maydan-e Abad
Doctor Habib-o-llah
Ostad Moeen
Shademani
Shahid Navab Safavy
Meydan-e Jahad
Rudaki
Komeyl
Baqeriah
Habib-e Ahmad
Toridi
Enghelab Sq
Imam Ali Univesity
Moniriyeh
Mahdiyeh
Hassan Abad
Saadi
Baharestan
Mellat
Imam Khomeini
Panzdah-e-Khordad
Khayyam

Sheykh-o-raeis
Piroozi
Nabard
Nimoon Hasaei
Shahid Kolahdooz
Basij

Rah Ahan
(for Central Train Station)
Javadiyeh
Zamzam
Shahrak-e Shariati
Abdol Abad
Nemat Abad
Azadegan

Mayda-e Mohammadiyeh
Shoush
Terminal-e-Jonoub
(for Southern Terminal)
Shahid Bokharaee
Ali Abad
Javanmard-e-Ghassab
Shahr-e-Rey
Palayeshgah

Besat
Dowlat Abad

Namayehgah Shahr Aftab
Shahed Bagher Shahr
Haram-e Motahhar
Imam Khomeini
International Airport
Kahrizak

KEY	
■□■■■■■■■■■■■■	Line 1
■□■■■■■■■■■■	Line 2
□□□□□□□□□□	Line 3
●○●■■■●○●■■■●	Line 4
++○++++++++++++	Line 5 (Tehran-Karaj-Mershahr Express-Line)
▬ ▬ ▬ ▬ ▬ ▬	Line 6
●○●●●●○●●●●●	Line 7

Tehran and the Road South   TEHRAN

3

95

of the Islamic Revolution in the late 1970s). The lobby is pleasant, but the décor is a little effete & old-fashioned. The outside garden is lovely, but the pool has regrettably fallen into disuse. The staff are polite & share with the hotel a slightly decadent charm. **$$$$**

🏠 **Raamtin Residence Hotel** [98 C2] (50 rooms) 2153 Valiasr St; ☎88722786, 88722788; **w** raamtinhotel.com. This business-style boutique hotel is simply classy & comes with excellent service. No opulence or frills here, but a sharp & minimalist interior. Rooms are spacious & comfortable & the basement restaurant offers great food in case you miss a good Western meal. The location is superb, just a few mins away from Saee Park in northern Tehran. **$$$$**

Above average

🏠 **Hoveyzeh Hotel** [98 D6] (178 rooms) 115 Taleqani St; ☎88804344–58. With exceptional views over the city & the mountains, this hotel was entirely redesigned & renovated in Dec 2015. Open spaces, unobstructed views; everything here is breathing modernity. The staff are professional & most pleasant. **$$$$**

🏠 **Iranshahr Hotel** [98 D6] (48 rooms) 81 Iranshahr St; ☎88310335, 88310337; **w** hotel-iranshahr.com. One of the best hotels in Tehran with a lot of character & super-smooth staff. The rooms, although a little dark, are impeccable & the location superb. **$$$$**

🏠 **Roudaki Residence** [98 C7] (50 rooms) 12 Shahriyar St; ☎66709421–2, 66706955–6; **w** roudaki-hotel.com. A charming & recently fully restored hotel in the cultural heart of the capital. Vahdat (formerly Roudaki) Hall is nearby & Tehran Theatre is just a few hundred metres away. Rooms are spacious in the form of SC apts & come with nice views over the bustling street. The hotel has a delightful old-fashioned feel about it. **$$$$**

Mid-range

🏠 **Ferdowsi Grand** [111 E2] (182 rooms) Ferdowsi St; ☎66727026, 66727031; **w** ferdowsihotel.com. Within walking distance of the National Archaeological Museum, the Golestan Palace, the Ministry of Foreign Affairs & the German & Turkish embassies, it boasts a rather glitzy lobby, but also a highly recommended, traditional restaurant run by the locally known

Mr Alizadeh. Also has a patisserie shop (with ice-cream sundaes!). Popular with tour groups. **$$$**

🏠 **Hotel Amir Kabir** [111 E3] (28 rooms) 220 Naser Khosrow St; ☎33978970; **w** amirkabirhotels.com. Formerly the famous Amir Kabir *mosafirkhaneh* on the Hippie Trail, there is, however, little left to identify it with the cult 1970s hotel. Entirely renovated, it now offers modern & simple rooms in the historic heart of Tehran. **$$$**

🏠 **Marlik Hotel** [99 E6] (84 rooms) 61 Somayeh Intersection, South Mofateh St; ☎88328001–9; **w** en.marlikhotel.ir. Opened in 1963, this charmingly furnished hotel was fully renovated in 2010 & offers impeccable rooms decorated with taste. Conveniently located in central Tehran a few hundred metres from Taleqani metro station, a large neon sign makes it unmissable. **$$$**

🏠 **Safir Hotel** [99 E6] (40 rooms) 10 Ardalan St, behind the former US embassy; ☎88300873; **e** info@indianhotelsafir.com. This small & cosy hotel is popular with businessmen from India & houses one of Iran's best Indian restaurants, Tandoor (see opposite). **$$$**

Lower mid-range

🏠 **Arman Hotel** [111 E3] (55 rooms) Ecbatana St; ☎33963421–25; **w** armanhotel.ir. Popular with Turkish & Iranian businessmen, this hotel offers clean & bright rooms. Cheaper rooms come with a shower, but no toilet facilities. Good option for a short stay. **$$**

🏠 **Khayyam Hotel** [111 F3] (45 rooms) 3 Navidi Alley, Amir Kabir St; ☎33911497, 33920218; **w** hotelkhayyam.com. In operation since 1976 & fully refurbished in 2016, it is not devoid of some old-fashioned charm. Rooms are small & a little dark, but pristine. **$$**

🏠 **Nader Hotel** [98 D4] (28 rooms) 22 Qaem Maqam Farahani St; **m** 0935 1303818. Reopened in spring 2019 after a major renovation, this simple hotel offers large albeit basic rooms in a superb location: 2mins' walk from the Haft-e Tir metro station & most city galleries. Lovely walk in the evening for a nearby ice cream & fresh juice is a must. There is regrettably no Wi-Fi & the main lobby is rather uninviting. **$$**

Budget and hostels

🏠 **Cedar Hostel** [111 D4] (2 private rooms, 2 dorms) 2nd cul-de-sac, Akbari Alley, Edalatkhah St; ☎55624761; **m** 0922 8603638;

w cedarhostel.com. Opened in Oct 2018, this simple hostel, tucked away off busy Tehrani alleys, has a large tranquil courtyard & with a capacity of only 14 guests, it offers a relaxing atmosphere away from the bustle of the city. Rooms are simple & fairly priced. **$–$$**

✳ 🏠 **Tehran Heritage Hostel** [111 F2] (10 private, 4 yurts & 7 dorms) 22 Kamal Al-Molk St, Baharestan Sq; ☎33988739; w heritage-hostel. com. The first Western-style hostel in Iran, Heritage offers a funky mix of modernity with tradition. Opened in Jan 2018, it has a spacious inner courtyard between 2 nicely refurbished historic buildings. Dorm beds are custom-designed & equipped with curtains to ensure privacy. Private accommodation inc yurts in the courtyard & on the rooftop. There is also a special heritage room in the basement, which in the old days functioned as *ab anbar* (water cistern) storage. **$–$$**

🏠 **Firouzeh Hotel** [111 F3] (26 rooms) Amir Kabir St, Dowlat Abadi Alley; ☎33113508; w firouzehhotel.com. Cheap & clean with old-fashioned décor & stylish staff. The clientele here is quite diverse: from photographers to backpackers. A good choice if you plan to spend most of your time outdoors. No en-suite rooms. **$**

🍴 **WHERE TO EAT AND DRINK** Apart from fancier restaurants, Tehran has a huge variety of traditional restaurants serving delicious and filling meals and fast-food eateries specialising in kebabs, pizzas, sandwiches and *morg-e sukhari* (crispy chicken pieces), as one of the favourites. The stretch of Si-ye Tir Street between Imam Khomeini and Jomhouri streets has been partially pedestrianised and converted into a lively **food street** with a variety of stalls and cuisines to choose from. The area around Teatr-e Shahr metro is awash with cheap sandwich bars. Café culture in Tehran is the best in Iran, in particular so-called book cafés, and apart from the selection of cafés below, there are many others in the vicinity of the University of Tehran. For a healthy budget snack and good coffee, drop into one of the numerous **Cluna** (often spelt Cluneh; w cluna.ir) branches across the city.

Luxury and above average

✳ 🍴 **Hestooran** [105 E3] 2nd floor, Royal Address Bd, Niloufar St, Fereshteh; ☎75426; w hestooran.com. Past the modern façade of the Royal Address, this exquisitely delightful restaurant with the décor of a Qajar summer veranda, is simply perfect. Menu diversity can appear baffling & the waiter's assistance is recommended for making a choice. Thick dough with crushed walnuts & herbs is a meal in itself & their *tahchin* crunchy rice cakes will blow your palate away. Service is excellent. Highly recommended for the ultimate dining experience in Iran. **$$$$**

🍴 **Nayeb** [98 C3] 2220 Valiasr St, across from Raamtin Hotel; ☎88713474; ⏱ lunch & dinner. This much-loved family-run restaurant (now part of a chain) features a traditional Iranian menu with emphasis on meats & kebabs & the food is served in style. The interior is modern with a touch of French glamour. **$$$**

✳ 🍴 **Rouhi Restaurant** [104 A6] 58 Sima-ye Iran St, Shahrak-e Garb; ☎88376080–90 (with branches in Bagh-e Negarestan; ☎33945460–1; & Astara Centre, Shahrdari St, off Tajrish Sq; ☎22708883–93); ⏱ 11.00–16.00 & 20.00–23.00 daily. Modern & stylish décor, grand lustres, wide wooden tables to accommodate family & group dining, or for single travellers to share with some friendly strangers, this is a very fine place indeed. Food is superb & served on traditional copper plates. Portions are generous & the welcome food served gratis does away with the need to order a starter. In short, an eating experience *comme il faut*. **$$–$$$**

🍴 **Gilar Restaurant** [105 F1] Niavaran St, before Majda crossroads; ☎22741665, 22741393; w gilarniavaran.ir; ⏱ noon–23.30. A 10min walk from Tajrish metro station, this restaurant, with rustic Gilani atmosphere & décor, is a gem. Wonderful homemade dishes, regional varieties, homemade dough & freshly baked bread. Try the salad buffet for lunch (from 13.00). Mouthwatering. **$$**

🍴 **Tandoor Restaurant** [99 E6] Basement of Safir Hotel (see opposite); ☎88820934; ⏱ noon–15.00 & 19.00–23.00. A wonderful Indian restaurant, serving probably the best 2-layer garlic naan bread you'll taste. Welcoming atmosphere & outdoor courtyard seating area with impeccable service. **$$**

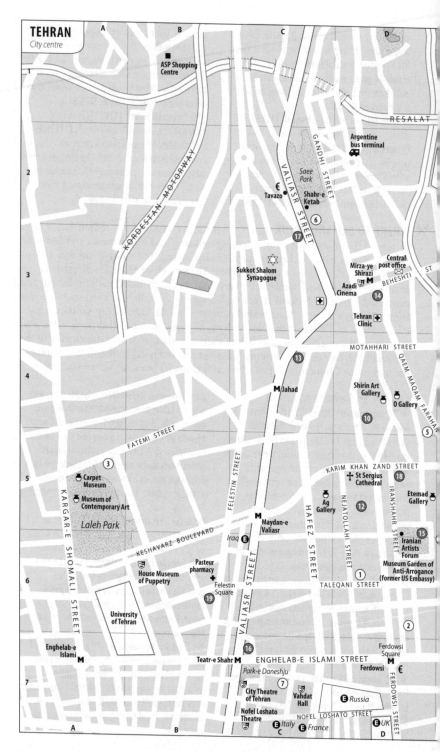

TEHRAN
City centre

ASP Shopping Centre

RESALAT

KORDESTAN MOTORWAY

GANDHI STREET

Saee Park

Argentine bus terminal

Tavazo

Shahr-e Ketab

VALIASR STREET

6

17

Sukkot Shalom Synagogue

Mirza-ye Shirazi M

Central post office

BEHESHTI ST

Azadi Cinema

14

Tehran Clinic

MOTAHHARI STREET

13

QAEM MAQAM FARAHAN

M Jahad

Shirin Art Gallery

O Gallery

10

5

FATEMI STREET

KARIM KHAN ZAND STREET

3

St Sergius Cathedral

18

Carpet Museum

Ag Gallery

12

Etemad Gallery

Museum of Contemporary Art

NEJATOLLAHI STREET

IRANSHAHR STREET

Laleh Park

FELESTIN STREET

M Maydan-e Valiasr

Iranian Artists Forum

15

KARGAR-E SHOMALI STREET

HAFEZ STREET

KESHAVARZ BOULEVARD

Iraq E

Museum Garden of Anti-Arrogance (former US Embassy)

Pasteur pharmacy

House Museum of Puppetry

Felestin Square

19

TALEQANI STREET

1

VALIASR STREET

University of Tehran

2

Enghelab-e Islami M

Ferdowsi Square

Teatr-e Shahr M

ENGHELAB-E ISLAMI STREET

Ferdowsi

FERDOWSI STREET

16

Park-e Daneshju

City Theatre of Tehran

7

Vahdat Hall

E Russia

Nofel Loshato Theatre

NOFEL LOSHATO STREET

E Italy

E France

E UK

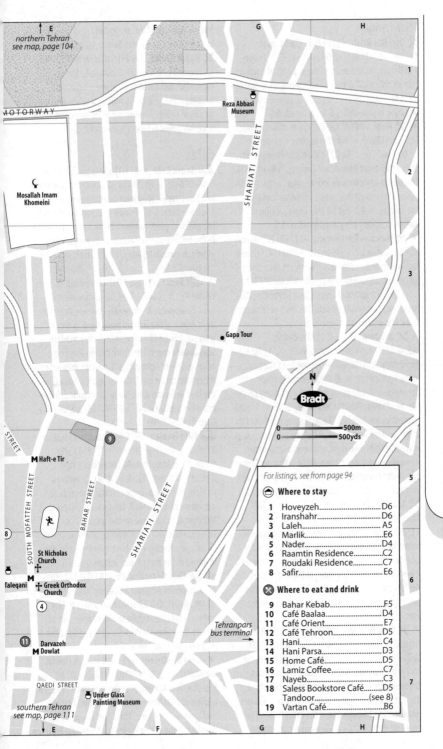

MOTORWAY

Reza Abbasi
Museum

SHARIATI STREET

Mosallah Imam
Khomeini

Gapa Tour

N

Bradt

0 ——————— 500m
0 ——————— 500yds

M Haft-e Tir

9

SOUTH MOFATTEH STREET

BAHAR STREET

SHARIATI STREET

8

St Nicholas
Church †

M

Taleqani   † Greek Orthodox
Church

4

11   Darvazeh
M Dowlat

QAEDI STREET

Under Glass
Painting Museum

Tehranpars
bus terminal →

For listings, see from page 94

🛏 **Where to stay**

1	Hoveyzeh	D6
2	Iranshahr	D6
3	Laleh	A5
4	Marlik	E6
5	Nader	D4
6	Raamtin Residence	C2
7	Roudaki Residence	C7
8	Safir	E6

✖ **Where to eat and drink**

9	Bahar Kebab	F5
10	Café Baalaa	D4
11	Café Orient	E7
12	Café Tehroon	D5
13	Hani	C4
14	Hani Parsa	D3
15	Home Café	D5
16	Lamiz Coffee	C7
17	Nayeb	C3
18	Saless Bookstore Café	D5
	Tandoor	(see 8)
19	Vartan Café	B6

Mid-range

✕ **Dizi Bar Atish** [105 E2] 82 Darbandi St, Tajrish; ✆22725981; m 0921 1664393; ⊕ noon–17.00 daily. Tucked away in the old part of northern Tehran, this small & cosy place specialises in one of Iran's favourite dishes – *dizzi* stew, served with a selection of side dishes & fresh bread. **$$**

✳ ✕ **Hani** [98 C4] Valiasr St, Cnr of Motahhari St; ✆88932020; w hanifoods.com; ⊕ noon–23.00; Hani Parsa [98 D3] (40 Shahid Beheshti St, across the street from Azadi Cinema; ✆88101581). This buffet-style local favourite offers a spectacular range of the most delicious traditional Iranian specialities. Watch out for that extra serving of saffron rice! Very busy during lunch. **$$**

✳ ✕ **Mesmes Restaurant** [111 F2] 22 Jomhuri St, Baharestan Sq; ✆33914819, 33902474. This new family-run restaurant has certainly set the standard for homemade cooking in southern Tehran. All food is served on traditional copper (*mes* in Persian; thus, the name) plates & their delicious *mast* with raisins alone is worth coming here. **$$**

✳ ✕ **Moslem** [111 E4] 15 Khordad St; ✆55602275; w moslemrestaurant.ir; ⊕ 11.00–18.00 daily. Join the queue outside, read the tiny menu handed over to all those excitedly waiting in the queue & slowly move forward, eventually up the narrow stairway into the hall where delicious Iranian specialities are ordered. The atmosphere is that of a communal canteen at a local factory, but is cosy & agreeable in its own right, although a little hectic. Avoid early lunch hour. Herbed rice with trout (*sabzi polo mahi*) is particularly delicious. Take-away is also available & is ordered from the counter outside. **$$**

✕ **Azari Restaurant** [90 C6] 1 Valiasr St, Rah Ahan Sq; ✆55489170–1, 55372402; ⊕ 06.00–11.00 & noon–23.00 daily. Great local atmosphere, meaty menu & long queues for lunch, attest to the quality of the food served. A very popular restaurant, it is a little far from the centre, at the last stop on the BRT bus line, but perfect to have a break while waiting for your train. Also offers live music in the eves. **$–$$**

✳ ✕ **Café Tehroon** [98 D5] 39 Khosrow Alley, Nejatollah (Vila) St; ✆88906813; ⊕ 08.30–22.00 daily. Previously located in Negarestan Garden, this cosy restaurant embodies the spirit of old Tehran & homemade cooking. You can enjoy a dish of the day outdoors in the café's leafy courtyard or indoors, while looking through one of the café's books. The eggplant dish (*kashk-e bademjan*) & herb-based

frittata (*kuku sabzi*) are particularly recommended. Ideal for b/fast on a sunny Sun morning. **$–$$**

✕ **Bahar Kebab** [99 F5] Bahar St; ✆77501953; ⊕ noon–15.30 & 19.00–23.00 daily. Basic & somewhat dull décor aside, there is otherwise nothing missing here. No frills or tourists, just succulent kebab; *kubideh* is particularly good, bread is freshly baked & service is excellent. **$**

Cafés

☕ **Reera Café** [111 D1] 5 Lolagar Cul-de-sac; ✆66707646; ⊕ 08.30–23.30 Sun–Fri. Stylish café in a fashionable alley with designer stores, Hanna boutique hotel & the French embassy nearby, this is a pleasant place to take a break from sightseeing in the historic part of Tehran. Coffee is excellent, although comparatively pricier than elsewhere in the city. **$$$**

✳ ☕ **Sam Café** [104 D3] 1 Fereshteh St, Sam Centre; ✆22653842; ⊕ 09.00–midnight. This new, fashionable & glitzy café is where the crème de la crème of the Tehrani wealthiest, & those who want to be like them, meet. Very modern Scandinavia meets New York design & décor, it offers excellent light meals & a drinks menu. Sam's refreshing cucumber *khiar sekanjabin* drink is the best in Tehran & highly recommended. Other branches are in Vanak (✆86092106) & Shahrak-e Garb (✆88579501). **$$–$$$**

☕ **Café Baalaa** [98 D4] Chamanara Museum, 11th Alley, Mirza-ye Shirazi St; ✆88813578; ⊕ 08.00–midnight daily. Located in a fine 2-storey mansion, this delightful café with an outdoor terrace has great cultural atmosphere & a good menu of drinks & light meals. Chamanara Museum & music store on the ground floor (⊕ 10.00–22.00) are in honour of a prominent Chamanara family, who have over the years been involved in the press & music business. **$$**

✳ ☕ **Café Golerezaiah** [111 D2] 172, 30 Tir St, opposite Abgineh Museum; ✆66707290; ⊕ 08.30–10.30 & 12.30–16.00 Sun–Fri. Tiny historical café/restaurant in the historic part of Tehran. Very popular with locals & tourists alike & gets very busy for lunch. **$$**

✳ ☕ **Café Orient** [99 E7] Darvazeh Dowlat metro station; ✆88347810; ⊕ 08.30–20.30 Sat–Thu. This Armenian café, open since 1942, has a lovely old-fashioned charm; you simply must find time to come here. Their homemade cakes are delicious & the coffee is excellent. The café features in the 2010 film *There Are Things You Don't Know* with Leila Hatami. $$

💻 **Home Café** [98 D5] Iranian Artists Forum; Iranshahr Park; 📞 88311906; ⏰ 11.00–23.00. Located in the artistic heart of Tehran, the café is divided into the terrace & mezzanine level & is a popular place for the alternative & modern Tehranis to meet up for a tea & a chat, inc some gently political discussions about Iran & beyond. $$

✴ 💻 **Inja** [111 D1] 4 Pedram Alley, off Nofel Loshato St; 📞 66727299; **w** inja.space; ⏰ 08.00–23.00 Sat–Thu. Looking for that alternative, underground artistic crowd? Tucked away in a narrow alley, Inja is the place to go. Delicious drinks & homemade food is served in the comfy 1970s design space or in the relaxed courtyard. $$

✴ 💻 **Lamiz Coffee** [98 C7] Valiasr St; metro Teatr-e Shahr; 📞 66462205; **w** lamizcoffee. com; ⏰ 08.00–midnight daily. A new café chain has taken Tehran by storm, with more than 13 locations around the city, inc Fatemeh Sq, Tajrish Sq & Vanak Sq. Very popular, with a great vibe & excellent selection of warm drinks. You can also leave your books here for others to enjoy. $$

💻 **Rayzan House** [105 F1] Niavaran St; 📞 22700614; **w** rayzanhouse.ir; ⏰ 10.00–23.00

daily. In operation since 2004, this cultural complex is home to a very nice café, excellent bookshop & a contemporary fashionable Shandiz restaurant. There are regular music & cultural events. $$

💻 **Ras Café** [105 E2] 6 Arefnasab St; 📞 22716010; ⏰ 09.00–23.00 daily. A pleasant outdoor café, bookstore & events centre all under 1 roof & in a beautiful garden awash with greenery of this exquisite mansion that once belonged to the Mossadeq family. $$

💻 **Vartan Café** [98 B6] 514 Taleqani St; **m** 66962914; ⏰ 09.00–midnight. A stylish café & very popular with students from nearby University of Tehran. $$

✴ 💻 **Haj Ali Tea House** [111 E4] Main bazaar, a few hundred metres from the main entrance. Tiny tea corner with a good vibe & welcoming owner. Make it your first stop on the visit to the bazaar. $

💻 **Saless Bookstore Café** [98 D5] 150 Karim Khan Zand Bd; 📞 88302437; **w** salesspublication. com; ⏰ 09.00–21.00 Sat–Thu, 16.00–21.00 Fri. A wonderful café on the 1st floor of renowned Saless Publishing House. It is also home to a gallery & a nice souvenir store. $

ENTERTAINMENT AND NIGHTLIFE Tehran boasts a number of theatres and music halls with an extensive cultural programme of traditional and modern performances. It is best to purchase tickets online (ask friends or hotel personnel to make a reservation; **w** iranconcert.com, tiwall.com), as good shows are often sold out within hours of going on sale. There are also music and street artists busking outside the Tehran Theatre in Park-e Daneshju, especially at weekends. For tickets and programmes, see the English-language website **w** theater.ir. Below are some of the best theatre and music hall suggestions:

🎭 **City Theatre of Tehran** [111 C1] Park-e Daneshju; 📞 66460592; **w** teatreshahr.com
🎭 **Nofel Loshato Theatre** [111 C1] 11 Nofel Loshato St; 📞 66483742
✴ 🎭 **Puppet Theatre** (*kheymeh shab bazi*) [98 B6] House Museum of Puppetry, 6 Shahed Alley, Vesal Shirazi St; 📞 88996273. No knowledge of Persian is required to enjoy this traditional Iranian art form. Performances are free of charge

& last 30mins. Held in the inner courtyard of a lovely traditional house converted into a pleasant restaurant & puppet museum (1st floor), find time to come here to enjoy a dinner or a refreshing drink while watching a show. Advance booking is required. Performances are held on different days & times, depending on the season (later during Ramadan).
🎭 **Vahdat Hall** [111 D1] (formerly Roudaki Hall) 📞 66731419; **w** bonyadroudaki.com

SHOPPING
Clothes and gifts The area near Park-e Daneshju [98 C7] between Valiasr and Hafez streets has a number of shops selling Iranian natural fabric **clothes and souvenirs**, while the stretch of Enghelab Street on the other side of the park is known for its good-quality **men's suit fabric**. The area around Baharestan metro station is the

place to buy musical instruments, while **sports stores** are all nicely packed on Valiasr Street between Khomeini Street and Moniriyeh Square. The area around Haft-e Tir is the place to shop for *manteaux*, and Ferdowsi Street in the vicinity of Ferdowsi metro station is awash with stores selling excellent-quality **leather goods**. For gift shopping, go to **Tavazo** [98 C2, 104 D3] for Iran's favourite *ajil* (assortment of nuts, pistachios, sweets, etc). It has been in business since 1915 and has branches all over Tehran.

Tehran boasts a number of luxurious **shopping malls** with food courts and local and international brands to choose from. **ASP Shopping Centre** is one of the nicest and characterful shopping centres in Tehran. Built in the 1960s as part of the ASP residential complex, it exudes minimalist Bauhaus-ish charm and boasts a refreshing selection of fusion Iranian and international restaurants, cafés and shops, including local designer boutiques. Popular with the elite and celebrities, this is the place for a clientele with good taste, in contrast to the boastful and flashy nouveau-riche shopping centres around Tajrish and Fereshteh. **Arg** [105 E2] in the vicinity of Tajrish and **Ava Shopping Centre** [105 H2] in Niavaran have excellent, albeit dear, **jewellery** stores. **Gold** in Iran is excellent quality, so do not hesitate, budget allowing. **Palladium** is a high-end expensive shopping mall, but has a good food court and a few good and practical stores to look through. For **electronics** and **mobile phones**, head to the Alladin mobile market [111 D2] on Jomhuri Street.

Souvenirs Nejatollahi Street (still sometimes referred to by its pre-revolutionary name, Vila Street) [98 D5/6], running south from the Cathedral of St Sergius, boasts a large number of souvenir shops, including an Iranian Handicrafts Organisation shop and a more exclusive Panj-e Tala, where you can order **custom-made jewellery**. Across the street from the former US embassy there are a number of **souvenir and handicrafts** shops to browse through.

Bazaars

Jomeh Bazaar [111 E2] Parvaneh car park, Jomhuri St; ⏰ 10.00–16.00 Fri. Here you can find anything & everything, from lovely fabrics, vintage Turkoman dresses to door handles. Those with a flair for antiques & good old curios will feel at home here.

Mowlana Bazaar [111 E4] Main bazaar. A full day could easily be spent here looking through great fabrics & much more.

Tajrish Bazaar [105 E2] Off Tajrish Sq. A lovely place to wander around & make a purchase or two.

Bookshops Iranians like to read: classics, modern, Persian or foreign literature, you name it. If you happen to be in Tehran from late April to early May, make sure to visit the Tehran International Book Fair (w tibf.ir). The area around Maydan-e Enghelab-e Islami is awash with bookshops, including English-language books about Iran. Haft-e Tir is home to numerous publishing houses, where you will find well-established Saless (page 101) and many others with an excellent choice of books, including in English, and local crafty souvenirs. There are also bookstores in some of the cafés listed on page 100.

Book Land 3rd floor; Palladium Shopping Centre [104 D3] & other branches in Ava Shopping Centre [105 H2] & Shiraz. Great selection, inc some English-language books.

Shahr-e Ketab (Book City) With branches on Niavaran St, nr Saee Park. A trendy, modern bookshop in central & northern Tehran with many books to leaf through.

OTHER PRACTICALITIES Friday prayer in Tehran is held in the University of Tehran [98 A6], which means that the area around Enghelab Square will be blocked off to traffic up until around 15.00.

✉ **Post offices** Tehran's central **post office** [98 D3] is located in the vicinity of Mirza-ye Shirazi metro station, & there is another one at Tajrish Sq.
$ Exchange kiosks Plentiful at the intersection of Jomhuri and Ferdowsi sts & around Fedows Garden on Valiasr St.

✚ **Hospitals** In the north **Erfan Hospital** [104 A4] (Riazi Bakhshayesh St) is convenient; **Tehran Clinic** [98 D3] (Qaem Maqam Farahani St; w tehranclinic.ir) is more central.
✚ **Pharmacies** There are numerous 24hr pharmacies, inc **Refah Pharmacy** [90 C5], **22 Farvardin Pharmacy** [111 B2] & **Pasteur Pharmacy** [98 B6].

WHAT TO SEE AND DO Tehran is not a pedestrian-friendly city and while major palace complexes are compact, other sites may be some distance apart. It is usually best to travel by metro or taxi between the sites. If you fancy a walk, leave it for one of the numerous city parks. The places listed below are arranged by their geographical location to make it easier to combine visits and move about and around.

Northern Tehran

Milad Tower برج میلاد ✳ [104 A7] (Sheikh Fazl Allah Nouri Expressway; w tehranmiladtower.ir; ⊕ 09.00–20.30 daily; entry 120,000–350,000 rials, depending on the deck you are visiting) Built in 2007, at 435m high the tower is the tallest in Iran and the fourth tallest in the world. It is easily seen from wherever you approach the city. The views of Tehran and the surrounding mountains (including the majestic Damavand peak), especially during sunset from the main observation deck at 276m, are breathtaking. At the base there is an international convention centre and a shopping centre with restaurants. The easiest way of getting here is by taxi, or by metro to Shahid Hemmat station and then along the motorway by taxi or bus. The bus stop is located on the motorway to your right after crossing the pedestrian bridge.

Saadabad Palace Complex مجموعه سعدآباد ✳ [105 E1] (Valiasr St, Taheri St; ☎ 22752031; w en.sadmu.ir; ⊕ 09.00–19.00 daily; 16 different museums with separate tickets; entry 80,000–300,000 rials each; 300,000 rials for the garden complex only) An enjoyable, unrushed half-day can be spent exploring Saadabad Palace and its 110ha of grounds, constructed to house the Pahlavi family and officials. If nothing else, such a visit reminds you how the late Mohammad Reza Shah (d1980) removed himself from the everyday life of Tehran. Today, of course, residential housing has spread on to this previously isolated hillside. Some of the palace-mansions now function as headquarters for various municipal services, others house art collections and before President Ahmadinejad took office, visiting VIPs were occasionally accommodated here, which meant certain areas were out of bounds, but currently such guests are housed elsewhere. If you do not have time to visit all the museums, do find time for the **Mellat Palace**, also known as the White Palace (*kakh-e sefid*), with a pair of giant bronze boots – all that remains of a huge statue of Reza Shah (d1941) – standing by the side of the steps. It was said that the army life so conditioned Reza Shah that he preferred sleeping on the floor rather than in a bed, and certainly this house does not feel lived in. During Nou Rouz outside the palace there are concerts and a small local market with a traditional tea house.

Further up the hill from Mellat Palace is **The Green Palace**, so called because it is faced with a distinctive special greenish-yellow marble, which reminded one visitor of 1950s Fablon plastic coverings. Reza Shah ordered this construction in 1925 and certainly his small office has a more personal ambience than the Mellat. Elsewhere the blue brocade silk curtains with silver-metal-thread fringes, the excess of mirror

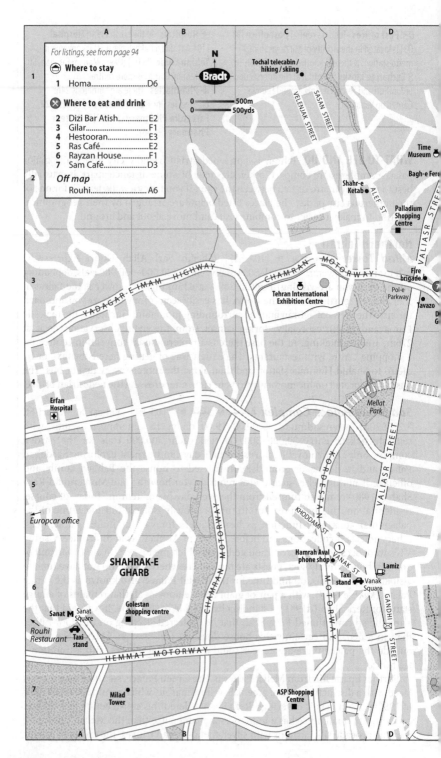

For listings, see from page 94

Where to stay

1 Homa...................D6

Where to eat and drink

2 Dizi Bar Atish...............E2
3 Gilar...........................F1
4 Hestooran....................E3
5 Ras Café.......................E2
6 Rayzan House..............F1
7 Sam Café.....................D3

Off map

Rouhi...........................A6

N

Bradt

0   500m
0   500yds

Tochal telecabin /
hiking / skiing

VELENJAK STREET

SASAN STREET

Time Museum

Bagh-e Fere

Shahr-e
Ketab

ALEF ST

Palladium
Shopping
Centre

VALIASR STREET

YADAGAR-E-IMAM HIGHWAY

CHAMRAN MOTORWAY

Fire
brigade

Pol-e
Parkway

Tehran International
Exhibition Centre

Tavazo

Di
G

Erfan
Hospital

Mellat
Park

VALIASR STREET

KORDESTAN MOTORWAY

Europcar office

KHODDAMI ST

SHAHRAK-E
GHARB

Hamrah Aval
phone shop

VANAK ST

Lamiz

Taxi
stand

Vanak
Square

GANDHI STREET

Sanat
Square

Sanat

Golestan
shopping centre

CHAMRAN MOTORWAY

Rouhi
Restaurant

Taxi
stand

HEMMAT MOTORWAY

Milad
Tower

ASP Shopping
Centre

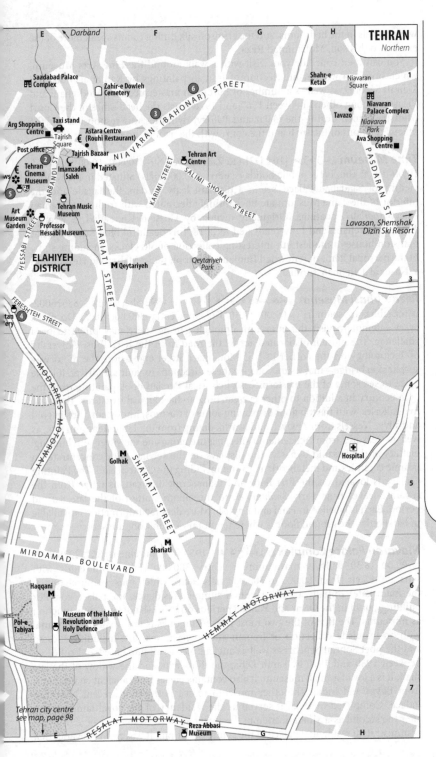

TEHRAN
Northern

Darband

Saadabad Palace
Complex

Zahir-e Dowleh
Cemetery

Shahr-e
Ketab

Niavaran
Square

6

3

Tavazo

Niavaran
Palace Complex

Niavaran
Park

Ava Shopping
Centre

Arg Shopping
Centre

Taxi stand

Tajrish
Square

Astara Centre
(Rouhi Restaurant)

Post office

Tajrish Bazaar

2

Tehran
Cinema
Museum

ws

Imamzadeh
Saleh

M Tajrish

Tehran Art
Centre

5

Art
Museum
Garden

Tehran Music
Museum

Professor
Hessabi Museum

**ELAHIYEH
DISTRICT**

M Qeytariyeh

Qeytariyeh
Park

Lavasan, Shemshak,
Dizin Ski Resort

3

FERESHTEH STREET

tan
ery

4

SHARIATI STREET

M
Golhak

Hospital

4

5

M
Shariati

MIRDAMAD BOULEVARD

Haqqani
M

Pol-e
Tabiyat

Museum of the Islamic
Revolution and
Holy Defence

6

HEMMAT MOTORWAY

7

Tehran city centre
see map, page 98

RESALAT MOTORWAY

Reza Abbasi
Museum

work, tassels in the bedrooms, and the crimson silk dining rooms speak more of the excesses of his son, Mohammad Reza.

You can then conclude your visit with a walk around the **Fine Arts Museum**, which houses a wonderful selection of Iranian paintings by Kamal al-Molk and Sohrab Sepehri, as well as a number of European masterpieces by Modigliani and Picasso, among others. Between 1967 and 1978 it was the head office of the Court Ministry, which during the Qajar and Pahlavi dynasties was responsible for the official relations of the shah and the court with the nation and *majles*.

Time Museum موزه زمان [104 D2] (12 Zaferaniyeh St; ⏰ 09.00–19.00 Sat–Wed, 10.00–19.00 Thu, Fri & public holidays; entry 300,000 rials) Situated in the relative vicinity of Saadabad Palace, set in a pleasant leafy garden, the façade and the interior of the Time Museum are enchantingly decorated with traditional Iranian stucco (*gajbori*) coatings. Originally owned by Hossein Khodadad, a wealthy Tehrani merchant, and fully renovated in 2018, this beautiful blue Rococo Qajar mansion houses a modest but interesting collection of old clocks, including some of the personal items of renowned Iranian nuclear physicist Mahmoud Hessabi and a 'Naser al-Din Shah' sundial.

Reza Abbasi Museum موزه رضا عباسی ✴ [99 G1] (892 Shariati St; ☎ 88513002; w rezaabbasimuseum.ir; ⏰ 09.00–17.30 Tue–Sun; entry 300,000 rials) Do make every attempt to visit this museum although getting there may prove to be a challenge. The museum is located across the road from the K H Toosi University of Technology on the corner of Mir Motahhari Street and before the motorway suspension bridge – make sure you give these directions to your taxi driver. It is the place to see some of the masterpieces of classical Persian book painting from the 14th century in addition to other eye-catching archaeological treasures. There are five galleries, with the top floor displaying some of the most important finds in gold and silver. Vessels from Ziwiyeh and Marlik dating from the 1st millennium BCE, as well as treasures from Achaemenid sites, feature alongside the silver-gilt 'hunting' platters of the Sasanid dynasty. The displays on the second floor concentrate on Islamic ceramics and metalwork up to and including the Qajar period. The Painting Gallery is located on the first floor and manuscript illustrations range from the separate leaves from early *Shahnameh* to the album studies of the late Safavid period. Each is labelled in Farsi and English. More detailed information is available in Farsi only. The ground floor is where temporary exhibitions are shown.

Niavaran Palace Complex کاخ نیاوران ✴ [105 H1] (Pourebtehaj St; ☎ 22282012; ⏰ 09.00–18.30 daily; w niavaranmu.ir; entry 300,000 rials; 7 museums with separate tickets (from 80,000 to 300,000 rials each), which must be purchased at the main gate) Initially a Fath Ali Shah summer residence, the palace complex buildings, built in the Qajar and Pahlavi periods on this 11ha of land, now function as museums. The first of the two most interesting ones is the small **Jahan Nama**, with an exquisite collection of Iranian and international art, including Picasso and the poet Sohran Sepehri as well as ancient pieces, all purchased and collected between 1960 and 1970 by Farah Diba, the third wife and the widow of the last shah. It is a joy of a small museum. It also contains pieces from ancient civilisations, from Egypt and India. The other museum to see is the more recent **Niavaran Palace**. Completed in 1968, it served as the residency of the royal family, when after the second assassination attempt the shah had decided to move here from his administrative residential palace in the centre of Tehran. It was from Niavaran that in January 1979 Shah Mohammad Reza Pahlavi went into exile, two weeks before the proclamation of the Islamic Republic. It is wonderfully modern, but the interior, designed by French architects, is classical. On the first floor there is fine French 18th-century tapestry and the Marc Chagal *Azure Shore* painting. The décor and the items belonging to the late shah have remained unchanged and in their original place. **Ahmad Shah Pavilion**, built during the final days of the Qajar dynasty as a private house for Ahmad Shah, the seventh and the last Qajar monarch, and subsequently used by Reza Pahlavi as his residence and office, is another must-see in this complex.

Tehran Cinema Museum موزه سینما تهران [105 E2] (Bagh-e Ferdows; ✆22705005; w cinemamuseum.ir; ◷ 09.00–19.00 Sun–Thu, 14.00–19.00 Fri & holidays; entry 500,000 rials) Located at the lower end of the very pleasant city park Bagh-e Ferdows, the museum occupies two floors of a beautiful Qajar-period mansion. Its front entrance veranda is a popular spot for selfies with the Alborz Mountains as the backdrop. If cinema generally and Iranian cinema in particular is of interest, a visit here is a must. The exhibits take the visitor on a journey through the history of film-making in Iran from the early 20th century, sketching a retrospective of the first films and then taking you to the Iranian hall of fame of the international achievements of Iranian actors and filmmakers, including the 1997 Abbas Kiarostami's Palm d'Or for the highly acclaimed *Taste of Cherry*. Moved here in 2002 from Lalehzar Street, the museum's collections are nicely arranged and accompanied with clear and informative labelling in English. The Bagh-e Ferdows itself is the place for the young and alternative Tehrani youth to spend their evenings leisurely.

Elahiyeh and Fereshteh From the Cinema Museum it is a short walk to Tehran's most expensive residential district **Elahiyeh**, also often referred to as **Fereshteh** after the main street. Hiding amid its luxurious apartment blocks and shopping centres, there are some of the most interesting museums of the capital, starting with the **Tehran Music Museum** (موزه موسیقی تهران) [105 E2] (✆22231708; w musicmuseum.ir; ◷ 09.00–16.00 daily; entry 300,000 rials). Located in a fine two-storey mansion surrounded by an immaculate garden, this wonderful museum houses an extensive collection of traditional Iranian musical instruments, both ethnic and classic, including Bakhtiari woodwind *sorna*, unusually shaped *yaruti* from Kerman, ancient bowed string *ghaychak* finely decorated in traditional Baluchi style, beautifully decorated and incised bowed string *kamancheh* from Lorestan and many others. First-floor exhibits include personal belongings of Iran's greatest composers and musicians, such as Homayun Khorram (1930–2013), Ahmad Ebadi (1906–93) and Colonel Alinaghi Vaziri (1886–1979). In the workshop at the basement level visitors can watch how these instruments are repaired, look through wood samples used in the process, as well as marvel at the museum's fine collection of *neys* (Iranian flutes), incised with traditional motifs, calligraphy images of *ney* masters, including Qajar-period Dariush Khan and Hossein Omoumi, scholar and teacher of Persian music. If music is your passion, make sure you have an Iranian SIM card with internet access so you can scan barcodes for more details.

A short walk from here, behind a decorative fence, lies the **Art Museum Garden** (باغ موزه هنر ایرانی) ✹ [105 E2] (◷ 08.30–22.30 daily; entry 30,000 rials) with its delightful water *jubs* (channels) and a collection of miniature must-see Iranian monuments, such as the Azadi Tower, Ali Qapu Palace and Soltaniyeh Mausoleum. There is also a **Plus Book** (✆26458979) shop with a good selection of art and travel books about Iran, the **Kohan Diyar Gallery** (✆ 22394263) with numerous antique carpets and souvenirs, as well as the excellent High Noon Restaurant with its alfresco seating area.

Just across the street is the **Professor Hessabi Museum** [105 E2] (✆ 22231676; w hessaby.com; ◑ 09.30–16.00 daily; entrance around the corner through the green gate; entry 100,000 rials), concealed behind a tall red-brick wall. This wonderful 600m² house was once the private residence of outstanding nuclear physicist and professor Mahmoud Hessabi (1903–92), the only Iranian student of Albert Einstein. Born into a prominent family – Hessabi's grandfather was Iran's ambassador to the Ottoman Empire – the family relocated to Beirut, where Mahmoud completed his engineering studies, then worked in Hama, Syria, eventually moving to France. In Iran he is known for his innovative engineering projects, such as the road from Bandar Lengeh to Bushehr, as well as for having established the first road construction school in Iran. The first-floor museum displays many of his personal items, revealing Hessabi's extraordinary personality. The 280S Mercedes parked in the house's courtyard belonged to the professor himself. The house's inner courtyard is a mini-zoo with birds singing and ducks washing their feathers in tiny ponds.

Central Tehran
Azadi ('Freedom') Monument برج آزادی ✳ [90 A4] (Western end of Azadi St, next to Azadi bus terminal; metro Ostad Moein; w azadi-tower.com; ◑ 09.00–17.00; entry 300,000 rials for the upper deck & ground-floor museum) Standing 45m high on a huge roundabout on the western approach road to Tehran, the monument is a conspicuous building. It was designed by an Iranian architect and built by a British construction team as part of the late shah's '2,500th' extravaganza in 1971. The influence of 14th-century Timurid architecture is evident in the intersecting rib network, while the turquoise-coloured glazed brick detail on the white Hamadan granite is derived from late 12th-century Seljuk decoration. On the ground floor there is a gallery and a souvenir shop. In the 1970s there were two museums in the building, a permanent display upstairs with visitors carried on a travelator, and temporary displays in the basement galleries. At present, however, the tower is visibly neglected and poorly maintained; it is suffering from humidity and internal water damage.

Carpet Museum موزه فرش ایران ✳ [98 A5] (Fatemi St, at the north end of Laleh Park, a short distance from Laleh Hotel; ✆ 88962703; w carpetmuseum. ir; ◑ 09.00–17.00 Tue–Sun; entry 250,000 rials) About 100 carpets and rugs are usually on show in this museum, which opened in 1977. The ground-floor display is arranged more or less in chronological sequence, working in an anticlockwise direction, beginning with a replica of the Pazyryk rug (c5th century BCE, the oldest known knotted carpet found in Altai, Siberia, in the 1940s, now in the Hermitage Museum, St Petersburg, Russia). It includes superb examples of 16th- and 17th-century Safavid rugs, including the so-called *polonaise* rugs, which caused a sensation at the 1867 Paris Universal Exhibition. There are now no more than 300 left worldwide. They were woven using silk, gold and silver thread as a special present for Polish rulers and aristocrats. But you may prefer decoding the 18th-century 'garden' carpets with their stylised irrigation channels (including fish) and chenar plane trees (see box, page 247). The impact of European art and taste on 19th-century Persian carpet design grows more marked as you walk around, whether it is the reproduction of a Watteau oil painting or a large 'family tree' of American presidents with a 1904–05 date (presumably made for the 1904

MODERN AND CONTEMPORARY ART IN TEHRAN

Iran has a vibrant art scene, with Tehran taking the lead thanks to its diversity of art galleries and the number of practising artists. A lot of the art, however, remains hidden from the eyes of tourists making their first trip to Iran, and familiarising yourself with modern and contemporary art in Tehran is highly rewarding and recommended. **Art Tour Tehran**, run by accomplished artist **Neda Zarf Saz** (m 0901 4242155; w artour.land), has since 2017 been organising personalised contemporary art and cultural tours in Tehran, including private visits to galleries and artist studios, giving tourists access to some of the most important museums and private collections in the country.

In Tehran, a large cluster of galleries is located in the vicinity of Haft-e Tir Square. Here, in Iranshahr Park, for example, the Iranian Artist Forum holds regular exhibitions throughout the year. Below are some of the recommended art galleries in the city:

Ag Gallery [98 C5] 43 Azodi St; 88802000; w aggalerie.com. Exclusive photography & video arts exhibitions.

Dastan Gallery [105 E3] 8 Beedar St; Fereshteh; w dastan.gallery.com. With branches on Felestin & Fereshteh sts, it is one of the most noteworthy galleries in Tehran.

Etemad Gallery [98 D5] 25 Shiroodi Cul-de-sac (also branch in Negarestan Garden); 88821271; w galleryetemad.com. Actively supporting emerging artists, this is one of the leading modern & contemporary art galleries in Tehran.

O Gallery [98 D4] 18 Shahin (Khedri) St, Sanaee St; 88324828; w ogallery.net. A new gallery with a focus on emerging Iranian artists.

Shirin Art Gallery [98 D4] 5, 13 Sanaee St, Karim Khan Zand Bd; 88823742, 88828482; w shiringallery.com. Modern gallery holding regular exhibitions.

Tehran Art Centre [105 F2] 26655590. Located in a pleasant garden in northern Tehran, the art centre houses a modern art gallery, a souvenir shop & a café with a good lunch menu.

Louisiana Purchase Exhibition in St Louis). The upstairs gallery serves as a temporary exhibition space, but generally includes more 'tribal' work. There is also a small cafeteria to the left of the entrance and a bookshop in the first gallery, both with the same opening hours as the museum.

Museum of Contemporary Art موزه هنرهای معاصر تهران [98 A5] (Laleh Park, Kargar-e Shomali St; 88965411; w tmoca.com; ⊕ 10.00–18.00 Sun–Thu, 15.00–18.00 Fri; entry 300,000 rials) Renovated in 2019, this gallery is always full of young people eager to hear your reactions to the paintings displayed both in the main galleries and in the temporary exhibition section in the basement; the latter houses shows organised by foreign cultural associations. Art students in Iran can major in 'traditional' or 'modern' schools or styles, though instruction and practice in both are encouraged. As Islamic art historically favoured two-dimensional work (some theologians argued against the relevance and legality of three-dimensional work outside architecture), it is not surprising to find the emphasis here is on oil painting rather than sculpture, but there is a wide diversity of approaches from the figural to the 'soft' abstract (ie: action painting is out but op art is in).

Museum of the Islamic Revolution and Holy Defence موزه انقلاب اسلامی و دفاع مقدس [105 E6] (Sarv St, metro Haqqani; 88657026; w iranhdm.ir; entry

300,000 rials) The term 'holy defence' refers to the arduous eight years of the Iran–Iraq War and the seven halls of this expansive hangar-style multi-media museum are devoted to various stages of the conflict. Starting with the video footage of historical events leading up to the Islamic Revolution, the emphasis is on the visual effect, as labelling is alas almost exclusively in Persian. The visit continues to a hall dominated by a picture of Saddam Hussein tearing a copy of the Algiers Agreement of 1975 which established borders between the two countries; then via various battle installations of some verisimilitude, leads into the martyrs' hall and the hall devoted to the international newspaper coverage of the end of the war. The tall wall to your right bears a seemingly infinite number of plaques indicating the total number of martyrs from each province in Iran. The row of tanks and military vehicles along the alley outside in front of the museum adds to the visual experience of the visit.

Museum Garden of Anti-Arrogance موزه سفارت آمریکا در تهران [98 D6] (Former US embassy; ◷ 09.00–12.30 & 14.00–18.30 Sat–Wed; entry 500,000 rials) Located in the former US embassy, with the US coat of arms still hanging above the main entrance, the rooms in the museum have been preserved in the state it was when it was a functioning building. Taking a guided tour is recommended, as labelling is minimal and requires imagination, in particular when picturing the use of the glass room for secret negotiations or the coding and electronic communication centre with all its extraordinary equipment. On the wall in the second hall the text in Persian above the English line 'There is no time for imperialism in Iran any more' is authentic and reads 'This spy nest must be closed' and 'Greetings to Khomeini'. Student Basij Organisation is the building next door.

Southern Tehran
Southern Tehran is the liveliest, most authentic and certainly most interesting area to visit. It is home to the city's oldest square – elegant Hassan Abad Square – which is warmly lit in the evenings, and the oldest theatre of Iran – Nasr Theatre – which reopened in 2019 after 30 years and is now a museum.

Moghadam Museum موزه مقدم ✳ [111 C3] (Khomeini St; ☎66463144; ◷ 09.00–17.00 Tue–Sun; entry 500,000 rials) One of the most opulent and splendid Qajar residences in Tehran, this mansion was built for Ehtesab al-Molk, a mayor of Tehran during the rule of Naser al-Din Shah. It was eventually inherited by his son, Mohsen Moghadam, and later opened as a museum under the auspices of the University of Tehran. With a wonderfully designed inner courtyard with arches, columns, *howzes* and tile decorations, the museum is divided into different sections, including a basement *howzkhaneh* room with Qajar-period plasterwork. The author of the emblem of the University of Tehran, Moghadam was an accomplished artist with a fine taste, attested by the design of the house and the private collections on display, including Safavid blue and white ceramics. His wife, Selma, was originally from Bulgaria and the house has a 'memory wall' with displays of some of her personal items of clothing and family pictures. The first-floor room houses an interesting collection of Bronze-Age pottery exhibits from some of the *tappehs* in Iran.

Ceramics and Glass Museum موزه آبگینه و سفالینه ایران [111 D2] (Si-ye Tir St; ☎6708153, 6708154, 6716930; w glasswaremuseum.ir; ◷ 09.00–17.00 Tue–Sun; entry 300,000 rials) Opened in 1980, the museum is housed in the 1915 mansion of a former prime minister in Reza Shah's government, and from 1953 to 1960 it functioned as the Egyptian embassy, so the building itself has architectural merit. There are two floors of displays that include dramatic 'Nishapur' slip-painted

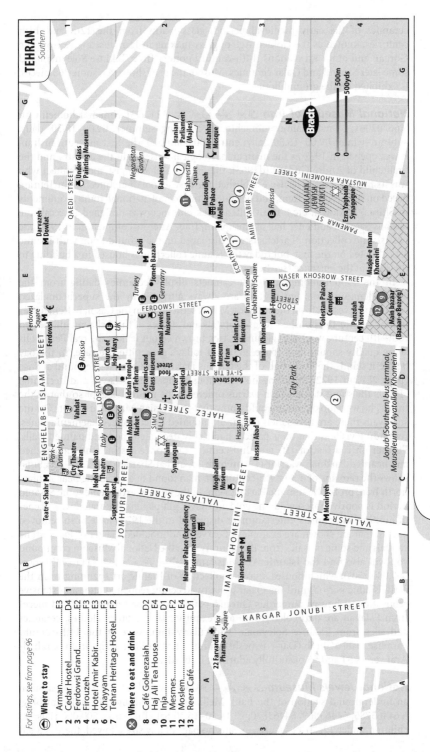

For listings, see from page 96

Where to stay

1 Arman..........................E3
2 Cedar Hostel.................D4
3 Ferdowsi Grand...............E2
4 Firouzeh.......................F3
5 Hotel Amir Kabir.............E3
6 Khayyam.......................F3
7 Tehran Heritage Hostel....F2

Where to eat and drink

8 Café Golerezaiah............D2
9 Haj Ali Tea House...........E4
10 Inja.............................D1
11 Mesmes.........................F2
12 Moslem.........................E4
13 Reera Café.....................D1

ceramics of the early medieval period, glass works from the 12th and 13th centuries, known as the Golden Age of glass-making in Iran, lustreware from the Gorgan and other excavations, 14th-century pottery from Takht-e Soleyman and some later Safavid and Qajar ceramics. Most of the glass, however, some 260 pieces, is exhibited on the ground floor.

National Museum of Iran موزهٔ ملی ایران ✳ [111 D3] (Imam Khomeini St; ☏66702061; w nationalmuseum.ichto.ir; ⊙ spring–summer 09.00–18.30 daily, autumn–winter 09.00–16.30 daily; entry 300,000 rials) The first museum in Iran, it was opened in 1937 as the main archaeological museum in the country and the brainchild of André Godard (d1965), the French archaeologist and architect who was its first director. (He also established the first school of architecture in Tehran, based on the French system, and designed a number of 'national' tomb monuments in Shiraz, Ferdowsi, etc.) The vaulted brick entrance was designed to recall the famous Sasanid audience hall at Ctesiphon, Iraq. After its completion in 1936, the pre-Islamic collection of artefacts was displayed on the ground floor, with Islamic art exhibited on the first, but today the Islamic collection is housed in a building to the right of the entrance (see below).

In the 1936 building, the first cabinets display ceramics dating from the 4th millennium BCE, but visitors are always attracted by the superb unglazed zoomorphic vessels from the 1000BCE Marlik settlement on the Caspian. Remember to look out for the polished reliefs, capitals and statues of the Achaemenid period (6th–4th century BCE); this gleaming, rich brown colour is how the real Persepolis stone quality should look (page 263); not today's grey, pitted surface. In the bay before it stands the lower half of the famous Darius the Great statue found at Susa (page 281) in 1972, recording his victorious campaigns in Egypt and declaring: 'This is the stone statue which Darius ordered to be made in Egypt so that in the future, he who looked on it would know that the Persian Man held Egypt.' On the side walls there are two panels of glazed, moulded brick from Achaemenid times, reminding visitors that their palaces had richly decorated tiled and painted walls. Further on is a feat of 1st- and 2nd-century CE bronze casting, the moustached and bearded Parthian warrior (1.94m high), found at Shami (page 287). A cabinet shows the remains of a 3th–4th-century CE man found in a salt mine near Zanjan, north Iran, probably from the Parthian era. In the current arrangement the Sasanid period is poorly represented: the gold and silver gilt platters decorated with scenes of hunting and courtly entertainment displayed in the 1970s have been removed and all that are shown are examples of carved and moulded plaster of Paris, stone capitals and some mosaics from Bishapur. Within the National Museum compound you will also find the **Islamic Art Museum** (موزه هنر اسلامی) ✳ [111 D3] (entry 500,000 rials), which houses a grand collection of Islamic art spanning from the early Islamic period until the Qajar dynasty. Recently reopened after an extensive renovation, it houses numerous Qurans, paintings, house textiles (Safavid pieces from Esfahan are particularly fine) and exquisite 10th-century clothes, ceramics and tiles from Takht-e Soleyman. Particularly impressive is the 14th-century Paradise Gate Mihrab (Dar-e Behesht) with the text in *Kufic* script from Surah al-Araf verses 54 and 55 beautifully adorning its borders.

National Jewels Museum موزه جواهرات ملی ایران ✳ [111 E2] (Ferdowsi St, in an underground section of the Bank Melli, entrance through the adjacent bldg; ☏64463785, 64463869, 64463870; ⊙ 14.00–16.30 Sat–Tue; entry 500,000 rials; no children under 12; strict security means no bags of any size allowed; there is a left luggage facility in situ) The labelling in English and Farsi is minimal and engraved on unpolished brass plaques, making it difficult to read, but the glitter and colour of the pieces set against a crimson fabric are eye-catching. Perhaps the most interesting pieces are the crowns, as you work out the historical artistic antecedents of the Kiani crown worn by Fath Ali Shah (d1834) with its 1,800 pearls (see box, below), and the one made for Reza Shah's coronation in 1925 with their clear allusions to Sasanid diadems (3rd–7th century CE). Another exhibit not to miss is the world's largest pink diamond (182 carats), the Darya-e Nur (Sea of Light), sister to the Kuh-e Nur in the British crown jewels; both were part of the booty plundered by Nader Shah Afshar during his 1739 Indian campaign.

Surely the most preposterous bejewelled object here is the Globe of Jewels made for Qajar shah Naser al-Din in 1869 or 1875. The wooden stand and frame are covered with gold sheet and smothered in jewels, while the globe itself has the land masses picked out in diamonds and rubies, and the oceans in emeralds; altogether there are over 51,000 gemstones totalling 18,200 carats.

Golestan Palace Complex کاخ گلستان ✳ [111 E4] (Arg Sq; ☎ 33113335–8; w golestanpalace.ir; ☉ 09.30–18.30 daily; garden entry only 300,000 rials, for all 10 museums & the garden 1,900,000 rials, for the garden, Talar-e Berelian (Brilliant Hall) & Negarkhaneh (art gallery) 460,000 rials) All traces of mid 18th-century construction by the Zand regime were almost totally obliterated by the early Qajar shahs and, rubbing salt into the wound, Agha Mohammad ordered the bones of Karim Khan Zand to be exhumed from his Shiraz grave and placed under the main threshold to be trodden on by all. The palace pavilions then built by Fath Ali Shah were in turn largely torn down during the extensive and lengthy construction programme (1867–92) of Naser al-Din Shah, although two main sections were saved: the Talar-e Divankhaneh or Audience Chamber of the Marble

BLAZING MAJESTY OF A QAJAR SHAH

Fath Ali Shah (d1834) was … one blaze of jewels, which literally dazzled the sight on first looking at him … A lofty tiara of three elevations was on his head, which shape appears to have been long peculiar to the crown of the Great King. It was entirely composed of thickly-set diamonds, pearls, rubies and emeralds, so exquisitely disposed, as to form a mixture of the most beautiful colours, in the brilliant light reflected from its surface … His vesture was of gold tissue, nearly covered with a similar disposition of jewellery; and, crossing the shoulders, were two strings of pearls, probably the largest in the world … But for the splendour, nothing could exceed the broad bracelets round his arms, and the belt which encircled his waist; they actually blazed like fire, when the rays of the sun met them … The jewelled band on the right arm was called The Mountain of Light; and that on the left, The Sea of Light; and which superb diamonds, the rapacious conquests of Nader Shah had placed in the Persian regalia … [There was the throne] platform of pure white marble, an apt emblem of peace, raised a few steps from the ground, and carpeted with shawls and cloth of gold, on which the King sat in the fashion of his country, while his back was supported by a large cushion encased in a net-work of pearls.

From R Ker Porter, *Travels in Georgia, Persia, Armenia* … 1821, vol I, pp 325–7, describing the Nou Rouz royal audience, Golestan Palace, in 1818.

Throne (Takht-e Marmar) and the Emarat-e Badgir (Wind Tower) in the south. But the work of that shah suffered too. The huge Taziyeh Hall, used for Moharram performance and inspired by the Royal Albert Hall in London (as seen by the shah during his 1876 state visit), was destroyed in 1946, and his 1891 Kakh-e Abyad (White Palace) was razed to make way for offices of the Ministry of Finance, the Bank Melli and the Ministry of Roads. Also inspired by the shah's 1873 visit to Europe, which included Versailles with its famous mirrored gallery, is the Hall of Mirrors within the Golestan complex, which served as the coronation room for both Reza Shah and his son; it remains intact.

If you do not have time to visit all ten museums, do buy a ticket for 460,000 rials covering the main sites and take a walk in the courtyard to look at the various tiled panels, all extremely decorative with the distinct Qajar palette of yellows, pinks and blues. There is a good but expensive gift shop next door to the Ethnographic Museum. The Marble Throne veranda (Ivan-e Takht-e Marmar), straight across the courtyard from the main gate, is decorated with mirrors and other goodies seized by Agha Mohammad from the Zand palace buildings. The throne-couch itself, not the most beautiful artefact made by man, was carved by Esfahani craftsmen in 1807 or 1841 (depending upon who you read) and was where the shah sat during public audiences; Reza Shah Pahlavi was the last ruler to receive birthday and Nou Rouz greetings from his courtiers on this throne. On the veranda a door leads into a small portrait chamber decorated with oil paintings of rulers, historic and mythical, a bevy of European women and garden scenes; Fath Ali Shah's portrait is over the chimney. The main art gallery (Negarkhaneh) is next door, including mainly 19th-century oils, some the work of Kamal al-Molk, the leading court painter to Naser al-Din Shah, and then come the 1875 hall of mirrors and the European Art Gallery. The twin-tower pavilion is the Shams al-Emerah built by Naser al-Din, which now houses a small collection of calligraphy (no labels in English) in a splendour of mirrors and plasterwork. This was the first five-storey building to be constructed in Tehran, which Lord Curzon described in 1892 as 'a very creditable specimen of the fanciful ingenuity that still lingers in modern Persian art'. Continuing around this gaily tiled courtyard you come across the photography gallery and archive, the Tent House, now used for conferences, and the so-called Diamond Room, a tea house and toilets.

Under Glass Painting Museum موزه نقاشی پشت شیشه [98 E7] (202 Qaedi St; ☏77526777; ⏰ 09.00–17.30 daily; entry 100,000 rials) This 1930s mansion, finely restored and fully refurbished in 2019, is home to a small collection of under glass or, as it is also known, reverse-glass paintings. Originating probably in ancient China, the oldest known example of an art piece painted using this technique dates from the 3rd or 4th century BCE and was discovered in Italy. The technique consists in painting, typically with a wide range of colours, over a piece of glass and then reversing it, whereby the viewer sees the image through the glass. It gives a somewhat unusual, matte and soft effect to the painting. There are no historical records to establish with certainty when under-glass painting first appeared in Iran, but it was popular during the Zand period (1750–94) and had predominantly religious, folkloric and *gol-o-morgh* (birds and flowers) motifs.

Negarestan Garden باغ موزه نگارستان [111 F2] (Shariatmadar St, metro Baharestan; ☏33119586; w negarestan.ut.ac.ir; ⏰ 10.00–18.00 Tue–Sun; entry 250,000 rials) Named after the numerous *negareh* 'paintings' of Fath Ali Shah and his court and hidden from the busy streets amid an idyllic garden, this historic mansion houses an extensive collection of modern Iranian art, including a beautiful selection of the works by renowned miniaturist Ali Esfarjani (1920–2005) and the spectacular 'Saff-e Salam' murals of Fath Ali Shah. Gracefully seated at the centre of this colossal painting and depicted as disproportionally larger, Fath Ali Shah is surrounded by his numerous sons standing at the upper rows and notables at the lower ones. Originally painted on the walls of a historic mansion in the vicinity of the **Hezrat-e Ma'sumeh shrine** (page 122), this treasure was carefully restored and eventually moved here from its temporary home in Golestan Palace.

Negarestan Garden also has a pleasant outdoor tea house and a branch of Rouhi Restaurant (page 97). Dating to the times of Fath Ali Shah, it was part of the Negarestan Palace, the intended Qajar summer capital outside Tehran. It is here that Iranian prime minister Ghaem Magham Farahani was killed in 1835 on the orders of Mohammad Shah Qajar. During the reign of Mozaffer al-Din, the house was converted into a school of agriculture and the School of Fine Arts under the direction of Kamal al-Molk. It was also the alma mater of some of Iran's greatest minds including Ali Akbar Dekhoda, author of the most comprehensive dictionary of the Persian language, who had also taught here. In 2013 one of the buildings was converted into a gallery of works by Kamal al-Molk and his disciples. There are currently around 180 paintings by the master himself.

Masoudiyeh Palace عمارت مسعودیه [111 F2] (Mellat St; ⊕ 09.00–16.00 daily; entry 300,000 rials) In spite of its sheer area of 4,000m², this vast Qajar-period palace complex with numerous buildings and green areas essentially remains overlooked by most visitors to Tehran. After the completion of the Negarestan Garden (see opposite) in 1807, a plot of land at its southern end was sold to Qajar prince Masoud Mirza known as Zell-e Soltan, who in 1879 built his residency here. The palace comprises five buildings that have each retained fine examples of Qajar plasterwork. One of the rooms in the palace was in 1887 converted into what became the first public library of Iran. During the years of the Constitutional Revolution, the palace was used as a base of the Constitutionalists and opponents of Mohammad Ali Shah.

Motahhari Mosque مسجد مطهری [111 F2] (formerly Masjed-e Sepahsalar, 'Commander in Chief') (East of Golestan Palace, on the south side of Maydan-e Baharestan, northeast of Maydan-e Imam Khomeini; admittance to the public is not allowed) This, along with its adjacent madrasa, is one of the most photogenic historic mosques in Tehran. The official policy promoted by Reza Shah Pahlavi in the 1930s led to most of Tehran's mosques closing down along with the madrasas; it has been estimated that by 1942 only 24 mosques were open and operating in the capital. That is certainly not the case today. As the Madraseh va Masjed-e Motahhari, it is now a fully functioning theological college again. The main entrance portal and the façade are quite distinctive Qajar style. Built by two high-ranking officials in the court of Naser al-Din Shah in 1879–81, when its location was just inside the city walls, for many years it was one of the largest four-*ivan* mosques in Tehran. Two massive minarets flank the recessed entrance, which leads into a courtyard surrounded by twin-storeyed arcades of college rooms; in all there are some 60 chambers. Tiles with full-blown floral motifs in typically flamboyant Qajar style decorate the courtyard, while a tile inscription band gives details of the original endowment. The prayer hall dome, 37m in height, is supported by 44 columns. Right behind the mosque is the new parliament (*majles*) building.

Bazaar and around ✻ [111 E4] The bazaar of Tehran was built on the prototype of Bazaar-e Amir in Tabriz. After Agha Mohammad Khan, the founder of the Qajar dynasty, moved the monarchy's capital to the small town of Tehran, Amir Kabir and Agha Mehdi Tabrizi (first King of Merchants of the Protected Domains of Iran; *malek ol-tojjar* in Persian) were appointed to modernise its bazaar. The caravanserai Saray-e Amir (originally known as Saray-e Dowlat) built in 1852 became one of their first projects. At that time, British merchants dominated trade and commerce in Iran and Saray-e Amir housed offices of foreign companies and wealthy merchants. Later on, following the dispute over Iran's first public shareholding company, founded by the son of Malek ol-Tojjar, commercial activities have moved to the streets and elsewhere in the neighbourhood.

The bazaar is located within the block edged by Khayyam Street (in the west), Panzdah Khordad Street (north) and Mostafa Khomeini Street (east). Traffic around this area is horrendous. The first higher-education establishment in Tehran, **Dar al-Fonun** [111 E3], founded in 1851 for upper-class Persians along the lines of the French *école polytechnique* where European teachers taught military studies, medicine, science and languages, is located nearby on Naser Khosrow Street. It is here that Iran's outstanding painter Kamal al-Molk started his career and famous writer Sadegh Hedayat went to school. The building is closed, but its tiled façade is unmissable.

Inside the main bazaar area, **Masjed-e Imam Khomeini** [111 E4] (formerly Masjed-e Shah) stands out as one of the area's most important historic buildings. The mosque was built according to inscriptions in the *qibla ivan* in 1808–13 on the orders of Fath Ali Shah (d1834); at that time it faced the main citadel. Much of the mosque, its central courtyard with the four-*ivan* layout and the *muqarnas* vaulting in the *ivans* recalls the royal buildings of 17th-century Esfahan, but the tile decoration is in the gloriously flamboyant Qajar style. It was repaired by Fath Ali Shah's grandson Naser al-Din Shah some 60 years later.

Religious minorities in Tehran Southern Tehran is also home to the largest cluster of churches, synagogues and Zoroastrian places of worship in the city. Although the main church in Tehran is the 19th-century Armenian **Cathedral of St Sergius** [98 D5] (north end of Nejatollahi Street, just south of Karim Khan Zand Bd; ⏲ 13.00–16.00 daily, best to come for a Sun service to hear the church bells ring & to smell the frankincense), the Armenian **Church of Holy Mary** [111 D2] built in 1938 for the growing Armenian community, is located off Jomhuri Street near the British embassy. Right across the road from it is the **Adrian Temple of Tehran** [111 D2] (⏲ 08.00–13.30 Sat–Wed, 08.00–noon Thu), completed in 1917 and housing the Zoroastrian Society of Tehran. If you cross the street and walk towards the Ceramics and Glass Museum you'll find **St Peter's Evangelical Church** [111 D2] (⏲ Fri for service only). Founded in 1876, it is the main place of worship for Korean embassy personnel and Korean students in Tehran. Another Armenian church, **St Thaddeus** [90 C5], is located in the southeast section of the bazaar, off Mostafa Khomeini, on Shahid Mostavi running west. Although the Russian community in Iran is tiny, across the road from the former US embassy there is a small Russian **St Nicholas Church** [99 E6] (⏲ 10.00–noon Sun only), built in 1945, with classical Russian-style onion-shaped domes. If the main door is closed, there is a side entrance in Atarod Alley.

Jewish Community in Tehran In Tehran there is a functioning **Sukkot Shalom Synagogue** [98 C3] (also known as Youssef Abad Synagogue owing to its location on Youssef Abad Street), opened in 1951 for the numerous Jewish residents in the

Youssef Abad neighbourhood. Drop in here on a Saturday for *shabbat* service. **Haim Synagogue** [111 C2] (Simu Alley, off 30 Tir St), of which only the sign in Hebrew on the main gate remains, was originally built in 1913 and was considered to be the first synagogue within the city limits. It had been used a place of worship for Ashkenazi Polish Jews deported to Iran during World War II and later by Iraqi Jews before their community emigrated to Israel. The late 19th-century Ezra Yaghoub Synagogue [111 F4] in the originally Jewish district of Oudlajan near the bazaar is still functioning. Tucked away in the tiny alley, it is usually open early on Saturday mornings.

Mausoleum of Ayatollah Khomeini آرامگاه روح الله خمینی [111 D4] (Behesht-e Zahra Cemetery, southwest Tehran, visibly unmissable when coming along the Besat motorway from Imam Khomeini International Airport, around 20km from Tehran; metro Haram-e Motahhar; entry free; shoes, bags, etc, must be left at the mausoleum entrance & photography is not allowed; women enter to the left, men to the right; no chador necessary) The complex is situated adjacent to the huge cemetery, Behesht-e Zahra, named after an epithet of Fatima, the Prophet's daughter and wife to Ali, the first imam. In the late 1970s, this cemetery became closely associated with the revolutionary movement against the Pahlavi regime, as many of those killed in the 1978 demonstrations were buried here; after the 8 September 1978 demonstration over 4,290 burial certificates were issued for this site. No wonder this was the place selected by Ayatollah Khomeini for his first public speech six months later. Many of the soldiers killed during the Iran–Iraq War were also buried here and photographs of the central fountain which once ran with blood-red-coloured water (symbolising the martyrs' sacrifice) featured on the front page of many Western newspapers.

The mausoleum of Khomeini dominates the landscape, particularly at night when the central golden-domed tomb and the surrounding buildings on each corner of an enormous 'terrace' are illuminated. The four minarets are each 91m high in honour of Khomeini's years of life and the cupola is adorned with 72 tulips in honour of the number of Karbala martyrs. The floor area of the actual tomb building is equivalent in size to twice that of London Heathrow's Terminal 4 check-in area, and has similar exposed pipes and structural girders. Acres of green onyx slabs cover the vast floor while a glass drum adorned with giant, fat, blood-red tulip motifs (blood of the martyrs) sits uneasily over the cenotaph grille.

AROUND TEHRAN

In proximity to the Iranian capital there are numerous mountain-hiking areas and ski resorts, where you can easily spend a full day walking or even stay overnight if you decide not to return to Tehran the same day. **Darband** (دربند), a small village fully absorbed into the northern outskirts of Tehran, lies at the end of Darband Street, approximately 2km north of Tajrish Square. A popular weekend getaway with fresh mountain air, it is a pleasant spot for family brunches and has a myriad traditional restaurants. For the best views over the village take a cable car (*telekabin* in Persian) (Kuhnavardi Sq; ⊕ 08.00–23.00 Sat–Wed, 06.00–23.000 Thu & Fri; 1-day/return 300,000/500,000 rials). Many hiking paths in the area start at Kuhnavardi Square and curl up around the slopes towards Tochal past **Pas Qaleh** (پس قلعه) village. Here you can overnight in **Osoun Hotel** (20 rooms; $$–$$$) with a nostalgic mountaineer atmosphere and delightful personnel. Rooms are simple, but views are breathtaking.

Walking further north and up, you reach **Tochal** (توچال) ski and hiking resort (☏ 24875000; w tochal.org). Known as *bam-e tehran*, 'the roof of Tehran', Tochal

3

(3,964m) is both the most popular and the most central Tehrani hiking spot. Getting here requires a taxi ride to the corner of Velenjak Street and Daneshju Boulevard. Consider this the '0' station. From here it is a short walk through the car park and past a café area to where you can take a minibus or walk around 2km to the first station. From there, yet again you can walk 3.5km up or take the cable car (⊕ 08.30–16.30 Sat–Wed, 07.00–17.30 Thu & Fri; 300,000 rials one-way) to the second station, where you need to change and purchase another ticket if you wish to continue on to the final, seventh station (return ticket from the first to the seventh station is 600,000 rials).

Higher yet again, around 1.98km from the seventh station is the famous **Tochal Hotel** (30 rooms; Shahid Chamran Expressway; ✆22418000; **$$$**), which is open for the seven to eight months during the year when the slopes are covered with snow. The total distance between the first station and the Tochal Hotel is 17.08km and there is a walking path all the way up for those in good shape and spirits. There are toilet facilities and a rest area at each of the stations. If you've left your skis at home, do at least come here for the stunning views over Tehran.

On the way back to Tehran, find time to visit **Zahir-e Dowleh Cemetery** [105 E1] (off Darband St; ⊕ for women 10.00–noon, for men 13.00–16.00 Thu only; entry free), dating back to the Qajar period. It is here where people come to pay homage to Iranian poets Forough Farrokhzad and Iraj Mirza, as well as many other outstanding intellectuals, including Ruhollah Khaleqi, the author of 'Oh Iran' – Iran's de facto national anthem. Many gravestones here bear the *tabarzin* ('dervish axe') incision in honour of the buried dervishes and followers of Ali Zahir-e Dowleh (born Mirza Ali Khan; 1864–1924), a high-ranking official under Naser al-Din Shah, known for his liberal and progressive (for his time) ideas.

Damavand (دماوند), at 5,610m, is Iran's highest summit, and covered with snow all year long. The area surrounding this volcanic mountain is rich in natural hot springs, and small rocks of volcanic formation scattered along the area's curvy roads are used in Iranian households. For tours up to the summit of Mount Damavand and for off-piste mountain ski touring, contact Ardeshir Soltani from **Mount Damavand Info** (m 0912 3856818; e solard@gmail.com; w damawand.de) or Advanture Iran (page 44), who can organise a number of trekking and hiking tours depending on the season. About 50km northeast from Tehran towards Damavand along the Haraz road lies a small ski resort and the affluent Tehrani holiday-home conglomeration of **Abadiyeh**. Continuing along the road you pass through **Imamzadeh Hashem**, famous for its kite games on account of strong winds at this altitude. The next town in the area is **Polur**, known for its freshwater trout and salmon hatcheries and a local fish market. One of the many fish restaurants here would be a good choice for lunch before you continue on towards the village of Rineh, where the Iranian army kept Iraqi prisoners of war. The town of **Larijan**, the namesake of the current chairman of the parliament of Iran, is known for its hot springs and has numerous apartment-style, essentially budget, hotels with a hot-spring bath. If returning to Tehran along the same road, stop at the **Latiyan Dam**, 10km away from the capital. Here you can take a break and have a picnic by the blue lake amid the mountain range.

SOUTH OF TEHRAN

REY AND AROUND Before the 19th century, biblical Rhages (a name of Greek origin), known in Iran as Shahr-e Rey, was a more important town than Tehran; it lies 16km south of the capital but Tehran has now engulfed it and the metro has stretched all the way from the city centre to here. Said to be the 12th city of the world

above   The eye-catching Shams al-Emarah in the Golestan Palace Complex was Tehran's tallest building when it was completed in 1892 (LA/S) page 114

below   Reaching towards the Alborz Mountains, the sprawl of modern Tehran can be seen from Milad Tower (MO) page 103

above   While Zoroastrians no longer use 'towers of silence' as vessels for placing dead bodies (instead of burying them), a few towers still remain around Yazd province (MK/S) page 317

left   The ancient Persian motif of a lion battling a bull is symbolic of springtime defeating winter, or Nou Rouz, one of the pillars of Iranian culture and tradition (AV/S) page 263

below   The monumental Gate of All Nations in Persepolis stands above the entrance steps to the ancient Achaemenid Empire's capital (BM/S) page 266

above   The massive brick stepped construction of Choga Zanbil is nearly 3,500 years old (MO) page 284

right   A Persian warrior, represented with his distinctive curly locks and beard, guards the Achaemenid kings in Persepolis (s/S) page 263

below   The Tomb of Cyrus the Great, founder of the Achaemenid Empire, is the centrepiece of Pasargadae, the ancient Persian capital that he constructed to attest to the majesty of Persian civilisation (LA/S) page 272

above left The Iranian textile industry is thousands of years old; shopping for fabrics is one of the most enjoyable things to do in cities across Iran (AB)

above Mosques and shrines in Iran are open to everyone for prayer, a minute of calm, or to exchange a few words with friends (SS)

below left Drop in to one of the numerous carpet shops in Shiraz's Vakil Bazaar for a cup of tea and a friendly chat with hospitable traders (AM/S) page 250

below The traditional Kashani weaving technique of *sha'rbafi* is now practised only in a few remaining workshops, such as in the Manouchehri House in Kashan (MO) page 152

above   Between visiting sites, stop in at one of Iran's numerous cafés, such as the Baharnarenj café in Esfahan, for a cup of tea or a glass of refreshing homemade lemonade (MO) page 186

right   A Qashqai woman spins wool in a traditional dwelling in northern Shiraz (AB)

below   Street bazaars across Iran have a fantastic vibe and often have wonderful antique pieces to browse through for souvenirs (AP)

above Maharlu Salt Lake, otherwise known as the Pink Lake, is a mere 20km away from Shiraz, and looks particularly splendid when seen from the air (MO) page 260

left The Iranian Persian Gulf coastline stretches for about 1,000km and has some spectacular and secluded beaches, such as this one at Banud (MO) page 297

below One of Iran's least explored natural wonders, Rageh Canyon's stunning 20km-long valley is an idyllic camping location (MO) page 320

top   Outside Varzaneh, the sunsets over some of Iran's highest dunes are spectacular and so too are the starry night skies (MO) page 162

above left   The reconstructed Robat-e Zayn al-Din caravanserai near Yazd offers comfortable accommodation to travellers, just like in the old days (MK/S) page 319

above right   Damavand is the king of the Alborz Mountains, the highest mountain in the Middle East and renowned for its wonderful nature (MI/S) page 118

below   Iran is home to a number of nomad groups scattered across the Iranian plateau, with most of them still leading a traditional lifestyle and migrating with the seasons (ME)

above The unique ecosystem of the Caspian Sea, the largest body of inland water in the world, helped to create rich woodlands in northern Iran (SS) page 193

left An Iranian *dhow* moored at Qeshm Island in the Persian Gulf (SS) page 301

below A catch of sturgeon off the coast of Iran (SS) page 200

to be created by Ahura Mazda, and the place where Tobias and the angel stopped after the wedding in Hamadan (page 133), the town was rebuilt and renamed as Europos by Seleucus Nikator (c300BCE), the same person responsible for Apamea and Dura Europos in Syria. There were important Parthian and Sasanid settlements here and Harun al-Rashid, the famous Abbasid caliph whose son was later to be involved in the sudden death of Imam Reza (see box, page 347), was born here in 763CE. It became an important administrative centre under the Seljuk sultanate when it became known as 'the most beautiful city of the East', second only to the Abbasid centre of the Islamic Empire, Baghdad. Very little of that remains, as Rey was almost totally obliterated by the Mongol armies in the 1220s.

Getting there and away Rey is located around 16km south from Tehran and is accessible by metro (Shahr-e Rey station on the red line). You can also order a taxi to take you there.

What to see and do To many Iranians, the most important monument in Rey is the **Shrine of (Shah) Abd al-Azim**, which houses the graves of the descendants of the second and fourth imams, and Hamzeh, a brother of the eighth imam. During the late shah's time, non-Muslims were not permitted to enter but could catch glimpses into the first courtyard from the 1950 concrete memorial-tomb of Reza Shah, who died during his South African exile, its monumental proportions reminiscent of certain Lodi tombs in Delhi, India; it was one of the first Pahlavi monuments to be destroyed in 1979. The shrine itself was lovingly repaired and decorated during the Safavid period, with additions including the mirror work in the 19th century. It was here, on leaving the shrine, that Naser al-Din Shah was assassinated in 1896.

To the north of the shrine are the heavily restored remains of a Seljuk tomb tower (entry 100,000 rials) known locally as **Toghrol** (برج طغرل) after the sultan Toghrol Beg (d1063), although it was built over 60 years later. It stands about 20m high, with a diameter of about 16.5m, but it has lost its original conical dome. In the hills behind is a Qajar rock-cut relief depicting the unfortunate Qajar shah Naser al-Din, with his ten sons, and another earlier panel showing Fath Ali Shah with some members of his enormous family (he was said to have fathered 189 children). This is **Cheshmeh Ali** (Water Spring of Ali) whose pure soft water ensured its reputation as a carpet-washing centre over the last two centuries.

It was near here that, during the 1920s and 1930s, American archaeological teams excavated the site of Nagarehkhaneh and found, among other items, remnants of woven silk fabrics, thought to date to around 900–1220CE. The textile world was astounded by the discoveries and when further pieces came on to the open market during and after World War II, they were eagerly snapped up by the major museums in the West; in the late 1970s scientific analyses revealed that many of the newly acquired 'Buyid' pieces were in fact clever forgeries. This is also the location of the Shrine of Bibi Shahrbanu. The story of this shrine is closely linked to that of a Zoroastrian shrine outside Yazd, in southeastern Iran (page 318), and similar to that of St Tikla of Maaloula, outside Damascus, Syria. It is said that a daughter of the last Sasanid shah, Yazdegerd III, married to the third imam, Hossein, grandson of the Prophet Mohammad, fled here to escape the overtures of an Umayyad general. At her behest, the mountain opened and then closed around her, saving her from a fate worse than death. Probably this was originally a shrine to Anahita, the Zoroastrian divinity. Evidence of 10th-century building work has largely disappeared under continuous rebuilding from the 15th century onwards.

Continuing south some 10km will bring you to the remains of a huge brick complex, **Tappeh Mil**, dating from Sasanid times. It is thought this was an important fire temple with royal audience halls and associate buildings. Little was readily identifiable in the mid 1970s and today it is more of a monument to modern reconstruction skills.

It is about 20km further on to **Varamin** (ورامین), which can also be reached by local train (departures every hour or two; see w ai.ir for exact timetable) from Tehran's main train station. Varamin is home to the heavily restored tomb tower of **Ala al-Din** (برج علاءالدین) (c1289) on Imam Khomeini Square, whose exterior is decorated with 32 angled flanges, and an early 14th-century masjed-e jame, built on the four-*ivan* plan. It is thought that the Ilkhanid ruler, Oljeitu, paid for this mosque, which was then completed by his successor in 1322. Almost a century later it needed attention as two panels in the prayer chamber refer to the Timurid ruler, Shah Rukh (see box, page 340). A great deal of restoration and rebuilding work was undertaken in the 1970s. Enough of the strap-brickwork decoration in turquoise and cobalt blue and the carved plasterwork remains to allow the imagination to picture the original scheme of decoration and the clean proportions. There are the remains of another Ilkhanid structure in Varamin, Imamzadeh Yahya, whose splendid tile-*mihrab*, now in the Hermitage Museum, St Petersburg, gives a late 13th-century date for the buildings itself.

QOM قم Located 154km southwest from Tehran, Qom (pronounced *Ghom*; population 1,200,000) is the second most sacred place in Iran after Mashhad, because it was here that Fatima, the sister of the eighth imam, Imam Reza (and not Fatima, the Prophet's daughter and wife of Ali) fell ill on her way to Mashhad and died in 816CE. Qom is also known to have become the first and distinctly Shi'a city in Iran when in the early 8th century a number of families from Kufa in Iraq settled here after fleeing from Umayyad persecution. In the 20th century Qom has been selected as a Shi'a theological centre and has since grown extensively, with a road and traffic system designed to cope with a daily influx of pilgrims and visitors.

When the town was established is unclear, for its water supply has always been poor and brackish so there was little logic for a settlement. Perhaps it was founded by the Arab Muslims after conquering the region in 644CE but possibly there was a sizeable settlement in existence then, for we know Zoroastrianism remained influential here until 901CE. By then Qom was also known for its Shi'a theologians although there was no sign of a special tomb to commemorate Fatima. It was rumoured this was the birthplace of that powerful political figure, Hassan al-Sabbah, leader of the Ismaili sect, the Assassins (see box, page 131). Perhaps that was why the Mongols exacted such a fierce revenge on the small town, as it was then, massacring most of the population in 1221. In the 14th century it was best known for its hunting, and many Iranian rulers wintered here; a shrine for Fatima was in existence, but it was a modest complex. All that changed with the Safavid regime (1501–1735). As champions of Ithna 'Ashari Shi'ism, the Safavid shahs undertook a programme of construction and repairs to the Qom shrine, as they would do with those of Karbala, Ardabil and Mashhad, perhaps hoping to persuade Iranians and other Shi'as to forego the hajj to Mecca and Medina. The rebel Afghans exacted their revenge and even with royal Qajar patronage, Qom's population in 1872 was a mere 4,000.

Today the population stands at approximately 1.2 million, owing much of its reputation as a theological teaching centre to the charismatic theologian, Ayatollah Haeri-Yazdi (d1935), one of Ayatollah Khomeini's teachers. As for the town's water, new reservoirs were constructed soon after the revolution.

Iran offers fantastic skiing opportunities and, contrary to a popular belief, neither slopes nor lifts are gender-segregated. Ski resorts are in fact the outposts of freedom for young Iranians; women here are not required to wear *manteaux* or hijab while skiing.

Dizin (w dizinskiresort.com; ☉ mid-Dec–May), about 100km north of Tehran and 15km off the Chalus Road (the turn is signposted) is unquestionably home to Iran's best pistes. Just the breathtaking views of Mount Damavand from the slopes make the trip worthwhile. It has two refurbished and pristinely clean hotels – Dizin 1 (70 rooms & chalet for 6 people; \026 35212978; **$$$**) and Dizin 2 (operated by Dizin 1), with Dizin 3 on the way. If you are planning to spend New Year's Eve in Dizin, think again – the resort is usually fully booked.

Hotel Dizin 1 is located right next to the slopes – the Dizin pad. A one-day ski pass costs 800,000 rials and a tourist pass is 350,000 rials. Ski lifts are numerous; but depending on the weather some may be closed. Ski-slope difficulty ranges from blue to black, with a number of people venturing off piste. There are a couple of good cafés and restaurants at the first level. The resort is very busy on Fridays and the first ski lift queue may take up to an hour.

Ski rentals are available in Dizin 2 Hotel (☉ 07.30–17.00; skis & boots 500,000 rials per day) and at the shop at the car park on arrival to the village (☉ 07.30–17.00; skis & boots 500,000–800,000 rials per day depending on how new the equipment is). Ski clothes rental is also possible. **Dizin Ski School** (☉ 08.00–16.00; prices start at 1,500,000 rials for a full day of lessons) is located across from the entrance to the ski lift.

Shemshak (شمشک) resort is a good alternative if Dizin is booked out. Shemshak mountain village is a picturesque retreat from the smog of Tehran and many affluent residents of the capital have their winter apartments and chalets here. On a good day the mountain road from Shemshak continues on towards Dizin, but do check the snow forecast before continuing further, as it might be closed. Other smaller ski slopes are in **Tochal** and **Ab Ali**, but their vicinity to Tehran means that these are best explored as a one-day trip from the city.

Iran's second-largest ski resort is **Pooladkaf** (پولادکف) (☉ Dec–Mar), 140km northwest of Shiraz near the village of Ardekan (also known by its more recent name Sepidan). The **Pooladkaf Hotel** (56 rooms; \071 36258025; w pooladkafhotel.com; **$$$**) is the only accommodation here and it is located at the entrance to the resort. Adventure tours in the nearby mountains, including a visit to the Margoon Waterfall, can be arranged in the hotel. The **ski rental** shop (300,000 rials for skis & boots for a full day) is located by the gondola ticket office (500,000 rials for a 1-day ticket, 100,000 rials will be refunded when returning the pass card at the end of the day) or in **Ardekan**. Ski lessons can be arranged at the **ski school** by the ticket office (m 0917 5563750; 360,000–570,000 rials per hr depending on the level).

Getting there and away Regular **buses** to Qom depart from Tehran's Terminal-e Jonub (Southern terminal). There is, however, no bus terminal in Qom and when returning or going further south the taxi will drop you at 72 Tan Square or Valiasr Square respectively, from where buses depart as soon as all seats are filled.

3

What to see and do The golden dome and twin minarets of Fatima's shrine, **Hezrat-e Ma'sumeh** (shrine of Fatima, sister of Imam Reza; see box, page 347) (⊕ always; grounds accessible to non-Muslims but women must wear a chador, available to rent in the women's entrance hall & must ensure that hair is covered entirely & at all times, otherwise it will not be long before one of the guardians points it out) dominate the skyline. It is, as Lord Curzon said, the 'Westminster Abbey of many of her kings', for the shrine houses the remains of four Safavid shahs (Safi I, Abbas II, Soleyman I and Sultan-Hossein) and two Qajar rulers, Fath Ali Shah (with two of his sons) and Mohammad Shah along with countless high officials of the Qajar court. There is a large *maydan* in front surrounded by a bazaar, souvenir shops and sweet shops selling the local delicacy, *sohan*, a thin butter 'brittle' with pistachios. Just before the main entrance to the first courtyard, the tiled doorway on the right marks the entrance into the madrasa where Ayatollah Khomeini studied. The city has been, and still is, witness to some of the most thought-provoking theological debates, discussing the role of the *ulama* (clergy) in revolutionary Iran.

A short description of the complex follows but note that it is based on information and maps published in the late 1970s; no account of any repairs or construction appears to have been published since then. An earlier arrangement of four courtyards in the complex was revised in Safavid times, when the Madrasa Faydiyeh was built over two of the courts, with a small hospital (Dar al-Shifa) behind. In the late 19th century a huge courtyard, Sahn-e Jadid, was constructed to cope with pilgrims. Several madrasas, including that of Jani Khan, were extensively repaired at this time, and the dome and drum over Fatima's cenotaph were gilded and the chamber extensively clad in mirror work. Such funding dried up as the Qajar regime faltered. Increasingly, during the first half of the 20th century, theological studies and the colleges involved in their teaching received markedly less royal patronage and funding. However, with increasing secularism in Ottoman and then Kemalist Turkey, Shi'a theologians returned to Iran, and particularly to Mashhad and Qom. Disused madrasas in the sacred precinct were repaired and reopened, and with the installation of Ayatollah Haeri-Yazdi from Arak and his numerous students, the rejuvenation of Qom as a teaching centre and a pilgrimage place really began.

From 1975 onwards, the main entrance has opened immediately into the Sahn-e Jadid, renamed Nou Atabaki, where the festival prayers are held. Directly opposite on the far side is the passageway, which leads to the Old Treasury. To the left is the tomb of Shah Safi (d1642) and, behind, that of Abbas II (d1666) along with the entrance into the Masjed-e Bala Sar, which formerly housed the museum. To the right a passage leads into the Sahn-e Kuhneh, where Fath Ali Shah is interred at the far end. Behind this courtyard are the Madrasa Faydiyeh and the Dar al-Shifa.

Some locals say that there are around 400 *imamzadehs* in Qom, but historical monuments here are few. The 8th-century **Gonbad-e Sabz** (the Green Domes Historical Complex) (Shahid Rouhani St; ⊕ 07.30–17.00) is across the road from **Imamzadeh Ali Ibn Jafar**, which was built in 1360 for a local amir and his family by a craftsman who went on to erect three other mausoleums. Its 12-sided exterior (but octagonal interior) once supported a double dome, hemispherical inside and tent-like on the outside, but today they have been replaced. The carved plasterwork on the exterior was originally colourfully painted.

From Qom, it is about 100km south to Kashan (page 151). Along this road, 6km from Qom is another important pilgrimage monument, the **Jamkaran Mosque**, built on the site where it is believed the 12th imam once appeared. When looking at a road map it is always intriguing to note the Iranian village given as Naufel

Le Chato on some early 1990s maps (the spelling on later maps is often 'Neufle'). This settlement wished to honour Ayatollah Khomeini, and so redesignated itself after the French town outside Paris where the Ayatollah lived in exile, Neauphle-le-Château.

Northwest of Qom is **Saveh** (ساوه), 112km from Tehran, associated with a type of lustre- and enamel-painted ceramics which was thought to have been made here in the 13th century, and more importantly for its double-spiral-staircased minaret in the centre of town, considered to be the earliest still standing in Iran, linked to the Masjed-e Maydan of 1062. Further down the same road is another early minaret with splendid brickwork patterning, this time belonging to the masjed-e jame of 1111. The prayer hall of this second mosque was probably constructed at the same time but much restoration and rebuilding was carried out in both the Mongol and later Safavid periods.

3

SEND US YOUR SNAPS!

We'd love to follow your adventures using our *Iran* guide – why not tag us in your photos and stories via Twitter (🐦 @BradtGuides) and Instagram (📷 @bradtguides)? Alternatively, you can upload your photos directly to the gallery on the Iran destination page via our website (w bradtguides.com/iran).

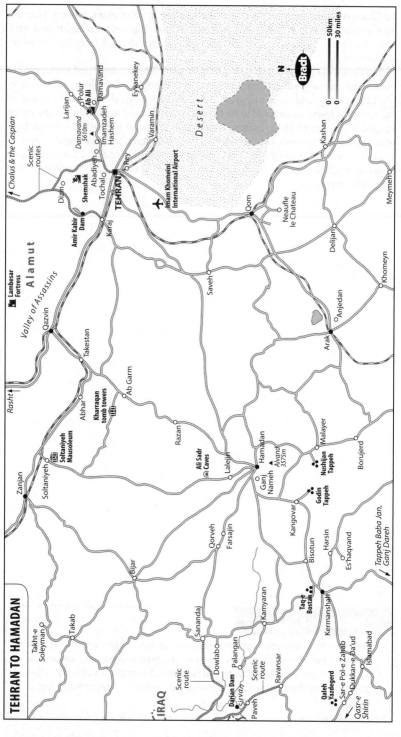

TEHRAN TO HAMADAN

N

Bradt

0   50km
0   30 miles

Chalus & the Caspian

Scenic
routes

Desert

Larijan
Polur
Ab Ali
Damavand
Eyvanekey
Damavand 5610m
Imamzadeh Hashem
Abadiyeh
Varamin
Rey
Dizino
Shemshak
Tochal
TEHRAN
Imam Khomeini International Airport
Karaj
Amir Kabir Dam
Kashan
Meymeh
Lambesar Fortress
V a l l e y   o f   A l a m u t
Qom
Neaufle le Chateau
Qazvin
Saveh
Delijan
Khomeyn
Rasht
Takestan
Anjedan
Abhar
Ab Garm
Kharraqan tomb towers
Razan
Arak
Soltaniyeh Mausoleum
Soltaniyeh
Ali Sadr Caves
Lalejin
Hamadan
Alvand 3575m
Nushijan Tappeh
Malayer
Borujerd
Zanjan
Ganj Nameh
Godin Tappeh
Qorveh
Farsajin
Kangovar
Bisotun
Harsin
Es'haqvand
Tappeh Baba Jan, Ganj Dareh
Bijar
Takht-e Soleyman
Takab
Sanandaj
Kamyaran
Taq-e Bostan
Kermanshah
Dowlabo
Palangan
Scenic route
Sirvan
Paveh
Ravansar
Dajian Dam
Qaleh Yazdegerd
Sar-e Pol-e Zahab
Dukkan-e Da'ud
Ishmabad
Qasr-e Shirin
IRAQ

4

West of Tehran: from Qazvin Onwards to Kurdistan and Beyond

QAZVIN قزوین *Telephone code 028*

About 152km west of Tehran lies Qazvin (pronounced *Ghazvin*, population 464,000), founded by the Sasanid shah Shapur I (d272) on the great central plain criss-crossed by caravan routes to the Zagros Mountains and Mesopotamia (Iraq), the Caucasus and the Caspian. The town quickly fell to the Arab Muslim armies in 644 and prospered, as the trade routes were made secure, with members of the Abbasid caliphate visiting the town en route to eastern Iran. In the 12th century the regional administration became destabilised as the Assassins established strongholds around Alamut to the north. Order was restored by the Seljuk sultanate, but then the city suffered at the hands of the Mongol armies in 1220 and 1256. The political rivalry between the Ottoman and Safavid empires in the early 16th century turned into military confrontation and Tabriz, the first Safavid capital, proved too close to the battlefield. The court moved down to Qazvin in 1555 until the Ottoman threat forced it to relocate to Esfahan in 1597, leaving behind the royal gardens, pavilions and offices. Even so, in 1628 foreign visitors reported that the city extended over 11km, with a population of about 150,000. By 1700 Ottoman incursions and earthquakes had left Qazvin in ruins, with few defences to withstand Afghan attacks against Safavid authority. Prosperity returned to a degree with Qajar rule, but again the city's location made it strategically important to Russian and then Soviet occupying forces during both world wars. The Qazvin Islamic Azad University, a popular choice among foreign students for studying Persian, is located here.

GETTING THERE AND AROUND Frequent *savari* taxis leave the Azadi (western) terminal in Tehran and get here within 90 minutes. Tickets cost 100,000–300,000 rials and can easily be purchased right before departure. **Buses** depart from the same terminal, but are less regular and you are more than likely to be intercepted by a *savari* section employee who will take you to the *savari* departures area. Buses from Hamadan are irregular (up to three services per day) and take up to 5 hours (250,000 rials), and the main city terminal is by the Tehran Gate. Once you are in Qazvin, as the town map on page 127 indicates, most of the sights are within walking distance of each other and the four hotels recommended are conveniently located near the historic city centre. Getting to Tehran from Qazvin, there are two *savari* departure points: the official yellow taxis depart from the bus terminal and the unofficial ones from the Valiasr intersection.

TOURIST INFORMATION Qazvin's **tourist office** is located in the Sadosaltaneh Caravanserai.

WHERE TO STAY AND EAT *Map, opposite, unless otherwise stated*

Qazvin is the best place to stay overnight if you wish to visit the Alamut region.

Alborz Hotel (36 rooms) Taleqani St; 33226631; e info@alborzhotel.com. No longer a budget option, this hotel has a large lobby with small balconies overlooking the main street. Each room is immaculate & spacious. B/fast is excellent & staff most accommodating & helpful. The best choice in town. **$$**

Hotel Marmar (50 rooms) Ayatollah Khamenei Bd; 33555771, 33555775; w marmarhotel.com. Described in their literature as 'the best & the largest city hotel' it has certainly seen more glorious days. Lobby décor is Qajar while at the same time trying to please tourists; rooms are large & clean, albeit a little dark. **$$**

Golshan Guesthouse [map, page 128] (55 rooms) 33222683; Imam Khomeini St. Simple guesthouse in the city centre. Furniture is very basic & toilets are shared, but it is overall very clean & has a certain old-fashioned charm. Ideal for shoestring travellers. **$**

Taleqani Guesthouse (24 rooms) Taleqani St (across the road from Alborz Hotel); 33224239,

33227698. Very clean, central & the best budget option in town. Offers different types of rooms, some en suite. Staff are friendly & helpful. **$**

Aghbali Restaurant Taleqani St; 33224990, 33222247; ⏰ 11.00–16.00 & 19.00–22.00. Despite the somewhat bland modern interior, this eatery nonetheless curries favour with the locals. Taste traditional Qazvini dish *qheymeh nesar*, rice mixed with beef & lamb, with a mix of sweet & sour *zereshk* to find out why. **$**

Sofrekhaneh Bazaar [map, page 128] 33234326; ⏰ 10.00–16.00. A tiny traditional & modest restaurant in the heart of the bazaar, serving b/fast & lunch. *Dizzi* is the reason to come here. **$**

Café Negarosaltaneh [map, page 128] Sadosaltaneh Caravanserai; 32247634; ⏰ 10.00–23.00 daily. A cosy café with a very hospitable atmosphere. A good cup of coffee & a light meal is exactly what one needs after a day of sightseeing. There are also a few books to leaf through while waiting. **$**

WHAT TO SEE AND DO Very little remains of the pre-20th-century walled town of Qazvin except for the Qajar-period **Tehran Gate**, decked out in its 19th-century yellow, blue and black tiling, looking rather lost and forlorn standing alone in the street. In 2015, however, one of the city's hidden treasures – Qajar-period **Sadosaltaneh Caravanserai** ✳, the largest inner-city caravanserai (see box, page 165) in the Middle East – got a facelift and was converted into one of Iran's nicest traditional roofed shopping and souvenir areas. In addition to numerous cafés and a traditional restaurant, it houses numerous galleries, souvenir stores and a carpet shop.

Most visitors make their way immediately to the **Imamzadeh Hossein**, which enshrines the remains of Hossein, a son of the eighth imam (passing at the top of the road, a *zurkhaneh* or wrestling gymnasium, see box, page 172, identified by the external tiled cornice of wrestlers and 'Indian clubs'). The main entrance vestibule into the *imamzadeh* is also decorated with 19th-century Qajar tiles in pastel shades depicting full-blown roses and other flowers. This brings the visitor into a huge octagonal courtyard (representing the four quarters of the world overset with the four gardens of paradise). In the centre stands the shrine with its mirrored-glass veranda. There should be no problem entering through the shrine's massive silver doors, women using the left-hand door and men the right, leaving shoes at the attendants' desks. Women must wear chadors, which are available for rent when

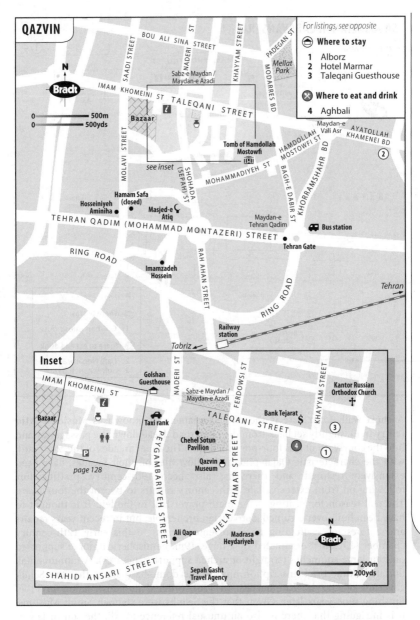

QAZVIN

BOU ALI SINA STREET

NADERI ST

KHAYYAM STREET

PADEGAN ST

MODARRES BD

Mellat Park

SAADI STREET

IMAM KHOMEINI ST

Sabz-e Maydan / Maydan-e Azadi

TALEQANI STREET

N

Bradt

0 ——— 500m
0 ——— 500yds

MOLAVI STREET

Bazaar

Tomb of Hamdollah Mostowfi

HAMDOLLAH MOSTOWFI ST

Maydan-e Vali Asr

AYATOLLAH KHAMENEI BD

2

see inset

SHOHADA (SEPAH) ST

MOHAMMADIYEH ST

BAGH-E DABIR ST

KHORRAMSHAHR BD

Hamam Safa (closed)

Hosseiniyeh Aminiha

Masjed-e Atiq

TEHRAN QADIM (MOHAMMAD MONTAZERI) STREET

RAH AHAN STREET

Maydan-e Tehran Qadim

Bus station

RING ROAD

Imamzadeh Hossein

Tehran Gate

RING ROAD

Tehran →

Railway station

Tabriz ←

For listings, see opposite

Where to stay
1 Alborz
2 Hotel Marmar
3 Taleqani Guesthouse

Where to eat and drink
4 Aghbali

Inset

IMAM KHOMEINI ST

NADERI ST

FERDOWSI ST

KHAYYAM STREET

Golshan Guesthouse

Sabz-e Maydan / Maydan-e Azadi

Kantor Russian Orthodox Church

Bazaar

Taxi rank

TALEQANI STREET

Bank Tejarat

3

PEYGAMBARIYEH STREET

page 128

P

Chehel Sotun Pavilion

Qazvin Museum

HELAL AHMAR STREET

4

1

Ali Qapu

Madrasa Heydariyeh

N

Bradt

0 ——— 200m
0 ——— 200yds

SHAHID ANSARI STREET

Sepah Gasht Travel Agency

West of Tehran: from Qazvin Onwards to Kurdistan and Beyond — QAZVIN — 4

passing through the main entrance. Note that no photography is allowed inside. The shrine was clearly active during Safavid times because an inscription records that a daughter of Shah Tahmasp I paid for restoration work in 1630, but most decoration is much later. On Fridays and holy days many families come here on pilgrimage, having lunch as they sit in the courtyard alcoves. As you walk around the exterior of the building, look at the paving stones, especially those to the left of the main veranda. Some of these are gravestones bearing emblems denoting the gender and profession of those commemorated.

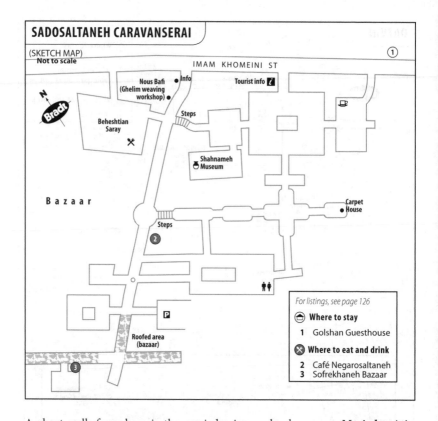

SADOSALTANEH CARAVANSERAI

(SKETCH MAP)
Not to scale ①

IMAM KHOMEINI ST

Nous Bafi ● Info
(Ghelim weaving
workshop) ●

Tourist info ℹ️

Steps

Beheshtian
Saray
✕

Shahnameh
Museum

Bazaar

Carpet
● House

Steps
②

♂️♀️

P

For listings, see page 126

🏠 **Where to stay**
1   Golshan Guesthouse

✕ **Where to eat and drink**
2   Café Negarosaltaneh
3   Sofrekhaneh Bazaar

Roofed area
(bazaar)

③

A short walk from here is the masjed-e jame, also known as **Masjed-e Atiq** (entry free), slightly set back from the main road. Head down the passageway and into the courtyard of this four-portal mosque. The inner arcades of the courtyard, with the characteristic Qajar pink and yellow tiles on their façades, have been extensively restored, and there has also been 19th-century 'prettification' following on from extensive late 17th-century repairs to two of the four *ivans*. The real reason for visiting is the main prayer hall to the left. It is thought to have been built over a ruined Zoroastrian fire temple, but in recent years repairs and a forest of scaffolding have prevented access to this early 12th-century chamber (15.25m²) dominated by a huge, 19m, hemispherical dome supported on four large squinches (straight or arched support structures). A monumental, floriated, *Kufic* brick inscription around the dome-base states that the Seljuk governor of Qazvin, Khumartash (d1136), ordered its construction in 1106, finishing nine years later. Given that the Seljuks were staunch Sunni Muslims, it is intriguing that there is also an unusual reference to Ali, the son-in-law of the Prophet Mohammad. Slowly the eye adjusts to the understated decoration of subtly coloured brickwork and carved plaster, once colourfully painted. A lengthy inscription band (Q3:133; Q27:40; Q16:34) snakes over three walls in a series of giant trilobed meanders, while other inscriptions record the list of endowments to the mosque over the years from shop rents, villages taxes and so on. The 19th-century winter hall downstairs has pleasing proportions but this has now been converted into a library for female students, who are happy to let foreign women (but not men) invade their space.

On Molavi Street is **Hosseiniyeh Aminiha** (◷ 09.00–13.00 & 16.00–18.00, ring the door on arrival), built during the 19th century to house the Moharram *taziyeh* 'passion play' that retells the story of Hossein's tragic death at Karbala and is performed every year. Turning north along Molavi Street takes one towards the bazaar and the 19th-century Masjed-e Nabi, and further east to the main square of Maydan-e Azadi. On its south side, almost concealed by bus shelters, is a small Safavid garden pavilion, the **Chehel Sotun**, constructed around 1545 possibly by or for Shah Tahmasp I (d1576) along with two other pavilions that haven't survived. This intimate building, originally open on four sides (now glassed in), and a chamber on the ground floor which since 2005 functions as the **Calligraphy Museum** (◷ 09.00–17.00; entry 80,000 rials, the garden is free), served as the 'coronation' hall of Shah Ismail II in 1576, and of Shah Abbas I 12 years later. In the 19th century, the local Qajar governor repaired the upper floor structure covering the exterior arches with exuberant tiling, but during the 1970s restoration, when the present garden was also laid out, some original Safavid decoration was discovered. Follow the large sign at the back of the garden to **Qazvin Museum** (◷ 09.00–18.00; entry 100,000 rials). Initially located in the Chehel Sotun pavilion, it was moved here in 2004. Its archaeological exhibits are worth a look if you are in the gardens already.

Close by is the only other Safavid building surviving in Qazvin, the 17th-century **Ali Qapu** (pronounced *ghapu*) or monumental entrance into the former palace complex. For over 40 years it has been the police headquarters. About 250m southeast and not far from the masjed-e jame, geographically and chronologically speaking, are the remains of a two-*ivan* **Madrasa Heydariyeh** located in a school yard. There is currently no access to the mosque, only during Nou Rouz when most sites are open to the public. Modern buttresses and a dome support the prayer hall, built c1115, probably just after the masjed-e jame, while a 'new' basement successfully combats rising damp (many restoration programmes have involved a generous use of concrete which has resulted in serious damp problems). Much remains of the early 12th-century brickwork with its subtly fired colouring, touches of turquoise and cobalt-glazed brick inserts, together with a fine plaster *mihrab* decorated with florid motifs and floriated *Kufic*. If time permits, the 14th-century **Tomb of Hamdollah Mostowfi** (entry 300,000 rials), not far from the Tehran Gate, is worth seeing. Although heavily restored, this tomb of a famous historian and geographer with its tiled, pointed, conical dome, has sufficient originality to satisfy the visitor.

One of the remnants of a more recent past is the Qajar-period **Kantor Russian Orthodox Church** (off Daraee St & just a 2min walk from the Alborz Hotel), known for its distinctive 11m-high bell tower and the two courtyard gravestones: one for a railway engineer, dated 1906, and the other for a Russian World War I pilot.

AROUND QAZVIN

ALAMUT الموت ✳ Approximately 60km northeast from Qazvin the Alamut region begins, encompassing fertile valleys, hillside villages and beautiful mountains. Mostly known outside Iran as the 'Valley of the Assassins' for its close association with the Ismaili Assassins under the leadership of Hassan Sabbah, it is today an idyllic place for hiking and marvelling at the breathtaking scenery of the Alborz Mountains. The 'eagle's nest', as the name 'Alamut' translates, is also famous for its delicious cherries and is equally beautiful in summer and winter.

Divided into Eastern and Western Alamut, with the valley in between two mountain ranges, Alamut is home to 500 small villages and settlements with approximately half of them inhabited all year around. In winter the only road here is from Qazvin, but in summer it is even possible to drive all the way to the Caspian Sea through here. The route is one of the most scenic in Iran and requires a good vehicle to cross over the mountains. There used to be approximately 50 castles, known as *qaleh* or 'fortress' in Persian, scattered around Alamut, but today the remains of only two, **Lambesar Fortress** and **Hassan Sabbah Fortress** (known mainly as **Alamut Castle**), are worthwhile tourist attractions.

Rajai Dasht is the first village you approach in the Alamut Valley as you cross over the mountain range from Qazvin and it is approximately 55km away from the provincial capital. It is here you would need to turn if travelling to **Lambesar Fortress** (30km away) in Western Alamut. The remains of this Ismaili fortress are accessible all year around and would take about 2 hours to visit, including some gentle hiking. When driving straight through Rajai Dasht to Eastern Alamut, up to **Moallem Kelayeh** (known to foreign tourists as Alamut Town), the first and only town here, the road goes down the valley. Here, after Shahrak village, it splits into two, one road heading to Garmarud to the Caspian Sea past **Hotel Navizar** (✆ 028 5839426; **$**) 14km further on, and the other going towards **Hassan Sabbah Fortress** (Qaleh Hassan Sabbah; ☉ 08.00–17.00 daily; entry 300,000 rials) further up. Also known as Dezh Alamut, the fortress is located roughly 8km from the village of Shotorkhan, right above the village of Gazorkhan, which in the past would serve as the main supplier of food to the fortress and its dwellers. Although its remains are scarce, what is left does offer an interesting insight into the life of the Ismailis, who called it home for 170 years.

The access to the fortress is officially closed after 17.00, but there is no gate to actually prevent anyone from going up. The hiking path to the top is suitable for novices, but in winter it can become slippery and it is important to exercise caution. The first structure you see by the main gate is a heavily restored **guardian's house** and there is a guardian here at all times. Walking 100m beyond this, you reach an *asbikhaneh* or stables and a watch point past the tunnel carved by the Ismailis to gain a view over Gazorkhan and for a better defence of the fortress. Walking further up, you reach the gate to the actual fortress. It originally had six watchtowers, which were built during the Safavid period on top of the Ismaili portal. Although heavy scaffolding makes it difficult to appreciate the extent of the inner rooms and spaces of the fortress, the 100m² courtyard with a mosque gives a good idea of the scale of this mountainous retreat. The height of the tallest remaining wall is 5m, but it is believed that the original reached 11m.

Tour guide

✳ **Gate of Alamut** m 0912 7821562; w gateofalamut.com. Run by an experienced & authorised guide, Hosein Farhady, the Gate of Alamut offers an extensive range of trip options, inc trekking, village life & adventure tours. While Hosein himself accompanies tourists on most routes, there is always another professional & certified guide present on more complex & intensive paths.

Where to stay and eat

🏠 **Alamut Eco Lodge** (10 rooms) Shahrak village; m 0910 0473101; e shahraki_hossein@ yahoo.com. Opened in 2014, this cosy & rustic guesthouse is probably the best accommodation option in the area. Atmospheric, rooms are traditionally decorated with locally made furniture & grouped around an inner courtyard. The guesthouse also runs a traditional restaurant (**$$**) with fresh homemade food. Try the local cherries. **$$**

QAZVIN TO HAMADAN If you are interested in patterned brickwork, there is a cluster of fine medieval examples near Qazvin. The first is in the outskirts of

Takestan (تاکستان), also known for its high-quality grapes (making their way into Iranians' homes for winemaking), southwest of Qazvin on the road to Hamadan. This is the **Pir-e Takestan** (also known as Imamzadeh Pir), built c1100 in what is a rather unattractive location. The plan is square both inside and out, with engaged columns flanking the single entrance and a single dome on squinches. Clearly the ground level around the *imamzadeh* has risen by over 1m because you have to walk down to see the north-facing frontage, grimy but still original. The interior, now firmly padlocked, should be covered with plaster decorated in strapwork designs, with details similar to those found in Qorveh's masjed-e jame, some 35km away, but we could make out only rows of bricks in the gloom. The second example is **Imamzadeh Abdullah**, a 15th-century tomb near the village of **Farsajin**, just before Qorveh. Its octagonal exterior is echoed on the inside, and it has a double dome, hemispherical over the interior and an external tent or pyramidal form. At some point an entrance portal and vestibule were added. In **Qorveh** (قروه)

THE ISMAILI ASSASSINS

As the Fatimid regime of Egypt and Syria began to crack and fragment in the 1060s, the Ismaili community in Iran began to dig in, securing strongholds to defend their villages and land. This valley soon gained an international reputation as the 'Valley of the Assassins', with its chain of impregnable fortresses dominating the trade routes, and its team of highly trained men willing to sacrifice their own lives to safeguard the leaders of the Ismaili community, such as Hassan Sabbah in Iran and Rashid al-Din Sinan in Syria (the 'Old Man of the Mountains' as described by the Crusader chronicler, Joinville). These were the young men whose clandestine activities spread terror among the Crusaders and Muslim military leaders as they infiltrated inner court circles to 'remove' those who threatened their own community – leaders like the Seljuk sultan and champion of Sunni Islam, Malik Shah (ruled 1072–92), his vizier Nizam al-Molk (assassinated in 1092) and Richard Coeur de Lion.

As recorded by Marco Polo, rumours spread that Hassan Sabbah could instil such loyalty and single-mindedness only by drugging his followers with hashish (who were then known as *hashashiyya*, from which comes 'assassin') and promising them the delights of paradise. The reality was that this was a tight-knit community with a rigid hierarchy under a charismatic leader – Hassan Sabbah – renowned for his scholarship and library. His death in 1124 resulted in serious disquiet within the community, and without the protection of the strongholds such as Alamut, perhaps its very survival would have been threatened. Later successors were more pragmatic, establishing links with neighbouring political powers, but the Mongol invasions changed all this. Circumstances allowed Hulagu, the Mongol commander, to seize and imprison the leader of the Iranian Ismailis in Qazvin in 1256, heralding a massacre in which the fortresses were surrendered.

The community scattered throughout Iran but in the 1770s it was in control of Kerman and Bam, with the blessing of the Zand family. The leader of the Ismailis was honoured with the title of Agha Khan by Fath Ali Shah, but by 1840 the religious atmosphere had so changed that most of the community left for India and the rest for central Asia, Pakistan and east Africa.

itself, ask for the **masjed-e jame**, to the northwest on the old Soltaniyeh–Zanjan road. A faded, painted inscription beneath its prayer dome dates this chamber and the two barrel-vaulted side rooms to 1023, perhaps re-using material from an earlier Sasanid fire temple judging from some very large bricks in the lower dome area. The *mihrab* probably also dates from the early 11th century, though alterations were made about two or three centuries later when repairs were made to the dome. Remains of painted plaster decoration in the drum and squinches supporting the dome probably relate to another inscription dated 1179. Like many early Islamic buildings in Iran, the visual impact is not immediate but its charms slowly reveal themselves.

The real delight, however, is on the horizon. Returning to the main Qazvin–Takestan–Hamadan road, drive about 35km towards Hamadan, turning west just before **Ab Garm** to **Hesar-e Armani** for **Kharraqan** (خرقان) ✳ (125km northeast of Hamadan). After about 30km on this recently upgraded asphalt road, two splendid Seljuk **Kharraqan tomb towers** (Gonbad-e Kharraqan) located in a small cemetery come into view. Both were badly damaged in the 2002 earthquake but prompt action by the local gendarmerie using available timber saved them from complete collapse. Just look at their superb brickwork patterning. First recorded only in 1963, the tower to the east was constructed in 1068 while its companion, also octagonal inside and out, is thought to be slightly later in date. A staircase in the buttress to the left of the door went from the crypt to the roof space between the two domes (approximately 7m in diameter) presumably for later repair work. Little remains now of the original painted plaster on the interior, which depicted hanging mosque lamps, a stylised tree with a bird stiffly sitting on each branch, and an inscription reading 'Blessings on its owner', but it is the external brick decoration that is such a joy. There are over 30 patterns in recessed and relief brick, including a Quranic inscription (Q59:21–4) and its date makes this one of the earliest (securely) dated double-dome constructions in Iran. The second tower, with even more glorious brick decoration and with each blind niche divided into three zones, was built in 1094. The Quranic quotations here are Q59:21–4 under the exterior dome, and Q23:115 on the door frame: 'What, did you think that We created you only for sport, and that you would not be returned to Us?' Again double-domed, it too has a staircase going up into the roof space concealed in a buttress. There is nothing to identify who was interred in either tomb but because of visual similarities with that 10th-century masterpiece of brickwork – the tomb of Ismail Samanid in Bukhara, Uzbekistan – scholars believe the Kharraqan towers were constructed for a local military commander, perhaps originating from central Asia, by a local Zanjani mason.

Back to the main road, another 65km towards Hamadan takes you through **Razan**, which possesses two more (so-called Darazin) tomb towers: the Gonbad-e Hud, thought to be Seljuk and the Azhar about 3km further east, possibly a Mongol/Ilkhanid construction. Continuing towards Hamadan, you might note the signs for Ali Sadr and Lalejin. The caves of **Ali Sadr** (🕐 10.00–17.00; entry 750,000 rials) were 'discovered' in the 1970s, although they were used in Safavid times to house refugees (perhaps fleeing from Ottoman incursions), and one hires a pedalo to view the magnificent natural beauty of stalagmites and stalactites. The underground lakes are at some sections 62m deep. The space is inhabited by a numerous colony of doves. You could also enjoy a visit to the local potteries of **Lalejin**, whose production was very well regarded in pre-revolutionary Tehran.

It is best to overnight in Hamadan (altitude 1,850m, 322km from Tehran), formerly the ancient 7th-century BCE Median stronghold and then the Achaemenid summer capital, Hagmatana/Ecbatana, at the foothills of the Zagros Mountains which link Iran with Iraq (Mesopotamia).

Its location near Mount Alvand (3,575m) and the pass across the Zagros always gave it a mercantile and strategic importance. In 550BCE the Achaemenid Cyrus the Great defeated the Medes and took control of the region and this city which, according to Herodotus, was defended by seven walls, the last two being of silver and gold (a clear allusion to great commercial prosperity). Alexander the Great was its next conqueror in 331BCE but he paid heavily with the death of his friend, Hephaestion. The city flourished under Parthian rule as an important cultural centre but then was neglected in Sasanid times. By 645CE, the Arab army had swept through bringing Islam; at first the town profited from the new political order but the 10th century brought a series of disasters: in 931CE large numbers of the inhabitants were massacred by a local warlord; 25 years later a serious earthquake caused great damage; and during religious riots in 962CE many lost their lives. However, it was also at this time that the city was home to one of the greatest medieval scholars, renowned in the west as Avicenna and known here as Bou Ali

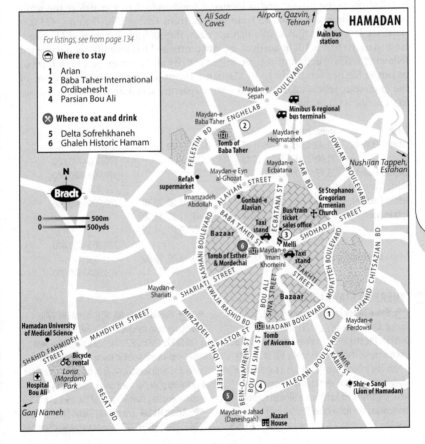

For listings, see from page 134

Where to stay

1 Arian
2 Baba Taher International
3 Ordibehesht
4 Parsian Bou Ali

Where to eat and drink

5 Delta Sofrehkhaneh
6 Ghaleh Historic Hamam

or Bou Ali Ibn Sina (d1037). Peace and prosperity were restored under Seljuk rule in 1100, but then the Mongol armies sacked the city in 1221 and again in 1224. Hamadan was later embroiled again in political and military conflict, first suffering under Timur Leng (d1405), then from the rivalry between the Aq and Qara Qoyunlu tribal confederations, and the Safavid–Ottoman conflicts. From 1724 the region was incorporated within the Ottoman Empire until Nader Shah Afshar retook it finally in 1732. Despite the English traveller Buckingham describing the city as 'a pile of ruins' in 1816, the population of Hamadan four years later stood at 40,000. This had halved by 1889. Today it stands at about 548,000, a little over 25% of the total population of Hamadan province, with a city plan largely laid out in 1928 by a German architect.

Its high altitude means Hamadan receives heavy snowfalls from November until mid-March. As a medieval Arab poet commented: 'Even the heat of the fire becomes frozen in Hamadan/And the cold there is a chronic evil.'

GETTING THERE AND AROUND You can reach Hamadan by intercity **bus** from Tehran, including daily bus connections from Esfahan, or any other large city. There are three bus stations in Hamadan: two local minibus stations are located north of the city; and the main interprovince terminal is further north between Mellat and Enghelab streets. The *savari* terminal for departures to Tehran (3hrs 30mins) is called *cheragh-e qermez* and is located a few hundred metres before the main bus station. There are up to two **train** services from Tehran (3hrs 30mins; 433,000 rials) via Saveh and regular, although not daily, **flights** from Tehran and Mashhad. Hamadan Airport is 10km north of the city centre and has recently been reopened following reconstruction. If you are within the city and looking for a *savari* taxi to go out to the bus terminals, go to Maydan-e Imam Khomeini and get into one of the numerous yellow taxis. Below is a bus departure schedule with selected times from major Iranian cities:

From	Departure	Price (rials)
Esfahan (Kaveh)	09.00; 12.45; 14.00; 15.30; 16.00; 16.30; 17.00; 20.30; 21.00; 22.45; 23.15; 23.45	370,000–480,000
Esfahan (Sofeh)	13.15; 23.00; 23.15	370,000–480,000
Shiraz (Karandish)	14.30	620,000
Tehran (southern)	06.15; 07.15; 08.15; 09.15; 10.30; 13.30; 15.00; 20.30	280,000–400,000
Tehran (western)	05.20; 07.00; 07.45; 09.30; 10.30; 11.45; 12.30; 13.30; 14.45; 15.30; 16.30; 17.30; 18.15; 19.15; 20.00; 21.15; 22.30; 23.30	280,000–400,000
Tehran (Beyhaghi)	01.00; 06.30; 08.30; 11.45; 15.00; 17.00; 18.00; 19.00; 20.30; 22.00	280,000–400,000

WHERE TO STAY AND EAT *Map, page 133*

🏠 **Baba Taher International Hotel** (135 rooms) Baba Taher Sq; 📞 34227180, 34227184. Don't let the sterile tinted glass façade put you off; this is a comfortable hotel slightly out of the city centre. The lobby is flashy, but has a comfortable seating area. Rooms are standard & come with some slightly aged furniture, although rooms overlooking the Baba Taher Tomb have lovely views over the park, square & mountains. **$$$–$$$$**

✳ 🏠 **Parsian Bou Ali** (36 rooms) Bou Ali Sina St, up from the Avicenna Tomb roundabout; 📞 38252822, 38252823; w buali.pih.ir. The best upper mid-range hotel in town, it is usually fully booked in high season. Wi-Fi in the rooms, outdoor swimming pool (for men only), shiny lobby & accommodating staff are part of the package. **$$$**

🏠 **Arian Hotel** (28 rooms) Takhti St; 📞 38261266, 38261277. One of the newer & better options in Hamadan. Although the décor has a touch of excessive modern Rococo, the staff are sharp & professional. Rooms are clean & spacious, albeit a little overheated, & there is a reading light by the beds, a rarity in Iranian hotels. There is alas no Wi-Fi. **$$**

✳ 🏠 **Ordibehesht Hotel** (15 rooms) Shohada St; ☎32522056. A small & very pleasant guesthouse in the heart of the city. Most rooms have at least 3 to 4 beds, but they can be let for single travellers or a couple. Staff are helpful & can arrange for a reasonably priced taxi to surrounding sites & Ali Sadr Caves. Wi-Fi is reliable. **$$**

✗ **Delta Sofrehkhaneh** Mirzadeh Eshqi St; ☎38262640; ⊕ 09.00–16.00 & 20.00–23.00.

Basement restaurant where you can lounge on day beds & enjoy traditional Iranian cuisine. **$**

✗ **Ghaleh Historic Hamam** Esther Alley, off Shariati St; ☎32511199; ⊕ noon–16.00 & 19.00–22.00 daily. Located a few hundred metres from the Tomb of Esther and Mordechai in the heart of the old city, this expansive (c700m²) traditional restaurant/ethnographic museum encompasses 4 halls in the refurbished late Qajar-period bathhouse, also known as Hamam-e Hajj Mohammad Saeed. Tourist-friendly atmosphere (your nation's flag is likely to adorn the tray with food) & traditional menu make it the most atmospheric place to dine in Hamadan. **$**

WHAT TO SEE AND DO Frankly, Hamadan has more historic interest for the visitor than aesthetic architectural delights, but the surrounding area has much to offer, whether you are keen on history, archaeology or crafts. The **Tomb of Avicenna** (Ibn al-Sina or Ibn Sina) (on the roundabout down from the Parsian Bou Ali Hotel; ⊕ autumn–winter 08.30–17.30, spring–summer 08.30–20.00; entry 300,000 rials) is a good example. This 10th-century Muslim scientist, who originated from Bukhara, central Asia, was mentioned in Chaucer's *Canterbury Tales* but the monument itself dates from 1952 and was clearly inspired by the early 11th-century Gonbad-e Qabus monument in northeastern Iran (page 206). The museum on the ground floor was once dull and uninformative, but it has been completely reorganised and is now a delight. Local artefacts are laid out in the first room to the left on entry, while the room to the right is a library with interesting displays of historical medical instruments, such as the glass blood-letting suction 'cuppers' and manuscripts, while the main hall with the memorial to Avicenna shows the herbs, plants and seeds (with their Latin names) used in pharmacy with labelling in English and Farsi. There is a good view of Mount Alvand from outside the upper platform, and the gardens are pleasant. Avicenna (born c980CE) fled from his enemies at court in Bukhara (present-day Uzbekistan), arriving in Hamadan in about 1015 to practise as a doctor for some nine years. He then moved to Rey and Esfahan, returning to Hamadan only to die of colic in 1037. Most of his 130 or so books have been lost but fragments remain to show he wrote knowledgeably on economics, poetry, philosophy (influencing St Thomas Aquinas) and music as well as physics, mathematics and astronomy. His *Book of Healing* and *Canon of Medicine* became the standard medical textbooks in Europe until the mid 17th century; it is from Avicenna and other Muslim scientists that we get such words as algebra, alchemy, alcohol and alkaline.

Another modern tomb (1951, repaired 1970) set in another pleasant garden commemorates **Baba Taher** (Baba Taher Park, Baba Taher Sq; ⊕ autumn–winter 08.30–17.30, spring–summer 08.30–20.00; entry 300,000 rials), author of metaphysical works but more renowned for his passionate mystical poetic quatrains which, it was said, could melt the snows of Alvand. No-one is sure when he lived or died other than it was sometime between 900 and 1300 but his Sufi love poetry remains a favourite and is still often set to music. Locals regularly come here to recite Baba Taher verses to the sounds of traditional musical instruments.

Hamadan is also of historical interest because its Jewish community used to be one of the largest in Iran and it is here that the most important Jewish site in the country lies – the **Tomb of Esther and Mordechai** (pronounced *mordekhai*; off the Maydan-e Imam Khomeini roundabout, set back behind a fence, but the entrance is through the bazaar behind it; ⊕ 08.00–noon & 15.00–18.00 daily except Sat; entry by donation to custodian). This small brick tomb is probably medieval in date with a (modern) devotional area below street level, but local tradition says it is much older, housing the graves of Esther and her uncle Mordechai of the Old Testament Book of Esther (despite the fact that an inscription was found naming the deceased as Elias and Samuel, sons of a certain Ismail Karlan). Another theory is that it was the tomb of Susan, the Jewish queen of the Sasanid shah Yazdegerd I (399–420CE). Entry into the tomb itself is through an old stone doorway (leaving shoes outside), which leads into various small prayer rooms and the main chamber with the two cenotaphs. The entrance is low and narrow so that those who enter bend their head in a sign of respect. The one to the right is said to be that of Esther (actual name Hadassah, but known as Esther, meaning 'star' in Hebrew, for her beauty), the Jewish consort of either Xerxes I (486–465BCE) or his successor Artaxerxes I (d424BCE), but actually both are ebony replicas of the 13th- or 14th-century cenotaphs destroyed by fire from pilgrims' candles; the actual graves are in the crypt below. You may remember the biblical story: at Susa in southern Iran a newly appointed Achaemenid court chamberlain, Haman, envious of the influence of Esther and her uncle, spread rumours that the Jewish community was conspiring against the emperor and argued for their extermination. Warned by Mordechai, Esther arranged a sumptuous royal banquet during which Haman was tricked into suggesting great rewards for Mordechai, thinking these were intended for him. At a second banquet he was denounced by Esther who then won royal permission for all the Jews to return from exile. At every Purim in the Jewish calendar, delicious pastries called 'Haman's ears' are still happily munched.

Before you leave Hamadan, visit the **Gonbad-e Alavian** (off Maydan Ain al-Qozzat in Shahdad Lane; ⊕ autumn–winter 08.30–17.30, spring–summer 08.30–20.00; entry 300,000 rials), a glorious if dusty tomb building; it is thought this was the mausoleum for members of the Alavian family, who controlled Hamadan for two centuries, but when it was built exactly is unclear. To some scholars its elaborately carved plaster of leaf and flower motifs resemble Seljuk decoration as found at Divrigi and elsewhere in Turkey – as well as on the 1148 mausoleum Gonbad-e Sorkh in Maragheh (page 235) – but others argue that the almost three-dimensional, lace-like 'Baroque' quality of its motifs is early 14th-century Ilkhanid work. The original roof has gone and much of the brick and plaster strapwork exterior has been restored but don't be put off by the present monochrome colour, dust and gloom; let the plasterwork speak to you. The Quranic inscriptions inside (Q53:1–35), on the *mihrab* (Q36:1–9), outside (Q76:1–9) and over the entrance (Q5:55–6) refer to rewards and punishments, death and paradise, the importance of prayer and charity giving – all very apposite for a mausoleum and possibly the plaster leaf and plant forms symbolise the gardens of paradise. A torch is useful for the interior. The basement vault, accessed via a narrow staircase from inside the tower, houses unidentified tombstones.

We must admit to less enthusiasm for the so-called **Lion of Hamadan** (Shir-e Sangi), located in a public square in the southeast of the town. The passage of time, together with the local tradition of kissing and greasing its nose to find a husband, mean much imagination is needed to identify this battered stone sculpture as a lion, but it is agreed that this could well be a Hellenistic memorial lion to Hephaestion, the beloved general and close companion of Alexander the Great, dating to the late 4th century BCE. Nothing else of Herodotus's Ecbatana is visible to the visitor, although archaeological excavations in the 1920s uncovered two tablets naming Darius the Great (d485BCE) and Artaxerxes II. In the 1970s, 25ha were acquired for archaeological excavations and the remains of a 9m-thick defensive wall were uncovered, which was originally protected with regularly placed towers. In 1974, 15 slipper coffins, probably 1st century BCE or CE, were uncovered in a Parthian cemetery, and since 1983 two stretches of the ancient city wall, along with houses and alleys, have been located. A 15-minute walk from here is **Nazari House** (باغ موزه نظری), formerly Ibn Sina Museum, from the late Qajar period. It currently houses the Iran Cultural Heritage Organisation and is closed for visits, but you are allowed to walk around its pleasant garden.

Hamadan previously had a large Christian community and a number of churches remain. The largest is **St Stephanos Gregorian Armenian Church**, built in 1676, although the present building dates only to 1936. Up the steps from it is St Stephanos Armenian Evangelical Church, built in 1886, and together the two function as the Applied Science Leaning Centre; lectures and workshops are held here on a regular basis.

AROUND HAMADAN

The real reason for staying in Hamadan is its proximity to other towns and attractions in the area – aside from the Ali Sadr Caves and the Lalejin potteries (page 132), which can be reached by taxi. Hamadan has two minibus stations, both a few minutes from the centre of town and across the road from each other (see map, page 133). One services departures southwest in the direction of Kermanshah and the other goes southeast towards Malayer. Minibuses depart as soon as they are filled and tickets are purchased on board.

About 10km west of Hamadan is **Ganj Nameh** ('Book of Treasures'). High up on a rock face, looking north, are two large panels carrying Achaemenid trilingual inscriptions recording the victories and lineage of Darius the Great and his son, Xerxes I (d465BCE), and giving thanks to the Zoroastrian deity Ahura Mazda. The area is a popular weekend and holiday spot with beautiful nature, a waterfall, restaurants and a cable car if you wish to spend half a day around here.

Going 60km in a southerly direction from Hamadan towards **Malayer** (ملایر) (population 177,000), you arrive at **Nushijan Tappeh** (⊕ 08.00–17.00; entry 100,000 rials), which lies approximately 10km north of Malayer. If travelling by bus to Malayer, ask the driver to drop you off at the turn towards the Nushijan Tappeh site. Alternatively, you can hire a return taxi to Nushijan Tappeh from Malayer itself. British archaeologists worked on this small Median site, about one-sixth the size of the main apadana platform at Persepolis, from 1967 to 1974. Four principal buildings were found on this outcrop: two temples, a fort and a columned hall with an enclosing wall. The central temple, probably constructed before 700BCE, had a narrow entrance leading into an antechamber possessing a stepped 'Maltese cross' groundplan and a spiral ramp (like Tappeh Baba Jan; page 149) to an upper level. It then led to a sanctuary with a triangular cella, or inner body of the temple and large blind windows with 'toothed' lintels decorating the walls. A brick fire altar (85cm high) with four steps was screened from the entrance and, perhaps to protect its sanctity from later squatters, the temple was filled with shale to a depth of 6m and carefully bricked in. This was a tremendously important find: perhaps the earliest temple with a fire altar in situ found in western Iran. The second temple, located just to the west, had similar rooms and a spiral ramp but with a different orientation and an asymmetrical groundplan. The fort measured 25m × 22m, approximately the size of the Gate of All Nations at Persepolis (page 266), with four long magazines and a guardroom with another spiral ramp for access to at least one other floor, while the hall with a slightly irregular groundplan was somewhat smaller with 12 columns supporting a flat roof. Very little stone was used in construction throughout the site but the bricks (especially in the vaults) were often carefully shaped. For some reason the site was then left largely unoccupied until the Parthian period (c1st century CE). At present the original structure is protected by an aesthetically unappealing steel roof, which regrettably spoils the authentic beauty of the site.

TOWARDS LORESTAN PROVINCE The road south takes you to **Borujerd** (بروجرد) (population 246,000) in Lorestan province, an important military town in the 19th century when the Qajars struggled to keep control over the local tribes. More recently it was the home of the famous theologian Ayatollah Hossein Tabatabai Borujerdi (d1962). Its masjed-e jame still retains its Seljuk domed prayer chamber among extensive 19th-century restoration work in the courtyard. In the same area is the Imamzadeh Jafar with a distinctive 'sugarloaf' dome, similar to those found in southern Iran, which looks very out of place this far north. The tombstone is dated 1108 but some scholars believe the tomb building is later.

About 110km to the southwest is **Khorramabad** (خرم‌آباد), the provincial capital famous for the remains of a massive Sasanid bridge (Pol-e Shekasteh or Pol-e Shapuri) spanning the river Kashkan, and a citadel **Falak al-Aflak** (entry 430,000) perched on an ancient hill in the centre of town. Originally called Dezh-e Shapurkhast (Shapur Fortress) and built probably during the Sasanid period, the fortress's current name dates to the Qajars. The Anthropology and Archaeology Museum in the fortress has, after the somewhat bland collection of ethnographic exhibits, a fine selection of ancient silver objects bearing cuneiform writing from Neo-Elamite and Achaemenid periods. The most interesting items include silver situla decorated with lion motifs. Neo-Elamite silver figures and a few examples of 1st- or 2nd-century BCE horse cheekpieces are particularly intriguing. There is a detailed Neo-Elamite or possibly Achaemenid statuette of a boar being hunted by a lioness, a motif frequently present in Persepolis. In the city itself there is also a free-standing **Seljuk minaret**.

Khorramabad is the best starting point for exploring the unspoilt and breathtaking mountainous area of Lorestan, which remains one of the least visited parts of Iran. Most sites, such as picturesque **Gahar Lake** (دریاچه گَهر) *,* located at 2,360m above sea level, and **Shirz Canyon** (تنگه شیرز) * can only be visited on a specially organised tour and advance planning is recommended. Gahar Lake, for example, is not accessible in winter owing to its high altitude and heavy snow.

From Khorramabad you can alternatively continue on towards **Khuzestan** (page 275). **Andimeshk** (اندیمشک) is the nearest and best-served destination with *savari* services leaving on a regular basis from Khorramabad western bus terminal. The scenic road to Andimeshk over the Zagros Mountains alone is worth making this journey.

Tour guide

* **Zandi Tours** 15 Abdolrazaq St, Esfahan; m 0913 2051561; w irantravelers.org. Farshid

Zandi Esfahani is a recommended English-speaking guide for the area.

Where to stay and eat

Azadi Hotel (28 rooms) Azadi Sq, Mojahediin Islam St, Khorramabad; ↘066 33327795. Spacious & modestly decorated rooms come either with Western-style or squat toilet facilities; ask in case of preference. Convenient location & passable b/fast make it an acceptable mid-range accommodation option. **$$**

Gap Traditional Tea House Gap Sq, old Bazaar, Khorramabad; ↘066 33339999; w gapcomplex.ir. 'Gap' means 'grand' in Persian & this place was once certainly a grand *hamam*, but the restored bathhouse below street level now houses a traditional restaurant serving hearty homemade meals & excellent *dough*. **$**

SOUTHEAST FROM HAMADAN The town of **Arak** (اراک) (population 536,000, 214km southeast from Hamadan and 100km east from Borujerd) is the capital of Markazi province and is known today for its aluminium smelter and a huge petrochemical factory (the brainchild of Rafsanjani), but in the 19th century its fame rested on carpet production. This was at Sultanabad, where an enormous complex, 'The Qaleh' (Fort), of carpet workshops was established in 1877 by the Ziegler company of Manchester, UK; it was possibly their representatives who brought the famous twin 16th-century 'Ardabil' carpets to London in the late 1880s. They are now in London's Victoria and Albert Museum and in Los Angeles' County Museum of Art. Readers with links to the Ismaili community (page 33) might make a short detour to **Anjedan**, 37km east of Arak. This village has long historical associations with Ismaili Shi'ism; even when the Assassins were thrown out of Alamut and lost any regional control, there was an active community here until the early 18th century. In the late 1970s it possessed two recorded historical monuments, both heavily restored: the 1480 tomb of Ismaili shah Qalandar and the tomb of Ismaili shah Garib, built eight years later.

Some 100km southeast towards Esfahan, passing the small town of **Khomeyn** (60km from Arak), closely associated with Ayatollah Khomeini ('of Khomeyn'), is the town of **Golpayegan** (گلپایگان), perhaps established by the Sasanids after the famous victory over the Parthians here in 224CE. Its masjed-e jame has a fine domed prayer hall dating from 1105–18, constructed on the order of the son of the Seljuk sultan, Malik Shah. The rest of the courtyard buildings are 19th-century additions, paid for by one of Fath Ali Shah's wives when her son was governor here. The brickwork inside this chamber is admittedly not the finest, nor are the proportions of the chamber, especially the narrow 'squeezed' corner squinches and the heavy piers, which led one writer to comment that it was 'a masterpiece of pessimism', but it is definitely well worth a few minutes' investigation. Leaving the chamber and the mosque by the right-hand portal, walk down (southeast) into the small, friendly bazaar by the main road. Almost directly opposite is a fine minaret, dated 1100, whose balconies were reached by two separate spiral staircases. At its base stand two later stone lions; rather gruesomely, the heads of their victims protrude from their mouths.

Back on the road again, the next pleasant stop is on the far southern outskirts of **Khansar** (خوانسار). If you have the luxury of time, take a walk in the shady streets of Khansar, edged with magnificent chenar trees. If you don't, be content with looking at the early 20th-century house across the stream, before leaving the town and heading towards Esfahan. The house has seen better days and is presently occupied by a number of families struggling to make ends meet, but it is still splendid with a clock (not working) over the main entrance, low reliefs of lions and Qajar soldiers, and slowly disintegrating balconies. The tiled spandrels give details of its 1910 construction and original owner, a local wealthy merchant who had made the pilgrimage to Mecca. If you can gain entry, the servants' quarters, storerooms and

4

cistern are off the main vestibule. Steep steps lead into the courtyard with a fine Qajar pool in the centre; today this court is occasionally used for the local Moharram ceremonies. The owner's quarters were located on the upper veranda level, as the remains of stained glass in intricate patterning over the doorways suggest.

WEST OF HAMADAN – TOWARDS KERMANSHAH AND KURDISTAN

The road west (Route 48 or A-2 although marked simply as 'To Kermanshah') from Hamadan towards Kermanshah passes some interesting sights. Travelling along this route by public transport would require extra time, with *savari* taxi being the fastest and preferable way of moving from one town to another.

TOUR GUIDE For tours in the area, in particular Kurdistan, contact Kaveh Padidar (m 0918 1710464; e kaveh.padidar@gmail.com), chairman of the local tour guides association and a very helpful guide.

WHAT TO SEE AND DO
Around Kangavar
Anahita Temple (Shohada St; entry 300,000 rials, or free of charge through the back gate in the small alley right before the mosque) is in the town of **Kangavar** (کنگاور) (population 53,000), some 95km from Hamadan and set back on the right (north) of the main road. Most bus services from Tehran in the direction of Kermanshah stop in Kangavar. The motorway passes through the town and if you are coming here by Kermanshah minibus/*savari* from Hamadan (there are no minibuses solely to Kangavar), you can get a local taxi to bring you to the temple. Alternatively, you could ask locals for directions, but it is a couple of kilometres' walk from where the minibus drops you off.

This was the ancient Concobar of the 1st century BCE, known for its temple to Artemis (the Greek version of the Zoroastrian Anahita) and later for the palace of the Sasanid shah Khosrow II. By medieval times its reputation among travelling merchants had sunk to being that of a place full of muggers and thieves. Many 19th-century European visitors suggested archaeological investigation around the standing columns and the immense stone platform, but extensive excavation was only undertaken from 1968 until 1977, with the final report published (in Farsi) in 1996 (and unfortunately unavailable). From brief reports of the 1970s, the first excavations revealed a plan similar to that of Persepolis, with double staircases up to the main terrace where a columned temple once stood; everything seemed to suggest an Achaemenid construction. However, as work progressed, the finds pointed instead to late Seleucid/early Parthian times, or even to Sasanid occupation with later Islamic buildings and workshops.

Today the site is largely overgrown, and there are no signs or a site map at the ticket office. The path from the ticket office leads to the remains of the double staircases fronted by some re-erected column shafts. Scrambling up the mound and looking back, you might make out the fired-brick walls of the Islamic workshops below. A little further up, to the extreme left, is a good view down on to more recent excavations, which have uncovered yet more columns and bases, while high up by the road fence a mosque rests on the original stone platform.

If archaeological sites are of interest, **Godin Tappeh** lies about 13km southeast of Kangavar (coming from Hamadan turn south just before Kangavar to the signposted township of Godin, which is located just south of the 30m-high *tappeh*) and as remains of certain mud-brick buildings have been consolidated, visitors can get a better understanding of the site. Located on the ancient High Road (Great

Hearing of the great beauty of Shirin, the Armenian princess, a young Sasanid prince (later Khosrow II) sent an artist bearing his portrait, mounted on his own wondrous horse, Shabdiz, to try to bring her to the Sasanid court. Falling in love with the picture, Shirin secretly stole away on Shabdiz, unaware that Khosrow was riding towards Armenia having quarrelled with his father. Their paths crossed (Khosrow even caught sight of Shirin bathing in a pool) but, neither recognising the other, they returned to their homes: Khosrow to succeed to the throne, and Shirin with her unrequited love. A rebellion then caused Khosrow to flee to Armenia where the two finally met and fell passionately in love. But the course of true love never does run smooth. Determined to regain his throne, Khosrow asked for help from the Byzantine emperor, cementing the agreement by marrying a Byzantine princess. Restored to power, he then begged Shirin to join him despite his recent marriage.

But Shirin, now queen in her own right and angry at his duplicity, sent a message of rejection from her palace, Qasr-e Shirin. Dejected and depressed, she yearned for fresh milk from her mountain pastures and commissioned a young engineer and mason, Farhad, who had the strength of two elephants, to carve a channel through the mountains. Head over heels in love with her, Farhad achieved this feat in weeks, but jealous Khosrow schemed to prevent any further liaison and to profit from Farhad's skills. Persuading Farhad to excavate a pass between the mountains at Bisotun, and carve a sculpture of Khosrow on Shabdiz at Taq-e Bostan, he promised Shirin would be Farhad's once these impossible tasks were achieved. Hearing this, Shirin visited Farhad who became so reinvigorated in his work that the king feared he would have to keep his promise; he lied to the engineer announcing that Shirin had suddenly died. Farhad killed himself and a shocked Shirin was at last persuaded to visit Khosrow's palace to hear his explanation. After many recriminations, the two lovers were reunited but only briefly. Khosrow, the story goes, was stabbed to death by a stepson maddened by the beauty and devotion of Queen Shirin and she, rejecting his advances, killed herself over Khosrow's body.

Khorasan Road) section of the Silk Road from Mesopotamia to the Far East, this was once an important trading centre. Canadian excavation work from 1965 until 1973 under the auspices of the Royal Ontario Museum revealed buildings dating to 2600–1600BCE, which included an eight-columned hall largely destroyed by earthquakes, and a later Median citadel (Level II) with a 30-columned audience hall, towers and magazines. At its pinnacle the citadel covered the area of 5,000m² and was protected by 3m-thick walls. Most of the residences had a raised square hearth in the main room with an elevated seat and footstool for the owner at one end and seating for guests along the side walls. Remnants of staircases showed houses had at least one upper floor, but for an idea of their external appearance, perhaps the Assyrian reliefs (at the British Museum, London) hold the key. The last season, in 1973, produced even more sensational dating evidence, pushing occupation of the site back to c4500BCE (Level X), with striking artefacts, a lot of which are now in the Royal Ontario Museum, uncovered from Level V (3200–3000BCE). Potteries from Godin Tappeh are similar to those found at Susa (page 281), suggesting a trading connection between these two important settlements. A particularly interesting discovery was that of almost 2,000 clay sling balls (*pellets*) dating to the late 5th millennium BCE found in various sites across Mesopotamia and Iran. These were part of the manufacturing standardisation process across the region to ensure that the combatant would not have to compensate for a different weight at every cast. In **Najafehabad** village 15km northeast of Godin Tappeh, the same archaeological team discovered the Najafehabad stela or memorial, kept in the National Museum of Iran, and bearing a carved image of Assyrian king Sargon II with the writing in the Neo-Assyrian dialect of Akkadian script, suggesting a possible connection between the Assyrians and the Medes.

Towards Bisotun and Taq-e Bostan
From Kangavar, the road leads towards Bisotun and Taq-e Bostan. All of this countryside is associated with Persian legend, and in late medieval book illustrations with the star-crossed royal lovers, Khosrow II and Shirin (see box, page 141). Among archaeologists, the region is famous for the exquisite (but frequently forged) Lorestan bronzes, some of which are displayed in the National Museum and the Reza Abbasi Museum, Tehran. Used to embellish horse equipment, as standard finials, etc, these cast bronzes with their powerful stylised animal forms were manufactured in this region from the 1st millennium until c600BCE, and some perhaps even date from the 3rd millennium BCE.

As you approach **Bisotun** (بیستون) *, you will see an immense rock relief, called by Ernst Herzfeld 'the gate of Asia' and the largest of its kind in Iran. Recording the victories of Darius the Great, it is the only Old Persian text commenting on specific historical events. The UNESCO-listed Bisotun relief regrettably remains hidden behind a massive scaffolding platform, but the surrounding area is worth exploring in detail (☉ 09.00–17.00; entry 500,000 rials; parking 30,000 rials). Just before Bisotun town, there is a Safavid bridge on the right, but drive on to the large layby on the left. The ticket office is a small kiosk past the car park and beyond here lies the extensive Bisotun archaeological park and modern recreation area. At (modern) road level on your right past the kiosk there is a small reclining statue concealed under a rusting canopy. Although emasculated in 1977 by thieves, he has now been provided with a new head. On close inspection you can just make out a club in the background and the lion skin under the figure: this is Herakles (Hercules) complete with a Greek inscription stating it was carved for Hyakin in 148BCE in honour of a local governor. But the most important set of inscriptions are about 10m to the left and very high up.

The modern road is on a much higher level than the original Royal Achaemenid road that ran from western Turkey across the Zagros Mountains to Hamadan and then south to Susa. Alexander the Great must have passed this way and presumably the significance of this enormous 18m × 7m carved panel was explained to him. However, later travellers variously described the panel as showing Shalmenezer and the ten captive tribes of Israel, Esther leading her community away, Jesus and his 12 disciples, a Sufi mystic with his followers, or a schoolmaster reprimanding his pupils. It actually depicts the Achaemenid emperor Darius the Great with his generals behind him, standing victorious on the rebel Gaumata who refused to accept the succession of Darius. Above, a winged figure, generally identified as Ahura Mazda of Zoroastrian belief, witnesses the submission of eight provincial governors who supported Gaumata's claim to the Achaemenid throne; the ninth figure of a Scythian chief with its inscription was added a few years after the main section was begun in 521BCE.

The ruins of the caravanserai were discovered by Abel Pinçon in 1598 and the panel inscriptions were first copied by Sir Henry Rawlinson in 1836, then advisor to the local governor, using ropes and ladders ('the interest of the occupation entirely did away with any sense of danger'). Like reading Egyptian hieroglyphs by means of the Rosetta Stone, their decipherment was fundamentally important to our understanding of the ancient languages of Babylonian, Old Persian and Elamite. Recording that Gaumata was killed near here at the Battle of Kundurush on 29 September 522BCE, Darius had carved: 'This is what I did by the favour of Ahura Mazda in one and the same year after that I became king [521BCE]. Nineteen battles I fought, by the favour of Ahura Mazda I smote them and took prisoner nine kings. One was Gaumata by name a Magian; he lied thus he said, "I am Smerdis the son of Cyrus"; he made Persia rebellious.' Darius's right to rule was emphasised: 'Eight of my family were kings before me. I am the ninth. We inherit kingship on both sides.' And promised: 'The man who co-operated with my house, him I rewarded well; who so did injury, him I punished well.' Its purpose is obvious but where did the idea of carving such a relief come from? Archaeologists point to Urartian rock carvings in Turkey and further east, but the nearest source of inspiration is the rock relief at Sarpol-e Zahab, 150km west (page 147).

Later rulers left their mark below Darius's proclamation, but to see these you have to get closer; just above the first set of steps is a worn low relief depicting the Parthian shah, Mithridates II, receiving the homage of four provincial governors while on the right his descendant, Shah Gotarzes II (c38–50CE), on his battle horse is lancing an enemy while a Roman-style Nike (Victory) Goddess flies overhead. Both have been damaged by the pious Sheikh Ali Han Zanganeh in 1684–85 as part of his expansion of the street under the rule of Shah Suleiman Safavi (1669–94). A 17th-century panel inscription describes the endowment of a nearby Safavid caravanserai, recently converted into the luxurious five-star **Laleh Bisotun Hotel** (20 rooms; ☏ 083 45883812; w lalehhotels.ir; **$$$$**). It lies at the foothills of the Farhad Tarash site (see below).

Continuing on the path beyond the main Bisotun inscription you will come to the enormous 200m-long and 33m-high unfinished wall carving, known as **Farhad Tarash** ('carved by Farhad'). The only part completed is the small face relief, which is believed to be that of Shirin, sculpted by Farhad (thus the name). Before leaving the site via the same entrance gate, turning left up the hill past the Hercules statue will bring you to the Parthian **Belash Relief**, an irregular quadrilateral rock with figures in high relief, including that of the Parthian king Belash, carved on each of its three sides. It now rests under the oddly shaped protection canopy, clearly visible from the modern road below.

Further on from Bisotun, 33km away towards Kermanshah, is the Sasanid *paradeisos* (hunting garden) of **Taq-e Bostan** (طاقبستان) ✳ (☏ 083 34218891; ⊕ 08.00–18.00; entry 300,000 rials). Approaching from the main road, to the right on the hillside rises a huge (undecorated) rock-cut surface that marks the remains of an immense platform. Legend has it that near here was an enormous reception area where the Sasanid rulers received envoys from the Chinese and Roman empires in great splendour.

A right turn leads to the two Sasanid '**grottoes**' of Taq-e Bostan. This is a popular lunch spot for local families and for pilgrims making the road journey to Karbala in Iraq. The entrance to the site is past the *chelo-kebab* cafés, at the far end of the pool; from here, it's a short walk to the first and larger 'grotto', among elaborately carved column capitals, some showing a Sasanid shah holding the diadem or Ring of Authority, brought here from the Bisotun locale. The surrounding area was renovated in spring 2013 and is pleasant to walk around. The word 'grotto' is inaccurate although there is an air of fantasy about this place. The exact function of these two manmade caves is unclear but the hunting scenes depicted on the two side walls suggest this was part of a favourite Sasanid royal hunting park or *paradeisos*. A stylised Tree of Life, perhaps symbolising the Zoroastrian Tree of All Seeds, from which all known plants apparently germinate, is carved either side of the main 'grotto' with Rubenesque victory angels above. At the back of the cave a huge, almost free-standing figure of rider and horse has been carved from the rock, while above stand (left to right) the Zoroastrian goddess Anahita pouring a libation, a kingly figure in the centre and Ahura Mazda. But which Sasanid shah is depicted here and below as the warrior-hero? The particular crown suggests it is Peroz I (r457–84CE) but this shah had a disastrous military career, culminating in his capture and ransom in central Asia after ordering a cavalry charge right into a concealed staked ditch: scarcely a record one would wish to have commemorated. The most likely candidate is Khosrow II (r590–628CE) with his legendary horse Shabdiz, who brought Byzantine Syria and Egypt under Sasanid control before his murder (see box, page 141). It is said he went hunting with 300 horses, 1,160 slaves with javelins, 1,040 slaves with swords and staves, 700 falconers, 300 riders with hunting panthers, 70 leopards, 700 hounds and 200 minstrels, and such scenes are beautifully depicted on both side walls. High up on the far left is a Qajar-period low relief of Mohammad Ali Mirza, son of Fath Ali Shah, recording his governorship of the region, dating from 1822.

The next 'grotto' contains the figure of Shapur III (r383–88CE) with his grandfather Shapur II (d378CE) on the right. The inscription just visible is in the Pahlavi script, largely abandoned after the Arab conquest in the 7th century. A little further along is a low relief of the investiture of Ardashir II (r379–83CE) with Ahura Mazda on the right, while Mithra, the Zoroastrian 'Lord of Covenant' or 'Justice', stands on a lotus dais, carrying a *barsom* of twigs for the sacred fire (see box, page 232). In Zoroastrian belief this manifestation of Ahura Mazda crossed the heavens daily in his sun-chariot (thus, his halo of sunrays) to check that all were keeping their word, but when he was adopted as a deity in his own right by Roman soldiery, his rituals were followed in secrecy in underground or windowless temples. Under the feet of Ardashir II lies a defeated enemy, probably a Roman emperor. It has been suggested that his beard identifies him as Julian the Apostate (responsible for reintroducing temple worship in the place of Christianity across the empire) who invaded Sasanid territory as far as Ctesiphon before being defeated and dying in 363CE. But this was 16 years before Ardashir came to the throne and furthermore Ardashir II led no campaigns against Rome during his reign; contemporary Roman rulers who might fit the bill in what was a period of turmoil are hard to establish. Just to the right of this panel is the natural spring that probably made this spot so appealing to the Sasanid shahs and explains the depiction of Anahita in the first 'grotto'.

KERMANSHAH کرمانشاه *Telephone code 083*

With a population of 857,000, Kermanshah (some early 1990s maps may show Bakhtaran; as the city was renamed for a short while after the revolution) is just 9km away from Taq-e Bostan. Probably dating from the Sasanid Empire, modern Kermanshah has little of historic or architectural interest, especially after constant Iraqi bombardment during the 1980s and subsequent rebuilding. Capital of Kermanshah province, this predominantly Kurdish city, with Sunnis making up 40% of its residents, is a good starting point for exploring Kurdistan and Kurdish villages to the north.

In Kermanshah itself there is the early 20th-century **Tekiyeh of Muavin al-Molk** (Hadad Abil St; 37214757; ◷ 08.00–14.00 & 13.00–18.00; entry 100,000 rials), with interesting tiled panels in the three performance areas. Those of the first courtyard reveal the function of the small complex with a large panel, to the right just after the entry, depicting a preacher reciting one of the Ashura eulogies about Hossein while veiled women sit at his feet, and men dressed in white flagellate themselves in the commemorative parades along the bottom section. In the main covered hall each panel shows an episode of the Karbala story (see box, page 73); look for the one depicting Zaynab, Hossein's sister, berating the Umayyad ruler in Damascus after the battle. Close by the throne, as if they were actively involved in 7th-century Umayyad politics, are European envoys in 19th-century dress, a reflection of Iranian Europhobia a century ago. The final open courtyard has a large panel showing a Sufi mystic with the ritual vessels and dress elements, while the back of the 'stage' is covered with moulded tiles alluding to Iranian archaeological monuments and historic or legendary figures: a visual delight for tired eyes. From here it is a short walk to the city's older **bazaar**, where you can try local delicacy *nun-e berenj*, prepared fresh from rice dough, or *ferni* dessert made from rice flour and milk.

GETTING THERE AND AWAY Kermanshah Airport is only 7km away from the city centre, off Imam Khomeini Square, the first roundabout on the approach from Hamadan and has regular **flights** from Tehran and Mashhad. Since March 2018 there is also a train service connecting Kermanshah to Mashhad via Tehran in 24 hours. The provincial capital has two **bus** stations: central Shahid Kaviani terminal servicing bus and *savari* departures to Sanandaj, Hamadan, Tehran and beyond lies approximately 2km after Imam Khomeini Square. The much smaller Rah-e Karbala terminal with *savari* and minibus departures in the direction of Qasr-e Shirin, lies on the other side of the city past the Flower Garden (Bagh-e Golha) park.

WHERE TO STAY AND EAT
Azadegan Hotel (70 rooms) Vahdat St; 34225591. Slightly away from the city centre, but with lovely views over the mountains, the building of the hotel has been recently given a fresh layer of paint. Rooms are spacious, although have a slightly nostalgic feel. **$$$**

Jamshid Hotel (50+ rooms) Taq Bostan Bd; 34296002. Opened in 2006, this 4-star hotel shaped as a Sasanid arch is conveniently located a few hundred metres from the entrance to the Taq-e Bostan site. Room décor is basic, but service is good. **$$$**

Parsian Kermanshah Hotel (100 rooms) Shahid Keshvari Bd; 34219151, 34219160; w kermanshah.pih.ir. A grand modern hotel

with facilities to match & spacious rooms, some overlooking the city's new stadium. Good value for money on the upper scale price range. **$$$**

Oak Hostel (4 rooms) 12 Naghibzadeh Alley; m 0912 4239737. Opened in early 2019, the first Western-style hostel in western Iran, Oak offers pristine & cosy dormitory-style accommodation as well as a reasonably priced double room. The real treat here, however, is the welcoming personnel & friendly atmosphere. **$–$$**

Haj Nasrollah Noori 2 Farhangiyan Faz; 14218166; ◷ 08.00–20.00 Sat–Thu. Local favourite bakery & supplier of fresh *nun-e berenj* biscuits. **$**

NORTH OF KERMANSHAH TOWARDS KURDISTAN PROVINCE

Early traveller accounts from Christian missionaries dating to the late 19th and early 20th centuries adamantly portray Kurds as lawless, rugged and uncultured. None of this is true. Kurdish loyalty and warmth are known throughout Iran, and Kurdish people are praised for their friendliness and hospitality. One observation dating to those earlier accounts was nonetheless accurate and remains true to date – the beauty of Kurdish women is extraordinary and so is the beauty of this land.

Iranian Kurdistan is predominantly mountainous and very scenic, dotted with attractive hill villages and serpentine roads. Nowhere else in the Middle East have Kurds so lovingly held on to their traditions and lifestyle and one of the first things a traveller through Iranian Kurdistan notices is the prevalence of traditional Kurdish dress with baggy trousers fitted at the ankles, known as *chuhoranak*. There are approximately 7–9 million Kurds living in Iran, or 12–15% of the entire population. Travelling around Kurdistan is most enjoyable in spring when nature comes to life and flowers start to blossom. The area is also famous for Nou Rouz celebrations held in villages across the region. As a souvenir, you may consider purchasing a traditional *faranji* gilet or handmade *kalash* shoes (the local version of *giveh*). Many Kurdish women work at home meticulously handweaving *kalash* both for sale and for use by men in the family.

The capital of Iranian Kurdistan is **Sanandaj** (سنندج), which in 2019 was named the Nou Rouz capital of Iran, a pleasant city of roughly 370,000 people. Well connected by *savari* taxis to Kermanshah and the surrounding area, you can overnight here in the **Shadi Hotel** (see opposite). It is otherwise a good transit point to the mountain villages of Kurdistan.

Approximately 32km south of Sanandaj (signposted 15km on the road to Kermanshah) lies the picturesque and secluded village of **Dowlab** (دولاب) ✳ or Dowlaw in Kurdish, whose name refers to 160 water springs scattered in the vicinity. Built on the mountainside in a 'stairway' fashion and set against the backdrop of Avalan Mountain (2,950m), Dowlab's 200 families spend most of their time working in the gardens, growing delicious fresh fruit, including the locally famous cherries and raisins. The village is also famous for its Sufi meeting place, Sheikh Mohammad and Sheikh Hadi Khanqah (or *tekiyeh*), holding the annual dervish *sama' qadriyeh* (or *zekr-e qiyam*) chant ceremony; alas for male spectators only. Dowlab has a number of traditional ecolodges with **Tishk** (see opposite) taking the lead role.

Dowlab is part of the greater region known as **Howramanat** (هورامان \ اورامانات) which consists essentially of four villages: Howraman-e Takht (the unofficial capital), Howraman-e Lahun, Howraman-e Shahu and Howraman-e Zhawerud and the mountainous areas in between. The cultural and traditional landscape of Howramanat is currently being studied by UNESCO for potential inclusion on the heritage list. **Howraman-e Takht**, located 75km southeast of Marivan, is one of the most picturesque and attractive villages in the whole of Kurdistan. Perched on the side of the mountain over the valley, it can be reached by *savari* taxi from Marivan bus terminal at Basij Square or the most intrepid can hike here over the mountains from Dowlab, but the route is demanding and time-consuming. Contact Adventure Iran (page 44) if trekking in this area is of interest. They organise a number of interesting routes nearby. Courtyards of Howraman houses are similarly located on the rooftops of the houses below in a 'stairway' fashion with narrow winding flights of steps and paths running in between the houses vertically and horizontally. Howraman is in particular famous for its annual **Pir Shaliar** celebrations, taking place on the last Wednesday and Thursday before 4 February (the date changes based on the Solar calendar), when the village transforms into the centre of music, family and social gatherings.

From Howraman you can either return by *savari* taxi to **Marivan** (مریوان) and explore the picturesque **Zarivar Lake** by unwinding in the **Marivan Tourist Inn** (see opposite), or continue on by private transport along the mountain road towards **Paveh** (پاوه). The real treat, however, is the road north of Paveh, towards **Noudesheh** village, 156km north of Kermanshah. Swerving up the mountains over the Sirvan River and the newly built **Darian Dam**, it is an enjoyable ride. Another spectacular village in Kurdistan is **Palangan** (پلنگان), which often adorns posters and postcards; it can be reached by private taxi from Kermanshah by turning left at **Kamyaran** on the road to Sanandaj.

WHERE TO STAY AND EAT There are no restaurants or cafés in Howraman. Kamaleh village nearby has a kebab restaurant open until 13.00, but otherwise the only food is that served in the Shadi Hotel, private homes or sold in local convenience stores. Fresh fruit and vegetables can be purchased from a Paykan truck driving around.

Shadi Hotel (Sanandaj) (82 rooms) Pasdaran St; \087 33625112, 33625114; w hotelshadi.com. Rooms are spacious & some come with a view over the surrounding hills. There is a pleasant lobby & a small green yard outside. **$$$**.

Marivan Tourist Inn (10 rooms) Zarivar Lake shore, Marivan; \087 34521626. The inn is perched on a hill & rooms are spacious & come with small terraces & stunning views over the lake & surrounding area. **$$–$$$**

Shadi Hotel (20 rooms) Howraman; \087 34883535. A low-key version of the 4-star Shadi

Hotel in Sanandaj, it was modestly refurbished in 2013. While the inner décor imitating a castle, is rather unimpressive, rooms are comfortable & well lit with windows facing the mountains. **$$**

Tishk (3 rooms) Dowlab; m 0910 9546333; w tishktravel.ir. Run by wonderful sisters Masta & Zara with excellent taste & eye for detail; the décor of this ecolodge is exceptional & warmly reflects local traditions. With stunning views to wake up to in the morning & delicious homemade meals, Tishk will most likely become your favourite place to stay. Advance booking is required. **$–$$**

WEST OF KERMANSHAH

The road west of Kermanshah in the direction of the Iraqi border crossing at **Khosravi** was historically part of the Sasanid Kermanshah to Qasr-e Shirin route and ancient wall remains are still visible on the approach to **Sarpol-e Zahab** (سرپل ذهاب), the largest town in the area with a population of 85,000, situated 149km west from Kermanshah. Very hot in the summer and often invisible behind the layers of dust brought by the wind from the Iraqi plains, it is best to explore the area in spring when the air is fresh and the surrounding mountains are green. In November 2017 Sarpol-e Zahab suffered a severe earthquake killing 620 people and injuring more than 8,000, forcing many to live in temporary accommodation and tents. Another earthquake in 2018 was less dramatic; there were no losses of life, but more than 700 people were injured. The drastic devaluation of the Iranian rial in summer 2018 made it next to impossible for people to purchase supplies, rebuild their homes and return to normal lives; many continue to live in tents.

Approaching Sarpol-e Zahab, past the decommissioned tank in the cemetery lies **Dakhmeh Dukkan-e Da'ud** ('David's Shop'), investigated by Rawlinson in 1836. The locals then said this tomb chamber carved high up out of the living rock housed the remains of a Jewish blacksmith who became a local ruler, but today some archaeologists argue it is Median or early Achaemenid in date, while others associate it with the Seleucid low-relief (1.5m × 0.9m) carved below the tomb, depicting a Zoroastrian priest holding a *barsom*. The tomb itself has two sections: the first functioned as a columned antechamber, 9.6m wide, with a door leading into the second, a narrower tomb chamber with a small ossuary pit dug out of the rock floor. Less than 5km away is another rock carving of greater interest to archaeologists and which probably inspired the Achaemenid stonemasons working for Darius the Great at Bisotun.

East of **Sarpol-e Zahab**, but still within the town limits, is the famous relief **Naqsh-e Anubanini**, dating from c2200–1900BCE. A local ruler, probably King

Anubanini of Lullubi, is shown standing on a platform supported by captives, with his foot firmly on the chest of a fallen enemy. Facing him is the goddess Ishtar or Inana, identified by her starred totem, presenting him with a ring or diadem while holding two roped prisoners. The relief is unfortunately heavily damaged and visibility of the image is impaired. (There are four other Bisotun-style reliefs relating to Lullubi rulers in the vicinity but they are much less accessible.) Below the Naqsh-e Anubanini relief you can just make out a Parthian carving, **Naqsh-e Gudraz Shah**, commemorating the victory of Shah Vologazes (II or III) over his rival Shah Mithdrates IV, c147CE.

Continuing approximately 10km on the same road past Naqsh-e Anubanini, brings you to the delightful village of **Piran** (پیران) awash with greenery, including fig, raspberry and pomegranate groves. Idyllic and ideal for hiking, the village is famous for its picturesque 180m-high **waterfall** (Abshar-e Piran), the highest in Iran. It is a 15-minute walk from the parking area. The path leading to the waterfall was almost entirely destroyed in the 2017 earthquake and good hiking shoes are a must to be able to reach it, but it is worth the effort. Another picturesque waterfall can be accessed from **Qaleh Yazdegerd**, badly damaged in the Iran–Iraq War. To come here, take the signposted turn to the right before Sarpol-e Zahab on the approach from Kermanshah. The extensive site of **Qaleh Yazdegerd** was excavated by the Royal Ontario Museum, Toronto, in 1975–78. The citadel's square towers were clearly 3rd-century Parthian in date but occupation of this hill citadel continued for another 1,000 years. Remains of fine wall-plaster decoration, carved, moulded and colourfully painted, were found. Some were patterned with stylised floral motifs, while other schemes contained scantily clad men and women, possibly entertainers, and cupid forms.

Before the turn to Qaleh Yazdegerd, the road to the left leads down to the valley towards **Taq-e Gara**, an arched gate and the only section surviving from a Sasanid caravanserai on the ancient Kermanshah–Qasr-e Shirin route. To the left in the valley the remains of original Sasanid walls are still visible. Back on the main road, about 1km further on, is a signposted turn to the picturesque village of **Pataq**, from where there are also good hiking opportunities and lovely views across the surrounding area.

Around 25km away further east is **Qasr-e Shirin** (population 18,000), or 'Castle of Shirin' (see box, page 141), and just before the city centre mounds of earth concealed the remains of a large Sasanid complex (known in Persian as 'Chahar Qapi') just visible before the 1980–88 Iran–Iraq War. Opinions were divided as to its form and function, some identifying it as an enormous, domed fire temple over 16m² set in gardens, while others argued it was a massive audience hall for Khosrow II. Nearby, another Sasanid complex known as Emarat-e Khosrow ('Refectory') was entered by a double staircase at the eastern end, and stables, storerooms and ten courtyards were identified mainly from drawings made in the 1930s; recently these drawings, and therefore these conclusions, have been questioned. What is clear is that the complex and the town of Qasr-e Shirin were severely damaged by the Byzantine emperor, Heraclius, in 628CE, and then by Arab armies some ten years later. Approximately 20km beyond Qasr-e Shirin lies the Khosravi Iraqi border crossing.

SOUTH OF KERMANSHAH AND TOWARDS ILAM PROVINCE

A little to the southeast of Kermanshah, 25km southwest of **Harsin** are the remains of Median rock-cut tombs (*gurdakhmeh*). Locating these is a little tricky and requires dedication. Signage is minimal and binoculars will be handy to know where to turn. Along route 35 towards Harsin, take the first turn to the right past the Gamasiab River

BASHMAGH BORDER CROSSING INTO IRAQI KURDISTAN

The border crossing between Iran and Iraqi Kurdistan lies approximately 20km northwest of Marivan and is a relatively straightforward and hassle-free experience once you have the paperwork in order. A taxi from Marivan to the border costs 500,000 rials and from the drop-off point you can either choose to walk for roughly 1km or take another taxi for 30,000 rials from the drop-off point to the passport control building. The crossing is usually open 24/7 (although it was closed during the 2017 Kurdistan referendum) and there is a prayer room to take a rest after a long journey, if required.

It is important to check in advance Kurdistan visa requirements with the Kurdistan authorities, as Iranian border police may not necessarily be up to date with any changes or developments for specific nationalities. European passport holders can as a rule obtain a 30-day tourist visa on arrival for 3,000 Iraqi dinars. Please note that the Kurdistan entry stamp is not valid for travel to Baghdad or anywhere outside the Peshmerga-controlled territory of Kurdistan. The same applies vice versa; the Iraqi visa issued by an Iraqi embassy in one's home country does not give an automatic right to travel to Iraqi Kurdistan. After the Bashmagh passport control and checkpoint there are shared taxis to Penjwen and from there to Soleymaniyeh.

and follow the road to the village of **Sorkheh Deh**. The first tomb (*gurdakhmeh sorkheh deh*) will come into view after the turn to your left. Keep an eye out for the faded metal sign. The niche is up above, 110cm wide and 85cm high. At the second site are three rock-cut tombs of **Es'haqvand** (اسحق وند) and associated locally with legendary Farhad, the engineer who loved Queen Shirin (see box, page 141). To reach these, continue along the same road to the village of **Deh Now** and from there keep your eyes to the left. The niches of the tombs are perched on the cliffs high up and can be approached by taking the gravel road and then walking up for roughly 300m. Judging by the low relief depicting a priest with uplifted hands in prayer, these Zoroastrian tombs, about 2m wide and 1.75m deep, date from the 4th or 3rd century BCE.

The drive further south from Kermanshah passes through lovely countryside. At Nurabad ask directions for the village of Morabad and **Tappeh Baba Jan**, excavated by a British team in 1966–69. You pass **Harsin**, and in this area at **Ganj Dareh** Canadian archaeologists found evidence of early Neolithic occupation with a suggested carbon-14 dating of c8450BCE. A severe fire around 7300BCE actually helped conserve certain artefacts and the mud-brick architecture, vitrifying the clay. The pottery was crude with no signs of imported trade goods but the walls, sometimes surviving up to 2m high, were carefully plastered. Some 30km further on, the main mound **Tappeh Baba Jan** revealed settlement from the 4th millennium BCE but the most important finds emerged from later levels, especially those from c900–700BCE. The groundplan and architectural details (such as blind niches and the arrow-slit forms) of these later buildings were similar to those found at Nushijan Tappeh (page 137) to the east and Hasanlu further north, incorporating defences to safeguard both the property and the inhabitants. The large-columned hall had side rooms and a portico under which a horse skeleton with harness and vessels was found. This burial probably dated from a destructive fire that swept the site, perhaps caused by invading Scythian tribesmen in the 7th century BCE. On the eastern *tappeh* nearby another fortified building with a central chamber (10.4m × 12.5m) was excavated. A spiral ramp led to a second storey, but what was striking was the rich painted plaster decorating the walls of the central chamber, and shards of painted ceiling tiles, decorated with squares or diamond forms. After the fire the site was not abandoned as there was some evidence of Achaemenid occupation, but for some reason everyone left before the Seleucids took control of the region.

A number of archaeological teams worked on various sites in this region down towards Ilam (Chavar, Tappeh Var Kabud and Bani Surmah) where remains of ancient palaces and extensive cemeteries were discovered, mostly dating from the 3rd millennium BCE. Three kinds of burial were uncovered: individual interment under the family house (as often found in Anatolia), mass interment in pits just outside the settlement, and thirdly, burial in large stone vaults constructed from beautifully dressed stone with luxurious grave goods to match.

ILAM PROVINCE ایلام

Ilam province is where nature reigns supreme and the only tourists you are likely to encounter will be pilgrims en route to or from Karbala in Iraq, less than 300km away. The Iranian **Payaneh Barakat** border crossing gets extraordinarily busy at the end of the Muslim month of Safar when hundreds of thousands of pilgrims from all over Iran stream on foot, in cars and buses across the border as part of the annual Arbaeen Shi'a pilgrimage.

The Ilam landscape is mountainous with rich green pastures, much appreciated by many nomads, and the spectacular **Kabir Kuh** mountain range (highest peak Kan Seifi at 3,050m) stretching 160km northwest to southeast, as if enveloping the province and marking its natural boundaries. Ilam is predominantly Kurdish with the Shi'a branch as the main denomination, unlike in Iranian Kurdistan. Historically part of the area of the ancient civilisation of Elam, the province has a few interesting archaeological sites to visit, although its splendid nature is the main reason for venturing this way.

The capital of the province bears the same name, **Ilam**, and has a population of approximately 200,000 people, a third of the entire population of the province. There a few interesting sites in the relative vicinity and in Ilam you can overnight in the basic **Khalash Hotel** (see below).

Only 10km south of Ilam, past the city's airport, the road splits into two, with the signposted turn to the right leading down to the spectacular **Ilam Dam Lake** with its turquoise-blue waters. Continuing on for another 20km without turning, concealed (literally) from visitors' eyes is the Assyrian **Ghel Ghel rock relief** (نقش برجسته گل گل), which is more than 3,000 years old and depicts an Assyrian soldier wearing a hat and a star carved above his head. The metal cage custom-built around the relief has alas made it impossible to discern the image. The site is signposted and necessitates a pleasant 10-minute hike along the mountain river flowing into the Ilam Dam.

Further south lies one of the highlights of a trip to the province, the spectacular **Raziyaneh Gorge** (تنگه رازیانه), which runs parallel to the Ilam–Bedreh road and starts approximately 50km past Ilam. In winter and early spring, the water running down the gorge is cold and plentiful, but in summer it is possible to hike unobstructively its entire length of 3km, coiling amid 15–30m-high walls at a width of up to 5m.

WHERE TO STAY AND EAT

Khalash Hotel (32 rooms) Heydari St; Keshvari Sq; 084 3333 6653; e khalash_hotel@ hotmail.com. With promising room décor (although the same cannot be said about the main lobby), en-suite toilets are surprisingly basic &

mainly squat-style, if opting for a budget room. The friendliness of the personnel & reliable heating – a must during cold winters – are the main reasons to overnight here. **$$**

5

From Kashan to Esfahan

KASHAN کاشان *Telephone code 031*

Kashan (232km from Tehran, 210km from Esfahan, population 294,000) will always be associated in Islamic art for its high-quality ceramics (*kashi*) production, which dates from the 12th century, even enduring the Mongol campaigns. It is also renowned for its manufacture of costly silks and carpets for the Safavid court. The 17th-century English merchant, Thomas Herbert, estimated there were then approximately 4,000 families in the town mainly involved in textiles, which would mean that the community was then 'in compass not less than York or Norwich … The houses are fairly built, many of which are pargeted and painted; the mosques and *hamams* are in their cupolas curiously ceruleated with a feigned turquoise.' Undoubtedly he would also have heard that Kashan was the place from which the Three Wise Men set out for Bethlehem. Almost 250 years later, other English travellers reported that Kashan boasted 24 caravanserais, 35 hotels for foreign merchants, 34 *hamams*, 18 large mosques, and 90 small shrines but in such a bad state that Lord Curzon commented, 'A more funereal place I had not yet seen.' Matters were made no better by its reputation for poisonous scorpions.

Kashan was once Iran's major silk-weaving centre, but the fine weaving technique known as *sha'rbafi* has only survived in a few workshops. There are fewer than ten traditional silk weaving mills (down from more than 200) left in the city and the high-quality produce is so dear that it is only sold in a limited number of exclusive shops (page 152).

Kashan is also at the very heart of Iran's rose-water production. Exported to 30 countries, including Saudi Arabia, UAE, China and South Korea, rose water is not only used in essence, but in treatment of depression and even for heart-related illnesses. Rose fields in Kashan lie at the foothills of the Karkas Mountains and flowers are harvested from the end of April until mid-July. Flowers and rose branches, which are believed to contain the best aroma, are then distilled in traditional workhouses and 68 factories in Kashan and the surrounding area.

Kashan's most recent political history has been primarily associated with the nuclear installation in Natanz, 89km southeast of the city. The details of the facility for enriching uranium were leaked in 2002 and subsequently confirmed by President Khatami's administration. It is the old merchant houses, however, that make this city special. A distinctive feature of Kashan architectural style is that the garden pits (*gowdal* in Persian) were dug so deep, that some of them lie 4m below street level to give easier access to underground *qanats* and create a naturally cool space to hide from the summer heat.

GETTING THERE AND AROUND The easiest way to reach Kashan is by intercity **bus** (3hrs from Tehran; 250,000 rials), which stops at the terminal north of the city, although the Tehran–Esfahan/Yazd–Kerman **train** service stops in the centre of town [155 D2]. From Tehran's Jonub terminal, buses leave every 30 minutes and if travelling from Esfahan, the only company operating the Esfahan–Kashan route (160,000 rials) is Levan Nour with departures from Kaveh terminal and their hourly service gets quickly filled up. Prior ticket reservation is recommended. Please note that travelling further south from Kashan is tiresome, as there are no bus services to Yazd or anywhere in that direction and you will either have to travel to Esfahan first or hitch a ride from one of the passing buses at the toll plaza (*avarezi* in Persian) outside Kashan. The Esfahan–Kashan motorway is a toll road (20,000 rials for a private car). There is also a multi-lane toll road (not used by intercity buses) that passes behind the Bagh-e Fin garden (page 157), from Tehran (3hrs) and on to Yazd (4–5hrs). When in Kashan, for reliable and reasonably priced **taxis** around and about, including to the village of Abyaneh, contact the friendly, family-run **Low Cost Taxi Reza** (m 0913 8190256, 8190276; e helen_arsenal@yahoo.com). *Savari* services to Meybod and Ardakan leave from Bahonar Square in Kashan.

WHERE TO STAY AND EAT Two or three days could happily be spent exploring Kashan with its beautiful merchant houses and the locale. There are a number of traditional houses converted into small boutique hotels (with good Wi-Fi) that also have traditional restaurants, but the next best alternative would be one of the numerous kebab restaurants along the main road outside the Bagh-e Fin.

Khaneh Ameriha [155 B1] (27 rooms) Alavi St; 55240220; w sarayeameriha.com. This traditional late 18th-century house was restored in 2013 & converted into an exclusive & luxurious 5-star hotel. Originally built by one of Kashan's wealthiest men & its Safavid governor, the hotel is flawless & faultless from the main entrance to the rooms. There are 2 inner courtyards, 1 for the guests & the other for visitors who are required to pay an entry fee of 50,000 rials, eventually refunded if ordering in the hotel's café. **$$$$**

Manouchehri House [155 C3] (19 rooms) 49 7th Emarat Alley, off Mohtasham St, follow green arrows on the houses; 55242617, 55245521; w manouchehrihouse.com. This exquisite 5-star hotel complex consists of 2 finely restored old merchant houses (section 2 opened in 2017). Connected by a narrow alley, each house has a classic Persian design, inner courtyard with a *howz* & a restaurant (**$$$–$$$$**) serving excellent Iranian fusion cuisine; service is so methodical it is almost mortifying. Each room is immaculate & individually decorated. The Iranian décor of the rooms & restaurant in the second mansion has a subtle Danish twist, but it nonetheless feels surprisingly authentic. The hotel houses a silk-weaving mill, whose exquisite

produce is sold in the hotel's exclusive shop. **$$$–$$$$**

Ehsan Historic Guesthouse [155 B3] (25 rooms) Fazl Naraqi St, across the street from the Agha Bozorg Madrasa; 55453030, 55446833; w ehsanhouse.com. The first historical house in Kashan to have been converted into a hotel. Utterly charming with a beautiful inner courtyard & traditional sitting benches under pomegranate trees, it offers a variety of rooms. Staff are friendly & accommodating. In front of the guesthouse is a small Sheibani's Museum of Fine Arts (⊕ 09.00–13.00 & 17.00–21.00; entry 20,000 rials). **$$**

Negin Historic Hotel [155 C3] (40 rooms) Shahidan Sabet Alley, off Mohtasham St, follow arrow signs on the houses; 55231783, 55235525; w negin.info. A traditional Qajar-period residence converted into a fine & modern traditional hotel with 5 different inner courtyards & a pleasant atmosphere. Rooms are simply decorated, but spacious & en suite. **$$**

Noghli Historic House [155 B4] (15 rooms) Pamenar Alley; 55233324; e info@noghlihouse.com; w noghlihouse.com. A friendly & cosy traditional hotel, spread over a number of properties in the historic part of Kashan. It has a spacious inner *gowdal* sunken courtyard, a

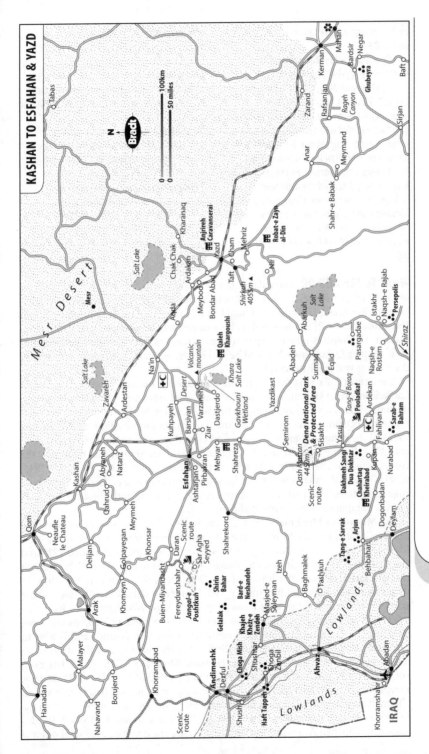

traditional vegetarian restaurant & a bicycle rental service. **$$**

☗ Puppet & Toy Museum and Guesthouse [155 A1] (5 private rooms & 2 dorms) 43 Allemeh Alley, in front of Tabatabaei House; `55225134; m 0902 3851485; w puppetmuseumhouse.com. This delightful guesthouse started with a private collection of unique & antique puppet dolls & the credit is all due to Amir Sohrabi for his efforts at reviving Iranian puppet toy traditions. Rooms are spacious & traditionally decorated; the inner courtyard is the place to relax & enjoy a homemade meal. *Kheymeh shab bazi* puppet theatre performances are regularly held in the in-house puppet & toy museum (⊕ 09.30–14.00 & 15.00–19.30 daily). **$$**

☗ Sayeh Saray [155 B3] (6 rooms, inc a 4-person dorm) 29th Farhang Alley; `55445828; m 0913 3617131; w sayehsaray.com. A tiny newly opened hotel/hostel in a traditional house with relaxing atmosphere & very pleasant staff. Rooms are on the smaller scale without any frills or luxuries. **$–$$**

✕ Khaneh Abbasian [155 B1] Alavi St; `55245764. A beautiful traditional restaurant located in historic Abbasian Hse. Offers excellent dishes, but can get a little crowded. **$$**

✕ Mozafferi Traditional Restaurant [155 A1] Around the corner from Tabatabai Hse; `55235300; m 0913 1626005, 9635383; ⊕ 10.00–23.00. Pleasant traditional restaurant, popular with tourists & locals, especially for w/end dinners. **$–$$**

WHAT TO SEE AND DO The Safavid family obviously had a soft spot for Kashan, as Shah Abbas I requested that he should be buried here in preference to Ardabil, Qom or Mashhad. His body is thought to lie in the 13th-century tomb of **Habib Ibn Musa** [155 C2], understood to be a descendant of seventh imam Musa Ibn Qasem. The tomb is now incorporated into a large mosque complex decorated in 19th-century Qajar times. You will be told his cenotaph is the black marble one to the right as you enter the crypt.

It is a short walk west from here into the extensive **bazaar** complex ✳ [155 C2] (closed on Fridays), which contains a number of interesting historical *hamams*, mosques, *khans* and *sarays*; many of the last function in the summer as open-air tea and coffee houses for both locals and tourists. As for the shops, under the fine vaults of the compact bazaar you can find everything and anything from spices to gold. One shop here is particularly recommended. **Zhee Showroom** ✳ (around the corner from Timcheh Amin al-Dowleh in the bazaar; `55442738; m 0912 3895843; ⊕ 09.00–21.00 daily) has one of the finest and most exquisite collections of antique rugs and kilims. The quality and fair prices make this one of the best carpet stores in Iran. Shipping can be arranged abroad.

The **Mosque of Mir Emad** [155 C2] (also known as Masjed-e Maydan, Masjed-e Maydan-e Sang, after the former name of the Maydan-e Mir Emad, or even Masjed-e Maydan-e Fayz) replaced the original Seljuk-period mosque built around 1218 and subsequently destroyed during the Mongol invasion. The mosque was then rebuilt in 1461 for Jahanshah, the leader of the Qara Qoyunlu tribal confederation. In its present state, however, it is mostly 19th century in date, when the local Qajar governor undertook large-scale restoration work. It is justly famous for its multi-layered plaster *muqarnas* decoration and its superb tiled *mihrab*, dating from 1226, which was in place until the beginning of the 20th century and is now in the Museum für Islamische Kunst, in Berlin. On the same side of the street, with a 19th-century tiled entrance, is the **Hamam Khan** [155 C2], which has been converted into a wonderful traditional tea house (`55452572; ⊕ 09.00–21.00 daily, except Fri; entry 20,000 rials if just to look around). It retains the basic original plan although there are some careless repairs and alterations. A short amble away on the same side is the 19th-century **Caravanserai Amin al-Dowleh** ✳ [155 C2/3] (also known as **Timcheh Amin al-Dowleh**), with its soaring dome painted with original

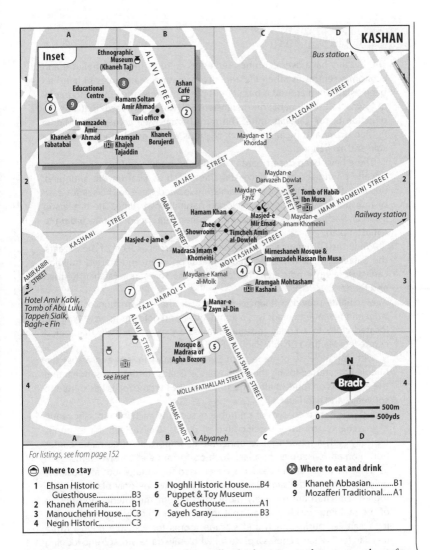

Inset

A | B | C | D

Ethnographic Museum (Khaneh Taj)

ALAVI STREET

Bus station

1

Educational Centre

Ashan Café

Hamam Soltan Amir Ahmad

Taxi office

Maydan-e 15 Khordad

TALEQANI STREET

Imamzadeh Amir Ahmad

Khaneh Tabatabai

Aramgah Khajeh Tajaddin

Khaneh Borujerdi

RAJAEI STREET

Maydan-e Darvazeh Dowlat

Tomb of Habib Ibn Musa

2

STREET

BABA AFZAL STREET

Maydan-e Fayz

ABBAZAR STREET

IMAM KHOMEINI STREET

2

Hamam Khan

Masjed-e Mir Emad

Maydan-e Imam Khomeini

Railway station

KASHANI STREET

Zhee Showroom

Timcheh Amin al-Dowleh

Masjed-e jame

Madrasa Imam Khomeini

MOHTASHAM STREET

Mirneshaneh Mosque & Imamzadeh Hassan Ibn Musa

AMIR KABIR STREET

1

Maydan-e Kamal al-Molk

4 3

3

7

FAZL NARAQI ST

Aramgah Mohtasham Kashani

Hotel Amir Kabir, Tomb of Abu Lulu, Tappeh Sialk, Bagh-e Fin

ALAVI STREET

Manar-e Zayn al-Din

HABIB ALLAH SHARIF STREET

see inset

Mosque & Madrasa of Agha Bozorg

5

4

MOLLA FATHALLAH STREET

N

Bradt

4

SHAMS ABAD ST

Abyaneh

0 500m
0 500yds

A | B | C | D

For listings, see from page 152

Where to stay

1 Ehsan Historic Guesthouse....................B3
2 Khaneh Ameriha............B1
3 Manouchehri House.....C3
4 Negin Historic................C3
5 Noghli Historic House......B4
6 Puppet & Toy Museum & Guesthouse..................A1
7 Sayeh Saray.......................B3

Where to eat and drink

8 Khaneh Abbasian............B1
9 Mozafferi Traditional.....A1

decoration. Here there is a spartan, but endlessly charming tea house, or rather a few tabourets around the central *howz* water pool and a lovely man with a moustache serving fresh black tea. It is a popular spot for tourists and bazaar dwellers alike.

Further on, you will find the **Madrasa Imam Khomeini** [155 B/C3] (formerly Madrasa Soltani), built between 1842 and 1850 with 52 student cells during the reign of Fath Ali Shah, and which is still functioning as a theological school. A few Seljuk monuments remain in the city. Continue walking through the bazaar until the main road is reached and turn right for the **masjed-e jame** [155 B3], extensively repaired in the 18th century, but still with its 1073 minaret. In August 2013 restoration and repairs had also begun in the mosque's courtyard and the basement. About 500m southeast from the mosque, the 12th-century **Manar-e Zayn al-Din** [155 B3] (Baba Afzal St) rises distinctively.

By retracing your steps to the bazaar entrance, this main road leads to the **Mosque and Madrasa of Agha Bozorg** ✳ [155 B3/4], named after a famous theologian and

The bazaars have over centuries served as cultural, religious, political and economic centres in urban life and city formation. Many cities in Iran had been established around a bazaar and not a mosque, thus the topography of towns and settlements on the ancient Silk Roads (eg: Yazd) matches the direction of the caravan route. The term bazaar itself comes from Middle Persian *wazar* and means a cluster of shops where goods and services are sold and exchanged.

There have been desert bazaars for nomad traders and seasonal bazaars outside pilgrimage sites. In coastal cities, such as Siraf (in the antiquity), Bushehr and Bandar Abbas, bazaars were located close to the sea for ease of transportation and have developed naturally over time. The bazaars in Esfahan, Kashan and Tabriz had on the other hand been built according to a master plan.

While the Ottomans emphasised the commercial aspects of the bazaars, the Safavids, their rivals, set geographical priorities and started building caravanserais in remote areas, having established bazaars in Esfahan, Kerman and Tabriz.

Merchants provided financial support for the construction of bazaars, *waqf* and revenue to madrasas and mosques, and goldsmiths were typically located close to a Friday mosque (masjed-e jame) or a main theological centre (eg: Madrasa Chahar Bagh in Esfahan).

With the increase of trade from Europe bazaars in Iran and across the Middle East started losing their importance. Guilds started to disappear and the emphasis on tourism after the 1970s meant that the focus has shifted to souvenirs and handicrafts.

A classic bazaar consists of a number of sections, each for a specific group of merchants and for a specific kind of goods. **Qeysariyeh**, for example, typically with a raised roof to underline its importance (the name comes from Roman 'Kaiser'), is the place to shop for more expensive items, such as gold. This part of the bazaar is never used for storage, but for business only. In north African *suqs* Qeysariyeh was usually the only place that was roofed. **Timcheh** are relatively more modest, but the interior and design of the buildings inside suggest that these were originally gathering places for wealthier businessmen and storage rooms for valuable goods. **Khan** (Persian for 'house') denotes a place for wholesale trade, storage and lodging for travelling merchants. In Iran most *khans* are two storeys (second for accommodation). Traditionally rectangular in shape, they were connected to the bazaar via a narrow passageway with a door locked at night for security. **Saray** serves the same purpose as *khan* and means effectively the same, but for more general goods.

jurist born in a neighbouring village and who was also known as Mehdi Naraqi (d1829). This 19th-century complex incorporates a deep sunken courtyard with a central ablution pool. The basement under the prayer hall acts as a winter assembly hall. Two wind towers, cunningly disguised as minarets, flank the main prayer *ivan*, dramatically accentuating the dome. Three 19th-century residences are nearby, all off Alavi Street.

Khaneh Borujerdi [155 B1] (⏱ 08.30–17.00; entry 300,000 rials), formerly the house of a Kashani tea dealer, is perhaps the best known residence, as its distinctive dome over the main audience *talar* appears on postcards and posters. **Khaneh Tabatabai** [155 A2] (⏰ 08.30–17.00; entry 300,000 rials) of 1834, hidden in a narrow alley next to Imamzadeh Amir Ahmad, is somewhat larger, with a clear division between the private family *anderuni* apartments by the main entrance, the servants' quarters (extreme right) and the public *biruni* rooms across the main court. The ornate plaster decoration, including some by the outstanding Kashani artist Kamal al-Molk, is grey and white augmented with lively landscape paintings in the two side chambers of the *talar* (veranda). But the real delight is **Khaneh Abbasian** [155 B1] (w abbasi-dh.ir; ⏰ 08.30–17.00; entry 300,000 rials), down the street from the Borujerdi House. This enormous complex, completed in 1823, was built to provide an equally ornate house for Tabatabai's daughter. With several levels, it is so extensive with numerous staircases, *talars*, five *godal-e bagcheh* (sunken courtyards) and chambers that you can become quickly disorientated. The richly carved plaster decoration is in high relief on a Wedgwood blue or pale terracotta ground, often complemented with coloured window glass set in highly patterned pierced screens: deliciously over the top. All three residences bring home to the visitor how rich and influential late 19th-century merchants were, so if you are thinking of buying a modern Kashan carpet, just remember that the Abbasian and Tabatabai families made their fortunes in carpet dealing. The nearby **Hamam Soltan Amir Ahmad** [155 B1] (⏰ 08.30–20.00; entry 300,000 rials) was the place to bathe and forget their commercial worries. Walking towards Fazel Naraqi Street there is another, although less glamorous, restored Qajar residence, **Khaneh Taj**, which is now Kashan's **Ethnographic Museum** [155 B1] (⏰ 08.30–20.00; entry 500,000 rials).

Halfway along the 8km route southwest of the centre, towards the gardens established by the Safavid shahs to break their occasional royal progresses, is the tiled pyramidic dome to the south side marking the **Tomb of Abu Lulu** [155 A3], honoured here in Iran for 'liquidating' Caliph Umar (d644ce), selected as caliph in preference to the Prophet's son-in-law, Ali, an insult to all Shi'a. As the tilework shows, it was extensively repaired in Safavid and then Qajar times. The tomb is permanently closed, reportedly due to pressure from Saudi Arabia. A little further, on the opposite side behind some houses, two mounds are visible, the larger being **Tappeh Sialk** [155 A3] (⏰ 09.00–16.30; entry 300,000 rials, the ticket is purchased at the small museum past the actual entrance to the right), excavated by the French during 1933–37. The elegant, long-spouted pottery vessels, shaped like stylised sandpiper birds, now in the National Museum, Tehran, were found here during archaeological work, while shell ornaments that were unearthed were proven to have been brought from the Persian Gulf, suggesting trading links between the two. The earliest level (Sialk I), which revealed stained red human remains buried underneath houses, has been dated to the 5th millennium bce, or perhaps earlier. The pottery finds from Level II, c4000bce, showed indisputable use of the potter's wheel, but for some unknown reason the residents then abandoned this site for the smaller mound. This second settlement was probably destroyed by fire around 3000bce, and there was then a gap of about 2,000 years before both sites were reinhabited. The new residents had other customs, employing stone foundations for their mud and wood buildings and burying their dead away from the town with the distinctive 'sandpiper' vessels as grave goods, along with trade items from the Persian Gulf. During the 9th and 8th centuries bce, a military attack caused the residents to flee, never to return. All the archaeological finds have been removed from the site, but the outlines of buildings are just visible.

The **Bagh-e Fin** باغ فین ✴ [155 A3] (Amir Kabir Rd; ⏰ 08.30–17.00; entry 500,000 rials; taxi fare from the centre of Kashan costs 70,000 rials) is at the end of the street (the toll road runs immediately behind) and is by far the most visually impressive Persian garden in Iran today. It still retains much of its Safavid layout, with a central pavilion placed over the artesian water channels, though repair and rebuilding work was carried out by Karim Khan Zand of Shiraz, then by Fath Ali Shah of the Qajar dynasty and again in early 2000. Majestic Shirazi cedars, of which some are 850 years old, add freshness and shade to this otherwise perfectly arranged space. A number of 19th-century foreign dignitaries, including the English envoy, Sir John Malcolm, broke their journeys here en route from Bushehr to the Tehran court. But there was a darker side to its history: in 1852 the much liked and progressive Iranian chief minister 'Amir Kabir' (see box, below) was assassinated here in the small *hamam* to the left. Banished from the Tehran court, he was told the shah planned to restore him to favour and, in preparing for the ceremony, he visited this *hamam*, ignorant that it was a royal plot to kill him. At the far end of the garden there is a pleasant tea house where you can enjoy a cup of tea or a cool refreshing drink.

AMIR KABIR (1807–52)

This 'Grand Commander' had lowly beginnings: his father was a cook in the royal palace when he himself started as a stable groom to the court. However, his abilities were quickly recognised and he was soon appointed a finance minister to the military in Iranian Azerbaijan. Aged 22, he joined the diplomatic team sent to St Petersburg and the Russian Caucasus, during which time he visited schools, factories, chambers of commerce and theatres. Only a handful of court officials had been sent abroad and these visits evidently had a lasting impact on him. He returned to the Caucasus in 1837, and spent four years in Erzincan (eastern Turkey) as an official negotiator, drawing up the Iranian–Ottoman frontier. These were the heady years of the Tanzimat period in Ottoman Turkey when the sultanate was yielding to constitutional demands, and undertaking reorganisation programmes affecting every aspect of economic and social life. On his return to Tehran in 1847, Amir Kabir was quickly promoted to tutor of the crown prince, then promoted again to chief army minister, and finally chief minister in 1848.

Iran was teetering on the edge of bankruptcy after paying a huge war indemnity to Russia (Treaty of Turkomanchay 1828), and he moved immediately to fill the state coffers by cutting civil service pay and pensions and ordering tax to be paid direct to Tehran instead of through court tax agents; palace officials were not amused. But the public loved him as he ordered investigations into government corruption and bribery and gave the go-ahead for the construction of bazaars, canals and factories, sending craftsmen to Russia and Ottoman Turkey for training. To stem the flood of imports, customs duties were increased while domestic manufacture and agriculture production were assisted. He was involved in everything, even actively sponsoring private citizens for small-scale contracts, instituting national prizes for art and design, and establishing the first state college organised on Western lines. But, with each project, the anger of his enemies at court intensified. On 16 November 1851 he was dismissed and exiled to Kashan, but that was not enough for his foes, who engineered his assassination in January 1852. With his removal, the reorganisation programme came to a shuddering halt for many decades.

On the old caravan road south to Esfahan is **Qohrud** (قهرود), about 45km away on the Meymeh road, with its masjed-e jame (formerly Masjed-e Ali). The mosque will be locked when you visit, as its lovely Kashan tiles produced in 1307 were stolen in the 1960s, even though they were subsequently recovered and reset in the *mihrab*. It also possesses a fine carved door dedicated to 'The Crown of the Community and Religion … the Seal of the Age', the work of an Esfahani woodworker.

Make every effort to visit **Abyaneh** (ابیانه) (altitude 2,500m) in the hills, some 70km southeast of Kashan, close to Natanz. A small 13th-century fortress (panoramic pictures of the village are best taken from the remains of this fortress) safeguarded this picturesque Zoroastrian village until Safavid sectarian intolerance drove many of the community to India. A ruined but extensive fire temple built in three stages, perhaps dating from the 3rd century CE, lies in the centre of the village, and nearby is the masjed-e jame with a Safavid entry portal and vestibule, with a Seljuk *minbar* and a 14th-century *mihrab* inside the prayer hall. However, the real joy is the vernacular architecture of red mud-brick houses with wooden balconies and decorated doors, in narrow alleyways. There are no buses going this way and you will need to hire a taxi from Kashan. The return journey costs approximately 1,000,000 rials. Alternatively, you can visit the village by taxi from Natanz as intercity Esfahan–Kashan buses should stop here, although not at Abyaneh (but do enquire at the bus station in advance). You can also stay overnight in Abyaneh if you wish to explore the area a little bit more. **Hotel Abyaneh** (30 rooms; ☏031 54282223, 54282230; w hotelabyaneh.com; **$$**), with pleasant staff and simple rooms, is the best choice available.

Alternatively, you could travel to Esfahan, taking the Kashan–Yazd road southeast and turning west at Na'in; this route allows you to see some beautiful monuments en route; see page 162. A short diversion west on this road at Bad leads to **Natanz** (نطنز), past numerous visible anti-aircraft military installations protecting the nearby Natanz nuclear facility. The town itself nestles in the foothills in a beautiful setting, with the remains of the pre-Islamic castle **Qaleh Vashaq** (قلعه وشاق) just to the north. A beautiful portal, decorated with turquoise and cobalt glazed inserts, dated 1317, is the first thing you see at the **masjed-e jame** complex, which dates mainly from post-Mongol times; this led into the *khanqah*, here to accommodate visiting sufis. A much smaller, insignificant doorway takes visitors into the four-*ivan* mosque, built 12 years before, incorporating an earlier Seljuk octagonal structure. The mausoleum of the Sufi sheikh Abd al-Samad al-Esfahani with its tiled tent dome was constructed some two years after. The *muqarnas* vaulting inside is beautiful as is the plasterwork throughout in the complex. Not far away in the northwest is the **Masjed-e Koucheh Mir**, which reportedly still retains a splendid carved plaster *mihrab* (Q11:114–5) dating to the 11th–12th centuries.

ALONG THE KASHAN–YAZD ROAD

Moving from Natanz southeast in the direction of Yazd, there are several interesting towns on the Kashan–Yazd road. Ardestan and, some 15km to the northeast, Zavareh (زواره) (branching off in the centre of Ardestan) are two of the best. **Zavareh** was an important centre on the trade routes from Sasanid times until the late 11th century, which explains the number of important monuments here. The way to the **masjed-e jame** (entry 100,000 rials) is through the covered bazaar, now largely empty. Turn immediately left on entry, passing at the far end a large *hosseiniyeh*

5

hall with great metal *alams* and drapes. This takes you very close to the masjed-e jame, which scholars consider to be one of the earliest-known mosques in Iran, built on the four-*ivan* courtyard plan in 1135, according to the *Kufic* inscription (Q9:18) running unusually around the court façade – such detail is generally placed inside the prayer chamber. Unfortunately, its gentle slide into decline noted in the late 1970s has accelerated, but enough remains of the prayer hall chamber and the occasional column decoration. It has a beautifully carved plaster *mihrab* with Quranic verses (Q7:52) in the angular *Kufic* script, and in cursive *naskhi* (Q9:18), while the dome, supported by trilobed squinches, was decorated with another inscription (Q3:187–8). Slightly to the southeast is the **Masjed-e Pa Menar** of 1069, according to the minaret inscription; this makes it one of the earliest firmly dated monuments to survive in Iran, although most of the mosque's plasterwork is 300 years later. In Zavareh there is at present no tourist accommodation, but Mohammad Abu Talebi (m 0912 4977502) can assist stranded travellers.

Ardestan (اردستان) was a strongly fortified town in the 10th century. Its **Masjed-e Imam Hassan** was founded during Seljuk times as a madrasa, perhaps the first in Iran built with a portal flanked by two minarets, although only one minaret has survived. But the purpose of the visit is the **masjed-e jame** whose domed prayer chamber was built, possibly on top of a fire temple, during the reign of Malik Shah (d1092; see box, page 131). Its main brick inscription concerns further building in 1158, and another in the prayer *ivan* of 1160 perhaps denotes the year when the present four-*ivan* layout was established. The plasterwork here is some of the best surviving in Iran, whether you look at the remains of the delicate trefoil and split palmettes once covering the prayer *ivan*, the deeply cut elegant inscription of the arch-soffits, or the richly carved *mihrab*, and well worth a visit. In the courtyard, there is access down two staircases to the winter prayer hall below, into which light is diffused through alabaster sheets incorporated in the courtyard pavement above.

NA'IN نائین *Telephone code 031*

Na'in (population 29,000), some 95km southeast of Ardestan and 145km east from Esfahan, is a pleasant old town that has managed to preserve some of its traditional charm with clay houses typical of the region. There are frequent buses here from both Yazd and Esfahan (Jey terminal), but it is advisable to book tickets in advance, especially if travelling from Yazd in the afternoon. Buses to and from Tehran also stop at a roundabout outside Na'in, making it a convenient transit point if travelling to smaller towns in the vicinity.

If you are staying overnight here and wish to explore the surrounding area in detail (which might not be a bad idea as most sites here are scattered around), contact local guide Mahmoud Mohammadipur (m 0939 8636090), who is also the author of the Wikitravel internet page on Na'in.

WHERE TO STAY AND EAT

Gol Nargez Hotel (28 rooms) Hossein Fatemi Bd; 46265830. Modern hotel located out of the city centre, but with parking facilities & very clean rooms. **$$**

Tourist Inn (9 rooms) Shahid Rajaie St; 46253088, 46253081. Traditional house with attractive large rooms, 2 inner courtyards & a good restaurant. **$$**

Gholami Guesthouse (11 rooms) Imam Khomeini St & Pirnia St crossroads; m 0913 2234667. Run by Vahid Gholami, the guesthouse offers simple & clean dormitories & en-suite rooms; ideal for a budget traveller. May be closed in low season. Ring to book in advance. **$**

WHAT TO SEE AND DO Most books on Islamic architecture refer to the **masjed-e jame** (off Shohada St; entry 300,000 rials) here, because something of its original 10th-century 'Arab' plan remains. This 'Arab' concept of positioning arcades running parallel to the enclosing walls quickly fell out of favour as more patrons plumped for an open court dominated by two or four tall *ivans*, and a domed prayer chamber. As well as the (much-restored) brick patterning of the courtyard piers, some lovely mid-10th-century plasterwork remains in the prayer chamber, but unfortunately a high wooden railing really limits access and viewing. In the soffits and spandrels of the arches large rosettes have been deeply carved, while some pillars are covered with plaster strapwork framing clusters of small mulberry-like fruits. If only one could get closer. Here and there a few 14th-century tiles enliven the brickwork. To the extreme left as you exit is the *hosseiniyeh* with a real stage for the performance of the Moharram play, and from its far doorway the remains of the town's citadel are visible.

Just across the small square is the local **Ethnographic Museum** in a traditional house (entry 300,000 rials). Mention an ethnographic display and we usually experience a sinking feeling, but this one is housed in a superb Safavid house of 1560. One enters to find a central sunken courtyard with rooms on both levels. Do persuade the knowledgeable curator, who speaks very good English, to take you round; his wife is a noted carpetmaker in the area. He has persuaded the townspeople to lend him interesting archival material, such as marriage contracts, as well as metalwork and ceramic objects. One display contains the *shalvar va qamis* (trousers and tunic) as worn by Zoroastrian women in the 19th century, which are comparable in quality to items in the Victoria and Albert Museum, London; those tiny motifs are not printed but handembroidered. The best is yet to come: the rooms on the right of the entrance are stunning with their mid-16th-century plaster decoration intact. The depictions on the *talar* walls and ceiling tell of the Prophet Yusuf (biblical Joseph), whose beauty was such that the pharaoh's female slaves cut their hands in amazement, and the Egyptian queen, Zulaykha, resorted to covering her bedroom walls with erotic paintings in an attempt to seduce him. Yusuf took to his heels and lived to tell the tale. The small sitting room next door is just as beautifully decorated. There is a striking correlation between this work and designs and compositions on famous Safavid court carpets in major Western museums, and of course Persian paintings of the same date. Behind the museum and visible from the small square in front are the remains of **Na'in Castle**, worth a picture, but there's nothing else to see.

Some 3km away in a northeasterly direction is **Mohammadiyeh**, now virtually absorbed into Na'in. It is known for its wind towers (*badgirs*), some of which serve to ventilate small underground weaving shops producing camel-hair and pure woollen fabrics, used mainly for religious clothing, exported to Syria and Lebanon. The doors are always open and you are welcome to have a look or even purchase. The whole suburb seems to be actively engaged in some form of textile manufacture and Na'in is well known for its weavers. Near Mohammadiyeh there is also an old **Rigareh Watermill** that consists of numerous underground *qanats*, but it can only be visited with a guide.

If you are here with time to spare, visit **Masjed-e Sar-e Kucheh** (ask for directions). The Sar-e Kucheh is (now) a small mosque that looks like a shrine because it has no courtyard, which is unusual for Iran. Both it and the alleyway may date from the 10th–11th century, because entry is through a side chamber into a tiny prayer room, with another side chamber on the other side. Its real claim to fame is the fine *Kufic* inscription painted along the interior walls and the base of the dome. Some of the inscription, especially around the *mihrab*, has now disappeared, but it has a specifically Sunni rather than Shi'a emphasis. This supports a late 11th-century dating, given that the Seljuks, the champions of Sunni Islam, were then in control. The inscription may look battered, but closer inspection reveals beautifully proportioned letters with elegantly curved 'swan-neck' hypostyles.

EN ROUTE FROM NA'IN TO ESFAHAN

The road from Na'in west to Esfahan is dotted with a number of well-preserved caravanserais and desert towns with traditional clay houses. In **Kuhpayeh** (کوهپایه), the **masjed-e jame** has one of the handful of tiled *minbars* still surviving, probably made in 1528 when the tiling scheme in the prayer chamber was installed (although some scholars consider the tiling to be from c1335).

From here one could continue southeast to visit **Varzaneh** (ورزنه), 105km from Esfahan. Coming here by car from Na'in, keep an eye for the sign to turn right after the Red Crescent station. It is roughly 40km from there. Alternatively, there are public buses (hourly between 07.00 & 18.00 daily except Fri, 50,000 rials) from Esfahan and four bus services per day from Varzaneh to Esfahan.

This pleasant agricultural area, with a myriad pigeon towers and beautiful nature, is well worth a few days' exploring. We suggest a two-day (time allowing) stay in Varzaneh's wonderful **Negaar Traditional Guest House** ✴ (page 164); Mohammad Ebrahimi, who runs it, can arrange trips to the stunning sand dunes, Khara Salt Lake and Gavkhouni wetland, famous for its flamingos. Varzaneh is possibly the only place where as you approach you can see three natural phenomena together – sand dunes, shimmering in the sun, on the white surface of the salt lake, the wetlands and a volcanic mountain rising in the middle. The basalt volcanic mountain (*kuh-e siyah* in Farsi) is climbable and views from the top are spectacular. Another interesting site in the vicinity is one of Iran's best-preserved caravanserais – **Qaleh Khargoushi** (Rabbit Castle), 54km away from Varzaneh. In **Negaar Guest House** you can book a sunrise/sunset tour of the caravanserai or simply order a delicious homemade meal if staying overnight or passing by.

You should arrive at Varzaneh's **masjed-e jame** in time for midday prayer (approximately 11.50 but seasonably variable). The reason you should aim for this timing is that the women of this township wear white chadors and seeing them gather for the midday prayer enveloped in their traditional attire creates the image of fluttering doves, going into and leaving the mosque. With a 20m-high minaret, the mosque was built c1100, although it was largely rebuilt in the Timurid 15th century. The tilework of the *ivan* leading to the prayer chamber incorporating the name of Shah Rukh (the son of Timur Leng who took Esfahan in 1417; see box, page 340) on the *minbar* and the *mihrab* is splendid. It is on the *mihrab* that the date 1444 is recorded, after the Quranic inscription (Q3:38–9). The different appearance of the north *ivan* results from 17th-century Safavid repairs. The guardian will suggest you walk behind the mosque, leaving by the left-hand door, facing the prayer chamber, so that you can see the exterior profile of the dome which still retains just a little of two bands of ceramic decoration around the zone of transition. Varzaneh has another treat for those interested in language because most of the residents, formerly a long-surviving Zoroastrian community, still speak a form of Pahlavi. In **Dastjerd** (دستجرد), 30km south of Varzaneh, there is a Zoroastrian *dakhmeh* with an Anahita temple and a clean-water hot spring (where travellers might like to take a plunge, women fully clothed of course).

Along the country road between Varzaneh and Esfahan there are a number of interesting sites to explore. The first is the village of **Ghurtan** (قورتان), with its more than 1,000-year-old citadel built from traditional adobe mud (*kheskt-o-ghel*) and enclosing a residential quarter, three mosques, *hamam* and a bazaar. Ghurtan is the only citadel in the province that is still inhabited.

Further along the road, there are three Seljuk minarets worth stopping for, in Barsiyan, Ziar and, a few kilometres before Esfahan, Jar. The one at **Barsiyan** (برسیان), about 45km southeast of Esfahan on the old caravan road to Yazd, was built in 1097, probably then a little taller than its present 35m. Its cylindrical base has a diameter of 5.75m but it tapers to 4.2m at the top, where there is a brick inscription (Q22:76–7) along with five bands of very fine brick patterning. The minaret and the domed prayer chamber of the mosque below are generally closed to visitors. The key is with the guardian, whose house is in front of the main gate; do not hesitate to knock. It is otherwise a functioning mosque. The inner section dates from the first half of the 12th century, the dome resting on four well-proportioned trilobed squinches and engaged colonettes, with a cut-brick inscription (now damaged); the actual dome, however, had to be rebuilt in 1421. The *mihrab* is from the 16th century with lovely patterned plaster star decoration. Little else remains standing of this structure, but go next door to the Abbasi caravanserai and walk up one or other of the two staircases off the main entrance to the roof and from there look down on to the mosque. It looks as if originally it was a two-*ivan* groundplan including the long, vaulted hall, with remains of two glorious 16th-century tile panels, leading into the domed prayer chamber. That tilework presumably dates from courtyard alterations carried out in the reign of Shah Tahmasp I (1524–76).

Across the river is **Ziar** (زیار), whose Safavid caravanserai was repaired in Qajar times and the amazing minaret here has provoked much discussion. Two very different dates, 1155 and 1289, have been given for this highly decorated shaft, some 50m high with its balcony intact, rising from a square plinth. Turquoise-glazed brick elements were used to pick out the Quranic inscription (Q41:33); these favour the later date. A similar wide dating span has been accorded to another minaret, the Manar-e Sarban in Esfahan (page 175), similarly decorated and with an identical Quranic verse. Here the names of the four caliphs after the death of the Prophet Mohammad are included, so this must be a Sunni, not a Shi'a, monument which strongly suggests it was built during the Seljuk period (eg: around 1155) and this Ziar minaret is now thought to be mid to late 12th century. To round off this collection, the **Jar** (جار) minaret on its octagonal base was built in 1122, according to its inscription, to serve the mosque endowed by Seyyed Reza Abu al-Qasem. Fields now surround it. Reportedly it has a double staircase, but the firmly padlocked door meant checking was impossible.

Some 25km closer to Esfahan on the road from Ziar (and some 75km from Varzaneh), passing through a countryside of wheat, rice and maize, just off the road to the west is **Aziran** (ازیران), where there is a domed mausoleum. It is now freestanding but it was clearly once part of a huge complex judging from the remains of mud- and fired-brick piers around. The dome rests on four lobed squinches similar to those 11th-century domes in the masjed-e jame in Esfahan, leading into a zone of transition composed of 16 blind niches, further decorated with lozenges of squared *Kufic*, but these are probably dated to 19th-century restoration work. There are remains of an elegant cursive *naskhi* inscription in the *mihrab*.

About 65km southeast of Na'in (towards Yazd) is **Aqda** (عقدا) (pronounced *aghda*), famous for its pomegranates, and which was once known as a strong Zoroastrian centre. There are no magnificent historic buildings here, but the village is well worth walking around. Its **masjed-e jame** is thought to date from the 14th century, but only the winter prayer chamber retains an echo of those Timurid proportions, while outside is a large *hosseiniyeh* (1875) for the Moharram ceremonies. A number of Aqda's other monuments have either been extensively rebuilt (eg: Masjed-e Shams 1679) or closed (*hamam* 1645 and cistern 1618). The police have at last vacated the 1846 caravanserai built by the merchant Hajji Abu al-Qasim Rashti, but no-one knows what will happen to the building now. Despite this, the village has a pleasing atmosphere and the locals are very happy but curious that visitors want to walk around exploring the narrow alleys, houses, city gate and so on.

⌂ WHERE TO STAY AND EAT

⌂ **Chapaker Traditional Guest House** (6 rooms) Varzaneh; ☏ 0 913 2030096; e khalilivarzaneh@gmail.com. If Negaar is booked out, this tiny guesthouse is worth trying. **$–$$**

❋ ⌂ **Negaar Traditional Guest House** (15 rooms) Varzaneh; m 0910 8682961; e varzanehtourism@gmail.com; w negaarhouse. com; see ad, page 192. This traditional mud-brick hotel with a courtyard & cosy common areas, inc a rooftop with beautiful views over the masjed-e jame, comes with comfortable en-suite rooms & the best menu in town. All dishes are homemade & you will certainly appreciate a special tea, which Mohammad, the hotel's owner, prepares with care from his collection of herbs. Here he can also organise a wide range of tours, inc to a local *hamam* & a traditional tea evening to learn about Persian & Islamic medicine. **$–$$**

ESFAHAN اصفهان *Telephone code 031*

Esfahan (421km from Tehran) is the most complete, so to speak, city in Iran, and can only be compared, according to André Malraux, French novelist and former minister for cultural affairs, to Florence and Beijing. It is simply remarkable: nowhere else in the country exists such a harmonious mix of modernity and history. Esfahan is truly 'half the world', as an Iranian proverb suggests, and it is impossible to do full justice to all of its historic monuments, but the most famous buildings and some of special interest have been included below.

HISTORY Bisected by the Zayandeh River (Zayandeh Rud) – the name comes from *sipahi*: soldier – Esfahan (altitude 1,585m; population 1.7 million; third-largest Iranian city after Tehran and Mashhad) has been an important trading centre since Parthian times, and possibly both the **Pol-e Shahrestan Bridge** and the **ateshkadeh** (fire temple) just on the outskirts are early Sasanid in construction, built when the city already had separate Jewish and Christian quarters. Esfahan initially was predominantly Jewish with small Zoroastrian and Christian communities. It fell to the Arab Muslims in 643CE and quickly gained a reputation for its textiles, becoming the capital of the Seljuk sultan Toghrol Beg (d1063). Bitter quarrels broke out among local Shi'a and Sunni communities, so its prosperity suffered and then plummeted as the Mongols invaded. Then it was the onslaught of Timur Leng's army, which slew at least 70,000 (and possibly 200,000) Esfahanis. The rivalry between the Aq Qoyunlu and Qara Qoyunlu tribal confederations in the 15th century prevented any sustained revival, but with the Safavid court's move from battle-threatened Tabriz and Qazvin to Esfahan in 1598, the city's fortunes changed.

Town planning began in earnest immediately with the Chahar Bagh gardens, and then the main square with its royal buildings was constructed. According to the French jeweller, Jean Chardin, by the 1660s Esfahan had 162 mosques, 1,802 caravanserais, 48 colleges and 273 public baths to serve a population the size of London's, then about 600,000. The sheer scale and the beauty of its buildings

Ancient Persia would have developed quite differently if not for the caravanserais (from Persian *caravan* 'travelling group' and *saray* for 'house/place'), synonymous with the Silk Road routes. These ancient inns or places of rest were built at intervals of 30–40km: the maximum distance that a caravan could travel in one day. Herodotus had recorded as early as the 5th century BCE the existence of such places welcoming travellers between Susa and Sardes along the 2,500km-long Royal Road built by the Achaemenids. *Khans*, caravanserais or *robats* were open to travellers from all over the world, of all religions and all trades. The system of underground *qanat* lines, which in 2016 were collectively designated as a UNESCO World Heritage Site, used for capturing underground water and transporting it to the valleys, would have usually run along the caravanserai route.

Over time caravanserais developed beyond their original function; they became economic and security hubs and religious places, particularly with the arrival of Islam, which had also brought the improvement in architecture. Original caravanserais were simple structures bearing no decoration, other than the grandiose main entrance, and comfort varied greatly. During Safavid rule caravanserai structure changed from stone to brick. Residential structures built around the central courtyard would often be two storeys with the ground floor used for storage of goods and the first floor for the actual residential quarters.

The end of the golden age of the Silk Road(s) and caravanserais arrived with the opening of trading sea routes. Nonetheless, in order to attract traders and travellers, Shah Abbas I ordered more caravanserais to be built, thus bringing the total number of active caravanserais to 3,000. With further decline in East–West trade and the subsequent emergence of steamboats and rail routes, it became impractical and unprofitable to run a caravanserai and although some have been restored and converted into luxurious hotels in recent years, most have been abandoned and destroyed over time. Caravanserai ruins now gracefully decorate the Iranian landscape, in particular around Yazd and Esfahan.

amazed most foreign visitors who marvelled at the turquoise domes and the dramatic minarets. But the Safavid regime was beginning to crack at the seams and in 1722 the capital was besieged for six months by Afghan rebels. Plague outbreaks and famine followed. Nader Qoli (later Nader Shah Afshar) ousted the Afghans but transferred the administration to Mashhad. By 1800 the population of Esfahan was probably only 120,000.

Esfahan today is a prosperous city with an incomparably beautiful main square and a rich culture of handicrafts. After 1960 the old gardens along Chahar Bagh were replaced with shopping areas and in 2018 the central part of this leafy avenue was pedestrianised, turning it into a very pleasant public space.

GETTING THERE AND AWAY There are daily **flights** from Istanbul and two flights weekly from Dubai (with Flydubai; page 48), as well as regular services from major cities in Iran. Esfahan has four bus terminals: Kaveh (North) [169 F1]; Sofeh (South) [169 E7]; Zayandeh Rud (West) [168 A6]; and Jey (East) [169 H2], and is well connected by numerous intercity **buses**. Check in advance with the bus driver as some buses arriving in Esfahan go to both Kaveh and Sofeh terminals. There is a service every half-hour from both Tehran's Southern and Eastern terminals and hourly departures from Shiraz (Karandish terminal).

You can reach the city by a daily **train** service from Tehran (page 61). Esfahan railway station [169 E7] is a few kilometres further along the road after Sofeh bus terminal. You can also arrive here by **taxi** directly from Imam Khomeini Airport in Tehran for around US$80. The taxi-hire desk is at the airport's arrivals floor.

GETTING AROUND Once in the city, the major Safavid buildings are located within **walking** distance of Naqsh-e Jahan or Imam Square [169 F3] (Maydan-e Naqsh-e Jahan or Maydan-e Imam in Persian), but for less-frequented monuments, it is best to hire a **taxi** especially for Pirbakran and Ashtarjan (page 189), or Varzaneh, Barsiyan, Ziar and Jar (page 163). To save money, avoid hiring a taxi anywhere around Naqsh-e Jahan Square. Taxi drivers take advantage of tourists unfamiliar with local prices and regularly quote double the actual fare. Do negotiate. As a pointer, a taxi drive across the whole city should cost 300,000–500,000 rials. **Snapp** phone app taxi service offers the best value for money.

A newly completed single-line **metro** (10,000 rials) is convenient and connects the two main Kaveh and Sofeh bus terminals. The official metro website is alas in Persian only and so is the map online. For metro stations, see map, page 168. Inner-city **bus** (15,000 rials) services are frequent and reliable. The **Esfahan Card** (w escard.ir) can be purchased and topped-up at ticket kiosks by most bus stops in the city or in the metro and can be used for all public transport in Esfahan. **Bicycle** rental kiosks (⊕ 08.00–14.00 & 15.00–18.30; 5,000 rials per 30mins; 100,000 rials for 30mins for electric bike) are located at main street intersections and tourist areas and although the rule says it that only men may rent bicycles, the further the kiosk from a mosque or a police station, the more likely female customers will be accommodated.

The centre of Esfahan is **pedestrian-friendly**, especially after the stretch of Chahar Bagh Street between Se-o-Se Pol and Darvazeh Dowlat Square was pedestrianised in 2018.

TOUR GUIDE AND TOURIST INFORMATION

Tourist information office [map, page 182]
Next to the entrance of the Ali Qapu Palace;
w isfahancht.ir; ⊕ 09.00–14.30 Sat–Wed,
09.00–12.30 Thu, longer hrs during Nou Rouz & in summer. Drop in for a free map of the city.
Alireza Damadzadeh m 0913 3049056;
e ardamadzadeh@gmail.com. English-speaking guide for the city, hiking & nature tours in Esfahan & beyond.

Shiva Khanbani m 0937 3968343; e chiva. khanbani@gmail.com. Recommended French-speaking guide for the city & environs.
Maryam Mirshafiee m 0935 6884054;
e mirshafiee.maryam@gmail.com. Offers well-organised & informative tours & visits in English & Italian.

 WHERE TO STAY Esfahan has a number of traditional historic houses that have been converted into boutique hotels. Some of them strive to preserve an air of exclusivity and self-importance, which at times makes booking a room or getting in touch somewhat tedious. Here we have selected some of the friendliest and most welcoming of them.

Luxury and above average

✳ 🏠 **Hotel Abbasi** [169 E4] (220 rooms)
Amadegah St; ☏ 32226010–19; w abbasihotel.
ir. Full of character & grandeur, this is one of

the best hotels in Iran. Rooms overlooking the inner courtyard come with small balconies & a large price tag. Cheaper options are substantially smaller. Staff wear traditional clothes & are exceptionally courteous. The abundant b/fast is served in the spectacular 1st-floor hall painted in traditional Persian style. In addition to an indoor swimming pool (⏱ 08.00–14.00 for women & 16.00–22.00 for men) there are various souvenir & carpet shops, & the tea house serves delicious tea with local Esfahani *gooshfil* sweets & *ash-e reshteh* winter noodle soup. **$$$$**

🏠 **Hotel Kowsar Parsian** [169 E5] (132 rooms) Mellat Bd; ☎ 350450; w hotelkowsar. com. Located by the Se-o-Se Pol bridge, this is a fine 4-star hotel with good service & excellent facilities. Rooms with a view of the river come with small balconies & the traditional tea house here is popular among Esfahani socialites. There is an outdoor swimming pool, which means it is for men only & closed in winter. **$$$$**

Mid-range

🏠 **Atigh Hotel** [169 G1] (30 rooms) 37 Alley, off Ibn Sina St; ☎ 34453328–9; w atighhotel.com. Opened in late 2013, the Atigh has been finely restored with 2 inner courtyards. All rooms are en suite, although double rooms are a little small; bulky beds take away some of the interior charm & space. Staff are, however, polite & very helpful. **$$$**

🏠 **Esfahan Traditional Hotel** [map, page 182] (15 rooms) Hakim St; ☎ 32236677. Opened in 2007, this pleasant hotel, located in a restored historic residence, offers spacious rooms & a welcoming inner courtyard. There is also a good restaurant ($–$$). **$$$**

🏠 **Keshish House** [168 A4] (11 rooms) Zeitoon Alley, Sangtarashsha St; ☎ 36255918; w keshishhouse.com. This former Safavid-period residence of a prominent local priest (hence the name *keshish* meaning 'priest' in Persian) was in spring 2019 converted into a delightful traditional hotel with a very spacious & leafy inner courtyard. Although gently commercial, its overall atmosphere is welcoming. Personnel are attentive & rooms are beautifully decorated. By far the best accommodation option in Jolfa. **$$$**

🏠 **Partikan Hotel** [map, page 182] (11 rooms) Saadi St; ☎ 32214291, 32214264; w partikanhotel.com. Modern, comfortable apt-style rooms, each at least 30m² in size. It is the location, though, just off Naqsh-e Jahan Sq that makes all the difference. **$$$**

🏠 **Sepahan Hotel** [169 G4] (42 rooms) Farshadi St; ☎ 32221235; w sepahanhotel.com.

Traditionally decorated & in good taste. The inner atrium gives the hotel an airy meringue feel. The Sepahan's highlight, however, is the 4th-floor 70-seat restaurant with spectacular views over the rooftops of Naqsh-e Jahan Sq & adjoining markets. The staff are pleasant & courteous & the walk there lies through the old market, if approaching from Naqsh-e Jahan Sq. **$$$**

Lower mid-range

✴ 🏠 **Howzak House** [169 G1] [(5 rooms) 31 Arabha Alley, behind masjed-e jame; m 0937 9652371; w howzak-house.com. Without exaggeration, the nicest hotel in Esfahan & probably the entire province, the Howzak epitomises taste, tradition & Iranian hospitality. Run by Nassim & Babak, who have carefully selected & taken care of every single detail in this wonderful traditional residence, rooms are delightful with custom-designed furniture & bed linen. With the exception of a few necessary changes, Howzak is warmly authentic. B/fast & homemade meals are excellent & so is the service from start to finish. Here you can also book highly recommended cultural, music & history tours. Member of the 'Mehmoun' association. **$$**

🏠 **Tourist Hotel** [169 E4] (25 rooms) Abbas Abad St; ☎ 32204437; w etouristhotel.com. A simple hotel with Wi-Fi & pleasant staff. Newly renovated lobby is tiny & rooms are standard, but location is good & so is value for money. **$$**

Basic and hostels

🏠 **Amir Kabir Hostel** [169 E2] (32 rooms; 100 beds) Takhti St, next door to the stadium; ☎ 32227273; e mrziaee@hotmail.com. Located in the bustling sports district of Esfahan, this central hostel has over the past few years lost some of its shine & old-fashioned charm. Offers clean & very basic dormitory-style accommodation or private rooms with or without bathroom. The inner courtyard is a cosy place to relax after a day of sightseeing. **$–$$**

🏠 **Mah Bibi Hostel** [169 G4] (8 rooms) Intersection of Chahar Bagh Khaju St & Felestin St; ☎ 32200777; m 0913 4067845; w mahbibihostel. com. A newly opened guesthouse/hostel offering single rooms & dorm-style accommodation in the city centre. There is a pleasant inner courtyard & the décor is a tasteful compromise between a traditional house & modernity. **$–$$**

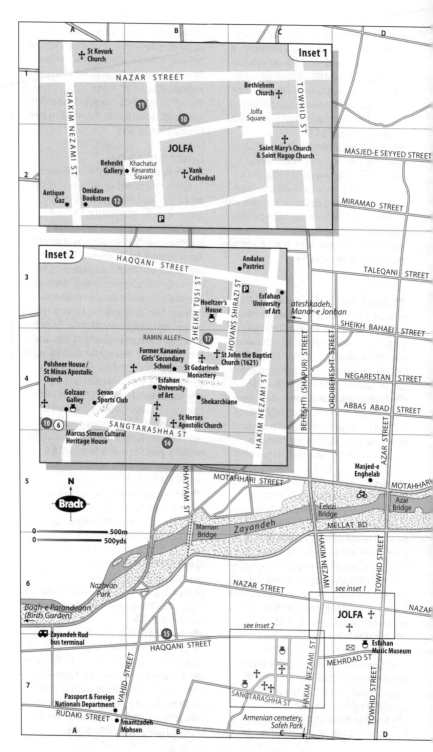

Inset 1

St Kevork Church

NAZAR STREET

HAKIM NEZAMI ST

Bethlehem Church

Jolfa Square

TOWHID ST

MASJED-E SEYYED STREET

⓫

⓾

JOLFA

Saint Mary's Church & Saint Hagop Church

Behesht Gallery

Khachatur Kesaratsi Square

Vank Cathedral

MIRAMAD STREET

Antique Gaz

Omidan Bookstore ⓬

P

Inset 2

HAQQANI STREET

Andalus Pastries

TALEQANI STREET

SHEIKH TUSI ST

HOVANS SHIRAZI ST

P

Hoeltzer's House

Esfahan University of Art

ateshkadeh, Manar-e Jonban

SHEIKH BAHAEI STREET

RAMIN ALLEY

⓱

Former Kananian Girls' Secondary School

St John the Baptist Church (1621)

St Gadarineh Monastery

BEHESHTI (SHAPUR) STREET

ORDIBEHESHT STREET

NEGARESTAN STREET

Polsheer House / St Minas Apostolic Church

Esfahan University of Art

Shekarchiane

HAKIM NEZAMI ST

ABBAS ABAD STREET

Golzaar Galley

Sevan Sports Club

AZAR STREET

⓾ ⑥

St Nerses Apostolic Church

SANGTARASHHA ST

Marcus Simon Cultural Heritage House

⓮

Masjed-e Enghelab

MOTAHHARI STREET

MOTAHHAR

N

Bradt

Felezi Bridge

Azar Bridge

Marnan Bridge

Zayandeh

MELLAT BD

0 ———— 500m
0 ———— 500yds

HAKIM NEZAMI

see inset 1

TOWHID STREET

Nazhvan Park

NAZAR STREET

JOLFA ✝

NAZAR

Bagh-e Parandegan (Birds Garden)

✝

Zayandeh Rud bus terminal

see inset 2

Esfahan Music Museum

HAQQANI STREET

⓯

VAHID STREET

MEHRDAD ST

Passport & Foreign Nationals Department

SANGTARASHHA ST

HAKIM NEZAMI ST

TOWHID STREET

RUDAKI STREET

Imamzadeh Mohsen

Armenian cemetery, Sofeh Park

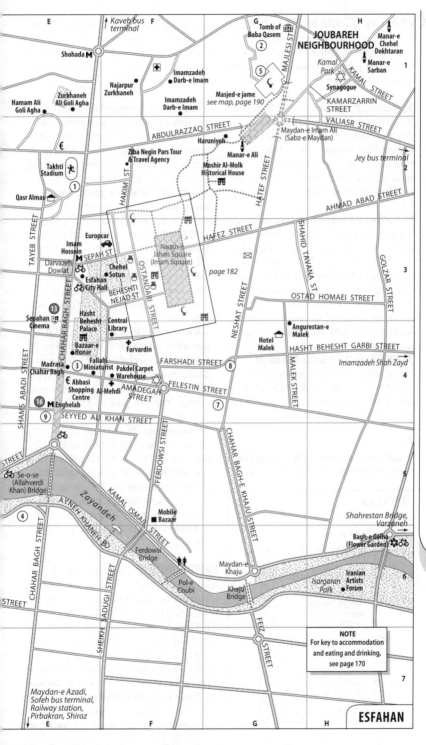

ESFAHAN

NOTE
For key to accommodation
and eating and drinking,
see page 170

✕ WHERE TO EAT AND DRINK Esfahan has a fantastic choice of cafés and restaurants and over the past few years a number of historic houses have been converted into atmospheric restaurants. A few very good cafés and restaurants are neatly packed within the **Jolfa Quarter** [168 D6] (page 185) and the area around Naqsh-e Jahan Square [map, page 182] is now bustling with very good coffee places.

✕ Shahrzad Restaurant [169 E4] Abbas Abad St; ☏ 32204490; ⊕ 11.30–22.30. In operation since 1967, this local favourite restaurant serves excellent & filling traditional dishes; lamb shank *mahicheh* is particularly delicious here. Large groups of tourists can alas be a little too noisy. One of the few places where leaving a tip is expected. **$$**

✕ Traditional Banquet Hall [map, page 182] Naqsh-e Jahan Restaurant, Naqsh-e Jahan Sq, through a small alley, past a tiny shopping yard & up on the 1st floor; ☏ 32200729; ⊕ noon–15.30 & 19.00–22.30. A delight of a place & an Iranian cuisine experience. Has indoor & outdoor seating areas overlooking the yard & the Sheikh Lotfallah Mosque. Try traditional Esfahani dish minced lamb *beryani* or *kofteh*, traditional meatballs. A little touristy, though. **$$**

✕ Jarchi Bashi Malek Soltan Restaurant [map, page 182] Masjed-e Hakim Alley; ☏ 32207418; w jarchibashi.ir; ⊕ noon–16.00 & 19.30–23.00 daily. An atmospheric traditional restaurant with a good choice of classic Iranian dishes. **$**

Cafés

☀ ☕ Café Radio [169 E3] Opposite Sepahan Cinema, Sepahan Alley; ☏ 32232701; ⊕ 08.00–

midnight. One of the most delightful cafés in Iran, serving delicious drinks & light meals. Iced coffee is particularly recommended. Atmosphere is excellent & Wi-Fi is reliable. Other branches are on Saadi St & Ostandari St (⊕ 08.00–midnight daily) next door to Hasht Behesht Gallery. **$$**

☀ ☕ Chah Haj Mirza Azadegan Tea House [map, page 182] Through the narrow alley at the top of Naqsh-e Jahan Sq; ⊕ 09.00–23.00 daily. This basement tea house has become an institution & a must when in Esfahan. Serves delicious *abgoosht* & tea or *dough* with *gooshfil*, as well as b/fast. Full of character & antique clocks, lamps, *kashkuls* & pictures suspended from the ceiling. Be discreet & avoid coming in large groups. **$$**

☕ Namakdan Café [map, page 182] Posht-e Matbakh St; ☏ 32247313; ⊕ 10.00–midnight daily. A new atmospheric café with an extensive menu of traditional dishes & drinks. Their beautiful outdoor courtyard is ideal for a glass of refreshing lemonade after a few hours' exploring the Naqsh-e Jahan Sq. **$$**

☕ Qeysariyeh Café [map, page 182] Qeysariyeh Bazaar; ☏ 32238230; ⊕ 09.00–21.00 daily; entry 300,000 rials. With the views hard to beat, under the vaults of Qeysariyeh Bazaar and the terrace overlooking Naqsh-e Jahan Sq, it is the location that is the main item on the menu here. Come in the eves, when the square is beautifully lit, & notice a glass of water will slowly turn into wine. **$$**

ENTERTAINMENT Esfahan city has a number of good *zurkhanehs* (wrestling gymnasiums; see box, page 172). In the northern part of the city, **Zurkhaneh Ali Goli Agha** [169 E1] (in the garden behind Hamam Ali Goli Agha) regularly hosts inter-province competitions. Performances are held daily at around 21.00 and female visitors are allowed in. There is no entrance fee, but you are welcome to make a small contribution to the guardian. Performances in **Najarpur**

Zurkhaneh [169 F1] (Sonbalsotun St 21, off Abdulrazzaq St) also start at 21.00. **Hassan Abad Zurkhaneh** (Ghasr Monshi Alley, near Naqsh-e Jahan Sq), established in 1897, is open to both female and male visitors between 18.00 and 23.00.

If modern and contemporary art is of interest, a number of small and private galleries in the Jolfa neighbourhood (page 185) hold regular exhibitions. Persian speakers may also like to attend a theatre performance in the small concert/cinema hall **Talar-e Sureh** on the lower ground level of the **Abbasi Shopping Centre** [169 E4]. Enquire inside for upcoming events.

SHOPPING There are a myriad workshops and small stores all around Naqsh-e Jahan Square selling handmade goods, silverware, etc, but for cash only. A handful of these places will accept credit cards and always at an extra charge of around 10%. For carpet shop suggestions, see box, page 180.

Books

Abbasi Shopping Centre [169 E4] Opposite Hotel Abbasi; 36681266; ⊕ 08.30–18.30 daily. The 2-storey shop has a wide range of books in Persian & some classics in English, & also houses the **Iranian Cultural Heritage, Handicrafts and Tourism Organisation shop** (street level), **Iran Travel Agency** & **IranAir** main sales office.

Omidan Bookstore [168 A2] Jolfa; 36266749; ⊕ 09.00–13.00 daily (except public holidays) (page 70). Specialising in English-language books, in particular Oxford University Press, & books for learning foreign languages.

Clothes

Dojdis Gallery [map, page 182] 64 Spadana Complex, Naqsh-e Jahan Sq; m 0936 8145143. This tiny store is the only one outside Tehran selling traditional handmade *giveh* shoes by Av Val (w avvalfootwear.com). The quality is superb & the price fair. Highly recommended souvenir.

Jewellery

Dayyani Gallery 21 Jahangiri Saray, Qeysariyeh Bazaar [map, page 182]; 32238306; m 0913 1196204; ⊕ 09.00–21.00 daily. For delicate & fine gold, silver & turquoise jewellery, this gallery is recommended.

Saee Art Gallery [map, page 182] 25 Saadi St; m 0913 1144326; e saeeartgallery@gmail.com; ⊕ 10.00–19.00 Sun–Thu. This is a family-run gallery making very fine & delicate silver jewellery & art pieces. Prices are a little higher than average, but the quality & work in the items is well worth the price tag.

Miniatures

Hossein Fallahi Miniaturist Shop Main store: 5 Saadi St [map, page 182], 51 Posht-e Matbakh [map, page 182] & 100 Amadegah St, opposite Hotel Abbasi [169 E4]; 32226733; w artacrafts. com; ⊕ 08.30–13.00 & 15.00–20.30. With easily the largest selection of miniature art pieces in Esfahan, this shop is highly recommended. The choice of works is superb & credit cards (with 5% extra charge) are accepted. They also run an online store with shipment possible worldwide.

Prints and postcards

Hasht Behesht Art Gallery [map, page 182] 149 Ostandari St, opposite Hasht Behesht St; m 0913 1115670; ⊕ 17.30–20.30 Sun–Wed. Run by a wonderfully pleasant artist, Soleiman Sassoon has lovely old prints & a nice selection of postcards.

OTHER PRACTICALITIES The central district for mobile-phone and **SIM card** services is Ahmad Abad Square, at the intersection with Bozorgmehr Street, where the first few rows of buildings are taken up by mobile-phone shops. Alternatively, there are a few shops around Esfahan Mobile Market at the bottom of Ferdowsi Street. The central **post office** is on Neshat Street [169 G3] and a smaller one [map, page 182] on Naqsh-e Jahan Square. Postcards and stamps are sold in the bazaar (especially around Sheikh Lotfallah Mosque) and some souvenir shops in larger and traditional hotels. A small kiosk at the entrance to the Chehel Sotun Palace

The sport of wrestling has always been popular in Iran. From ancient times, a special form of spiritual fighting developed in the so-called *zurkhanehs* (literally 'houses of strength') which became widespread at the time of the Arab invasion. People escaped to caves and trained clandestinely in stylised military movements in preparation for resistance to the approaching invaders.

Wealthy merchants and court officials traditionally sponsored wrestling teams and patronised the *zurkhanehs* where the athletes practised calisthenic exercises. Traditionally, a young man has to be at least 16 years old, with a beard growth thick enough to support a comb, before being accepted for training. There are some 50 holds to learn and two tests to pass before being recognised as a junior athlete, and progress is shown in the ways the wrap is worn around the hips. Only a select few have ever been acknowledged as champion, or *pahlavan* (one reason why Reza Khan chose this title as his dynastic name in 1925).

The exercise and wrestling place is one and the same: a sunken area (*gowd* in Persian), often octagonal in shape, large enough to hold 12 to 18 men during their exercising. One English visitor in 1833 described it with 'seats for the spectators … the roof, which was plastered, was painted all over with fierce figures of *pahlavans* performing their various feats of strength'. Today the *zurkhaneh* walls are usually decorated with photographs of past and present wrestlers, and objects strongly identified with Sufi and dervish fraternities, like *kashkul* beggar's bowls, axes, a sheepskin mat and posters of Imam Ali, the shrines of Karbala and Mashhad. This association with Ali and his descendants is stressed as the *morshid* (leader) beats out the rhythm for each exercise while shouting out Shi'a sayings. Each calisthenic exercise builds up the muscles: a wooden board to strengthen the shield arm, 'Indian' clubs (*mil* in Persian) weighing anything from 4kg to 40kg substituting for heavy warclubs, and an iron bow to exercise shoulder muscles. The gymnasts' strength is publicly recognised every year when they are asked to carry the heavy *alam* standards in the Moharram parades, but in the 1960s–70s many *zurkhanehs* were closed down as the late shah grew nervous about their members' loyalty to the crown.

also has a good choice of postcards. **Pharmacies** and **medical centres** are all closely packed on Amadegah Street, where there is an all-night pharmacy Al-Mehdi [169 F4]. There is also a Farvardin pharmacy [map, page 182] (⊕ 08.00–midnight) in the Farhanghian Clinic (⊕ 24/7) on Hasht Behesht Street. To arrange an extension to your visa, go to the **Passport & Foreign Nationals Department** [168 A7] (Rudaki St; ⊕ 07.30–13.30 Sat–Wed, 07.30–11.30 Thu). In central Esfahan there are several **exchange** kiosks, in particular on Sepah Street and Ostandari Street [both map, page 182]. The central **tourist police office** [map, page 182] is the small glass kiosk-building on Naqsh-e Jahan Square.

WHAT TO SEE AND DO Esfahan is simply splendid. The Naqsh-e Jahan Square (at present also known as Imam Square, but formerly Shah Abbas Square) will most likely be the first place you visit here and is visually breathtaking. Esfahanis are also perhaps the most craft-minded bunch in the country, as certified by the abundant workshops and exquisite carpet stores, but they are also notoriously most difficult to bargain with. Do not count on any serious discounts.

It is the history and its remnants, unlike Shiraz that has witnessed the destruction of most of its historical heritage in earthquakes, that make this city the gem of Iran. Esfahan is also by far the most religiously and culturally diverse Iranian city. If you intend to visit as many sites here as possible, then you will need at least a week. The list below is not exhaustive; places that are particularly worth a visit are marked with ✳. You may also want to leave a day aside for shopping: Esfahan is a great place to buy souvenirs or carpets. For special and unique pieces, book an arts tour with Howzak House (page 167) to visit some of the city's best workshops.

Driving to Esfahan from the west Just 7km from the centre, visitors see a rocky outcrop with the remains of a 13th-century citadel and so-called **Sasanid ateshkadeh** or fire temple (off Saremiyeh St; ⊕ 08.30–17.00; entry 300,000 rials) on top. It is best seen at sunset; the view over the surrounding area is glorious. About 1km further on (on the same side), is a garden with a small building, the **Manar-e Jonban** ('Shaking Minarets') (Saremiyeh St; ⊕ 08.30–17.00, closed for lunch; entry 300,000 rials). Unless you have extra time, both can be ignored particularly because neither is on a direct bus route from the city centre. However, as both are often promoted as tourist highspots, a few details are included here. The energetic can climb up the Ateshkadeh Hill for a panoramic view, smog permitting, but take care as there is no defined path. Apart from the huge concrete cistern, the visible remains probably date no earlier than the 13th/14th century, when it was a signal tower in the city defences. As for the shaking minarets, this small building over a tomb takes its name from its two small towers, one or other of which is, at certain times, clasped in a firm embrace by an attendant at roof level and rocked back and forth; it and the other clearly move. For onlookers at ground level, it is quite dramatic as deep cracks in the towers and walls visibly open. Lord Curzon wryly reported in 1892 that many travellers 'have exhausted their ingenuity' trying to explain this phenomenon: an underground chain linking the two minarets; an inner vertical beam in each tower resting in a socle; or a horizontal beam within the arch brickwork on which the minarets are 'balanced'. We prefer the theory that it is the Sufi sheikh Amu Abdallah in his 1317 grave beneath the building, shaking with fury at being disturbed yet again.

Believe us, a **pigeon tower** (*borj-e kabutar*) is far, far more interesting and spectacular. There are plenty of them scattered around the province. There is a Sasanid example dating back to the 16th or 17th century in Esfahan on Mardovich Square south of the Zayandeh River. It is well preserved with pigeons still nesting inside. A very kind guardian will let you climb up to the rooftop, but do leave a small donation before leaving. There are also marvellous examples of pigeon towers near Pirbakran (page 188) so you could combine visits to this, Pirbakran itself and also Ashtarjan by hiring a taxi for half a day.

The northern historic neighbourhoods of Esfahan The highlight of this area is the UNESCO-listed **masjed-e jame** ✳ [169 G1] (Majlesi St; ⊕ 08.00–11.00 & 13.00–17.00; entry 500,000 rials; free during prayer times & religious holidays), an architectural treasure in its own right. Just beyond the ticket office is a small room displaying a scale model of the complex and photographs of the Italian archaeological finds of the 1970s. The rather dusty, insignificant-looking pillars with decorated brick-plugs to one side date back to the 10th century when a small 'Arab'-style mosque was built here on the remains of a fire temple. Then, between 1072 and 1092, work began in earnest: two huge domed chambers were constructed, one inside the complex, the other just outside. After a serious attack by the Assassins (see box, page 131) in 1122, as recorded on the northeast door, the mosque was reorganised according to a four-*ivan* plan, and then two centuries later extensively redecorated and repaired by the Mongol Ilkhanids. Some 50 years later the local Muzaffarid rulers extended the mosque, bringing the second Seljuk domed chamber into the enclosure. Thereafter, work in the mosque was more or less confined to replacing tile and plasterwork.

From the main entrance, rather than continuing down to the central courtyard, cross over and walk through the arcades in a clockwise direction and you'll soon realise how beautiful (and subtly coloured) brickwork can be, and how quickly your film is disappearing or your memory card being filled up. A yellow tile panel, far left, describes repair work after Iraqi bomb damage in the 1980s. This is the way to the first of two magnificent, 11th-century **'true' domes**, covering the south chamber, constructed on the order of the Seljuk vizier and scholar Nizam al-Molk (d1092) around 1087, judging from the titles used in the dome inscription. Let your eyes become accustomed to the darkness; what remains of the 10th-century plasterwork was probably once richly painted like the interior of Southwark Cathedral, London. Huge brick pillars support this glorious dome (diameter c17m), the four massive trilobed squinches and the 16-sided zone of transition. Ideally, the thickness of the 'perfect dome' at its apex should be $^1/_{45}$ of the diameter; here it is $^1/_{42}$. To meet the lateral thrust of the dome, the inclination should be 5:1; here it is 4.5:1. Compare this with St Paul's Cathedral, London, which was built some 600 years later and its dome is conical. As one architectural historian wrote: 'The Seljuks ... solved the difficulties which [Sir Christopher] Wren avoided.'

If you want to see yet more brick-patterned vaults, continue walking through, skirting the courtyard. At the far end is a small 'shrine', in the past boarded up by the authorities as 'un-Islamic'; the thick soot betrays years of candle burning. Moving into the courtyard, you pass the second large 'teachers' *ivan*' decorated on the order of Shah Hossein, later murdered in the madrasa near to the Hotel Abbasi. The small door to its right takes you into a mid-15th-century chamber containing the famous 1310 carved plaster *mihrab*, constructed in honour of the Ilkhanid ruler, Oljeitu (page 236). Its long inscription surprisingly contains no Quranic verses, but eulogises Oljeitu alongside references to Ali, the first imam – so it clearly dates from before Oljeitu's conversion to Sunni Islam. From this room another door leads down to the Safavid **winter mosque** with transverse vaulting springing from floor level. You will have to ask the guardian to unlock it and, more importantly, switch on the lights.

In the courtyard again, walk down to the next (north) *ivan*, known as the *sofeh* ('meeting or sitting area') of the dervishes. Its elegant plaster cartouches and lozenge-shaped decorations were part of the 1682 repairs undertaken during the reign of Safavid shah Soleyman. A new door to the right takes you to the other dome chamber (c22m high, diameter c11m), built by Taj al-Molk, Nizam al-Molk's bitter political rival, and perhaps designed by the famous poet-mathematician, Omar Khayyam. Built in 1089 and at that time *outside* the mosque, it perhaps functioned as a robing, meditation or judicial chamber for the Seljuk ruler. Its proportions are so pleasing to the Western eye, relating as they do to the golden mean (the ratio of the shorter side to the longer in the golden rectangle – 1:1.6180339887 – usually called by the Greek letter phi (f)) used by architects of Renaissance Europe. The dome inscription (Q7:52, 54), describing the creation of the world in six days ends with 'Is it not His to create and govern?' before immediately giving the Seljuk vizier's Persian titles and date; the implication is undeniable. The 32 blind niches in the zone of transition have short inscriptions, each specifying a name or quality of the Almighty, while those across the large niche panels are Quranic (Q17:79–81).

After taking photographs of the courtyard, most visitors leave, but if time allows, look at the small madrasa behind the 'students' *ivan*' with its fine mid-14th-century mosaic tile decoration. Because the Muzaffarid ruler who paid for the work was Sunni, the star motifs in the vault include references to the first three caliphs (after the death of the Prophet) recognised by the Sunnis but not Shi'as. Returning to the courtyard *ivan*, on the far back wall, a grille protects other Sunni formulae. As you leave the complex, a little before the ticket office, tucked back on the right in deep shadow, you will find another elaborate plaster *mihrab*, presumably dating from the early 14th century.

We should say a word about the mosque gates. The present main (southeast) entrance was repaired in 1804 according to its inscription, while the southwest one is dated 1591. The north gate, usually locked, carries a lengthy Quranic inscription (Q76:1–27) describing the delights and rewards in paradise, while that on the northeastern entrance (Q2:114) clearly refers to repairs after the Assassins' attack in 1121: 'Who is more wicked than the men who seek to destroy the mosques of Allah?'

East of masjed-e jame Across Majlesi Street lies **Joubareh** (محله جویباره) [169 H1], a Jewish neighbourhood, where on Kamarzarrin Street there are still a number of functioning synagogues. The Jewish community in Esfahan dates from the 7th century BCE and is the largest in Iran. Many Jews also moved here in the early 17th century with the resettlement of Armenians and established their homes in New Jolfa (page 185) south of the Zayandeh River. At present, however, there are only 12 synagogues left (down from 20 in 1972) and the community is mainly active around Kamarzarrin Street and near the Jewish Association of Esfahan on Felestine Square behind the blue gates and tall yellow brick walls. Walking down Kamarzarrin Street from Kamal Street, Jewish buildings are recognisable by their low entrances and distinctive glazed domes. Starting from Kamal Park, the first is the Qajar-period **Synagogue of Rabbi Yaakov Zayil**, located at the back of the tomb of Esfahani poet Kamal al-Din Ismail, which was restored in 2000. Walking a few hundred metres down on the opposite side of the street is **Synagogue of Moshe Haia**. Further down to the left in the centre of an open space used as a car park, stands another Qajar-period **Synagogue of Hajji Eliyahu**. A much larger, but somewhat desolate looking on the opposite side of Kamarzarrin Street is **Synagogue Hannisen and his wife Haninin**, dating to 1916. The stone plaque above the entrance below street level, bears the Hebrew tombstone inscription *tantzava* meaning 'The soul of my lord shall be bound in the bundle of life' (1 Samuel 25:29, King James Bible), suggesting perhaps the location of a tomb. Next door to this is Vali Asr theological school (Imam Hassan Askari centre). If you would like to attend a *shabbat* service, walk around the area to see which of the synagogues is open. Be discreet and arrive at around 05.00 on Saturday; most services are over by 09.00.

In the northern part of Joubareh (see above), is the **Manar-e Sarban** (منار ساربان) [169 H1] ('camel-driver's minaret'), a fine minaret, possibly Seljuk mid 12th century, amid small houses whose front doors often have two knockers, each with a distinctive shape and sound so those inside could know if a male or female visitor was calling. This phenomenon may also be observed in traditional quarters elsewhere in Iran. The mosque has long gone, but the doorway (through which you can see the spiral staircase) some 5m up probably marked the connection with the mosque roof. Standing about 30m high, it still possesses after seven centuries good brick patterns and glazed inserts, although its balcony has gone. From here you can see the **Manar-e Chehel Dokhtaran** (مناره چهل دختران) [169 H1] (off

Maydan-e Qods (formerly Tughchi) Soroush St), which has also lost its mosque, but the staircase doorway remains. There are no coloured glazed inserts, but just look at the richness of the brickwork. Up the cylindrical shaft (24m high) there are more than seven patterned zones of rhomboids, lozenges, octagons and six-pointed stars, picked out in recessed and relief brick. Near its base, a six-line *Kufic* inscription panel gives the construction date (1108), making this one of the earliest minarets to survive in Iran.

Just off the Baba Qasem intersection nearby is the 1880 tiled tent-roof of the small, rather neglected **Tomb of Baba Qasem** (مقبره بابا قاسم) [169 G1] (pronounced *ghasem*), built by a certain Soleyman Abdul Hassan Tahit al-Damghani in 1341 'with the intention of honouring the theologian who has departed for Paradise'. The key is held by the man in the shop next door to a very new shrine which itself lies in a former shop. This visit brings home how just 20-odd years can affect a building which previously survived for over six centuries with comparatively little damage. There is now no sign of its tiled portal inscription, noted in the mid 1970s, recording that Baba Qasem of Esfahan had been a devout Sunni. The original door has recently been blocked up and now entry is directly into the second chamber. In here there should be a *mihrab* decorated with Quranic verses (Q9:18–22) which emphasised the difference between devout Muslims and those who pay lip service to Islam, and indeed local tradition had it that liars and perjurers met horrid deaths at this shrine. The *mihrab* has gone, however, as has the mosaic tilework (Q17:1–6) embellishing the dome base; two cenotaphs, one commemorating a local wrestler hero (d1577), remain, though, but are shoved against the walls. Nearby was Baba Qasem's four-portal madrasa, built in 1325.

Mosques in Iran can be empty places except on Fridays. One Esfahani shrine, however, is always crowded on account of its association with Imam Hossein and the establishment of Shi'a Islam as the official religion under the Safavids but its diminutive size makes it totally unsuitable for tour groups. It will mean a taxi drive to the eastern part of the city, off Hasht Behesht Sharqi Street; take a camera in (the unlikely) case it is deserted, but don't attempt to use it otherwise. Esfahanis call the shrine the **Imamzadeh Shah Zayd** (امامزاده شاه زید) [169 H4] (Hasht Behesht Sharqi St, walking south along Pozorgmehr St from the Soroush Quarter), but happily admit the actual name is Zayn al-Din. A small courtyard precedes the entry portal (women enter to the right; men to the left). Its tiled frieze records repairs to the shrine in 1686, so perhaps this was when the paintings inside, depicting the harrowing tale of Hossein's last moments at Karbala, were executed, but they are probably later, dating from the late 19th century. Protected by (grubby) glass screens, the scenes are arranged in an approximate sequence, showing Abbas bringing life-restoring water to the imam, his family and supporters (he lost both hands in the process); the womenfolk are clearly depicted, including Rukayya, whose popular tomb-shrine is in Cairo. Look for a horse wounded by so many arrows that it looks like a pincushion; this is Hossein's steed and he is shown veiled with a halo. The lion underneath recalls the miracle of a certain Sultan Qays who, attacked by a lion in India, invoked the help of Hossein just as the imam was fighting for his own life in Iraq. Miraculously, Hossein was momentarily transported to India, causing the lion to cower in submission, while the imam reappeared at Karbala only to be slain himself.

Staying in the northern part of the city, you may also like to visit a cluster of interesting monuments in the vicinity of the Amin Hospital for Leukaemia, between masjed-e jame and Chahar Bagh Street or to be more precise off the Maydan-e Shohada. Most people around here know where the **Imamzadeh Darb-e Imam** (امامزاده درب امام) [169 F1] (also referred to as the Darb-e Islam, Abdulrazzaq

St, Bazzarcheh Haj Mohammad Jafar) is, but there are no road signs. Much of this building, including the two domes, was restored in the 17th and 18th centuries, but the *ivan* portal, with its fine mosaic tile decoration guarded by yet another stone lion, the vestibule and mausoleum dates from 1453, the year when Constantinople fell to the Ottoman Turks. Constructed on the order of Jahan Shah of the Black Sheep confederation two years after taking Esfahan, the building houses his mother, but was dedicated to two imams, Ibrahim Tabatabai (or Batha) and Zayn al-Abidin, the fourth imam; in time so many were buried here that the original door was closed by a grille. Lines of Sufi poetry frame the portal telling the visitor:

> From the roof of this house of the world [eg: heaven] seek not the image of faithfulness
> At its coming be not glad, nor grieve at its going
> See with the eye of understanding, how that building whose *ivan* Passed above the
> seventh heaven [Saturn] fell to earth.

An inscription on the far left records that the man in charge of its construction suddenly disappeared, never to return. A large second courtyard gives access to the shrine itself, a series of rooms, some evidently restored, and a storeroom for some magnificent *alam* standards used in the Moharram parades.

Across Chahar Bagh Street from here, through the narrow alleys you will arrive at **Hamam Ali Goli Agha** [169 E1] (Bid Abadi St; ⊕ summer 08.30–14.30 & 15.30–18.00, winter 08.30–13.30 & 14.30–17.00 Sat–Thu, 09.00–13.00 Fri; entry 300,000 rials), located in the small bazaar of the same name. Built during the late Safavid period in 1713 and subsequently enhanced under the Qajar and Pahlavi dynasties, this historic *hamam* is presently a museum, covering an area of around 1,200m² and consisting of two sections, large and small *hamams* (*hamam-e bozorg* and *hamam-e kuchek* respectively).

South of masjed-e jame

The route towards the main bazaar lies via the vast, but mostly empty **Maydan-e Imam Ali**. With the layout designed to resemble Naqsh-e Jahan Square, its commercial spaces have remained mostly idle, to the joy of local boys who can unobstructively play football here. Walking through one of the arches (all exits and directions are clearly signposted) brings you to the shrine and mausoleum of Harun-e Vilayet, known as **Haruniyeh** [169 G2] or **Imamzadeh Harun-e Vilayet** (امامزاده هارون ولایت), built in 1513 and restored in 1656. Before the revolution, a stone lion thought to possess powers to cure sterility stood in the courtyard; today he has been banished to the exterior and a birth-control clinic operates in his place. A small door leads into the public part of the shrine; leave your shoes at the door. Inside, 17th-century or later wall paintings of Ali, Fatima, and their two sons, Hassan and Hossein, introduce the main tomb chamber honouring Harun, whose life and attributes are cloaked in mystery; perhaps he was a son of one of the Twelve Imams. Outside, the two enormous paintings of modern-day theologians have been replaced since 2006 with ceramic tiles depicting the faces of Khomeini and the present spiritual leader of Iran, Ayatollah Khamenei. Also represented is Dr Beheshti, formerly of Esfahan, who was the head of the judiciary and lost his life in 1981 in the bomb attack on the Tehran headquarters of the Islamic Revolutionary Party. In all, about 100 were killed but here a clear reference is made to the 72 people who died with Hossein at Karbala. As you leave the shrine courtyard, turn right and you'll soon find the lion looking into the shrine and also visual proof that the tiled plaster *muqarnas* decorating the semi-dome were literally suspended from the main brick structure.

Across the alley rises the tall **Manar-e Ali** (مناره علی), now about 48m high but probably originally 2m taller. Built around 1200 (or perhaps 1235), the minaret has three main bands of brick decoration with blue-glazed elements, although only two can be seen from street level, with inscriptions declaring that there is no god but Allah and that all power belongs to Him, along with a Quranic verse (Q3:16). Masjed-e Ali, housing the minaret, was repaired extensively in the Safavid period according to the inscriptions, and its portal was constructed around 1522.

Moshir Al-Molk Historical House Museum of Islamic Heritage

خانه مشیرالملک ✳ (A few hundred metres down from Manar-e Ali along Haruniyeh Alley; ☏32223230; ⊕ 08.00–16.00 daily; entry 100,000 rials) This former Safavid residence is the only remaining one of the original seven mansions grouped together as one palace. During Qajar rule it functioned as the consulate of Prussia and numerous European-style paintings were added to the interior of the building. The unique feature of this house is the largest and the oldest sash window in Iran (with nine panes of glass) in the slightly raised central *shahneshin* room. Below it is a room with distinctive *shobbak or* blue-tile glazed windows for looking into the courtyard from the inside to preserve privacy. Winter (*zamestanneshin*) and summer (*tabestanneshin*) rooms are to each side of the *shahneshin* and enclose the charming inner courtyard with a pool in the middle. The smaller room – *howzkhaneh* – with a tiny water pool was used for ceremonies with the lower section reserved for men and the upper for women.

Naqsh-e Jahan Square میدان نقش جهان ✳ [169 F3] As for Esfahan itself, a

minimum of 4 hours is needed in and around the enormous public square now known as Maydan-e Naqsh-e Jahan (formerly Maydan-e Shah or simply Imam) Square, laid out by the Safavid Shah Abbas I (d1628), and an evening walk around is recommended as the square and the monuments are often floodlit. Said to be three times the size of St Mark's Square in Venice, this immense open space (500m × 160m) now has lawns and fountains but was once the royal parade ground, where the shahs watched military equestrian exercises, wrestling bouts and polo matches (stone goalposts used to stand in front of the Qeysariyeh Bazaar and Masjed-e Imam, with the remains of the latter still visible). *Chogan*, as the game of polo is known in Persian, is originally an Iranian game, first played more than 2,500 years go. At the north end is the main entry into the Qeysariyeh Bazaar, facing the Masjed-e Imam, with the coffee-coloured dome of Masjed-e Sheikh Lotfallah to the east, and opposite the Ali Qapu, the 17th-century ceremonial entrance into the royal palace compound: each is described below.

Shah Abbas I ordered the building of the **Masjed-e Imam** (مسجد امام) ✳ [map, page 182] (formerly Masjed-e Shah) (⊕ 08.30–17.00, closed 11.00–13.00 Fri; entry 500,000 rials, free daily in the evenings during prayer) in memory of his ancestor Shah Tahmasp I (d1576). Work began in 1612 and finished in 1638, ten years after his death. Growing impatient at the length of building time, so we are told, Abbas I demanded that the labour-intensive technique of 'mosaic' tilework used for the main entrance be abandoned for the time-saving underglazed painted tile squares seen elsewhere in the mosque. The best tilework, with a purity of glaze, colour and motif design, is indeed present on the majestically tall entrance portal flanked by soaring minarets, facing on to the *maydan*. Incidentally, it has been suggested that the two peacock motifs below the central grille window were a Safavid dynastic device as they also feature at the Ardabil and Mashhad shrines. Through the great silver doors of 1636, you'll see the courtyard is set at a 45° angle necessary for the correct direction towards Mecca, so clearly Shah Abbas I was primarily concerned that the *maydan* had a north–south orientation. The call to prayer was never made from the mosque's tall minarets because, according to Lord Curzon writing in the 1890s, the shahs were fearful that the *muezzins* would have a clear uncensored view into the royal gardens. Instead the call was made from the little roof-pavilion over the *ivan* to the right of the central courtyard.

Walking slowly around the mosque allows the visitor to see the vistas as they open out, and the astonishing range in the tile colouring and pattern on the walls, vaults and side domes become apparent. Sadly, modern tiles of inferior quality are increasingly replacing original ones. Either side of the main prayer hall, set back in a small courtyard, is a small madrasa where students were taught until the late 19th century. But before entering the main prayer hall, do look at the bulbous shape and decoration of its exterior dome (54m high) because, inside, the dome has a different shape. This is a splendid example of a double dome, the inner one absorbing and distributing the structural load so allowing the outer dome to have a more eye-catching outline. At the apex there is a 14m gap between the two, the outer shell being supported on huge spars embedded into the inner dome. Peace and calm rarely prevail in this hall as visitors stand on a central floor slab and clap to hear the resounding echo. Perhaps Bradt travellers could establish a quieter tradition – just as effective – of tearing a piece of paper. If you have a camera which has a slow shutter release and a non-automatic flash, switch the latter off, alter the shutter speed to ½ or one second (check the light meter), and place the camera on the floor and you should achieve a good shot.

The Masjed-e Imam's angled entrance is best photographed from the **Ali Qapu Palace** (عالی قاپو) ✳ (⏰ 08.00–17.00; entry 500,000 rials), constructed around 1600. Described disparagingly as a brick boot-box by Robert Byron (and even Della Valle in the 17th century called it 'pretty rather than magnificent'), the Ali Qapu is often called the Safavid palace, but it was actually the High Door (*qapu*: door) into the royal compound, from where the shah and his court viewed parades and celebrations in the *maydan*. The staircase with steep steps rising to the four floors is to the left of the small ticket office and lead up to the viewing area, or *talar*, added around 1644. The scaffolding that had been in place since late 2007 was finally removed in 2018 to reveal the beautiful decoration beneath, including delicately carved, pink plaster friezes, although their original gilded top layer has been largely lost over the centuries.

After enjoying both the breeze and view from the *talar*, continue up to the so-called music rooms. The floors of these rooms appear uneven but this is a result of inserting H-girders during the extensive repair programme; similarly the *talar* columns now have metal cores. The intricate plaster ceilings were devised to assist acoustics for court musicians, or to display *objets d'art* as in the Ardabil shrine (page 216) and certain Mughal and Rajput palaces in northern India.

Across the square demurely stands the portal of the **Masjed-e Sheikh Lotfallah** (مسجد شیخ لطف الله) (Sheikh Lotfallah Mosque) ✳ [map, page 182] (⏰ 09.00–17.00, shorter opening times in winter; entry 500,000 rials), named after a famous preacher. Rather than being a 'public' mosque, it possibly functioned as the mosque for the women of the royal harem; the portal dedication certainly emphasises the explicit Shi'a role of the shah as 'reviver of the virtues of his pure ancestors, and propagator of the doctrine of the pure Imams'. It also records that the decoration was started in 1603 but finished about 15 years later, the extra time needed to complete the amazing ceramic tilework throughout the building. A narrow corridor, angled to attain the correct orientation, leads into the prayer hall, where the simple square groundplan

The quality of Iranian carpet is unparalleled and the choice is bewildering. More than 400 tonnes of handwoven carpets are produced annually in Iran, of which approximately 80% are exported and sold at much higher prices abroad.

If you decide to buy a Persian carpet, and we suggest you do budget allowing, Esfahan is perhaps the best place to do it. Prices in Kashan are fairer, but the choice is far smaller, especially if you are after a silk carpet, and shops in Yazd are few and unjustifiably expensive.

Generally speaking there are two types of carpet: city carpets (Esfahan, Qom, etc) with often similar reproduced designs but nonetheless more expensive due to the weaver's higher fees; and nomadic carpets (Sarakhs, Qashqai, etc) without a pre-defined design.

Carpet shops in Esfahan (can on condition) accept Visa or MasterCard and you will need it. The credit-card charge is usually 4% (it may, however, vary from 2% to 15%, though more likely to be on the lower scale for expensive carpet purchases), but sellers do prefer cash or bank transfer from abroad to a predefined account, not necessarily located in Iran. They will give you all the details you need and will trust you enough to leave Iran with a carpet. There is no bargaining as such, but expect to get up to US$100 off a carpet worth around US$1,000, especially if you pay cash.

The most expensive carpets and also the most manageable to bring back home are 100%-silk carpets, which cost approximately US$2,000 apiece (1m wide × 1.30m long). Sarakhs, Ferdowsi and Qom regions are well-known centres. Do make sure, however, that the silk is 100% Iranian and not imported. This affects the price and most importantly the value of your purchase. The next two points to bear in mind are whether the carpet is two-sided and whether the pattern is geometric. When looking from different angles silk carpets change slightly in

is forgotten as the impact of the decoration kicks in. The surface patterns of ceramic shapes, sometimes set into unglazed brick, disguise massively thick walls which support the single-shell dome (diameter 13m) while giant turquoise barley-twist cables outlining the full-length squinches lead the eye into the dome. We always wonder how the pattern designer calculated for the diminishing size of the motifs on the dome's concave surface. No wonder geometry, algebra and mathematics developed in the Islamic world. By employing the same technique as suggested with the Masjed-e Imam above, very successful photographs of the dome pattern can be taken, but to see the winter prayer hall below, with its *mihrab* of 1602, you must descend by the staircase near the main entrance.

Qeysariyeh Bazaar بازار قیصریه * [map, page 182] (pronounced *gheisariyeh*) Since 1998 many more shops, including one or two selling the famous Esfahani *gaz* or nougat, have reopened in the covered arcade running all around the square. Before walking through the main 17th-century door of the bazaar, look up and you'll see a Sagittarius figure and Shah Abbas I victorious over the Uzbek enemy, as described by Jean Chardin in the late 17th century. The cleaning has also revealed a depiction of Europeans playing chess high up on the right. Above, there was a gallery where musicians banged and trumpeted every sunset, causing foreign merchants to suffer violent headaches, and a Portuguese bronze bell marking the Safavid conquest of Hormuz (page 302). Just inside the door, immediately on the right, a narrow alley leads into a small courtyard of **cotton block-printing**

colour; so have a careful look from all sides and do see more than one sample. The choice is harder to make than you think.

If you are lucky and a friend or a guide happens to know a local weaver, you can purchase more cheaply directly from him or her. You can contact Mohammad Ebrahimi (page 162), who can make the necessary arrangements.

Finally, customs is not a problem: 100%-silk carpets when folded fit into a standard luggage bag and you are allowed up to 12m² of customs-free goods. If your carpet is too big or you still cannot bring it with you, the seller will gladly take care of all the customs formalities and ship the carpet to you free of charge.

Bazaars in Esfahan, Shiraz and Tehran have separate carpet sections and coming here is a must, but the choice may prove too overwhelming. Below are some carpet shop suggestions in Iran:

ESFAHAN
Iran Pazirik Carpet [map, page 182] 195 Ostandari St; ℡ 32201408–9; w iranpazirik. com. Not known to be the friendliest bunch in town, but their customers include some famous & powerful international persona, testifying to the value & quality of some of the items sold by Iran Pazirik Carpet.

KASHAN
Zhee Showroom [155 C2] ℡ 55442738; m 0912 3895843; ◷ 09.00–21.00 daily. In the older part of the Kashan Bazaar, this showroom has an exquisite collection of antique rugs & kilims. Knowledgeable personnel will assist in making the right purchase.

TEHRAN
Kohan Diyar Gallery Art Museum Garden, Fereshteh; ℡ 22394263; ◷ 08.30–22.30. This is a relatively small carpet shop & gallery with a nice variety of mainly older carpets. Otherwise, the Tehran Bazaar is the place to do your carpet shopping.

workshops. There is an endless variety of printed cottons; prices depend on size, quality of the fabric and the colour complexity of the design. Dealers now greatly outnumber the makers and just one or two of them are retained to show tourists the basic technique. The bazaar runs northwards and eastwards intermittently. The main **carpet quarter** is situated to the far left (west) away from the main street; a short walk through here will raise serious doubts in your mind whether there are enough homes worldwide to house all these carpets.

East of Naqsh-e Jahan Square
Here you will find the beautiful mansion **Angurestan-e Malek** (انگورستان ملک) [169 G4] (Malek St; ◷ 09.00–14.00; entry 300,000 rials). The grape ('angur') garden that the house is named after is long since gone and the inner courtyard requires serious maintenance work. The mansion is also the venue for international Quranic reading competitions and access cannot always be guaranteed. Refurbishment has also meant much of the original decoration has been replaced. The original garden has also been ripped up to install new pools and paving, but the entrance doorway and four-porch columns have escaped unscathed. Through the main door you enter the first room, with its Bohemian chandeliers and Qajar sash windows opening on to the garden, while a screened upper gallery allowed the women of the household to view visitors in secret. This room leads into a chamber, now rapidly disappearing under new highly varnished wood panelling. At its far end is a small room decorated with early 20th-century plasterwork and mirrored glass, which contains the grave of Mohammad

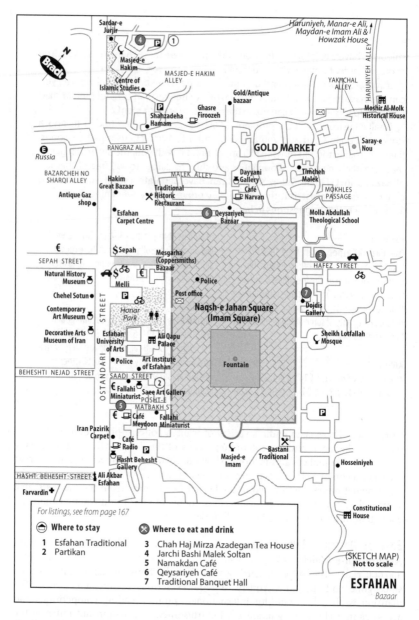

Sardar-e
Jurjir

4 P **1**

Haruniyeh, Manar-e Ali,
Maydan-e Imam Ali &
Howzak House

Masjed-e
Hakim

MASJED-E HAKIM
ALLEY

Centre of
Islamic Studies

YAKHCHAL
ALLEY

Gold/Antique
bazaar

Moshir Al-Molk
Historical House

Shahzadeha
Hamam

P

Ghasre
Firoozeh

RANGRAZ ALLEY

GOLD MARKET

Saray-e
Nou

E
Russia

BAZARCHEH NO
SHARQI ALLEY

Hakim
Great Bazaar

MALEK ALLEY

Traditional
Historic
Restaurant

Dayyani
Gallery

Café
Narvan

Timcheh
Malek

MOKHLES
PASSAGE

Antique Gaz
shop

Esfahan
Carpet Centre

6 Qeysariyeh
Bazaar

Molla Abdullah
Theological School

€

$ Sepah

Mesgarha
(Coppersmiths)
Bazaar

3

SEPAH STREET

Natural History
Museum

Melli

P

Chehel Sotun

Honar
Park

Contemporary
Art Museum

Decorative Arts
Museum of Iran

Esfahan
University
of Arts

Ali Qapu
Palace

Police

Post office

**Naqsh-e Jahan Square
(Imam Square)**

HAFEZ STREET

7
Dojdis
Gallery

Sheikh Lotfallah
Mosque

BEHESHTI NEJAD STREET

Police

Art Institute
of Esfahan

SAADI STREET

€ Fallahi
Miniaturist

Saee Art Gallery

2

POSHT-E
5 MATBAKH ST

Fountain

Café
Meydoon

Fallahi
Miniaturist

Iran Pazirik
Carpet

€

Café
Radio

P

Hasht Behesht
Gallery

Ali Akbar
Esfahan

P

HASHT BEHESHT STREET

Farvardin

Masjed-e
Imam

Bastani
Traditional

Hosseiniyeh

Constitutional
House

(SKETCH MAP)
Not to scale

ESFAHAN
Bazaar

For listings, see from page 167

⊖ **Where to stay**

1 Esfahan Traditional
2 Partikan

⊗ **Where to eat and drink**

3 Chah Haj Mirza Azadegan Tea House
4 Jarchi Bashi Malek Soltan
5 Namakdan Café
6 Qeysariyeh Café
7 Traditional Banquet Hall

Ibrahim Malek (d1922), the former owner. Theological permission for interment within the home is rarely given, but this Esfahani merchant was so renowned for his good works, feeding the poor and finding work for the unemployed, that an exception was made.

West of the bazaar From the carpet quarter, or walking (west) down the tarmac road parallel to the main bazaar street and then along the Masjed Hakim alley, the small entry to your left opens into the airy *ivan* of **Masjed-e Hakim** (مسجد حكيم)

182

[map, page 182]. Continue walking the alley with the mosque walls to your left and you will come to the beautiful portal, known as *sardar-e jurjir*. Discovered during 1955 repair work, this patterned (Q3:16–18) doorway is all that remains of the late 10th-century Mosque of Sahib al-Kufa, a vizier (d995CE) known for his writings on theology, history and poetry. Everything else, which included a dervish centre, library, colleges, accommodation and assembly rooms and a tall minaret, was destroyed to make way for this Safavid Mosque of al-Hakim (built 1660–63), named after Shah Safi's physician Da'ud. After leaving the Esfahani court under a cloud, Da'ud made his fortune in India attending the Mughal emperor, Aurangzeb (d1707). Perhaps it is no coincidence that some of the Quranic verses used in the Taj Mahal are also included here on the 1660 *mihrab*. The prayer *ivan* has a calligraphic frieze (Q2:256) suggesting Da'ud was a (possibly Jewish) convert to Islam, while another quotation (Q62:9) around the base of the dome tells people (perhaps like today's carpet dealers) to forget business and attend the Friday prayer. The architect of the mosque is believed to be Mohammad Ali Ibn Ostad Ali Beg Esfahani.

Walking back along Hakim Street, turn left into Sepah Street, at the intersection with Ostandari Street; set inside railings a large white building with a tall vaulted entrance originates from the 15th century, but was converted into an officers' club in Pahlavi times and had until recently functioned as the **Natural History Museum**, which explains the dinosaur and aged lion sculptures on the front steps.

Just next to the Natural History Museum is the most important surviving Safavid palace, **Chehel Sotun** (چهل ستون) ✳ [169 F3] (40 columns) (Ostandari St; ☉ 09.00–17.00; entry 500,000 rials; no flash photography), taking its name from the reflection of its 20 columns in the algae-rich pond in front of the main *talar*. As suggested by the wall paintings all around the outside of the pavilion, this was where the Safavid rulers received foreign envoys and where Shah Soleyman was invested in 1668, some 20 years after its construction. The 16m-high columns, once painted and gilded, used to be hung with curtains sprayed with rose water to perfume the air, and the *talar* walls still retain some mirror work, originally imported from Venice at great expense.

The rooms either side of the *talar* have small, minimally labelled displays of Safavid (and later) ceramics, metalwork and textiles, but most visitors go straight into the main hall. On entry, immediately facing you is a huge 19th-century painting of Shah Ismail I attacking the Ottoman Janissaries (note the different headgear and dress details) during the famous 1514 Battle of Chaldiran, eastern Turkey, which was a resounding defeat for the Safavid army, although here Ismail looks victorious. Either side are 17th-century paintings: on the left, the royal reception held c1543 by Shah Tahmasp I for the exiled Mughal ruler Humayun, and on the right, Shah Abbas I entertaining the ruler of Bukhara, Vali Mohammad Khan; both guests seem ill at ease with their surroundings. Over the main door another 19th-century picture portrays Nader Shah, the Afghan general who seized control in 1735, in typical battle mode, this time in India. To the left there's a Safavid painting of Shah Abbas II receiving another central Asian ruler, and on the other side, Ismail II on a hennaed horse fighting Uzbeks; the sense of perspective suggests a European artist at work.

The exit by the small door to the far right leads into a gallery reopened in 1998. Despite the depiction of a scantily clad female looking somewhat flirtatious among flames, the wall painting on the right continues the theme of battles; it perhaps records the 1649 capture of Qandahar, Afghanistan, or more exactly the wife of the city commander, killed in action, about to immolate herself on his funeral pyre.

On leaving the pavilion, take the trouble to walk round the building to view the exterior murals, painted by both court painters and, it is thought, the 17th-century artists who accompanied the various European and Russian trade delegations, eager to purchase Persian silk.

To the right of the **Chehel Sotun** palace you will take delight in visiting the Esfahan **Contemporary Art Museum** [map, page 182] (🕘 09.00–17.00; entry 500,000 rials), housing wonderful examples of modern and contemporary Iranian art and, photography, and regularly hosting temporary art exhibitions. Right next to it is the **Decorative Arts Museum of Iran** [map, page 182] (🕘 09.00–17.00; entry 300,000 rials). Continue walking further down and turning on to Hasht Behesht Street will take you to a small public park and the intimate Safavid **Hasht Behesht Palace** (هشت بهشت) ✳ [169 E4] ('Eight Paradises') (🕘 09.00–16.00; entry 300,000 rials), built in 1669. In the 17th century an English traveller described how the court was entertained in its gardens by the re-enactment of naval battles in the water channels, while Jean Chardin a few years later waxed lyrical over the place 'expressly made for love … one's heart is melted … one always leaves with a very ill grace'; many young couples today share the sentiment. The palace has 17th-century tiled panels decorating the external arches, a main domed ceiling set with mirror work, and remnants of wall paintings, the best-preserved surfaces being in the small rooms in each corner.

The southern perimeter of the park is marked by a tall brick wall of the Abbasi Hotel caravanserai. Proceeding into Chahar Bagh Avenue from here, immediately on your left is the entrance to the single-aisled 18th-century **Bazaar-e Honar** [169 E4] (🕘 17.00–21.30 Sat–Thu) whose shop rents once provided an endowment to the nearby madrasa to cover salaries, repairs, etc; it now houses jewellery shops. The **Madrasa Chahar Bagh** (مدرسه چهارباغ) [169 E4] (also known as Madrasa Imam Sadegh) (1706–14) (🕘 to the public only during Nou Rouz when pupils are on holiday) is next door. It is on the corner of Amadegah Street with **Chahar Bagh** ('four gardens' in Persian after the traditional Persian garden design alignment) where centuries ago with 'Night drawing on, all the pride of Esfahan was met … and the Grandees were airing themselves, prancing about with their numerous trains, striving to outvie each other in Pomp and Generosity' (Fryer, c1680). Before the revolution it was possible to enter the madrasa (formerly Madrasa Madar-e Shah). Built in honour of Shah Hossein's mother (as its original name suggests), its sun-yellow, patterned-tiled vaults, 160 rooms and a peaceful 'Persian' garden disguise a violent history, for Hossein was decapitated here in 1722 by the Afghan rebels. It is now a fully operational theological college once more.

On Amadegah Street itself, right next to Madrasa Chahar Bagh, is the **Hotel Abbasi** ✳ [169 E4]. Here in its main courtyard you can take a well-deserved tea break; ice creams are also very good. This was an early 18th-century caravanserai built, along with a small bazaar behind, to finance the madrasa before being converted into a hotel in 1955. It was one of the late shah's favourite hotels and several tour groups in the 1970s returned after a day's sightseeing to find their luggage in reception, as the royal retinue had unexpectedly commandeered their rooms. Guests have the evening meal on the ground floor amid painted 'Safavid' beauties, or in the garden, while breakfast is always served in the upper restaurant section decorated in a 'Qajar' style.

Zayandehrud bridges
A walk down the now-pedestrianised Chahar Bagh towards the river takes you to the **Allahverdi Khan Bridge**, built in 1603, so named after its patron (d1613), a famous kingmaker, ethnic Georgian (page 191), provincial governor and the first commander-in-chief of the Safavid army (page 14); the bridge is mainly known as the **Se-o-se Pol** (which stands for number 33 in

Persian, referring to its 33 arches). The 360m-long × 14m-wide Allahverdi Khan Bridge, on piers some 4m thick, with its two levels and high walls to protect camel trains from wind buffeting, connected Chahar Bagh Street with the Armenian Christian Quarter across the river. Greatly admired in the 17th century – 'truly a very neat piece of architecture if I may say the neatest in all Persia' (Tavernier) – it is still a favourite place to walk and take tea. A walk along the river is especially recommended in the evening, when Se-o-se Pol and the Khaju Bridge are also illuminated, but during the day it is a pleasure seeing young people enjoying themselves in pedalos on the river (when the river is not dry, that is). In order to support the tile and agriculture in Yazd province, the Zayandehrud is now essentially almost continuously dammed upstream towards Yazd.

Further down after the modern Ferdowsi Bridge is a less touristy, but equally charming **Pol-e Chubi**, built initially as an aqueduct to supply water to royal gardens on the north side of the river. The next is **Khaju Bridge** *, built in the 1660s by Shah Abbas II to join up with the old Shiraz road, with 24 arches and a central, two-storey, octagonal kiosk. Described by Engelbert Kaempfer (a late 17th-century German physician who visited Persia attached to a Swedish mission before joining the Dutch East India Company) as 'more superb [when] compared with other buildings', it probably functioned as a toll bridge and also provided a spectacular water cascade when its channels were blocked by angled wooden boards. It is a popular place for young musicians and singers, gathering under one of its arches, to practise their music skills. On the south side, 36m away, a stone lion stands looking at the river. The carved symbols on its chest and side show it was a gravestone or tomb marker of a local champion wrestler, as the same types of exercise equipment are still used in today's *zurkhanehs* (see box, page 172). Initially called Pol-e Shahi (royal bridge) it is now known as Khaju after the city neighbourhood it is located in.

From behind the next bridge, Pol-e Bozorgmehr, opens up the **Bagh-e Golha** (Flower Garden) [169 H6] (⊕ 07.00–20.00; entry 300,000 rials), with some of the most beautiful flowers and garden arrangements in Iran. It has a tea shop and peaceful gazebo to take a pause in.

To see the third historic and the oldest bridge in Esfahan will entail a taxi ride to **Shahrestan Bridge** [169 H5] (by the Esfahan International Fair), which dates from the Sasanid period but with pre-Islamic-era foundations. Rebuilt by the Seljuks, and with a toll station added in the 17th century, it too acted as a weir, but the river has long been diverted.

Jolfa neighbourhood جلفا *

Don't leave Esfahan without visiting the Armenian Quarter south of the river, known as (**New**) **Jolfa**, and its churches, cafés and art galleries. The area is essentially divided into a busier touristy part between Nazar Street and Mehrdad (Shahid Ghandi) Street and quieter residential Sangtarashha area, west of Hakim Nezami Street. Many locals gather in the evenings at **Jolfa Square** around the bust of Zaven Ghokasian (d2015), famous Armenian-Iranian writer and filmmaker. The neighbourhood is home to the **Esfahan University of Art** occupying three historic mansions – one on the corner of Nezami Street, the second a former French school established originally on Chahar Bagh Street in 1902 and relocated here in 1956, where it now houses the Faculty of Visual Arts, and the third a fine mansion on Sangtarashha Street, off Davudiha Alley.

Across the small park from the former French school is the former **Kananian Girls Secondary School**, established in 1901. The Sangtarashha area is in itself an artistic bubble with two music schools – the Arpa Music Academy next door to **Saint Gadarineh Monastery** (1623) and the School of Fine Arts and Music within 200m radius from here. On Sangtarashha Street is the **Saint Nerses Apostolic Church** dating from 1660. A few doors down past Gozaar Gallery is the **Marcus Simon Cultural Heritage House** built in 1893. **Saint Minas Apostolic Church** (1659) is just down the street in the cosy courtyard of **Polsheer House** that it shares with Polsheer Architects, one of Iran's most prestigious architectural groups. Returning to Haqqani Street bustling with stores and barber shops, turn right to find a former Armenian school, built in 1893 during the rule of Naser al-Din Shah; only the marble door arch modestly hiding amid shop signs suggests where its entrance had once been.

✖ Where to eat and drink

✖ **Arabo** [168 A1] Vank Church Alley; ⏲ 11.00–midnight daily. So famous that even Tehranis vising Esfahan make a beeline for here. A tiny sandwich shop, where on a summer evening customers block the street queuing to order Arabo's succulent roast beef sandwich (for a whopping 750,000 rials) that would easily feed 2 hungry tourists. $$

✖ **Monsieur Arakel** [168 B5] Sangtarashha St; 📞36243714; ⏲ 09.00–23.00 daily. Opened in early 2019 in a historic mansion, its lovely inner courtyard is an inviting place to enjoy a hearty lunch; portions here are very generous. The menu is a mix between Iranian & Western cuisine & their *tahchin* rice cake is delicious. $$

✳ ✖ **Toranj Traditional Restaurant** [168 C7] Hovans Historical Hse, off Hovans Shirazi St; 📞36293788; ⏲ noon–midnight daily. In the heart of Jolfa, a finely restored historic residence, with live music & great menu to match. Popular with locals for special occasion dining. $$

🖵 **Ani** With branches opposite Vank Cathedral [168 B1] & Sangtarashha St [168 A4]; w cateani. com; ⏲ 09.00–midnight daily. This is the most popular café in Jolfa & a great place for a sandwich & a cup of good coffee. $$

🖵 **Baharnarenj** [168 A2] Church St; ⏲ 09.00–midnight daily. Beautiful cosy interior with traditional Persian motifs makes this tiny café an ideal place to stop for a cup of coffee or *damnush* herbal tea. $$

🖵 **Safavi House** [168 B6] Haqqani St; m 0912 0194728; w safavihouse.com; ⏲ 09.00–23.00 daily. A centre of various exhibitions, art space & café/restaurant all under the vaults of the restored Safavid Hse; there is also a charming courtyard. $$

Shopping In Jolfa there are a few shops, including a curious cluster on tiny **Khachatur Kesaratsi Square** (with the statue of Archbishop Khachatur Kesaratsi the founder of the first printing house in Iran in the centre):

Behesht Gallery [168 B2] Khachatur Kesaratsi Sq; 📞36245473; m 0937 5045146; w beheshtjewelry.com; ⏲ 09.00–22.00 daily. Part of a popular chain selling Iranian-made jewellery. **Omidan Bookstore** [168 A2] Church St; 📞3626674; ⏲ 09.00–13.00 daily (except public holidays). Sells a good collection of Englishlanguage books.

Shekarchiane Shop [168 B4] Sheikh Tusi St; ⏲ 09.00–13.00 & 17.30–21.00. Sells sweets & delicious Armenian *gata* bread.

Galleries and museums

Golzaar Galley Sangtarashha St; w gozaargallery.com; ⏲ 10.00–20.00 daily. This tiny contemporary art gallery regularly hosts exhibitions by local artists as well as varied cultural events.

Hoeltzer's House 18 Shokofeh cul-de-sac, off Khaqqani St. This beautiful private house, formerly owned by German telegraphist & photographer Ernst Hoeltzer, was in 2019 converted into a small gallery, café & arts shop.

What to see and do

All Saviours' (or Vank) Cathedral کلیسای وانک ✳ [168 B1] (Kelisa St; ⏲ 08.30–17.30 daily; Nou Rouz 09.00–20.15 daily; entry including museum 300,000 rials;

authorisation to visit the well-kept Armenian Cemetery is obtained here) Around 1603 the Safavid shah ordered the resettlement of some 10,000 Armenian families from the Caucasus into this quarter and nearby villages, probably to ensure their skills in silk trading remained in Safavid hands, and to thwart any Armenian schemes of siding with the Ottomans to get autonomy. The community was allowed freedom of worship, and Abbas I himself, we are told, attended Epiphany celebrations and commanded important Christian relics – such as the arm of St Gregory the Illuminator, who converted Armenia in 301CE – to be brought here; it was returned to Echtmiadzin, Armenia, in 1637. By 1701 this quarter boasted about 30 churches but now only about 13 survive, and the community has shrunk considerably from 100,000 in the mid 1960s to approximately 7,000 in 1995 and it has not changed since. Several of the 18th-century **merchants' houses** with interesting painted decoration were open in the 1970s but as many now function as government offices, official permission is required. The Jani House close to All Saviours' Cathedral, for example, is now the art college.

Construction of All Saviours' began in 1606 but it was largely rebuilt during the years 1650–63, with the bell tower added in 1764. The decorative plaster and paintings covering the interior date from 1660–70, the gift of an Armenian merchant, Avandich, but the tiles are somewhat later. In the east dome, the story of the Creation, the Expulsion and the Killing of Abel are depicted, but elsewhere the painted decoration is arranged to show episodes from the Old Testament, with related New Testament themes below. So Abraham and the Angels is paired with the Annunciation, Hagar and Ismail with the Nativity, and almost opposite the entrance, Moses and the Tablets above the Transfiguration. Over the door itself a huge Last Judgement fills the space; centuries' worth of candle soot and incense accumulation has now been removed to reveal the vibrant colours of the original. It is not known whether the artists were Esfahani Armenians or Europeans attached to the various East India companies resident in this quarter, but clearly they had seen engravings by the contemporary Dutch artist, Van Sichem. At shoulder level, small panels gruesomely retell the tortures faced by the early Armenian Christians, the costume and textile details proving that these too are 17th century. One near the main door depicts St Gregory the Illuminator curing the Armenian king who had been transformed into a pig (or wolf according to some traditions) as a punishment for lusting after and torturing Christian maidens (or nuns). The murals go on to show the conversion of the king and the people in 301CE, and the honouring of the saint. On the left side of the small west door you see that St Gregory went through a particularly nasty form of colonic irrigation as part of his torture cycle.

Behind the west wall in the courtyard lie a few gravestones of British missionaries, their families and soldiers who died in the Esfahani and Yazdikast areas. Underneath the canopy another 19th-century grave is decorated with the famous bathing episode of Shirin, the Armenian princess, watched by Shah Khosrow II who bites the 'finger of astonishment' (see box, page 141). Directly opposite is a striking monument, erected in 1975, marking the early 20th-century Ottoman atrocities. Further down is the museum building with displays (labelling in English) on two floors of rich liturgical vestments and objects, illuminated and illustrated manuscripts, oil paintings, the first (1636) printing press in Iran, historic documents, etc. The small museum shop at the main entrance usually has pamphlets and books.

Other churches If All Saviours' Cathedral is crowded, a short walk takes you to **Bethlehem Church** [168 B1] (Nazar St; ⊕ 08.30–17.30 daily; entry 100,000 rials), built in 1628, which lies immediately to the northeast behind the cathedral. The decorative scheme is very similar to All Saviours', but perhaps some 30 years earlier in date and in a strange sequence. The donor's picture is on the north wall, and horrific scenes on the west wall illustrate the tortures inflicted on St Gregory the Illuminator, St Sergius, St Mercurius and St Theodore. In the narrow alley behind Bethlehem Church there are two more churches: **Saint Mary's** [168 B1], built in 1613, which has fine 17th-century tiles, and some paintings, including the Beheading of John the Baptist, with a figure of the donor in the bottom left; and **Saint Hagop**, built in 1607. Both are closed to the general public and can only be visited at 09.00–11.30 on Sundays during services. Another Armenian church, **Saint Kevork** [168 A1], dating back to 1611, is only open for Saturday service between 16.30 and 20.30.

Esfahan Music Museum [168 D7] (74 Mehrdad (Shahid Ghandi) St; ☏ 36256912; w isfahanmusicmuseum.com; ⊕ 09.00–21.00 daily; entry 300,000 rials) is a lovely museum of musical instruments offering a very special insight into Iranian musical tradition. Its collection of ethnic, national and regional instruments, such as *kamancheh* displayed in its different shapes, makes it easy to compare and learn about various forms of Iranian musical culture. Other exhibits include the unusual Kurdish instrument *dozaleh* and a *neyanban* bagpipe from southern Iran, or a *robabeh* made from a metal oil container. To learn more about Iranian music, book a music tour with Howzak House (page 167).

Armenian Cemetery [168 C7] (⊕ 08.30–16.30) The cemetery is located off Sepahan Road near to al-Zahra Hospital (Shiraz direction), but visiting permission is needed from the cathedral authorities (page 186). Here are the graves of Rodolph Stadler (d1637), the Swiss watchmaker to Shah Safi I, and Claudius James Rich, the British Resident (Consul) in the early 19th century, among many others. Further up from the cemetery is Sofeh Park [168 C7], popular for weekend strolls and great views over the city. A cable car (600,000 rials) is operational when not too windy.

FURTHER AFIELD

About 30km south of Esfahan, off the Zobahan (ذوبآهن) (Steel Factory) Highway, is the town of **Pirbakran** (پیربکران), in an area once strongly associated with the Jewish community and, in early medieval times, overshadowed by several Assassin (see box, page 131) castles from where attacks on Esfahan were conducted. Around here is grown the famous small-grained Linjan rice, with its distinctive flavour. Set aside half a day (and around 500,000 rials for taxi hire) for a visit to Pirbakran and the surrounding area.

There is no direct access from the main road to the early 14th-century building which gives the township its name, so walk past with the enclosing wall on the left and then double back along the alley below. Many of the houses along here have the characteristic two door knockers, one for female, the other for male visitors. The children are helpful and will fetch the guardian to unlock the gate. Walk straight through, into the small tomb chamber at the back, pushing away a grimy curtain into a small domed chamber with faint depictions of cypresses or minarets on the walls. This was probably the actual teaching room of the famous Sufi sheikh Mohammad Ibn Bakran, known as *pir*, namely 'revealer of the secrets of the Truth, venerated Master of the Way', as the inscriptions here repeatedly describe him. Shortly after his death in 1304, the small tomb chamber with its massive cenotaph was constructed and decorated in turquoise and cobalt blue tilework, but sticky fingers since World War II have removed most of the tiles. A steep slope behind the teaching room precluded any further building at that end, so in 1312 a lofty prayer hall was constructed in front of the tomb. It too was once covered in early 14th-century moulded tiles in two shades of blue and a few dusty ones remain, too high up to be stolen. But fortunately most of the marvellously carved plasterwork is intact, whether calligraphic *Kufic* 'seal-squares' resembling Chinese chop marks, 'Baroque' leaf forms carved through several levels, once all highly coloured, or the beautifully patterned brick end plugs. The *mihrab* is splendid. Look for the rock jutting out from floor level; this is where the horse of the prophet Elijah set down his hoof before he rode into the heavens. This *ivan* extension of 1312 meant a new entry passage which didn't interfere with the *qibla* orientation and a *mihrab* had to be constructed; as you leave, take time to look at its decoration, somewhat damaged but still fine.

In the township itself there is an old **Jewish synagogue** and **cemetery**, known locally as Esther Khatun (Lady Esther). You need permission from the Jewish authorities in Esfahan to visit both. Enquire at the tourist police office (page 172). The complex bears signs of vandalism but pilgrims still come here, leaving small stones on the gravestones, as a sign that someone has visited the grave. The synagogue has rooms for pilgrims, but it is doubtful whether these are now much used. The main room, a domed chamber with the Torah stand, is at ground level, while above there are small prayer rooms with stone panels carved with Hebrew texts. In a small garden behind is a free-standing domed chamber where Esther (or Sarah, who has also been mentioned) disappeared into the walls. (The Jewish community in Esfahan, which was once the largest in Iran, is now mainly based around the Joubareh neighbourhood north of the city.)

Along the road to **Ashtarjan** (اشترجان) about 5km away in agricultural land are two fine **pigeon towers**. Just as the towers come into view, turn down a narrow road to the right, and then left, which takes you up to the larger tower. Hover, and hopefully a key will materialise to allow you in, but even if it doesn't this is a splendid building even when viewed from the outside.

You will be just as awestruck by these immense edifices as the 17th-century traveller Jean Chardin was, amazed that they were 'six times as big as the biggest we have: they are built with Brick overlaid with Plaister and Lime'. Looking like giant chess pieces, they provide multi-storeyed nesting boxes inside for pigeons, not for breeding and eating (the birds have traditional sacred connotations) but for the guano used to fertilise the local melon fields; a cynic would argue that the pigeons destroyed more crops with their voracious appetites than they helped grow. To prevent snakes from getting in, there are no windows and only one door opened once a year to collect the guano. Nothing prepares you for the size of these towers, and the simple grandeur of their interiors. Even without a torch, the impact is sensational, almost as good as any Gothic cathedral. Stairs go up to the roof but some of the steps are damaged.

You could complete this half-day trip with Ashtarjan (signposted as Oshtarjan), 35km southwest of Esfahan, for the little **masjed-e jame**, gifted by a local man in 1305, and there is the *imamzadeh* of Rabia Khatun close by, dated 1308. While waiting for the mosque guardian, as perhaps the famous Arab geographer Ibn Battuta did during his visit in 1327, have a look at the exterior doorways. This small two-*ivan* mosque is quiet and serene, with exquisite decoration with numerous chinoiserie motifs. It has seen better days, but remains of painting show the detailed plasterwork and the dome interior was once brilliantly coloured, complementing the plain brick and coloured tilework (the work of Hajji Mohammad of Tabriz) and

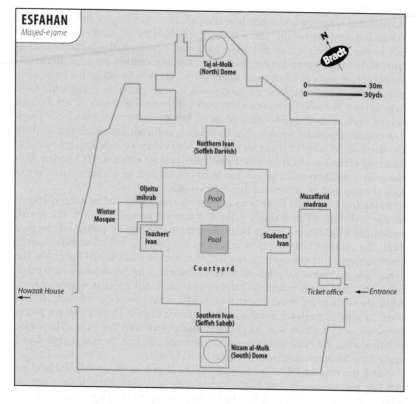

ESFAHAN
Masjed-e jame

Taj al-Molk
(North) Dome

0 ———— 30m
0 ———— 30yds

Northern Ivan
(Soffeh Darvish)

Oljeitu
mihrab

Pool

Muzaffarid
madrasa

Winter
Mosque

Teachers'
Ivan

Pool

Students'
Ivan

Courtyard

Howzak House

Ticket office ← Entrance

Southern Ivan
(Soffeh Saheb)

Nizam al-Molk
(South) Dome

a lovely *mihrab*. The *qibla ivan* is dominated with a large lozenge motif giving the names of the Twelve Imams, edged with *Kufic* inscription (Q36:1–9) on one side, and on the other wall another containing the 99 names of God, edged with more calligraphy (Q59:23–4). Around the dome inside, more Quranic verses (Q48:1–6) ask for forgiveness of past faults, and the reward of paradise in richly plaited *Kufic*, while the *mihrab* records the date of completion as 1316. A carved stone panel on one of the courtyard piers states: 'In the time of the caliphate of his majesty, the Emperor of Islam, the greatest Sultan, Lord over the necks of the peoples … Uzun Hassan [of the Aq Qoyunlu 1453–78] … the repair of this masjed-e jame [was undertaken by a local Sufi master] at his own personal expense.'

The road from Esfahan to Shiraz or to Yazd via Abadeh and Abarkuh runs through interesting scenery scattered with the remains of walled villages and caravanserais. There is one well-preserved caravanserai in Mahyar, 30km south of Esfahan, which up until ten years ago functioned as a prison. Some 50km further along the same road is **Shahreza** (شهرضا) with its *imamzadeh*, built in Safavid times and then greatly reworked in the 19th century; there are clean toilets here in the new small hotel set back from the row of shops just below the shrine. Just before **Izadkhast** (ایزدخواست) in Fars province 60km further on, there is a dirt spur road to the right (notionally west), which leads directly to the old fortress that controlled the main caravan route to the southeast. Built on Sasanid foundations, judging from the substructure, this fort is splendid despite its ruined appearance; even the remains of the old drawbridge are still visible. Sometimes the guardian can be found, who will unlock the drawbridge door. Inside is a jumble of rooms and as usual with a castle, the function of most is unclear except for the well house with the bathhouse opposite, and the bread ovens. If the guardian is not available, never mind; backtrack a little from the drawbridge and turn left along the narrow alley which will lead to a vantage place for a superb view across the old river valley and the Safavid caravanserai on the other side. Below are the ruins of houses. In the 19th century the regional governor ordered the killing of all the menfolk (by throwing them down into the valley) as punishment for non-payment of taxes, and it was here that two young army officers buried in the All Saviours' courtyard, Esfahan, lost their lives. Izadkhast traditionally had another claim to fame as a 17th-century French traveller recorded: 'That to live happy, a man must have a wife of Yazd, eat the bread of Izadkhast, and drink the wine of Shiraz.'

EAST OF ESFAHAN PROVINCE

Northeast of Esfahan, towards the picturesque villages at the Zagros Mountains foothills lies one of the most culturally diverse and well-kept secrets of the province, the town of **Buien-Miyandasht** (بوئین و میاندشت). Together with **Fereydunshahr** (فریدونشهر) a few kilometres away, it is the only place in Iran with an ethnic Georgian community. Little information is available about the Georgians who were forcibly brought here during the Safavid campaigns in the Caucasus. Then, many towns were looted, many people were killed and approximately 300,000 Georgians were moved to Esfahan and then resettled in the surrounding area. Known for their bravura and military skill, Georgians have always been valued as able fighters. Unlike Armenians, however, who had been granted certain freedoms and exemptions in recognition of their artisan skills, Georgians were never allowed to develop their cultural identity and language, for fear that it would jeopardise discipline in the military ranks. They were forced to convert to Islam and although the few Georgian families that still live in the area speak Georgian, their language has not changed since the 15th century, giving it a certain charm.

BAKHTIARI PEOPLE AND NOMADIC MIGRATION

Bakhtiari people, numbering approximately 600,000, are originally nomad people residing predominantly in the Zagros Mountains. Those who do still lead a nomad lifestyle migrate in winter from the highlands of Chahar Mahal and Bakhtiari and Lorestan provinces towards the warmer climate of Khuzestan. The journey takes up to 15 days and the most daring and fit travellers are welcome to follow the migration (known in Persian as *kuch*) either from start to finish or in parts and it will undoubtedly become the highlight of your trip to Iran. Although no special permission is required, it is recommended to arrange such travel via **Nomad Tours** (page 43).

Bakhtiari men's traditional attire consists of a *chuqah*, a white coat with black stripes, made of sheep wool, black trousers known as *dabid*, which are similar to Kurdish but differ in that these are not tight at the ankle, and a hat, simply known as *kollah* (hat in Persian), which is made from woollen goat hair. Bakhtiaris wear traditional handwoven *giveh* shoes, but also rubber shoes in which most of them cross at times very challenging mountain terrain.

When visiting Bakhtiari villages, make sure to try their herbal teas. Locals here drink celery (*kerafs*) tea, which is believed to reduce blood pressure.

Here there is also a small Armenian community and more than 30 Armenian churches, including three in the village of **Khoygan** (خویگان), 3km away from Buien-Miyandasht, where the Qajar-period **St Mariam Church** built in 1892 has been restored thanks to the efforts of Anahid. This wonderful and softly spoken woman moved here from Tehran to restore her family's house and give support to the local Armenian community. With 12 inner columns in honour of the Twelve Apostles, it is a charming church and is well looked after.

The mountainous area southwest of Fereydunshahr is best explored on an organised tour and with a good off-road vehicle. Winters are cold here and mountain roads often get blocked. Alternatively, you can continue further north towards Khorramabad, the capital of Lorestan province (page 138), the land of waterfalls and spectacular mountains or join nomads on their migration across the Zagros (see box, page 191).

TOUR GUIDE

✳ **Zandi Tours** 15 Abdulrazaq St, Esfahan; m 0913 2051561; e zanditours@gmail. com; w irantravelers.org. Based in Esfahan, the recommended tour guide is Farshid Zandi Esfahani; he can organise 2-day & longer trips & accommodation in Jangal-e Poshtkuh & Kuh Rang mountain areas dotted with Bakhtiari villages, such as secluded **Durak** & more popular & touristy **Sar Agha Seyyed**.

 ## WHERE TO STAY AND EAT

✳ **Javaheri Ecolodge** (5 rooms) Buien-Miyandasht; m 0913 3722513. To explore the area, we recommend spending a night or two here. Opened in 2017, this ecolodge offers comfortable & spacious rooms, traditionally & tastefully decorated. Homemade food is delicious & walnuts in the *kashk-e bademjun* will probably be from one of the walnut trees in the ecolodge's courtyard. Mehdi Javaheri, its friendly owner, will happily show you around & take you to some of the traditional Georgian houses in the area. Member of the 'Mehmoun' association. **$$**

6

The Caspian Region

The road from Tehran to the shores of the Caspian Sea (the Lake of Khazar in Persian) is surely one of the most beautiful in Iran, with lush greenery, tree-covered mountains and valleys. One route runs via Qazvin towards Rasht, through the town of Manjil, also known as the 'windy city' owing to its geographical location and the largest windfarm in Iran, and the other is the spectacular Karaj–Chalus road via the lake on the Amir Kabir Dam.

The Caspian region has been a favourite royal hunting ground over the centuries, while from the 15th century onwards, foreign visitors knew it for the breeding and usage of silkworms, with all the associated processing. This was the source of the silk eagerly snapped up by Western and Russian merchant adventurers until the mid 19th century when pebrine, a disease of silkworms, struck. Attempts to revive the industry were made but by 1870 the Suez Canal was bringing cheaper Japanese, Chinese and Indian silk to the West. Another Caspian luxury product has since fared badly: caviar. And again the fault did not lie at Iran's door, but this time with inadequate Soviet and post-Soviet control of water pollution and poaching, which have largely killed off the sturgeon.

The severe earthquake of 1991, which killed some 40,000 in the Caspian region, and the comparatively few foreign visitors to this area have meant development priorities have lain elsewhere, such as with building of holiday apartments and villas for Tehranis eager to escape the capital. The region, however, has a wonderful tradition of hospitality and you can be sure that hotel staff will be most welcoming here. Finding accommodation, especially during the Nou Rouz holiday, can be a problem. For further details of places to stay and eat, see the relevant towns within the chapter.

The Caspian region comprises three provinces: Gilan (stretching towards the border with Azerbaijan), Golestan (bordering Turkmenistan); and Mazandaran in between the two and to the north of Tehran.

GETTING THERE AND AWAY

Apart from daily 1-hour **flights** to Rasht from Tehran and a regular train connecting the two cities, there are 'express' **rail** services from Tehran, especially towards Mashhad, that pass via Shahrud in the province of Semnan. There are plans to link Rasht with Baku via a new railway line expected to run along the shores of the Caspian Sea, but construction has not started yet. Road transport, however, offers the greatest opportunity to enjoy the scenery and some of the sites. Daily intercity **buses** and *savari* services run north from Tehran to Rasht via Qazvin and to Chalus from the Western bus terminal at Azadi Square. The two-lane Karaj–Chalus road gets exceptionally busy on weekends and on certain

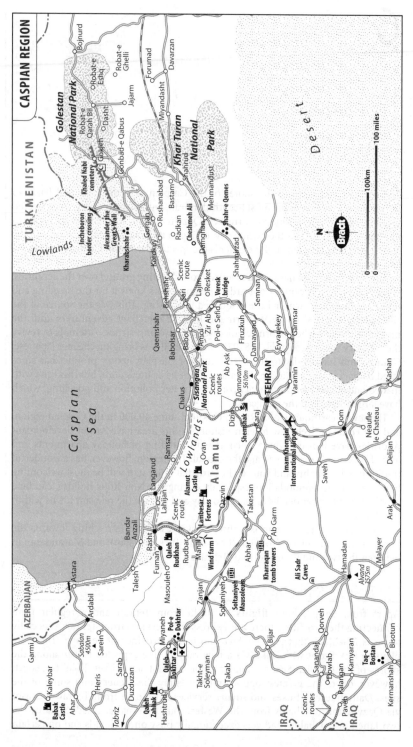

AZERBAIJAN

TURKMENISTAN

Lowlands

Caspian Sea

Golestan *National Park*

Khar Turan *National Park*

Desert

Bojnurd
Robat-e Ghelli
Robat-e Eshq
Robat-e Qarah Bil
Gomen
Dasht
Jajarm
Forumad
Davarzan
Miyandasht

Khaled Nabi cemetery
Incheboron border crossing
Alexander the Great's Wall
Kharabshahr
Gonbad-e Qabus
Gorgan
Kordkuy
Rushanabad
Radkan
Bastam
Shahrud
Mehmandust
Shahr-e Qomes

Sari
Behshahr
Scenic route
Qaemshahr
Babolsar
Babol
Amol
Zir Ab
Pol-e Sefid
Resket
Lajim
Veresk bridge
Cheshmeh Ali
Damghan
Shahmirzad
Semnan

Bandar Anzali
Rasht
Fuman
Talesh
Astara
Ardabil
Lahijan
Langarud
Ramsar
Chalus
Lowlands

Sisangan *National Park*
Scenic routes
Ab Ask
Ab Ask
Damavand 5670m
Shenshak
Dizin
Karaj
TEHRAN
Firuzkuh
Damavand
Eyvanekey
Garmsar
Varamin

Qaleh Rudkhan
Masouleh
Scenic route
Ovan
Alamut Castle
Alamut
Lambesar Fortress
Wind farm
Manjil
Rudbar
Qazvin
Takestan
Ab Garm
Abhar

Imam Khomeini International Airport

Takht-e Soleyman
Takab
Zanjan
Soltaniyeh
Soltaniyeh Mausoleum
Kharraqan tomb towers
Ali Sadr Caves
Bijar
Hamadan
Alvand 3575m
Malayer

Miyaneh
Pol-e Dokhtar
Qaleh Dokhtar
Qaleh Dokhtar
Hashtrud
Qaleh Zahhak
Tabriz
Babak Castle
Kaleybar
Ahar
Duzduzan
Heris
Sarab
Sarein
Sabalan 4500m
Garmi

Saveh
Delijan
Qom
Neaufle le Chateau
Kashan
Arak

IRAQ
IRAQ
Scenic routes
Paveh
Palangan
Kamyaran
Sanandaj
Qorveh
Ravansar
Kermanshah
Bisotun
Taq-e Bostan

Bradt

N

0 ___ 100km
0 ___ 100 miles

days (eg: Friday afternoons); both lanes are used for one-way traffic in the direction of Tehran. Comparatively few non-Iranians come this way, as historic monuments are few and far between, but do go to this region before its distinctive village character is completely swamped in holiday apartment complexes, which are taking over the shoreline. The roads are good and well engineered, but the hundreds of Tehrani families travelling to and from the region to their holiday homes mean the driving can be as mindless and dangerous as in the capital itself. The coastal road running along the Caspian Sea all the way from Astara to Chalus will not leave you disappointed. Here it is also reasonably easy to hitch a *savari* taxi passing by at great speed.

If there is no time to explore the whole of this region, there are three choices from Tehran: due north to Chalus; northwest to Gilan (this route runs through Qazvin, which is the best stopover if visiting Alamut; page 129); or east and subsequently northeast to Mazandaran and Golestan provinces. For the third option the Tehran–Sari train journey is particularly recommended (see box, page 204).

TOWARDS GILAN

The motorway towards Gilan province curves in a northeasterly direction after Qazvin and stretches a further 114km to the town of **Rudbar** (رودبار) (65km before reaching Rasht), which lies to the northwest and is famous locally for its olives. It is here that the tree-lined hillsides and the distinctive high-gabled roofs of Gilan's houses begin. The whole area is associated with the marvellous finds from the **Marlik** royal necropolis, locally known as Cheragh Ali Tappeh, excavated during 1961–66 by the Iranian authorities and already overgrown by the mid 1970s. Although most of the 53 stone-slab tombs excavated had been looted by grave robbers (probably a major source of the so-called Amlash artefacts sold in the West), enough survives to show that this site continued to be used for burials over two or three centuries from about the 1st millennium BCE. The grave goods, some on display at Tehran's Reza Abbasi Museum, fall into three groupings: bronze weapons and ornament, belonging to 'warrior kings'; jewellery and figurines associated with their womenfolk; and more domestic artefacts, which the archaeologists associated with servants. For those interested in the transmission of beliefs about the afterlife, it is fascinating to note that tombs with horse skeletons were also uncovered, which immediately recalls burial traditions found across Asia from northern Cyprus to China and southern Siberia. Noting similarities in the finds with those from the Sialk, Ziwiyeh and Hasanlu excavations and the striking parallels with Assyrian motifs, the Iranian archaeologists suggest that the population for some reason moved from Marlik to resettle at Sialk (Level VI) around 900BCE. A number of other archaeological settlements similarly dated have been identified in the region, for example Rostamabad, some 15km north of Rudbar. In this region were the valley strongholds associated with the medieval Assassins, the scourge of Crusader and Muslim leaders alike, but it is best to approach the so-called Valley of the Assassins from Qazvin (see box, page 131), and also overnight there (page 130).

RASHT رشت *Telephone code 013*

The regional capital (current population 698,000) since Safavid times, Rasht in the 19th century was renowned for its high-quality patchwork (Rasht work) used for wall-hangings, saddlecloths, floor coverings and for the gloriously coloured tents used in court circles when hunting. Like the Ottoman tents currently displayed in the Military Museum, Istanbul, these Qajar tents bore no resemblance to the canvas tents of early 20th-century Europe but were glorious architectural statements in rainbow colours with eye-catching designs composed of patchwork decorated with chain-stitch embroidery. Today, Rasht is known only for its reputation as perhaps the wettest place in Iran, its good food (one well-known restaurant is Moharram, close to the new masjed-e jame) and a more relaxed attitude to the separation of the genders. It is also the birthplace of Mirza Kuchek Khan, founder of the revolutionary, early 20th-century Forest Movement (Nehzat-e Jangal) and who is considered a national hero in Iran. His former house is a **museum** now (Ostad Sara St; ⊕ 09.00–21.00; entry 300,000 rials), and well worth a visit. The tomb of Mirza Kuchek Khan is some distance away at the **Soleyman Darab Cemetery** on the outskirts of Rasht.

The city boasts very few historic buildings, as Russian forces ran amok in 1668 slaughtering the population and destroying everything that stood in their way, even sinking the Persian navy on the Caspian Sea before ransacking Rasht. Further occupation during World War I caused more damage, with the total destruction of the bazaar by the Bolsheviks in 1920. The 1991 earthquake brought down anything that had survived, including the former masjed-e jame, now rebuilt to a new design, an unhappy mixture of 'classical Safavid' and Gilani vernacular styles. That said, Rasht is quite atmospheric. Its traditional central bazaar with freshly caught fish on sale and always-smiling locals is reason enough to come here. The more modern and upmarket Golsar district is the place to head for cafés and nightlife. Rasht and its wonderful city character were well captured in the beautifully nostalgic film *What is the time in your world?* (2014) with Leila Hatami.

Getting there and away
Below is a bus departure schedule with selected times from Tehran:

From	Departure	Price (rials)
Tehran (Beyhaghi)	00.30; 01.00; 05.00; 08.00; 10.00; 10.30; 11.00; 13.30; 14.00; 15.00; 17.00; 18.00; 19.00; 20.00; 21.00; 22.00; 23.00	200,000–350,000
Tehran (southern)	06.45	200,000–350,000
Tehran (western)	00.30; 06.00; hourly between 07.00 & 22.00	200,000–350,000

🏠 Where to stay and eat
🏠 **Pardis Hotel** (50 rooms) Emam Bd; ☎ 33231101, 33231105; w rashtpardishotel.com. Opened in 1985 & located just a few blocks down the road from Grand Kadus Hotel, this is a pleasant place with an inviting lobby & reception area. The staff are helpful & polite. Smallish rooms are pristine & come with little balconies, but unfortunately not all have Western-style toilets. $$$

🏠 **Rasht Grand Kadus Hotel** (100+ rooms) Azadi Bd; ☎ 33365072; w kadus-hotel.ir. A self-proclaimed 4-star option located at the edge of the city centre. Comes with amenities such as tennis court & outdoor pool, but the décor is standard & rather lacking in flair, although rooms facing the street come with small balconies. $$$

✳ 🏠 **Hotel Ordibehesht** (30 rooms) Shahrdari Sq; ☎ 33229210, 33229211. Charming, central & a little old-fashioned, the hotel has large rooms & equally large bathrooms. Reception welcomes with a cosy velvety seating area where you can have a cup of tea & use Wi-Fi, which is not available in the rooms. Staff are friendly & there are a few traditional restaurants in the area. $$

✗ **Restaurant Moharram** Imam Bd, near Pardis Hotel; ☎ 33666090; w moharamrestaurant.com. The décor is more suitable to a fast-food restaurant, but the smallish local specialities menu is really good & well served with a small starter of Gilan olives. Fried Caspian white fish is recommended. $$

Café de Paris Gilan Bd, Golsar; 33772680; 17.00–midnight. A modern café with cosy atmosphere. Dim lighting gives it a smoky feel. There is a good choice of drinks & cakes. **$$**

MASOULEH ماسوله ✳ In this region is the attractive hill village of Masouleh, over 1,000 years old and 56km west of Rasht via Fuman (فومن), which is regularly cut off by snow during the winter months. When in Fuman, make sure to try the traditional freshly baked and still-warm *kolucheh* biscuits filled with soft walnut paste. These are also sold in shops around Rasht and even Tehran, but are really the best in Fuman. Masouleh has managed to retain its charm, thanks to its welcoming residents and stunning natural scenery, despite crowds of young tourists coming here in groups to smoke *qalian* and relax in one of the local cafés. Go up to the cemetery on the opposite hill for better views of the village. Some 25km southwest from Fuman up in the mountain forests is the visually impressive and well-preserved Ismaili fort **Qaleh Rudkhan** (قلعه رودخان) ✳ (09.00–17.00; entry 300,000 rials), which was rebuilt during Seljuk times. It boasts 65 well-preserved towers and its outer walls stretch 1,500m. The walk up here is a pleasant 4km climb; steps are reasonably good, but at times steep. Take a large bottle of water with you and watch out, especially if it has rained recently; it can get slippery. You could spend a whole day here and perhaps stay overnight (there are a few guesthouses under construction in the rest area at the bottom of the climb).

Getting there and away Take a *savari* from Rasht to Fuman 30km away and another one from there to Masouleh, around 32km or 45 minutes from Fuman. Alternatively, a *darbast* **taxi** from Rasht to Masouleh costs around 1,000,000 rials. Similarly, you can reach Qaleh Rudkhan by travelling to Fuman, 21km away, and then hiring a taxi. Below is a bus departure schedule with selected times from Tehran to Fuman:

From	Departure	Price (rials)
Tehran (western)	Hourly between 06.30 & 12.30; 17.00; 19.45; 22.30; 23.15	310,000–380,000

Where to stay and eat

Mehran Hotel (10 rooms) There is no specific address, so arrange for a hotel staff member to come & fetch you; 013 34752096. Towards the back of the village, rooms come with kitchenette & terraces with beautiful views. Excellent & clean mountain accommodation. **$$**

Monfared Hotel (25 rooms) There is no specific address, but the hotel is located at the edge of the village; 013 37572374. Simple but clean budget hotel, albeit with a little less character than the Mehran Hotel. English is spoken. **$$**

Khaneh Moallem Restaurant Located behind the Monfared Hotel. Has excellent local dishes. **$**

BANDAR ANZALI بندرانزلی *Telephone code 013*
The road to Bandar Anzali, the main commercial port of the Iranian Caspian (40km away from Rasht), celebrated in its former name, Bandar Pahlavi, passes through more green hills spotted with sharply angled thatched farm buildings. Development began as early as the 15th century, but major improvements were made to the port facilities during the 1920s and 1930s. By all reports the Saturday market is very good. The town itself is divided by an inlet: the easterly section is the commercial port area, while the west is less developed.

Getting there and away Below is a bus departure schedule with selected times from Tehran:

From	Departure	Price (rials)
Tehran (Beyhaghi)	01.00; 02.00; 05.00; 08.35; 10.30; 16.30; 19.00; 22.00; 23.00; 23.59	320,000–400,000
Tehran (western)	06.30 (via Rasht); 08.00 (via Rasht); 09.30 (via Rasht); 10.30; 11.30; 12.30; 13.00; 14.00; 15.30; 16.00 (via Rasht); 17.30 (via Rasht); 19.30 (via Rasht); 20.30 (via Rasht); 22.15 (via Rasht); 23.00; 23.30 (via Rasht)	320,000–400,000

Where to stay and eat You may prefer to stay in Bandar Anzali, as Rasht's hotels are a little more expensive. Most hotels here are located in buildings more than 80 years old and do not lack a certain charm.

Gol-e Sang Hotel (19 rooms) Imam Sq; 44543910. Very central & charming, the hotel is located in an early 20th-century Russian building with high ceilings & matching wooden doors. Has a traditional restaurant ($) on the ground floor. $$

Hotel Iran (40 rooms) Motahhari St; 44542524. A pleasant old-fashioned hotel right by the port & a park. Rooms come with sea view & antique furniture. Staff are chatty & knowledgeable about the area. $$

WEST AND SOUTHWEST OF BANDAR ANZALI

TALESH تالش From Bandar Anzali it is an attractive drive among conifers, beeches and rice fields along a good road westwards following the coastline. Some 15km on, and again 7km before Talesh (also called Hashtpar) and 65km from Bandar Anzali, there are roadside displays of colourful *ghelims* made in the hill villages, adding yet more colour to the vibrant greens of the rice fields. Keep an eye open for the low, long, thatched **silkworm sheds** set within mulberry plantations, and the steeply dipping storage roofs supported by chunky stone pillars.

Getting there and away Below is a bus departure schedule for Astara with selected times from Tehran:

From	Departure	Price (rials)
Tehran (western)	08.00; 08.30; 10.00; 12.30; 15.45; 17.00; 17.45; 19.45; 22.30; 23.15	420,000–500,000

Where to stay and eat Accommodation in Talesh is either very basic or expensive, but if you do decide to stay, there are a few choices here or in **Astara** (آستارا), the frontier with the Republic of Azerbaijan. If continuing on towards Baku, you can walk to the border station to cross into Azerbaijan (make sure you have the visa in advance). If staying at the Espinas Astara, a turn-off west into the mountains leads to the famous shrine of **Ardabil** (page 216), which is strongly linked with the Safavid dynasty.

Espinas Astara (160 rooms) Lake Estil; 013 44856801, 44856805; w espinashotels.com. This is a more luxurious option near Astara; it is a resort on the shore of Lake Estil with stunning views of the lake and mountains, 5km from Astara. $$$

Astara Tourist Inn (40 rooms) Hakim Nezami St, Astara; 013 4816063, 4822134, 4822135. A clean & central inn. $$

Rastin Hotel (25 rooms) Talesh, off motorway 49; 013 44252499; w hotelrastin.

Chinese histories record how central Asia finally managed to learn the secrets of silkworm rearing and how to acquire the eggs. About 1,600 years ago a central Asian ruler was cunning enough to warn his Chinese princess bride-to-be that as silkworms were unknown in his country, she could never have new silk robes to wear unless she brought her own supply. Knowing that imperial customs officials would search her luggage but never her person, she smuggled silkworm eggs out of the country in her headdress to her wedding. By the early 9th century the shores of the Caspian were famous for the quantity and quality of their raw silk, and plantations of mulberries were being harvested to feed the silkworms. There are no medieval descriptions of the 'nursery' huts but very probably they were essentially the same as they are today: long, low-lying huts with thatched roofs to maintain a shaded, warm but humid atmosphere to ensure that the eggs hatch in the large flat trays in which they are kept. The worms feed greedily and very noisily on white mulberry leaves, growing noticeably in size over the course of six weeks before beginning their cocoon spinning over the next ten days. Some are kept aside to complete the full cycle, turning into the moth and producing eggs, but for most of the cocoons the end comes quickly. They are subjected to full sunlight or hot water, which kills the pupa before it breaks out of its silk protection (which damages the length of silk filament to be harvested). The natural gumminess of the cocoon is water soluble so a stick or fingers are used to gather up the fine filament, which is then reeled off, each up to a kilometre long.

To counterweigh the import of silkworms from China and India, Iran has been working on expanding local production. As of 2019, 30 out of 31 Iranian provinces were in some shape or form involved in silkworm production, which has since 2009 increased by 55%. More than 34% of all silkworms are cultivated in Gilan.

com. Although located on the outskirts of Talesh, it offers comfortable apt-style rooms with a warm old-fashioned décor. **$$**

🏠 **Vasli Hotel** (15 rooms) Down the road from the Astara Tourist Inn; 📞 013 4815806. A more basic establishment than the Astara Tourist Inn. **$**

EAST OF BANDAR ANZALI

LAHIJAN لاهیجان The road eastwards from Bandar Anzali similarly follows the coastline. Many of the Qajar kings and princes built retreats here as bases for hunting expeditions but, with the exception of Lahijan, you need to travel further east if historic monuments are of interest. Lahijan, 79km from Bandar Anzali, was where the young Safavid prince Ismail (r1501–24) was brought up secretly for five years, to protect him from further imprisonment and possible assassination by the Aq Qoyunlu. Today it is known for tea growing and processing. In its thriving western bazaar area, just off the *maydan* bearing the same local name, is the **Masjed-e Chahar Padeshah** (Four Kings), more correctly called Chahar Oleyeh and better described as a mausoleum. Despite the name, only three cenotaphs of the Sadat-e Keyeh family are housed here in two main rooms under a low gabled roof. It has been suggested that the mausoleum dates from early Mongol times but nothing

The Caspian Sea is the source of 90% of caviar produced in the world and is home to the greatest variety (six out of 27 species worldwide) of sturgeon. Iran is one of the leading producers of caviar and the decline in species, caused by poaching, overfishing and pollution, is of serious cultural and economic concern to the Islamic Republic. Thus, ever-increasing emphasis is being placed on the development of fish hatcheries to restore depleted stocks. In 2013, the International Sturgeon Research Institute based in Bandar Anzali confirmed that after 18 years of research it had successfully applied biotechnology to fish farming and achieved the artificial reproduction of all sturgeon species from the Caspian Sea.

Around one tonne of farmed sturgeon caviar was produced in Iran in 2013 and more than 50% of it was exported to Europe and the rest of the world. Furthermore, in 2012 and equally in 2013, the Iranian Fisheries Organisation, Shilat, in charge of production and distribution of Iranian caviar, has released more than 5 million sturgeon fry into the Caspian Sea.

The potential for sturgeon fish farming in Iran, with its 900km of coastline, remains, however, underdeveloped. Sturgeon could be farmed in 16 out of 31 provinces. The Gomishan area of Golestan province, with its numerous shrimp farms, offers some of the best conditions for sturgeon farming.

about the building indicates that. The exterior wall paintings, depicting Abu Fazl Abbas riding off to find water for Hossein's supporters and their families at Karbala, are late 19th century, as are the colourful dado tiles; both schemes bear 1920s–30s repair dates. The beautiful wooden doors that once graced its main entrance from the bazaar have been removed to the new Islamic section of the Tehran Archaeological Museum. In the opposite (east) direction, about 3km outside the town, set up on the hillside from the main coast road, is the **Bogheh Sheikh Zahid Gilani** (بقعه شیخ زاهد گیلانی), a square mausoleum honouring the spiritual advisor to Sheikh Safi al-Din, founder of the Safavid dynasty. A carved inscription gives a construction date of 1419 but there is nothing 15th century about the present building and its unusual tiered, pyramidal tent roof tiled in turquoise and yellow. Not unlike many other towns along the Caspian coast Lahijan has a telecabin (250,000 rials return trip) up to the **Bam-e Sabz**, where you can have a cup of tea and *qalian* while enjoying the spectacular views.

Getting there and away Below is a bus departure schedule for Lahijan with selected times from Tehran:

From	Departure	Price (rials)
Tehran (Beyhaghi)	01.30; 07.15; 08.30; 10.00; 11.30; 13.30; 15.00; 17.30; 21.00	220,000–380,000
Tehran (western)	Hourly between 06.30 & 23.30	220,000–380,000

LANGARUD AND RAMSAR Some 10km further east by the coast is **Langarud** (لنگرود), famous for its late 19th- to early 20th-century wall paintings decorating the Mahalla shrine of **Agha Seyyed Hossein** and Ibrahim, largely rebuilt in the 18th century. Just outside the town, in the village of Lisehrud, amid sweet and bitter orange groves and tea plantations, lies **Dasbagh Ecofarmstay** (see opposite)

Started as a sustainable farming project, this is the first ecofarm tourism centre in Iran.

Approximately 40km away along the coastal road, in the village of **Ghasem Abad Sofla** (قاسم آباد سفلا) lies Gilan's first ecolodge, **Gileboom** (see below). Locals in the town are now well used to tourists and will in no time assist a stranger lost amid narrow alleys, to find their way to the ecolodge.

About 16km on, continuing eastwards, is **Ramsar** (رامسر), a town of 30,000 people, and formerly a favourite haunt of the two Pahlavi rulers. Mazandaran province starts on the outskirts of the city, at the Ramsar telecabin. In 1971, the Ramsar Convention was signed here by 21 nations. The number of signatory parties today stands at 170. For more details, see w ramsar.org. Next to the Ramsar hotels, two exquisite **villas** will catch your eye. Formerly Reza Shah's property, these are now completely abandoned. Ramsar itself is thriving thanks to the Tehran holiday trade, with many shops now catering for their custom.

Where to stay and eat

New Ramsar Parsian Azadi Hotel (121 rooms) Rajaie St, Ramsar; ℓ011 55223593, 55223595; e info@ramsarhotel.ir. At the foothills of the Alborz Mountains, this is the best place to overnight in Ramsar. Although common areas & the lobby are in need of some freshening up, & in the rooms a hook or two could be screwed in a little tighter, the hotel is overall a treat. Rooms are impeccable with the furniture in the right place & large bathrooms. The **Grand Hotel** next door, which was commissioned by Reza Shah in the 1930s, echoing the furnishings of Istanbul's Khedive Palace on the Bosphorus, functions as a museum & is testimony to its past glory. The garden at the back is open to the public & New Ramsar Hotel guests. **$$$**

Gileboom (5 rooms) Ghasem Abad Sofla; m 0919 6396185; w gileboom.info. Run by Mahin & Khosrow on the premise of sustainable use of the nature's resources, everything here exudes local charm & traditions. Hiking & nature tours, as well as visits to the local *chadorchabbafi* textile-weaving workshop, can be arranged here. **$$**

✷ **Dasbagh Ecofarmstay** (5 rooms; unlimited camping) Lisehrud; m 0935 2424957. Run by friendly Reyhan & Ali, this venture started as a sustainable farming project; it is the first ecofarm tourism centre in Iran. Both travellers & volunteers are welcome to stay in the authentically restored 2-storey rural house & practise their farming skills or simply enjoy the beauty of the area. **$–$$**

What to see and do

Ramsar Palace Museum and Garden ✷ (Rajaie St, a few hundred metres up from the New Ramsar Hotel; ℓ011 55225374, 011 55225375; entry 300,000 rials) Formerly the property and leisure palace of the Pahlavi monarchs, the museum complex comprises a number of detached buildings surrounded by the immaculate gardens of orange trees.

One of the main buildings here is the **Marble Palace** (*kakh-r marmar*) (کاخ مرمر) built of red marble in 1938. The entrance door opens into the opulent **living room** with chandeliers, rich carpets and Baroque-style mirrors on the walls. Next is the **reading room**, equally European in style; the only Iranian item here is the floor carpet from Mashhad. The Pahlavis had clearly preferred Western décor, mostly French.

During the reign of Mohammad Reza Shah, the palace was used for ceremonial purposes only, which meant that it has remained unchanged since the late 1930s. Outside the palace there is a pool with two beluga sturgeons, symbolising the wealth of the Caspian Sea. Behind the Marble Palace is a small **traditional bath museum**, built in 1937 to be used by the first Pahlavi monarch as a spa. All the tiles are original and the furnishings are German-made.

The **Iran Ivory Museum (kakh-e kaj)** (کاخ کاج) (East of the Marble Palace; entry 300,000 rials; paid at the entrance to the gardens) is a true highlight of the visit here. It is the first museum dedicated to ivory in the western part of Asia with the collection featuring 300 rare and exquisite elephant ivory pieces from India, China and Africa. It offers insight both into the fine art of ivory cutting and the exuberant taste of royalty. All exhibits are clearly referenced in both Persian and English. Most statuettes date to mid-20th-century China and India, but there are some other interesting items such as daggers from Russia's Republic of Dagestan, which until the early 19th century was under Persian rule.

Set towards the back of the ivory museum is the tiny, but interesting **Ramsar Museum of Anthropology of Northern Iran**. On display, there are old schoolbooks, as well as some school pictures of Reza Shah. There is an over 100-year-old wooden milk and *mast* measurement gauge and a 250-year-old metal Sufi *kashkul* beggar's bowl, bearing inscriptions and supplications in Arabic and Persian.

Mijran Dam سد میجران In the vicinity of Ramsar, approximately 10km further along the coastal road to Chalus, and 5km inland from the **Mar Mountain** (*markuh*), amid lush forests lies the picturesque **Mijran Dam Lake** on the Nasa River (*nasarud*). Constructed in early 2004, the dam supplies much-needed water to the surrounding fields.

MOVING ON Travelling further along the coast towards Tonekabon, you arrive at **Chalus** (چالوس). If returning to Tehran from here, find time to visit the village of **Kandalous** (کندلوس), located roughly 42km into the mountains off the Chalus–Tehran road. The setting and the surrounding scenery have inspired master artist Kamal al-Molk to paint some of his works here.

A number of local residents rent rooms in their private houses to wandering travellers, but the village gets completely booked out on 5th Khordad (end July) for the annual Ferdinmasho Festival of Music and Dance. There is no restaurant in the village, but you can purchase homemade meals from the central kitchen (⊕ noon–22.00 daily), which is located down the steps from the main parking area and the convenience store.

AMOL AND AROUND

While Mazandaran province is similar to Gilan geographically, it is a little more traditional in terms of dress code and the further east you move in the direction of Mashhad, the more noticeable the differences between the two will appear. From Chalus, the more southerly road leads to **Amol** (آمل) (population 222,000), once the capital of medieval Tabaristan province and famous for a certain kind of 13th-century pottery that was, perhaps, produced here. The settlement was destroyed by Mongol forces, so its monuments post-date their ravages. The easiest to find is the **Imamzadeh Ibrahim** set within a cemetery enclosure on the northern outskirts. Locals understand this 'Ibrahim' to be the son of Imam Musa, but the 1519 wooden cenotaph – now totally cloth-covered – suggests another (unidentified) Ibrahim was interred here along with his brother Yahya and their mother. A large modern ambulatory has been constructed around the square tomb tower (c1426), but modern repairs and decoration have cheerfully ignored the historic architecture. Inside the actual tomb tower a riot of rainbow gloss paint overshadows remnants of 15th-century wall painting, while flat mirror glass and highly varnished wooden pillars confidently detract any merit from the new construction. In the same cemetery is another 15th-century mausoleum, built to honour **Hajji Namdar**, who reportedly travelled from eastern Iran to repair his friend Ibrahim's tomb but died before completion. Judging from the exterior, more remains of the original building, but it now serves as the local headquarters for the Revolutionary Guard and is totally inaccessible.

In the bazaar, off Mostafa Khomeini and Bahonar streets, is a modern complex, **Mashhad Mir Bozorg**, which includes a 17th-century building, possibly a *khanqah*, with some external tiling in place. Having read about the early 15th-century **Imamzadeh Qasem** 'located behind the main bazaar … adjoining a modern mosque', whose octagonal exterior was described as having rich plasterwork, we tried to find it. Finally we were directed 3km west outside the town, to a clump of trees shielding a sad cemetery with many unmarked graves, the final resting place of local *mujahedins* killed during the early years of the revolution. Only recently have relatives been allowed to place some gravestones, but dried rose petals and burned candles show they are remembered as family rather than for any political activity. As for the *imamzadeh*, nothing about the small building there accorded with the published description. A case of mistaken identity? Or is the 'original' Qasem now known by a different name? Three more 15th-century **tomb towers** survive in Amol, all near to each other: that of **Naser al-Haqq** (also known as Gonbad-e Seyyed Sadaf) has a square plan inside and out with an eight-sided tent-dome, as does the **Gonbad-e Gabri** (or Shams-e Rasul), but the **Imamzadeh Seh Tan** ('three bodies') is octagonal in plan.

If travelling to Amol in spring, en route from Tehran, find time to stop by the village of **Ab Ask**, which is famous for its 600-year-old *varf chal* ceremony (literally meaning 'snow storing'); it involves local men carrying frozen snow cubes and dropping them into a 10m-deep pit in the belief that once melted it would provide fresh water for animals and thirsty passers-by.

About 50km further east from Amol is **Babol** (بابل), which in the last 70 or so years has lost many of its architectural treasures and now just two 15th-century *imamzadehs* remain. One is set just back on the main Amol–Sari road, built to honour the dervish, Fakhr al-Din, in 1430. Its basic circular form and tent roof, separated by two rows of blind niches with light and dark blue tiles in the drum, is reminiscent of the Galata Tower, Istanbul, though of course it is much smaller. The other tomb tower stands some 4km to the north of the Amol road. It was built in 1471 to commemorate **Sultan Mohammad Tahir Ibn Musa Qasem** by his two sons, using the architect Shams al-Din Ibn Nasrallah Motahhari according to the cenotaph inscription. One set of doors records another date 20 years after, which perhaps was the completion date.

A quick glance at the map and you could confuse Babol with the town of **Babolsar** (بابلسر), some 30km north, by the Caspian coast. This too has a couple of 15th-century octagonal **tomb towers**, which have seen better days. One was built to honour Ibrahim Abu Javeh – or rather his head, which is all that is buried here; he was a son of Imam Musa and the brother of Imam Reza (see box, page 347), and some 300m away is another *imamzadeh* marking the burial place of Bibi Sakineh, a sister of Imam Reza.

 WHERE TO STAY AND EAT You may stay in Chalus, or in Babol. Better hotels are all located along the Caspian coast.

Marjan Hotel (60 rooms) Keshvari Sq, Babol; ☎011 32252186, 32252189. Very basic, but clean, conveniently located across the road from the *savari* terminal for Sari & beyond. **$$**

With a population of around 300,000, a **Saturday market** day in Sari buzzes, with money and people coming from the many rice and tea plantations in the area. It was one of the last important Iranian towns to fall to the Muslim Arabs in the 7th century, and a strong Zoroastrian community lasted here until the 19th century. Like many towns in this area, Sari, 72km east from Amol, suffered badly from both the Mongol and then Timurid campaigns sweeping through the eastern provinces. So, although the small local **museum** houses some Sasanid gold and silver artefacts found locally, its three historic buildings date from the Timurid period and once again they are tomb towers. The **Imamzadeh Yahya** is situated in the bazaar southwest of the **Maydan-e Saat** (Clock Square). The shrine has at its hub a cylindrical tower with a 12-sided tent roof, built in 1442–46 to house the remains of a descendant of Imam Musa, but is now faced by a modern brick portico and its beautiful pair of doors has been removed for safe keeping to Tehran. Just behind it is a slightly later square tower with an eight-sided tent-like dome, the **Imamzadeh Seyyed Zaynolabeddin** (though Jamal and Kamal are also named in the tile inscription); in some publications the monument is given as Seyyed Mohammad Reza. Originally constructed in 1448–50, the tomb retains some of its 15th-century *cuerda seca* tiling inside, and on the exterior some turquoise brick inserts survive in the zone of transition. Just off Enghelab Street down from the Maydan-e Saat, you will find the Qajar-period **Kolbadi House** (*emarat-e kolbadi)* (entry 100,000 rials), presently a museum and formerly the private house of Manuchehr Khan Kolbadi, a member of the parliament of Iran. Walk past it and you will come across an old, possibly Qajar-period, *ab-e anbar* (traditional reservoir).

Some 3km from the centre, off Imam Reza Boulevard, stands the **Imamzadeh Abbas** in a small garden. Its beautifully carved cenotaph dates the octagonal tomb tower with its eight-sided tent roof to 1492, stating that it was constructed after Imam Abbas, a son of Imam Musa, appeared here in a vision in 1424; an inverted Safavid blue and white bowl marks the apex of the inner hemispherical dome. A low-lying brick building has been added to the front; a young guardian who takes great pride in keeping the place immaculate sprinkles rose water on the paving and rugs.

GETTING THERE AND AWAY Below is a bus departure schedule with selected times from Tehran to Sari:

From	Departure	Price (rials)
Tehran (Beyhaghi)	08.30; 10.00; noon; 14.00; 16.00; 18.00; 21.30; 23.00; 23.59	260,000–350,000
Tehran (Pars)	01.00; 02.00; 04.30; hourly between 08.00 & 19.00; 22.30	260,000–350,000

TRAIN JOURNEY FROM TEHRAN TO SARI

Built by German, Danish and Austrian engineers more than 80 years ago, this scenic train route lies through the Alborz Mountains northeast of Tehran, passing by Firuzkuh and climbing slowly up the mountains and then down again via the spectacular Veresk arch bridge built in 1936, towards the rice fields of Mazandaran.

The train makes a few stops en route, including in Firuzkuh, Veresk, Pol-e Sefid and Shirgah and leaves Tehran central station daily at 06.30. It takes 7 hours to reach Sari, with the return service departing at 17.00, but timetables are seasonal and may vary. Prices start at approximately 300,000 rials per person for a six-person compartment.

WHERE TO STAY AND EAT

Asram Hotel (60 rooms) ☎011 33255090. Very reasonable & clean central hotel. Rooms are spacious & come with small balconies. There is also a travel agency, run by the hotel, which can organise tours around Sari. **$$**

EXCURSIONS FROM SARI If time allows, it is worth making a detour from Sari, dropping south via Qaemshahr (قائمشهر), formerly Shahi (or alternatively, a longer drive north from Semnan via Firuzkuh), to **Zir Ab** for the tomb tower at **Lajim** 29km further east, and another in the village of **Resket**, around 36km from Pol-e Sefid. Locally known as the **Imamzadeh Abdullah**, the Lajim tower was probably erected in 1023 and – although Iran had then been under Muslim rule for almost four centuries – the patron had the brick inscription for her beloved son, Shahriyar Ibn al-Abbas Ibn Shahriyar, written in pre-Islamic Pahlavi script as well as Arabic. So it's interesting on two counts: firstly, the Pahlavi script and, secondly, this is the earliest known building commissioned by a female patron in this part of Iran; she was possibly related through marriage to the famous tomb-tower builder Qabus Ibn Wushmagir (page 207).

To see the tomb tower at Resket (*borj-e resket*), it is probably best to backtrack and continue to the village of Duab, just before Pol-e Sefid, although some prefer to walk the 2km or more cross-country. It is now thought the Resket tomb tower dates from c1106, during the first years of rule by the Seljuk sultan, Sanjar (r1097–1157), and once again Pahlavi script occurs even at this late date, this time in the names of the two brothers interred here, Hormuzd and Hdyer. Yet at the same time there is the *shahada* ('There is no God but God. Mohammad is the messenger of God.') recorded in the plaster door-plaque, and Quranic floriated *Kufic* inscriptions relating to death (Q1:36) running around the cylindrical exterior, below the dome and the elaborate decoration.

From Sari, the road continues northeastwards through woodlands, orange groves and rice fields towards **Behshahr** (بهشهر). Archaeological investigation carried out in the 1950s by a Pennsylvanian team in the limestone cliff caves to the south, at **Turujan Tappeh**, between Gelin and Fars Abad, proved the place had been settled around 9500BCE. Besides pottery shards and evidence of seal fishing, the Neolithic skeleton of a teenage girl was found, whose bones had been ritually painted red after removal of the flesh. Signs of even earlier settlements were found in other caves, just south of Behshahr itself, by Cambridge (UK) archaeologists in 1964, pushing the date back another millennium. Behshahr, earlier known as Ashraf, has a royal **Abbas Abad pavilion and gardens**, established in Safavid times, which were heavily restored in the 1930s by Reza Shah, high in the hills overlooking the town. Abbas Abad is one of the nine Iranian gardens on UNESCO's Persian Garden World Heritage List.

Some 40km further east, past Gaz, is **Kharabshahr** ('ruined city'), the 9th-century city of Tammisha, excavated in the mid 1960s by a London University team. In the Sasanid period, probably around the 550s CE, thick defence walls were constructed to protect the townspeople from tribal raids launched from the central Asian steppes. It became the administrative centre for a local warlord with a Friday mosque and citadel, until destroyed by the first Mongol wave in 1220. From here, stretching eastwards along the minor road to Gokjeh and passing **Hajji Qushan** (on some maps, Hajehlar) are the remains of the huge brick walls – originally over 170km long with some 33 fortresses – known locally as **Alexander the Great's Wall** (*divar-e iskandar*), although it probably dates from Parthian times (eg: late 2nd century BCE). Thirteenth-century Iranian chroniclers and artists understood that it had been built to hold back those great enemies of civilisation, Gog and Magog. Stretching east from Gumishan to Mount Pishkamer and perhaps continuing into present-day Turkmenistan, it consisted of a ditch, some 3m wide, before the wall, defended by towers and forts. On the Iranian side, field cultivation came up to the wall line so the contrast between the wild steppe and settled agriculture would have been obvious.

Fifteen kilometres south of Kordkuy near the village of **Radkan** (رادکان) is an 11th-century cylindrical tomb tower 35m high, referred to as 'Radkan West' in academic publications. The two inscriptions, one above the door and the other just below the dome, in Arabic, plaited *Kufic* and also in Pahlavi, identify that a certain Abu Jafar Mohammad Ibn Wandarin was a local warlord whose Bawanid family had controlled the eastern Caspian region from around 665CE until it fragmented in 1349, having converted to Islam in 854CE. He ordered its construction in 1016, to house his remains after death.

Imamzadeh Roshanabad is located within a cemetery near the village of Sarkolateh, 41km west of Gorgan. It was constructed by Hajji Abdullah in 1460 according to the doors, although some scholars have suggested 1420. A long prayer hall introduces the tomb tower, which is described as possessing an 'extraordinary use of glazed tiles' and 'unique painting' on the interior depicting buildings, perhaps symbolising the Ardabil shrine, Mecca or Medina.

The main road continues to **Gorgan** (گرگان) (population 344,000), where the occasional Turkoman woman still wears her distinctive colourful shawl with a floral dress. The medieval town was famous for its amazing lustre-decorated pottery vessels; excavation work 4km west of the modern city between 1970 and 1977 found superb examples. Today most visitors come to visit the tomb tower **Gonbad-e Qabus** (also pronounced *qavus*), located some 80km away on the outskirts of Gonbad town. But Gorgan itself is worth a couple of hours' exploration, if only to look out for late 19th-century shops and houses which retain their traditional brick, wood and terracotta tiling, despite a severe earthquake in 1928. Buried in the vegetable and fruit section of the bazaar, near to Maydan-e Wahdat, there is the two-*ivan* **masjed-e jame**, with the remains of a Seljuk minaret over the main entrance, but the courtyard tilework dates from the 20th century. The helpful guardian will unlock the *ivan* to the far left of the main entrance which contains some exuberant Qajar plasterwork as well as the original mosque doors, moved here some years ago for their preservation. The lower carving has been worn away by the worshippers kissing and stroking the panels, but in the upper section the exquisite 15th-century work is clearly visible despite the thick modern varnish. Also here is a walnut *minbar*, gloriously unvarnished and decorated with the names of the Twelve Imams; across the front section is a date corresponding to 1609 (this area is only accessible to men). A 5-minute walk behind this mosque and straight through the bazaar, passing some lovely houses with overhanging eaves, leads to the **Imamzadeh Nur** (or Ishaq Ibn Musa Ibn Jafar). Although this 12-sided tomb tower has lost its original roof, its brick patterning is still attractive, and inside a little of the original, deeply carved plaster decoration remains, especially in the *mihrab*. Although the original doors have now vanished, one had a date corresponding to 1453 carved into it. If you stay here, 9km south of Gorgan town there is a **Tourist Inn** (67 rooms; ☏017 32540034; **$$**), located in a lovely forested area.

GONBAD-E QABUS گنبد کاووس

This UNESCO World Heritage monument (⏰ 08.00–20.00; entry 500,000 rials; the actual tower is closed, but ask a soldier on duty to let you have a quick look inside) is always mentioned in books on Iranian Islamic architecture. Robert Byron described

Gonbad-e Qabus as one of the 'great buildings of the world'. Its staggering size and strength of form look very out of place in the fragile, pretty garden now surrounding it. Two weary *kibitkas* or domed trellis tents stand by its side. We know something of the man who had it built in 1006 as a suitable family mausoleum. This was before he was deposed in 1012 and deliberately left to freeze to death in the Gorgan winter snows. He was the military commander, Amir Qabus Ibn Wushmagir, a famous calligrapher, known scholar (the famous medieval polymath al-Biruni dedicated his multi-volume *Chronology of Ancient Nations* to him), patron of the arts and renowned, bloodthirsty warlord. An artificial mound conceals the formidable foundations (late 19th-century Russian archaeologists gave up digging down after 10m) for this 51m-high tower of coffee-coloured brick. The basic circular plan, 17m in diameter, is quickly broken by ten soaring angular flanges and one small door. Two brick inscriptions run around the shaft in between the angled buttresses, one low down and the other high up, under the superbly 'tailored' conical dome which was once in grey-green brick, though what you see now is a modern replacement; both refer to the promise of paradise awaiting the true believer. There is just one small window in the roof, positioned to catch the rising sun which would illuminate, according to local legend, a suspended rock-crystal coffin holding the body of Qabus (not quite the cheap wooden coffin recommended in Islamic law).

South of here, Cambridge (UK) archaeologists excavating caves found evidence that people had inhabited the region from at least 40000BCE and possibly much earlier (65000BCE), hunting, working flint and living off bears, rhinoceros and also horses. This last point is interesting: the Caspian and Turkoman regions were once known for two special types of horse (see box, below). If you are staying here there is the simple **Qavus Hotel** (18 rooms; Imam Ali St; **$$**), where you may consider spending the night before continuing your journey.

AROUND GONBAD-E QABUS Just as intriguing, but very different, is **Khaled Nabi Cemetery** (گورستان خالد نبی) about 86km northeast of Gonbad-e Qabus, named after a tomb to a certain Khaled Nabi, near to the mountain called Gokjeh Dagh; up a steep,

CASPIAN AND TURKOMAN HORSES

The Caspian horse is similar but far from identical to the stocky Turkoman horse, the sturdy mount of the 12th-century Seljuk Turks and later Turkoman tribesmen. The Caspian stands about 11 or 13 hands high, but is narrower in width across the back, with a pronounced forehead and small ears, a distinctive oval hoof, which needs infrequent shoeing, and a unique haemoglobin structure. A small stud was established in 1965 near Shiraz, and later in Tehran, and immediately after the Islamic Revolution this section of the then-royal stables came under the Ministry of Jihad, but it is not known whether that stud still exists. The breed continues in the USA, Australia and also in the UK, as a mare and stallion were presented to Philip, Duke of Edinburgh, in 1971.

The Turkoman horse continues today in the modern breed known as Akhal Teke, often pale gold or possibly grey or bay in colour. It stands taller than the Caspian, at about 15 hands with a narrow chest, flat ribs and long back. The tail is comparatively short and the mane even more so. Its well-known stamina and ability to go without water for over 300km in desert conditions are put down to a distinct, constructed diet, low in bulk and high in protein, often made with animal fat and eggs mixed with barley.

largely unmetalled road. No-one knows who Khaled Nabi was, let alone if he was Muslim, but the real mystery is the 600-odd standing stones. Some are cylindrical and anything from 1m to 5m high, while others are rectangular with two upper lobes. There are no dating inscriptions, but a conservative guess is that these date from the 17th or 18th century and may mark a traditional Turkoman tribal burial site.

MOVING ON From Gorgan, most travellers continue towards Mashhad, or indeed to the Irano-Turkmenistan frontier (see box, page 351), but if you have to return to Tehran there is no need to backtrack – go by the 'southern' road via Shahrud and Semnan, as detailed below.

Shahrud شاهرود (population 166,000) is on the main road from Mashhad to Tehran. Train and daily bus services to and from Mashhad stop here. If you want to visit the masjed-e jame and famous shrine at Bastam, 12km to the north, you can stay in Bastam itself in the conveniently located Tourist Inn (see opposite), just a few metres up from the site. But do note that there is nothing else of historical interest around here and you might prefer to continue on to Damghan instead. There are numerous *savari* taxis and the journey between the two towns takes around an hour. But if you are indeed staying here and completely bored, around 15km past Bastam in the small village of Qaleh Mirza Soleyman there is a mausoleum of Sheikh Abu al-Hassan Kharaghani, a prominent 10th-century Iranian Sufi mystic.

BASTAM بسطام AND AROUND

BAYAZID HISTORICAL COMPLEX Like many other pilgrims, Oljeitu, then the local governor, came to pay homage to the grave of the famous Sufi charismatic mystic, Sheikh Bayazid al-Bastami (d874), and was initiated as a Sufi here in 1300. He later undertook a massive programme of rebuilding, enlarging the **shrine complex** and became Ilkhanid ruler of Iran (d1317). Today you enter into a large court and to the immediate right (north) is a **tomb tower**, often referred to as that of Sheikh Bayazid, although his actual grave is in the courtyard immediately in front of the main shrine building alongside a later one of Azam Khan Afghani; it now functions as an office. Rather than walking ahead, bear left and walk through an east-facing portal, beautifully embellished with turquoise strapwork and moulded brick-plugs, leading into a long hall. Constructed in 1313 perhaps as the main entrance, it now has an almost central position in the extended enclosure. High on the inside walls is a lengthy, elegant plaster inscription, the work of a Damghani master craftsman, naming Oljeitu and his brother, Ghazan Khan 'Sultan of the land of the East and China, king of the servants of the horizons' (r1295–1304) as patrons. At the end, not only does Bayazid's tower come into view but also another lofty *ivan* for teaching, also decorated with turquoise-blue tile inserts. On the left, a small locked door – peek through the side window – gives entry into one of two small 'hermitages' which served as a *chehelkhaneh*, both richly decorated with soot-blackened, early 14th-century plasterwork.

In the main building, there is an *imamzadeh* shrine immediately to the right with a grilled cenotaph commemorating Mohammad Ibn Jafar; women have to don a chador. The hexagonal, tiled dado is much earlier in date than the painted decoration of the walls and dome, restored in 1894. Viewed from the outside, this shrine is underneath a tiled tent roof with a brick-patterned minaret of 1120, its lower section incorporated into the hall further into the building. This vaulted hall was constructed after the decorative brick wall of the little mosque, with two intricately carved 14th-century doors now behind glass. In the late 15th century the roof of this mosque fell in and a wooden roof was installed but the carved plaster *mihrab*, dated 1314, the work of Mohammad Ibn Hossein Abi Talib al-Mohandis, was saved. Some beautiful plasterwork also remains in the winter prayer hall next door but its *mihrab* has been removed.

To get to the **masjed-e jame**, leave the complex by the main gate and walk southwest, keeping the shrine on the left. The mosque is down a side road nearby. At its back is a large 13.6m circular tomb tower of 1313, again the work of Mohammad al-Damghani, with some 26 vertical flanges and remains of glazed inserts in the two inscription bands under the roof. Inside, it is 12-sided (possibly to symbolise the Twelve Imams) with blind niches in three zones accentuating the height. Its door, firmly locked, is located within the mosque at the end of a small vestibule decorated with 14th-century carved plaster and well hidden behind a curtain. Very little of the original masjed-e jame remains but do wait for the guardian to let you into the *mihrab* area as it still retains some wonderful plasterwork, exquisitely carved in 1306 with unusually shaped arch profiles, akin to upturned pagoda eaves. This decoration was clearly applied on to an earlier structure, and above the *mihrab* the Qajar ruler Fath Ali Shah recorded his own 1809 repairs to the building.

WEST OF BASTAM AND SHAHRUD About 55km west from Shahrud is **Mehmandust** (مهماندوست), where the Safavids finally defeated the Afghan rebels in 1729. In a cemetery on the southern outskirts stands another lovely tomb tower, popularly known as Imamzadeh Qasem, a son of the seventh imam, despite the fact that its *Kufic* inscription above the bird-like frieze clearly stated it was made for a commander, Abu Jafar Mohammad, 'the hospitable *mehmandust*' (thus the name of the township), before modern restoration messed up the reading. Built in 1097, the tower (external diameter c10m) was about 21m high but its original conical roof has not survived. The number of flanges, 12 in all, was probably deliberate symbolism (Twelve Imams) as the verse (Q41:31) in the inscription has strong Shi'a connotations.

Nearer Damghan (altitude 1,120m) **Qaleh Gerdkuh** (گردکوه) comes into view. Known for its Ismaili connections as early as the 10th century, this is where the Assassins (see box, page 131) constructed a fortress so well defended that Hulagu, the grandson of Genghis Khan, laid siege for many months before finally taking it in 1256. By all reports, sections of the enclosing walls, the gatehouse and cisterns remain; as yet no archaeological survey has been undertaken. Access is through the village of Qaleh Gerdkuh, and may still be difficult.

🔺 Where to stay and eat

🔺 **Tourist Inn** (25 rooms) Bolvar Park, Ferdowsi St; ☏ 023 32226078; w ittic.com. Rooms are standard, clean & with Western toilet facilities.

Has a lovely outdoor garden & seating area as well as a reasonable restaurant ($). **$$**

DAMGHAN دامغان

It is thought Damghan (population 65,000) was originally known as Deh-e Magi (Village of the Magi/Zoroastrian Priests), and in the past some scholars wondered if it was Hecatompylos (also known as Sad Darvazeh or 'The City of 100 Gates'), the ancient Parthian capital under the Arsacid dynasty (248BCE–224CE). Finds from excavations at Shahr-e Qomes in the 1970s have established that Hecatompylos was indeed located in the area (page 211).

Damghan was a prosperous walled city in Sasanid times as confirmed by American archaeological excavations in the early 1930s (the Philadelphia Museum of Art,

USA, has decorative plaster from the Sasanid palace at Tappeh Hesar, southeast of the present town) and possibly its importance then was linked to certain Zoroastrian sacred fires in the region, although there had been occupation from at least 2,000 years before. The earthquake of 856CE destroyed the Sasanid defensive walls, killing about 45,000 people by some reports, so there was massive rebuilding in the 920s. As local warlords and governors battled for control, real authority rested in the Assassins' fortress above and Hassan al-Sabbah (see box, page 131) felt safe enough to enter the city itself. With the Mongol conquest, the power struggle continued with the rulers of Khwarizm (present-day Turkmenistan) also intervening. The city was taken by Timur Leng in 1381 but raids and massacres continued for the next 50 years. In 1528 the Safavid regime brought a measure of stability to the region, ended by Afghan incursions in the 1720s. By the time Nader Shah finished bombarding the town in 1729, its population had shrunk to 3,000. Prosperity slowly returned with the Qajar dynasty (Fath Ali Shah was born here in 1772), but the town was torn apart in 1911 when pro-constitutionalist activists met their opponents head-on; hundreds were left dead. In 1929 the town had a population of 5,000 and today it is over 50,000.

If you are approaching Damghan from the Sari direction, you are likely to drive past **Cheshmeh Ali** ('Spring of Ali'), 35km north of Damghan, but do not confuse it with Cheshmeh Ali in Rey (page 119). This is one of the permanent springs in the area, drawing on water from the mountains in the north.

WHERE TO STAY AND EAT

Tourist Inn (14 rooms) Laleh Intersection, Shomali Bd; \023 35242070; w ittic.com. Renovated, & central, this 1-storey inn offers spacious rooms with high vaulted ceilings & large bathrooms. B/fast is a little poor, but the whole place is comfortable enough & has a restaurant ($). **$$**

WHAT TO SEE AND DO Despite its turbulent history, the city boasts some important historic buildings. About 500m southeast of the main square, Maydan-e Imam Khomeini, is the **Masjed-e Tarik Khaneh** (also known as Masjed-e Chehel Sotun) (Motahhari St; ⊕ 08.30–13.00 & 15.00–17.00 Sat–Thu; entry 300,000 rials), thought to be the second-oldest mosque surviving in Iran. A very helpful Persian-speaking guardian, Emadi Bozorgheh, holds the key to Pir-e Alamdar (see opposite) and can direct you to Tappeh Hesar. He can also arrange for you to visit the underground section of the masjed-e jame. This is a 'majestically simple' mosque, retaining something of its 8th-century 'Arab' plan, a design that quickly fell out of favour with Iranian patrons. The arrangement of arches running parallel to the enclosing walls and some of the fat, stumpy brick piers are from the original 760CE construction, but the remains of the brick and plaster patterning are from an 11th-century Seljuk restoration. Its **minaret**, just outside the mosque, 25m high, was erected in 1028, making it the earliest Iranian minaret still standing. Its inscription among the six bands of brick set in relief and recess records that the mason was the man who built the Semnan minaret (page 212) while the costs were met by the governor who before his appointment also paid for the Pir-e Alamdar tomb tower nearby.

From here it takes about 8 minutes to walk to the **masjed-e jame** (also called Masjed-e Imam Hossein), crossing the main road and going northeast. You've come here just for the **Seljuk minaret**, constructed sometime between 1031 and 1035, which has ten lovely brick-pattern zones still retaining some glazed inserts, including the Quranic verse (Q24:35) which talks of the message of Islam burning brightly in a glass lamp, very apposite for Imam Hossein, often represented by a lighted candle. Presently it is about 27m high but the upper section was destroyed in 1933. Check out the handles on the old door leading up to the mosque courtyard.

The one with the circle is for women and the other is for men to knock. Each makes a different sound thus signalling to the person inside the mosque whom to expect. About 100m away is the 16m-high **tomb tower of Pir-e Alamdar** (remember to get the keyholder to come from the Masjed-e Tarik Khaneh) of 1027. It no longer has its original exterior tent roof, but the brickwork with the main inscription below the dome is still lovely, recording that it was built for the then governor of Damghan, Abu Jafar Mohammad Ibn Ibrahim, by his son who was also responsible for the Tarik Khaneh minaret described opposite. But the best work is inside: a splendidly ornate plaited *Kufic* band running around the interior (Q39:53–4) in blue, and justly described as 'a tour de force', speaks of God's forgiveness.

Also near the Maydan-e Imam Khomeini there is the historical **Khanqah of Shah Rukh**, but locals are unlikely to be familiar with this name. The site is commonly known as Imamzadeh Jafar. The first building is a much-restored tomb presently known as **Imamzadeh Mohammad Ibn Musa Kazem** but the Sufi meeting place, which gives the complex its name, is a small square building with a 15th-century Timurid tile panel high over the door, recording that Shah Rukh, Timur Leng's son (see box, page 340), paid for extensive repairs. Today in its crypt it houses another Shah Rukh, a relative of Nader Shah Afshar, killed by the first Qajar ruler in 1796. Adjoining it is the large **Imamzadeh Jafar**, still retaining its Seljuk inner dome, probably the reason for establishing a *khanqah* here. It commemorates Jafar Ibn Ali (d901), a descendant of the third imam. Just behind is a cylindrical tomb tower standing 14.8m high called the **Chehel Dokhtaran** (40 Maidens) but, as its two inscriptions used to record before modern restoration, it was built in 1055, by and for the military commander Abu Shuja 'Asfar Beg 'preparing for his sleep a tomb for himself and his sons'. Resembling the Pir-e Alamdar above, it is the second-earliest dated tomb tower surviving in Iran.

Just 5km southeast of Damghan, close to the railway line, archaeological work at **Tappeh Hesar** uncovered not only the remains of a 6th-century Sasanid palace, but also evidence of settlement from at least the early 2nd millennium BCE with charred remains of skeletons and weapons. The main excavations were undertaken during the two world wars when splendid conical bowls bearing fine black-painted motifs (now in the National Museum, Tehran; page 112) were uncovered alongside finely modelled rams' heads in gold foil for textile decoration. Road widening in 1995 has presumably put paid to further discoveries.

Again south of the main road from Damghan to Semnan another interesting archaeological site was found: **Shahr-e Qomes** (قومس). Excavation work here in 1967 revealed rich Parthian finds from mud-brick vaulted tombs (c70BCE), and evidence of a Parthian fortified encampment. Part of the 28km² site was then inhabited into Seljuk times, before its destruction by the Mongols in the early 13th century. But, importantly, the archaeologists left the excavation convinced that indeed they had found Hecatompylos or 'The City of a Hundred Gates' where Alexander the Great broke the news to his soldiers that they were not returning home, but carrying on into India.

SEMNAN سمنان

The next major city on the road back towards Tehran is Semnan (population 163,000), 226km east from the capital. There are eight daily train departures from Tehran that will bring you here in 3 hours (100,000–500,000 rials). Centuries ago its wealth came from the trade caravans passing to and from central Asia and Afghanistan via Mashhad going west, but now it is a centre for light industry and serves as the provincial capital; it lies on the main railway from Tehran to Mashhad and several of the trains stop there.

WHERE TO STAY AND EAT

🏠 **Tourist Inn** (36 rooms) Basij Bd, after Amir Kabir Bridge; ☎ 023 33459122. Provides a more than adequate stay. **$$**

WHAT TO SEE AND DO Famous for its pistachios, Semnan also has a couple of interesting buildings as well as the remains of the mud-brick **citadel** which once defended the city. Its **masjed-e jame,** on the western outskirts off the Maydan-e Motahhari, was established in the 8th century but the only visual evidence of this is the restored fat brick pillars and a boarded-up *mihrab* in the arcade opposite the excessively tall prayer *ivan*. That main *ivan* is part of the major Timurid rebuilding programme undertaken by Shah Rukh around 1424, and the large underground winter prayer hall may also date from this period or later, though locals think it is Seljuk work. What is clearly Seljuk is the prayer chamber itself. At first sight its proportions – height of walls to dome, squinches and zone of transition, etc – seem illogical and the only explanation is that for some reason the later Timurid repairs involved raising the original ground level of this chamber considerably. The **minaret**, standing over 28m high, is also Seljuk, constructed in 1031–35 by the same man responsible for the minaret at Tarik Khaneh, Damghan. It has at least eight pattern zones, including two bands of inscription (including Q41:33) and an attractive wooden balcony. Within easy walking distance through the bazaar, about 200m northeast, is the 19th-century **Masjed-e Imam Khomeini** (formerly Masjed-e Shah), proof of the city's prosperity in the Qajar period. Somewhat understated for Qajar religious buildings, the exuberant tiling and colouring dating from the reign of Fath Ali Shah are delicious. Another Qajar monument, the **Darvazeh Arg-e Semnan** (Semnan Citadel Gate) dated 1884, once marked an entrance gate into the town but is now transformed into a busy roundabout. Its tile panels feature armed soldiers and a cannon. Semnan's **bazaar** is also worth stopping by. Its historic *hamam* is now a museum (entry 300,000 rials) with some interesting historic artefacts from the area.

About 28km north of Semnan is the small village of **Shahmirzad** (شهميرزاد) with its distinctive rustic architecture; spend some time here in the fresh air to escape the summer heat of the city.

SEMNAN TO TEHRAN

From Semnan, there are two routes to Tehran: the more southerly route goes through Garmsar, while the other heads off via Firuzkuh and passes close to the town of **Damavand**, named after the mountain standing 5,610m high to the north. The area is dotted with the ruins of numerous fortresses, strongholds of the Assassins in the late medieval period. Close to Damavand's masjed-e jame is a tomb tower known locally as the **tomb of Sheikh Shibli**, a Sunni mystic and former local deputy governor before his death in Baghdad in 945CE. His actual tomb still survives there, though it was probably built for someone completely different as its style suggests the late 11th century. It has an octagonal exterior with a rounded buttress at each corner, decorated in brick patterns with octagons, lozenges, eight-pointed stars and an octagonal flanged tent roof.

The road from **Eyvanekey** (ایوان کی), 25km west of Garmsar, into Tehran goes through marvellous scenery with spectacularly coloured rocks. But this route, known locally as 'Alexander's [the Great] Gate', still has some sharp hairpin bends (despite improvements) which Tehrani drivers acknowledge only at the last moment.

7

Iranian Azerbaijan

For centuries this region formed a major gateway into both Europe and Asia, with merchants and armies travelling the trade routes along the foothills of the Caucasus separating modern-day Turkey and Iran from the republics of Georgia, Armenia and Azerbaijan, and through the Zagros Mountains dividing Iraq and Iran. Today's political frontiers are only a century old, so unsurprisingly excavations in this region of Iran frequently reveal archaeological proof of strong cultural links with ancient civilisations associated with Anatolia, Mesopotamia and across the Caucasus.

The main language spoken in Iranian Azerbaijan is a form of Turkish Azeri, which dates back to the 9th century, when Turkic people first started moving and settling here in large numbers. Under Seljuk rule the region enjoyed a certain autonomy and Tabriz emerged untouched following the arrival of the Mongols in the 13th century. Timur Leng (Tamerlane) conquered Azerbaijan in 1386, prompting the growth of the influence of Turkomans.

Because of its location, surrounded on two sides by mountains and with the Caspian Sea to the east, the region was a battle arena in more recent times, including 400 years of conflict against the Ottoman armies. In 1590, Shah Abbas I conceded to the Ottoman Empire large parts of Iran's possessions in the area, including further north in Armenia, Georgia and Qarabag, in order to solidify Safavid rule in central and eastern Iran. Just 20 years later, however, he managed to take back a lot of the territories, including Tabriz. Fighting and hostilities between the two great rivals continued until 1639. It was only in 1794 that Agha Mohammad Khan, the founder of the Qajar dynasty, conquered Azerbaijan; this was the start of the area's eventual integration into modern-day Iran. The weakness of the Qajars and the Russian (and Bolshevik/Soviet) campaigns in the 19th and 20th centuries, however, meant that the boundaries shifted yet again.

The region was always known for its Christian communities, which before World War I made up over 30% of the local population. Western missionaries came here in the 19th and early 20th centuries, establishing medical centres and schools, and fired with the wish to 'convert' the Nestorians and Armenian Gregorians, to join various Protestant denominations. Russia followed suit in 1897 by establishing a Russian Orthodox mission in Orumiyeh with the purpose of spreading faith among local Assyrians. Although tolerated by the central administration as long as there was no evidence of Muslim conversions, such activity caused problems to all layers of Iranian society and fuelled xenophobic anxieties. The region, however, has retained some of the most beautiful and well-preserved churches in Iran, in particular in the vicinity of Maku and Jolfa. Eastern Azerbaijan is ideal for hill walking and mountain trekking. There is good budget accommodation in smaller towns and **Alp Tour Iran** with its head office in Tabriz (✆041 33310340; m 0901 4211647; e alptouriran@ yahoo.com) can arrange all kinds of travel activities in the area.

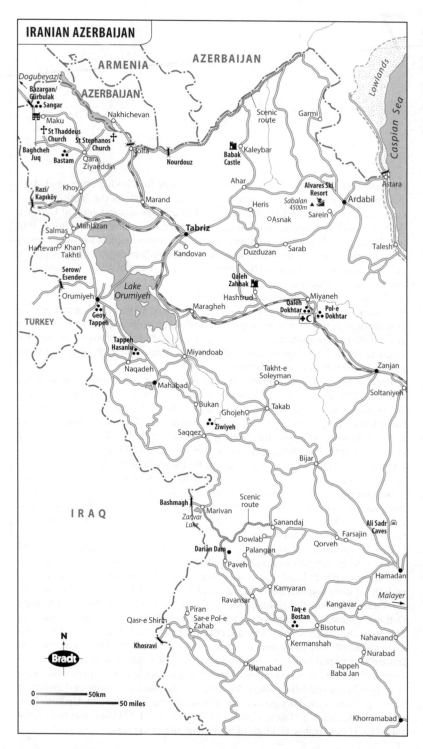

IRANIAN AZERBAIJAN

ARMENIA

AZERBAIJAN

AZERBAIJAN

Dogubeyazit

Bazargan/
Gürbulak
Sangar

Maku

Nakhichevan

Scenic
route

Garmi

Caspian Sea

Lowlands

☩ St Thaddeus
Church

St Stephanos ☩
Church

Jolfa

Nourdouz

Babak
Castle

Kaleybar

Baghcheh
Juq

Bastam

Qara
Ziyaeddin

Ahar

Alvares Ski
Resort

Astara

Razi/
Kapıköy

Khoy

Marand

Heris

Sabalan
4500m

Sarein

Ardabil

Salmas

Mahlazan

Tabriz

Kandovan

Duzduzan

Sarab

Talesh

Hartevan

Khan
Takhti

Asnak

Serow/
Esendere

Lake
Orumiyeh

Qaleh
Zahhak

Hashtrud

Miyaneh

Orumiyeh

Maragheh

Qaleh
Dokhtar

Pol-e
Dokhtar

Geoy
Tappeh

C

TURKEY

Tappeh
Hasanlu

Miyandoab

Zanjan

Naqadeh

Takht-e
Soleyman

Soltaniyeh

Mahabad

Bukan

Takab

Saqqez

Ghojeh

Ziwiyeh

Bijar

IRAQ

Bashmagh

Zarivar
Lake

Marivan

Scenic
route

Sanandaj

Farsajin

Ali Sadr
Caves

Dowlab

Qorveh

Darian Dam

Palangan

Paveh

Hamadan

Kamyaran

Malayer

Ravansar

Kangavar

Qasr-e Shirin

Piran

Sar-e Pol-e
Zahab

Taq-e
Bostan

Bisotun

Nahavand

Khosravi

Kermanshah

Nurabad

N

Islamabad

Tappeh
Baba Jan

Bradt

0   50km
0   50 miles

Khorramabad

GETTING THERE AND AROUND

The main highway northwest from Tehran to the provincial capital Tabriz (about 215km; altitude 1,340m) is good, taking about 12 hours by express **bus**. If you wish to visit places such as Soltaniyeh and Zanjan, the slower 'old' road will have to be used in part. To avoid returning on the same route, why not travel from Tehran to Bandar Anzali (page 197), staying there for the night and then continue up the western shores of the Caspian to visit Ardabil? There are regular bus services from there to Tabriz (270km away). After visiting various sites to the north, you could then make your way back to Tehran. See the individual towns for bus departure times.

ARDABIL اردبیل *Telephone code 045*

With the establishment of the Safavid Empire (1501–c1735), Ardabil (altitude 1,300m) became increasingly important. Five centuries earlier it had been a walled town, but in such a ruinous, filthy state that the Arab geographer al-Muqaddasi (flourished 967–85CE) described it as 'one of the latrines of the world'. Local campaigns against the Georgian princes in 1208, which resulted in the sacking of Ani (eastern Turkey) and the deaths of 12,000 Christians, led to swift and violent retribution in 1209 when over 12,000 Ardabil citizens were slain. Later, the conflict between the two great tribal confederations – the Qara and Aq Qoyunlu – had repercussions on the local economy. But once the Safavid leader Ismail I took control in 1501, the town's future became more secure, for this was the burial place of the Sufi teacher, Sheikh Safi al-Din (1251–1334), considered to be the founder of the dynastic family. It also benefited from its proximity to the new Safavid capital, Tabriz, until the court moved south to Qazvin and later Esfahan. Time and money were lavished on Ardabil, especially on the tomb of Safi al-Din, as the shahs sought to emphasise their lineage and championship of the Ithna 'Ashari branch of Shi'a Islam. By 1656 the shrine and town were crown domain, endowed with superb costly carpets like the Ardabil carpet (now in the Victoria and Albert Museum, London) and its twin (Los Angeles County Museum of Art, USA), and a magnificent collection of Chinese porcelain including celadon (mostly in the Islamic section of the Archaeological Museum, Tehran but some displayed here in Ardabil and yet other pieces in the Azerbaijan Museum, Tabriz (page 223)). It also had a vast library, but this was ransacked during the Irano-Russian wars of 1826–28 when Ardabil was occupied by Russian troops, and anything valuable was taken back to St Petersburg.

Former Iranian president Mahmoud Ahmadinejad was the governor of the province from 1993 until 1997. Ardabil is now a large city of 485,000 people and as with many other cities in the region it has, in recent years, seen a rise in the number of Azerbaijanis coming from across the border for medical treatment. The city itself has few historical sites and the main tourist attraction here is the UNESCO World Heritage Site Sheikh Safi al-Din Mausoleum. Among Iranians, however, the area is appreciated more for its clean air, beautiful surroundings and natural springs.

GETTING THERE AND AROUND There are several **flights** a day from Tehran with a journey time of just over an hour, and there are a few flights each week to and from Mashhad. The city is also well served by long-distance **buses**. However, if you are coming from Astara on the border with Azerbaijan, a *savari* is the best option. There are no direct buses, only the passing Tehran–Ardabil service, if you're lucky.

Ardabil has two bus terminals, one central (terminal) and the other local, as well as one *savari* terminal at Basij Square. Buses from the terminal stop at the *savari* stop as well to pick up passengers. Below is a departure schedule with selected times from major Iranian cities:

From	Departure	Price (rials)
Esfahan (Kaveh)	16.30; 17.30	750,000
Esfahan (Sofeh)	15.45	750,000
Tabriz (central)	Hourly between 06.00 & 19.45	140,000
Tehran (southern)	21.30; 22.00	520,000–630,000
Tehran (western)	Hourly between 07.00 & 23.45	520,000–630,000

 WHERE TO STAY AND EAT

Hotel Negin (33 rooms) Simetri St; 33235671, 33235673. Just a 2min walk from Sheikh Safi al-Din Mausoleum, it offers very clean, although not the most aesthetically original rooms. Excellent location & price make it a good option, nonetheless. **$$**

Hotel Shorabil (40 rooms) On the banks of Lake Shorabil, 4km southeast of the centre; 33513096. Rooms are basic with oldish furniture. The décor is suggestive of initially grander ambitions, but at present it's a simple hotel with friendly & caring staff. **$$**

WHAT TO SEE AND DO

Sheikh Safi al-Din Mausoleum (Sheikh Safi al-Din Ardabili St; ⏰ 08.00–18.00; entry 500,000 rials) It was Sheikh Safi al-Din himself who established a *khanqah* in the 13th century, perhaps on the site of the present *chinikhaneh* (porcelain room). After his death, his followers built a tomb to honour him and thereafter over the centuries, buildings were added, torn down or converted. The main entrance into the shrine complex dates from 1926 when the four or so shops either side were built, their rents going towards the upkeep of the shrine. This leads directly into a garden laid out in c1834, which today is a favourite meeting place for elderly gentlemen. At the other end a porch from 1629 (heavily restored), leads into a courtyard with 'very fair and spacious vault[s] arched above, paved without with green and blue [tile] stones', as seen by one European traveller in 1637. The domed structure immediately on the left, hidden by a large wooden grille, was originally constructed on the orders of Shah Tahmasp I around 1540, perhaps as another *khanqah*, and it is possible that the two Ardabil carpets (if they were ever here; page 14) were made for this octagonal building. By 1843 it was in a sorry state, having lost its dome, and it was perhaps at this point it was turned into a mosque, the Jannat Sura; major repairs were undertaken from 1935 onwards to this building and in fact to all the tiled façades in this courtyard.

A small door takes the visitor into the main building and a long prayer hall known as the *qandilkhaneh* (lantern hall); the endowments paid for teams of Quran readers to sit and intone before the tombs. When visiting the *qandilkhaneh*, take off your shoes before entering. The portal inscription stresses the importance of reading the Holy Book, and it has long been assumed the door and hall were part of Tahmasp's building programme. However, recent research suggests perhaps both were constructed two centuries earlier. For a number of years, it housed a huge vertical loom, as the authorities decided a copy of the Ardabil carpet should be made but, like many projects in the new republic, resources were diverted elsewhere and progress was painfully slow. The massive silver doors were a royal gift in 1602–03, and then ten years later Shah Abbas I ordered the hall to be painted and gilded, and silver grilles erected.

A doorway immediately on the left leads into the *chinikhaneh*, a large octagonal room with plasterwork niches, which once held some of the fine Chinese porcelain pieces from the Safavid court. In all, over 1,160 pieces of costly, rare Chinese blue and white porcelain and celadon vessels were given by the Safavid shahs, some probably taken as battle spoils from the defeated Uzun Hassan, leader of the Aq Qoyunlu (d1478). In the 1930s about half of these were moved to Tehran for safe keeping. A number of dishes are displayed alongside manuscripts and other historical artefacts. Most of the structure dates from the Safavid rebuilding programme of 1607–11 but, as you will spot, the domed roof is more recent, dating from 1971.

Returning to the *qandilkhaneh*, you can explore the other small rooms off to the left housing numerous cenotaphs marking interments in the crypts below. Thick but fine-quality 'inlaid' patterned felts cover the floors, getting dirtier and more moth-eaten every year. Important members of the Safavid court, military generals and the royal ladies rest here, including Shah Ismail's mother and the shah himself with a magnificent cenotaph, presented, so the locals say, by the Indian Mughal emperor, Humayun, in about 1530, in gratitude for giving him refuge during his exile from India.

The *haramkhaneh* should, as the name suggests, contain the cenotaphs of the royal ladies but as one scholar has noted, at least one of the deceased was the eldest son of Sheikh Safi al-Din, who died in 1324 when the room was probably constructed and not, as first thought, the wife of Safi. The tomb chamber nearest that of the sheikh himself contains Ismail's large cenotaph and little else, other than deep cobalt-blue tiles with stencilled fired gold patterns and smoke-damaged wall decoration. Next door, at the end of the prayer hall, once decorated with costly rugs and gold lamps but ransacked over a century ago, is the circular tomb chamber of Sheikh Safi al-Din himself, constructed in 1334 and extensively repaired (on the outside) in 1949. Before you leave the courtyard outside, don't forget to walk round to see the exteriors of these tomb chambers with their tile decoration.

AROUND ARDABIL

Sarein سرعین Just 20km west of Ardabil, and at the foothills of Sabalan (4,811m), the highest mountain in the region, Sarein, is a popular getaway for Iranians on account of its natural springs (*ab garm*).

🏠 **Where to stay and eat** There are more hotels per square kilometre here than anywhere else in the country. Enquire about discounts; in low season even the most expensive hotels may offer up to 40% off the price.

🏠 **Laleh International Hotel** (97 rooms) ☏045 32222750–6; w lalehhotels.ir. Conveniently located opposite Sabalan Hydrotherapy Complex, this large holiday resort has a traditional restaurant, coffee shop & Wi-Fi. Staff are spot-on & the service is excellent. **$$$**

What to see and do Various natural spring baths are all within walking distance and centrally located. **Sabalan Hydrotherapy Complex** is the biggest (across the road from Laleh Hotel; ☏045 32224060; ⏲ 09.00–23.00; entry 210,000 rials). In operation since 1997, this 7,200m² centre can accommodate up to 400 male and 200 female customers at a time. An older, but cheaper option is **Ab Garm Pahanlu** (⏲ 06.30–midnight). Right behind it is a hotel and natural springs bath **Ershad**. In the vicinity, 23km beyond Sarein is the **Alvares Ski Resort**. The drive is scenic, but the 1,250m-long cable car does not have a fixed schedule. Opening times depend on the weather. Ask your hotel to ring in advance before making the journey up.

WEST OF ARDABIL There is an interesting mosque about 75km to the west, on either the Ahar (north) road or that going through Sarab. Near the village of Mehraban (south of Heris, north of Duzduzan, west of Sarab) is **Asnak**, whose **masjed-e jame** is remarkably fashioned of red stone. It was built around 1333 on the so-called 'Arab' hypostyle plan with wooden columns inside and a flat wooden roof. Very unusual for this pre-Safavid date, the foundation inscription under the left window of the entrance portal is in Persian, written in the Arabic script, recording that: 'Malik Shah … made all its decoration with the point of an adze, may his hand be steady and may Allah preserve him.'

About 60km north of Ahar is **Kaleybar** (کلیبر), which can also be approached directly from Tabriz further west. The town is known for its well-preserved fortress **Babak Castle** (*qaleh babak*) (قلعه بابک) at an altitude of 2,300m, some 3km from the town. Note that there is a 50,000 rials municipal charge when driving up here in your own vehicle. This Sasanid castle is named after Babak Khorramdin, the warlord and leader of the Khorramdini uprising, the first rebellion against the invading Arabs, which lasted over 22 years and ended in 839CE. Almost a mythical figure in Iranian history, little is known about Babak's private life and the available accounts are unreliable at best. The uprising originally started as a popular, religious and political movement. Founded by Javidan, son of Sahl, it was based on Mazdakist Zoroastrian ideas and the idea of the communal division of property. Following Javidan's death, Babak took the leadership position and fought against the Abbasids, which was considered to be the first real Iranian attempt to resist Arab dominion.

In the ruins of the rooms and corridors of the Babak Castle, pottery and coins dating from the 13th century have been found by Iranian archaeologists and restoration teams, working here since 1998. Access is difficult, but the scenery is stunning, involving an arduous uphill walk from the base of what used to be the Babak Hotel (may reopen in the future), taking over 2 hours each way. You can arrange for a guide to accompany you (contact Alp Tour Iran, page 213) or hire a short 4×4 Nissan Patrol ride at the tourist camping site by the old Babak Hotel. You are also welcome to pitch your tent here at no additional charge, if camping. The drive shortens the 3km walk up by about 1km. Alternatively, bring a few bottles of water with you and have a good breakfast beforehand. The walk starts at the camping site. Access to the castle will most likely be blocked by winter snow until early May. Visits are best made in summer around 10 July when Iranians celebrate the birthday of the national hero, Babak. The town gets very busy and advance accommodation booking is recommended.

🏠 Where to stay and eat

🏠 **Paradise International Hotel** (35 rooms) Start of Kaleybar Rd, Kaleybar; ☎041 44441012, 44441013; e info@paradisehotel.ir. Opened in 2015, this is a comfortable, although a little flashy, hotel. Rooms are spacious & staff are caring. **$$$**

🏠 **Anza Hotel** (17 rooms/apts) Off Farmandari St, Kaleybar; ☎041 44444202, 44444209. An unexpectedly glitzy & modern hotel with spacious rooms & bathrooms. The staff, however, seem a little unsure as to their purpose there; be patient. **$$**

TABRIZ تبریز *Telephone code 041*

Tabriz, said to have been founded by Khosrow Arshakid (Arsacid) of Armenia in c220CE, has been hit by earthquakes many times during its history, with those in 858CE and 1042 wiping out any structures from the pre-Islamic period. The most recent earthquake in 2012 left 308 people dead and more than 3,000 wounded.

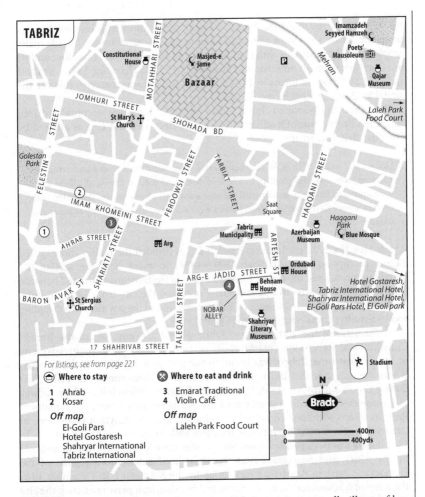

TABRIZ

Imamzadeh Seyyed Hamzeh

Poets' Mausoleum

Qajar Museum

Constitutional House

Masjed-e jame

Bazaar

MOTAHHARI STREET

MEHRAN

JOMHURI STREET

St Mary's Church

SHOHADA BD

Laleh Park Food Court

Golestan Park

FELESTIN STREET

FERDOWSI STREET

TARBIAT STREET

HAQQANI STREET

IMAM KHOMEINI STREET

Saat Square

Haqqani Park

Tabriz Municipality

Azerbaijan Museum

Blue Mosque

AHRAB STREET

SHARIATI ST

Arg

ARTESH ST

Ordubadi House

BARON AVAK ST

St Sergius Church

ARG-E JADID STREET

Behnam House

Hotel Gostaresh, Tabriz International Hotel, Shahryar International Hotel, El-Goli Pars Hotel, El Goli park

TALEQANI STREET

NOBAR ALLEY

Shahriyar Literary Museum

17 SHAHRIVAR STREET

Stadium

For listings, see from page 221

⊖ **Where to stay**

1 Ahrab
2 Kosar

Off map
El-Goli Pars
Hotel Gostaresh
Shahryar International
Tabriz International

⊗ **Where to eat and drink**

3 Emarat Traditional
4 Violin Café

Off map
Laleh Park Food Court

N

Bradt

0 ————— 400m
0 ————— 400yds

HISTORY At the time of the Arab invasion, Tabriz was just a small village, of less importance than Ardabil and Orumiyeh. By the end of the 10th century, however, it had become such a prosperous trading centre that it was selected as the venue for the marriage celebrations of the Seljuk sultan Toghrol Beg (d1063) and a daughter of the Baghdad caliph. Known for the business acumen of its traders who rioted over the introduction of paper money to replace coinage, Tabriz achieved the status of a 'royal' capital first with the Mongol Ilkhanid ruler Abaqa (r1265–81). His descendant Ghazan Khan (r1295–1304) kept Tabriz as his capital and ordered the building of the city walls and defences, the bazaars and an enormous mausoleum, spending a vast amount, but sadly nothing of this has remained. Moreover, Ghazan's conversion to Islam was marked by persecution of all non-Muslims in the region and within Tabriz itself all churches, synagogues and fire temples were razed to the ground. From the mid 14th century, the city and the surrounding area came under the control of various warlords, until the Qara Qoyunlu tribal chiefs made Tabriz their capital from 1436–67, after which it came into the Aq Qoyunlu domain.

Shah Ismail I, founder of the Safavid dynasty, entered Tabriz in 1501 and having taken on the title of Shah of Iran, made the city into his capital. During this time, out of Tabriz's 300,000 inhabitants, 200,000 were Sunni Muslim and Ismail's proclamation of Shi'ism as the state religion caused rebellions in which many people died. The hostilities with the Ottoman Empire became too close for comfort and from this moment onwards also assumed a religious character. Tabriz was first occupied by Ottoman forces in 1514 and Shah Ismail I was forced to relocate the capital to Qazvin, where he died in 1523.

The Ottomans occupied Tabriz again in 1585, but were eventually driven out; when fleeing from Qezelbash troops, they destroyed the city, as attested by Eskandar Beit Turkaman:

> Houses decorated with gold and lapis lazuli were destroyed. Doors and windows adorned with beautiful paintings were torn down and used as firewood; all the trees were uprooted from the gardens; all the shops and two-storey houses decorated with ceramics were destroyed and dead bodies were scattered across the city squares and bazaars.

A year after the 1721 earthquake, Russian forces invaded the region and attacked Tabriz, prompting Fath Ali Shah (1797–1834) to move here the seat of the hereditary prince and the troops for the defence of the territories disputed between Iran and Russia. Tsarist troops eventually occupied the city from 1826–28 until, under the terms of the 1828 Peace of Turkomanchay and the payment of a crippling war indemnity, it was returned to the Qajars.

At the start of the 20th century, Tabriz played a major role in the Iranian Constitutional Revolution (*mashrutiyat*) of 1905–11. The most progressive city in Iran at that time, Tabriz was home to the first printing press in the country. It was the only city that did not surrender itself to Mohammad Ali Shah Qajar during the *mashrutiyat* period. In 1916 the Russian Tbilisi–Jolfa–Tabriz railway was completed and with the advent of the Bolshevik Revolution, the remaining Russian troops withdrew completely, leaving the arms to Assyrian Christians, so Ottoman forces moved in until the frontiers with Turkey were finally settled. In 1941 Tabriz was occupied by Soviet forces, after Reza Shah was forced to abdicate by the Allies, and four years later the short-lived autonomous regime of the Democratic Party in Azerbaijan was set up by the Bolsheviks. In December 1946 the army of Mohammad Reza Shah, assisted by American personnel, took the city and all Bolshevik and communist elements were purged.

Tabriz now has more than 1.5 million residents and is a major transit point on the movement of goods between Turkey and Iran as well as a major travel destination for Azerbaijanis coming here in huge numbers (more than 1 million per year) for medical treatment. In 2018, the city was the tourist capital of the Muslim world and local businessmen and manufacturers are still known throughout Iran for their commercial acumen. So, the historic bazaar is probably the best place from where to start exploring the city.

GETTING THERE AND AROUND The **airport** in Tabriz is classed as international and there is a daily flight from Istanbul in Turkey; there are also domestic services from Tehran and Mashhad with a number of different airlines depending on the day of the week. There are regular national and international **bus** routes, including to Turkey, Armenia, Azerbaijan and Georgia. Tickets can be purchased at the stations or ticket sales offices in major cities. There are also frequent **train** connections. The Tehran–Ankara train (via Tabriz) service resumed in June 2019 and takes 24 hours; the Tehran–Tabriz rail line was one of the first to be completed in Iran. Both rail (west of the city) and bus (south of the city) terminals are located outside the city centre, approximately 10 minutes from the bazaar area by taxi.

Tabriz is a vast metropolis with hilly streets and you are strongly recommended to hire a **taxi** or take the **metro** (10,000 rials) to move around. The official Tabriz metro website is alas in Persian only and so is the online map. The historical part is relatively small and walkable, but the main park – El Goli – is not reachable on foot. Below is a bus departure schedule with selected times from major Iranian cities to Tabriz:

From	Departure	Price (rials)
Esfahan (Kaveh)	09.00; 17.00; 18.00; 19.00	618,000–790,000
Esfahan (Sofeh)	16.15; 18.00	618,000–790,000
Shiraz (Karandish)	14.30	1,000,000
Tehran (southern)	Hourly between 07.15 & 10.15; 21.30; 23.00	470,000–550,000
Tehran (western)	Hourly between 06.00 & 23.59	470,000–550,000
Tehran (Beyhaghi)	09.00; 10.30; 12.30; 14.30; 20.00; 21.00; 22.00; 23.00; 23.59	470,000–550,000

 WHERE TO STAY AND EAT   *Map, page 219*

Tabriz hotels enjoy high season all year round thanks to Azerbaijanis coming here for medical treatment. Accommodation is thus priced accordingly. Decent budget hotels are few, but plenty of cheap last-resort *mehmanpazirs*, of which a few are located in the vicinity of the Ahrab Hotel.

El-Goli Pars Hotel (180 rooms) El Goli St, in a park around 8km away from city centre; ☎33807820, 33807830; w pars-hotels.com. The best hotel in Tabriz & the best of the Pars chain (6 hotels in total). Spacious rooms are decorated in good taste & come with excellent views, but you need to pay extra to have windows overlooking the park. Service is good & staff are polite & well mannered. **$$$$**

Shahryar International Hotel (200 rooms) El Goli St; ☎33291420–29; w shahryar-hotel.com. This hotel – named after a renowned 20th-century poet – has a good range of facilities & several restaurants, as well as a Turkish Airlines office on the ground floor. A little more central than El-Goli. **$$$$**

Hotel Gostaresh (150 rooms) Imam St, intersection with Azadi Bd; ☎33366590, 33366599; w gostareshhotel.com. In operation since 1960, this 13-storey hotel was the first high-rise structure built in Tabriz. Fairly priced & in a good location, rooms are spacious with minimal & tasteful décor. **$$$**

Tabriz International (130 rooms) Imam St; ☎33341081, 33341089; e tabrizhotel@yahoo.com. Good hotel with decent-sized clean & bright rooms & accommodating personnel. The lobby is a little crowded & has a somewhat disorientating layout, but the rest of the building is tranquil. **$$$**

Ahrab Hotel (50 rooms) ☎35515116, 35515119; w ahrab-hotel.com. This new hotel is centrally located & is by far the best accommodation option in Tabriz within this price range. Interior décor is modest, but rooms are spacious & have everything you need for a comfortable stay. Personnel are helpful & courteous. There is also a traditional restaurant ($) & a good b/fast. **$$–$$$**

Kosar Hotel (24 rooms) Imam St, opposite Farhangiyan Cinema; ☎35537691–3. A reasonable & unpretentious budget hotel in central Tabriz. Rooms overlooking Imam St come with old-fashioned & cosy balconies. Staff are caring & helpful. **$–$$**

✕ **Laleh Park Food Court** ⏱ 10.00–23.45 daily. Located on the top floor of the city's most luxurious & modern Park Laleh Mall, the food court has a number of international & quite good Iranian restaurants serving local speciality *kofteh tabrizi* meatballs. The location is alas not very convenient, being a good 15min taxi drive away, but it is a good option nonetheless. **$$**

✕ **Emarat Traditional Restaurant** Shariati St intersection; ☎35538591; ⏱ noon–16.00 & 19.00–23.30. A newly opened traditional basement restaurant featuring a classic Iranian menu. $

🖵Violin Café Nobar Alley; ☎35578123; ⏰ 11.00–23.00 daily. A cosy place for a warm cup of tea or coffee. The owner is a violinist, which explains the choice of the name. Tabriz Islamic Art University Faculty of Culture & Urbanism is just across the street & the café gets busy in the eves. $

WHAT TO SEE AND DO The extensive UNESCO World Heritage-listed bazaar, parts of which date from the 15th century, is arranged very compactly across two main roads and has over the centuries been the single most important element contributing to the growth and development of the city.

Arguably, the most famous monument in town is the **Arg** (Citadel) (entrance from Imam Khomeini St) as it is locally known. In fact, only the massive walls remain of what was not a fort but the enormous four-*ivan* **Masjed-e Shah** (or Masjed-e Ali Shah), once smothered with tile panels. This structure of 1312–22 was the brainchild of a 14th-century vizier serving in Oljeitu's court (page 236) who obviously wanted to build bigger and better than anyone else. Judging from the surviving height (26m) and thickness (10.5m) of the walls, it is thought the *ivan* leading to the prayer chamber stood about 66m high, with the vault springing starting around 24.5m, across a staggering span of almost 31m (wider than anything attempted in 14th-century Europe). Chronicles described the mosque as having a huge 285m × 228m marble-paved courtyard, surrounded by an alabaster-columned arcade and with an ablution pool so large that, two centuries later, Shah Ismail I would sail across it in a beautiful barge. Its minarets, probably soaring over 60m high, were said to have so impressed envoys from the Mamluk Court of Cairo that they influenced the design of those built in 1330 at the no-longer extant Mosque of Amir Qarasunqur in Cairo. By the 17th century the mosque was in ruins, although there was enough cover for the Friday prayer still to be conducted. In 1809 the Qajar governor took over the building, turning it into a citadel (an earlier Arg built elsewhere under Ottoman occupation had been destroyed in 1603), with a defensive ditch. Even so, some original mosque tilework was seen in situ by the English envoy, Ker Porter, ten years later but shortly afterwards Tabriz fell to the Russians. The Arg's defences were finally dismantled in the late 19th century and by then not one tile panel remained.

Continuing on along the street, at Saat Square look up at the distinctive **clock tower**. This is the Tabriz Municipality building, built in 1934 under the supervision of German architects.

Across the road a few hundred metres down the same street, is the so-called **Blue Mosque** (*masjed-e kabud*) (مسجد کبود) (Imam Khomeini St; ⏰ 08.00–17.00, closed Fri; entry 300,000 rials), known in Iran for centuries as the 'Turquoise of Islam' because of its tilework. This mosque was built on the orders of Saliha Khanum, the daughter of Jahan Shah, chief of the Qara Qoyunlu, or of his wife, Khatun Jan. It was finished in 1465, two years before Jahan Shah was killed in an Aq Qoyunlu ambush in 1467. A severe earthquake in 1776 caused some of the building to collapse, but an extensive and sympathetic rebuilding programme between 1950 and 1966 allows today's visitors to gain an accurate idea of the original layout, scale and proportions, and also to inspect the incredible 'mosaic' tilework inside and out. The main entrance portal still stands with its rich cable moulding and tiling, but otherwise much of the exterior façade has been rebuilt. This leads into a five-domed 'corridor' which in turn leads to two domed side aisles and a large central domed chamber (diameter 16m) supported by eight piers, which had internal staircases that led to an upper gallery. Essentially it is a fine example of the 'covered mosque' plan of nine domes, including the main central one, which is more usually found in early Ottoman architecture, for instance in Bursa, Turkey. But there's something else: behind the *qibla* wall and down a few steps there is another domed chamber, so the actual groundplan is similar to the so-called 'T-shaped' mosques of 15th-century Bursa (eg: 1414–20 Yeşil Cami), but function, emphasis and proportions are different. Only a fraction of the mid-15th-century tilework remains, but the impact is sensational, with the jewel-like intensity and depth of colour modern glazes rarely matching. The second domed chamber behind was also at some point covered in cobalt-blue tiles embellished with a gilded pattern, but only a few remain. The impact must have been dramatic, but perhaps lightened by the calm grey of the marble panelling with its elegantly carved inscriptions (Q26, 36, 48), some still in situ. The selection of the Quranic chapters is interesting: aside from describing the joys of paradise (suggesting, perhaps, that this was intended to be a tomb chamber), there is a clear allusion to the then large Christian community in the region.

The **Azerbaijan Museum** (Imam Khomeini St; ⊕ 08.00–17.30; entry 500,000 rials) is located nearby. This is the second most important archaeological museum in Iran after that of Tehran with important material including both Achaemenid and Sasanid metalwork and some of Shah Abass's porcelain donation to the shrine of Ardabil. The museum also holds regular historical and archaeological exhibitions. A 10-minute walk from here is **Shahriyar Literary Museum** (31 Nobar St; ⊕ 09.00–18.30 Sat–Thu, 09.00–13.00 Fri; entry free), located in the house that the celebrated poet had once called home. Visitors are welcomed into this cosy space by the statue of Shahriyar (pen name of Seyyed Mohammad Hossein Behjat-Tabrizi) himself, gracing the courtyard, before proceeding to the displays of numerous books by and about the poet, as well as of his personal belongings. Explanations are in Persian only and it is recommended to familiarise yourself with his works before coming to the museum.

A lovingly and carefully restored **Behnam House** (خانه بهنام) (⊕ 08.00–20.00 daily; entry 300,000 rials) is just 200m away. This maze of Qajar-period historical houses, courtyards and rooms operates under the auspices of Tabriz Islamic Art University and is open for visitors to wander around.

Another testament to those turbulent and historically important *mashrutiyat* years is **Constitutional House** (خانه مشروطه) (Motahhari St; ⊕ 08.00–17.00, closed Sat; entry 300,000 rials). Located near the bazaar, it was built in 1868, the late Qajar period, by a local architect and used by many of the Constitutionalists. The first owner of the house was Hajji Mehdi Kuzeh Konani, a merchant and a revolutionary activist, known as *Abolmeleh*, meaning 'father of the nation'. The house was a meeting place and an important point for decisions that were part of the Constitutional Revolution of 1905–11. Across the road is the **masjed-e jame** and the central **bazaar area**, which is interesting to walk around because some sections are from the 18th and 19th centuries and even earlier.

There are approximately six churches still in the locale, but most of them are closed or in ruins. The oldest **St Mary's Armenian Church** (1785), at the corner of Shariati Street on Namaz Square, will open its doors to a guide from the tourist office, but **St Sergius** (Sarkis), extensively renovated in 1845, is the only church still functioning and is open for service on Sundays from 10.30 to 13.00. Please bear in mind that the community is protective of its privacy and permission from the local patriarch is required to attend the service.

Do, however, take a walk in this central part of town, for there are innumerable early 20th-century houses and businesses with patterned brickwork decoration around the windows and doors, especially around the Maydan-e Saat (formerly Maydan-e Shahrdari), **Tarbiat** (look up at the old city gate Darb-e Nobar at the start of this pedestrian area) and Mahabeh streets. Not on a par with the Kharraqan tomb towers (page 132) or the brick vaults of the masjed-e jame, Esfahan (page 173), maybe, but still worth a look.

Of interest to lovers of Persian poetry is the **Poets' Mausoleum** (sho'ara) (مقبره الشعرای) (Seyyed Hamzeh St, next to Imamzadeh Seyyed Hamzeh; ⏱ 08.00–20.00 except holidays; entry free), where 400 famous Iranian poets are buried. Built in 1971, it is located in a park in the Sorkhab historical district of Tabriz. Once here, make sure to visit the nearby **Qajar Museum** (Sheshgelan Alley; ⏱ 09.00–18.30; entry 300,000 rials) located in the historical Amirnezam House which was built during the rule of Naser Al-Din Shah. Spanning an area of 1,500m² with a spacious courtyard, the museum exhibits, including Qajar glass and porcelain objects, tiles and gunpowder horns as well as some rare and beautiful items of clothing, are nicely displayed over two floors and a number of small galleries.

In fine weather many Tabrizi families will spend the day in the 53,000m² central **Golestan Park** (Bagh-e Golestan), established in the 1930s, or they'll go 8km south of the city to the slightly larger **Bagh-e Melli Park** (known locally as El Goli, previously called Shah Goli) with its artificial 12m-deep lake, perhaps first constructed in the 15th century but definitely extended in the Safavid period. Consider renting a pedalo (100,000 rials pp) here on a warm summer day.

SOUTH AND SOUTHEAST OF TABRIZ

The historic troglodyte village of **Kandovan** (کندوان) is located 55km from Tabriz and 22km southeast from Osku, and offers a unique insight into traditional rock-house living in Iran. The geology of the area is similar to that of Cappadocia in Turkey and some of the houses here are more than 800 years old and are still inhabited. The village has a natural spring and pleasant rest areas by the river, as well as one of the most luxurious and expensive hotels in Iran. There are unfortunately no buses to get here from Tabriz. Hiring a taxi is the only option and a return journey will cost around 1,000,000 rials. During Nou Rouz and public holidays, Kandovan becomes a magnet for local mass tourism, doing away with the otherwise charming and laid-back atmosphere of the village.

 WHERE TO STAY AND EAT

🏠 **Laleh Kandovan International Rock Hotel** (16 rooms) ☎041 33224951–7; e hotel. laleh.kandowan@gmail.com. The cave hotel is the only one of its kind in Iran & is designed

& decorated to international standards, with luxurious spa bathrooms, underfloor heating & simple rooms with tribal rugs & Persian carpets. **$$$$**

WHAT TO SEE AND DO Further southeast near the town of **Hashtrud** (هشترود), approximately 164km from Tabriz (savari taxis for Hashtrud leave from Darvazeh Tehran in Tabriz), are the remains of **Qaleh Zahhak** (قلعه ضحاک), discovered by a British colonel in 1830. Named after a despotic ruler from Ferdowsi's Shahnameh (see box, page 349), it is believed that the citadel was either an official building or a fire temple dating to the Parthian dynasty. The site is famous for its plasterwork, including reliefs of Mithra, the God of the Covenant and the Lord of Fire, which have since been removed to the Azerbaijan Museum in Tabriz. The view from the citadel over the surrounding area and the gorge is breathtaking, and so is the steep walk up to it. It takes approximately an hour to reach the qaleh and the remains of two brick structures that were probably used for religious ceremonies, but their exact purpose remains unknown.

The nearby area is famous for its high-quality limestone. The town of **Miyaneh** (میانه), 67km east of Hashtrud on the old road, is the first stop en route to the Sasanid bridge, **Pol-e Dokhtar** (پل دختر), over the Qezel Ozan River, flowing from the Zagros Mountains in Kurdistan. On the night of 10 December 1946, Pol-e Dokhtar together with the nearby rail bridge and motorway, was exploded with dynamite by the Azerbaijan Democratic Party forces, to stop the advance of the central government troops.

Past the Red Crescent station facing the bridge, the mountain road starts coiling up towards the remains of the ancient fortress **Qaleh Dokhtar** (قلعه دختر). The short walk to its spectacular setting is easily manageable and the area offers very good hiking opportunities.

NORTH OF TABRIZ

Travelling north takes you into the region once heavily populated by Armenian Christians. It was from here that Shah Abbas I took tens of thousands of Armenians to Esfahan in the 17th century to exploit their expertise in silk trading with European and Russian merchants, and it was here that many 19th-century European and American missionaries came, hoping to introduce such Monophysite Christians into the Baptist, Methodist or other Protestant churches. In 1946–47 most of the Armenians were 'repatriated' into Soviet Armenia. There are, however, still some beautiful but austere Armenian churches surviving in this mountainous area, the most famous being St Stephanos near Jolfa, close to the Azerbaijani frontier, and the Qara Kelisa ('Black Church'), near Maku.

The road to **Jolfa** (جلفا) goes through **Marand** (مرند), 70km from Tabriz, whose **masjed-e jame** was established in Seljuk times and then rebuilt in the 14th century; it has a splendid plaster *mihrab*. Some 10km further north is a caravanserai built around 1330 but badly damaged in the mid 19th century. It is another 55km or so to Jolfa. If you are going to explore the Armenian heritage of this area, you may contemplate staying here. There is the simple, but comfortable **Jolfa Tourist Inn** (23 rooms; Beheshti Sq, Imam Khomeini St; ☏041 42022220; **$$**). The border crossing to Nakhichevan (Azerbaijan; ⏰ 24/7) is in Jolfa itself.

From Jolfa, a further 16km west and 3km from the Aras River, brings you to the UNESCO World Heritage Site of **St Stephanos** (⏰ opening hours vary with the season, but best to arrive here between 10.00 & 15.00; at the approach to the church there is also an area with restaurants & cafés, but these are closed in winter & early spring; entry 500,000 rials), named after the first Christian martyr. In the past foreign visitors needed to obtain a letter from the Armenian cathedral authorities in Esfahan, or a gendarmerie permit, west of Jolfa, but this authorisation is no longer required. The monastery church is said to have been founded by St Bartholomew around 62CE, with the late 9th-century King of Armenia, Ashot, ordering its construction, but most of the present structure dates from the 16th century. The large church faces east with a long cloister along the north side, but surprisingly it does not possess the usual large *gavit* (where the congregation stood) seen in most medieval churches in the Armenian Republic. Instead, the layout bears a closer resemblance to 10th-century Armenian churches in present-day Turkey (eg: Ani and Akdamar), of a single nave form, with a tall belfry in the south wall. The exterior 'prismatic' tent-like dome (and the interior hemispherical one) in red and white stone, along with the *muqarnas* portal, date from the 16th century and the numerous stone carvings of saints and patriarchs, especially on the drum, are reminiscent of churches at Akdamar, which were decorated some 600 years earlier.

A few kilometres further west down by the Aras River, your eyes will catch the sight of **Nana Maryam Church**. It is unfortunately not accessible, and you can only see it from the road. As it lies close to the Aras free-trade zone there is a military presence in the area; be careful when taking photos of the church. 08.00–17.00;

A visit to another UNESCO World Heritage Site, **St Thaddeus Church** (*qara kelisa*) (قره کلیسا) (⏰ 08.00–17.00; your taxi driver will help you find the man with the key in the nearby village; entry 500,000 rials), 45km from Maku, deep in the hills is also recommended, but take some refreshments with you as there is no tea house (or toilets) here. Nothing seems to have survived from the first church built here to fulfil the dream of St Gregory the Illuminator (page 187) to commemorate the martyrdom of St Thaddeus, whose death (c68CE) was ordered by King Abgar of Edessa on revoking his brief conversion to Christianity. Part of the 10th-century church remains specifically in the area around the altar, to the right of which the saint is said to be interred, and the dome. The rest was destroyed by earthquakes in 1329 and in 1689, so most of the fortified church seen today dates from the rebuilding, with the exterior decoration added about two centuries later. Very few visitors come here except in the summer to celebrate the movable Feast of St Thaddeus (usually July) when pilgrims come and camp out. The guardian kindly allows people to explore the buildings (formerly refectory, kitchens, flour mill, stores and dormitories) around the huge courtyard, and to climb up to roof level to take photographs of the church façade. Why it is called the Black Church is a mystery. It is indeed very gloomy inside, with the austere walls covered in soot from the thousands of candles lit over the centuries, and the 10th-century eastern section is clad in dark tuff, but the exterior church walls are a wonderful creamy-yellow limestone, decorated with a lively narrow frieze running around the building, depicting scenes from the *Shahnameh* (see box, page 349) among which are musket-bearing hunters taking potshots at wild animals. There is a similarity to the highly carved exterior of the 10th-century church of Akdamar on Lake Van, Turkey, perhaps because of early close links to that diocese, and to the deeply worked decoration of the Ishak Pasha palace, Doğubayazit, eastern Turkey, which throughout the 18th century controlled the trade routes west to east. The Akdamar architectural details resemble Georgian church decoration, but the sombre interior of St Thaddeus is totally in the manner of the massive stone churches across the Caucasus in the Armenian Republic.

Exploring the area or if travelling to Turkey via the Bazargan/Gürbulak border crossing (page 229), you may consider staying overnight in **Maku**, which has a pleasant and clean **Maku Tourist Inn** (30 rooms; Imam Khomeini St; ☎044 34223185, 4223212; **$$**), with spacious and comfortable rooms.

Between Maku and the Turkish border crossing at Bazargan and just off the main road in the village of Baghcheh Juq you will find the Qajar-period **Baghcheh Juq** (باغچه جوق) palace fully renovated in 2019 (⏰ 09.00–18.00 Tue–Sun). It was built for a commander of Shah Muzaffar al-Din (r1896–1907) and is surrounded by 11ha of gardens (*baghcheh* in Persian means 'small garden'). The building exhibits a mixture of European and local styles and is embellished with plaster decoration, mirror work and paintings. The mountain road past Baghcheh Juq continues to the main treat, a visit to Maku, the Armenian **Chapel of Dzordzor** (also known as St Maryam Church). Located roughly 40km from Maku and overlooking the Barun Dam Lake, this chapel is all that remains of the 14th-century monastery,

Today, Mount Ararat forms the frontier between Turkey and the Republic of Armenia, but the kingdom of Urartu, or Ararat, is mentioned in Assyrian texts dating from 1275BCE and also in the Bible (Jeremiah 51:27; II Kings 19). European scholars became very interested in this civilisation after the decipherment of a lengthy cuneiform inscription from the citadel of Van, Turkey, in the 1840s, but it was almost a century later before serious archaeological investigations started in (then) Soviet Armenia, followed by British work around Van in the 1950s and in northwest Iran by German scholars in the late 1960s.

Urartian power grew during the reign of Sarduri (also spelt Sardusi) II, c760–735BCE, whose successful military expeditions were recorded in the Van text; from just one campaign his armies captured over 21,000 people, 1,600 horses, 16,500 cattle and nearly 40,000 sheep. Urartian merchants came to control the major trade routes across Anatolia and the Caucasus into the Mediterranean, as shown by finds of huge Urartian bronze cauldrons in excavations in France, Greece and Italy. Although increasingly threatened by the Assyrian Empire to the south, Rusa I (735–714BCE) undertook such major irrigation schemes that even Sargon II of Assyria grudgingly admitted he 'changed the entire surface of its unproductive region into meadowland and the fresh green grass of spring'. Much time and effort went into the construction of palace-citadels, carving down into the bedrock, and working ashlar stone blocks so accurately that a sheet of paper cannot be inserted between them. Attention was given to temple buildings to honour the Urartian pantheon of some 50 gods, dominated by three deities with their consorts, each requiring a daily sacrifice of at least six bulls and sheep: Khaldi the warrior 'father' god often depicted standing on a bull; the rain god Tesheba; and Shivini of the sun, always shown holding a winged disc.

After fending off Assyrian attacks, Urartu negotiated peace in 650BCE, which should have guaranteed its survival, but the 605BCE Battle of Carcemish marked the end of the great Assyrian Empire. Without this ally, the days of the Urartian kingdom were numbered. A Scythian attack from the north c590BCE and the rise of the Medians in the south dealt the final blows.

a renowned calligraphy centre under Mongol rule. The chapel is UNESCO-listed together with St Thaddeus and St Stephanos churches (page 225).

In this region close to the frontiers with Turkey and the Caucasian republics, archaeologists have identified over 50 Urartian settlements, such as the 8th-century BCE citadel of **Sangar** (سنگر) or the Historical Sangar Complex, 10km northwest of Maku (signposted), with its rock-cut chambers and steps cut from the bedrock. The present state of the site, in particular the inner walls of the rock-cut chambers, known as the stone crypt of Farhad (page 141), might leave an avid historian disappointed, but the view of the two glorious Ararats in the distance will justify a quick visit here. Perhaps you have visited Cavus Tappeh, east of Lake Van, Turkey; the stoneworking in that palace-citadel site and the presence of bichrome, recessed 'blind' windows have prompted more than one archaeologist to suggest an Urartian influence at Pasargadae and Naqsh-e Rostam (pages 269 and 272).

The main road **south from Maku** passes many other Urartian sites, including the important **Bastam** (بسطام), near Qara Ziyaeddin. This excavation site, 70km southeast from Maku and not far from St Thaddeus Church on the old road, should not be confused with Bastam to the east of the Caspian (page 208). This one was the Urartian 'town' of Ruzu-Urutur, associated in the histories with the famous king, Rusa II (685–645BCE). The German archaeological team that worked here from 1968 until the late 1970s found the site extended over an area 850m × 400m, and something of the huge stone walls, once topped by mud-brick galleries and ramparts, may still be seen in their present restored state. A citadel was constructed by the north gate from the 8th century BCE but then, possibly due to political instability after Rusa's death in 645BCE, it was dismantled in preference for a new defensive structure near the south gate, with stables, barracks and storerooms. Above was the palace area with the remains of a 14m² tower temple (somewhat like those at Pasargadae and Naqsh-e Rostam) dedicated to the god Khaldi, and a large audience hall with 14 column bases. Banqueting was obviously important in court life and one chamber served as a meat store judging from the cuneiform tablets listing the stock found there. The site continued to be occupied in Median and Achaemenid times until the 13th century when, recognising its strategic importance on the trade routes, an Armenian warlord built a fortress here. The Mongol invasion put paid to his activities and the site was abandoned to the nasty local black spiders.

Khoy (خوی), 136km north of Orumiyeh, is probably the best place for restaurants if you are continuing your journey southwest towards Orumiyeh. A Safavid gateway, an unusual Armenian church and the Shams Tabrizi minaret are the only reminders of Khoy's turbulent past, when it was a walled town belonging to local warlords. Shams Tabrizi (d1248) was a Sufi mystic who introduced Mawlana Jalal al-Din, otherwise known as Rumi, to Islamic mysticism. After some years with Rumi, Shams left him and came to Khoy where he died and was buried; the rather unusual minaret, with its protruding ram's horns, is associated with the tomb.

The area around Khoy and further south once had a strong Christian presence, as testified by a great number of churches, some closed and in ruins and others still operational, albeit without regular opening hours. Approximately 15km north of Khoy, driving past the village of **Mahlazan** (ماهلازان), you catch sight of the humble dome of **Mahlazan Church**, entirely void of any writings or decorations on the inside. While there are no historic records to suggest when it was built, it was probably during the Mongol period. The **St Serkis Church** in Khoy itself, however, can be dated to the 4th and 9th centuries. With rectangular 6m-high outer walls, the interior has six columns and two entrances, southern and western, in line with Iranian temple design. According to historical records, it was fully repaired in Safavid times.

About 47km south of Khoy and surrounded by mountains lies **Salmas** (سلماس), a town with a mixed Azerbaijani and Kurdish population, but once also numbering many Armenians and Assyrians. On its southern outskirts a Manchester University (UK) archaeological team undertook excavations from 1968–78 at Butan Tappeh, near the village of **Haftavan** (هفتوان). Apart from signs of settlement since the 4th century BCE and buildings and artefacts from around 2000BCE, remains of an Urartian citadel were found. Occupation continued during the Median and Achaemenid periods, continuing up to Sasanid times when the settlement was walled. Here there are also numerous churches scattered across small villages and often hidden amid newly built alleys and structures. Haftavan has a functioning 18th-century Armenian **St George Church**. With a rectangular groundplan and only one entrance, the church rests in a large courtyard, which it shares with the remaining façade of the former Haftavan theatre, built in 1914 during the Russian occupation. In the nearby village of Malham, tall stone walls encircle the ruins of **Nana Maryam Church** and only the carving above the metal gate, probably depicting heaven and hell, together with a cross and the date of 1895 suggest it had once been a church.

Some 18km south of Salmas in the direction of Orumiyeh and on the main road, those with sharp eyesight might see a **Sasanid relief** (*khan takhti*) of Ardashir I and his son, later Shapur I, recording his victories in this region. Above are the remains of the Urartian fort of **Qaleh Vaseriyeh**.

ORUMIYEH AND BEYOND (TO THE SOUTH AND SOUTHEAST)

ORUMIYEH ارومیه *Telephone code 044*

Formerly known as Rezaiyeh, Orumiyeh or Urmia (altitude 1,330m; population 670,000) was a city of Christians in the 19th century, mainly Nestorian and Armenian Monophysite Orthodox along with Western missionaries. However, its ancient history bears a tradition that it was the birthplace of Zarathustra, founder of Zoroastrianism. Its geographical position led later to its being contested territory, passing at various times between Kurdish and Turkish tribes before being controlled by the Safavids in the 17th century. The first Qajar ruler of Iran, Agha Mohammad Khan, was crowned here in 1795.

Getting there and around There are a few daily direct **flights** from/to Tehran with a journey time of 1½ hours. From Orumiyeh **central bus station** there are regular services to and from major Iranian cities as well as Turkey, Azerbaijan, Armenia and Georgia. The company operating *savari* taxis is furthest to the left in the terminal. Once in the city walking is manageable, but **taxis** are convenient and reasonably priced. **Buses** to and from the central bus station (terminal) stop by/across the road from the Park International Hotel. It is also possible to rent a **bicycle** (first 30mins free, 5,000–10,000 rials for the following 30mins; w traffic. urmia.ir) from rental kiosks in touristy areas. Below is a bus departure schedule with selected times from major Iranian cities:

From	Departure	Price (rials)
Esfahan (Kaveh)	15.45; 16.00; 17.00; 17.15	1,080,000
Esfahan (Sofeh)	16.15	1,080,000
Shiraz (Karandish)	13.30	1,600,000
Tabriz (central)	Every 30mins between 05.30 and 19.30	160,000
Tehran (southern)	09.00; 09.30; 10.00; 12.10; 13.30; 14.30; 13.30; 16.45; 17.45; 19.00; 19.30; 20.00; 21.00; 21.30; 22.00; 23.30	765,000–850,000
Tehran (Beyhaghi)	20.00; 21.00; 22.30	765,000–850,000

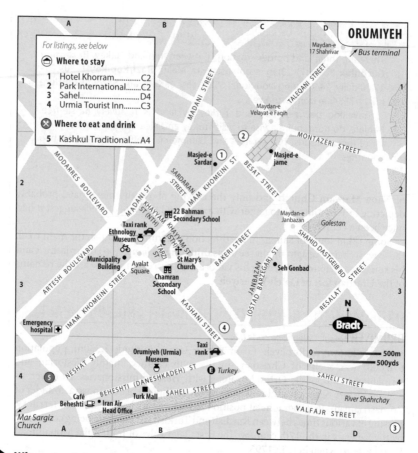

For listings, see below

Where to stay

1	Hotel Khorram	C2
2	Park International	C2
3	Sahel	D4
4	Urmia Tourist Inn	C3

Where to eat and drink

| 5 | Kashkul Traditional | A4 |

ORUMIYEH

🏠 **Where to stay and eat** Hotels in Orumiyeh are numerous, and so are tourists from Turkey and Iraq. For food, the bazaar has numerous spartan eateries and there are many kebab and sandwich shops in the centre, especially around Khayyam Street.

🏠 **Park International Hotel** [230 C2] (77 rooms) Imam St; ☎32245926, 32245932; w parkhotel.co. Flashy & a little expensive, this hotel, located in the vicinity of the bazaar, has comfortable, spacious & very bright rooms with modern & tasteful décor. **$$$$**

🏠 **Sahel Hotel** [230 D4] (60 rooms) Valfajr St; ☎33369970. Slightly away from the centre, but by the river & parks. The interior is gently old-fashioned but brightened up with traditional Iranian hospitality. Swimming pool (⏰ 09.00–18.00 for women & 18.00–23.00 for men). **$$$**

🏠 **Urmia Tourist Inn** [230 C3] (74 rooms) Kashani St, opposite Mellat Bank; ☎32223070, 32222230; e info@ittic.com. Offers all the perks of an expensive, luxurious hotel, excellent service & very spacious rooms. Although cheaper than the Park International Hotel, it is probably the most expensive tourist inn in Iran. It also has a simple & welcoming café with good Wi-Fi. **$$$**

🏠 **Hotel Khorram** [230 C2] (30 rooms) Imam St, behind Sardar Mosque; ☎32225444. Very clean & central, possibly the best budget option in town. Serves good b/fast & has caring personnel. **$$**

✖ **Kashkul Traditional Restaurant** [230 A4] Barq St; ☎33456666, 33473333; ⏰ noon–16.30 daily. Open for lunch only, this delightful traditional restaurant specialises in meaty dishes & serves excellent *dizzi*. **$$**

What to see and do

Orumiyeh (Urmia) Museum [230 B4] (Shahid Beheshti (Daneshkadeh) St; ☎ 33489851, 33489853; w urmiachto.ir; ⊕ 09.00–19.00 daily; entry 300,000 rials) This small museum houses quite an impressive collection of pottery, bronze and other items from various archaeological *tappehs* in the province. The exhibits are displayed in chronological order, starting with bowls from the 5th millennium BCE, pottery from the Neolithic period and concluding with Safavid brass and copper and Qajar glassware. Particularly eye-catching is the 1st millennium BCE rhyton pottery and hairpins as well as tiny bronze lions, revealing the variety and spectrum of items produced at Tappeh Hasanlu (page 232), one of the most important ancient settlements in the area. There are also some fine examples of Sasanid glassware. Considered ritually pure by Zoroastrians, production of glass was widespread across the entire Sasanid Empire. The real treats, however, are the 1st millennium BCE glazed clinker bricks with mythical animal patterns from Rabat Tappeh and Ghalaychi and a grand collection of very intricate seal impressions from the same era. These were first used in northern Mesopotamia in the 5th millennium BCE to prevent tampering with containers. The 'seized by' annotation on labelling refers to the items that were seized from smugglers across the border.

Ethnology Museum [230 B3] (Enghelab-e Islami (Ialat) Sq; ☎ 33489851, 33489853; w urmiachto.ir; ⊕ 09.00–19.00 daily; entry 300,000 rials) Established in 2013, the museum's ethnographic collection, housed in a characteristic mansion, includes classic ethnographic exhibits, such as farming tools, copies of historic marriage certificates with transliteration and a collection of lenses, watches, cinema equipment and effectively everything and anything else to familiarise the visitor with the life and traditions of the province.

Masjed-e jame [230 C2] (Bazaar area) Perhaps built in the Seljuk period with a domed prayer chamber over the remains of a Zoroastrian fire temple, the masjed-e jame has a beautiful plaster *mihrab* dated to 1277, one of the earliest post-Mongol architectural remains. On the southwestern outskirts is the **Seh Gonbad** (⊕ 09.00–13.00, entry 300,000 rials) tomb tower, standing 9m high; built in 1184, it has some fine plasterwork and *muqarnas* details. In the centre, the modern Assyrian **St Mary's Church** (1960s) (*kelisa hazrat-e maryam*) (⊕ 09.00–13.00 & 15.00–20.00 daily), replaces a much older shrine. Currently known as the Assyrian Church of the East, the original location is believed to have been chosen by the three Magi, who were in fact Zoroastrian, having indicated the building of the new church on the place of a Zoroastrian fire temple.

Mar Sargiz Church [230 A4] (Outskirts of Orumiyeh; ⊕ Sun) This church is only a short drive from the city centre. The man with the key to the entrance gate lives in the house by the entrance. The church is essentially closed during the week, but comes to life on Sundays. This part of the city is a popular weekend retreat with a cable car under construction.

SOUTH OF ORUMIYEH Approximately 7km south of Orumiyeh lies the important archaeological site of **Geoy Tappeh** (گوی‌تپه). Although of no striking visual interest for the visitor, the mound is historically significant. Excavated first by British archaeologists in 1948, it was an important manufacturing centre of early Transcaucasian ware, a distinctive handmade ceramic with a glossy black surface and

The idea that Zoroastrians are 'fire worshippers' is technically incorrect but traditionally great reverence has always been shown to this, surely the most important 'gift' to humanity. Prayer, for instance, is always made towards a fire or other light source such as a lamp, the sun or the moon. To devout Zoroastrians even domestic fires should be treated with care, their embers taken to the temple every third day for cleansing of any accidental pollution by adding cold embers from the temple fires. Every ninth day fires of blacksmiths had to be cleansed nine times before those embers could be taken to the temple for such renewal.

It is held that there were four great sacred fires, each later associated with a social class. The **Azargoshnasp** fire originated near or in Lake Orumiyeh in the lands of the Medes. In around 400CE it was transported to Takht-e Soleyman where it became firmly associated with royalty and warriors. The second, the Azar barzea fire of the agricultural class, was known to exist in the 3rd century CE in Parthian lands, perhaps in a major temple complex between Shahrud and Sabzevar or further east on Mount Revand, near Borzinan. The Zoroastrian priests understood the third Azarfarnbag fire to be their special fire, which had been brought into southwest Iran from central Asia. To protect its survival during the Arab Muslim conquests, this fire was divided into two, one being kept in Fasa and the other transported to Sharifabad, north of Yazd. The fourth fire, Azarkarkuy (or Azar Karkuy), is associated with Kuh-e Khajeh, near Lake Hamun in Sistan, where the oldest known fire temple in Iran stands.

The Zoroastrian priest is the only person to attend the temple fire, during which he wears a white cotton robe and mouth-mask to prevent his breath polluting the sacred flames, which are fed five times a day. In ancient times a *barsom* bundle of pomegranate twigs was offered to the flame but today a bunch of brass or silver wire replaces this. However, fires at shrines (eg: at Chak Chak, page 318) are tended by laymen because they are used only in a minor role, such as cooking the special *dron* – unleavened cakes – used for certain Zoroastrian services.

thick walls (sides of a pot), which was characteristic of the 3rd millennium BCE and widely spread from Anatolia all the way to Godin Tappeh near present-day Hamadan.

Tappeh Hasanlu تپه حسنلو The road further south from Orumiyeh passes several important archaeological sites such as this one (probably Manaai in the Assyrian texts) about 5km north of **Naqadeh** (نقده). The main excavations carried out during 1956–74 by Pennsylvania University (US) and then the Metropolitan Museum of Art showed that Hasanlu was settled from the 6th millennium BCE. Carbon-14 tests in the 1980s suggested that the main period of occupation was c1350–1150BCE. Around 1000BCE an impressive citadel, some 200m in diameter with defence walls, towers and gates, was built, along with multi-storey housing whose interiors were decorated with Assyrian-style tiles. At this point the earlier (outer) settlement became the city cemetery. A fierce attack (Level III) caused the collapse of the eastern citadel gate, causing the death of some 40 people, mainly women, and at least another 30 met a violent end on the roof of a porticoed building to the north, one skeleton still holding a beautifully worked gold vessel. The walls were rebuilt on the charred remains of the citadel with Cyclopean stonework. The excavations yielded bronze horse trappings, helmets and mace heads alongside delicate ivory carvings. Soviet archaeologists argued that the Assyrian attack in 714BCE, as recorded in cuneiform texts, caused the Urartian occupants to flee. However, using data from further carbon-14 tests, the American archaeological team have since offered another sequence: the attack and fire occurred earlier (c850–800BCE), perpetrated by Urartian forces, who then took over the citadel, rebuilding the defence walls using their distinctive masonry skills. This occupation continued and survived the Assyrian attack of 714BCE, when the then-famous temple mentioned in the Kul-e Shin stele (southwest of Ushnuyeh/Oshnaviyeh) was destroyed. This stele and also the six-line Urartian cuneiform inscription found at Qalatgeh (just before the archaeological site of Dinkh Tappeh), west of Hasanlu, supports the theory of Urartian campaigning in this area around 800BCE.

Ziwiyeh زيويه South of Naqadeh and 40km before Saqqez, is the famous archaeological site of **Ziwiyeh** where in 1947 a treasure of gold, silver and ivory was found by a shepherd boy; today these finds are divided between Tehran (Reza Abbasi Museum), New York (Metropolitan Museum of Art) and Cincinnati, Ohio (Art Museum). Archaeological investigation revealed that the main period of occupation was 800–600BCE when, as indicated by finds of Scythian arrowheads, the occupants fled their citadel. Illicit digging has since destroyed much of the site, but an Iranian archaeological team restarted work in 1994.

Mahabad مهاباد Continuing south you reach the town of **Mahabad**, also known as Mukrivan, but this historic name only lingers in a few local shop signs. Predominantly Kurdish, it was the capital of the short-lived Republic of Mahabad that managed to hold Kurdish aspirations for autonomy alive from 22 January until 15 December 1946. Tourist attractions are not plentiful here, but if you are planning an overnight stop, while travelling further to Iranian Kurdistan, for example, and have some time to spare, a walk through the bazaar and a visit to the local **Mirza Rasul Hamam (Anthropology Museum)** (🕐 08.00–14.30, closed Fri; entry 300,000 rials) in the restored Safavid will be enjoyable.

About 15km north of Mahabad, there is an example of a modest Median rock-cut tomb, **Fakhrigah** (فقرگاه). The turn is signposted and the road lies past Kani Barazan Wildlife Refuge. The surrounding hilly area is pleasant, particularly in spring. Driving along the winding Mahabad–Bukan road, about 43km away, you might like to stop at the **Saholan Water Cave** (🕐 08.00–17.30 daily; entry 300,000 rials). Although not a patch on the spectacular Ali Sadr Caves (page 132), it is nevertheless impressive, with the depth of underground water channels reaching 62m.

Where to stay and eat

Hotel Afshar (21 rooms) Jam-e Jam St, opposite TV & radio station, Mahabad; ⎆044

42225886, 42230700; w hotelafsharmahabad. com. A hotel offering basic accommodation. **$**

SOUTHEAST OF ORUMIYEH Much more is visible at the UNESCO World Heritage Site of **Takht-e Soleyman** (تخت سليمان) (🕐 summer 08.00–20.00, winter 09.00–17.00 but best visited early in the morning; entry 500,000 rials), which can be approached from **Miyandoab** (میاندوآب) by travelling around 200km southeast to Takab (pronounced *Tekab*). The road twists and turns, but the surface is good and there is little traffic along this route. You can overnight in Takab in the simple but clean **Hotel**

Ranji (27 rooms; Enghelab St; ☏044 45523179; you can eat dinner here but order in advance; **$$**) and take a taxi to Takht-e Soleyman 40km away in the morning. A return taxi trip will cost 1,000,000 rials. If you are camping, you are welcome to set a tent up on the hills overlooking the walls of the actual archaeological site at its main entrance. It is perfectly safe and increasingly more people are camping in the area. Alternatively, you could drive from Zanjan (see opposite). The location of Takht-e Soleyman is dramatic, up in the mountains at over 2,600m with a large volcanic lake in the centre. The depth of the lake remains unknown. Exercise caution: a few years ago a young man drowned here. Swimming is strictly prohibited. The asphalt road leads right up to the north entrance. The enclosing walls, built in early Sasanid (or possibly Parthian) times to honour this place, is home to one of the four important sacred fires of Zoroastrianism, the **Azargoshnasp** (آتشکده آذرگشنسب) or Royal Warrior Fire (see box, page 232). Its reputation may even date from the Achaemenid period, as there is evidence of occupation around the small dead volcano rising 2,200m, 3km northwest of the walled site. You can easily climb it for beautiful views over the area and the Takht-e Soleyman complex. It is thought that the Sasanid shahs always came here after their investiture at Ctesiphon, Iraq, to pay their respects to this fire, and there are the remains of at least two fire temples along the processional way from the north gate to the lakeshore: the Hasht Taq with its eight arches of fine stonework to the east, and the main temple marked by four huge brick piers facing the lake. A small shrine lies behind a columned hall, 'Khosrow's Palace', to the west of the main temple.

The German archaeologists working here in 1959–77 discovered that, during the last quarter of the 13th century, the largely abandoned site measuring some 550m × 400m was reoccupied as a summer palace by the Ilkhanid ruler, Abaqa, when the main temple building was used for a royal reception hall and the columned hall for private rooms. At this time certain alterations (eg: blind niche forms) were made to the structure of the large west *ivan*. A south gate was also constructed and arcading erected all around the lake. A 12-sided hall, perhaps inspired by the nomadic felt domed tent, is located just south of the two western octagonal buildings on the northwest corner of the arcading. This, it is suggested, possibly functioned as a storehouse where the wife of Abaqa kept the royal treasures for her grandson, the later Ghazan Khan. Numerous splendid examples of 13th-century tiles (which must have decorated the walls), remains of marble flooring and – an important find for Islamic architectural history – a carved stone slab detailing a *muqarnas* pattern composition were all found. Here finally was proof of how medieval masons calculated and devised the intricate arrangements of various three-dimensional architectural elements. Remains of kilns and a pottery workshop were unearthed behind the main north palace hall, to the northeast.

If time allows, a short diversion to the southeastern corner of Lake Orumiyeh should be made. This is where you'll find **Maragheh** (مراغه), famous in the late medieval histories for its 'state-of-the-art' astronomical observatory, constructed on the order of Hulagu (r1256–65), grandson of Genghis Khan, the scourge of all Asia. Hulagu used this Star House, as it was called, to develop a strong interest in philosophy and astrology. He was married to a Christian woman and under her influence, ordered for the mosques and Buddhist temples in the area to be converted to churches, albeit for a short period of time. Nothing now remains of his Star House, but it was from here that the scientist Naser al-Din Tusi (d1274) solved the seeming incompatibility between Ptolemy's planetary model and Aristotelian theory about planetary movement, which was then taken up and developed by

Copernicus. The city still possesses three fine tomb towers. The **Gonbad-e Sorkh** (also known as Gonbad-e Qermez), built in 1148 for a local prince, a certain Abd al-Aziz, has been described by one scholar as 'the most beautiful example of brickwork known'. We are not convinced. The square brick mausoleum rises from a stone base and then the brick patterns begin, 'contained' within two blind niche frames on three of the four external sides, including the foliated *Kufic* inscription over the door and over the blind niche frames. Twelve sizes of interlocking brick units were used, with some glazed strips inserted for highlights. The original, eight-sided tent-like roof has gone, but the octagonal drum and the inner dome remain, though much restored.

Slightly to the north is the 12-sided blue **Gonbad-e Kabud** of 1197. Standing 14.5m high, it has long been associated with Hulagu as local people thought the tomb was built to honour either his mother or his daughter, though there is nothing to prove this assumption. It has lost its original roof but retains much of its very ornate exterior decoration consisting of intersecting turquoise blue 'strap' brickwork of hexagons and six-pointed stars. Just under the exterior cornice is an inscription band (Q2:255) while inside around the dome is another (Q67:1): 'Blessed be He to whom all sovereignty belongs; He has power over all things', while downstairs in the crypt there is another inscription (Q55:26–7) alluding to death and paradise. Nearby is an anonymous tomb tower, circular in plan, built around 1330 and known locally as **Koyborj**, looking more like a defence tower than a mausoleum. Also in the northern outskirts in a Sufichay riverside of Ghaffariyeh park, is a 14th-century tomb tower known as the **Gonbad-e Ghaffariyeh**, which in its decorative scheme includes a heraldic device of two polo sticks, indicating the bearer was Master of the Royal Polo; he was Amir Qara Sunghur, who worked for both the Egyptian Mamluk regime and then the Ilkhanids, as a local governor at a time when Maragheh was known as 'Little Damascus'. The Tabriz–Tehran train makes a stop in Maragheh and from here you can make an overnight journey to the Iranian capital or otherwise continue by regional buses or *savari* elsewhere in the province.

It is known that Hulagu built a palace (or at least reception rooms) on the largest island in **Lake Orumiyeh**, Jazir-e Kabudi (formerly shah's island), and indeed he and his successor are said to have been buried here. Like the water of Takht-e Soleyman, this lake, also known in ancient times as the Lower Lake of Nairi, has a high mineral content, which, although good for rheumatism, means fish and other wildlife are limited. The lake's salinity levels are at a present record high of 340 grams per litre and the lake is in a very fragile state, having lost nearly 90% of its mass since 1970. The desiccation has been caused by poorly planned manmade projects and natural factors. Despite some improvement recorded in late 2015, when 700km² of the southern bed of the lake were again covered with water, largely owing to heavy rains, the lake remains severely endangered.

ZANJAN زنجان *Telephone code 024*

Capital (population 389,000) of the province of the same name, the town was allegedly founded in Sasanid times. Its main claims to fame are its close associations with the Bahai faith in 1851 and today its proximity to the World Heritage Site of Soltaniyeh. Its handicraft traditions are unfortunately in decline but it is still known for its distinctive, colourful, animal-covered *sumak* (warp-wrapped) rugs, high-quality and expensive handmade knives and its thriving bazaar. Zanjan is just off the motorway that runs between Tehran and Tabriz and is only 340km from the

Iranian capital. Admittedly not a town known for historic monuments, it still has the richly tiled **Khanum Mosque** built in 1905 on the order of Jamileh Khanum, the daughter of a local tribal chief. Ring the bell at the main door to be let in. Once in Zanjan, you may also consider visiting the Qajar-period **Rakhtshooy Khaneh** (entry 300,000 rials). Built originally as a house for women to wash clothes, it currently functions as the regional ethnographic museum.

GETTING THERE AND AWAY The best connections are by the long-distance **bus** network, but **trains** en route to Tabriz and places beyond also call here. There are a few daily trains from Tehran, the price depending on the level of comfort. If you are travelling here from Takab, around 226km away, the picturesque route lies through Bijar and takes around 4 hours by bus. There are two daily buses from Takab to Tehran (10.00 and 14.00) that pass by Zanjan as well.

 WHERE TO STAY AND EAT

Zanjan Grand Hotel (48 rooms) Basij Sq; 33788190–5; w zanjangrandhotel.com. Facilities are quite good & there is a restaurant ($$). Rooms have Wi-Fi, but the hotel is a distance from the centre & a little pricey. $$$$

Tourist Inn (17 rooms) Down the road from the Grand Hotel towards the centre; 33771930, 33771910. Located in a green & quiet area. Less glamorous than its neighbouring competitor,

the rooms are nonetheless adequate & en suite. $$–$$$

Hajj Dadash Traditional Restaurant Zanjan Bazaar; 33322020. Small & cosy, under the Zanjan bazaar arcade this pleasant venue serves mouthwatering dishes & has traditional live music in the evenings. *Gheymeh bademjun* meat stew with eggplant is recommended. $$

WHAT TO SEE AND DO

Soltaniyeh (سلطانیه) Zanjan is without doubt the most convenient place from which to visit Soltaniyeh, but you will have to hire a taxi to get there. Alternatively, you can arrive here by train from Tehran and get off at Soltaniyeh train station, approximately 10km from the centre, or equally get here on a bus bound for Tehran and get off on the motorway at the turn for Soltaniyeh, 10km south. From here you would have to walk or hitch a ride towards the centre of the town, but this is not recommended. The mausoleum is clearly visible from the motorway and is unmissable. From Soltaniyeh, it is about 100km to Qazvin (page 125) to the southeast.

Mausoleum of Oljeitu (also known as Gonbad-e Soltaniyeh) (⏰ 08.00–17.00; entry 300,000 rials) Do make an effort to visit this 14th-century World Heritage Site, which was constructed in just 11 years (1306–17). This huge mausoleum proudly stands on a fertile plain on the old road to Zanjan with a backdrop of purple-blue mountains and is clearly visible from the surrounding area. Its turquoise-blue dome is the earliest existing example of the double-shelled dome in Iran. Nothing else remains of the 14th-century walled town although recent excavations have revealed foundations of a mosque, madrasa, *khanqah*, palace pavilions and other buildings, all part of Oljeitu's plan to make this small town his capital.

Oljeitu (r1304–17) was a descendant of Genghis Khan. Historical records state that after sending architect-engineers to survey the vast palace audience hall of the Sasanid shahs at Ctesiphon, Iraq, he employed 10,000 men to lay the foundations of this tomb and the surrounding structures, as well as 500 carpenters and 5,000 marble-masons. His idea, it was said, was not to build a funerary monument for himself, but rather to bring the remains of Imam Ali and Imam Hossein, the third imam, from Karbala to this place; he had already procured a lock of the Prophet's hair, but gave up on the idea after in a dream Imam Ali told him to. Oljeitu, also known as the conqueror of the impregnable Gilan, had been slow to accept Islam, preferring at first Buddhism and then Christianity, the faith of his mother, before adopting Shi'a Islam; he finally (c1313) decided on Sunni Islam and a Muslim name Mohammad Khodabandeh ('God's slave'). It was at this point, so some argue, that he announced that the brick mausoleum was to be his own memorial.

Its size and scale are immense. The huge egg-shaped dome (interior diameter 26m) rests on eight internal piers but their massive size is disguised by their soaring, tapering height, high arches and a rhythmic arrangement of connecting galleries. From the floor to the apex of the dome is a staggering 52m. And viewing from the outside, forget the untidy brick infills and imagine continuous open galleries all around. When completed, this turquoise-tiled dome, framed with eight slender 'minarets' around the roof, must have appeared to be magically balanced on a graceful network of arches and vaults. Indeed, certain Italian scholars are sure it influenced the work of Brunelleschi, the Renaissance architect, and in particular his Santa Maria del Fiore in Florence. Inside, two different layers of decoration are apparent here and there: glazed brick strapwork and also patterned plasterwork, perhaps visual evidence of Oljeitu's change of faith from Shi'a to Sunni Islam. Access to the crypt, housing three tombs, lies to the south.

On his travels across Iran, Robert Byron described the mausoleum in the following terms:

Against the flat desert, pressed about by mud hovels, this gigantic memorial of the Mongol Empire bears witness to that Central Asian virility which produced, under the Seljuks, Mongols, and Timurids the happiest inspirations of Persian architecture. Certainly, this is façade-architecture: the prototype of the Taj and a hundred other shrines. But it still breathes power and content, while its offspring achieve only scenic refinement. It has the audacity of true invention; the graces are sacrificed to the idea, and the result, imperfect as it may be, represents the triumph of the idea over technical limitations. Much great architecture is of this kind.

An internal staircase near the entrance leads up to the galleries, where the 'openness' and inner proportions of the building become much more apparent. In places, the intricate decoration of these galleries still survives, but for the best work another narrow and steep staircase to the exterior galleries has to be tackled. Here you'll find the richest, most exquisitely carved and painted plasterwork on the vaulted ceilings – quite mouthwateringly superb. There are also wonderful views over the countryside, despite the higgledy-piggledy housing at ground level.

A short walk around the building means you can see some of the original tilework, along with some scattered 14th-century ceramic shards found during excavation work.

In the town, around 1km away diagonally opposite the tomb, there is another historic site of interest. The blue-domed, but much smaller **Molla Hassan Kashi Tomb** (آرامگاه ملاحسن کاشی), built in honour of one of the poets and gnostics of the Oljeitu court. The building of the tomb itself is closed, but the site with the mountains as a backdrop is spectacular.

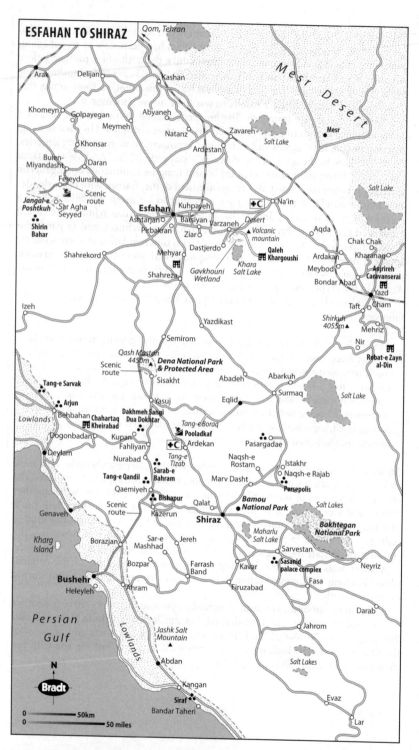

ESFAHAN TO SHIRAZ

Qom, Tehran

Mesr Desert

Arak
Delijan
Kashan
Khomeyn
Golpayegan
Abyaneh
Zavareh
Salt Lake
Mesr
Meymeh
Natanz
Khonsar
Ardestan
Bulen-Miyandasht
Daran
Salt Lake
Fereydunshahr
Jangal-e Poshtkuh
Scenic route
Sar Agha Seyyed
Esfahan
Kuhpayeh
+C Na'in
Shirin Bahar
Ashtarjan
Baksiyan
Varzaneh
Desert
Aqda
Pirbakran
Ziar
Dastjerdo
▲ Volcanic mountain
Chak Chak
Shahrekord
Mehyar
Qaleh Khargoushi
Ardakan
Kharanaq
Dastjerdo
Khara Salt Lake
Meybod
Anjireh Caravanserai
Shahreza
Gavkhouni Wetland
Bondar Abad
Yazd
Taft
Cham
Yazdikast
Shirkuh 4055m ▲
Mehriz
Semirom
Nir
Qash Masten 4450m
Dena National Park & Protected Area
Abadeh
Abarkuh
Robat-e Zayn al-Din
Scenic route
Sisakht
Surmaq
Salt Lake
Tang-e Sarvak
Yasuj
Eqlid
Arjun
Behbahan
Chahartaq Kheirabad
Dakhmeh Sangi Dua Dokhtar
Tang-e Boraq
Dogonbadan
Kupan
Pooladkaf
Pasargadae
Deylam
Fahliyan
+C Ardekan
Nurabad
Tang-e Tizab
Naqsh-e Rostam
Istakhr
Tang-e Qandil
Sarab-e Bahram
Naqsh-e Rajab
Qaemiyeh
Marv Dasht
Persepolis
Genaveh
Bishapur
Qalat
Salt Lakes
Scenic route
Kazerun
Shiraz
Bamou National Park
Bakhtegan National Park
Kharg Island
Borazjan
Sar-e Mashhad
Jereh
Maharlu Salt Lake
Sarvestan
Lowlands
Bozpar
Farrash Band
Kavar
Sasanid palace complex
Neyriz
Bushehr
Heleyleh
Ahram
Firuzabad
Fasa
Darab
Persian Gulf
Jashk Salt Mountain ▲
Jahrom
N
Abdan
Salt Lakes
Bradt
Kangan
Evaz
Siraf
Bandar Taheri
Lar

0 ——— 50km
0 ——— 50 miles

Shiraz and Around

SHIRAZ شیراز *Telephone code 071*

Shiraz (altitude 1,600m, 910km south of Tehran), with its long and rich history, friendliness and the laid-back attitude of its inhabitants, is one of the nicest and most welcoming cities in Iran. As the Iranian saying goes, 'Esfahan for the head, but Shiraz for the heart'. Despite dramatic growth in the last two decades to a population of around 1.5 million and the resultant traffic nightmare, Shiraz has miraculously managed to preserve the relaxed atmosphere of a provincial town, despite the daily assault on both its infrastructure and the nerves of its inhabitants. It has an excellent university, which annually floods the city with an appealing wave of young, educated and friendly Iranians, who provide the real energy driving this fine city. Many foreign visitors are surprised that Shiraz itself has so few surviving historical monuments when there are such archaeological treasures in the neighbouring countryside, but earthquakes over the centuries have taken a heavy toll, along with the less excusable 'urban development plans' of the Pahlavis (for whom Shiraz was an unfortunate target of their dubious vision and largesse).

Shiraz is a place to stroll in fine gardens and see the Azadi Park Ferris wheel and roundabouts crowded with excited schoolgirls, chadors flying in the breeze. Both in the bazaar and in the major shrine, Shah Cheragh, you may glimpse the darker complexions of men and women from various nomad and tribal clans such as the Qashqai, the Qash Kuli and the Khamseh, visiting the city for provisions, clothing and jewellery. Older men often wear a beige, hemispherical felt cap with a tall upturned rim, while women cover their immense skirts and glittering lurex tabards with black chadors; both caps and skirts are made in the bazaar. Many of these families still retain a migratory lifestyle, travelling with goats and sheep from Hamadan to Shiraz and the south in late autumn, returning in the spring, but some are now at least partially settled in outlying villages. If you wish to see the rugs and carpets associated with such clans, the Shiraz Bazaar is a good place to look, but prices are no longer low and quality is variable since such work was highly acclaimed in the West during the 1976 World of Islam exhibitions in the UK.

HISTORY Shiraz was once the route from Susa to Persepolis and there are tentative whispers in the archaeological record of an Elamite settlement on the site of modern Shiraz, with further occupation during the Achaemenid dynasty (reputedly the site of a depository of Achaemenid imperial records), but settlement here truly prospered from the early Islamic era, burgeoning quickly into a grand walled city. Predictable rivalries between local warlords during the 11th and 12th centuries created significant problems, but Shiraz miraculously escaped severe damage from the Mongol armies by a tactical surrender. This successful tactic was again adopted when the city was confronted by the armies of Timur Leng in 1395, and such foresightedness by the city elders was rewarded with significant investment and prosperity under Leng's grandson's governorship. But good times never last forever, and in 1668 severe flooding – almost impossible to comprehend when glimpsing the almost permanently dry bed of the river Khoshk (meaning 'dry') running through the city – brought death and outbreaks of plague. Shiraz's traumatised citizens had barely recovered from this disaster when Afghan rebels, bent on destroying the remnants of Safavid authority, set about massacring the population with gusto in 1725. However, order and stability brought to the city through the rule of Karim Khan Zand (d1779, and still remembered with great affection today) and his descendants meant that Shiraz regained its former prosperity as the Zand capital for some 20 years in the second half of the 18th century. Yet even those days of tolerance were sadly short-lived; 15% of the population were Jewish in the early 19th century, but few Jews remain today. Shiraz was also the home of Bahaism in Iran (page 37), but mass executions of members of the community in 1852, followed by the forced exile of the leader, sadly denuded Shiraz's rich cultural garden of one of its most intriguing blooms.

Today the city is still the best place in Iran to smell beautiful Shiraz roses, buy perfume and locally distilled rose water, but thanks to the 1979 revolution, it's no longer possible to enjoy the world-famous Shirazi wine grape, except as fruit – unless, that is, you are fortunate enough to be invited to a party by enterprising locals, and try a surprisingly good home-brewed hooch, which is 100% natural and most delicious.

GETTING THERE AND AROUND There are regular **flights** from major Iranian cities and abroad; Turkish Airlines have daily flights from Istanbul, and in high season Flydubai offers flights from Dubai. Shiraz is connected by numerous intercity **bus** links and has three bus terminals: Karandish [241 G3] (for Esfahan and Tehran); Modarres [241 G4] (southern direction, including Firuzabad); and Amir Kabir [241 A3] (western destinations, including Bishapur and Bushehr). For Yasuj there is a *savari* Shahid Mohammad Reza Tabaee terminal outside the city near Shiraz train station. There is at present no train service between Shiraz and Esfahan, but there are regular trains to/from Tehran via Kashan.

You can arrange **taxi** trips around and outside the city at your hotel, from a taxi driver directly or from any of the guides listed below. Shiraz has a one-line **metro** system (w shirazmetro.ir; ⊕ 06.30–22.30; fare 10,000 rials) stretching from the airport via the city centre towards Ehsan Square in its northern neighbourhoods. City **transport cards** can be purchased at metro stations (70,000 rials) and can also be used for **buses** (10,000 rials) around the city.

LOCAL GUIDES

Hossein Ghahramani m 0917 3116225; w persiapopulartours.com. Experienced & knowledgeable, Hossein has been working as a guide since 2007; he speaks fluent English, works closely with many independent tour guides across Iran & can arrange for a variety of customised tours.
Aria Gojerati m 0917 3135938; e ariagojerati@yahoo.com. An independent guide in Shiraz who

can easily organise a car for the day (or even a helicopter trip).
Azadeh Khademi m 0917 1052191; e tbs-azadehkhademi@hotmail.com. Fluent in both French & English. Recommended female guide.
Elaheh Khademi m 0937 5861118; e elahehkhademi1@gmail.com. Sister of Azadeh Khademi (see above) & also a recommended female guide. She leads German & English tours.

SHIRAZ

Qasr Dasht Street

Chamran Street

→ Railway station, Qalat,
Pooladkaf Ski Resort, Yasuj

Valiasar Street

Afif Abad Street

Sattar Khan Street

Besat Boulevard

Amir Kabir
bus terminal

Aban Gallery

Afif Abad Garden

Qasr Dasht Street

M Motahhari

Bradt

N

0   500m
0   500yds

Namazi Hospital

Namazi M

Maydan-e Namazi

Molla Sadra Street

Eram Street

Bagh-e Eram

Jomhuri Islami BD

Khoshk River

Mezra-e Fatimeh Zahra

Karim Khan Zand

Neshat Street

Trip to Persia

Felestin Street

Qasr Dasht Street

Zolanvar St

Azadi Boulevard

Maydan-e Azadi

Azadi Park

Meshkinfam Street

Enghelab Bazaar

Ordibehesht Street

Moadel Street

Haft-e Tir Street

Faghihi (Sarbaz) Street

Engheab Islami Street

Maydan-e Imam Hossein

Vasale-e Shirazi

Jomhuri Islami BD

Qajar rock reliefs

Quran Gate

Jam Art Gallery

Shiraz Grand

Iran Burger

Haft Street

Hafez Street

Haft Tanan Museum

Jahan Nama Garden

National Library

Ershad-e Islami

Maydan-e Ghaem (Attasi)

page 244

Tomb of Saadi,
Bagh-e Delgosha →

Karandish bus terminal

Golestan Boulevard

Chehel Magham

Saheli Boulevard

Valiasr Square

Modarres BD →

Immigration & Passport Office
Modarres bus terminal, Airport, Firuzabad →

Barm-e Delak →

Tomb of Hafez

Khoshk River

Ferdowsi Street

Rudaki St

Maydan-e Shohada

Karim Khan Zand Boulevard

Lotf Ali Khan Zand Street

Piruzi Street

Bazaar Vakil

SANG-E SIYAH

Esfahan, Persepolis →

For listings, see from page 242

Where to stay
1 Homa.........................E2
2 Pars International.......C2
3 Royal Hotel Shiraz.....F1

Where to eat and drink
4 Book Land..................D2
5 Café Forte..................A1
6 Haft Khan Restaurant
    Complex...................F1
7 Shater Abbas..............D1

Shiraz and Around   SHIRAZ

8

241

Bahman Mardanloo m 0917 9100943; w bahmanzagrosmountainstours.wordpress.com. A local specialist in Qashqai nomad tours & can arrange for hiking & trekking in the Zagros Mountains.
MrPersepolis/Peyman Soodmand m 0936 9173113; e mrpersepolis1@gmail.com; w mrpersepolis.com; see ad, page 262. Recommended for tours to Persepolis & Naqsh-e Rostam. Peyman also organises historical tours around Shiraz & free walking city tours. He is the person to ask if Sufism is of interest. He volunteers for the *khanqah* Ahmadi charity in Sang-e Siyah.

TOUR OPERATORS

Gasht Tour [244 B1] Ferdowsi St; ☎ 32236542–3; w irangashttour.com; or via Dr Harry McQuillan in New Zealand: e zagros@ts.co.nz. For visas to Iran, hotel booking assistance & tours around Shiraz. With prior notice, Gasht Tour can also organise tours by English-speaking wildlife & birdwatching specialists.
Pars Mehregan Tour & Travel Agency [244 B2] Ground floor of the historically important, first ever built 2-storey building in Shiraz; ☎ 32224488.

Centrally located in Shiraz, the wonderfully hospitable staff can help book bus/train & flight tickets (without commission).
Trip to Persia [241 C2] Zand Bd, Shiraz; ☎ 32301316; e contact@triptopersia.com; w triptopersia.com. Offers tour packages varying from 4 to 21 days, cooking & nature tours, as well as day trips out of Shiraz, Tehran, Esfahan, Yazd, Ahvaz & Kerman. Also provides visa assistance, hotel reservation & transportation across Iran.

TOURIST INFORMATION If you are simply looking for some friendly advice and information about the sites in Shiraz and around, contact the main **tourist office** [241 E3], located in a small kiosk outside Arg-e Karim Khan Zand.

 WHERE TO STAY Shiraz has easily the largest choice of hotels in southern Iran. A number of small traditional houses have over the past few years been converted into charming basic and mid-range hotels and these are often located in clusters of three and more in the vicinity of each other in the *baft-e tarikhi* (old part of the city). The most recommended from this category are reviewed and other nearby options are listed for convenience. Rooms in traditional hotels are located on two levels, slightly under and slightly over the ground level. Rooms with Western-style beds are usually less spacious, as the traditional design envisaged sleeping on the floor and then packing bedding into colourful sacks by the walls for extra space. Otherwise, Rudaki Street is awash with modern and comfortable hotels, popular with tourists from the Persian Gulf.

Above average

🏠 **Homa Hotel** [241 E2] (200+ rooms) Meshkinfam St, nr Azadi Park; ☎ 32288000, 32288009; w homahotels.com. The Homa (in its pre-revolutionary incarnation as the Hilton) was *the* hotel to stay in when visiting Shiraz, under the Pahlavis. Beautiful gardens, which double as an alfresco dining area during good weather, are to the rear of the hotel, overlooking Azadi Park. It has souvenir & coffee shops, a sauna, tennis courts (with lessons available: check out Shiraz's 'ladies who lunch' popping in for their lunchtime lessons), a barber shop & 3 restaurants ($$). $$$$
🏠 **Pars International Hotel** [241 C2] (150+ rooms) Karim Khan Zand Bd; ☎ 32332255; w parsinternationalhotel.com. Rooms here are bland but comfortable &, unlike the Homa, the management are politically conservative, so BBC is not available in the rooms. However, hotel staff are both efficient & friendly. $$$$
🏠 **Royal Hotel Shiraz** [241 F1] (80 rooms) Ghoram Bd; ☎ 32274356; w royalshirazhotel.com. Pleasant on the inside, although hefty-looking on the outside, the Royal offers good 4-star accommodation. Rooms are decorated with taste & some come with great views over Shiraz. A little out of the city centre, but next to the Haft Khan Restaurant Complex. $$$$
🏠 **Zandiyeh Hotel** [244 C1] (75 rooms) Saadi St; ☎ 32234234; w zandiyehhotel.com. One of the

latest 5-star additions to the Shirazi hotel scene. A very nice hotel, with spacious rooms & a bright & welcoming lobby. There is a swimming pool & sauna & staff are most obliging & caring. **$$$$**

Mid-range

🏠 **Hotel Aryo Barzan** [244 B1] (50+ rooms) Roudaki St; ☎32247182; w aryobarzanhotel.ir. Rooms are kept pristine, & the Aryo Barzan is a popular choice with businessmen from the Persian Gulf & group tours, so book ahead. Some rooms are let down by tiny bathrooms. On-site travel agency. **$$$**

🏠 **Karim Khan Hotel** [244 B1] (56 rooms) Roudaki St; ☎32235001; w karimkhanhotel. com. Opened in 2014, the hotel is a pleasant addition to the Shirazi hotel scene. Rooms are modern & alas a little dark. Staff wear traditional clothes & attend to the comfort of guests in style. **$$$**

🏠 **Panjdari** [map, page 254] (10 rooms) 9 Dey St; ☎37395214; e hotel5dari@gmail. com; w hotel5dari.com. Opened in 2017, this traditional hotel has a very spacious inner courtyard, with surprisingly few rooms in the hotel itself, ensuring some privacy for the guests. There are alas no single rooms & individual travellers would need to pay for a double room or ask for a discount, but the location is otherwise good, rooms are spacious & personnel attentive. **$$$**

Lower mid-range

🏠 **Forough Traditional Hotel** [map, page 254] (16 rooms) Sang-e Siyah; ☎32225877; e foroughhotel@gmail.com. Opened in 2016, this nicely finished traditional hotel has a pleasant open courtyard & comfortable rooms. **$$**

🏠 **Golshan Guesthouse** [244 C4] (8 rooms) 15 Alley St, off Lotf Ali Khan Zand St; ☎32220715; w golshanhostel.com. A friendly & busy backpacker-style traditional guesthouse with private rooms & dorms. Comes with a leafy inner courtyard & jolly atmosphere. Conveniently located near the bazaar. **$$**

✳ 🏠 **Mahmonir** [244 D4] (7 rooms) Through the alley past Zinat al-Molk's house, a little further up from the Toranjestan hotel; m 0917 6800010. This is one of the nicest traditional hotels in Shiraz with a very pleasant atmosphere & excellent service. **$$**

🏠 **BB Heritage Hostel** [map, page 254] (11 rooms) Sang-e Siyah, behind Bibi Dokhtaran; ☎32248698; w shirazbbhostel.com. A cosy & laidback hostel popular with budget travellers & backpackers, it has the charm & comfort for a few nights' stay. **$–$$**

🏠 **Toranjestan** [244 D4] (7 rooms) Through the alley past Zinat al-Molk's house; m 0921 2586977. Opened in 2018, this family-run traditional hotel has a leafy inner courtyard & rooftop seating area. Rooms are comfortable & all en suite. Popular with foreigners & Iranians alike. **$–$$**

✗ **WHERE TO EAT AND DRINK** In addition to the numerous fast-food places, such as **Iran Burger** [241 F1] (Quran Gate; ☎32289162) or corner shops selling soups and sandwiches, Shiraz has a number of very good restaurants. Below are some of the recommendations.

✳ ✗ **Haft Khan Restaurant Complex** [241 F1] Nr the Quran Gate; ☎32270000, 32280000; w haftkhanco.com; ⊕ all day, except for the traditional Iranian restaurant in the basement, which is open for dinner from 19.00. Opened in 2011, this Persian- & international-cuisine 5-storey complex is popular with the Shirazi middle class. The décor is fancy & modern. Tables by the window have great views; traditional seating area in the basement not so much. Food is excellent; *marasseh polo* is particularly recommended. 9% service charge applies. **$$$**

✗ **Parhami Traditional Restaurant** [244 D4] (6 rooms) Off Lotf Ali Khan Zand St; follow street signs from the main street; ☎32232015; e soroushparhami@gmail.com. Opened in 2014, this cosy & charming restaurant offers excellent homemade traditional lunch & dinners. **$$$**

✳ ✗ **Shater Abbas** [241 D1] Khahshenasi St; ☎32261370, 32261371; w shaterabbas.org; ⊕ 11.30–23.30 daily. In operation since 1982, this traditional restaurant serves excellent Iranian food. The *mahicheh* lamb shank is particularly good. **$$$**

✳ ✗ **Balo Café & Restaurant** [map, page 254] Located in a newly restored traditional house, near Soofi restaurant; ☎32245364; ⊕ 08.00–23.00

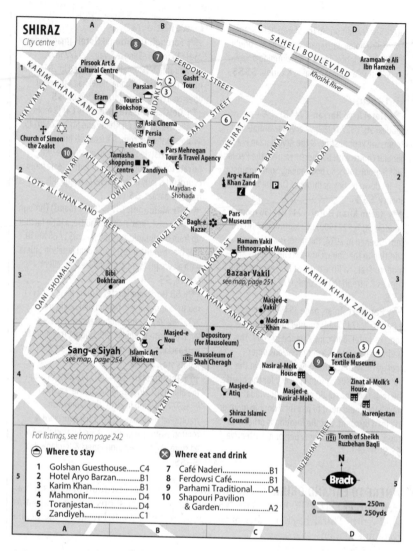

SHIRAZ
City centre

Aramgah-e Ali Ibn Hamzeh

SAHELI BOULEVARD

Khoshk River

Pirsook Art & Cultural Centre

FERDOWSI STREET

KHAYYAM ST

KARIM KHAN ZAND BD

Eram

Tourist Bookshop

Parsian

Gasht Tour

RUDAKI ST

SAADI STREET

Asia Cinema

Persia

Felestin

Church of Simon the Zealot

ANVARI ST

AHLI STREET

Tamasha shopping centre

Zandiyeh

Pars Mehregan Tour & Travel Agency

HEJRAT ST

22 BAHMAN ST

26 ROAD

LOTF ALI KHAN ZAND STREET

TOWHID ST

Maydan-e Shohada

Arg-e Karim Khan Zand

Pars Museum

Bagh-e Nazar

PIRUZI STREET

Hamam Vakil Ethnographic Museum

TALEQANI ST

Bazaar Vakil
see map, page 251

KARIM KHAN ZAND BD

QANI SHOMALI ST

Bibi Dokhtaran

Masjed-e Nou

Depository (for Mausoleum)

Masjed-e Vakil

Madrasa Khan

9 DEY ST

Sang-e Siyah
see map, page 254

Islamic Art Museum

Mausoleum of Shah Cheragh

Nasir al-Molk House

Fars Coin & Textile Museums

Zinat al-Molk's House

HAZRATI ST

Masjed-e Atiq

Masjed-e Nasir al-Molk

Narenjestan

Shiraz Islamic Council

RUZBEHAN STREET

Tomb of Sheikh Ruzbehan Baqli

N

Bradt

0 ————— 250m
0 ————— 250yds

For listings, see from page 242

Where to stay

1	Golshan Guesthouse.......C4
2	Hotel Aryo Barzan.............B1
3	Karim Khan.......................B1
4	Mahmonir.........................D4
5	Toranjestan......................D4
6	Zandiyeh..........................C1

Where eat and drink

7	Café Naderi.......................B1
8	Ferdowsi Café..................B1
9	Parhami Traditional.........D4
10	Shapouri Pavilion & Garden.........................A2

daily. This is a very nice restaurant serving hearty Persian dishes; it's also an ideal place to relax with a refreshing lemonade on a hot summer day. $$

✻ ✗ **Qavam Traditional Restaurant** [map, page 251] Original branch at end of Rudaki St; ☏32359271; Vakil Bazaar branch; ☏32223585, 32231710; ⏲ 11.30–23.30 daily. Authentic & cosy restaurant serving the most delicious & mouth-watering homemade dishes. *Halim bademjun* recommended. $$

✗ **Saray-e Ayneh** [map, page 251] Close to Saray-e Moshir; 📱 0930 2100620; ⏲ 09.00–23.00 daily. Slightly off the tourist track, this delightful

café/restaurant is worth locating. Atmospheric & authentic, it is the place for a light lunch or tea either in the inner leafy courtyard or in a beautiful room with exquisite Qajar-period mirrorwork on the walls & ornate wooden ceilings. $$

✗ **Saray-e Mehr Restaurant** [map, page 251] Saray-e Moshir Bazaar, signposted at the entrance to Rouhollah Bazaar, when exiting the south wing of the Vakil Bazaar; ⏲ Vakil Bazaar opening hrs. Lovely traditional restaurant serving good *dizzi*. $$

✗ **Sharzeh Traditional Restaurant** [map, page 251] Vakil St, in the basement of the shopping centre across the square from the Vakil

Bazaar entrance; ⏰ noon–15.00 & 19.00–midnight. Popular Shirazi restaurant, serving excellent local *kalam polo* (cabbage with rice) & famous Shirazi salad with verjuice, which you must try. There is often live traditional music. $$

✗ **Vakil Traditional Restaurant** [map, page 251] Taleqani St, at the front of Department of Finance; ☎32243977, 2228312; ⏰ noon–23.00. A good, reasonable option on the tourist path in central Shiraz. The menu is comprehensive & prices are reasonable. $$

Cafés

🍽 **Book Land** [241 D2] 1 Eram St; ☎32250974; w book-land.ir; ⏰ 10.00–23.00 daily. This popular bookshop & café has cosy indoor & outdoor seating areas as well as a good selection of books, stationery & souvenirs. $$

✳ 🍽 **Cafe Forte** [241 A1] 54 Qasr Dasht St; ⏰ 09.00–23.00 daily. This tiny cafe serves superb coffee in all varieties. Connoisseurs will appreciate the effort of the owner & guests will simply enjoy the taste. Not the place to spend hours while reading a book, but definitely stop by to savour what modern Shirazis come here for. $$

✳ 🍽 **Ferdowsi Café** [244 B1] Ferdowsi St, opposite Arian Apartment Hotel; ⏰ 09.00–23.00 Sat–Thu, 17.30–23.00 Fri. The best café in Shiraz, with character, excellent drinks, light meals &

great vibe. This is the place to meet & chat with young & upbeat Shirazis. $$

🍽 **Joulep Café** [map, page 251] Opposite the entrance to Vakil Bazaar; ☎32246980, 32246982; ⏰ 08.30–23.00 daily. Airy café in the square near Vakil Bazaar. Coffee here is excellent & Wi-Fi reliable. $$

🍽 **Shapouri Pavilion & Garden** [244 A2] Anvari St; ☎32347491; w shapourigarden. com; ⏰ 07.30–23.30 daily; garden entry 50,000 rials. This beautiful garden & residence built in the 1930s are ideal for an atmospheric coffee experience or b/fast. $$

🍽 **Syrah Café Gallery** [map, page 254] Sang-e Siyah, beside St Mary's Church; ☎37362476; m 0912 7262253; e syrah.gallery@gmail.com; ⏰ 10.00–22.00 daily. A photo gallery & a cosy café in the courtyard & on the rooftop of the finely restored residence. $$

🍽 **Café Naderi** [244 B1] Ferdowsi St; m 0917 3041952; ⏰ until late daily. Head here in the evening for a game of backgammon & a good cup of coffee. A nice place with more seating opened in summer across the road. $

🍽 **Old Bazaar Tea House** [map, page 251] To the right when leaving Vakil Bazaar in the direction of the Baba Khan madrasa. This historic & rustic tea house with outdoor tables is a popular local meeting place & serves b/fast & tea with *qalian* waterpipe. $

GALLERIES AND ENTERTAINMENT

Aban Gallery [241 A2] Afif Abad St; m 0902 3112310; ⏰ 09.00–noon & 17.00–22.00 daily. A new & modern art & photography gallery in the middle of a bustling district in between Afif Abad & Sattar Khan sts.

Jam Art Galley [241 F2] 225 Rabbani Bd; ☎32285845. Holds a variety of exhibitions from jewellery & handicrafts to paintings & sculpture. Enquire in advance.

✳ **National Library** (کتابخانه ملی) [241 F2] Hafez St; ☎32263513. Located in a new & finely

designed park, there is a cinema, gallery, café & cultural ambience all around.

✳ **Pirsook Art & Cultural Centre** [244 A1] 11, 38th Karim Khan Zand Bd; ☎32314870; w pirsook.ir. A modern & popular cultural space with a garden & café, hidden behind solid turquoise-coloured gates. There is also a bookstore with postcards & a gallery. There are regular movie screenings, inc European cinema days.

OTHER PRACTICALITIES In central Shiraz on Rudaki Street there is a good **Tourist Bookshop** [244 B1] (Rezadarb Bldg, 1st floor; ☎32338200; w farhanghonar.com; ⏰ 09.00–14.00 & 16.00–22.00). Here in the same building next to a fruit stall you can also purchase an **Iranian telephone SIM card** from the Irancell store. Alternatively, Irancell and Hamrah Aval SIM cards are sold in the Tamasha Shopping Centre [244 A2] by the pedestrian bridge. The best choice for **souvenirs** is the main bazaar (page 250) and **Enghelab Bazaar** [241 D2] near the Homa Hotel if you are after musical instruments.

The central **post office** [241 F2] (Hejrat St; ☉ 07.15–14.00 Sat–Wed, 07.15–13.00 Thu) is behind the Arg. Pharmacies in Shiraz are plentiful, especially along Karim Khan Zand Boulevard and there is an **all-night pharmacy** at Maydan-e Valiasr [241 F4], which is also the address for the **Immigration and Passport Office** for visa extensions (Alley 57, Modarres Bd; ☉ 08.00–13.30 Sat–Wed, 07.30–11.30 Thu); there is a photocopy kiosk on its premises if you forgot to bring copies of documents with you. Alternatively, there are a few photocopy and picture shops on Karim Khan Zand Boulevard between Rudaki and Saadi streets. Shiraz has a number of private and government **hospitals**; most central is Namazi Hospital [241 C1] (Namazi Sq; ☎36474332). **Foreign exchange shops** [241 E3] are nicely packed on Karim Khan Zand Boulevard between Hejrat and Saadi streets and there is also an exchange shop on Taleqani Street near Vakil Bazaar [map, page 251] (☉ 09.00–19.00 Sat–Wed, 09.00–13.30 Thu; closed Fri). For permission to visit the synagogue or the church you need to go to **Ershad-e Islami** [241 F2] (Hafeziyeh Crossroads; ☉ 08.00–14.00) or try using your charm outside the main gates, usually open when there is a service inside.

WHAT TO SEE AND DO

Approaching from the north Entering Shiraz from the north (Esfahan) or northeast (Persepolis), the first visible monument is the **Quran Gate** (*darvazeh quran*) [241 G1], originally built in the 10th century in the city walls. It was a benign Karim Khan Zand who ordered a Quran to be placed in the gatehouse so that travellers would be blessed as they left for the open road. In the 1950s increased traffic dictated a new road and the demolition of the original gate, whereupon a pious Shirazi citizen paid for it to be rebuilt in its present location.

Halfway up the hillside, above the gate, is the tomb of one of Shiraz's famous poets, Khajeh Kermani (d1352), and one of the eight known **Qajar rock-reliefs** [241 G1], c1824, showing Fath Ali Shah on a throne dais supported by two angels, with two of his numerous sons in attendance. The hillsides have been landscaped with terraces, water cascades, the odd kiosk and a tea house, 'the Khaju', while many Iranian families camp out here, in *Tardis*-like tiny tents. While offering unparalleled views of the city lights at night, the traffic noise and pollution can be overwhelming and the views are not enhanced by the *Thunderbirds*-style 'Shiraz Grand Hotel 5 Star', which clings to the upper rock face.

In an easterly direction, some 10km further on, is **Barm-e Delak** (برم دلک), where there are two battered Sasanid rock reliefs 6.5m above ground level. The larger one depicts a shah offering a flower to a lady, perhaps the divine Anahita, although some scholars think it portrays Shah Narseh (d301) making a peace offering to the consort of either Bahram II or III. The other panel shows Bahram II raising his hand, with the (infamous) high priest Kartir lurking off to one side. There is, alas, no sign pointing to the location but if you are coming by car from Shiraz, look for an area with trees to the left side of the road, opposite a car-repair workshop.

At the foothills of Chehel Maqham Mountain, approximately 1km down Haft Tanan Boulevard from the Quran Gate, shying away from the tourist eye behind tall brick walls is **Haft Tanan Museum** [241 G2] (☉ spring–summer 07.30–20.00, autumn–winter 08.00–18.00; entry 300,000 rials). On Karim Khan Zand's orders, the northern section of this tranquil garden was fitted with a fine house consisting of an elevated *ivan* terrace with two monolithic columns and two side rooms. The oil paintings by Agha Sadeq on the walls of the *ivan* also date to the Zand period (1751–94) and depict in a clockwise direction a dervish with a beggar's bowl

Completed in the 1960s, the Amir Kabir Dam and the picturesque lake it has formed lie about 60km from Tehran on the scenic road to Chalus (MO) page 193

above   An ancient necropolis for Persian kings, breathtaking Naqsh-e Rostam is a can't-miss stopover en route to Persepolis (PL) page 269

below   The lush mountains of Northern Iran are dotted with fortresses and picturesque mountain villages, like Masouleh (a/S) page 197

above left The whole of Iran is an open-air museum, where the lifestyle has remained unchanged for many residents in rural parts of the country (ML/S)

above right Bazaars in Iran are mesmerising with the spices, smells and tastes on offer. It is to the bazaars that many cities owe their foundation and continuing existence (EA/S)

below Ali Shariati, a brilliant intellectual, was one of the founding fathers of the theory behind the Islamic Revolution. His ideas are still celebrated by many, irrespective of their political views (MO) page 366

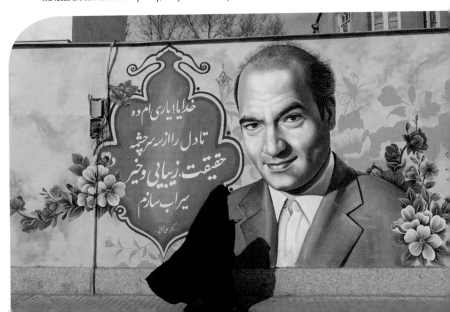

above   The Zagros Mountains area, northwest of Esfahan, is rich in natural wonders (MO) page 3

below   Kerman province, with its snowy mountain peaks and villages set amid lush greenery, is one of the least explored in Iran (aM/S) page 320

MEHMOUN
en route to tales & tastes

We are inviting you to stay in each one of our traditional houses and to immerse yourself in Persian art and culture.

www.mehmoun.com
info@mehmoun.com
call/whatsapp +989022004210

Ⓕ Ⓞ Ⓢ Ⓓ *mehmounroute*

Trip To Persia

We listen to you and respond to your wishes.

We offer a full range of tailor-made tours unbounded by time or space, all while respecting your budget. You are free to focus on culture, history, eco & adventure, or any combination.Discover the richness of Iran's culture and its people.

Grab the opportunity to experience the best that our country has to offer.
We invite you to join Trip to Persia for a real taste of Iran.

Incoming@TriptoPersia.com   +989174441652   TriptoPersia.com (*kashkul*) and axe (*tabarzin*), Moses the shepherd with a herd of sheep, Sheikh Sanan and the Christian maiden, the sacrifice of Ismael by Abraham and lastly a young dervish. Formerly used as a *khanqah* or Sufi meeting place, the garden is also known as *tekiyeh haft tanan* or the 'mourning place of seven tombs or bodies' after the tombs of seven mystics buried in front of the building. It was Karim Khan Zand who ordered large stones without inscriptions to be placed here on top of the original anonymous graves.

Just a few hundred metres away from Haft Tanan Museum lies an idyllic **Jahan Nama Garden** (باغ جهان نما) ✳ [241 F2/G2] (Hafez St; ⊕ 08.00–21.00; entry 500,000 rials). Considered to be the oldest garden in Shiraz, Jahan Nama, with its 3,500m² of green areas, was already a blossoming retreat during Timur Leng's occupation of the city. Its classic garden design with rows of majestic cypresses and *narenj* bitter orange trees and flower beds is crowned in the centre with a two-storey summer residence. This hexagon-shaped brick structure, consisting of four *shahneshin* rooms, was finely restored and like the current arrangement of the garden dates from the period of Karim Khan Zand's rule. Few tourists find time for a visit here, making it one of the most secluded and pleasant places for an evening stroll. In the summer, the garden is open until as late as 23.00.

There are three other major gardens in Shiraz although two are 20th-century constructions, owing little to the classical Persian garden layout, but pleasant places to

THE PERSIAN GARDEN

From Achaemenid and Sasanid times, rulers and princes established formal gardens with stone watercourses feeding pools, shaded terraces and pavilions. This was the essential plan which spread across the Muslim world to Spain and north Africa and eastwards to north India, for this is the image of the heavenly paradise as described in the Quran (Q55:45ff). In the 'classical' Persian garden, known as *chahar bagh* or fourfold garden design, mud-brick walls kept the desert out while providing support for climbing plants and shade from the fierce midday sun. The English visitor, Thomas Herbert, in 1628 described the Shirazi gardens as:

Safeguarded with walls fourteen feet high and four feet thick; and which from their spaciousness and plenty of trees resemble groves or wildernesses … they abound in lofty pyramidic cypresses, broad-spreading chenars, tough elm, straight ash, knotty pines, fragrant mastics, kingly oaks, sweet myrtles, useful maples … also flowers rare to the eye, sweet to the smell, and useful in physic.

To Persian poets the cypress was like a young Muslim man, evergreen and enduring in his faith, while the chenar tree with its open five-fingered leaves was the prayer leader for all plants in the garden. Around the wall were planted climbing roses, whose very fragrance came from a bead of perspiration falling from the Prophet Mohammad's brow, jasmine and pomegranates. Fruit trees such as cherries (whose scented blossom was as short-lived as a woman's beauty), oranges, limes, apples and quinces were also placed by the walls or in raised beds divided by straight water channels in which fish, ducks and swans swam. Or the beds were planted with sweet-smelling herbs, or spring bulbs such as hyacinths, whose heavy scent reminded the poets of the beloved's hair, narcissi ('red-eyed' like a weeping lover) and red tulips (willingly shedding blood for the beloved). All would lower their heads in worship on hearing the nightingale's song (Quranic verses) on the evening breeze.

visit nonetheless, and perfect for trying to envision the Shiraz that so entranced 18th-century European visitors. One garden surrounds the **Tomb of Hafez** (حافظیه) ✳ [241 F2] (*hafeziyeh*) [241 F2] (Golestan Bd; ☉ 08.00–21.30; entry 500,000 rials), the great Shirazi poet (1326–c90) who wrote lyrical poems about love and the beloved, which are understood to be imbued with deep Sufi mystical meaning; his epithet 'Hafez' is an honorific title bestowed because of his memorising of the Quran by heart as a small child. Because of Hafez's Sufi associations, one or two dervishes still come here on Wednesdays and Thursdays, while families and visitors enjoy the small garden and take tea in the ugly modern tea house in the far right corner (sadly, the lovely 18th-century *chaykhaneh* (tea house) closed in a 2008 dispute with the government over taxation and smoking, and hasn't yet reopened). Karim Khan Zand ordered a suitable tomb to be built in 1773 to honour this most famous son of Shiraz, but it was torn down in 1938 to erect the present octagonal kiosk. Further embellishments were made for the 1971 Pahlavi extravaganza. The bookshop at the far end of the terrace often has a good selection of history and art books in English, as well as maps and postcards, but the English translations of Hafez on sale mostly render the beauty of Hafez's poetry into something opaque and incomprehensible. Before leaving, why not have your fortune told? For a small sum, a copy of Hafez's best-known anthology, the *Divan*, will be opened randomly by a canary or budgerigar, which plucks out a card inscribed with couplets; the proffered verses offer a portent to the future.

Nearby, down from an 18th-century bridge over the river Khoshk, is the **Aramgah-e Ali Ibn Hamzeh** (آرامگاه علی ابن حمزه) [244 D1] (☉ dawn to dusk), probably constructed in the 9th century CE to honour one of the innumerable relatives of the fourth imam. Its two minarets, exterior dome, entrance vestibule and courtyard rooms, however, date from the late 18th and 19th centuries. If a visit to the Shah Cheragh shrine (page 252) is not possible during your stay, this shrine possesses similar extensive Qajar mirror work on its interior walls and vaults. There is one entrance into the shrine sanctuary (women are asked to don a chador) and as the *qibla* wall is immediately to the right on entry, you should move quickly to one or other side to minimise disruption to anyone praying (although you will see many worshippers happily chatting to family and friends on their mobile phones).

The **Tomb of Saadi** (سعدیه) ✳ (*saadiyeh*) [241 G2] (Bustan Bd; ☉ 08.00–20.30; entry 500,000 rials) is set in similar grounds near to the Hafez garden. Born around 1185 or 1208 (or possibly 1215) and dying around 1292, Saadi fled the Mongol invasions, travelling on to Baghdad and then Syria, where he was imprisoned by Crusaders. Ransomed by an Aleppan man, he felt duty-bound to marry the man's daughter, a deeply unhappy decision he later commemorated in a couplet: 'A bad wife comes with a good man to dwell / She soon converts his earthly heaven to hell.'

Saadi's two major poetic works are the *Golestan*, a series of anecdotes composed in 1257, and the *Bustan* (1258) in which he wittily and humorously expounded his thoughts on justice and government. One of his most famous verses – a version of which adorns the United Nations building in New York – has prompted comparisons with the 16th–17th-century English poet, John Donne:

> The sons of man are limbs of one another,
> Created of the same stuff, and none other.
> One limb by turn of time and fate distressed,
> The others feel its pain and cannot rest.
> Who unperturbed another's grief can scan
> Is no more worthy of the name of man.

Again, like the tomb of Hafez, the mausoleum of Saadi is quite an elegant product of 1950s Modernist architecture, replacing an earlier 18th-century Zand building. To the left of the tomb is an intriguing underground structure, which now contains a *chaykhaneh* (tea house) and is often packed with visitors. The main attractions are the deep, subterranean spring, into which visitors throw coins for good luck, and the strange, grey fish that haunt the depths, coming up to nibble on crumbs. The spring also provides water to the garden surrounding the tomb and, traditionally, the surrounding houses too. The most interesting element of this structure is that when the spring and *qanat* (underground water channel) were dredged during the 1950s, Sasanid pottery and coins were discovered, hinting at its use as a possible cultic site, probably dedicated to Anahita. As with early Christian sites in Europe, often constructed over pagan religious locations, many pre-Islamic sites in Iran show a similar and shadowy continuity with earlier traditions, here in the modern visitor 'dedicating' coins to the well and the fish (both associated with Anahita herself).

Also suggested is a visit to the nearby **Bagh-e Delgosha** (باغ دلگشا) (Garden of Heart's Ease) [241 G2] (☉ 07.30–22.00; entry 500,000 rials). The extensive grounds broadly retain their 1820 layout (actually originally set out in 1790), although the water channels have been relined with tacky modern turquoise tiles and the original mud-brick walls were destroyed in 2000. In the centre stands a pavilion from late Zand or early Qajar times, in a dramatic setting, with surrounding hills and tall cypresses. Together with the Bagh-e Eram, this garden and a small one within the Arg of Karim Khan Zand (page 250) are the best examples of the 'classical' Persian garden outside Mahan (page 329) and Kashan (page 157).

A short taxi drive away from here is one of Shiraz's jewels, the beautiful **Bagh-e Eram** (باغ ارم) ✳ [241 C1] (Eram Bd; ☉ 08.00–12.30 & 14.30–17.30; entry 500,000 rials), a garden named after one of the four gardens of paradise described in the Quran. The garden and grand house were originally created by a chief of the Qashqai clan around 1823, with the house later rebuilt by Hajji Mohammad Hassan Mi'mar, following his successful pilgrimage to Mecca, to include fine reception rooms, an orangery, stables and pavilion. Both garden and buildings were confiscated in 1953 and given to the late shah for his private use; this was when the original mud-brick enclosing walls were torn down and replaced by metal fencing. Later, Shiraz University was permitted to establish a botanical garden. After the fall of the Pahlavi regime it was returned to the Qashqai family, but then handed over in its entirety to the university, and today houses the **Law Faculty**. Some small areas of the lower garden are out of bounds; the garden doubles as the Shiraz municipal nursery (where all those ornamental cabbages, decorating roundabouts, are propagated), but otherwise visitors have freedom to range and explore the rock gardens, traditional *chahar bagh* (fourfold garden) and rose garden, which was entirely replanted in 2010. Almost all the specimens of plants and trees are labelled with their Farsi, Latin and common English names, and this is a popular location for parties of young schoolchildren larking about on day trips, older university students quietly flirting away from prying eyes and Shirazis simply escaping the noise and traffic of the city.

Entry into the main rooms of the actual house itself is not permitted (except for the bathrooms and a small tea house, which is usually closed anyway), but the exterior is photogenic enough, with stunning late 19th-century tiling under the roof. The central main panel shows the legendary Sasanid king, Khosrow II, coming across the Armenian princess Shirin bathing (see box, page 141) while to the right is the Quranic/biblical story describing how the beauty of the prophet Yusuf (Joseph)

8

caused the ladies in the pharaoh's court to gasp in thrilled delight and cut their fingers, distracted, while peeling fruit. Above is depicted the famous meeting of King Soleyman (Solomon) and the Queen of Sheba, Bilqis, with all of the protagonists depicted in a curious melange of 'traditional' and 19th-century clothing.

City centre The citadel, **Arg-e Karim Khan Zand** (ارگ کریم خان زند) ☀ [244 C2] (Shohada Sq; ☉ spring–summer 07.30–21.00, autumn–winter 08.00–20.00; entry 500,000 rials), was constructed around 1767 and is perhaps the best-preserved 18th-century example of urban fortification in Iran. Used from the 1930s as a police station and prison, access was long impossible, but in autumn 1999 the primary courtyard and surrounding rooms were opened to visitors and now regularly house temporary art and photographic exhibitions, such as a display of early 20th-century photographs of Shiraz in 2011. Four 15m round towers with good brick patterning mark the corners of the enclosure joined by 12m-high walls which, in Zand times, surrounded an audience hall, barracks, bathhouse and a garden with two pools. When a Qajar prince used the Arg as his official governor's residence, further building and decoration were undertaken. Over the main entrance is a huge tiled panel depicting an episode from the *Shahnameh* in which the famous Persian warrior, Rostam, fights the white Deev (demon or devil; *div-e sepid*), who is known to throw poison to blind people to prevent them from seeing the reality.

The entry vestibule leads into the main Zand court and it's a very pleasant walk around the central, four-garden layout (note the original stone water channels in the paving). Restoration work means it takes but little effort to imagine colourful 18th-century public audiences held under the painted *talar* verandas, with waterpipes and tea prepared with hot coals from the numerous fireplaces. A suite of rooms that once housed the Cultural Heritage Organisation is now a museum of daily life of the period, complete with atrocious waxwork dummies. Restorers from the organisation still regularly bring work from their offices at the rear of the Arg into the garden itself, and are very happy to chat with visitors.

Outside, across the street is the small octagonal reception pavilion of Karim Khan Zand, **Bagh-e Nazar** (باغ نظر) [244 C2] (☉ 08.00–13.30 & 14.30–18.00; entry 300,000 rials, inclusive of a visit to Pars Museum; see below). Set in a small garden gloriously smothered in bougainvillea and roses, it offers another peaceful haven away from Shiraz's traffic and crowds. At its centre is an octagonal pavilion, home to **Pars Museum** [244 C2], which houses a small collection of mainly 18th- and 19th-century items. Most of its original interior is intact and the tiled panels outside are mainly contemporary with the building. Karim Khan must have loved this place, as it was chosen as his mausoleum. However, he was not allowed to rest in peace: Agha Mohammad Qajar (not particularly renowned for his generosity of spirit) ordered the remains to be exhumed and sent to Tehran, where they were reburied in the Golestan Palace, so that every time the Qajar shah and his ministers crossed the threshold they trod on Karim Khan. Reza Shah Pahlavi stopped this practice in 1925, allowing the Zand family to reinter his unfortunate remains.

Vakil Bazaar [map, page 251] (☉ usually 08.00–20.00 Sat–Thu) is within walking distance of the Arg and within 5 minutes' walk of the entrance to Bagh-e Nazar. As the name suggests, its construction formed part of the extensive building programme undertaken by Karim Khan, the so-called *vakil* (regent) to the last Safavids. The bazaar maintains much of its late 18th-century character with a northeast–southwest orientation (the direction of Mecca) laid out about a century earlier. Originally, it was one long street with four large caravanserais to accommodate merchants, but in the 20th century a main road was constructed across the street and two of the

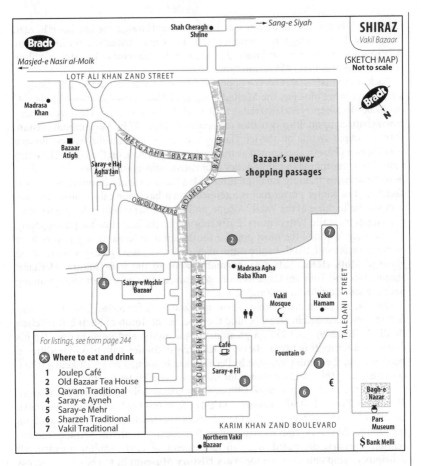

For listings, see from page 244

☒ Where to eat and drink
1 Joulep Café
2 Old Bazaar Tea House
3 Qavam Traditional
4 Saray-e Ayneh
5 Saray-e Mehr
6 Sharzeh Traditional
7 Vakil Traditional

four caravanserais were demolished in an unfortunate Pahlavi city modernising scheme. Rents from the bazaar and its *hamam* endowed the **Masjed-e Vakil** [244 C3] (⊕ 08.30–18.00; entry 300,000 rials), constructed around 1773 and for many years out of bounds to foreign tourists. It retains a sense of intimacy despite its large size and is organised on the two-*ivan* plan. Forty-eight stumpy stone columns, each carved in a barley-sugar spiral, mark the sanctuary area, producing a space vaguely reminiscent of Durham Cathedral. The original *mihrab* of 1634, which suggested that an earlier mosque had been demolished, is no longer in place, but the 18th-century, 14-stepped *minbar* cut from one huge block of marble, is still standing. Some idea of the tile decoration inside can be imagined from the exterior panels. Purists may raise eyebrows at the flamboyant flower motifs and the colourful pastel palette but our spirits soar at such cheerful ornateness. Not all the tiles are original, as some restoration was carried out in 1828 and later years.

Next door towards the main road is the bathhouse, converted in 2001 into a tea house and restaurant but then closed again by the authorities. It now functions as the **Hamam Vakil Ethnographic Museum** [244 C3] (⊕ 08.00–18.00; entry 300,000 rials).

Exiting the bazaar at Lotf Ali Khan Zand Street via Rouhollah Bazaar, walk left then turn left into a small alley where, set back a little, is the **Madrasa Khan**

[244 C3]. You can also find your way here walking through the Moshir-e Bazaar. Originally the building was a warehouse, as the name suggests, built in 1615 by Allahverdi Khan and his son Imam Qoli Khan, although most of its extensive tiling scheme dates from an 1833 restoration.

Back at the main street on the opposite side of the road, a narrow alley leads to a truly charming mosque, the **Masjed-e Nasir al-Molk** (مسجد نصیرالملک) [244 C4] (⏰ 07.00–16.30; entry 500,000 rials), which feels like a personal and secret discovery when chanced upon. It's a two-*ivan* mosque built 1876–87 by Mohammad Hassan, with a covered arcade on the left (facing the sanctuary) and the winter mosque (*shabestan-e gharbi*), also known as the western prayer hall, on the right. The entry vestibule is smothered in painted tiles (not *cuerda seca* as sometimes described) of floral ornaments framing small pictures of landscapes clearly inspired by Russian sketches. The winter prayer hall is interesting as it has stone cable-spiral columns very similar to those of the Vakil Mosque, and most of the vividly coloured window glass dates from the 19th century. Early morning is the best time for photography. The mosque is one of the most popular tourist spots in Shiraz and gets very busy between 08.00 and 10.00. In the same alley (Alley 37) is a Qajar-period restored **Nasir al-Molk House** [244 C4], currently home to the Iran Cultural Heritage, Handicrafts and Tourism Organisation; you can see this on the left when walking back towards Lotf Ali Khan Zand Street.

On Lotf Ali Khan Zand Street, turn right and walk for 300m. Less than 100m further down Ruzbehan Street behind the fence is the **Tomb of Sheikh Ruzbehan Baqli** (1128–1209) [244 D5], a prominent Sufi mystic and poet, known for his diaries and accounts of his revelations. Delicately decorated with tiles in traditional Persian style, the tomb (*aramgah* in Persian) sits in a small and well-kept garden, demonstrating the attention shown for the mystic and his teachings.

Across the road are two large 19th-century houses behind massive brick walls. The first is **Zinat al-Molk's House** [244 D4] (⏰ 08.00–19.00; entry 300,000 rials), completed in 1885 after more than ten years of construction. The mirror work on the ground-floor reception rooms is pure 19th century, as are the painted wooden ceilings upstairs, decorated with an assortment of coyly smiling women, all deliciously camp and over the top. **Fars History Museum** in the basement across the entire perimeter of the house displays ethnographic exhibits of important historical figures (eg: Atoosa, daughter of Cyrus the Great) as well as replicas of the Persepolis stairways and the Cyrus cylinder.

The other house is the **Narenjestan** (نارنجستان) (Orangery) [244 D4] (Lotf Ali Khan Zand St; ⏰ 08.00–20.00; entry 500,000 rials), home of the famous Asia Institute, organised by the American Iranologist Arthur Upham Pope during the 1960s and 1970s. The house was built in the late 1870s by Mohammad Reza and Ibrahim Qavam al-Molk, a former mayor and tax agent of Shiraz, as their public reception rooms, connected by a tunnel to Zinat al-Molk's House, which functioned as the *anderuni* or private quarters. A vestibule leads into a small walled garden, essentially 19th century in character, with tiled panels of attendants bearing platters of fruits. The house itself is sparsely furnished but the mirrors and floor tiles, the latter decorated to look like ikat fabrics, especially on the ground floor and *talar*, are decoration enough, with crude imitations of Persepolis reliefs decorating the lower exterior wall. A small Museum of Antique Objects has been opened in the basement. Walking along the alley between the two houses brings you to the **Fars Coin Museum** [244 D4] and **Fars Textile Museum** [244 D4] (closed at the time of writing).

Most strangers to the city, whatever their nationality, aspire to visit the **Mausoleum of Shah Cheragh** (شاه چراغ) [244 B4] ('King of the Lamp'). (The modern wing & entrance are off Lotf Ali Khan Zand St. Here there is also a depository for clothes, computers & pretty much everything else you will not be allowed with into the shrine; ⊕ 24hrs; chadors are provided at the entrance. A reader reports that visitors with cameras may need to be accompanied by an official guide.) From early October 2002, after a noisy and disruptive visit by a foreign group, non-Muslims were not allowed entry even into the courtyard, but now there are even guided tours and access is unlimited. Visitors are permitted to carry and use cameras but, if you do so, you may be escorted around the site by a representative of the International Affairs Office. The most popular shrine is the large one to the right after entering the courtyard, which commemorates the brother of the eighth imam Reza, Seyyed Amir Ahmad, while the tomb of another brother, Seyyed Mir Mohammad, is situated further down on the left. Seyyed Amir Ahmad came to Shiraz in 808CE and died here in 835CE. Only a *mihrab* remains from the mausoleum and madrasa built to honour him in the 1340s by the mother of the then local ruler, as the shrine was largely rebuilt in 1506, then extensively repaired after an earthquake in 1588. Its local reputation was such that Nader Shah Afshar, despite being a Sunni Muslim, ordered further repair work in 1729, and Karim Khan Zand added further repairs in 1765. What is seen today is essentially 19th century, especially the mirror work smothering the interior, the silver doors and tilework, but the exterior dome is a 1959 fantasy, and the minaret dates from around 1970. On entry, note that men enter the shrine from the far left while women access on the right.

Across the courtyard to the left is the mausoleum to Shah Cheragh's brother, which has retained more of its 16th-century structure, but the decoration is again predominately Qajar in date. For some undefined reason, this tomb always has fewer visitors, as does the mausoleum of a third brother, Seyyed Ala al-Din, situated in the southwest of the city. This is also a 16th-century structure on an earlier 14th-century building, but extensively repaired and covered with mirror work in the 19th century.

The gate to its far right leads into the Qashqai Bazaar or to the Masjed-e Nasir al-Molk. Nearby are two mosques, much repaired after the 1852 earthquake. The **Masjed-e Nou** (مسجد نو) [244 B4] (meaning 'new mosque', referring to its status as the new Friday mosque) is also known as the Atabak Mosque after its patron, the military governor (*atabeg*) of Shiraz, Sa'd Ibn Zangi. To mark his sick child's miraculous recovery, he had this mosque, possibly with the largest courtyard (220m × 100m) in Iran, built on the site of his palace in 1201. The mosque was extensively repaired in Safavid times and then practically reconstructed after 1852. It now acts as the Friday mosque, so entry on Fridays is restricted from noon. Masjed-e Nou is considered to be historically the second most important mosque in Shiraz, after the Masjed-e Atiq (see below). Masjed-e Vakil is the third most important historically (page 251).

Some 300m southeast is the **Masjed-e Atiq** (مسجد عتیق) [244 C4] (⊕ irregularly), which functioned as the masjed-e jame until the Islamic Revolution. It can be accessed from the Mausoleum of Shah Cheragh (see opposite). Nothing remains of the original structure of 894CE, and the little free-standing building in the courtyard, thought to date from 1351, has been reassessed. This is the Beit al-Mashaf (or the Khodakhaneh (God's house), echoing the shape of the Ka'ba in Mecca, and which once housed the mosque's Qurans and other manuscripts. Its tiled portico inscription gives the 1351 foundation date, but recent conservation work has revealed that its present appearance is largely a result of an extensive post-1935 repair programme. Originally the complex had a madrasa, two hostels for visiting scholars, a reading room and hospital, but its dilapidated state persuaded

Shah Abbas I in 1567 to rebuild in this present four-*ivan* layout, with large sections of the west and north sides reconstructed 50 years later. This was also when the main avenue of the bazaar was constructed along the processional way used by the Safavid and then Zand rulers riding from their residences for the Friday prayer. Such occasions offered one of the few regular times when the public were certain of seeing the ruler, and Islamic history is dotted by assassination attempts during the Friday procession: two 20th-century victims were King Feisal of Iraq and King Abdullah I of Jordan.

Before crossing 9 Dey Street into the historic district of **Sang-e Siyah** (سنگ سیاه), stop by the **Islamic Art Museum** [244 B4] (Hazrati St; ⏰ 08.30–13.30 & 16.30–19.30; entry 70,000 rials), cosily housed in the Qajar-period Manteghinezhad House (خانه تاریخی منطقی نژاد). Right across the street, behind the disproportionately large Soofi restaurant sign, is the Sufi meeting place (*khanqah*) Ahmadi, known and well respected in the city for its free medical assistance (contact local guide Peyman Soodmand for details; page 242), which explains the number of people waiting outside in the alley to be seen by the doctor. The *khanqah* also holds regular free dinners for the poor.

The Sang-e Siyah ('Black Stone') [map, below] itself, named so after the large 600-year-old black stone in the courtyard of the **Sibuvey Cultural House**, located herein, is a maze of narrow alleys, historic houses and is the place to wander around on a sunny afternoon. The main gate to the neighbourhood lies opposite the public bus terminal and the first site you walk past is **Imamzadeh Bibi Dokhtaran** (b1358–84). Continue walking to the end of the narrow alley where you arrive at the square with Qajar-period **Masjed-e Moshir** on your right and **St Mary's Church** (see map, below) a little further up on your left. Continuing straight, in between high brick walls of the alley ahead, do not miss the door to your right, to the historic **Saadat House** with its beautiful *shahneshin*-tiled portal gently peeking from above the 2m-high brick walls. Built in 1923, this mansion is currently used

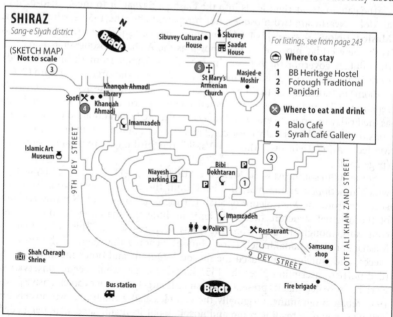

SHIRAZ
Sang-e Siyah district

(SKETCH MAP)
Not to scale

Sibuvey Cultural House
Sibuvey
Saadat House

St Mary's Armenian Church
Masjed-e Moshir

Khanqah Ahmadi
library
Spofi
Khanqah Ahmadi
Imamzadeh

Islamic Art Museum

9TH DEY STREET

Niayesh parking

Bibi Dokhtaran

Imamzadeh

Police

Restaurant

LOTF ALI KHAN ZAND STREET

Samsung shop

Shah Cheragh Shrine

9 DEY STREET

Bus station

Fire brigade

For listings, see from page 243

Where to stay
1   BB Heritage Hostel
2   Forough Traditional
3   Panjdari

Where to eat and drink
4   Balo Café
5   Syrah Café Gallery

as a handicrafts workshop. Do enter to look closely at the fine *shir-o-khorshid haft rang* decorative tile arrangement. The statue at the square at the end of the alley is that of Sibuvey himself. It was installed here in 2016 right in front of the scientist's mausoleum (*aramgah*) inside the **Sibuvey Cultural House** to the left side of the square. There are still Christians, Jews and Zoroastrians living in Shiraz but these communities have shrunk dramatically during the last three decades. Some of their places of worship are closed, but others are still functioning and can be visited. The Armenian **St Mary's Church** in the heart of the Sang-e Siyah neighbourhood was built during the reign of the Safavid Shah Abbas II (d1666) and not unlike the rest of the city, sustained major damage in the earthquakes. It remains essentially closed except on religious holidays. Knock on the door and if you are lucky its guardian Sooren will open and show you around. Inside, it has ornate wooden ceiling panes decorated in classic Persian style and a number of historical memorial plaques for British civilian and military personnel. A more recent **Church of Simon the Zealot** (*kelisa-e moghaddas-e qaur*) [244 D3] (Alley 39, off Zand St, past Keyvan Bookshop), dating to the Pahlavi dynasty is *in theory* open to all-comers on Sundays, but it was closed on each occasion we stopped by; according to a local tradition, Simon was martyred in Iran. Right across the street from it is **Rabi Zadeh synagogue** [244 A2], one of several in the city. Built around 70–80 years ago, it is open on Saturdays and Sunday mornings for *shabbat* service. The Jewish community are friendly and welcoming, but you still need a permit from Ershad-e Islami to explore it in detail. Few will admit to knowing the whereabouts of the original house of the Bab, the founder of the Bahai movement (page 37), but Canadian sources say it is located near Beit al-Mahdi, Shahid Dastgheyb Street, 100m from the Shah Cheragh shrine. Most people, however, do not know its precise location. It is best to come here with someone who knows exactly where the house is.

Slightly less central is the **Afif Abad Garden** (باغ عفیف آباد) [241 A2] (Bagh-e Afif Abad; ⊕ 08.00–12.30 & 15.00–17.30; entry 300,000 rials) with a military museum inside. The garden itself is lovely and is less touristy than other places in Shiraz, but it is the guns displayed here that you really come to see.

AROUND SHIRAZ

Most visitors stay in Shiraz in order to visit Sasanid Bishapur and Firuzabad, and most importantly the Achaemenid palace complex of Persepolis – situated in the west, south and northeast respectively. To visit all three will entail a minimum three-night stay, and even then this leaves little time for exploring Shiraz itself. A taxi to go to either Bishapur or Firuzabad and return to Shiraz will cost 1,000,000 rials, and slightly more in the 'tourist' season. Alternatively, you will need to use public transport, which will take longer. Avoid setting a limited number of hours for either of the towns as visiting various sites may take longer than expected.

For those dedicated to exploring Fars province in its entirety, the area north of Shiraz in the direction of Yasuj is dotted with spectacular mountain gorges or canyons (*tang* in Persian) with cool rivers and spectacular scenery. Two are particularly recommended and offer excellent swimming opportunities and idyllic picnic locations. **Tang-e Tizab**, 130km northwest of Shiraz is less touristy, while **Tang-e Boraq**, 166km further northwest, gets very busy on weekends.

BISHAPUR بیشاپور The historical city of Bishapur (139km west of Shiraz; ⊕ 08.00–18.00; entry 500,000 rials; museum 300,000 rials) lies off the Kazerun Road, which passes through some dramatic scenery, climbing up to and then through the 'Old

Woman' Gorge. Other than Kazerun there is no place to buy lunch in this area, so take the bulk of a picnic with you, and buy fresh bread en route. With a very early start it should be possible to incorporate a short visit to the bird sanctuary at Lake Parisan (formerly Famur), if you are there during the spring or autumn migrating seasons. The road is asphalted but there is little shade. This diversion takes you past a small bridge, Pol-e Abgineh, and a Qajar rock relief of 1829, depicting the prince-governor conquering a lion. This commemorated the reopening of the road in 1824, after a severe earthquake. The prince, a grandson of Shah Fath Ali Shah, had to flee to England in 1834 after his father's unsuccessful attempt to seize the throne on the shah's death. Also in this area is the Safavid caravanserai of Mian Kotal, for many years a police post but now open for general exploration and scrambling around.

Getting there and around There is no direct bus service from Shiraz. If travelling by public transport, take a **bus** from Amir Kabir bus station to Kazerun and from there take a taxi to Bishapur, 20km away. A one-way **taxi** journey from Kazerun will cost around 500,000 rials, but you should negotiate a return fare as the historical site is on the outskirts of the town and taxis here are few. Mountain scenery along the Kazerun Road, which was built by the Germans during the last Iranian monarchy, is simply stunning, passing via the spectacular gorge Tang-e Abolhayat.

What to see and do Bishapur was a **palace-town complex**, built in 266CE (according to dedicatory column inscriptions) on a Hellenistic–Roman grid system rather than the circular plan traditionally favoured by the Parthians and early Sasanids. The city was the creation of Shapur I, using Roman prisoners of war. There was a decade of archaeological work here before World War II, carried out by the French, and then from 1968 by the Iranian Archaeological Service, but these excavations involved only 3% of a site that probably housed over 50,000 townspeople. It is best to visit these ruins first, remembering to take a torch. Then have a picnic by the river, looking at the low reliefs either side of the gorge.

On entering the site, there are Sasanid walls surviving up to about 3m high with solid round towers, but at some point one in three was demolished, perhaps contributing to its capture by the Arab armies around 637CE. The place has a rather desolate air as it was stripped bare of all its sculptures, mosaics, decorative plaster and other treasures; most went to the Louvre, Paris, with a few pieces going to Tehran's National Museum. Before visiting the main buildings of the excavated site, head towards the museum building (closed at present) from where you'll see in the distance, straight ahead, a votive column; this marks the centre of the original city. None of that vast area in front of you has been excavated.

Returning to the excavated area, the main building, some 20m² with its stepped cruciform plan and four huge *ivans* or portals, probably functioned as the **royal audience chamber**. Opinions are much divided as to whether it was covered by a huge dome or left open to the skies, but there is no evidence of springing high on the walls. Thick wall plaster remains in places, but you have to imagine the deeply carved, moulded and painted decoration. Behind, and close to the walls, is a stone-lined chamber below ground level; several masons' marks are still visible on the ashlar blocks. This chamber was 'identified' by the French archaeologist as the prison of Valerian.

Retracing your steps to the audience hall, west of this on the same ground level is another chamber entered through a triple-arched doorway. This was where most of the 'mosaic' work was found, depicting entertainers and courtiers, and some small tesserae can be seen close by the doorways. The way the walls meet the ground level strongly suggests that radical alterations were made at some time. This is just one reason why modern archaeologists question the early conclusions, which were reached after digging in such a small sector of the whole site.

There is an intriguing building to the north with high-quality, honey-coloured ashlar stonework. The staircase down is restored but 15m of the original walls remain, forming four faces of a central courtyard, with a covered ambulatory behind. This was in fact a huge shallow pool, as inside the interior ambulatory (the reason for bringing a torch) there are narrow water channels with blocking or damming devices. This was probably a **temple to Anahita**, the Zoroastrian deity associated with battle, fertility and water, an identification further supported by the two (damaged) bull capitals found nearby and now incorporated high on the wall opposite the stairs, for bull sacrifices were regular offerings at various other Anahita shrines. As the Sasanid shahs traced their lineage back to a high priest at the Istakhr Temple of Anahita, near Persepolis (page 271), what could be more logical than Shapur I, victorious over Rome, honouring this goddess by constructing a temple in his new city by the river?

A short walk away are the remains of a small **mosque** built, possibly, over a small fire temple, as a fire altar was found incorporated into the structure. French archaeologists believed the entire site was abandoned in the 10th century, but with so little of the site excavated it is impossible to be certain.

Leaving the site, look up into the hills on the immediate right: all that rubble was originally **defence walls** and towers guarding the approach to the city of Bishapur. The minor tarmac road on the right-hand riverbank brings you to the first of the **rock reliefs** (open site; entry free). It is badly damaged, but enough survives to identify the characters as the Zoroastrian uncreated god, Ahura Mazda, on the left, investing Shah Shapur I (c240–72CE) on the right; note that in a motif possibly drawn from the West, the ring of authority is carried by a putto. Both are on horseback, but there is a prone figure under Shapur's mount, probably the Roman emperor, Gordianus III, killed by his own men after their defeat on the Euphrates in 243CE. The kneeling Roman is thought to be Philip the Arab (r244–49CE), who paid 500,000 gold denarii to secure peace terms a year later. His monumental buildings, with their exquisite mosaics (sadly looted in 2011 in the chaos of the Syrian conflict), still standing in his birthplace Philippopolis (today's Shahba) south of Damascus, Syria, reveal nothing of this ignominious submission. Further along this road, but set up high, is another panel in better condition, once plastered and painted. In billowing drapery, Shapur grips the wrist of a Roman emperor, probably Valerian (r253–60CE) who was captured by the Sasanid army in Edessa (today's Sanliurfa, southeast Turkey), an event that drew the opportunistic Queen Zenoubia of Palmyra into the conflict. Shapur's horse tramples on a fallen enemy, thought to represent the unfortunate Gordianus III again, while the kneeling figure is Philip the Arab; this panel therefore records royal victories over a span of 20 years and was probably a commemoration panel for Shapur's funeral. Behind the shah are courtiers and generals, while figures behind Philip may represent the Roman governor of Syria and a court archivist witnessing the submission. To the right are two rows of figures, one set carrying the sacred *barsom* to feed the fire, the others, perhaps builders of Bishapur, carrying swords and spades.

On the left bank in the open area called **Tang-e Chogan** (تنگ چوگان) (⏱ 08.00–18.00; entry 300,000 rials; picnic area crowded with locals on Fri) are several further rock reliefs in better condition, also once plastered and painted. The first **low relief** again depicts Shapur I with his three sons victorious over the same three Roman emperors, with five splendidly depicted rows of soldiers, elephants, lions and chariots, in all numbering over 200 figures. It probably dates from 260–73CE. All of the figures are badly stained by water seepage. The next panel shows Bahram II (r274–91CE) receiving the submission of rebellious Arab tribesmen whose thumbs have been removed to prevent them drawing bows again; this may commemorate his famous victory at Mesene (in modern-day Iraq), around 282CE. Further on there's a low relief of Ahura Mazda, on the left, handing over the ring of authority to Bahram I (r271–74CE). However, Bahram's brother Narseh (r292–301CE) later had his own name inscribed in Pahlavi, top right, presumably still smarting that Bahram I selected his son and not him as successor. In removing the water conduit in 1975, a figure lying under the horse's hooves was revealed, possibly representing the troublesome Bahram (later III) or his advisor Wahnam, who persuaded him to seize power after his father's death (Bahram II); both caused Narseh several sleepless nights.

The last relief, with two rows of figures, looks very crude, but perhaps was never finished. Who the centrally placed shah is, is unclear. Probably it is either Shapur I accepting the submission of central Asian rebels or Shapur II (309–79CE), the grandson of Narseh, celebrating his victories in eastern Iran over certain Indian tribes. There are altogether over 200 human figures, along with elephants, carved into the rocks, some carrying decapitated heads.

From the path on the right bank of the stream, look up across the Bishapur River to the far hills. Close to the top ridge you will spot a large cave, the **Gar-e Shapur** (غار شاپور) (entry free), so named because a free-standing statue over 7m high of Shapur I was carved from the living rock, perhaps to mark his (as yet unlocated) tomb. The statue collapsed some years ago but has been re-erected. In order to visit, keep on this river road past the Qashqai village of Abdallah Khan. Turn left (following handwritten signs in Persian) and drive over the bridge and then walk for about another hour. There are 329 steps up to the cave and it is advisable to climb these in the afternoon. It takes around an hour to make the climb; be sure to bring water with you.

In all, the trip around Bishapur archaeological site takes 4 hours, so such an expedition may mean spending more than a day in the Bishapur area. In the village of Kashkuli, near Bishapur, there is a lovely traditional Bishapur *bumgardi* (5 rooms; m 0917 3219271) with a spacious courtyard and very friendly atmosphere. This is the best place to stay overnight to explore the area.

NORTH OF BISHAPUR Some 10km northwest of Bishapur in the village of Qandil, is **Tang-e Qandil** (تنگ قندیل) (possibly 'Gorge of the Hanging Lamp'; 25km south of Nurabad, to the left of the main road). After the village, the road is unpaved. Bear right at the water cistern and follow the dirt track by the dry riverbed for 400m; the boulder bearing the carving is in the riverbed. This relief is one of the most well preserved in Iran. Scholars cannot agree who is represented here, but Western archaeologists generally identify the king as Bahram II being offered a lotus flower by his queen, with the crown prince, later Bahram III, holding the ring of authority. Such family portraits are rare in Sasanid relief tradition. The only other known example is Barm-e Delak (page 246), where it is the king, on the other hand, offering a flower to the queen. Nearby, just 5km from Nurabad there is another Sasanid rock panel, 2.9m wide and 4.8m long, known locally as **Sarab-e Bahram**, which depicts Bahram II with an attendant on either side; the one at the shah's right is clearly Kartir, as his cap carries the distinctive 'scissor' motif. There is no sign pointing here from the main road. When approaching from Shiraz, turn right at the police station and then walk for about 300m through the bushes. The relief is, alas, in poor condition.

Some 20km further on, west of Nurabad, the remains of a possible Parthian fire temple **Mil-e Izhdeha**, resembling those at Naqsh-e Rostam and Pasargadae (pages 269 and 272 respectively), were found and about 10km further on (5km northwest of **Fahliyan**) Sir Aurel Stein, famous for his archaeological discoveries along the Chinese Silk Road, discovered column bases of an Achaemenid palace. About 10km north of Fahliyan are the Elamite rock reliefs of **Kurangun**, located high up the hillside (you will need a local guide to find them), close to Seh Talu, and, to the east, **Tel-e Sefid**, an Elamite settlement dating from c1500BCE to 1000BCE. It was a local route across the mountains that took Alexander the Great behind Achaemenid defence lines to capture Persepolis. The main Kurangun panel shows two divine – or perhaps regal – figures, one sitting on a throne like a coiled serpent pouring a libation. Their date is disputed, some scholars arguing for c2400BCE, while others prefer 16th–15th century BCE. Most agree, however, that the second section, depicting three rows of worshippers returning from the libation ceremony, was carved much later, probably during the 8th century BCE. Nearby and off the main road to the right stop briefly to view the vast and impressive Sasanid bridge at **Basht** where there are also the remains of an ancient fire temple on the escarpment from where one may look down on the bridge.

Approximately 20km northeast of Basht near the village of Bahrehana is **Dakhmeh Sangi Dua Dokhtar** (also known as *Dei Dua* in Lori language, meaning 'Mother and daughter'). This is a rock-cut tomb now thought to date from the Seleucid or possibly early Parthian period because there are visual similarities in the carved columns 'supporting' a crenellated frieze to those of the rock tombs at Naqsh-e Rostam, although they remind the author of the Nabatean tombs at Mada'in Saleh, Saudi Arabia, and Petra, Jordan. The tomb was comprehensively identified as an Achaemenid construction when first recorded during the late 1920s. Some believe it was built for Ario Barzan (d330BCE), also known as Ariobarzanes the Brave, Achaemenid military commander and *satrap*, who commanded the Persian army in the Battle of the Persian Gate against the Macedonian army, led by Alexander the Great.

SOUTH OF BISHAPUR A dirt track leads southwest of Jereh (55km south of Kazerun) via Hassan Abad to **Sar-e Mashhad** (otherwise, from Firuzabad, turn northwest at Farrash Band) to a rock panel depicting the Sasanid Bahram II (r274–91CE) protecting his wife and son from a lion attack, with a lengthy Pahlavi inscription detailing Zoroastrian religious teachings and rituals; four figures, one of whom may represent Anahita, witness the actions of the 'Hero King'. Some 12km further south along another dirt track (which may require a 4x4 vehicle) is **Bozpar**, famous among archaeologists for one small building, the **Gur-e Dokhtar** ('daughter's tomb'), discovered in 1960 by Belgian archaeologist Louis Vandenberg. A small limestone tomb with a gabled roof stands on a three-tiered platform, bearing remarkable similarity to Cyrus the Great's tomb at Pasargadae (page 272), 125km northeast of Shiraz. This is smaller, being 4.45m high, 5.10m long and 4.40m wide (Cyrus's tomb at Pasargadae is 10.6m × 13.2m × 12.2m). It was first thought that this was the resting place of Cyrus's grandfather, but the metal clamps holding the stone blocks suggest not a 7th-century BCE date after all but a 5th-century one, so perhaps it was the final resting place of Cyrus the Younger (d401BCE), killed in battle nearby. Others believe it was the tomb of Mandana, mother of Cyrus the Great, or his daughter Atossa, which explains the name of the actual structure.

FIRUZABAD فیروزآباد About 110km south of Shiraz, Firuzabad makes for an enjoyable day trip through striking and dramatic scenery. The 2-hour bus journey swerves past the large salt lake of **Maharlu** with its salt pans, some 20km after leaving Shiraz. Emerging from the second road tunnel, about 15km before reaching Firuzabad, look for the well-preserved Sasanid fortress on the cliff top on your left. This is the palace complex known as **Qaleh Dokhtar** (Daughter's Castle; entry 300,000 rials), from the local legend that a girl continually carried a young heifer from birth to maturity up to the castle and down to the river (the *Shahnameh* contains a related story linked with the Sasanid shah Bahram V). Access is possible but entails about 40 minutes' hard walking of 250 steps, the path snaking upwards opposite (and just past) the roadside rest stop (with bathrooms) on the bend of the road. The cable car to the top is alas not in service. A German archaeological survey in the late 1960s identified a three-terraced complex, with a large circular tower, visible from the road, and a central square chamber dominated by a barrel-vaulted hall and series of chambers, all originally set within a garden. Given the neighbouring rock reliefs depicting Shah Ardashir I (d242CE), it seems likely the palace was constructed for him between 212CE and 224CE, but Shapur I (d272CE) has also been suggested. There is a parking place just past the rest stop, and a short walk down below the road allows you to see the remains of a Sasanid bridge, which presumably once connected a small fort on the other bank with the palace. Back on the main road, continue walking to see an eroded Sasanid **rock relief** on the far bank, showing Ardashir standing before a fire altar with three sons and a page, all facing Ahura Mazda on the left. About 1km further on, but very difficult to spot, is another relief (18m wide × 4m high), depicting Ardashir unseating the last Parthian ruler, Artabanus V, from his horse in 224CE, while his son Shapur tackles the Parthian vizier and a Sasanid courtier dispatches another opponent.

Driving further towards Firuzabad, the remains of a huge Sasanid palace **Kakh-e Ardashir** (approximately 105m × 55m), also known as the fire temple (*ateshkadeh*) of Firuzabad (☉ 08.00–18.00; entry 300,000 rials) soon come into view on the right, but to visit it you have to drive down into Firuzabad itself and approach by a parallel road, so you can also visit the remains of the Sasanid city of Ardashir Khurreh (The Glory of Ardashir), known as **Gur**. In Gur turn right at the roundabout bearing a gas flame, taking the left fork at the cemetery. On the town outskirts, opposite a small cluster of light industrial buildings, is a dirt track leading through what remains of the massive circular defence walls of Gur, to the far right of the solitary ruined tower. Follow this until it threatens to take you into a farmhouse, then swing on to the left, over a pot-holed track which leads closer to the ruined tower. The last 1km or so must be walked. Even in its overgrown state, Gur visitors can make out the ruins of city walls, buildings, wells and water channels, and Sasanid pot shards litter the track. Archaeologists think this circular city, over 2km in diameter, was originally a Parthian settlement, but tradition says that Ardashir I built it to mark his victory over the Parthian regime. A deep ditch and huge ramparts with four gates protected it. The centrally placed solitary tower, with traces of an external spiral staircase, was probably a huge fire altar standing some 30m high and 10m square. To one side in the near distance a 25m² stone terrace is visible, on which stood a cruciform domed chamber with side rooms, perhaps functioning as the main temple compound.

Retrace the rough drive to get to the Kakh-e Ardashir that lours conspicuously over the flat plain. Continue past the light industrial building, keeping the tower of Gur on the right, and eventually the road leads right up to the site. The present-day entrance is not the original one, so walk from the small car park to view the little lake and the huge *ivan* opening on to it, once the official palace entry. The thick stone walls, relieved by groups of three engaged columns, look unprepossessing without their top layer of plaster, once painted and decorated. The modern entrance leads immediately into a series of huge domed chambers with early examples of squinches; tall blind niches decorated with Pharaonic-looking cornices elegantly spaced along the walls accentuate the vast space. The doorways go either to the audience *ivan*, once decorated like the royal 'coronation' *ivan* at the Sasanid capital of Ctesiphon (near Baghdad), Iraq, which had a huge jewelled crown suspended from the apex and a rich bejewelled, gold and silver floor carpet; or, in the opposite direction, to a courtyard surrounded by rooms and passageways. A spiral staircase connects with the upper floor and roof, and this can usually be accessed with a polite word to the site guardian. The local Cultural Heritage Organisation staff have always been very generous, and although eating within the boundaries of the site is not officially allowed, with a polite word it is often possible to get permission to enjoy a picnic by the pool at the front of the palace, which marked the original entrance. Few experiences make history as pleasurable as a languid alfresco lunch at this site: a watermelon cooling in the water, mongooses scurrying around in the underbrush, and birds and frogs chattering as the sun climbs high over the palace allow the lucky visitor to picture the Sasanid court at play and marvel at the fact that they are among the few guests at this remarkable site. If you are lucky, a security guard may let you (for a small tip) climb up to the upper levels of the palace.

Where to stay and eat In modern Firuzabad, a well-known trading centre until the 11th century, there's a simple but clean **Tourist Inn** (10 rooms; Enghelab St; 071 38723699; e info@ittic.com; **$$**) set in a small garden to one side of the gas flame roundabout. It has basic accommodation and good food, but be sure to make advance reservations.

SARVESTAN (سروستان) AND BEYOND From Shiraz, a main road leads southeast to Sarvestan (80km). The small town has a mausoleum, the **Imamzadeh Pol** (known also as Mazar-e Sheikh Yusuf Sarvestani), with a 1282 dating inscription that seems at odds with its form, which resembles a Zoroastrian fire temple. But the real reason for stopping is the restored **Sasanid palace** complex (⊕ no specific opening hrs; entry free), part of the eight sites from the UNESCO-listed Sasanid Archaeological Landscape of Fars Region. To reach the mausoleum, turn right after approximately 5km past Sarvestan at the Momen Abad village mosque, then continue until the signposted turn to the right towards the complex itself past pistachio groves. A triple-arched portico formed the entrance, the two smaller arches leading into a series of halls with interesting vaulted systems, which connected to other smaller rooms. The central arch opens directly into the main brick-domed chamber, a large central courtyard and then other rooms, each architecturally different from the other. Perhaps built for Bahram V (r420–38CE), it might have functioned as a royal hunting lodge and surrounding walled *paradeisos*. Surface pottery shards litter the ground everywhere and the palace is splendidly illuminated by night.

From Sarvestan, it is approximately 140km due east to **Neyriz** (and eventually **Sirjan**) with its **masjed-e jame**, important for its single-barrel-vaulted *ivan*, which is thought to be the oldest to survive in Iran. This section of the present building could well date from 951CE when the mosque was constructed over the remains of a fire temple, or perhaps 20 years later, as its Seljuk plaster *mihrab* refers to further work here begun in 972CE. The south *ivan* and side arcades were added during the Seljuk period. The small gardens and sleepy atmosphere make this an excellent picnic lunch stop if travelling to Shiraz from Yazd. For accommodation options in Sirjan, about 100km east of Neyriz, see page 327.

Fasa (فسا) is no longer the sleepy village seen by Sylvia Matheson in the late 1970s but a thriving township with the municipality busily landscaping its historic mounds into leisure areas. The road continues to **Darab** (275km from Shiraz) and neighbouring **Darabgerd**, 8km southwest, known for its Sasanid remains. Before being abandoned in the 12th or early 13th century, the circular fortress Qaleh Dahyeh measured 1,850m in diameter with a 55m-wide defensive ditch, and walls at least 12m high with four gates. On the hillside nearby is the rock-relief known locally as **Naqsh-e Rostam Darab**. It depicts a Sasanid shah on horseback, with rows of courtiers behind receiving the submission of two important men, while a third lies on the ground and rows of Roman captives line up to the right. Opinions are divided over who is depicted: the shah's crown suggests it is Ardashir I, once regional governor here, recording his victory in 230CE over the Roman emperors, Severus Alexander and Maximinus Thrax, before overthrowing the Parthians, but the depiction could as easily be Shapur I giving Valerian and Philip the Arab another good kicking. Be aware that this site is not easy to find and was sadly sprayed with graffiti in 2008. About 5km further to the southeast is a rock-cut chamber. Although it has a *mihrab* dating from 1254 and is known locally as **Masjed-e Sangi**, the presence of a narthex and a cruciform chamber has led some archaeologists to associate it with the 3rd-century Nestorian bishopric in the locale.

NORTH OF SHIRAZ Travelling in the direction of the Zagros Mountains, approximately 35km away from the city, lies the small village of **Qalat** (قلات) (pronounced *ghalat*), much liked by Shirazis for its fresh air and moderate temperatures. The beautiful setting amid leafy mountain foothills by the river, with historical buildings, including remains of an Armenian church, and numerous cafés, makes Qalat ideal for a day trip from Shiraz, but preferably on a weekday because it gets very busy at weekends. Continuing for another 147km north brings you to **Jasuj** (یاسوج), capital of the predominantly Lori-speaking Kohgiluyeh and Boyer-Ahmad province. The route becomes increasingly more scenic as it climbs further up the Zagros Mountains. Jasuj is the starting point for exploring this stunning area. **Dena National Park and Protected Area**, covering 43,285ha, starts from the town of **Sisakht** (سیسخت), reachable by a *savari* taxi from Yasuj in 40 minutes. Here you can overnight in **Raeeis Ecolodge** (5 rooms; m 0911 2077375; **$$**) and arrange for a local guide to accompany you on hiking around the area. Adventure Iran (page 44) also organises professional hiking and trekking tours in this part of Iran and are highly recommended.

9

Persepolis and the Surrounding Area

PERSEPOLIS تخت جمشید

More than any other ancient site in Iran, Persepolis (Takht-e Jamshid) embodies all the glory – and the demise – of the Persian Empire. It was here that the Achaemenid kings received their subjects, celebrated the New Year and ran their empire before Alexander the Great burned the whole thing to the ground as he conquered the world. To date, it remains a mystery whether he did it on purpose or it was an accident. And while we may never find out the truth, the remains of Persepolis testify to the glory of the world's greatest empire. It is also at Persepolis that the first signs of Achaemenid art appear in 510BCE, and only afterwards at Bisotun and then in Pasargadae.

GETTING THERE AND AWAY Transport to Persepolis and nearby sites is a problem. There is a scheduled **bus** service between Shiraz and Marv Dasht but not to and from Persepolis itself, so the easiest solution is to hire (and retain for the return trip) a **taxi**, if not from Shiraz (50km southwest) then from Marv Dasht about 15km away, but the latter option might in the end prove more expensive. It is also possible to arrange a taxi or tour leaving from Shiraz to Yazd or Kerman or in the opposite direction, stopping at Persepolis and other sites in this chapter. If ordering a taxi from Shiraz on a one-day tour, be aware of the eager drivers offering to take you to Persepolis and back for a reasonable price. To get business the quoted fare will most likely be exclusive of the visits to Naqsh-e Rostam and Pasargadae, although all three sites are usually covered on the same full-day trip. The recommended option, however, is to arrange for a one-day trip with one of the tour guides listed on page 242.

WHERE TO STAY AND EAT

Apadana Hotel (17 rooms) Opposite the site; ✆ 072 84432636, 072 84432637; 📘. Expensive, because it can cash in on its favourable position. Has a certain charm, but overall rather standard both in service & facilities on offer. **$$$**

Tourist Inn (22 rooms) Takht-e Jamshid St; ✆ 072 84474001; e info@ittic.com. With detached villas & a number of dble bedrooms, it is just a few mins' walk from the site & has a very nice alfresco tea house. **$$**

✗ Parsian Restaurant Takht-e Jamshid St; ✆ 072 84473555. This restaurant has a cave-like interior & reliable meals. **$**

WHAT TO SEE AND DO

The site of Persepolis (⏰ autumn–winter 08.00–17.00, spring–summer 07.30–20.00; entry 500,000 rials, museum 300,000 rials) Archaeological excavations began

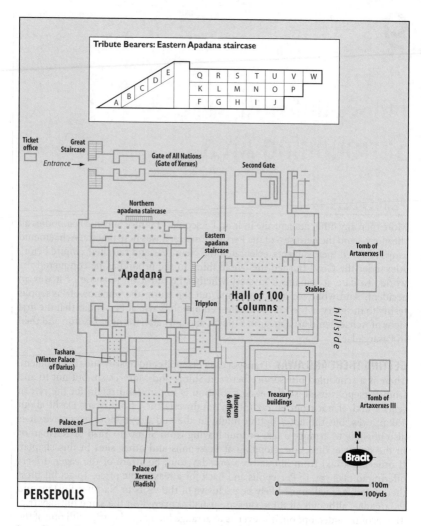

Tribute Bearers: Eastern Apadana staircase

		Q	R	S	T	U	V	W
		K	L	M	N	O	P
E		F	G	H	I	J

Ticket office
Great Staircase
Entrance →
Gate of All Nations (Gate of Xerxes)
Second Gate
Northern apadana staircase
Eastern apadana staircase
Tomb of Artaxerxes II
Apadana
Tripylon
Hall of 100 Columns
Stables
hillside
Tashara (Winter Palace of Darius)
Museum & offices
Treasury buildings
Tomb of Artaxerxes III
Palace of Artaxerxes III
Palace of Xerxes (Hadish)
N
Bradt
0 ——— 100m
0 ——— 100yds

PERSEPOLIS

here for the first time in 1931 by the Archaeological Expedition from the Oriental Institute of the University of Chicago and have continued on and off ever since. The immense scale and grandeur of this site (over 13ha) has long been recognised and in 1979 it was awarded the status of UNESCO World Heritage Site. Locals thought it could only be the throne dais (*takht*) of Jamshid, a legendary figure in the *Shahnameh* (see box, page 349), while in the 14th century it was known as Chehel Manar (40 Minarets), from the standing columns seen from a distance. Between 1964 and 1972 the site and its monuments were being restored by a dedicated team from the Italian Institute for Middle and Far East (IsMEO) and their Iranian colleagues. In the early 1980s hysterical reports in the Western media announced that revolutionary zealots had destroyed much of this pre-Islamic site. Nonsense. Admittedly few visitors appreciate the installed 'protection measures', such as covering the stone stairs with wooden ones and roping off access to parts of the complex as well as 'guiding' visitors along prescribed paths, but there has been no gratuitous damage.

KEY TO EASTERN APADANA STAIRCASE RELIEFS

FIRST RISE UPWARDS
A Ethiopians bringing a giraffe or okapi
B 'People of the Punt', probably Libyans, with an antelope and chariot
C People of the eastern regions, possibly the so-called Carians, with a bull
D Arabs leading a dromedary camel
E Unidentified, but possibly Skudrians, wearing pointed caps and offering a horse

PANELS AT GROUND LEVEL, LEFT TO RIGHT
F Indians from Sind wearing skirt wraps, bringing an ass
G Parthians leading a Bactrian camel and carrying metal objects
H Ionians holding cloth and honeycombs or balls of yarn
I Cappadocians carrying garments and leading horses
J Lydians (or possibly Syrians) with a chariot

MIDDLE ROW, LEFT TO RIGHT
K Soghdians (today's Samarkand region) with gifts of a horse and metalwork
L People of Gandhara (Pakistan) with a humped bull
M Scythians with a distinctive pointed cap, bearing clothing
N Assyrians with sheep
O Babylonians with a fringed cloth and a humped bull
P Armenians, bringing a horse and double-handled ewer

TOP ROW, LEFT TO RIGHT
Q Possibly Median people or Sagartians with a horse and textiles
R Bactrians with a Bactrian camel
S Egyptians (very fragmentary)
T Drangianans (north of Afghanistan) bringing a Bactrian camel
U Arians (Baluchestan) with a Bactrian camel and a lion skin
V Elamite archers from Susa bringing a lioness – the only female form in Persepolis – and two cubs
W Medians with metal objects and clothing

According to the archaeological evidence the earliest remains of Persepolis date to around 518BCE, four years after Darius the Great's accession to the Achaemenid throne. His successors added further buildings, but the site was still unfinished when, in early 330BCE, Alexander the Great burned it to the ground after looting the city, seven years before his death. It took him, according to Plutarch, 10,000 mules and 5,000 camels to carry away the booty from this revenge attack for the Achaemenid firing of Athens. The stone came from nearby quarries but the labourers came from all over the Achaemenid Empire including Greece, as the marks of the Greek toothed chisel testifies. Gold and silver foundation tablets (now in Tehran's National Museum) were found on the site but more fascinating, for their wealth of detailed information, were the uncovered 30,000-odd clay tablets. The complex consisted of military quarters, treasury stores, small private rooms and huge reception areas, but its exact function remains an intriguing mystery. Susa was the Achaemenid winter capital and Hamadan the summer residence, while Pasargadae was perhaps built to commemorate Cyrus the Great's victory over the Medians. But Persepolis?

On the evidence of low reliefs showing visitors bearing gifts, and lions attacking bulls (Leo ascendant over Taurus suggesting spring pushing winter away), many assume Persepolis was used once a year to celebrate Nou Rouz, the spring equinox. Frequent use of the lotus flower motif with its 12 leaves possibly symbolises the 12 months of the year and the always-green cypress tree could also be interpreted to refer to Nou Rouz, but such festivities are not mentioned in Achaemenid and later sources. There seem to have been only two occasions when the Achaemenid ruler received gifts: on the official imperial birthday, and the annual sacrifice to Mithra. The bull may also be depicted to represent a cow, a symbol of fertility and a guardian of nomad people.

Orientation and facilities The only access to the site is at the end of the main road. A new glass ticket building with electronic ticket machines has been erected some 150m before the Achaemenid terrace wall. Cars, taxis, tourist buses, etc, have to stop and park a few hundred metres before this new development, and visitors have to walk from here to the ancient site.

If possible, two visits should be made: in early morning to explore when the light is much 'whiter', and about 90 minutes before sunset, when the stone takes on a softer, golden colour. Most of the stone now has a rough grey appearance, a result of wind-blown dust over the millennia, so do make a point of visiting the National Museum in Tehran to see the 'waxed' reliefs and column ensemble from Persepolis. This rich, dark-brown stone set alongside a creamy limestone was the original colouring. If you are limited to one visit, it will take 3 hours or so to walk around and take photographs, especially if you plan to walk up to the Achaemenid royal tombs behind for a magnificent view over the site. Take a telephoto lens or binoculars for viewing these tombs; these will also be useful if you're going to Naqsh-e Rostam (usually included on the same day).

Guided tour of the ruins Most tourists arrive with a guide from Shiraz or a driver who does not enter the site with them, so they have to rely on a book such as this or the excellent local one by Dr Alireza Shapour Shahbazi, *The Authoritative Guide to Persepolis*, Tehran, 2004. Digital 3D glasses recreating the original walls and buildings can be rented at the ticket sales point (500,000 rials) but will most probably distract you from enjoying the beauty of the site. The great double staircase with low risers, perhaps to allow horses to be ridden up, leads to the monumental **Gate of All Nations** (also known as the Gate of Xerxes), constructed c475BCE on the order of Xerxes I, successor to Darius the Great. Here trumpeters would have sounded a welcome as visitors walked through enormous wooden doors flanked by giant sculptures of two quadrupeds, while two huge human-headed winged bulls in the Assyrian style face into the palace area. High over the sculptures is a trilingual cuneiform inscription proclaiming:

> I am Xerxes, the great king, King of Kings, King of the lands of many people, King of this great earth far and wide … By Ahura Mazda's favour I have had made this Gate of All Nations. Much that is beautiful has been built in this [region] which I and my father have built. All that has been built and appears beautiful … we have built by the favour of Ahura Mazda.

It is one of the 110 inscriptions here, many of which reaffirm belief in the Zoroastrian creator God. Please resist the temptation to add your name to all the graffiti, which include Stanley (of Dr Livingstone fame).

When Cyrus the Great died in 529BCE, both north and south Iran had been brought together under Achaemenid rule and most of Libya, Sudan and Egypt were added by the military campaigns of his son, Cambyses II, before his own death in Egypt in 522BCE. Having just quelled an uprising against Cambyses, a small group of courtiers including Darius, a close relative, agreed that Cambyses's successor should be chosen by supernatural forces: the owner of the first horse to neigh at dawn would be crowned. Darius's groom decided to assist the gods and Darius was selected, only to be immediately faced with an Elamite revolt in southern Iran and uprisings in the northern regions. Order was restored, and Darius then campaigned successfully in India, returning with cargo loads of booty. Four years later the Achaemenid Empire was further extended by moving into Anatolia, crossing the Bosphorus and marching into the Balkans and along the river Danube, although a Greek revolt in 500BCE regained some ground. By the time of his death in 486BCE, he had consolidated the foundations of an empire of 23 peoples that was to last for another 200 years, using an efficient administration with standardised weights and measures run from at least three major centres: Ecbatana, Susa and Persepolis. His legal code, only fragments of which have survived, was praised by Plato. Merchants and others travelled safely along the patrolled Royal Road from Sardis in modern-day Turkey to Susa, and sailors navigated through the ancient Suez Canal, started and abandoned by the Egyptian pharaoh Necho but completed by Darius. As the Persepolis apadana foundation tablet proudly recorded: 'This is the kingdom which I hold from Saka beyond Soghdia to Ethiopia, from India to Sardis, which Ahura Mazda greatest of the gods presented me.' As his name suggested, he was the 'Holder of Good'.

Past the gate, on the left, are examples of bird-headed 'push-me-pull-you' addorsed animal capitals designed to carry ceiling crossbeams of Lebanese cedars; this *homa* bird is used as the logo of IranAir. Further on is the **Unfinished Gate**, which was probably one of the latest monuments to be erected on the terrace during Achaemenid rule, but the tour usually swerves to the right after the Gate of All Nations along the route the royal guests would have followed in the official processions. Their soldiers would continue straight ahead towards the Unfinished Gate.

The greatest palace on the site is the square-shaped **apadana** whose construction started in 515BCE and took 30 years to complete. The original 72 columns (36 interior and 36 exterior), of which only 13 remain, were styled as animal sculptures of two-headed bulls, lions and eagles, and were joined by oak and cedar beams. Two symmetrical staircases were built on the northern and eastern sides of the palace, and if the light is good you may wish to go immediately towards the right to photograph the **northern apadana staircase**. The informality of the carved figures, the Medes in their rounded caps and knee-length tunics, and the Persians with distinctive 'Victoria sponge finger' caps and long pleated robes, is charming. They slowly ascend up the left side chatting, carrying lotus buds, touching arms or holding hands. In the 19th century Lord Curzon must have felt very jaded to comment wearily, 'It is all the same, and the same again, and yet again … there is no variation in their steady, ceremonious tramp.'

Most visitors, however, continue past the sound and light seating to the second gate or doorway flanked by unfinished horse figures, once the formal entrance into the **Hall of 100 Columns** (70m²) and probably constructed c480–460BCE. These unfinished pieces show how the blocks were brought, set up and then carved in situ. Also note the unfinished column shafts and square bases. Having borne the brunt of Alexander the Great's arson attack, the hall no longer possesses the thick brick walls, once colourfully decorated with painted plaster or glazed tiles (as displayed in the National Museum, Tehran, and the Louvre, Paris) between the stone window and door frames. The far door-jamb reliefs, showing the enthroned Achaemenid ruler protected by his Median and Persian guards, suggest this was where the envoys presented their gifts, which were then stored in the Treasury beyond. Above, as on reliefs here and elsewhere (eg: Bisotun, Naqsh-e Rostam), a winged composition hovers over the royal canopy; it represents Ahura Mazda, the one uncreated God according to Zoroastrian scriptures, and/or the spirit of the royal ancestors holding out the ring of authority. The door jambs of the hall's side chambers are carved with a giant male figure, perhaps the emperor as the Perfect Hero, slaying evil spirits. Similar images are repeated on the doorways of the **Palace of Xerxes** near the museum.

To the far right is the famous main **eastern apadana staircase**, which can be glimpsed through rusting supports of an enormous canopy. Erected at the same time as the glass entrance, the canopy's purpose is likewise totally unclear. It is a badly designed, corroding eyesore, casting slanting shadows so infuriating for photographers. Furthermore, the reliefs are roped off, preventing close examination of the fine sculpted detail.

This staircase was uncovered in 1932, so it has the best-preserved reliefs. The right-hand section has lines of Medes and Persians representing the famous 10,000 Immortals, the imperial bodyguards, and attendants leading small horses, some with Elamite chariots, or carrying intricately worked furniture and textiles, etc. To the left side, the panels depict envoys from the 23 subject nations in fine detail, right down to the cuticles of their fingernails, bringing gifts. They are usually identified as in the key in the box on page 265.

Neither this nor the northern staircase still possesses its original centre panel of the enthroned ruler in situ. The central panel of the northern staircase is now in Tehran's National Museum, but the one from this eastern staircase is here albeit in the Treasury building near the site museum (see opposite). But both staircases retain their dramatic depictions of a voracious lion sinking its teeth and claws into the neck of a bull, which cause some to think Persepolis was used in Nou Rouz festivities symbolically representing the astrological season.

On reaching the **apadana** level, look back at the low central section of the eastern staircase, to see various stages of stone carving in the row of shield-bearing guards. The vast platform was the floor of an enormous audience hall capable of holding 10,000 people, covered with a timber roof supported by 36 interior columns, each 20m high, surmounted by a huge addorsed animal capital. Tall cedars from newly conquered Lebanon permitted Achaemenid masons to space out the column bases, unlike the more closely grouped ones seen at Pasargadae (page 272).

To the south, on a terrace some 2m higher, is the **Winter Palace of Darius** (Tashara, as given in the trilingual cuneiform inscription), built around 486BCE. It is entered by a western staircase ordered by Artaxerxes III, decorated with figures of servants (or possibly priests, as some appear to wear a *padam* – a white mask used to avoid polluting the sacred fire) carrying food, vessels and lambs. As with the apadana's bell-shaped column bases with lotus designs, there are echoes of Egyptian architectural detail here with the curved mouldings over the doors. The intimate scale of this room, the polished stone, the remains of a red plaster floor and the low reliefs showing royal attendants with parasol, fly whisk, towel and perfume box have led some archaeologists to identify these rooms as royal private apartments with a bath. In the central area Darius I, again as the Perfect Hero, is depicted slaying legendary animals trying to enter. The now empty spaces between window and door frames would have been filled with mud-brick walls decorated with painted plaster or glazed brick.

Across the courtyard, due south, lies the **Palace of Artaxerxes III** (c359–338BCE), entered from staircases carved with further figures of delegates and attendants. A keen eye will spot the marks on stones at ground level left by the Achaemenid masons for positioning columns and corner stones. To the left (east) is the Hadish or **Palace of Xerxes** ('Ruling over Heroes') with its 36 columns and five doorways with low reliefs showing Xerxes himself. According to legend, the fire that destroyed Persepolis started in the Hadish. To its northeast is the small building known as the **Tripylon** because of its three doors. This is where the polished staircase, now in the National Museum, came from. On the eastern doorway, Xerxes is shown standing behind Darius who is seated on a throne, supported by representatives of the subject nations. Down in the hollow is the small **museum** (entry 500,000 rials) constructed in the Achaemenid style over the foundations of a building identified on very slim evidence as the **Harem** (Queen's apartments). It houses a number of the smaller treasures found on site, including an Achaemenid trumpet, and has a small book-cum-gift shop. To the far right of the entrance (exterior) are toilets, and facing the museum door a small cafeteria selling drinks.

In front of the hillside, low walls mark the **Treasury** buildings where tens of thousands of clay tablets were unearthed, recording, among other things, the numbers, nationalities and wages of the palace labourers. Its main feature today is the **central relief panel** from the eastern apadana staircase, moved here in late Achaemenid times. This damaged panel shows an enthroned Achaemenid emperor, perhaps Darius I or Xerxes, holding the royal staff and a lotus flower. Behind him are the crown prince, a court eunuch and an official, while in front a general pays homage.

If there's time (and especially if you aren't visiting nearby Naqsh-e Rostam; see below), walk up the hillside for a good panoramic view and a close-up of two of the four **royal tombs** cut into the rock. There are stairs behind the Treasury and paths to the side of the sound and light seating, the latter an easier path. The tomb above the Hall of 100 Columns is thought to have housed the bones of Artaxerxes II (d358BCE); the other further on behind the Treasury was perhaps constructed for Artaxerxes III (d338BCE), but the owners of the other two concealed from immediate view are not known. (The title Artaxerxes meant 'Ruling through Truth'.)

NAQSH-E ROSTAM نقش رستم

A 3km drive northwards from Persepolis across the main Shiraz to Esfahan road brings you to **Naqsh-e Rostam** (⊕ autumn–winter 08.00–17.00, spring–summer 07.30–20.00; entry 500,000 rials). Take your binoculars or telephoto lens. The words *naqsh* (picture) and 'Rostam', a legendary Persian warrior (see Matthew Arnold's poem *Sohrab and Rostam*), were given to this place by locals seeing the Sasanid rock reliefs of jousting and investiture scenes, which they had thought represented Rostam, but the **four Achaemenid tombs** carved high into the rock face are more dramatic for today's visitors.

The first, on the left, was probably the tomb for Darius II (d405BCE); the next for Artaxerxes I (d424BCE); the third, and most imposing, held the remains of Darius the Great (d486BCE); and the last, on the adjoining rock face, was carved for Xerxes

I (d465BCE) or possibly Xerxes II (d423BCE). Why the rock face was worked in such a cruciform shape is unclear. Perhaps it symbolised the empire, covering the four quarters of the known world, the four cardinal points or perhaps an abstract stylisation of the Ahura Mazda figure (the head and torso, the protective wings, etc) and symbolising four central elements in Zoroastrianism – water, wind, earth and fire. Or perhaps the surfaces were prepared for inscription panels, as at Bisotun, which were never added.

As with the Persepolis tombs, the Achaemenid ruler is depicted as if standing above a columned portico, making an offering to the fire altar with the composite Ahura Mazda figure flying above, depicting most probably the coronation (*taj gozari*) ceremony. He stands on a platform (which, incidentally, has the same proportions as Solomon's dais, as mentioned in Chronicles II) held up by representatives of the subject nations. Their inclusion is deliberate, for the Darius tomb inscription states: 'If now you shall think: how many are the countries which King Darius held? Look at the sculpture.'

Before going over to the rock reliefs below the tombs, walk over to the half-submerged stone cube building to appreciate the original ground level. Known locally as the **Kaba-ye Zardosht** ('Zoroaster's Ka'ba' or 'shrine'), it is a single-storey building with one entrance and no windows, standing 12.6m high. Perhaps inspired by earlier (Anatolian) Urartian architecture, it is clearly Achaemenid but its function is a mystery, although it is far better preserved than its Pasargadae cousin (page 273). It could not have been a fire temple as there is no smoke vent. Perhaps it held royal archives or royal battle standards or served as a mortuary chamber. According to another theory, 12 larger and 365 smaller square carvings across the perimeter of its four walls, suggest that the building functioned as a solar calendar. There is a long inscription along the bottom at the far right of the staircase, but this is Sasanid, added by the high priest Kartir recording the victories of Shapur I, including his own name wherever possible, stating that he, Kartir, was responsible for establishing fire temples in Cappadocia, Syria, Armenia and Georgia.

Clearly the Sasanid shahs wanted to associate themselves, historically and visually, with the Achaemenid monuments in this place. Apart from this inscription there are **seven Sasanid panels**. Starting on the far left by the boundary fence, they are as follows:

A Ardashir I on the left with a courtier behind is invested with the ring of authority by Ahura Mazda, holding the sacred *barsom* of twigs (for tending the sacred fire), carved near the end of his reign in c240CE. Here, as on other Sasanid reliefs, the shah sees himself as the equal, physically at least, of the deity. His horse tramples on the last Parthian king, while Ahura Mazda's steed crushes Ahriman, the evil one.

B The next relief on a convex surface shows Bahram II (d291CE) with his courtiers, each with distinctive headgear. This was carved over a much earlier panel, c9th century BCE, of which the figure of an Elamite king is clearly visible on the far right, whereas to the far left the crowned head of his queen is less distinct.

C Under the first tomb and opposite the stone building is an unidentified Sasanid jousting scene.

D Under the second tomb is another jousting scene, possibly showing Bahram V causing his opponent to fall dramatically from his horse.

E Below Darius's tomb, slightly to the left, Shapur I on horseback holds captive the Roman emperor Valerian, while a kneeling Philip the Arab sues for peace (page 257). Behind is the bust of his vizier, the high priest Kartir, responsible for collating the remains of the Zoroastrian scriptures after Alexander the Great burned the Achaemenid library, and who initiated official persecution of Christians and Jews in the Sasanid Empire.

F Directly under the tomb are two Sasanid equestrian battles, one over the other. The shah lancing the enemy's horse is probably Hormuzd II (r302–09CE) or perhaps Bahram II.

G A relief showing Shah Narseh (d301CE) with two attendants, invested with the ring of authority by the Zoroastrian divinity, Anahita; between them the small figure is, perhaps, the crown prince. The depiction of Anahita, the goddess of fertility and also of war, indirectly supports the theory that the Kaba-e Zardosht was a depository for battle flags. One of her main temples was located at Istakhr nearby (see below).

If you have a free hour, walk up the hill to view the two fire altars still standing on the top. The path is situated behind the first Sasanid relief (A) but outside the perimeter fence.

Return to the main Shiraz–Esfahan road. Opposite the junction is a lay-by in front of **Naqsh-e Rajab** (نقش رجب) (⊕ 08.00–18.00; entry 300,000 rials), so called after a former local café owner. The site was first mentioned in 1763 by Carsten Niebuhr on his journey to Arabia Felix. Only since late 2001 has the metal fence been erected. The ticket booth is occasionally unmanned and locked, as is the gate. Exactly why these important Sasanid investiture reliefs are carved here is unclear. The first relief on the left, possibly worked in c250CE, shows Shapur I on horseback, with his distinctive crown and a bilingual inscription on his chest, while behind him are courtiers and perhaps the crown prince. On the panel almost opposite he is shown again, taking the ring of authority from Ahura Mazda on the left, so perhaps this relief commemorates Shapur's investiture in March 242CE. As at Naqsh-e Rostam, both god and shah are shown as equal in size. The last relief at the back depicts Shapur's father, Ardashir I, the first of the dynasty, with Ahura Mazda on the right handing him the ring while holding a *barsom* for the sacred fire. The figure behind Ardashir is probably Shapur, then the crown prince, and behind him – and clearly added later – the *éminence grise* (high priest Kartir), crooking his finger in respect. In the inscription his hand is pointing at heaven and hell, thereby proclaiming Kartir's view on the afterlife. Between Ardashir and his god are children, perhaps the shah's grandsons. Two female figures to the far right complete the panel: these are thought to represent the queen, or Ardashir's mother with an attendant, but it is a mystery why they are depicted apparently leaving the scene.

✗ **WHERE TO EAT AND DRINK** You could ponder over the mystery of the Naqsh-e Rajab reliefs in the pleasant nearby garden restaurant, **Laneh-e Tavoos** (m 0917 1280057; $), identified by a white stone porch just set back from the main road, on the same side of the road as Naqsh-e Rajab. It often caters for tour groups so service is efficient, with reliably good food. There is usually one English-speaking member of staff on duty, and the toilets are spotless.

ISTAKHR اصطخر

The place perhaps most associated with the Sasanid dynasty is Istakhr, 7km north of Persepolis. An ancestor served as high priest at Istakhr's Temple of Anahita, which following the Arab conquest had to give way to a mosque, and it is possible the shahs' investitures were celebrated here. But as only one column and a few corner blocks remain standing, the site requires a great deal of imagination. Preliminary excavation many years ago revealed a vast walled enclosure (1,400m × 650m), with stone blocks re-used from Persepolis. Taken by the Arabs in 643CE, it was later totally sacked as punishment for a local rebellion, and by the 11th century only a village of 100 inhabitants remained. The site is totally overgrown but lots of Sasanid shards of the distinctive turquoise-blue glazed earthenware still lie on the surface. Foreign visitors rarely stop here, so expect any passing police or army vehicle to drive over to check you out.

PASARGADAE پاسارگاد

About 115km further on towards Esfahan, past brick kilns, is the turn-off for Pasargadae. Some 4km from the village of Kord-e Shul, the site is not regularly served by any intercity bus. There is a **Pasargad Restaurant** (✆071 43582660; w pasargadrestaurant.com; ⏲ b/fast, lunch & dinner), located just off the main road well before the village, which offers a good and filling buffet. Go through the village, bearing left at the fork, until the road is barred; the **ticket office** (with toilets) is on the right.

Undoubtedly, Persepolis was a ceremonial centre fit for an emperor, but **Pasargadae** (classified as a World Heritage Site in 2004) (⏲ autumn–winter 08.00–17.00, spring–summer 07.30–20.00; entry 500,000 rials), the first capital of the Achaemenids, was built on a more intimate, smaller scale, as if catering for a warlord about to emerge on the world stage. Founded in around 546BCE by Cyrus II as his own and entirely Persian capital, Pasargadae (possibly meaning 'the camp of the Persians') was not finished before his death in 530 or 529BCE and had remained the capital of the empire until the construction of Persepolis.

The first European to have come here was the Venetian, Josafat Barbaro, who visited Pasargadae in 1474. Subsequent travellers left numerous accounts and descriptions of the site, but it was only in 1949–54 that excavation work started here. It was continued by the British Institute of Persian Studies in the 1960s, when the full extent of the site was realised. The first monument to be seen is the **Tomb of Cyrus the Great** (d529BCE) standing on its three-stepped platforms, the lowest one measuring 13.5m × 12.2m. Alexander the Great came here during his conquest of Persia and the tomb is the only monument at Pasargadae described by the Greeks who followed him. The tomb chamber has a simple almost square form (5.25m², 6m high) with a gabled roof. Its form has reminded scholars of Mesopotamian work, Turkish Phrygian or 7th-century BCE Urartian buildings (perhaps Cavustepe, by Lake Van in eastern Turkey). A few of the lead and iron swallow-tail clamps remain in situ, but the small entry doors have long gone, as have all the precious treasures they protected. Nor can you see from ground level the simple rosette form carved on top of the roof gable; such multi-petalled motifs, perhaps symbolising fertility, prosperity or the wingless disc of Ahura Mazda, are repeated throughout Persepolis. And there is no sign either of the tomb inscription recorded by Strabo: 'O man, I am Cyrus who founded the empire of the Persians and was king of Asia. Grudge me not this monument.'

The stone used to build the Tomb of Cyrus and most of the monuments at Pasargadae is white arenaceous limestone. Originating in the mountain quarries northwest of the village of Sivand, some 50km from Pasargadae, it could not be procured in time for the Shah's 1971 monarchy celebrations and cheaper materials had to be purchased from Shiraz merchants. The stone eventually used for repairs contained great amounts of sand and the chalk-white colour had to be given a patina. The stone, however, did not take on the colour evenly and dark spots can still be seen on the tomb's surface.

Follow the road into the site. In the hills immediately in front a huge retaining wall and terrace are still visible, known locally since the 15th century as **Takht-e Madar-e Soleyman** (Throne of Solomon's Mother) or Tel-e Takht ('hill of the throne'), and similarly Cyrus's tomb was locally attributed to her. This was the main **citadel** area, occupied until its destruction by the Seleucids in 280BCE; across from it is a platform with two stone **fire altars**.

In the foreground at ground level, looking like a Hollywood film-set prop supported by scaffolding (this time essential) is all that remains of a single-storey building, known locally as the **Zendan-e Soleyman** (Solomon's Prison). It probably pre-dates its cousin at Naqsh-e Rostam (page 270), as here there is no sign of marks left by the Greek toothed chisel, but its function is just as enigmatic. The total height of the structure including the plinth is 14m. The two blind windows had once been decorated with black limestone, but none of it has remained. Interestingly, this building and an identical one in Naqsh-e Rostam are the only two examples of this construction style, making it difficult to establish their exact functionality.

The road to the right leads eventually to ruins of a **gatehouse**, a small chamber whose huge stone corner blocks once supported mud-brick walls. The eight large column bases are set remarkably close together, suggesting construction pre-dated the Achaemenid conquest of Lebanon and easy access to its famous cedars used for ceiling beams. The four doorways were once embellished by human-headed bull sculptures as in Persepolis, but their present whereabouts (since the late 1930s) is unknown. However, one low relief remains to fox the archaeologists. It features a standing, winged genie figure facing into the building; its headgear is Egyptian in form, its robe Elamite and its four-winged stance is Assyrian. Perhaps it symbolises the submission and offerings of these conquered peoples entering into the Achaemenid stronghold.

Retracing your steps on the road, there is the first of two audience halls, known as the **Palace with the Column** or the **Palace of Audience,** whose columns, except for one, were removed to build a mosque near Cyrus's tomb. Again, huge corner blocks once supported the walls, one with a trilingual cuneiform inscription recording: 'I Cyrus, the king, the Achaemenid, built this.' Around the eight-columned central hall on all four sides were porticoes with stone doorways. Their carved decoration suggests to some visitors that this was a temple rather than an audience hall; only the feet and ankles have survived but one set appears to belong to a priest in a fish-like costume accompanied by standing bulls and huge bird forms. In Persepolis a similar combination, but much more confrontational, can be found (page 267).

Further on to the right are the remains of a larger audience hall known as the **Private Palace** or the **Residential Palace of Cyrus the Great** with some 30 central column bases and two porticoes, one originally stretching the length of the building. Its flooring is worth looking at, a veritable jigsaw of limestone slabs with small repairs to imperfections. Polished, it would have served Fred Astaire and Ginger Rogers splendidly. Facing into the building from this portico, the corner block to the left carries another of the 24 trilingual inscriptions found on the site, which records 'Cyrus the Great King the Achaemenid'; the omission of the personal pronoun leads some scholars to suggest that a successor, perhaps Darius, ordered the carving. At the far end a doorway relief, to the height of 1.5m, showing a standing figure in a pleated robe inscribed with cuneiform characters, again reads 'Cyrus, the Great King'. There are small drilled holes, perhaps to carry jewels or gold plaques as at Persepolis. Next to the palaces are the remains of the earliest known example of the Persian fourfold garden design – *chahar bagh*. Some scholars have even suggested that the splendour of Pasargadae at its zenith decorated with architectural motifs from Babylonia and Egypt would have surpassed the grandeur of Persepolis itself.

Walking back to the tarmac surface, look for signs of stone water channels. In 1963 David Stronach found evidence of a garden with a pavilion, and unearthed a jar containing jewellery, beads and charms, hidden in Achaemenid times perhaps to foil Alexander's men. Classical literature suggests that even the Tomb of Cyrus the Great was once surrounded by a luxuriant garden.

10

The South Coast

For centuries this mainly Arabic-speaking region was one of the most prosperous in all Iran, handling the cargoes and supplying the ships calling in for water, food and repairs on their voyages to and from Europe and Asia. Many locals here are ethnically Arab and speak Arabic or a local Arabic-based dialect as their first language. The Arab invasion of Iran started from Khuzestan province and followed on from the Battle of al-Qadissiyah (modern-day Iraq, near Kufa) in 636; it was the most significant and defining stage of the Arab advancement into Iranian territory.

The 'discovery' of the sea route around Africa by Vasco da Gama resulted in a certain loss of trade, and Shah Abbas I battled endlessly to promote the advantages of shipping Persian silk and Indian chintzes from these Iranian ports on the south coast. He had limited success, possibly because European merchants and sailors found the high humidity and extreme summer temperatures very difficult, and because once the cargoes were unloaded traders were still faced by tortuous journeys into the interior. Caravans and travellers also had to contend with raids by tribesmen; even in the 1920s and 1930s foreign oil companies paid protection money to the tribes to prevent damage to the oil lines and installations. The one wide river, the Karun, was not navigable until 19th-century British soldiers took matters into their own hands and blew obstructing rocks and boulders out of the water. At present it remains the only navigable river in Iran and the only river that is not seasonal.

The Iran–Iraq War set back the oil, petroleum and natural gas industrial development in this region, but now a number of projects, in particular the world's largest South Pars natural gas field (accounting for 8% of the world's gas reserves) with the facilities in the port of Asalouyeh, are back on track despite some setbacks, including Total's withdrawal in 2018 from the South Pars project under pressure from the US. In addition to its wealth of natural resources, the region is also famous for high-quality dates; 40% of the Iranian export of this delicacy is produced in Khuzestan province. Khuzestan is also home to Iran's community of Mandaeans, numbering between 5,000 and 10,000 people. The origins of this Gnostic group are dated to pre-Christian times and their belief focuses on John the Baptist, hence the importance of baptism to their practices and traditions.

Once in this part of Iran, unless you are travelling between late October/ November and February/early March when temperatures are moderate, do leave very early in the morning. Remember Strabo's words: 'Although Susa is fertile, it has a hot and scorching atmosphere', and there is little shade.

AHVAZ اهواز *Telephone code 061*

Ahvaz, also spelt Ahwaz (altitude 17m; population 1.4 million) once witnessed Achaemenid ships unloading goods for transportation on the 'Royal Road' to Susa

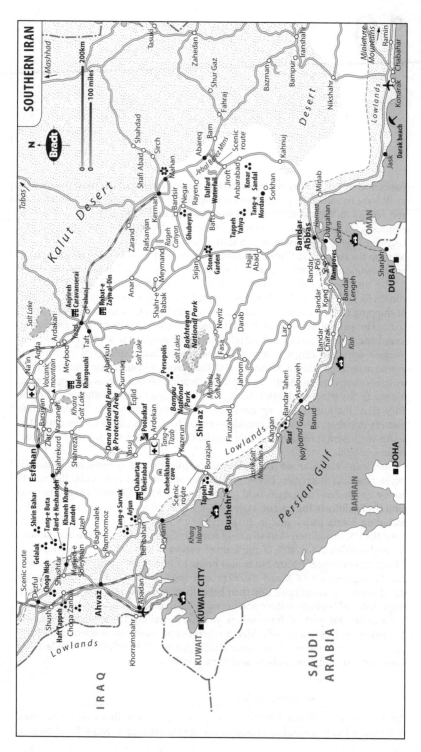

and Persepolis, and later the fleets of Alexander the Great moored here on their return from the Indian campaign. The port and town centre were developed by the early Sasanid shahs and an extensive Christian community here had its own bishop by 410CE. Its fortunes declined in the 630s CE after the Arab conquests, and uprisings against the Abbasid regime in Baghdad in the 9th century brought further retribution. Matters did not improve, with the Mongol armies blamed for the destruction of the 9th-century bridge-cum-dam, and by the 14th century Ahvaz had an unhealthy reputation for voracious mosquitoes and jaundice. The local economy revived a little in 1857 when Anglo-Indian troops were stationed there during the Anglo–Persian War; and the opening up of the lower Karun River area in 1888, which facilitated water transport, led to a new settlement, but still the population was estimated at a mere 700 people.

Then oil production started in the Masjed-e Soleyman area and Ahvaz was established as the provincial capital in 1926. In fact, the so-called Chah-e shomareh Yek ('well number one') in Masjed-e Soleyman was the first oil well dug in the Middle East. It was completed in 1908 when oil exploration in the area was under the command of the Englishman George Bernard Reynolds. The discovery of oil here was reportedly the cornerstone of the formation of the Anglo-Persian Oil Company (presently known as BP). With the disruption of the late 1970s, many of the 330,000 inhabitants left and did so again in the 1980s because of the Iran–Iraq War, when on 22 September 1980 the Iraqi Air Force started its attack on the city. However, Ahvaz was not extensively bombed (unlike Dezful) because, it was rumoured, Saddam Hussein's mother-in-law came from Ahvaz. The 1986 census (during the war) gave the population as 580,000. Ahvaz is the capital of Khuzestan province, which is locally known as 'the land of the sun and water'. The city today is arranged on a grid plan with a tortuous one-way system. Foreign visitors come to Ahvaz for business purposes, or to see the archaeological sites in the region; the city itself is modern and otherwise has little to offer.

GETTING THERE AND AWAY The quickest and easiest way to Ahvaz is **by air** from Tehran. There are numerous daily 1½-hour flights with various Iranian airlines, including Mahan Air and Aseman. The airport here is also linked by frequent flights to other Iranian cities, such as Esfahan, Shiraz and Mashhad. The availability of flights to Dubai from Ahvaz fluctuates in line with the state of the Iranian economy and US sanctions. Flydubai no longer operates flights to the UAE, but Kish Air and Qeshm Air still fly to Dubai from Ahvaz up to four times a week. The same is valid for IranAir flying once a week to Kuwait. There are plans to relocate the existing airport 15km from the city due to the discovery of oil deposits under the runway, but no schedule has been finalised at the time of writing. The National Iranian Oil Company confirmed the purchase of the airport in 2012.

There are up to four daily **train** services from Tehran but the journey takes more than 15 hours (560,000–800,000 rials). Ahvaz is also served by frequent intercity **buses** from the major centres, including convenient overnight VIP services. The city has a number of **bus stations**, depending on the destination. Siyahat terminal (also known as Seh Rah Khorramshahr) [278 A3] caters for both Esfahan and Tehran, as well as Shush and Shushtar; head for the right wing of the terminal. Buses for Abadan leave from Abadan–Shadegan terminal [278 B4], a good 10-minute taxi ride away. Please note that no public transport operates on Fridays. The main **roads** are good but the lorries and oil tankers plying between Ahvaz, Abadan or Bushehr and the interior mean congestion is inevitable. An oil pipeline runs next to the

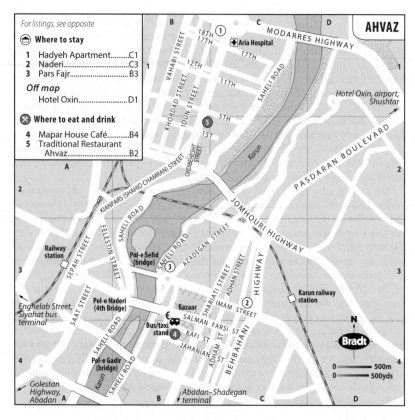

For listings, see opposite

Where to stay

1 Hadyeh Apartment..........C1
2 Naderi.............................C3
3 Pars Fajr.........................B3

Off map
Hotel Oxin.......................D1

Where to eat and drink

4 Mapar House Café...........B4
5 Traditional Restaurant
   Ahvaz...........................B2

AHVAZ

Aria Hospital

Hotel Oxin, airport, Shushtar

MODARRES HIGHWAY

PASDARAN BOULEVARD

JOMHOURI HIGHWAY

Railway station

Pol-e Sefid (bridge)

Pol-e Naderi (4th Bridge)

Enghelab Street, Siyahat bus terminal

Bazaar

Bus/taxi stand

Karun railway station

Pol-e Gadir (bridge)

Golestan Highway, Abadan

Abadan–Shadegan terminal

0 ——— 500m
0 ——— 500yds

N

Bradt

motorway, and approaching Ahvaz from the south you will be welcomed to this region by numerous oil rigs with gas flares. Below is a bus departure schedule with selected times from major Iranian cities:

From	Departure	Price (rials)
Esfahan (Kaveh)	08.00; 09.00; 11.00; 13.00; 14.00; 17.30; 19.30; 20.30; 21.00; 21.30; 22.00; 22.45; 23.00	500,000–650,000
Esfahan (Sofeh)	00.30; 08.30; 09.15; 10.15; 11.45; 12.30; 13.30; 14.40; 18.30; 20.15; 21.15; 22.00; 22.45; 23.15; 23.45	500,000–650,000
Shiraz (Karandish)	16.00; 17.30; 20.00; 21.30	350,000–650,000
Tehran (southern)	08.10; 09.00; 11.15; noon; 12.30; 13.30; 14.00; 15.00; 16.00; 16.30; 17.00; 18.00; 18.30; 19.30; 20.00; 21.30; 22.00; 22.30	500,000–820,000

GETTING AROUND Once **in the city**, the best mode of transport is a **taxi**. Ahvaz still has no metro system, despite some suggestions to the contrary. Unless travelling on business, you will probably be here because you want to explore the **surrounding area**, which in spring turns a distinctive yellow from *golza* (oilseed rape) fields – it is a memorable feature of the province. From Shushtar, about an hour's drive away, you could continue to Shush (115km from Ahvaz; about 60km from Shushtar) and then visit Choga Zanbil. We would suggest this order of visits as you might well feel disappointed with the Susa excavation site.

TOUR GUIDE A very helpful and knowledgeable English-speaking guide who could take you, or organise tours, to the many interesting sites detailed in this chapter is Ahvaz-based **Ashkan Nezampour** (m 0916 6114373; w travelguide.ir). His assistance is particularly invaluable and recommended on the trips to the numerous ancient rock reliefs, particularly around Izeh and Behbahan.

WHERE TO STAY AND EAT A vibrant city, Ahvaz has nonetheless an exceptionally poor choice of hotels, and all activities within the city are limited to Kianpars (Shahid Chamran) Street or the main bazaar area in the old town.

Pars Fajr Hotel [278 B3] (130 rooms) Shahid Abedi St; 32234999; w pars-hotels. com. Founded in 1968, this hotel has welcome AC, & is near the river & well-known suspension bridge, known as Sefid (white) Bridge. By far the best in town among the very poor bunch. It has 2 traditional restaurants (**$$**). **$$$$**

Hadyeh Apartment Hotel [278 C1] (24 rooms/apts) 20th Alley, Kianpars St; 33914551; e info@hadyehcenter.com. The only accommodation in the vicinity of Kianpars, this hotel with a tiny lobby offers large & clean self-contained apts for up to 5 guests. **$$$**

Hotel Oxin [278 D1] (51 rooms) Pasdaran Bd, close to Airport Rd; 34474721; w oxinhotel. com. Close to the airport, but quite a distance away from the city centre, with modern facilities & service with a smile. **$$$**

Naderi Hotel [278 C3] (115 rooms) Imam Khomeini St; 32213081, 32213083, 32225757; w naderihotel.ir. Located in the old part of town near the central bazaar, the hotel caters for

business travellers from around the Persian Gulf. Not devoid of old-fashioned charm, it has pristine & smallish, but regrettably somewhat windowless rooms. The staff are friendly & Wi-Fi is reliable. **$$$**

Mapar House Café & Restaurant [278 B4] Ferdowsi St, between Kafi & Jahanian sts; ⏰ 09.00–midnight. With a cosy café in the inner courtyard & a restaurant at basement level, Mapar is a much-needed addition to the Ahvazian eating-out scene. Opened in 2017, this historic, but heavily restored mansion still oozes some of its original charm. The menu is extensive & includes Persian classics with a local twist of extra spices & sauces. Fish dishes are particularly recommended. **$$**

Traditional Restaurant Ahvaz [278 B2] Kianpars St; 33921811, 33921709. A locally known restaurant serving good Iranian food & freshly baked *tanuri* bread. Although in need of a little extra maintenance, the food is good. **$$**

SHUSHTAR شوشتر *Telephone code 061*

Shushtar (approximately 100km north of Ahvaz) was once famous for its exquisite silks and other luxury textiles, one orator comparing the fabrics with 'every flowering plant in spring, the dewy freshness on the cheek of his mistress'. The Karun River splits in two in the north of the city at Sasanid dam **Band-e Meyzan** (بند میزان), and surrounds Shushtar. This then creates an island between its western and eastern flows that merge approximately 50km further on at **Band-e Qyer** (بند قیر) dam.

Shushtar first appears to have come to prominence in the Ilam due to its proximity to Choga Zanbil. It was an important centre under the Sasanids, who built the city's extensive system of channels. There are a few remains of the great dams-cum-bridges and channels, constructed by Roman prisoners of war in the 3rd century. One barrage of dressed stone and concrete (**Band-e Qeysar** or Valerian's Bridge) is seen when arriving from Dezful. Also visible high up on an outcrop are the ruins of the upper citadel with 18th-century walls on Sasanid foundations, with 3rd-century, rock-cut tunnels to provide agricultural irrigation. Further along the road on an outcrop, with its white sugarloaf dome

10

and two minarets, is the **Shrine of Khajeh Khezr-e Zendeh** (خواجه خضر زنده) (the 'Green Man'), reputedly the anonymous friend of the Prophet Moses described in the Quran (Q18:59–81). Local tradition holds that Hajji Khezr took a boat to Abadan, telling the boatman to accompany him as he walked. The boatman refused but the boat followed, recognising his saintliness, and its anchor is kept as a relic in his shrine at Abadan (page 291).

In Shushtar itself there is the mid-9th-century **masjed-e jame**, one of a dozen or so in Iran retaining something of its early 'Arab' plan, evident in the fat piers placed parallel to the enclosing walls. A major rebuilding scheme was completed c1125 when its *minbar* and *mihrab* were probably installed. The minaret, with its glazed bricks spelling out the word Allah, was built in 1419. The courtyard is now full of girders and this structure is covered in corrugated iron. The space is divided in two for gender separation to increase the prayer space, but the old interior is somewhat decayed and the *mihrab* has disappeared.

The town has a pleasant welcoming atmosphere. On the northern outskirts the road passes over a small modern dam, **Abshar** ('waterfall'), built on Sasanid foundations, which are part of the UNESCO World Heritage-protected dam complex (entry 500,000 rials). A narrow staircase to one side heads down to impressive archaeological remains of the mill races, drop towers, rock-cut steps and carved rock channels to the left and right. In the 1930s there were some 40 mills here grinding silica (for glass making), sugarcane and cereals. Only a few mills remain in private hands, and the Sasanid bridge has been destroyed, but the area is being imaginatively landscaped as a park. Some mills have been restored as museums.

There are also the remains of Iran's second electricity supply station, Mostofizadeh, built here in 1941 and a traditional two-sided *jajim* rug-weaving workshop run by Haj Rajabali Forozan Zadeh (m 0936 7914488).

Perched high above the watermills and accessed by a flight of steps from inside the site, is the Qajar-period **Marashi's Historical House** (⊕ 09.00–14.00 daily; entry free). Originally owned by Seyyed Mohammad Hassan Khan from an influential Marashi family, the house is open to the public to marvel at the traditional *khavun chini* brickwork on the walls.

Also in this region is the site of **Gelalak** (about 77km northeast of Masjed-e Soleyman, in the mountains; latitude 32.38, longitude 49.71), excavated since 1986 by the Iran Cultural Heritage Organisation. Five splendid brick tombs, one with a pottery sarcophagus decorated with vines and garlands, have reportedly been found, along with burial finds thought to date from the Parthian period (1st–2nd century CE).

TOUR GUIDE Local tour guide and driver **Mehran Saadi** (m 0939 0565959; w mehransaadi.com) is based at Tabib Traditional Hotel (see below) and can arrange interesting and informative tours in the surrounding area, the entire province and the city itself.

WHERE TO STAY AND EAT

🏠 Tabib Traditional Hotel & Afzal Hotel (15 rooms) Imam Khomeini intersection, Sangfarsh St, next to Afzal Caravanserai; ☎36227474, 36227477; w tabib.house. 2 adjacent traditional hotels operating under the same management. Built by the affluent Afzal family of merchants, this Qajar property was eventually sold to the Tabib family trading in medicine & perfume. It is now a traditional hotel tucked away in the quieter section of the bazaar area & offers a variety of rooms from mid-range to more expensive options in the Tabib section that also has a lovely & relaxing inner courtyard. **$$–$$$**

Mostofi Restaurant 36210909; 11.30–23.00 daily. This architecturally interesting historic house, encompassing a mosque, *hamam* & even a bridge, was once owned by a prominent merchant family from Shushtar. Now it is a traditional restaurant indoors with a very pleasant outdoors seating area overlooking the remains of the Band-e Qaisar bridge across the Karun River. **$$**

SHUSH شوش *Telephone code 061*

The town of Shush (population 87,000) is located 197km north of Ahvaz and is reachable by regular *savari* service from the Shush/Shushtar terminal. The journey takes around 1 hour. The town's main claim to fame is the remains of the ancient city of **Susa** (also called Shush in Persian) in its centre that it has effectively grown to incorporate. Shush suffered during the Iran–Iraq War, when at times the front line was a mere 4km away. Few scars are now visible, but the extensive archaeological site has over recent years suffered some wear and tear due to it being used as a public park.

HISTORY OF SUSA It was a British amateur archaeologist, William Loftus, who in the 1850s first identified Susa with the biblical Shushan and located some Achaemenid palace remains, but Sir Henry Rawlinson persuaded the British Museum that the site had little to offer. So French archaeological teams took over from 1885 and this is why such a wonderful range of artefacts from Susa is displayed in the Louvre Museum, Paris, instead of London. Arguably, the most significant find they made was the black stele containing the Code of Hammurabi, unearthed in 1901. Archaeological work is still continuing.

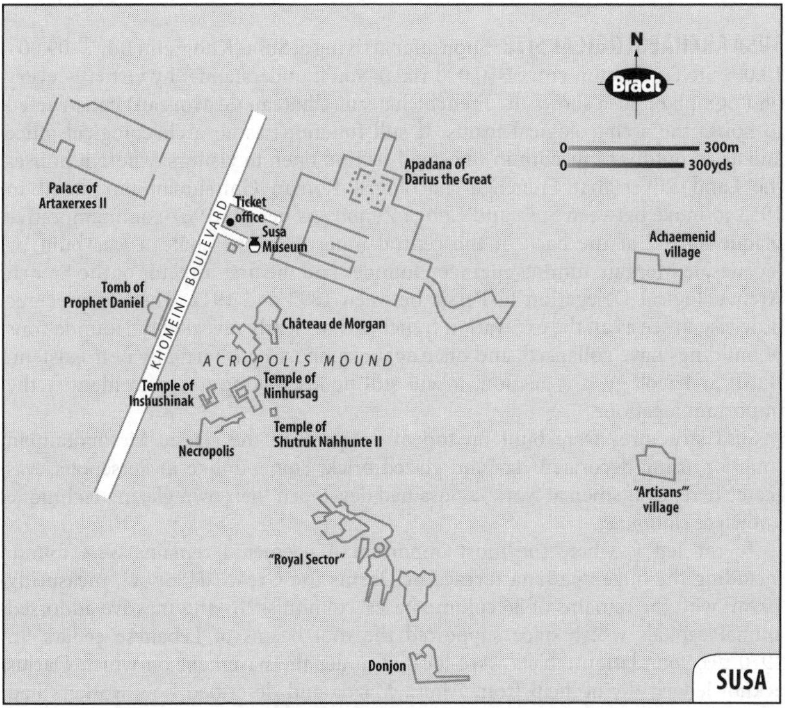

The earliest carbon-14 dating, c4300–3500BCE, was recorded from finds mainly discovered in the *massif funéraire* (funerary mound) with numerous burials and the *haute terrasse*, a mud-brick platform known as the Acropolis sector, suggesting that Susa was already an important religious and ceremonial centre.

It was from the Acropolis sector that a bronze and copper statue of Queen Napirasu, wife of Untash Napirisha (r1359–1333BCE) known from Choga Zanbil, was uncovered in 1903 in the **Temple of the Goddess Ninhursag**. Weighing 1,750kg, it stands now headless 1.29m high, inscribed with a warning to anyone causing it damage that 'his name shall become extinct, that his offspring be barren'. Unlike Choga Zanbil, where construction ceased after Nebuchadnezzar's invasion, new buildings at Susa were erected, perhaps to mark the victories of the Susan ruler against the Babylonians, and to exploit a new ceramic technology in making glazed moulded bricks. Then the city declined into obscurity, only to be devastated by the Assyrian armies in c640BCE, in a sacking that continued for over 50 days.

About a century later it was rebuilt by the Achaemenid rulers as their winter capital, and it is this settlement that is associated with the story of Esther and her uncle Mordechai (page 136), the biblical Shushan king 'Ahasuerus' being either Darius the Great's son and successor, Xerxes I, or possibly Artaxerxes I, his grandson. It was from Susa that Xerxes set out against Greece and Athens, an action that later provided Alexander the Great with a motive to destroy Persepolis (page 263). Alexander's generals continued to reside here after his death in 323BCE, as did the Parthians, but the final battle between the Parthian, Artabanus V, and the Sasanid leader, Ardashir I, in 224CE resulted in great damage. Further destruction followed in c339CE, possibly linked to Shapur II's persecution of Christians in the town.

SUSA ARCHAEOLOGICAL SITE Soon after arriving at Susa (Khomeini Bd; ⊕ 09.00–18.00; site & museum entry 350,000 rials), you'll understand why virtually every photograph of Susa shows the French château (**Château de Morgan**) constructed to house the archaeological teams. It still functions as an archaeological office and as an outdoor museum in the small section open to visitors, where it houses the Land Rover that French archaeologist Roman Ghirshman purchased in 1953 to move between Susa and Choga Zanbil. As per the 1967 commemorative plaque affixed at the back of the central inner gate, the château was built by Jacques de Morgan, mining engineer, founder and the first director of the French Archaeological Delegation in Persia between 1897 and 1912. There is precious little else to see as all the excavation trenches that clearly revealed the foundations of buildings have collapsed, and once again signposting is virtually non-existent. But if archaeology is a passion, it will still be fascinating to try to identify the important locations.

Susa structures were built on top of a *tappeh* in the classic Mesopotamian tradition using decorated clay and glazed brick. Stone, unlike in Persepolis, was scarce here. Craftsmen at work in Susa had developed their own glazing technique known as *cloisonné*.

To the left is where the most important Achaemenid remains were found, including the huge **apadana terrace of Darius the Great** (d486BCE), measuring 109m² with the remains of 36 column bases, column shafts and massive addorsed animal capitals which once supported the roof beams of Lebanese cedars. In 1970 two foundation tablets were located under the pavement on which Darius acknowledged divine help from Ahura Mazda and described how workers had come from all over the empire – Babylonian brickmakers, Assyrian carpenters, Egyptians and others – as indeed had the treasures, such as gold from Anatolia and Afghanistan, lapis lazuli, turquoise and cornelian from central Asia, silver from Egypt and ivory from Ethiopia and India. Your imagination will have to go into overdrive to envisage the colour and ornateness of the original decoration of the ceiling and walls. Any surviving painted plaster and glazed brick panels of pacing animals and motionless military guards and attendants were all removed to Paris, with a few examples going to Tehran.

Was it here or in the enormous Palace of Darius (246m × 155m) to the south that Esther revealed the duplicity of the minister Haman, plotting to kill all the Jews, and was it here that Alexander the Great held the celebrations in 324BCE to mark the wedding of 10,000 of his soldiers to Persian women? Did either of these legendary figures enter through the monumental doorway (40m × 30m) where the fragmented granite statue of Darius, now in Tehran (page 112), was found in 1972, its quadrilingual inscription recording his victories in Egypt? The mounds far behind the château mark the so-called **Royal Sector**, an area which the site guardian is unlikely to allow you to approach, where the French found evidence of at least 15 layers of occupation, reaching from 2700BCE up to the Islamic period. Remains of the streets and buildings uncovered dated from the Elamite period, c1900BCE, but this section, especially House A, proved to be rich in Seleucid figurines so this was probably where the Seleucid military garrison was stationed after the death of Alexander the Great. Various Seleucid inscriptions suggest that, as with Dura Europos in eastern Syria, a stadium, gymnasium, archive and law court were constructed along with at least three temples: to Apollo, to the Mesopotamian goddess Nanaya and to Ma, an Anatolian deity. Later this area was occupied in the Sasanid and early Islamic periods, up to the 10th century CE.

To the east in the distance is the '**Artisans' village**' where clear evidence of Seleucid and Parthian workshops, and an early Islamic mosque, were discovered. Immediately south of the château was the Acropolis where a mass burial place was found and the Elamite temples uncovered. It doesn't seem possible that from such a jumble of lumps and humps, such unique and fascinating artefacts were uncovered in such a marvellous state of preservation. Make a mental note to visit the Louvre in Paris to admire the surviving treasures.

Across the road from the Acropolis, the white sugarloaf conical roof of the **Tomb of the Prophet Daniel** (⏰ 08.00 until late evening; women & men use separate entrances; women must wear a chador – available to borrow in the courtyard of the site) is visible at the far end of a late Qajar courtyard. Many pilgrims throughout the centuries came here, especially during times of drought to pray for rain. This association with water goes back at least to the 12th century when the Seljuk ruler decreed that Daniel's body be put into a (rock) crystal coffin and suspended from the bridge. The present shrine has been carefully restored following serious damage by Iraqi bombardment, and prior to that, as a result of floods in 1869. The interior has mirror work and a shallow dome and the current shrine is also Qajar in style.

The remains of another Achaemenid palace came to light during ploughing in 1969, across the Shaur River to the northwest. Excavation uncovered an **apadana** of 64 wooden columns, probably constructed on the order of Artaxerxes II (d359BCE) because the cuneiform inscriptions on certain column bases on the earlier apadana of Darius record Artaxerxes's rebuilding works after a fire there during his predecessor's reign.

From Shush the road northwest goes towards Kermanshah, Khorramabad and Hamadan (page 133). Just south of **Dezful** (دزفول), itself almost obliterated during the Iran–Iraq War, there are two sites of textbook interest to the archaeologist and historian, but a very knowledgeable taxi driver or, even better, the very pleasant guide Ashkan Nezampour (page 279), is needed to find both: Choga Mish (about 25km south) and 6km further on, the Sasanid site of Gundeshapur. **Choga Mish** was first excavated in the early 1960s by the University of California (US). Besides Achaemenid and Parthian remains, the real interest lay in the early Elamite defence walls, platform and private houses, with a drainage system dating from the Proto-Elamite period (c3000BCE). Subsequently the team found evidence of earlier settlement, perhaps dating back to 7000BCE. Carbon deposits showed a serious fire caused damage around 4500BCE, and shortly afterwards about two-thirds of the site was abandoned, perhaps to be resettled at Choga Zanbil.

Jondi Shapur was a city rebuilt to a grid plan to accommodate the many Roman captives taken by the Sasanid shah Shapur I (r240–72CE), and it was perhaps here that the Emperor Valerian died, as did the founder of Manichaeism, Mani, in 276CE (see box, page 286). It was a Sasanid winter palace until the first half of the 4th century, but its real reputation came from Shapur's famous hospital, run on Hippocratic lines, which endured until 869CE when Baghdad became the centre for medical science. The city is mentioned in Syriac Christian documents, in the Talmud (eg: Beth Lapat, etc), and by the Byzantine chronicler, Procopius. The numerous surface Islamic pot shards on the site, described in the 1970s as 'indistinct clusters of low mounds', show it had been a cultural centre of some standing, with a strong Nestorian Christian community and housing the metropolitan bishop until 1318.

SOUTHEAST OF SHUSH/SUSA

CHOGA ZANBIL (چغازنبیل) ✳ (🕐 07.00–18.00; entry 500,000 rials) From Susa/Shush a short drive (30km) due south and then east will take you to Choga Zanbil, the Elamite city of Dur-Untash, which dates from around 1340BCE and was classified as a UNESCO World Heritage Site in 1979. The site was spotted from the air by oil survey engineers in 1935 and archaeologists were quickly sent in, but the main excavation campaign was delayed until 1950, lasting 12 years and recommencing after 1965.

The visitor is immediately struck by the huge brick-stepped construction nearly 3,500 years old, surrounded by remains of a vast walled precinct (1,200m × 800m) originally with seven gates. This ziggurat (105m²), originally with four, now three, terraces connected by external staircases, was surmounted by a temple dedicated to the god Inshushinak, 'Lord of Shush'; its total height was probably 53m. The similarity with ancient Mesopotamian ziggurats is striking but archaeological work has shown that this one at Choga Zanbil has a different construction, erected from the centre outwards; in other words, the highest (now vanished) section was built first and then each of the 'steps' built around to a lower height. All around the lower terrace there are, in every 11th row or so, bricks inscribed in Elamite cuneiform giving the name of Untash Napirisha (r1359–1333BCE), the king who ordered its building. The numerous remains of glazed brick, glass and ivory suggest that the exterior of the temple was richly decorated about two centuries later, and at least one wall (northeast) had moulded glazed tiles forming the figure of a huge winged bull, the symbol of Inshushinak, guarding the main staircase at ground

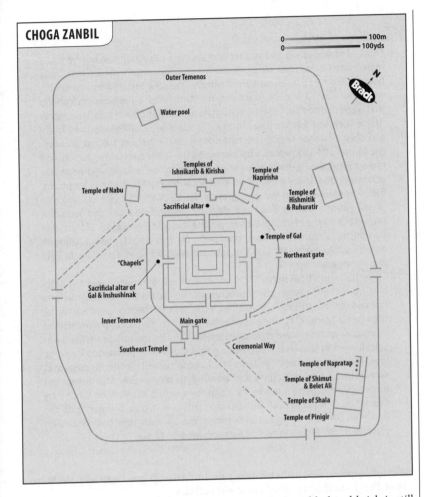

CHOGA ZANBIL

Outer Temenos

Water pool

Temples of Ishnikarib & Kirisha

Temple of Napirisha

Temple of Nabu

Temple of Hishmitik & Ruhuratir

Sacrificial altar

Temple of Gal

"Chapels"

Northeast gate

Sacrificial altar of Gal & Inshushinak

Inner Temenos

Main gate

Southeast Temple

Ceremonial Way

Temple of Napratap

Temple of Shimut & Belet Ali

Temple of Shala

Temple of Pinigir

level. Here and there, especially on the eastern wall, the odd glazed brick is still visible. At ground level there are still signs of the original sacrificial tables and a pit, presumably to catch the blood of the slain animals. A 12th-century BCE bronze tableau found at Susa, now in the Louvre, depicts two naked priests or worshippers kneeling between such tables and trees, preparing a sacrificial offering, one pouring water on to his colleague's outstretched hands. Just next to the brick construction, identified as a sacrificial altar plinth of Gal and Inshushinak, there is a footprint in the clay pavement, presumably that of an Elamite worker.

Iranian archaeological work from 1965 found yet more evidence that this was not the only temple within the precinct. In all, the remains of some 11 sanctuaries were identified along with three palaces, an elaborate water system of a reservoir and channels, tombs and tunnels, but everything suggests that after the invasion of Nebuchadnezzar I (r1125–1104BCE), all building stopped. The final end for this 'holy city' came around 640BCE with Ashurbanipal, the Assyrian ruler, who devastated the region, proudly recording: 'I levelled the whole of Elam, I deprived its fields of the sound of human voices, the tread of cattle and sheep, the refrain of joyous harvest songs.' Visitors are restricted to certain areas of the ground level and

MANI AND MANICHAEISM

Think of St Augustine and you think of an early Church father, but he was a Manichaean for at least nine years before his conversion. Mani himself was born in 216CE in southwest Iran of princely parents. Inspired by revelations when he was 12 and 24 years old, he formulated a religious philosophy that appealed to many in Iran, central Asia, China and west into Syria, north Africa, Italy and Roman Gaul. To him the essence of all religion was Truth, and that existence was a constant cosmic battle between Good and Evil, the former offering peaceful harmony and the latter constant agitation. The importance of such religious leaders as the Buddha, Zoroaster and Jesus was acknowledged, but their roles defined according to Manichaean scriptures. Believers were divided into two groups: the Elect and the Hearers. The role of the hearers was to assist the elect by performing tasks that would, if carried out by the elect themselves, pollute them, in the manner of Hinayana Buddhism. Circumcision was practised, as was vegetarianism (though hearers could eat meat), and the Sabbath kept, while in devotions St Paul was abhorred.

On his return from India, Mani converted the brother of Shapur I in 242CE and from then was greatly honoured at the Sasanid court. At this time Zoroastrianism, although influential, especially in the figure of Kartir the high priest (page 271), was not officially the state religion and Mani gained many converts in eastern and northwestern Iran. On Shapur's death Mani was still allowed to preach but succeeding shahs, probably persuaded by Kartir, were increasingly hostile. In 276CE Mani, accompanied by two disciples, was summoned before Bahram II and arrested, to die horribly in captivity. His followers were persecuted in Iran, and then across the Roman Empire by Diocletian, but pockets of Manichaeans survived in Iran and Iraq until the mid 10th century, dying out in Europe some 50 years later but continuing until the 15th century in central Asia and western China.

must follow prescribed paths between roped-off areas. A good spot with shady trees about 2km from the site would allow you to picnic.

HAFT TAPPEH (هفت‌تپه) (⏱ 08.00–17.00; entry to museum 300,000 rials) On the way here and on the return to the main Shush–Ahvaz road, 30km from Choga Zanbil, you will have passed the turn-off to Haft Tappeh, where the Iranian Archaeological Service excavated during 1965–78. The royal tombs are quite clearly signposted by the side of the road.

The **small museum** (air-conditioned and UNESCO-sponsored) on the 30ha site, opened in 1973, is used to display some of the finds from this site and Choga Zanbil and is by far the best museum in the area; there is labelling in Farsi and English and it is set in pleasant gardens. The two main 'royal' tombs are protected with corrugated iron roofs as are two small ziggurats to the left of the tombs. Archaeological work revealed remains of ziggurats (much smaller than at Choga Zanbil), temples, palaces with water channels and little bridges, and the royal tombs. The first settlement appears to date back some 8,000 years and parts of the enclosing walls were constructed before the early 3rd millennium BCE, with numerous finds produced c1500–1300BCE, from the Proto-Elamite period according to the archaeologists. The larger of the two **tombs**, measuring about 10m × 3m, contained 21 skeletons on a raised platform, while the other adjoining it held in all 23 bodies, with nine others bundled unceremoniously in the doorway. Their brick vaulting system caused much excitement in archaeological circles as it pre-dated that at Choga Zanbil, as well as the stone vaulted passages at Bögazköy, central Turkey and at Ugarit, northern Syria, which were probably constructed a hundred or so years later.

EAST OF SHUSH/SUSA

AROUND MASJED-E SOLEYMAN
If time allows, the region east in the direction of Izeh (population 120,000) around 360km away, has interesting sites, such as Bard-e Neshandeh and Sar-e Masjed detailed below. The faster motorway lies through Ahvaz, but the slower and more picturesque route passes Masjed-e Soleyman.

Where to stay and eat There used to be no tourist hotels in the area, but now, in Masjed-e Soleyman (مسجد سليمان), an important oil exploration region, there is one. Alternatively, you could continue on to Esfahan via Shahr-e Kord on a new fast (but long) road, or return to Ahvaz for the night.

Tourist Inn (30+ rooms) Panj Bangeleh Sq; \061 43263985. Comfortable enough for 1 night, geared to visiting oil workers. Do not expect Wi-Fi connection, but the staff are helpful & friendly. **$**

What to see and do Some 35km beyond Masjed-e Soleyman, in the centre of the local oilfields, is the Seleucid–Elymaian–Parthian site of **Bard-e Neshandeh**, perched dramatically above the town. Its name ('Raised Stone' in Lori language) comes from the huge stone platform or terrace, about 54m × 91m, reached by staircases to the north (the best preserved), south and east. A cult niche and crudely carved relief of a king offering a *barsom* of sacred twigs to the fire altar were found, which supported the theory that a Parthian temple once stood on this terrace, but the numerous Seleucid/Elymaian figurines, pilgrim flasks and coins found under and around this platform strongly suggest it was constructed in pre-Parthian times. In 2005 the headless statue of a Parthian 'princess' was unearthed.

To the south of Masjed-e Soleyman, at **ateshkadeh Sar-e Masjed** ('Sar-e Masjed' Fire Temple), were found fragments of a larger-than-life-size statue of Herakles (Hercules) with the Nemean lion on a platform surrounded by remains of a porticoed temple, probably Parthian in date, although the defence walls are thought to be older. Most of the finds, including this statue and other beautifully carved heads from the first site (often clearly deliberately smashed, perhaps in post-Sasanid times), were moved in the 1960s to the Susa Museum for safe keeping. Also in this region, a discovery of a Parthian rock carving was made in 1999 at **Shirin Bahar**. Although known by the local Bakhtiari tribespeople, it was unknown to scholars because of the area's distance from population centres. The relief (2m × 1.45m high), shows three frontal figures: the one on the left carrying a lance sits on a throne; another appears to raise his right arm towards the seated figure; while the one on the right is depicted with his arms crossed. It may be an investiture scene but it's difficult to ascertain as the surface is very worn.

Further south lies Izeh, with its important Elamite remains, and to its north (via Peyan and Mehrenanis) is **Shami**. This is where the superb bronze Parthian king or warrior (possibly the general described by Plutarch, called Surena), of the late 1st century BCE and now in Tehran's National Museum was found in 1934 by the famous archaeologist, Sir Aurel Stein, on an artificial terrace in a building which had been torched. The scattered fragments of stone slab tombs below suggests it was a royal Elymaian (not to be confused with Elamite) cemetery. Elymais was a semi-independent kingdom with the capital in Susa, which was conquered and absorbed by the Parthians in the 2nd century BCE. Further on in the same direction, some 60km northeast of Masjed-e Soleyman, near the town of Andika, is **Tang-e Buta** (تنگ بتا), where rock reliefs depict four investiture scenes and a portrayal of Herakles (Hercules).

IZEH ایذه
Izeh was once the capital of the Lori people whose name is perpetuated in the nearby Lorestan province. There is no suitable accommodation in the area and you are advised to stay overnight in Masjed-e Soleyman, Dezful or Ahvaz.

What to see and do If coming from Ramhormoz in the south, the village of Gonbad-e Loran is famous for the nearby 'Fire Mountain' or **Tashkuh** (تاشکوه). Flames coming from under the ground that have been burning for thousands of years make it look as if the actual mountain is on fire. The *Shahnameh*'s mythical hero Esfandiar killed the dragon here, which suggests an association with fire in this region from ancient times. The effect is caused by hydrogen sulphide mixing with natural gas present in the surrounding area. The Abul Farez oilfield is just a few kilometres away. Further along the road past Baghmalek to the south, about 25km before Izeh, keep an eye out for a **cemetery** on the left which contains three or more standing stone lions thought to mark the graves of Bakhtiari tribal chiefs. An even better collection of **lion tomb markers** is to be found on the other side of town just off the road towards Esfahan. After 2km turn right, opposite a car salesroom and follow the road through three villages until it becomes a dirt track; some 500m further on at the base of the mountain is a large cemetery with more than 33 stone lion tomb markers.

Just on the southwest outskirts of Izeh itself is the grotto of **Eshkaft-e Salman** (اشکفت سلمان). The Izeh municipality has really made an effort here, planting trees and landscaping the hillside. It has since become a popular wedding picture backdrop. Inside the shallow cave, two badly eroded **Elamite reliefs** commemorate a local 8th-century BCE ruler, Prince Hanni, and his consort. A large notice provides the full inscription in Farsi, giving Hanni's royal lineage, listing the villages and areas under his authority and dedicating the grotto to an Elamite goddess. High on the right-hand rock face is the carved figure of Hanni and his queen and another showing, according to some scholars, his chief minister and family, facing the grotto. Purists will dislike the modern plaster animals scattered around but young children adore them.

Kul-e Farah (کول فرح), a site with Neo-Elamite rock reliefs is straight across town from here, 7km to the northeast. It is more accessible than Tang-e Buta (see above) – but wear comfortable, tough shoes as the ground is very stony. The rock-cut reliefs clearly formed an open-air sanctuary of deep religious significance for local Elamite rulers. At the far end of the tarmac road is the village, in a hollow at the foot of the hills, now totally deserted after a dam cut off its water supply. A series of Elamite rock reliefs, the megaron layout of the village houses, and the evident re-use of old stone columns to support roofs and floors, makes the village interesting to explore. As one faces the village, the reliefs are to the far left (east). One cluster is high on the limestone rock, with attendants facing into a deep crack, while on the other face a larger regal figure, Prince Hanni again, mirrors the direction. Despite severe erosion, the multiplicity of figures is amazing and some retain considerable fine details. On another surface the prince is shown seated witnessing animal sacrifices. From here, walk downwards and towards a dried-up stream. You're looking for a massive boulder carrying reliefs on all sides, carved probably in the 8th century BCE. One side depicts a religious procession featuring nearly 200 human figures and 21 other animals, with a (badly eroded) kingly figure welcoming a cult image carried by four priests. On another side the prince is attended by three rows of courtiers, priests with vessels and harpists. Their hands held at the waist presumably denote a posture of prayer or reverence. Another face of the boulder depicts the priests dispatching the sacrificial animals. If the proposed dating for this and all the other carvings is accurate, this place held sacred connotations for the worship of the Elamite deities of Tepti, Tirutur, Napir and others for some 400 years.

Hung-e Azhdar (Tang-e Nourouzi) (خونگ اژدر \ تنگ نوروزی) (some 6km north), among other villages in this area, has similar representations, but these are generally thought to have a much earlier date, c1950–1800BCE. Alongside it is a Parthian investiture scene, first attributed to Mithridates I (171–138BCE), but this is no longer accepted. Also in the locality of Izeh, some 30km east, a rock relief depicting four reclining figures was discovered in 1987, but there are no details of its exact location; it is thought to date from the Parthian or Sasanid period.

SOUTH OF AHVAZ

ABADAN آبادان *Telephone code 061*

Business affairs often take foreigners, but very few tourists, to Abadan (altitude a mere 3m; population 230,000), 150km south of Ahvaz. The heat here is fierce during the summer months (58°C has been recorded) and the humidity can be as high as 99%.

Since at least the 4th century CE its location at the junction of the rivers Tigris, Euphrates, Karun, and the Persian Gulf gave Abadan a significant commercial importance and is presently the 'capital' of the Armand Tax Free Zone.

The grid layout of the city dates from the early 20th century when the oil and petroleum refineries were constructed and urban expansion went hand in hand with increases in output; it has been described as the Surbiton of Iran. At the time of the nationalisation of Iranian oil in 1951, the Abadan refinery was the biggest in the world. Needless to say, the refinery was a prime target for Iraqi bombing during the 1980–88 Iran–Iraq War, but it has since been entirely rebuilt.

On 19 August 1978 a fire at the Rex Cinema killed at least 370 people and proved to be one of the turning points in the pre-revolutionary movement, as the shah's SAVAK security service were accused of instigating it.

In the first half of the 20th century Abadan was home to a large Armenian population who lived in the same residential area with oil refinery workers, mainly from Britain, in the exclusive Breim and Bavardeh districts. The bustling life of these communities is wittily narrated by the Iranian writer and Abadan native Zoya Pirzad in her semi-biographical novels (page 370).

Getting there and around From **Khalij Fars Marine Terminal** in Khorramshahr 8km from Abadan, there are two weekly departures (Sat & Wed) to Kuwait and two weekly return sailings (Sun & Thu), leaving at 10.00 and operated by Valfajr (w valfajr.ir; ticket price 4,520,000–8,000,000 rials). There are at least five direct **flights** per day from Tehran to Abadan (approximately 3,500,000 rials one way), as well as flights from several other centres, such as Esfahan, Mashhad and Shiraz. Abadan International Airport is around 12km from the city and the only way of getting to the city centre is by taxi. The **rail** network links Tehran to nearby Khorramshahr daily and there is the usual selection of long-distance **buses** connecting the area to the main population centres. Buses arriving from the north leave passengers at the end of the Ahvaz–Abadan motorway, northern bus terminal. Ahvaz is only 106km away and there are regular *savari* departures. Within the city, as always, **taxi** is probably the best option for the visitor. Below is a bus departure schedule with selected times from major Iranian cities:

From	Departure	Price (rials)
Esfahan (Kaveh)	09.30; 17.30; 19.30; 20.30; 21.30; 22.00; 22.30	420,000–720,000
Esfahan (Sofeh)	10.15; 18.15; 20.15; 21.15; 22.15; 22.45; 23.15	420,000–720,000
Shiraz (Karandish)	10.30; 20.00; 20.30; 21.00; 21.30; 22.00	350,000–650,000
Tehran (southern)	11.15; 12.30; 13.30; 14.45; 16.00; 16.30; 17.45; 18.00; 18.30; 19.00; 20.30; 21.15	550,000–920,000

Where to stay and eat

⌂ Abadan Caravansara Pars Hotel (95 rooms) International Airport, Breim district; ☏53264002, 53264009; w pars-hotels.com. Built with reference to traditional architecture, though mixed with plenty of 1970s glamour. Busy with Iranian & foreign oil delegations. **$$$$**

⌂ Keivan Hotel (38 rooms) Montazeri St; ☏53220490, 53220493. On the upper scale of the price range & easily the best of the poor bunch. Conveniently located by the port & Imam Khomeini St. Some rooms overlook the refinery. **$$$**

⌂ Azadi Hotel (30 rooms) Taleqani St; ☏53226598, 53231505. Central, near the bazaar & city activities. A bit neglected. Last resort for an adventurous traveller. **$$**

✳ ✘ Pakistan Central Restaurant Imam Khomeini St; ☏53242437; ⊕ noon–16.00 & 19.00–23.00 daily. Local favourite since 1942, it serves classic Iranian & some spicy Pakistani *beryani* dishes. Always busy. **$$**

What to see and do The most interesting attraction in the city is the somewhat misleadingly named **Abadan Artisan School Museum** ✳ (Opposite Takhti Sports Stadium; ⊕ 08.00–20.00 daily; entry free). Perhaps best described as the oil museum of Abadan, this is what any museum should be – an informative experience. The 4,276m-large hangar-shaped workshop and artisan school for oil machinery and tools is divided into various sections, corresponding to the learning courses that had at one time been taught here. The pump shop, for example, displays various pumps made by a now-defunct British manufacturer, Worthington-Simpson, that oil refinery employees were trained on. All exhibits date to the pre-World War II period and are in excellent condition.

The older brick section of the school, the building to the left as you enter the main gate, was built in 1933 and is now dedicated to the history of oil exploration in Iran. Labelling is alas in Persian only, but the timeline starts from the establishment of the Qajar dynasty by Naser al-Din Shah in the 1850s. The 1950s were marked by the nationalisation of the Iranian oil industry by Prime Minister Mohammad Mossadeq and the death of Joseph Stalin. The timeline terminates with the uprisings in the Arab states in 2010. Pictures in the frames above provide a visual accompaniment for the ease of cross-reference. Here there are more maquettes of learning and technical equipment used by the apprentices at the school, followed by learning certificates awarded at the end of their studies and official meeting minutes, including from 1994 attesting to the change of the school's name.

In the city centre, the fine Pahlavi **Ranguniha Mosque** (essentially closed, unless you are in luck & there is a special event on), built in 1921 in the Indian style, most probably for Indian and Bangladeshi workers, is just across the street from the refinery. For some fresh fish you might like to visit the **fish market** (*bazaar-e mahi*), although it is relatively modest for a port city. Within walking distance of the fish market is **St Karapet Church**, built in 1958, but heavily damaged during the Iran–Iraq War to be eventually rebuilt in 1991. Adjacent to the church is the all boys' Damavand school (formerly the Armenian secondary school) with a 1915 Armenian Genocide memorial in its courtyard. The church is permanently closed, locked and the key is with its guardian, in Esfahan.

Some 15km from the city, the **Shrine of Khezr** (the 'Green Man') was a popular pilgrimage site in medieval times, but it is hardly a highlight. Consider instead visiting the small town of **Khorramshahr** (خرمشهر), 8km northwest of Abadan, which is closely and tragically associated with the Iran–Iraq War. Effectively now a satellite suburb of Abadan, the town lies at the spot where the Karun River joins Arvand and marks the border between Iran and Iraq. The reason for coming here is the **Museum (Cultural Centre) of the Holy Defence of Khorramshahr** (063242; 07.00–18.00 daily; entry free). Built in 1930, it had initially served as the British oil company headquarters. Most of the sections of the original 10,000m² space were destroyed during the Iran–Iraq War in 1980–88 and the remaining parts were preserved and converted in the mid 1990s into the museum it is today. A visit with a guide is recommended, as the labelling is in Persian only and aside from the visual effect of the photographs, it is otherwise not easy to navigate through the museum's five halls, each dedicated to a different aspect of the resistance of Abadan and to the lives of the martyrs. The city fell to Iraqi forces on 26 October 1980 after 35 days of ferocious resistance and remained occupied for 19 months, during which time the museum building was used by Iraqi soldiers as their military base.

EASTWARDS

A slight detour along the coast road from Abadan, or on the eastern route from Ahvaz to Bushehr will take you to the town of **Behbahan** (بهبهان), famous for its narcissus flower festival, high-quality dairy products and beautiful mountain scenery with numerous rock reliefs and picturesque villages. Established by settled nomads, Behbahan, with a population of 123,000, lies on the route from Esfahan to the Khuzestan Plain and is a relatively important trading centre. In the town's compact historic district there is the wonderful family-run **Khaneh Mohseniha** ecolodge (7 rooms; m 0916 5856686; **$$**), which is by far the best accommodation option in the area. Rooms are spacious and in most *lahaf toshak* roll-up mattresses are used for sleeping. The ecolodge also houses a popular local restaurant ($), serving delicious meals and freshly baked bread. Visits to the nearby sites can be arranged from here.

About 10km northeast of Behbahan is **Arjun**, where a 9th–8th-century BCE stone burial chamber was found during construction work for a dam in 1982. Inside was a U-shaped coffin and the remains of a body with grave goods including ornate gold jewellery, a bronze lamp stand, and daggers. A magnificent decoratively patterned bronze platter, over 43cm in diameter, is engraved with over 100 human figures, 66 animals of 33 kinds, trees and rock formations in scenes of banqueting, hunting and harvesting, processions and musical performances. The deceased, according to an inscription on a beautifully worked bracelet in the grave, was the Elamite ruler Hutran, son of Korlash. All these treasures are now in the National Museum,

Tehran, but unfortunately not on public display. The main reason for coming here, however, is **Tang-e Sarvak** (تنگ سروک) (locally known as Tang-e Soulak; 54km northwest of Behbahan), where boulders are carved with Elymaian or Parthian reliefs dating from c200BCE onwards. The gorge is picturesque with pine and walnut trees dotting the hills and necessitates a 1-hour hike from the closest parking spot to reach the first rock relief. Registers of standing figures attend a figure reclining on a couch, while another rock face depicts a ruler and his family. Elsewhere the representation of a priest standing by a fire altar is carved alongside depictions of hunting activities. Some scholars believe this to be the site of the Nanaya-Artemis temple referred to by Strabo.

Another interesting historic site is the location of the remains of the Sasanid *ateshkadeh* (Zoroastrian fire temple), **Chahartaq-e Kheirabad** (چهارطاقی خیرآباد) near Dogonbadan, approximately 72km southeast of Behbahan on the road to Yasuj. Although the dome of this four-arch structure has been destroyed, the bearing four columns stand a solid 11.07m high as a testament to the classic Persian architectural style known as *chahartaqi* or 'four-way arch'. This fire temple is believed by some to have been built together with other structures to commemorate Ardeshir Babakan's victory over Artabanus V (Ardavan V) of Parthia, on the Ramhormoz Plain, and lies on the ancient trade route from Fars to Khuzestan.

If travelling around this area by public transport, there are regular *savari* departures (a 1-hour shared taxi fare ranges from 300,000 to 500,000 rials) from Ahvaz to Behbahan, from where you can continue by bus to Shiraz or Esfahan or by *savari* from Zeydun Square in Behbahan towards **Deylam** (دیلم) or Genaveh (pronounced *Ghenaveh*) and from there to Bushehr.

BUSHEHR بوشهر *Telephone code 077*

The history of Bushehr (population 300,000) goes back to the Ilam period, when the original settlement was known as Lian. During Sasanid rule, the city was named Bukht-e Ardeshir after the founder of the empire and at a later stage known as Rio Ardeshir or simply Rishehr.

Bushehr first became a major port when in 1734 Nader Shah Afshar made it his principal commercial and military naval transportation hub. Some 25 years later, with the decline of the Dutch East India dominion over foreign trade in Persia and the Persian Gulf, the area came under British influence. Following the granting of the monopoly on foreign trade by Karim Khan Zand, the British East India Company set up its 'factory' (headquarters) here, while operating from its Bandar Abbas base. It was only later in 1857 that Bushehr came under Qajar authority and became the Qajars' most important commercial port. It was also then that Bushehr became the fourth city in Iran to have a printing press; the first national satirical magazine, *Tolu* (*Sunrise* in Persian) was established here. British forces left Bushehr in 1919 and after the construction of the railway line to Khorramshahr, the importance of the city started to dwindle.

Bushehr is now famous mainly for its nuclear power plant, located approximately 17km southeast of the city in the fishing harbour of **Bandargah**. Conceived by Mohammad Reza Shah in the 1970s and initially developed by Siemens, the plant was almost entirely redesigned and completed in 2010 by Russia. At present the Russian State Atomic Energy Corporation (ROSATOM) operates it jointly with Iran and is scheduled to complete construction of units II and III in 2024 and 2026 respectively.

Bushehr is also still known for its shipbuilding industry, although teak has been replaced by fibreglass as the building material due to increasing wood maintenance costs. The city's location in the seismic zone has meant that much of its sites have been destroyed, particularly in the severe 1806 earthquake. The 6.3-magnitude earthquake that in 2013 killed over 30 people and injured around 800 did not affect the city itself. With its epicentre 91km south of Bushehr, the shockwaves were felt in various parts of the country, including Shiraz, and across the Persian Gulf. The 5.9-magnitude earthquake that hit the area in April 2018 luckily caused no damage.

Located about 350km southwest of Shiraz on the coast of the Persian Gulf, Bushehr is stiflingly hot and humid in the summer months. The best time to visit is late winter when days are sunny and evenings are mildly cool. As Bushehr is stretched along the coast, it has a very pleasant sea promenade. The old city *baft-e tarikhi* is tiny and is enjoyable to wander around and marvel at its unique architecture and historical houses. A lot of activity is centred around Enghelab Square and West Lian Street. Gold and exchange shops are also located here.

In mid-March Bushehr takes centre stage for a week-long popular **Koocheh Music Festival** (w koochehfestival.ir) of traditional music from all over Iran. Performances are held in the cosy atmosphere of the inner courtyard of Haj Raeis Traditional Hotel, but the music spills on to the streets of the old city as well. Advance accommodation booking is highly recommended during this period.

Getting there and around Bushehr is a major centre for oil development projects (on and offshore) in Iran and there are numerous daily 2-hour **flights** from Tehran to Bushehr and other cities in Iran. The city is also well served by long-distance **bus** services from the major cities arriving at the Bushehr bus terminal southeast of the city near the airport, but it can be difficult to get here from Kish by public transport. The journey over the mountains to and from Shiraz is particularly scenic, although it gets busy with lorry traffic. Below is a bus departure schedule with selected times from major Iranian cities:

From	Departure	Price (rials)
Esfahan (Kaveh)	10.00; 11.00; 18.00; 20.30	760,000
Esfahan (Sofeh)	21.30	760,000
Shiraz (Amir Kabir)	00.30; 01.00; 06.00; 07.30; 08.45; 09.15; 10.15; 11.15; 12.20; 13.00; 14.00; 15.00; 16.15; 17.15; 18.20; 19.30; 22.00; 23.15	360,000
Shiraz (Karandish)	05.45; 21.15	360,000
Tehran (southern)	11.30; 11.45; 14.15; 15.00; 16.00; 17.00; 18.00; 19.00; 20.00	988,000–1,235,000
Tehran (Beyhaghi)	15.30	988,000–1,235,000

Within the city, the **historic part** is an enjoyable walkable maze of alleys and within greater Bushehr **taxis** are your best option. The standard rate is approximately 50,000 rials for a short trip. Some parts of the city may be off-limits, as central Bushehr is home to the Iranian Air Force base.

Where to stay and eat Bushehr now has two wonderful traditional hotels, but otherwise the choice of accommodation is limited, as visitors prefer so-called apartment hotels with up to five rooms. Good restaurants are few, but the Haj Raeis Traditional Hotel now has an excellent traditional restaurant, serving local dishes, albeit for lunch only. Shrimps are particularly good here; Bushehr province accounts for 60% of Iran's shrimp produce.

✳ 🏠 Haj Raeis Traditional Hotel (7 rooms) Old city, off Enghelab (Kelisa) St; 📞 33341229; 📱 0936 6104550. Opened in 2019 & run by welcoming Edris Abdipur, the creative mind behind the Haj Raeis (Bushehr) Café in the alley in front of the hotel. Rooms in this traditional Bushehri mansion are spacious with high ceilings & cosily decorated in local style. There is regular live music, in particular traditional Bushehri *khayyamkhani*, in the hotel's airy inner courtyard & the traditional restaurant ($$) serves excellent local specialities for lunch only. $$–$$$

✳ 🏠 Maan Hamishe Sabz (3 rooms) Old city, off Khalij-e Fars St; 📱 0917 7730642. The first ecolodge in Bushehr, this tiny traditional guesthouse is a gem of a place run by Mohsen Pournabi. In the old part of the city, with a terrace overlooking the Persian Gulf, the location is hard to beat & so is the quality of accommodation & service. B/fast is excellent. $$–$$$

🏠 Hotel Delvar (known as Tourist Inn) (56 rooms) Shahrdari Sq; 📞 33326342, 33326346.

Located on the square adorned by the statue of Raeis Ali Delvari, a national hero who fought against the British in World War I, this is a good, central mid-range hotel near the seafront. It has good facilities & large rooms that come with balconies. Its 1970s décor is welcoming; the staff are pleasant & professional & Wi-Fi is fast. $$

✳ ✕ Ghavam Restaurant Sahali St; 📞 32530700, 2521790; e ghavam.restaurant@ gmail.com; ⏰ noon–15.00 & 19.00–23.00. Fashioned from a restored water cistern, this is one of the best restaurants in Iran, serving home-baked bread & delicious food. Do note, however, that the local cuisine is spicy. $$

✳ ✕ Haj Raeis (Bushehr) Tea House Opposite Haj Raeis Traditional Hotel, Old city, off Enghelab (Kelisa) St; ⏰ 18.00–midnight daily. This is the place to be in the evenings, exchange the news of the day, catch up with old friends & simply spend time in good company. The vibe is excellent & tea is always fresh & ready to be served. $

Other practicalities

$ Foreign exchange In the old city there is a foreign exchange shop on Enghelab Sq next to the row of jewellery stores.

✚ Hospital Shohada Khalij Fars Hospital (Taleqani Bd; 📞 33455375, 33455388; w mpgh.

bpums.ac.ir/en) comes clearly into view on arrival in Bushehr.

✚ Pharmacy Dr Rezaei Pharmacy (Dehdashti Alley, Old city; 📞 33337266) is open 24/7.

What to see and do There are the remains of two large merchant houses here, one of which is the Qajar-period **Emarat-e Malak** (former residency of the famous merchant Mohammad Mehdi Malak), which was built under the supervision of French engineers. The other is the **Emarat-e Haj Raeis,** also built under the Qajar dynasty for Haj Abdul Rasul Talebi, known as Raeis the Merchant. Both of these tradesmen made their fortunes in trade to India and Pakistan. A more central **Emarat-e Amiriyeh** in the old part of Bushehr is now the seat of the Bushehr Islamic Council. Also in the vicinity is the historic building of **Saadat Secondary School** (Imam St, opposite Moallem Sq), the first modern school in southern Iran, established in 1900 with financial help from Muzaffar al-Din Shah; it functions as a Cultural and Historic Centre with a small museum dedicated to the history of the school.

The **British Cemetery**, located 7km south of the city at Bahmani, is closed and there does not seem to be anyone removing the weeds. Nearby, the site and the building of the pre-revolutionary **British Consulate** have been converted into a museum.

A few kilometres further on are the remains of the original port of **Rishehr** (ریشهر), which got its name either from the Elamite word meaning 'great' (*rishair*) or from a Sasanid fortress here, **Rev-Ardashir** – named after the first Sasanid ruler – which was later built over by the Portuguese and Safavid occupiers. Elamite remains have been found: there are foundations of a town near to the original port and about 14km away (4km from **Saadabad**) the site of an Elamite temple has been identified. French archaeologists concluded the main period of settlement was c2500–1200BCE, and possibly a millennium earlier.

The old quarter still has some good examples of traditional architecture with wooden doors and overhanging balconies with lattice windows that allow the women of the household to view the streets below without being seen. Do try to visit this quarter before it disappears in the zeal for modernisation. The Corniche is a popular family retreat in the evenings with bands playing; all swim here at the city's public beach but women enter the sea fully clothed. Further south, the coast between Bushehr and the shimmering white dome of the nuclear power plant, in particular at the village of Heleyleh, has some deserted pristine **sandy beaches**. Women must nonetheless remember to be fully clothed, as there are regular police controls here owing to the sensitive nature of the area. You are otherwise completely undisturbed and welcome to enjoy the Persian Gulf at its best.

EAST OF BUSHEHR Driving from Bushehr towards Shiraz via Kazerun gives the opportunity of seeing a series of rock-cut caves on the old medieval road which have intrigued several archaeologists, who have suggested they functioned as Christian or possibly Buddhist monastic dwellings. **Chehelkhaneh** with, as its name suggests, some 40 caves (*chehel*: 'forty'), is situated 17km northwest of Borazjan (itself 70km from Bushehr). South is **Kalat-e Heydari**, where there is another cluster of caves with intersecting passages, and rectangular and 'domed' chambers on two levels. In the early 1970s, some 5km before Chehelkhaneh, the remains of an **Achaemenid palace** (Kakh-e Sang-e Siyah) were found. Its layout (the closeness of the column bases) and the use of black and white limestone suggested it was constructed during the reign of Cyrus the Great (c529BCE) but abandoned after his death. Nearby on the large **Tappeh Mor** (also known as Tel-e Mor), traces of an Elamite fortress were located.

KHARG ISLAND جزیره خارک About 31 nautical miles northwest off Bushehr (page 292) is Kharg Island (Jazir-e Kharg), whose oil-pumping facilities suffered such serious bomb damage during the 1980–88 Iran–Iraq War that French engineers asserted that the Kharg Fire Brigade was the most experienced in the world. It has a population of some 15,000, mostly employed in the oil industry as 90% of Iran's oil exports pass through these facilities.

In the 1950s archaeological finds of bricks with cuneiform inscriptions proved the island was under Elamite authority during the 3rd millennium BCE, but the two megalithic tombs found probably date back only to c1000BCE. Thirty years later, a marble figurine, probably of Sumerian manufacture, was uncovered suggesting the importance of the island to maritime trade. Strabo, writing in the 1st century BCE, was probably referring to this island when he reported the remains of a large temple to Apollo with an oracle, and two centuries later Pliny recorded that Kharg was 'sacred to Neptune'; the ruins of a Roman temple may relate to this. On top of this complex a Sasanid fire temple, dated by a coin find to the early 4th century, was built, and then a mosque was later constructed. Today there stands a mosque and shrine of Mir Mohammad, both surmounted with a 'sugarloaf' dome, characteristic of the region. Nearby more than 80 rock-cut tombs were found, probably carved in Sasanid times for Zoroastrian use, though Christian crosses have been carved on some doorways. Two hypogea for multiple interments were located, which the French archaeologists thought suggested Palmyran merchant occupation. To the west, extensive remains of a Nestorian monastery and a basilica church were uncovered. The 60 cells, each containing three stone-and-plaster bed-couches, suggest a community of over 150 monks.

The island's strategic position between India and Arabia resulted in occupation by the Portuguese and then the Dutch East India Company after it closed down its Basra operations in 1752. The remains of the **Dutch Fort** (Qaleh Holandiha) built in 1747 on the northeastern tip of the island, testify to the once-thriving Dutch trade in the Persian Gulf. The French then moved in with the blessing of Karim Khan Zand (page 15) but the island was returned to the Qajar dynasty in 1809, and again in 1857 after a brief British occupation. As recently as 2007 an Achaemenid cuneiform inscription praising one who brought water was discovered, but this was vandalised soon after.

Getting there and away There are daily round trips to Kharg Island from Bushehr, but these are for workers and residents only (no accommodation is available for visitors). Permission (and invitation) is necessary in order to visit. During Nou Rouz there are tours for Iranians (holding permits). Foreigners must apply to the governorate in Bushehr, but it is likely to be a lengthy process, which may well not result in permission. Students at the university on the island are issued with a commuting card.

FURTHER ALONG THE COAST ROAD

The main road from Bushehr towards Hormozgan province lies in between mountains and the Persian Gulf, as if converging at the narrowest point at the port of **Asalouyeh** (عسلویه) in the Pars Special Economic Energy Zone (PSEEZ). One of the first sites en route, but a few kilometres inland, is the visually striking and colourful **Jashk Salt Mountain** (کوه نمک جاشک). Made entirely of salt, its quirky formations of red, grey, yellow and red colour are shaped by the rainwater running down through the mountain in the winter and spring. A few kilometres away, the first town you reach is **Abdan** (آبدن), famous for its delicious tomatoes. The rule has it that passers-by are welcome to pick and taste one or two of the delicious tomatoes, but do avoid taking advantage of this friendly tradition and filling up a basketful for the following day. The fishing port of **Kangan** (کنگان) is 36km further southeast.

Almost due south from Shiraz (although there is no direct road) is **Bandar Siraf** (بندر سیراف) (the modern part of the port is also known as Bandar Taheri, 220km southeast of Bushehr), where British archaeologists excavated the important medieval port of **Siraf** for over nine years from 1966. According to the histories, **Siraf** was trading with India and China, and by 950CE its population approximated to that of Shiraz. However, a severe earthquake in 977CE caused many to leave, and by 1200 most of the trade had been transferred to the eastern port of Qais. The final report describing the excavations on this enormous 250ha site and its finds was finally published in 2010 after a 30-year delay. The quantities of Chinese ceramic shards uncovered in the first season of work proved the accuracy of the medieval historians. It was discovered that the large ruined mosque noted in 1930 had been built on top of a large Sasanid fort constructed shortly after 804CE, and which was then altered some five times before the site was abandoned c1263. Nearby, a six-roomed *hamam* with hypocaust system had been in operation, along with the workshops and warehouses of a bazaar, some clearly involved in metalworking. Remains of about 30 pottery kilns were found with their shelf-support systems still largely intact. Streets with residential buildings, often incorporating a well for drinking water, were also identified, and a large cemetery with late Sasanid 9th- and 10th-century tombs was located.

Past Asalouyeh and the myriad flare stacks, turn right towards the idyllic and picturesque **Nayband Gulf**; although the area has clearly suffered from mass tourism, the view over the Persian Gulf from the cliffs is breathtaking, especially during sunset. Just a few kilometres further down, past the village of **Banud** (بنود), lies a tiny stretch of the most pristine and secluded Persian Gulf coast. A protected area for turtle breeding, it is open for tourists, although on a limited basis.

KISH ISLAND جزيره كيش *Telephone code 076*

From Bandar Taheri there is a good road eastwards along the coast to **Bandar Charak** (بندر چارک) from where ferries leave for the island of Kish (Jazir-e Kish). In the past, like Hormuz (page 302), it had a lively trading community over ten times as large as now, and was known for its pearls and beautiful women. The late shah had a large villa with an airstrip, and desalination plants (for drinking water) constructed here. The Kish Free Zone Organisation (KFZO), which answers only to the president, is currently targeting foreign companies for investment, promoting the island as an offshore banking centre, and a number of the official regulations (eg: partnership with an Iranian representative) were removed in spring 2000. Many Iranians come here to shop, as, reputedly, the prices are lower than in Dubai, or to visit the Kish Dolphin Park.

A visa waiver system operates for foreigners wishing to visit Kish, but this is not valid for further mainland travel; a tourist visa for the rest of Iran can usually be issued here, however. A number of Dubai workers come here to wait for their Emirati visa renewal.

Getting there and around Kish Air connects the island to major cities in Iran and operates four weekly international **flights** from Dubai to Kish (9,000,000 rials) and two flights a week from Muscat in Oman; the airline also has daily services from Tehran and Esfahan and six flights per week from Shiraz. Regular comfortable **ferries** leave from the nearby mainland ports of Bandar Charak (from where the journey takes 90 minutes) and Bandar Lengeh further down the coast (less frequent departures and longer journey time). Make sure to have your passport with you as it will be checked when buying a ferry ticket. To move around the island and visit the sites, consider hiring a **taxi** for a day.

Where to stay and eat There are no budget hotels on the island, despite the fact that some hotels have different classes of accommodation on the same site. Room prices tend to vary with the season. All the hotel complexes and shopping malls have a variety of restaurants, but for a cool evening venue try the **Payab Restaurant** (near the underground water reservoir; ✆44423638; **$$**) for fish and other specialities.

🏠 **Dariush Grand Hotel** (163 rooms) Dariush Sq; ✆44444900; w dariushgrandhotel.com. One of Iran's most luxurious hotels with the front façade built to resemble Persepolis & the Gate of All Nations. Completed in 2003, it simply stuns with its nonchalant flamboyance. If you are lucky, you might even be able to snatch a room with a sea view. There is a swimming pool for women, but the beach for female guests is a distance away & necessitates a taxi ride. **$$$$**

🏠 **Sadaf International Hotel** (54 rooms) Amir Kabir Sq; ✆44420590. Friendly staff, shiny lobby, clean rooms & facilities, which include an internet café, pool room & sauna & jacuzzi, not to mention the restaurant built into a 'mountain'. **$$$**

🏠 **Shayan International Hotel** (193 rooms) Sahel Sq; ✆44422771. The late shah's original concrete hotel, now a homage to retro kitsch. **$$$**
🏠 **Kish Parsian Hotel** (90 rooms) Between Trade Centre & Zeitoon malls; ✆44423616. A little expensive for what you get. The rooms are standard & the lobby is flashy & touristy. The staff are not very attentive & even somewhat indifferent. **$$**

What to see and do There are a couple of places of interest here, but they can all be visited in one day. All tourist groups are guided alike and if you are looking for a romantic moment to share the sunset with your other half, you will probably end up sharing it with hundreds of others. Hotel buses drive everyone around along the same route. **The Underground City of Kish** (کاریز کیش) (Kariz; ⊕ 09.00–22.00; entry 500,000 rials), which is made of a series of interconnected underground passageways built around subterranean water channels, is effectively a place for walking around, exploring the ancient system of canals, some light souvenir shopping and enjoying a bite to eat in its lively open-pit traditional restaurant and music venue.

The main attraction is of course still the duty-free shopping, but the beached **Greek ship** (*keshti yunani*) is also very popular. Otherwise, perhaps the turtle colony and scuba diving (for men only) may be of interest. Although it is very cheap to dive here, diving equipment is not easy to find on the island. Windsurfing, jet skis and waterskiing are also available. There is a beach for women only near the ferry terminal; enquire at your hotel for directions.

In the northern corner of the island, between Saffeyn and the New Jetty, there are a few remains of the **palace and fort complex** built in the 11th–12th century when, according to the chronicler Benjamin of Tudela, Kish was an important and prosperous trading port with large Jewish and Indian communities. In 1135 the ruler of Kish felt strong enough to attack Aden, and 15 years later it is known that his navy consisted of 50 vessels, each capable of carrying 200 men. Its wealth attracted the attention of the ruler of Hormuz who seized the island in 1229, only to divert traffic away. There was a brief period of prosperity from 1292 when Kish became a major port for the Ilkhanids (page 13), but again Hormuz acted to stop trade in 1330, and the island never recovered. An archaeological survey in 1974 recorded a number of cisterns and kilns, while surface finds of 13th–14th-century Chinese pottery shards revealed a busy trade with medieval China. In the early 1990s archaeological excavations in the **Harireh** historic port uncovered evidence of workshops, a mosque and a bathhouse from Ilkhanid and Timurid periods, and plotted the coastal location of numerous manmade loading bays, with rock-cut steps to serve the trading dhows in these waters. For shows with dolphins and white whales, visit the 70ha **Kish Dolphin Park** (shows 16.30–21.00 daily; 1,350,000 rials), built in 2000. It has a lovely garden and tea house. Your hotel will book a show ticket for you on request.

BANDAR ABBAS بندرعباس *Telephone code 076*

As with the rest of the south coast of Iran, the best time to visit Bandar Abbas (altitude 3m; population 449,000) is during the winter months, November to April. Summer temperatures often soar over 45°C, with the humidity of a Turkish bath; 18th-century English sailors used to moan that 'there was but an Inch-deal betwixt Gombroon [Bandar Abbas] and Hell'. Bandar Abbas was the name given to the medieval port of Gameron in 1615 by the Safavid Shah Abbas I after forcing the Portuguese out from their forts here and on Hormuz Island in 1622, ending both their occupation and their strategic and commercial control of the Straits of Hormuz that had lasted since 1515 with the permission of Shah Ismail I. He saw the possibility of circumventing the Ottoman embargo on Persian silk passing through its empire by sending bales by sea, as well as the potential of pearl fishing, and it was probably this commercial connection which led the English in particular to refer to Bandar Abbas as 'Gombroon' (Turkish for 'customs house'), a name later given to the high-quality soft paste porcelain ware from Iran so avidly collected in 19th-century Europe. A preliminary archaeological survey undertaken near Tiab, southeast of the present city, shows this trade had a long history; over 2,000 shards of fine 13th–14th-century Chinese porcelain from the site are now at the Ashmolean Museum, Oxford (UK). Like much of Iran, the area is subject to earthquakes: there was a serious one in 2005 measuring 5.6 on the Richter scale and a slightly stronger one in September 2008 which affected the island of Qeshm quite severely.

Work on port facilities in 1964–67, and then the setting up of the Iranian naval headquarters in 1973, meant increased business, and an international deep-water port was constructed in 1976–86. Now Bandar Abbas is the main port of Iran. The traditional dhow boats can still be seen in the old port, plying their trade between India, Zanzibar and Dubai, carrying tyres, oil drums, children's bicycles, spices and bales of cloth.

Bandar Abbas came to international attention at the end of the Iran–Iraq War when on 3 July 1988, US warship, USS *Vincennes*, the 'supership' of the Persian Gulf, shot down IranAir 655 Airbus A300 on a regular civilian flight from Bandar Abbas to Dubai. All 290 passengers and crew were killed. In the atmosphere of heightened tension between the two countries, the United States government never admitted responsibility, but agreed to compensate the families of the victims. The Iranian government, in return, refused to accept that what had happened had been an accident.

Getting there and around There are several daily **flights** from Tehran and a daily service to Shiraz as well as flights from other cities. Flydubai has two services per week to the city of Lar (241km away), which may be a convenient option if coming here on business to the surrounding extensive maritime area. As a port, daily **sailings** link Bandar Abbas with Hormuz and Qeshm. There is also an international service twice a week (Thu & Sun) from Sharjah (UAE) operated by Valfajr Shipping Company (w valfajr.ir). The ferry departs at 21.00 and arrives in Bandar Abbas (Shahid Bahonar Port) at 09.00. The ticket is purchased from Al Hili Marine Services (Al Khan Rd, Sharjah Ground Floor, Al Ikhias Tower; \0097 165288575). The price per person is approximately 5,200,000 rials one way and includes dinner and breakfast. No advance booking is possible and you have to make your way to the Al Hili head office in Sharjah to purchase the ticket. Women have to remember to cover their heads once on board. Intercity **bus** connections run between the major cities, such as Shiraz and Kerman, but you must count on a minimum of 8 hours' travel time even to reach Shiraz. The road from Shiraz and the north (1,050km to Tehran) is good, but as it is the main route from the coast to the interior there is a constant stream of lorries and tankers. To this tedium must be added the heat in the coastal regions. Below is a bus departure schedule with selected times from major Iranian cities:

From	Departure	Price (rials)
Esfahan (Kaveh)	16.00; 16.30; 17.00; 17.30; 18.00; 19.15; 20.15; 20.45; 21.00	720,000
Esfahan (Sofeh)	17.00; 18.30; 19.00; 20.00; 21.00	720,000
Shiraz (Karandish)	08.00; 08.30; 10.00; 10.30; 11.30; noon; 12.25; 18.00; 18.30; 20.00; 21.00; 21.15; 21.30; 22.00; 22.30; 23.00	530,000
Tehran (southern)	noon; 13.00; 14.30; 14.50; 15.50; 16.30; 17.00; 17.30; 17.50; 19.05; 19.30; 20.05; 20.30; 21.30	630,000–1,060,000

It is also possible to reach Bandar Abbas by **train**; the service is good, but it takes a minimum of 19 hours from Tehran via Yazd. Within the city **taxis** are available.

Where to stay and eat
Hotels in this part of Iran are more expensive, even in low season, and there are no budget options here. For eating out try the old bazaar or the fish market (*bazaar-e mahi*).

Homa Hotel (formerly Gameron) (180 rooms) Meraj St, Pasdaran Bd; 35553080, 35553089; w homahotels.com. Located by the sea in a lush green garden with a tennis court & a good traditional restaurant ($$). The staff are exceptionally helpful & rooms are excellent. **$$$$**

Hormoz Hotel (345 rooms) Enghelab Sq; 763210; w hormozhotel.com. With several restaurants ($$), indoor swimming pool & a central location, this is by far the fanciest place to stay in Bandar Abbas. Some rooms come with a view of the Persian Gulf. **$$$$**

Amin Hotel (53 rooms) Taleqani St, beside jetty for Qeshm & Hormuz; 32244305, 32244309; Basic & clean, although rooms are a little dark & small & the level of maintenance has alas reduced in quality over the past few years. **$$**

Qeshm Guesthouse (20 rooms) Behdar Jonubi St; 32240797, 32247536. Friendly & very proper guesthouse. Rooms are not en suite, but common areas are clean. Well worth considering if travelling on a budget. **$**

Qasr-e Honar Restaurant Shohada (Yadbud) Sq, upper level of Pasazh Shahrdari shopping centre; 32237475; ⏱ 11.30–15.30 & 19.00–23.30. Decorated in traditional style, it serves tasty dishes & homemade *dough*. There is also live music daily after 21.00. **$$**

Samco Restaurant Imam Hossein Bd, next to Samco petrol station; 33731743, 33731744; ⏱ 11.00–15.00 & 18.00–23.00 daily. Out of the city centre, this small restaurant is locally famous for excellent seafood. You will need to arrange a taxi to take you here & to bring you back. **$$**

What to see and do
It has to be said, there is not a multiplicity of tourist attractions in the city; even in 1622 one Portuguese diplomat described it as 'more of an emporium than a town', while his English counterparts remarked that the town's fame rested on its *panj* ('five') or punch, made of *arak* (date alcohol), lemon juice, sugar, nutmeg and water, which 'occasions a Guddiness in the Head, Feavers and Fluxes, and is so corrosive that some, who have drunk immoderately of it, died'. The much-vaunted **Hindu temple** is a small stone and concrete building set back from the main boulevard, but as it is no longer a functioning place of worship, all the temple ornaments, statuary and images have been removed. The temple was built in 1888 to serve a large Indian community working for the British East India Company. Its 'factors' or merchants had withdrawn from Bandar Abbas after the fall of the Safavid dynasty c1735, but they returned in 1793 to administer the port and Hormuz on behalf of the ruler of Oman who had seized control. The temple dome is decorated with 72 small decorative towers. And as for the little **Masjed-e Khezr** (Green Mosque) in the grounds of the Homa Hotel, it has been heavily repaired inside and outside with a new glass- and metal-frame extension. There is also a Qajar-period **Galedary Bathhouse**, the only historical *hamam* in the city located behind the Amin Hotel but, alas, it remains closed.

The thriving, bustling **bazaars** of Bandar Abbas are fun, offering a very different range of goods imported mainly from the Far East; sunglasses are very good buys. Also on sale are the distinctive red cloth or leather facemasks and heavily machine-embroidered tight-legged trousers (*shalvar-e bandari*) worn by women in the region. Bazaar-e Ruz is the best place to purchase a pair as a souvenir; prices start from 500,000 rials. You pick the design and the lady behind the counter will measure your ankle and have the trousers ready for the following day. Offering different but just as colourful and fantastic produce is the small **fish market** at the western end of the coastal promenade. It seems a shame there is no good fish restaurant next door. Here there are also spartan eateries to taste freshly cooked fish.

QESHM ISLAND جزیره قشم *Telephone code 076*

Some 150km further east along the coast, the large island of Qeshm (pronounced *gheshm*; 1,330km²) (w qeshmgeopark.ir), with a population of 100,000, comes into view, but the landing point is on the far eastern tip of the island, easily reached by ferry from Bandar Abbas less than an hour away. There's also a daily direct bus from Esfahan and Shiraz that takes you all the way to the island through the narrowest point between the mainland at Bandar Pol and the island at Bandar Laft. An international airport on the island has connections to Dubai as well as daily flights to Tehran with a journey time of just over 2 hours. Tickets are best purchased from any Kish Air sales office located in every major city.

The vast resources of natural gas here have led the government to promote the island as an industrial free and duty-free zone since 1990. In the 1970s, preliminary archaeological surveys recorded an Achaemenid and Sasanid settlement and for centuries many cargo ships docked here for supplies and cargo, as recorded by Marco Polo.

Although the tourist potential for watersports, diving and recreation on the island has remained largely undeveloped, there is excellent turtle-, dolphin- or birdwatching to be enjoyed on the island, justifying a day trip here. The Iranian Paragliding Association gathers here in the summer both to show their skills and to take tourists up in the air at very reasonable prices (from 800,000 rials).

Qeshm is a much livelier and a less glamorous island than Kish, but with more sites to attract foreign tourists looking for an authentic experience. It was Kish, in fact, that was intended to become Iran's Dubai, which explains the myriad luxurious hotels and cars on the island. All residents on Qeshm, on the other hand, have maintained their traditions and use Arabic and Persian interchangeably with older generations conversing essentially in Arabic. Although the Iranian rial is the official currency here, the UAE dirham is widely used in more upmarket restaurants and hotels. Qeshm is a transit point for many workers heading to Dubai or waiting for their UAE visa renewal.

Getting there and around The town of Dargahan, 15km from the town of Qeshm, is the commercial centre of the island and is the terminal for long-distance **buses** arriving from the mainland (crossing at Bandar Pol). From here, take a **taxi** to Qeshm, the actual capital and the ferry terminal for Bandar Abbas and Hormuz. Here you can hire a taxi for a day for approximately US$50 to explore the island and all the attractions it has to offer. Below is a bus departure schedule from Esfahan and Shiraz:

From	Departure	Price (rials)
Esfahan (Kaveh)	14.00; 15.30; 16.30; 17.00; 18.00	1,120,000
Esfahan (Sofeh)	16.15; 17.45; 18.45	1,120,000
Shiraz (Karandish)	21.30	775,000

Where to stay and eat

 Golden Beach Hotel (54 rooms) Simin Beach Resort, South Saheli Rd, beside Shah Shahid holy shrine; 35342900, 35342907. The nearest thing to a resort hotel is a few kilometres out of town, with bungalows, a restaurant (**$$**) & dive shop where you can hire equipment & book courses. **$$–$$$**

Hotel Alvand (25 rooms) Saadi Sq; ☏35228805, 35228809; **w** hotelalvand.com. A relatively new hotel, decorated in a modern & somewhat lifeless taste. A little pricey for the services on offer, but rooms are spacious & bright. **$$**

★ **Dehkhoda Coludang Guesthouse** (8 rooms) ☏58389319; **m** 0930 6665256. A charming & family-run traditional guesthouse in the village of Dehkhoda, 22km from Bandar Laft. Rooms are basic, but pleasant & you will certainly appreciate a homemade meal in the airy courtyard. **$–$$**

Diplomat Hotel (25 rooms) Azadegan St, beside the Red Crescent; ☏35225557, 35225558; **e** diplomat_hotel@yahoo.com. Catering mainly for foreigners, this hotel offers clean accommodation in a good location. **$–$$**

Park Hotel (34 rooms) Azadegan St; ☏35221459. Popular with Iranians & offers accommodation in semi-detached houses grouped around a pleasant inner courtyard. Best budget option & the in-house Alvand Restaurant ($) compensates with its views over the town & the shimmering sea. **$–$$**

✗ **Golden Nights Beach Restaurant** (Shabhaye Talai) Zeytoun Park; **m** 0936 3974103; **w** shabhayetalai.com; ⏰ 17.00–01.00 daily. A traditional restaurant in the beachside Zeytoun Park. The setting is excellent & the food is good. **$$**

What to see and do

Qeshm has wonderful clean beaches and natural scenery that will not leave you disappointed. The ruins of the **Portuguese fort**, built in the early 16th century in order to exert their control over the island, will most likely be the first site you visit. The castle remained in Portuguese hands until its takeover by the Safavid army under the command of Imam Gholi Khan.

Around 15km further along the coast, passing by the Golden Beach Resort and the **Khorbas Caves** (⏰ 07.00–17.00; entry 300,000 rials), the tourist route leads towards the **Stars Valley** (Darreh Setaregan) (entry 300,000 rials including small museum at the entrance). This spectacular rock plateau, formed around 2 million years ago as a result of wind and rain, and not by falling stars as the name suggests, is by far the most picturesque place on the island. A few kilometres along the coast lie the **Naz Islands**, accessible on foot at low tide.

Qeshm also boasts the world's longest water cave, **Tirian**, located at the western tip of the island. Discovered in 2006–07 by Polish and University of Shiraz adventurers, the cave is still being studied and is closed to tourists. There are two other caves in the vicinity that can be accessed, but you are not advised to venture here alone.

On the opposite shore of Qeshm and amid the oil rigs lies the famous **Mangrove Forest** (*jangal-e hara*) where you can hire a boat (700,000 rials per boat) for about an hour's sail amid these amazing trees. It is also near here that you can visit dhow-building yards, such as the Lancheh Sazi Azad Shipping Yard and another yard near the town of Douhab.

HORMUZ ISLAND (JAZIR-E HORMOZ) جزیره هرمز

It's an enjoyable half-day trip from Bandar Abbas to Hormuz, about 18km away from the Iranian coast and only 85km from Oman. Today it has a population of about 4,000 but, in times of political upheaval and military confrontation, ten times this number have sought temporary refuge on the island, despite the limited freshwater supplies; today water is piped over.

Getting there and away By fibreglass **speedboat** from the main jetty in Bandar Abbas (Shahid Haghani Passenger Terminal near Hotel Amin) to the quay (Iskel-e Qadim), the journey takes approximately 45 minutes (**w** hamdticket.ir; 100,000 rials each way). For groups, it should be possible, with prior notice, to hire a dhow (traditional sailing vessel), but the sailing time will be much longer. From Hormuz you can sail on to Queshm (90,000 rials) and from there either take the bus towards Fars province or sail back to Bandar Abbas.

What to see and do The best and, in fact, the only way to explore the whole island is to hire one of the local guides waiting on their pick-up motorcycles (500,000 rials/hr) or rickshaws (300,000 rials/hr) at the boat terminal. The driver will take you first to the **Portuguese sea fort** located on the northern tip (far left) of Hormuz Island. It is clearly visible to your left from the ferry landing. The fortress was built from local pink, brown and green coral shortly after the island was taken by the Portuguese military hero, Alfonzo Albuquerque, in 1515, quickly taking advantage of the severe Safavid military defeat at Chaldiran (page 183) to maintain and extend Portuguese control of the sea trading routes from India and the East Indies to Europe. Portuguese military history tells of an 8-hour battle by a few hundred soldiers against 30,000 islanders and defence troops, but Persian records state Albuquerque took the island by bribery and treachery. The Ottoman navy tried but failed to seize the island in 1550, but after Shah Abbas I took control of Suru and renamed it Bandar Abbas in 1615, it was only a matter of time before the Portuguese were pushed out of Hormuz, in 1622, for in the 1580s only seven or eight soldiers defended the castle. As the English had assisted the shah in this action, the fort and all of the 40km-odd island, along with 50% of the customs dues, were ceded to the British East India Company, but the gradual collapse of Safavid authority, advancing rebel Afghan forces, and changes to the customs levies led 18th-century European merchants to move trading activities further west to Bushehr. It was not until 1868 that the Qajar shah regained authority, but it was too late, for the newly opened Suez Canal was causing most shipping companies to reroute their vessels. By 1893, life on the island was described by the British consul as 'miserable', with just 200 residents. Matters improved from the mid 1960s, when Bandar Abbas received development funds, and it later became the naval headquarters.

Originally the fortress was completely surrounded by water, but now the sea laps around less than half of the walls. By the main entrance are the **prison dungeons** but you need a torch to explore. A walk across the main courtyard leads to the **underground church**, whose cross-groined vaults are supported on great columns; the altar must have stood where the entry now is. From here it is a short walk to the splendid **underground cistern**, built with an inner walkway around it. It's easy to imagine off-duty Portuguese soldiers sitting, talking, smoking and drinking here in the delicious cool. There is no spring water on the island to speak of, so rainwater would have filtered through the coral stone to collect in this and other cisterns throughout the fortress. Other than the remains of a tower (now one floor) with windows and cannons, there are just the ramparts left to explore.

From the loading quays, the driver will then drive you along the sea walls past a pink stone building with a pseudo-Portuguese frontage. It had once served as an **army post** built as a residence for Mohammad Reza Shah, but is closed at present with no military personnel around. The exterior wall is decorated with paintings of military officers and their relatives, some of whom were killed while on hajj to Mecca in the 1980s. Further on are fishermen's houses with nets placed ready for the evening fishing, and children playing table tennis on rusting metal doors. Some archaeological excavation was undertaken in 1977 during which 14th- to 17th-century pottery kilns and also shards, including Chinese export ware, came to light. It is known that the famous 14th-century Arab geographer, Ibn Battuta, stayed in the Ziyarat-e Khezr, located in the main cemetery alongside the Ziyarat-e Mollah, but little remains.

The highlight of the island's natural beauty, however, is the multi-coloured salt **rock formations**, covering large areas of Hormuz. Your driver will willingly accompany you through the rocky landscape and show you around. Salt and associated sedimentary and igneous rocks with seawater running through have over the centuries created a remarkable landscape, locally known as **Kuh-e Namak** (salt mountains). One of the pick-up motorcycle guides will also take you to salt mountain caves and the most beautiful beaches on the island. Swimming is allowed, but women, unfortunately, have to be fully dressed. It is the pristine beaches of Hormuz and the sense of being cast away far from the restrictions of the mainland, that over the past few years have attracted large numbers of young Iranians to travel and camp around the island. Cars are still essentially non-existent, but it makes Hormuz that more authentic than the commerce-driven Qeshm a few miles away.

BACK ON THE MAINLAND The road north from Bandar Abbas leads directly to Kerman but this is a very busy road, especially the first 150km climbing up into the mountains, crowded with lorries and tankers. But this route does take you past **Sirjan** (سیرجان) (page 327) where a British team found the remains of a Sasanid palace in the 1970s. Less tortuous, and with almost as dramatic scenery, is the road east towards **Minab** (میناب) (famous for its Thursday market where local women wear traditional clothes and masks locally known as *laqab* or *borkeh*) and then north via Kahnuj and Sabzvaran. The shelters for the Baluchi migratory families in this region are very distinctive, reminiscent of **reed huts** in the Iraqi delta area. Tall reeds are bent over to form a long barrel vault and covered with palm fronds, so making a shaded but well-ventilated shelter.

11

En Route to Yazd and Kerman

Yazd is the most historically interesting Zoroastrian city in Iran and is a must-see site for its wind towers, minarets and the nearby 'towers of silence'. However, the smaller city of Kerman is also worth a visit – not only for its architecture that reflects 1,700 years of settlement, but also for Iran's most glorious Persian garden in Mahan as well as for the carpets and jewellery on sale in its sprawling bazaar. The motorway south runs from Tehran past Yazd, and continues on to Kerman and beyond.

COMING TO YAZD FROM THE SOUTHWEST

ABARKUH ابرکوه From the crossroads at Surmaq, on the south–north route from Shiraz to Esfahan, the road to the northeast goes through Abarkuh (meaning 'On the Mountain' in Persian) 45km away. The town itself had once been a famous textile and trading centre in medieval times, but it never recovered from being devastated by rebel Afghan troops in the early 18th century. However, there is still plenty for the interested traveller to see.

Getting there and away The town (population 31,000) is best visited by **car** or rented **taxi** from Shiraz or Yazd. Alternatively, there are a number of regular **bus** services from the main cities at the times below:

(From Abarkuh)	Departure	(To Abarkuh)	Departure	Price (rials)
Esfahan (Sofeh)	19.00	Esfahan (Sofeh)	16.45	140,000
Shiraz (Karandish)	07.00; 12.30	Shiraz (Karandish)*	12.15; 12.30; 18.00	300,000
Tehran (Jonub)	19.00	Tehran (Jonub)	18.00	400,000
Yazd	05.30; 07.00; noon; 15.30	Yazd	noon; 13.00; 17.00	100,000

Many Shiraz–Yazd bus services also stop in Abarkuh. Enquire in advance.

🏠 Where to stay and eat

🏠 **Aghazadeh Boutique Hotel** (11 rooms) Shahid Bahonar St; 📞035 32827677; w aghazadeh. org. The iconic merchant house of Abarkuh, whose *badgir* adorns the 20,000 rials banknote, is now the most luxurious accommodation option in town. Beautifully restored with opulent rooms, excellent service & location in the historic centre make Aghazadeh a very attractive hotel indeed. **$$$$**

🏠 **Sarv-e Kohan Abarkuh** (8 rooms) Historic district; 📞035 32828681; e sarv.

tourismvillage@gmail.com. Opened in early 2016, this pleasant ecolodge in the historic part of Abarkuh offers comfortable rooms grouped around an inner courtyard with pomegranate trees & a freshwater brook. Here you can also taste the local rice dish with tomatoes (*kateh gujeh*) or simply enjoy the fresh air & a good sleep. **$$**

✕ **Koomeh Bibi Seyed Traditional Restaurant** Sarv St; 📞035 32828246; m 0913

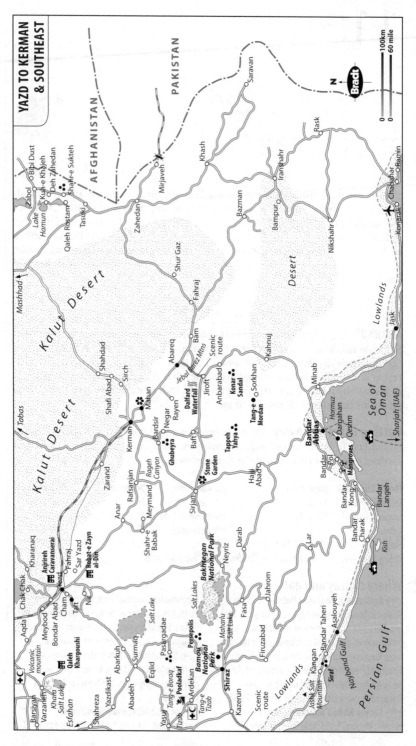

AFGHANISTAN

PAKISTAN

Kalut Desert

Kalut Desert

Kalut Desert

Desert

Sea of
Oman

Persian Gulf

Noyband Gulf

Lowlands

Lowlands

N

0   100km
0   60 mile

Lake
Hamun

Zabol
Bibi Dust
Kuh-e Khajeh
Deh Zahedan
Shahr-e Sukteh
Qaleh Rostam
Tasuki

Mirjaveh
Khash
Saravan
Rask

Mashhad

Tabas

Shahdad
Sirch
Shafi Abad
Mahan
Negar
Rayen
Dalfard
Waterfall
Abareq
Jebal Barez Mtns
Scenic
route
Jiroft
Anbarabad
Konar
Sandal
Tang-e
Mordan
Sorkhan
Bam
Kahnuj
Bazman
Bampur
Iranshahr
Nikshahr
Jask

Zahedan
Shur Gaz
Fahraj

Kerman
Bardsir
Ghubeyra
Baft
Tappeh
Yahya
Stone
Garden
Hajji
Abad
Minab
Hormuz
Dargahan
Qeshm
Bandar
Abbas
Bandar
Pol
Mangroves
Bandar
Kong
Bandar
Langeh
Bandar
Charak
Kish

Sharjah (UAE)

Zarand
Rafsanjan
Anar
Meymand
Rageh
Canyon
Shahr-e
Babak
Sirjan
Darab
Neyriz
Lar
Bandar
Taheri
Asalouyeh
Siraf
Kangan
Bandar Taheri

Kharanaq
Anjireh
Robat-e Zayn
al-Din
Pahraj
Sar Yazd
Yazd
Fahraj
Cham
Taft
Niriz

Bakhtegan
National Park
Salt Lakes
Mahan
Salt Lake
Fasa
Jahrom
Firuzabad

Aqda
Volcanic
mountain
Meybod
Bondar Abad
Chak Chak
Qaleh
Khargoushi
Barsiyan
Varzaneh
Khara
Salt Lake
Esfahan

Abarkuh
Surmaq
Eqlid
Abadeh
Yazdikast
Shahreza

Pasargadae
Persepolis
Bamou
National
Park
Shiraz
Ardekan
Pooladkaf
Tang-e
Tizab
Tizb
Yasuj
Tang-e Boraq
Tang-e Tizab

Kazerun
Scenic
route

Jashk Salt
Mountain
Bandar Kong

Maharlu
Salt Lake
Salt Lake

Bradt

306

3592390; ⏱ noon–16.00 & 20.00–23.00 daily. Excellent traditional restaurant serving a variety of local dishes & delicious tandoor bread baked in the clay oven. $–$$

What to see and do In the centre of town is the **masjed-e jame** with a classic four-*ivan* groundplan, probably established in the 14th century when its 'Baroque' plaster *mihrab* (1338) was installed in the left (on entering) *ivan*, although the domed prayer chamber could be from 12th-century Seljuk times. Today the town is most famous for its immense and reportedly 1,000-year-old **cypress tree** (*sarv*) and its traditional merchant houses, including the Qajar-period **Khaneh Aghazadeh** (now a boutique hotel), which adorns the 20,000 rial banknote. The house has been finely restored and its *badgir* is said to be the tallest in Iran. From the rooftop the vista opens into the inner courtyards of other adjacent mansions, which together served as a single residential quarter for wealthy merchants. The **Iran Cultural Heritage, Handicrafts and Tourism Organisation** is located in another traditional house nearby (⏱ 07.00–14.00 & 17.00–18.00; entry 300,000 rials) and is well worth a visit. It is currently a museum and houses some rare curios, including government-issued opium prescriptions. In Abarkuh there is also an interesting and engaging **Dasvareh Handicrafts Centre and Workshop** (Khaneh Ghayumi, Shahid Mohammad Ali Najafi Alley; m 0913 2509246), run by talented Hamed Akrami, who has been carefully and lovingly reviving local weaving techniques, including that of the traditional *sofrehpambeh* tablecloth. **Shahrasb** (شهراسب) village on the outskirts of Abarkuh is famous for its caravanserai and old houses made of sun-dried and fired bricks, known in Persian as *khesht*. The same material was used for a number of once-beautiful 14th-century tombs in the vicinity. In particular, archaeologists pointed to tombs such as the Mausoleum of Pir-e Hamza Sabz Push, with its lovely Ilkhanid *mihrab*, and the 1315 **Tomb of Hassan Ibn Kaikhosrow** (also known as Mazar-e Tavus) with its decorated interior. This mausoleum, one of the earliest tomb towers surviving in Iran, is on the hillside just to the south as you leave Abarkuh for Yazd before Shahrasb. Small, austere and (over) restored, this octagonal Gonbad-e Ali was built for a local warlord, 'the illustrious, the pure, the happy …' Omid al-Din Shams al-Dawleh and his wife, by their son in 1057, according to the brick inscription around the exterior. From here there is a superb view across the plateau from which the local ice houses can easily be spotted.

If you are keen on good vernacular architecture, do examine the layout and arrangement of an **ice house** (*yakhchal*) while in this region. There is a fine example here at the entrance of Abarkuh, coming from Esfahan or Shiraz or, if this is not convenient, there is a restored one near Azadi Square in Kerman. As with the cisterns and wind towers, these are made of fired brick and probably those that have survived are no earlier than 19th century in date. The basic plan is that of a large brick-dome chamber set deep into the ground, with a single door for access. Outside, there should be the remains of a long high mud-brick wall facing south to keep the lower dome section in shade. Beneath, there may still be signs of shallow beds along the wall. In winter months, 15–25cm of water was let in to flood these beds and freeze overnight. The ice was then broken up into blocks for storage, and insulated with straw in the chamber for summer use. Simple but very effective.

After the last roundabout on the very outskirts of Abarkuh (in the direction of Yazd), there is a huge brick complex set back to the right (notionally south). This was the family house of a politician who served in a pre-revolutionary parliament, and nearby there is a small fort with thick corner towers. The late 19th- and early 20th-century residence, known locally as **Amidsalar**, is ruined; the ground floor has a large and high central room surrounded by small chambers, while a well-worn exterior staircase at the back gives access to the first floor. To get into the **fort**, known by the same name, it is possible to scramble around the walls but, as its entrance is on the other side, it's quicker and easier to return to the main road and continue to the next (metalled) turning, which takes you almost directly to the entry gate. It is well worth exploring; you'll find the latrines, stables, bread ovens and a mosque, as well as the corner watchtowers.

In the south of the town is the **Masjed-e Birun** near the cemetery. It has a two-*ivan* plan with a domed sanctuary, which could be earlier in date than its (ruined) Timurid minaret and repair work. The prayer chamber area was heavily restored in the 18th century.

THE ROAD TO YAZD Travelling on to Yazd, the road traverses a 'desert' area with a salt lake lying to the south; there has been systematic planting of camel thorn and other desert shrubs here in an attempt to prevent the spread of the saline earth. Approaching Yazd, between the two chains of hills (especially if you are flying in during daylight hours) you will see lines of holes, like ruined giant anthills coming from the hillside across the land. These are inspection holes marking *qanats*, which brought water to irrigate the fields. The knowledge and skill needed to locate the right spot in the hills to tap into the water table, to angle and construct the tunnels to obtain the correct flow, beggar belief. In 2016 UNESCO collectively inscribed the *qanats* of Iran into their World Heritage List. Every year the *qanats* were checked for damage, removal of debris, etc, and although modern irrigation systems are fast taking over, just occasionally you still see a windlass device resting on top of an inspection hole.

Taft (تفت), 26km southwest of Yazd, has an important Safavid building, which is now the **Taft Anthropology Museum** (⊕ 09.30–13.30 daily; entry 300,000 rials). This late 15th-century *khanqah* and Mausoleum of Shah Khalilullah and the adjoining Masjed-e Shah Vali were built by the sister of the Safavid shah Tahmasp I. The famous Sufi mystic, Ne'matullah Vali Kermani (page 329) was responsible either directly or indirectly for persuading the provincial governor to allocate four years of tax revenue to this complex, and since then it has always been important for Sufis of the Ne'matollah order. Later embellishments were paid for by Tahmasp's sister in the 16th century.

Taft once had a vibrant Zoroastrian community, but their numbers have since dwindled. Young couple Tina and Ramtin are one of the few who still live in this rural town in between the mountains and have since 2016 been welcoming guests into their family home, **Nartitee Ecolodge** ✳ (9 rooms; ☎ 035 32622853; m 0919 4057118; w nartitee.ir; $–$$), converted into one of the most charming and authentic ecolodges in Iran. A member of the 'Mehmoun' association of traditional ecolodges, this traditional Zoroastrian house with a vast pomegranate garden is the place to spend a few days to unwind. Rooms are cosy, the rooftop is sunny and the tea is always fresh and promptly served to all guests. There are bicycles available for rent and hiking trips to Shirkuh Mountain (4,055m) can be arranged with the welcoming hosts. Situated within walking distance from Nartitee is **Sadri Namir Garden**. Originally a pomegranate grove, it is now a restaurant without alas any regular opening hours, but visitors are welcome to stroll around the pool on a hot summer day.

In the 14th century the Sufi movement evidently had a great following in this area as, some 30km from Nir at **Bidakhavid** (بيداخويد), 57km southwest of Yazd, there are two shrines facing each other. One is the mosque-shrine of a Sufi sheikh, Taj al-Din

Binyaman, identified and dated (1379) by his elaborately carved tombstone and consisting of three elements: a courtyard, a mosque and the tomb. As the shrine is a little larger than the mosque, it seems likely that this was originally built as a *khanqah* or meeting place for his disciples, and then became his tomb after his death. The other complex is the masjed-e jame, which possesses the unusual upper gallery arrangement in the square domed prayer hall, as seen in Yazd (page 314). Its stone *mihrab* is decorated with Quranic verses (Q3:38–40) and dated 1437, perhaps marking the completion of the building works.

Right before the police checkpoint 20km southwest on the approach to Yazd lies the small Zoroastrian village of **Cham** (چم) (signposted). Drive past the first group of houses along the tarmac road towards the hill with its *dakhmeh,* a Zoroastrian 'tower of silence'. Its platform is nicely laid out of stone, unlike the two examples in Yazd (page 317).

YAZD یزد *Telephone code 035*

The compact and friendly city of Yazd (altitude 1,215m; 677km southeast of Tehran) was already in the 9th and 10th centuries known as a centre of commerce and its dwellers today are still perceived as able tradesmen, albeit a little conservative in their spending habits. The population of Yazd has grown dramatically over the last century, from a mere 93,241 in 1966 to 551,000 today.

The city has long been associated with Zoroastrianism, and the production of textiles. It fell to the Arab invaders in 642CE but the Zoroastrian community remained strong until the late 17th century. There were still plenty of adherents left in the early 19th century when the city enjoyed a period of prosperity and relative calm. Official persecution has, however, subsequently caused many to flee to India or to Tehran, where the presence of foreign diplomatic missions offered more protection. Today, Zoroastrians represent less than 10% of the city's population; in 1995 there were an estimated 12,000 or fewer, mainly based in the Posht-e Khan Ali Quarter.

When Marco Polo visited in 1272, noting its fine textiles and its strategic location on trade routes from India and central Asia, this 'Good and Noble city' was walled, but undoubtedly today he would get hopelessly lost in the confusion of ring roads and roundabouts that have since been built. Yazd has an unusual topography, the result of the desert climate with its reliance on the *qanats* (underground water channels), all of which have unfortunately since completely dried up, and the trade routes. The city's orientation matches the alignment of the road to Shiraz and to Kerman towards India. Major urban changes in the 1930s and 1940s have, however, completely redefined the city street grid. Imam Khomeini Street (formerly Pahlavi Street) was built in 1935 to connect the government district of Narin Qaleh to the city centre.

Today Yazd is one of the most tourist-friendly cities in Iran, and offers excellent souvenir-shopping opportunities. Traditional hotels are abundant and conveniently located in the old part of town. Look through the workshops selling handwoven silk cloth *termeh,* produced solely in Yazd or try to visit one of the few still remaining *daraii* weaving mills. The city is also known as the *hosseiniyeh* of Iran, the centre of the Imam Hossein commemorative celebrations. Numerous *nakhl* (date palm litter) used for Moharram processions patiently wait on city squares to be carried again in the processions the following year. A number of historic houses functioning as museums also offer a glimpse into the *qanat* system that had once sustained the city.

GETTING THERE AND AROUND There are up to six daily **flights** from Tehran to Yazd, operated by various Iranian airline companies (3,000,000–5,000,000 rials) with a flying time of only 1 hour. There are daily overnight **buses** and **train** connections from the Iranian capital and most major population centres to Yazd. Below is a bus departure schedule with selected times from major Iranian cities:

From	Departure	Price (rials)
Esfahan (Kaveh)	06.30; 07.30 (hourly); 14.00; 16.30; 18.30; 20.30; 23.30	170,000
Esfahan (Sofeh)	12.25; 14.15; 15.55; 18.00	170,000
Esfahan (Jey)	01.30; 05.30; 06.00; 07.00 (hourly); 12.40; 16.15; 20.15; 23.59	170,000
Shiraz (Karandish)	08.00; 08.30; 10.15; 11.30; 14.30; 15.30; 17.00; 21.00; 23.00; 23.30; 23.55	330,000–430,000
Tehran (southern)	08.00; 08.30; 10.30; 12.30; 13.00; 14.30; 15.30; 16.00; 16.30; 17.00; 17.30; 18.30; 19.00; 20.30; 21.00; 23.30	300,000–590,000
Tehran (western)	10.15; 16.45; 17.00; 19.15; 20.00; 20.30; 21.30; 22.15; 23.00	300,000–590,000
Tehran (Beyhaghi)	20.30; 22.30; 23.00; 23.30	300,000–590,000

If coming from Varzaneh and Na'in, hop on one of the passing buses at the police post outside Na'in. Note that the main bus terminal in Yazd is quite far from the centre and a taxi to Imam Street will cost approximately 120,000 rials. Within the town, **walking** is best in the historic centre. To travel to and from the airport (10km from the city) and the railway station, as well as for excursions to the hinterland, **taxis** are available. When in Yazd, it is best to negotiate a price with taxi drivers. It is not recommended, in particular for single female travellers, to walk unaccompanied in the old town quarter after dark. For **bus**, **train** or **flight** tickets, go to **OGE Tour and Travel** (321 Imam St; ✆ 36229070, 36229074; w ogetravel.com). Avoid tourist-focused agencies; these often charge commission and do not always have the most up-to-date bus timetables. Your hotel can also assist in booking or even purchasing a ticket for you.

TOURIST INFORMATION The **tourist information office** (opposite Zendan-e Eskandar) can assist in hiring a taxi and has a wide range of maps and information leaflets about nearby attractions.

TOUR GUIDES

Atefeh Dehghan m 0913 3565234. With more than 11 years' experience in tourism, Atefeh is a very professional & recommended tour guide.
Esmaeil Tours m 0913 3520268; w yazdvoyage. com. For those with an interest in cycling & off-road travel, experienced & friendly Esmaeil offers a wide range of well-organised & interesting trips in Yazd & beyond, inc combined tours to Persepolis & Shiraz. He also runs a bicycle-rental shop on Vaqt-o Saat Sq.

Mohsen Hajisaeid m 0913 3514460; w iranpersiatour.com. For personalised & guided tours, contact this very knowledgeable English-speaking guide, who is also the President of the Iran Federation of Tourist Guide Associations.
Pegah Latifi m 0913 3524460. Wife of Mohsen Hajisaeid, Pegah also gives personalised & guided tours, specialising in culinary tours.

 WHERE TO STAY All hotels are located in traditional houses with bedrooms generally below street level in order to remain cool in hot weather and hence have no 'view'. Each hotel, however, has a good, traditional restaurant. New,

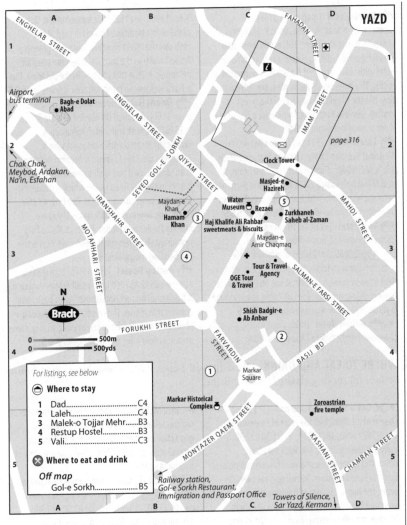

page 316

For listings, see below

⌂ **Where to stay**

1 Dad......................................C4
2 Laleh..................................C4
3 Malek-o Tojjar Mehr.......B3
4 Restup Hostel...................B3
5 Vali....................................C3

✕ **Where to eat and drink**

Off map
Gol-e Sorkh.....................B5

smaller and more spartan hotels have over the past three years sprung up in narrow old city alleys, making it very affordable to overnight in the historic centre. During the low season expensive hotels are more accommodating and offer reasonable discounts (up to 40%). A number of traditional and slightly more expensive hotels operate under the Mehr chain. For more information, see w mehrchainhotels.com.

⌂ **Malek-o Tojjar Mehr Hotel** [311 B3] (10 rooms) Inside the Panjeh Ali Bazaar; ◟36224060. Qajar-era home converted to an atmospheric traditional hotel with a small reception area & a lovely inner courtyard. It might prove to be a challenge to locate the hotel, as you have to walk through the bazaar itself. **$$$$**

⌂ **Dad Hotel** [311 C4] (61 rooms) 214 Farvardin St; ◟36229400; w dadhotel.com. The largest & one of the more expensive traditional hotels, it is located in a former 19th-century house & still managed by the descendants of the person who made it into a hotel more than 80 years ago. **$$$**

11

🏠 **Fazeli Hotel** [map, page 316] (16 rooms) Vaqt-o Saat Sq; ☎ 36208955, 36208956; e fazelihotel@yahoo.com. This nicely renovated Safavid-period building is now a cosy traditional hotel with medium-sized & tastefully decorated rooms. The inner courtyard is pleasant, although tiny, but the hotel café has one of the nicest rooftop views in Yazd. Drop in here for a cup of tea, if not staying overnight. **$$$**

🏠 **Laleh Hotel** [311 C4] (38 rooms) Next to Ab Anbar Golshan (water cistern), Taal area, Basij Bd; ☎ 36225048; e info@yazdlalehhotel.com. A traditional hotel since 2004, its design is perhaps excessively modern, which at times overshadows the historic Qajar residence the hotel is in. **$$$**

🏠 **Vali Hotel** [311 C3] (16 rooms) Off Imam Khomeini St, across from Shahzadeh Fazl; ☎ 36228050, 36228053; e info@valihotel.com. Popular with locals, this hotel is somewhat neglected by foreign tourists. It has one of the nicer inner roofed courtyards you will come across in Yazd & staff are pleasant & accommodating. **$$$**

✳ 🏠 **Kohan Hotel** [map, page 316] (22 rooms) Right before Alexander's Prison; ☎ 36212485, 36211297; w kohanhotel.ir. One of the oldest traditional hotels in Yazd, it has probably the nicest courtyard awash in greenery & spectacular in the summer when the trees are blooming. A little tricky to find in the old town, but it has a welcoming reception area & polite staff. **$$**

🏠 **Orient Hotel (Hotel Shargh)** [map, page 316] (20 rooms) Off Masjed-e Jame St; ☎ 36267783; e shargh.hotel@gmail.com. Excellently located with a pleasant vibe & consistent quality of service & accommodation. It is an ideal place if you wish to avoid the backpacker banter in the Silk Road Hotel, which is incidentally under the same management. The Orient's dble rooms are, however, a little small, if you are looking for extra leg room. Rooftop Marco Polo restaurant ($) offers great views over Yazd & the surrounding mountains. **$$**

🏠 **Restup Hostel** [311 B3] (4 rooms) Saadi Alley; m 0912 1510861; w yazdhostelrestup.com. A traditional budget hotel/hostel with basic, but comfortable rooms. The comfortable & relaxing atmosphere makes it a pleasant place to stay, some distance away from the touristy areas. **$$**

✗ **WHERE TO EAT AND DRINK** All traditional hotels listed above have an in-house restaurant serving classic Iranian cuisine.

✳ ✗ **Gol-e Sorkh Restaurant** [311 B5] Qasem Abad district, at the start of Ferdowsi Bd; ☎ 38211090, 38219010; ⏱ 11.30–23.30 daily. Off the touristy track, with very basic décor, this is nonetheless a local favourite & gets busy for lunch & dinner. In business for over 20 years, the menu consists of traditional dishes prepared exactly in the way Iranians like them. Try their mouthwatering *shirin polo* dish of rice with candied citrus zest, sweet carrots, almonds, pistachios & raisins on top. **$$**

✳ 🖵 **Art House Café** [map, page 316] m 0919 2115966; e yazd.arthouse@gmail.com; ⏱ 08.00–23.00 daily. Located in the historic house of Mehdi Malek Zadeh, the view from the rooftop terrace is the best in Yazd & there is a good choice of drinks & vegetarian dishes. The ground-floor souvenir shop offers a nice variety of handmade curios. **$**

🖵 **Tourist Library** [map, page 316] Rafeieian Historic Hse; ☎ 36208699; ⏱ spring–summer 08.30–21.00, autumn–winter 08.30–19.30; rooftop entry 120,000 rials. A café with an excellent selection of books about Iran in a variety of languages to leaf through. A little commercial, but with a lot of items & souvenirs to look around. The building itself, dating to the early Qajar period, is worth seeing. **$**

ENTERTAINMENT

✳ **Traditional Persian Night** m 0935 9357123; w tpersiannight.com. A special treat awaits visitors to Yazd, *shab neshini* or a traditional Persian night gathering, where guests have the pleasure of listening to a Persian story being recited to a *setar* accompaniment, followed by tea & a delicious dinner. Organised by Masoud Seyedhassani & held in the Kohan Hotel (see above), this unique & very special event offers an invaluable insight into Iranian culture, traditions & literature & is highly recommended.

Zurkhaneh Saheb al-Zaman [311 C3] ⏱ performance times: 06.00; 16.30, 17.30 & 19.00 Sat–Thu, 17.00 Fri; 300,000 rials. Popular with tourists, although less authentic than the more traditional *zurkhanehs*, which alas do not allow female visitors. Opened more than 20 years ago, it is located in a small alley off Amir Chaqmaq Sq

(look for the bldg with 5 *badgirs* or wind towers) around a 500-year-old *ab anbar* (water cistern). In the past it collected water from 7 *qanats,* which have since completely dried up.

SHOPPING
Handwoven cloth
Yazd is world famous for its intricate handwoven cloth, *termeh*, available in most shops across the city.

Rezaei [311 C3] (est in 1942) Stores on the cnr of Qiyam & Imam sts; 36270707; 09.30–22.00 daily; & Atlasi Bazaar; 38242073, 38242684; w termehrezaei.ir. One of the oldest suppliers of handwoven cloth.

Pottery, ceramics and carpets
Desert Handicrafts [map, page 316] In the vicinity of Alexander's Prison; m 0914 0333547; 09.00–21.00 daily. Recommended for carpets, colourful tiles, ceramics & antiques.
Oasis Gallery [311 C3] In the arcade under the Amir Chaqmaq façade vaults; 36227580;

m 0913 2589156; w oasisgallery.ir; 09.00–21.00 Sat–Thu, 10.30–21.00 Fri. Has a fine collection of pottery, ceramics & carpets.
Sarv-e Sefid Handicraft [map, page 316] In the vicinity of Alexander's Prison; m 0913 3593500; 09.00–21.00. Has a lovely selection of handmade ceramics.

Sweetmeats and biscuits
Haj Khalife Ali Rahbar [311 C3] On the cnr of Amir Chaqmaq Sq; 08.00–20.00 daily. In 2016, the shop celebrated its 100th-year anniversary. If you have a sweet tooth, this is the store to buy a box of Yazd's famous sweetmeats & biscuits. Alternatively, you can treat yourself to a piece of local sweet bread, *soruk*, from one of the bakeries in town.

OTHER PRACTICALITIES
$ **Foreign exchange shop** [map, page 316] Imam St; 36205560, 36205561
Historic City of Yazd Cultural Heritage Base [map, page 316] Old city. Head here to get a general idea of the topography of Yazd; here you will find old city pictures & maquettes.
 Hospital [311 D1] Seyyed al-Shohada, Imam St; 36210010, 36210015. There are also a number of late-night pharmacies on the same street.
Immigration and Passport Office [311 B5] Near Qasem Sq; 08.00–13.00. Only a short taxi

ride from the city centre; visa extensions can be processed in a day.
Iran Cultural Heritage, Handicrafts and Tourism Organisation Building [map, page 316] Imam St. This dates to the Pahlavi period & has a distinctive façade.
 Pharmacy [311 C3] There are a few pharmacies in the city centre & Chamran Pharmacy (Farokhi St; 36266900) is open 24hrs.
 Post office Main post office [map, page 316] next to the Melli Bank on Imam St; 08.00–14.30 daily

WHAT TO SEE AND DO   Although it does not possess any royal monuments like those at Persepolis, Shiraz and Esfahan, Yazd is renowned for its **vernacular buildings**, including ice houses, water cisterns (*ab anbars*), domestic houses and spectacular wind towers (*badgirs*). Such windcatchers were once common in cities and towns throughout the Middle East, and while quite a few of them now survive in Iran, they serve more as a decoration since residents prefer electric air conditioners. The idea is simple: a brick tower is built – anything from 30cm high upwards – with one or more openings at the top and directional vents to catch the prevailing wind. The air is funnelled into the building, either at ground-floor level or lower, and perhaps passed over a small pool and fountain to cool it further before travelling through the rooms.

Yazd boasts one of the tallest *badgirs* in the world at 33.8m, gracing the (former) governor's pavilion in the **Bagh-e Dolat Abad** [311 A2] (07.30–17.00

(times may vary; the garden is sometimes open till 23.00); entry 500,000 rials). Although the garden is associated with a 1718 endowment, which included the construction of a school, bath, caravanserais and *qanats* over 60km in length, the layout is one typically associated with a late 18th-century date. A long avenue of cypresses leads down to the main building (now private property), but the pavilion on the right after entering the garden is open to the public. This small, two-storey building has been carefully repaired. Both of the main chambers had fountains, each filling a large stone basin, which fed others and also reflected the colourful window glass. If you walk through to the back room, you can look up the 'chimney' to see the wind ventilation system. Bagh-e Dolat Abad is one of the nine Persian gardens, which were in 2011 were collectively inscribed on the UNESCO World Heritage List.

The traditional water cistern (*ab anbar*) also employed wind towers. One well-known Yazd example is the **Shish Badgir-e Ab Anbar** (Six Wind Tower Cistern) [311 C4] located on the north side of Shahid Beheshti Street (the extension of Ayatollah Kashani Street) behind the shops. It is no longer used by the community, so to prevent rubbish being thrown in, a padlocked gate has been erected.

An interesting cluster of historic buildings lies in the **city centre** around the **masjed-e jame** [map, page 316], which was founded by the local Seljuk commander in 1119 over a ruined Sasanid fire temple, and largely rebuilt during the 14th century. Visitors to the mosque are immediately struck by the disproportionately high minarets over the entrance, which render the (double) dome almost insignificant. These are the first indication of 14th-century work, along with the 1324–28 entrance vestibule decorated with numerous plaques recording local decrees, taxes and endowments. Most of the splendid ceramic patterning in the main prayer hall beyond was put in place 40 or so years later. The work is worth looking at, whether for the geometric strapwork in turquoise against a brick surface with intricately cut and moulded plaster infills, or the 'mosaic' jigsaw panels of the magnificent 1375 *mihrab* – although each year it seems more replacement tile pieces have been inserted. The prayer hall has an unusual gallery arrangement (for women?) occasionally seen in other late 14th-century mosques, but here the heavy piers and vaulting system disperse the weight, allowing the side walls to be pierced by windows, bringing shafts of light into the chamber. On the right is a large winter prayer hall built in the 16th century by the Safavid architect Saad Ibn Mohammad Kaduk. The bare whitewashed walls make the beautiful proportions and transverse vaulting fully apparent. In the courtyard (104m × 99m) there are steps on this side, leading down to an underground room with a disused *qanat*.

Leaving by the same entrance, take the second left in the parking area and nearby, on your immediate right, is the small entrance into the popular shrine **Aramgah Rokna al-Din** (آرامگاه سید رکن الدین) [map, page 316] (⏲ 08.00–13.00 & 16.00–20.00 Sat–Tue & Thu, 08.00–13.00 Fri, 08.00–20.00 Wed; only women are allowed in on Wed (remember to put on one of the chadors available at the entrance). Little, but enough, remains of the original complex of school and library that was once renowned for its mechanical sciences. Its minarets were surmounted with automata such as a bird, which turned to face the sun, and chroniclers described a huge circular wall calendar whose rings and sections constantly moved to show the passage of time. The exterior still retains some exquisite detail, which is easily overlooked. Inside the gloomy, single-domed chamber housing the cenotaph is a mass of low-relief plasterwork carved and painted (and originally gilded) in strong 14th-century central Asian style, akin to that of the architecture in Samarkand and Shahr-e Sabz, Uzbekistan. The high walls are decorated with plaster moulding in blind niche forms of varying size in rows, and panels of plaited *Kufic* calligraphy. Huge teardrop medallions in plaster embellish the dome interior (diameter 12m) and underneath is the silver-gilt grille protecting the cenotaph.

Continue along this alley, crossing the modern *hosseiniyeh* space (if in doubt bear left), and eventually you will reach **Zendan-e Eskandar** (Alexander's Prison) [map, page 316] (Zaiee Sq; ☉ autumn–& winter 08.00–17.00, spring–summer 08.00–20.00; entry 500,000 rials), tucked back in the same open space as the **Davazdah Imam** (Twelve Imams) [map, page 316]. Safavid history tells that Alexander the Great built a castle in Yazd (then known as Kasah), but local tradition says he was actually imprisoned here in the extensive underground chamber beneath the courtyard. The present building is much later, finished in 1305, and is now used as a theological college. It was largely rebuilt in 1671, although the domed prayer hall to the right of the entrance retains some 14th-century decorative plaster. Davazdah Imam nearby, is in theory open for tourists, but remains essentially closed. The oldest historical structure in Yazd, it dates from 1038 and is known for having fine-quality plasterwork in the *mihrab* and dome but, despite its name, none of the imams or their relatives was interred here. It is thought the two Shi'a brothers who paid for the construction meant it to be purely a commemorative building, for the painted Quranic inscriptions (including Q2:158, 163, 255–6; Q40:65, 67) stress belief in the Imamate and are clearly a personal selection. You could walk north from here, asking directions to the **Khaneh Lariha** [map, page 316] (☉ autumn–winter 08.00–17.00, spring–summer 08.00–20.00; entry 300,000 rials), a conserved and repaired 19th-century merchant's house. It has a charming atmosphere with a large pool in the central courtyard over which sits a huge, gently disintegrating wooden *charpoy*. All explanations inside the house are in Farsi only. Just a few hundred metres away is **Yazd Heydarzadeh Coins & Anthropology Museum** [map, page 316] (☉ 08.00–20.00 daily; entry 500,000 rials). This Qajar-period Arabzadeh mansion, located in the Fahadan district of the old city, has certainly seen better days, but its exhibits of coins from 42 historical epochs, starting with the Achaemenid Empire, justify a quick visit here. The Parthian coins are particularly interesting. The underground *qanat* room accessed via a long stairway suggests it had once been a wealthy household with private access to a clean water supply.

In the bazaar area around **Maydan-e Amir Chaqmaq** [311 C3], you could visit the **Amir Chaqmaq** complex and the Mosque of Amir Chaqmaq, both named after the former ruler of Yazd. The mosque (☉ during prayer times only) was constructed in 1437, along with a hostel, cistern and *qanat*, bath, caravanserai and the square itself, built by a local Timurid prince Amir Chaqmaq and his wife Seti Fatemeh, who was linked to the central Asian family of Timur Leng (d1405); only the mosque and her tomb remain. The mosque layout, with its 16m² courtyard, two *ivans* and the prayer chamber with an upper gallery like the masjed-e jame are original, as is the 'mosaic' tilework in the prayer chamber and on the *mihrab*. The eastern section, on the other hand, was extensively repaired in the 19th century.

Most visitors, however, are attracted by the multi-storey building at the end of the *maydan*. Like the Palace of the Winds, Jaipur (north India), it is pure **façade**, constructed in the 19th century on early 15th-century foundations to provide a viewing stand for city parades and ceremonies, especially those of Moharram. A huge wooden *nakhl*, shaped like a giant (palm) leaf, stands on the right, waiting to be draped in black cloth and carried by 70 or so young men the following year. The central gateway, its northern entrance, was until the 1930s connected to the main bazaar area. The façade's southern gate opens into Salman Farsi (formerly Soraya) Street, built in 1946 as part of the major urban development in the city.

Turning away from the Amir Chaqmaq complex façade, walk ahead towards the main crossroads and look up for the large sign for the **Water Museum** [311 C3] (⊕ 08.00–13.30 & 14.30–19.00 daily; entry 300,000 rials), located in a traditional merchant house of about 1890. There is good plasterwork especially in the audience platform area and the exhibition showing the system of cooling and underground living is in the basement with good information and colour pictures of *qanat* construction and repair, along with the tools; there are some English captions.

After the crossroads on the other side of the road are some high-quality nut and dried fruit shops. Walking down this side takes you past a marvellously understated pair of **wooden doors** dating from the Safavid period; the detail is superb. On the opposite side of the busy road are passageways into the fabric, furnishings and gold shops of the bazaar, but continue for another 400m or so and ask directions to **Maydan-e Khan** [311 B3], the fruit and vegetable market. At the far end of this huge courtyard is a small office of a *naqqash* (traditional textile designer) with his cartoons and drawings (for carpet making) ready for sale or hire. The narrow passage to its immediate right leads to the **Hamam Khan** [311 B3] of 1797, a former bathhouse. It is now a traditional restaurant run by the Iranian Touring & Tourism Investment Co (ITTIC), but you can drop in to have a walk around.

Southwest of the city centre
The **Markar Historical Complex** (Off Markar Sq, Milad Alley; ☏ 36270039; m 0913 5246477; w markarmuseum.com; ⊕ 09.00–13.00 & 16.00–20.00 Sat–Thu, 09.00–13.00 Fri; entry 160,000 rials) offers the most detailed and comprehensive insight into the traditions and customs of Zoroastrians. Originally an orphanage built in 1934, it is named after its founder Peshotan Dossabhai Markar, member of a prominent Parsi (Zoroastrian) family from India. Profoundly interested in Iran and Iranian culture, Markar had over his lifetime established a number of schools and educational endowments both in Iran and India.

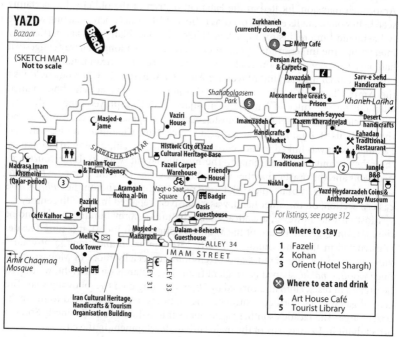

YAZD
Bazaar

(SKETCH MAP)
Not to scale

Zurkhaneh (currently closed)
4 ☐ Mehr Café
Persian Arts & Carpets
Davazdah Imam
Sarv-e Sefid Handicrafts
Alexander the Great's Prison
Khaneh Lariha
Shahabolqasem Park 5
Zurkhaneh Sayyed Kazem Kheradnejad
Desert handicrafts
Masjed-e Jame
Vaziri House
Imamzadeh
Handicrafts Market
Fahadan Traditional Restaurant
Historic City of Yazd Cultural Heritage Base
Koroush Traditional
SARRAFHA BAZAAR
Iranian Tour & Travel Agency
Fazeli Carpet Warehouse
Friendly House
Jungle B&B 2
Madrasa Imam Khomeini (Qajar-period) 3
Aramgah Rokna al-Din
Vaqt-o Saat Square 1
Badgir
Nakhl
Yazd Heydarzadeh Coins & Anthropology Museum
Pazirik Carpet
Oasis Guesthouse
Café Kalhor
Melli
Clock Tower
Masjed-e Manargoli
Dalam-e Behesht Guesthouse
ALLEY 34
IMAM STREET
Amir Chaqmaq Mosque
Badgir
ALLEY 31
ALLEY 33
Iran Cultural Heritage, Handicrafts & Tourism Organisation Building

For listings, see page 312

☐ Where to stay
1 Fazeli
2 Kohan
3 Orient (Hotel Shargh)

✖ Where to eat and drink
4 Art House Café
5 Tourist Library

Central museum exhibits are displayed in the basement of the main building of the complex, and provide an informative overview of the history of the orphanage and its founder. Information is clearly presented in both Persian and English, making it easy to follow, but museum employees will gladly show you around. Of particular interest to the visitor is the Zoroastrian tradition of table arrangement (*sofreh*) for various celebrations, such as *sedreh pooshi* (Zoroastrian religious initiation ceremony) and *gavahgiri* (marriage contract). Each *sofreh* carries a set number of items considered holy, symbolic and important to the specific event or celebration. This ancient tradition has made its way into modern Iranian homes in the form of the Nou Rouz table arrangement of *haft-sin* (page 71). Other exhibits in the museum include a traditional Zoroastrian *koshti* belt-weaving machine. The Markar Historical Complex consists of a number of other interesting buildings, such as an old-style *hamam* and *ab anbar* (water cistern) and in addition to its cultural activities, it offers weekly Zoroastrian religious classes. The **Markar Clock Tower** (originally called the Ferdowsi Clock Tower) built in 1942 is in a nearby city square. No journey through the history and tradition of Zoroastrianism will be complete without a visit to the central **Zoroastrian fire temple** (*ateshkadeh*) [311 D5] (Kashani St; ☉ 08.00–17.00; entry 300,000 rials). Located in a side street off Ayatollah Kashani Street, it has the appearance of a family house set within a garden. Accommodation for pilgrims is located in the main section, which, as with the actual temple area, is off-limits to casual visitors. Nevertheless, the sight of the sacred fire burning in a huge steel vessel brings the philosophy and history of Zoroastrianism home. This fire, protected by a glass screen to prevent pollution from people's breath, has been burning since 470CE (see box, page 232). In all there are some 18 fire temples operating in Yazd itself and the surrounding villages.

Two **dakhmeh** (Zoroastrian 'towers of silence') are situated a little south of town, after the Safaiyeh Hotel. A taxi from the centre will cost around 100,000 rials. In accordance with Zoroastrian laws governing the sanctity of earth, fire, air and water, in Achaemenid times the dead were exposed and their bones later gathered to be placed in ossuaries or tombs in rock. But in later centuries large circular stone walls were built on rock and the bodies of Zoroastrian men, women and children were placed on their designated, paved zone on the open stone platform inside. A small central pit, filled with sand, charcoal and phosphorus to prevent pollution of the earth, acted as the drain. These towers are no longer in use (Zoroastrians are now interred in the nearby cemetery within a concrete chamber to avoid pollution of the earth), so with time and energy visitors may climb up – the smaller, lower one on the right entailing a marginally shorter, easier clamber with access high up. Access into the other *dakhmeh* is best made from the gentle rise on the extreme left rather than the track on the extreme right. These towers were constructed according to strict observance of prayer and ritual, so please treat them accordingly, even though others clearly have not. Below, there is a collection of buildings, a water cistern with two wind towers and rooms for mourners. There is also a mortuary reception area, where the body would be cleansed and dressed in a clean but old sacred shirt (*sudreh*), before being tied to a metal bier by the sacred girdle (*kusti*) for carrying to the platform. The local authorities have turned a blind eye to vandalism of these buildings, which only serves to fuel foreigners' negative perceptions of religious tolerance in modern Iran. If you come here for sunset, climb up the lower of the two towers as the top platform on the higher *dakhmeh* has high side walls blocking the view.

North of Yazd A day trip from Yazd can be combined to visit **Meybod** (ميبد), 50km northwest, with the remains of the mud-brick **Narin Fort** (entry 300,000 rials) that once protected the old caravan route and the town itself. As the name suggests, this used to be a strong Zoroastrian centre (*moabed*: priest). A nicely restored caravanserai with traditional double-cloth *zilu* workshops is well worth the 5-minute taxi ride from the fort. Adjacent to the caravanserai you find a welcoming **post office museum** (entry 300,000 rials), located in what used to be one of the 99 similar post office stations, known as *chaparkhaneh*, around Iran. This is the last one remaining. Here you can also ask for the key to the *yakhchal* (ice house) right across the road. Meybod is known as a production centre for domestic pottery incorporating 'traditional' patterns and colouring. It also possesses a 15th-century masjed-e jame (in the mid 1970s the mosque still owned a historic *zilu* or floor-covering with a woven date corresponding to 1405).

In the adjacent town of Ardakan you can overnight in the newly opened and family-run **Kheshtomah** traditional hotel (8 rooms; 44 Haj Ahmadi Alley, old town; m 0937 6061021; w kheshtomah.com). Young couple Samaneh and Habib, who run this cosy place, ensure that all guests have a wonderful stay and learn about the history of the area. Make sure to visit the underground *qanat* (entry 500,000 rials), which has only recently opened to tourists.

In **Bondar Abad** (بندرآباد), 35km northwest of Yazd, there is a 14th-century complex honouring the Sufi sheikh Taq al-Din Dada Mohammad (d1301), buried here in 1321. It has one of Iran's mere handful of tiled *minbars*, patterned with eight- and 12-star motifs, probably made and installed at the same time as a carved marble panel, in 1473.

Northeast of Yazd there are various **desert camps**, such as Haft Sang or Sinbad, that offer basic facilities, seating around a bonfire and some company, if overnighting in solitude in the desert is not something you look forward to. Further on in the direction of Tabas lies a nicely restored Safavid-period **Anjireh Caravanserai**, which in 2016 was converted into a hotel (10 rooms) and takes guests on advance booking. To make a reservation, contact Esmaeil from Esmaeil Tours (m 0913 3520268) in Yazd. Just a few kilometres away is the town of **Kharanaq** (خرانق) which you should consider visiting for the ruined Safavid village and its shaking minaret.

You must find time for **Chak Chak** (چک چک) (Shrine of Pir-e Sabz), some 50km northeast of Yazd (turning at Hossein Abad), to visit the **shrine of Banu Pars**, dedicated to the goddess Anahita. Zoroastrians from all over Iran and even from abroad gather here every year in mid-June (between 24 and 26 Khordad of the Solar calendar) for the annual pilgrimage and celebration. The taxi will drop you off at the parking area to let you climb the numerous flights of steps up to reach the small grotto shrine. This is no living village; rather a desolate collection of houses and communal kitchens to accommodate pilgrims. Only a few families look after the place, including a reticent shrine attendant who ensures all visitors remove their shoes. The shrine itself is understated, consisting of a grotto housing an ancient *chenar* (oriental plane) tree with the marble grotto floor covered in water dripping from the mountain (in Persian *chak chak* means the sound of water dripping). The doors and walls date only from the early 1960s but it is known that pilgrims have come here in June since 1626, if not earlier. According to Islamic chronicles, however, this was the place where a daughter of the last Sasanid shah, Yazdegerd III (d651CE), pursued by the invading Arabs, begged for help. Desperately thirsty, she was offered a bowl of milk, only for it to be overturned by a cow before she could drink it (Anahita was traditionally offered bull sacrifices). Terrified for her life, she prayed that the rock face would open up for her and she disappeared into it; similar stories are connected with the shrine near Rey (page 119) and further afield in Maaloula near Damascus, Syria, at the grotto of St Tikla.

Towards Kerman Approximately 30km southeast of Yazd lies the small town of **Fahraj** (فهرج) (population 16,500), whose masjed-e jame is believed to be the oldest in Iran. Located in the centre of town, it is built from sun-dried bricks in a simple style with some decorative elements, characteristic of the Sasanid period. The minaret of the mosque dates back to the 10th or 11th century. If staying here overnight, there is a pleasant, albeit a little pricey, traditional hotel, the **Farvardinn Desert Inn** (9 rooms, most rooms en suite; in an alley behind the post office & Fahraj Castle; **m** 0913 3524723; **w** farvardinn.com. **$$**).

Around 40km southeast along the same road, but turning towards Mehriz, lies the small village of **Sar Yazd**, with the remains of what is known as the Fortress of Sar Yazd and a number of other examples of Sasanid architecture, including water cisterns, a post office and a caravanserai. **Mehriz** (مهریز) itself boasts a delightful **Pahlavanpour Persian Garden** (**w** persiangarden.org; ⏰ 08.00–18.00 daily; entry 500,000 rials). Guarded by a tall wall and a watchtower at the entrance, this magnificent garden, with sycamore trees and water streams from the 600-year-old Hassan Abad *qanat*, should not be missed. A light meal in its traditional restaurant in the summer is particularly recommended.

Further south on the road to Kerman, the most visible monuments are caravanserais, the first standing to the west of the main road about 55km from Yazd, the other approximately 65km further on and almost straddling the modern highway. The first is known as the **Robat-e Zayn al-Din** (entry 100,000 rials), built by a Safavid governor of Kerman. It consists of a circular enclosing wall with five towers and a monumental entrance. Inside, the accommodation and relaxation areas were arranged around a 12-sided court with a large hall opposite the main door. The whole building has been so extensively restored that the functions of the various rooms can no longer be distinguished, but in a caravanserai of this size there should have been a small mosque, kitchen area and perhaps a *hamam*. About 100m away is the ruined, two-storey stable block with its mangers still intact. Heavily vitrified bricks in the broken dome of the small corner chamber, with two broken fireboxes in the extreme right corner of the courtyard, suggest to us that this was the blacksmith's forge for making horseshoes and the like. The caravanserai is privately owned and functions as a hotel (35 rooms; ☏ 035 38243338; **m** 0912 4500124; **e** zeinodin2003@yahoo.com; US$50 pp per night including HB) and a restaurant. The people in charge of its day-to-day management are friendly and caring. Cyclists are welcome to use the toilet facilities and eat at a special price. In the evening hotel staff can arrange star watching with Reza Tameri for guests.

The second caravanserai before Anar (which translates as 'pomegranate' in Persian, suggesting the speciality of this area) is thought to be earlier in date. The smaller section on one side of the building perhaps acted as a toll house, levying dues from passing merchant trains, while the main building offered accommodation and stabling.

The road to Kerman lies via **Rafsanjan** (رفسنجان), from where the former Iranian president Akbar Hashemi Rafsanjani (d2017) takes his name. The city itself is of little historical interest, but the **Presidential Museum of Rafsanjan** (⏰ 07.30–15.00 Sun–Fri; entry 10,000 rials) dedicated to the late president is worth a brief visit. Museum exhibits are spread over a number of rooms on the first floor of a large oval building and include mainly personal gifts and presents bestowed to Rafsanjani from world leaders and various organisations over his 40-year-long career, including two presidential terms. Labelling is scarce and in Persian only, but photographs of Rafsanjani's life speak for themselves. Moving anticlockwise, an interesting item in the very first hall is a fine mother-of-pearl *incrustation* of the Dome of the Rock mosque in Jerusalem, a present from the late Palestinian leader Yasser Arafat. The actual maquette of the Dome of the Rock is a gift from the ambassador of Jordan to Iran. The room with pictures of Rafsanjani's meetings with world leaders contains a maquette of his coffin, but the late president is buried at the Behesht-e Zahra Cemetery outside Tehran. For lunch, there is a good **Tavakkol Restaurant** you could try (98 Baft-e Tarikhi, Shahid Beheshti St; \ 034 34269097; ⊕ noon–midnight daily; $). Formerly a *hamam*, it is now the only traditional restaurant in Rafsanjan and has a great menu at very reasonable prices. About 6km east of Rafsanjan is **Khaneh Haj Agha Ali** (⊕ 08.00–14.00 & 16.00–20.00 daily; entry 300,000 rials), the world's largest house built of sun-dried mud bricks (*khesht*). This historical mansion from 1757 took a number of years to be restored, but its long-awaited conversion into a hotel and a traditional restaurant is alas still pending.

The area around Rafsanjan is mainly known for numerous groves of pistachio trees. It is not a dramatic landscape but the real reason for coming here is **Rageh Canyon** (دره راگه), a stunning 20km-long valley, created by erosion and shaped by the waters of the Guivdary River and the wind. This natural attraction is a well-kept secret in Iran; very few people have been here or know about it, which makes it ideal for camping and trekking. There are still a number of *qanats* running through the valley, carrying water to the pistachio groves. If you are driving, finding the way here may be a little tricky. Just 5km from Rafsanjan towards Kerman turn right towards Nasriyeh village off the main road after the Almas Kavir tile factory. From here it is another 20km along a gravel road; you'll need a 4x4 vehicle to reach the canyon. It is otherwise best to contact Reza Sadeghzadeh (m 0913 1936912; w rageh.ir), who can arrange trips and camping in the canyon.

KERMAN کرمان *Telephone code 034*

Perhaps founded by the Sasanid shah Ardashir I in the early 3rd century (it was called Beh-e Ardashir until Safavid times), the town of Kerman (987km south of Tehran) quickly succumbed to the Arab armies in 642ce. Thereafter, all the major regimes in the region were eager to control this important town linking the old caravan routes from Afghanistan, India and the south coast into the Iranian heartlands. It came under Seljuk authority in 1041, but severe damage by Turkoman tribesmen in 1187 resulted in Zarand (87km northwest) becoming the provincial centre, and this opened the way for a Mongol general to establish a short-lived principality here. The town continued to pass from hand to hand – Muzaffarid authority to Timurid (until that empire fragmented) to the Qara Qoyunlu and then the Aq Qoyonlu tribal confederations – until Iran was united under Safavid control. Kerman had always had a large Zoroastrian community, but in the last years of the 17th century the Safavid shah Soleyman yielded to theological demands that its adherents be relocated to the north of the city. By the mid 19th century, perhaps only 150 Zoroastrian families remained in Kerman itself. From 1750 until 1792 the region, including Bam, was controlled by the Ismailis with the agreement of the Zand family. With the Qajar advance and takeover of Zand authority, the Ismaili community left for Tehran and then migrated to Pakistan and India. Kerman was the site of the tragic culmination of the Zand dynasty. It was here in 1794 that the last of the Zand rulers, Lotf Ali Khan, died in a siege against Agha Mohammad. The inhabitants of Kerman stood firm against the barbaric Qajars and paid a high price for their bravery. Tens of thousands were killed, blinded or taken into slavery and it took the city decades to recover.

Despite such a troubled political history, the region had a long-established reputation in textile production, especially carpet weaving, even before the Safavid Shah Abbas I established a royal carpet workshop here. Marco Polo

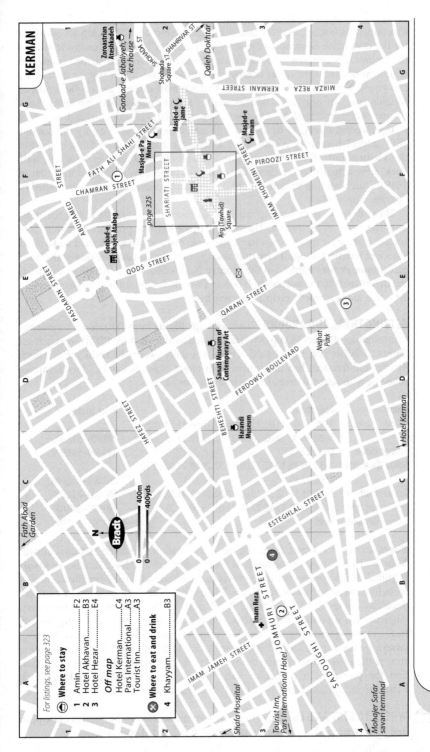

KERMAN

For listings, see page 323

ⓘ **Where to stay**
1 Amin..........................F2
2 Hotel Akhavan..............B3
3 Hotel Hezar..................E4

Off map
Hotel Kerman..................C4
Pars International...............A3
Tourist Inn.....................A3

✗ **Where to eat and drink**
4 Khayyam.....................B3

Fath Abad
Garden

N

Bradt

0   400m
0   400yds

Shafa Hospital

Tourist Inn,
Pars International Hotel

Mohajer Safar
savari terminal

PASDARAN STREET

HAFEZ STREET

ABUHAMED STREET

CHAMRAN STREET

FATH ALI SHAHI STREET

QODS STREET

Gonbad-e
Khajeh Atabeg

Masjed-e Pa
Menar

page 325

SHARIATI STREET

Arg (Towhid)
Square

QARANI STREET

FERDOWSI BOULEVARD

Sanati Museum of
Contemporary Art

Harandi
Museum

BEHESHTI STREET

ESTEGHLAL STREET

IMAM JAMEH STREET

Imam Reza

JOMHURI STREET

SADOUGHI STREET

Neshat
Park

Hotel Kerman

IMAM KHOMEINI STREET

PIROOZI STREET

Masjed-e
jame

Masjed-e
Imam

Shohada
Square 17 SHAHRIVAR ST

SHAHI ST

Zoroastrian
Ateshkadeh

*Gonbad-e Jabaliyeh,
ice house →*

MIRZA REZA   KERMANI STREET

Qaleh Dokhtar

mentioned its leather workers and silk embroiderers in 1271. Keep an eye open for the distinctive Kerman embroidery of chain-stitch and *tambour* (referring to the embroidery patterns made on fabric stretched over a drum-shaped frame) on scarlet wool cloth (but reject cheaper manmade fabrics); you pay for quality. Its rug production achieved such quality that Kerman carpets graced the imperial Mughal court of northern India as well as Safavid palaces and pavilions. Such carpets were described by Engelbert Kaempfer (d1716), doctor and secretary to the Swedish envoy, as decorated with animal motifs, so possibly the famous 16th- and 17th-century 'Animal' and 'Hunting' carpets (such as those housed in the Victoria and Albert Museum, London, and the Metropolitan Museum, New York) were actually woven here. The quality of produce was so good here that in 1659 a Dutch trading station opened in Kerman to purchase wool. It remained in operation until 1744.

These days Kerman has a population of more than 621,000 and is the most important city in the region. The capital city of Kerman province, where 80% of Iranian pistachios are grown, it has a lovely old town with a vast bazaar and a good choice of jewellery shops. Kerman is also the best place to explore one of the most picturesque Persian gardens in the country, Bagh-e Shahzadeh in Mahan, as well as the desert areas to the northeast. It boasts a wonderful museum of modern Persian art – that alone is worth a trip all the way here.

GETTING THERE AND AROUND There are daily **flights** from Tehran, with a journey time of under 2 hours (4,000,000 rials) as well as at least three flights weekly from Shiraz, Esfahan and Kish Island. There is a daily overnight **train** service from Tehran and frequent **bus** departures from major cities. Below is a bus departure schedule with selected times from major Iranian cities:

From	Departure	Price (rials)
Esfahan (Kaveh)	09.00; 10.00; 11.00; 11.30; 13.00; 15.00; 15.30; 16.30;	
	17.00; 18.00; 20.00; 20.30; 21.30; 22.30; 23.15	340,000–588,000
Esfahan (Sofeh)	21.30; 22.15	340,000–588,000
Shiraz (Karandish)	08.30; 09.30; 10.30; 11.00; 12.30; 20.00; 21.00; 21.30;	
	22.00; 22.30	250,000–500,000
Tehran (southern)	15.45; 16.30; 18.30; 19.00; 20.00; 21.00; 21.30; 22.30	500,000–830,000
Tehran (western)	14.30; 15.00; 15.30; 17.30; 18.00; 19.30; 21.30	500,000–830,000
Tehran (Beyhaghi)	18.00	500,000–830,000

Buses arrive and depart from the main bus station – Adineh terminal (Imam Khomeini Motorway) in the south of the city. Kerman also has a number of *savari* terminals for destinations in the province. Southbound *savaris* (eg: Jiroft) depart from Beyram Abad Square; for Sirjan, Shahr-e Babak and Rafsanjan from 'Mohajer Safar' *savari* terminal on Tehran Road next to the post office headquarters. Alternatively, if coming from Shiraz, you can hire a private taxi, leaving the city in the morning and driving through Persepolis, Pasargadae and Naqsh-e Rostam, covering a distance of around 800km for around US$100, including driver waiting time at the above sites. Tipping in this case is recommended. For **tours** in Kerman and the province, in particular Kalut desert, contact English-speaking guide Mansour Sadeghizadeh (m 0913 3461191; w irankalut.com).

 WHERE TO STAY AND EAT The choice of accommodation in Kerman is quite poor and it's recommended you stay in one of the hotels listed opposite.

🏠 **Pars International Hotel** [321 A3] (265 rooms) Jomhuri Islami Bd; 📞 32119301, 32119332; **w** pars-hotels.com. Popular with business tourists, this is by far the best hotel in town, but is unfortunately not good value for money. While the rooms are large & Wi-Fi is working, the staff are scatty. There is also an apparent lack of maintenance of the public areas. **$$$$**

🏠 **Hotel Akhavan** [321 B3] (40 rooms) Sadoughi St; 📞 32441411. Privately owned by 2 friendly & helpful brothers (the name of the hotel means 'Brothers'), with a good restaurant (**$**). Has a pleasant homely atmosphere & a large lobby. Rooms are spacious, albeit the décor is a little old-fashioned. The hotel is overall well maintained & popular with both group tours & individual travellers. **$$$**

🏠 **Hotel Hezar** [321 E4] (42 rooms) 5 Neshat Park; 📞 32260040. An expensive & very modern hotel with simple, but clean rooms. In the northwest outskirts of the town on the way to a restored ice house (page 326). **$$$**

🏠 **Tourist Inn** [321 A3] (53 rooms) Jomhuri Islami Bd; 📞 32445205. Rooms have been renovated but tend to be on the small side. Overall, reliable ITTIC hospitality. **$$$**

🏠 **Amin Hotel** [321 F2] (16 rooms) Chamran St; 📞 32250865, 32250866; **e** aminhotel@yahoo.com. Simple & central, cheapest of the very, very poor bunch. Old-fashioned & somewhat neglected, but staff are polite & helpful. **$$**

🏠 **Hotel Kerman** [321 C4] (40 rooms) Qods Bd; 📞 32515065, 32515066; **w** kermanhotel.com. Not without charm, in early 2019 the hotel was given a facelift & the walls a fresh coat of paint. Easily the best mid-range hotel in town, rooms are spacious & pristine & Wi-Fi is working. There is also parking. **$$**

✕ **Hamam-e Vakil Restaurant** [map, page 325] Bazaar Vakil; 📞 32254493, 32235259; 🕐 08.30–20.30 daily. Order & pay at the entrance, including a 30,000 rials entrance fee. Beautiful 19th-century underground tea house, easily the most atmospheric place to eat & often there is live traditional Sufi drumming at lunchtime. Try local *kolompeh*, walnut-&-date-filled baked biscuit. The café is the first room when entering the *hamam* & the restaurant is at the back. **$–$$$**

✕ **Khayyam Restaurant** [321 B3] Sadoughi St; 🕐 after 19.00. The somewhat bland décor aside, it is one of the best restaurants in Kerman. There is

---

THE *HAMAM*

Here is the account of an early 19th-century traveller's reaction to bathing, Persian-style:

The bather having undressed in the outer room, and retaining nothing about him but a piece of loose cloth around his waist, is conducted by the proper attendant into the hall of the bath; a large white sheet is then spread on the floor, on which the bather extends himself [and warm water is poured over him] … The attendant then takes his employer's head upon his knees, and rubs in with all his might, a sort of wet paste of henna plant, into the mustachios and beard … Again he has recourse to the little pail, and showers upon his quiescent patient another torrent of warm water. Then putting on a glove made of soft hair, yet possessing some of the scrubbing-brush qualities, he first takes the limbs, and then the body, rubbing them hard for three quarters of an hour [after which, follows pumicing] … To this succeeds the shampooing, which is done by pinching, pulling, and rubbing, with so much force and pressure as to produce a violent glow over the whole frame. Some of the natives delight in having every joint in their bodies strained till they crack … that the very vertebrae of the back are made to ring a peal in rapid succession … This over, the shampooed body, reduced again to its prostrate state, is rubbed all over with a preparation of soap confined in a bag, till he is one mass of lather. The soap is then washed off with warm water, when a complete ablution succeeds by his being led to the cistern, and plunged in.

From R Ker Porter, *Travels in Georgia, Persia, Armenia …*, 1821, vol I, pp231–2 traditional music in the evenings & a wide range of Iranian dishes on offer. $–$$

✕ **Zir Bazarcheh Traditional Restaurant** [map, page 325] Bazaar Vakil; ↳32222622;

⊕ 09.00–20.00 daily. A traditional restaurant with a pleasant atmosphere & caring staff. A good alternative to the Hamam-e Vakil Restaurant. $–$$

OTHER PRACTICALITIES The main **post office** [321 E3] in Kerman is on Edalat Street and the central **hospital** is the Shafa Hospital [321 A3] (Shafa Bd; ↳32115793). In the city centre there is an all-night **Imam Reza pharmacy** [321 B3] (Cnr of Jomhuri & Imam Jameh sts) and the most convenient **foreign exchange shop** [map, page 325] is on Arg (Towhid) Square or there is also one in front of the Pars International Hotel.

WHAT TO SEE AND DO Comparatively few foreign tourists make it to Kerman, and those that do have mostly come to visit Bam, which necessitates a day trip (page 330). Yet Kerman itself holds a few pleasant surprises up its sleeve. Inside the **Bazaar-e Bozorg** [map, page 325] (also called Bazaar Vakil) is the Safavid **Ganj Ali Khan** complex, essentially 17th century in date, which includes a mint, a caravanserai and a *hamam*. The last is now an **Ethnographic Museum** [map, page 325] (⊕ 09.00–17.00 Tue–Sun; entry 300,000 rials), displaying all the accoutrements needed to visit the bathhouse in Safavid times; the exterior painted decoration is some two centuries later in date. There is an opportunity for men to go to an operating bath nearby, the 1817 **Hamam Ibrahim Khan** [map, page 325], whose rents, with those of the neighbouring *khan*, went to endow the madrasa next door, both built and colourfully decorated by a local governor (and son-in-law) of the Qajar shah, Fath Ali Shah. Much of the bazaar was constructed in Safavid times but as its other name, Bazaar Vakil, suggests, many of the *khans* off the main passages were part of extensive rebuilding by another energetic Qajar governor (*vakil*), Mohammad Ismail Khan (1859–66). A caravanserai bearing the name Vakil is still in use as offices for local merchants. Drop in for a cup of tea to the nearby **Hamam-e Vakil Restaurant** and further down the main gallery from here, on the opposite side, look out for a richly ornamented doorway in Qajar style. Its blue-tiled panel identifies it as the 19th-century education and endowments office, which dealt with locals wishing to make the hajj pilgrimage to Mecca. The building currently functions as the **Banoo Hayati Museum** [map, page 325] (↳32254889; ⊕ 09.00–12.30 & 16.00–19.00 Tue–Thu, Sat & Sun, 09.30–13.00 Fri, closed Mon; entry 300,000 rials) of urban lifestyle and handicrafts. The **masjed-e jame** [321 G2] is located just off the main Maydan-e Shohada. The basic four-*ivan* plan dates from its construction in 1349 by Mubariz al-Din (r1314–58), the founder of the Muzaffarid regime (1314–93), but there have been extensive repairs since the 16th century. The modern additions (glazing in the courtyard, etc) are cheap and nasty, but some splendid tilework in both 'mosaic' and *cuerda seca* techniques remains in the prayer chamber. Visitors are usually riveted by the intriguing notices written in English, and the Farsi notices are just as confusing. Some 200m northwest is the **Masjed-e Pa Menar** [321 F2] (Fath Ali Shahi St), which is heavily restored. Its 1390 entrance portal did have (note the past tense) splendid 14th-century tile decorations which were still in situ in the late 1970s; visit, if only to mourn the substitution of such bad-quality work.

But the **Masjed-e Imam** [321 F3] (formerly the Masjed-e Malek), with just a stub (7.5m) of its original Seljuk minaret standing, is worth some time. The main domed prayer chamber dates from the late 11th century, perhaps slightly post-dating the essential four-*ivan* plan, but the prayer *ivan* and portal, with its geometrical brick patterns and fragmentary inscription in deep relief, date from about a hundred

For listings, see from page 323

❌ **Where to eat and drink**
1 Hamam-e Vakil
2 Zir Bazarcheh Traditional

CHAMRAN ST

N

Bradt

SHARIATI STREET

(SKETCH MAP)
Not to scale

SHAHID MAHMOUD TAJALLI STREET

Arcades

€

🏠 Badgir

Mirza Hossein
Caravanserai

P

● Zarrab Khaneh
Ganj Ali Khan

Ab Anbar ●

Ganj Ali Khan
Complex & Mosque
☪

Hamam
Ibrahim Khan
●

Vakil
Caravanserai

Arg (Towhid)
Square

🕯 Ganj Ali Khan

Golshan
Caravanserai ①

Arcades

Caravanserai
Chahar Suq

Hamam Ganj Ali Khan
(Ethnographic Museum)
②

Madrasa
Mahmoodiyeh ●

Chahar Suq
tea house ◱

P

Banqo Hayati 🏺
Museum

Ganj Ali Khan
⌂ Hamam for Ladies

Golamali Mosque ☪
(Qajar period)

Caravanserai
Haj Mehdi

Caravanserai
Hindu

P

KERMAN'S BAZAAR-E BOZORG

years later. Even a cursory glance at the tilework reveals wide-ranging repairs in the Safavid period, and the essentially black and pink tiling with yellow inscription in the prayer hall can only be 19th-century Qajar work. Publications of the 1970s mention 12th-century stucco *mihrabs* in the prayer hall, but these have now been relocated to the roof. To see them, first pay the custodian 50,000 rials, then find the narrow staircase to the extreme left (facing the prayer *ivan*) and, emerging at roof level, look for a metal canopy to the left. The three carved *mihrabs* are there, damaged and dusty but lovely. Another interesting – and obviously early – *mihrab* is now kept behind locked doors downstairs, so you need to find the knowledgeable building supervisor, who clearly loves the place. He thinks this fourth *mihrab* is pre-Seljuk and describes how local tradition says it was visited by Hassan, Ali's son (the second imam). The whole complex is undoubtedly Seljuk but now so heavily restored that little of its original glory is visible.

The 12th-century Seljuk tomb tower **Gonbad-e Khajeh Atabeg (Bazghush)** [321 E1] lies on the ground not far from Abuhamed Street, behind the bazaar. It has been renovated after collapsing in an earthquake in 1897 and the dome was eventually rebuilt. As a result of the years of neglect the octagonal exterior has been shorn of its decorative patterned brickwork highlighted with coloured ceramic tile elements. The tomb itself is closed, but you can see inside through the fenced door.

Kerman postcards often show a simple octagonal mausoleum, the **Gonbad-e Jabaliyeh** [321 G2] (⊕ 09.00–19.00 Tue–Sun; entry 300,000 rials), located in a cemetery, east of the Maydan-e Arg on the outskirts of town. Some scholars consider it to be one of the earliest surviving tombs with a double dome in Iran, but it is debatable if anything of the original fabric now remains; it is located in a park and serves as a museum of grave markers. There is a Safavid-period **ice house** [321 G2] (*yakhchal*), somewhat heavily restored, close to a restored section of city wall with views of the citadel. But another reason for making this short journey is to see the extensive remains of the old Sasanid fortifications, the **Qaleh Dokhtar** [321 G2], built by Ardashir I, whose castle is situated on the other side of the road, up on the hill behind the houses before the mausoleum. There is also a well-preserved *yakhchal* on the way here.

Nearby is Kerman's **Zoroastrian Ateshkadeh and Museum** [321 G2] (Ateshkadeh Alley, off Shohada Sq; ☏33126686; ⊕ 08.00–noon & 15.00–18.00 daily, without lunch break in Nou Rouz; entry 100,000 rials), also functioning as the cultural centre for approximately 1,000 members of the Zoroastrian community still living in the city. The museum holds a small collection of holy books, pictures and displays of traditional *sofreh* table arrangements laid out for various Zoroastrian festivals celebrated in accordance with Yasna, the sacred liturgical texts of the Avesta. The actual fire temple (*ateshkadeh*), with the sacred fire hidden behind a glass window, is the building furthest to the right after having walked in through the main gate.

Kerman boasts an excellent museum of contemporary art, which you should consider visiting. The **Sanati Museum of Contemporary Art** [321 D2] (Beheshti St; ⊕ 09.00–noon & 17.00–19.00; entry 300,000 rials) used to be an orphanage established by a Kermani philanthropist Hajj Akbar Sanatizadeh and is now home to numerous works by renowned Iranian artists such as Ali Akbar Sanati (d2006), Sohrab Sepehri (d1980) and Kamal al-Molk (d1940). Most labels are alas in Farsi only. In this part of the city there also used to be an Anglican Church of St Andrew (Kelisa Moqaddasi), as in the 19th century Kerman was an important centre for Western Christian missionary work. Coming up towards the museum you will pass by a well-preserved *yakhchal*. Another fine museum here is the **Harandi Museum** [321 D3] (Bagh-e Muzeh Harandi) (Ferdowsi St; ⊕ 09.00–19.00 Tue–Sun; entry 300,000 rials), located in a formerly private Qajar home of the Harandi family. Reza Shah Pahlavi himself stayed here whenever he visited Kerman. The ground-floor displays are dedicated to music and traditional musical instruments such as *tar, barbat* and *tombak*, but the first floor is the main reason to visit, with objects ranging from metalwork to sculpture from Jiroft (page 328) and Shahdad. In the vicinity of Kerman, approximately 25km northwest of the city, lies the picturesque and beautifully restored Qajar-period **Fath Abad Garden** (باغ فتح آباد) [321 B1] (⊕ 08.00–20.00 daily; entry 300,000 rials). Although of no particular historical significance, the mansion is so atmospheric and finely lit during evening hours that a taxi ride there, particularly at dusk, is recommended.

AROUND KERMAN

EAST OF KERMAN There are a few interesting historical and natural sites east of Kerman, which can all be visited in a day trip. The first stop along the desert road to Mashhad is the village of **Sirch**, which lies on the earthquake fault line of the province. Driving in the direction of **Shahdad**, 95km from Kerman, past the small village of **Shafi Abad** with the remains of a Qajar-period caravanserai and its unusual towers, you finally arrive at the start of the vast and spectacular desert **Kalut** (Kavir-e or Dasht-e Lut), which often features on posters around Kerman and in 2016 was included on the UNESCO World Heritage List.

SOUTH OF KERMAN To the southwest, past Kerman Airport on the road to Sirjan, is **Bardsir** with the **Tel-e Eblis** (Devil's Mound); American-funded archaeological work here in the mid 1960s found evidence of continuous settlement from c4400BCE to 400BCE, and proof that both copper smelting and ceramic production were in operation. And in Bardsir itself there is the 13th-century tomb of **Seyyed Mohammad**, with later buildings around. It has a double dome, good plasterwork and fine *muqarnas* along with three historical cenotaphs.

Returning to the Sirjan road, continue for another 20km to **Negar**, off a side road. Here there are the remains of a Seljuk citadel and a minaret probably from 1216 with a brick inscription from the Quran (Q97); glazed infills provide colour to the patterning. Both the mosque and the old *hamam* nearby could be Seljuk in plan. This village is on the centuries-old migration route, so there is a possibility of seeing families and flocks on the move in the spring and autumn. About 23km east of here is **Ghubeyra**, an Islamic site probably destroyed by Timur Leng's armies in 1393. It was excavated in the early 1970s by a British team of archaeologists.

SIRJAN سيرجان A further 100km along the main road, Sirjan itself was a regional capital from Sasanid times until the 10th century, and before the revolution the British Institute of Persian Studies undertook preliminary excavations that revealed an important medieval complex which, judging by the richness of its decorative plasterwork, could have housed the governor. The town is otherwise famous for its unusual ship-funnel-shaped **Chopoghi Badgir** (windcatcher), rising above Agha Seyyed Ali Asghar Razavi historic mansion. If staying overnight in Sirjan, the **Tourist Inn** (30 rooms; Khayyam St; ✆034 42236417; **$$**) is ITTIC recommended. It is situated in a pine grove and offers clean accommodation with good, simple food available by arrangement.

Some 5km past Sirjan, on the road to Baft you should catch sight of **Qaleh Sang** ('Stone Fortress'), a huge medieval fortress which managed to resist Timur Leng for two years. It lies off the main road behind the newly built Imamzadeh Ali; the path to the actual fortress passes through pistachio groves. About 37km further along the same road, past the village of Balvar, you will arrive at a visually unusual place – the small **Bagh-e Sangi** ('Stone Garden') where huge rocks hang off the branches of dried trees. The story has it that the garden was 'planted' by a deaf and mute man named Darvish Khan Esfandiarpour (1924–2007), who lost most of his lands to the Pahlavi land reforms and eventually his garden to drought. It took him 50 years to 'build' this garden, bringing rocks from the nearby mountains, in protest and defiance at the injustice he had suffered. Esfandiarpour is buried here, where his house still stands and his descendants still live. Iranian film director Parviz Kimiavi won the Silver Bear at Berlin in 1976 for his film *The Garden of Stones*, about Darvish Khan.

Continuing further south towards Bandar Abbas, and before reaching Hajji Abad (approximately 300km from Kerman), turn left at Aliabad on the road leading to Dolat Abad; 30km further on is the site of **Tappeh Yahya** (تپه یحیی), first systematically excavated by the Peabody Museum of Harvard University (US) in the late 1960s. Some seven distinct layers were identified, the earliest dating from c4500–3800BCE, when the inhabitants were evidently growing cereals and raising domesticated animals. By 3500BCE the settlement was prosperous enough to import turquoise, alabaster and ingots of copper. Occupation of the site continued without a break until the late Parthian or Sasanid period. The latest level and Period 2 (second level down) is clearly Achaemenid date, leading scholars to believe this was Carmania, where Alexander the Great stationed his men returning from the India campaign. About another 100km further east near to the town of Sorkhan, is the gorge, **Tang-e Mordan**, again associated with the Macedonian warrior, with rock reliefs and a 'fantastic number of cairn burials' according to Sylvia Matheson.

A handful of similar cairn tombs at Sar-e Asiab, 40km north of Kerman, were also excavated by the Peabody Museum. The finds ranged widely in date, even up to the 7th century CE, although it is generally considered the cairns, originally standing perhaps 2.5m high, were erected in prehistoric times.

If you have had the time and the inclination to view the archaeological finds in the Sanati and Harandi museums in Kerman (page 326), you will probably be drawn to visiting **Jiroft** (جيرفت) itself, a site that was largely a chance discovery occasioned by flash floods in 2000. It may prove, according to Yousef Majidzadeh, the Iranian archaeologist in charge of the excavations here, to be the lost Bronze-Age city of Aratta mentioned in Sumerian records from c2100BCE. The visit can be undertaken from Kerman (the *savari* terminal is at Beyram Abad Square southeast of the city) by travelling down the road towards Bam and then turning right at Abareq, from where the scenic route lies across the Jebal Barez Mountains. Time allowing, make a stop at the picturesque **Dalfard Waterfall**, some 40km before Jiroft. The reason for coming here is **Jiroft Archaeological Museum** (Halil Bd; ✆034 43217553; ⊕ 09.00–19.00 daily; entry 300,000 rials) displaying some of the objects, largely in a greenish soft stone called chlorite, excavated from the principal site at the village of Konar Sandal, 28km south of Jiroft. The artefacts are extremely lively with vegetal, zoomorphic and anthropological representations. **Konar Sandal** has two ancient hills, north and south. The northern hill has been dated to c3rd millennium BCE and appears to have consisted of a multi-storey, ziggurat-type religious building of mud brick, clay and straw plaster. The southern mound, some 1,300m from the other hill, revealed the remains of a large structure, possibly a local ruler's residence, on older remains. Artefacts such as bowls appear to have been exported to all regions of Mesopotamia. Large parts of the site are still untouched with many shards littering the surface. There are good views from the tops of the mounds, but these would otherwise appear unexciting, if archaeology is not a passion.

The fact that the early years of the 21st century saw the arrival on the European market of many artefacts extracted or trafficked illegally from this site, prompted the Dutch in particular to take an active part in convincing the authorities to protect the site and display the finds. This Bronze-Age culture, now dubbed 'Jiroft Culture', is agreed to be widespread in the Halil river basin. Some evidence of writing has also been found although the script has not yet been deciphered.

WEST OF KERMAN Some 27km from Shahr-e Babak is the ancient rock village of Meymand (ميمند), which in 2015 was inscribed in the UNESCO World Heritage List as a Cultural Landscape. The village has around 140 residents who continue the semi-nomadic lifestyle maintained by their ancestors over the past few thousand years. They are mainly involved in animal husbandry and spend the first four months of the year with their cattle on the plains, four months engaged in horticulture and then return to Meymand for the winter. The village's cave houses were built on the mountain, 2,200m above sea level, without the use of any modern house-building tools and are similar to those in Kandovan village near Tabriz (page 224). The Meymand mosque, more than 150 years old, is the most recently built structure here and it is the only building in the village with white inner walls, as there has never been a fire lit inside it. Meymand's residents are camera shy, so be sensitive when taking pictures. In the village there is a 'Mehmoun' association **Maymandmoon Ecolodge** ✳ (m 0912 3715120; e maymandmoon@gmail.com) which organises troglodyte accommodation and tours in the village. Their €20 per person fee also covers the 500,000 rials tourist entrance fee for Meymand.

NORTHWEST OF KERMAN The road to the northwest of Kerman leads to **Zarand** (زرند) (87km), which at the end of the 12th century superseded Kerman as the provincial centre, and was also famous for its textile manufacture. Its **masjed-e jame** was founded in the 10th century but, other than the remains of a minaret constructed sometime before 1074, the present building is 18th century. Just a little backtracking on the main road brings you on to a main highway to Mashhad.

MAHAN ماهان

From Kerman, most foreign visitors head southeast for **Bam**, stopping en route to see the shrine and gardens at **Mahan**, which takes a full day. Arguably Mahan, 40km from Kerman, is best visited in the evening, perhaps on the return journey from Bam, for during the summer the **Qajar Garden** and pavilion, the **Bagh-e Shahzadeh** (⊕ 09.00–21.00, until 23.00 in summer; entry 500,000 rials), are open and illuminated at night. Set back about 2km from the main road, the layout of this restored garden is one of the few in Iran that retains its original plan. A series of terraces descends the hillside with main and side water channels. On occasion the fountains are switched on, to the enjoyment of both ducks and visitors. The 19th-century pavilion offers a splendid place to take and enjoy both a *qalian* (page 54) and the lovely view over the garden.

Mahan itself is known for the famous shrine complex of (Shah) **Ne'matullah Vali Kermani** (d1430), the Sufi mystic poet-saint who spent his last 25 years here after residing in Mecca, Karbala and Samarkand, where he had incurred the wrath of Timur Leng. Called the Iranian Nostradamus, he is said to have foretold the rise of the Safavid regime, the separation of Bangladesh from Pakistan and the Islamic Revolution in Iran.

The main entrance has bright yellow and blue tiles from Qajar restoration work in 1871, as recorded on the floral tiles in the shrine doorway. A courtyard with reflecting pool and trees leads to the main shrine complex. The original silver grilles of the cenotaph and an enormous gold-inlaid steel *kashkul* (dervish begging-bowl) presented to the shrine by a Safavid shah are kept in the centre. Apart from a large gift- and bookshop, all other rooms in this courtyard offer basic accommodation for pilgrims.

The actual shrine building itself is an engaging mixture of architectural and decorative styles. If it is not crowded, do enlist the help of the kind and very knowledgeable guardian, who will also willingly (for a small fee at your discretion) let you go up to the roof to enjoy wonderful views (a goodwill gesture reserved for foreigners only). The inner square chamber dates from 1436 and its inner walls are still decorated with high-quality Timurid 'mosaic' tilework, while a steel and glass screen protects the Sufi's cenotaph. Off the upper left-hand corner of this central space is the tomb of the original patron, a student of the Sufi. The room is painted, has relief plasterwork and the dome is in the shape of the Sufi's hat. There are signs of flood damage on the lower part of these walls. The doorway into this area opposite the main door has a 19th-century three-images-in-one glass picture on each wall, one with different verses of the Quran, and the other showing Hossein's head, his tent at Karbala and his desecrated body. The carpets to the left are of Mahan production, incorporating the saint's poetry in the long cartouches. Walking anticlockwise – so the cenotaph chamber is on the left – look at the vaulting. The superbly proportioned fan of intersecting ribs was constructed in 1436 on the order of Ahmed I Bahmani, ruler of Bidar, a state in the Indian Deccan and a devotee of this Sufi master. Halfway round, the Safavid alterations are visible to the right of the cenotaph chamber, where the Timurid tiling disappears under a later Safavid wall constructed to support the vaulting system. On the outer wall are double wooden doors, which the guardian will proudly open to allow you to inspect them and see how the complex was enlarged in the 19th century to make it symmetrical. Returning to the central area, the room in the next corner is richly decorated with magnificent early 17th-century calligraphy arranged in a giant sun whirl around the vault; this was the *chehelkhaneh* where, as the name suggests, Sufis spent 40 nights in spiritual devotions.

The next door leads outside the shrine complex to a photogenic view of the shrine's exterior. Back within the building, look for a wooden door further along. Small figures along the top depict Sufi sheikh Abu al-Hassan Kharaghani (d1033; page 208), known for his miraculous abilities to tame wild animals, riding a lion and using a snake as a whip. A simple, small chamber in this final section is the resting place of the master. Currently behind the complex is a large caravanserai, which was originally at the front of the building; it is currently being restored.

A detour to 'mini-Bam' in **Rayen** (راین) just southwest of the main road about 50km beyond Mahan, will enable you to explore a similar fort city, the **Arg-e Rayen** (⊕ 09.00–18.00; entry 300,000 rials), though it is unlikely to be as ancient. It too consists of a vast walled complex of linked buildings constructed of sun-dried brick with the usual *qanat* and cooling systems characteristic of this desert region. As in Bam, a small *zurkhaneh* survives (see box, page 172). If you have time to spare, 13km east from Arg-e Rayen there is a picturesque waterfall with a picnic area.

BAM بم

From Mahan it is about 170km to Bam (*vahma*: glorification, prayer; population 126,000), which was struck by a severe earthquake on 26 December 2003. It is thought to be the city of Haftvad mentioned in the Iranian epic, the *Shahnameh*. The story goes that Haftvad's daughter was spinning cotton with friends when she spotted a worm in her apple. Refusing to kill it, she found her output magically increased as the worm munched and grew in size. As it brought great wealth to her family and town, a citadel was built to protect it, but this only aroused the interest of the Sasanid shah, Shapur. Eventually killing the giant worm by forcing hot metal down its throat, he took the city and its riches. This sounds purely the stuff of legend, but we know that, according to Iranian tradition, it was Shapur I (or perhaps Shapur II) who destroyed the Chinese silk monopoly, by actively promoting silkworm cultivation and silk production in Iran and promoting Bam as a trading station for eastern caravan routes. Furthermore, in silk processing, to avoid the pupa damaging its silk cocoon, it is killed by heat of which there is plenty in the sunshine of the area (see box, page 199).

Aerial photographs taken shortly after the devastating earthquake have revealed the complexity of the medieval *qanat* system, and evidence that the site was occupied as early as 2600BCE. The town was an important frontier and commercial post, trading in dates, cotton and other textiles until it fell to rebel Afghan forces in 1719. Its economy never fully recovered. Then the citadel's defences were partially dismantled in the 19th century, following Agha Mohammad Qajar's capture of the Zand ruler, Lotf Ali Khan (page 15) in 1794. More local trouble in 1838 caused the Qajar shah to take direct control, and many of the townspeople were moved to a new residential area to the south. By 1958 most families had left the old walled town, and the site was declared an open-air museum. It was the new town that suffered most in the 2003 earthquake but the historic walled city was also gravely damaged. Since 2004, Bam has been included on the UNESCO World Heritage List.

Although the ongoing repair work on the citadel at Bam aims, with the aid of photos, to restore it to its earlier form, as has happened with mud-brick structures through the ages, some parts remain propped up by scaffolding and the rather grotesque newly installed benches all across the perimeter seem more forced than authentic.

Similarly to Kerman, Bam used to have a Zoroastrian community and the remains of the Qajar-period Zoroastrian bazaar and official quarter, all destroyed in the 2003 earthquake, attested to that.

GETTING THERE AND AWAY There is an airport to the east of the town, now repaired and with up to three **flights** a week to and from Tehran Mehrabad Airport (2,860,000–3,165,000 rials one way). In common with other Iranian cities, there are hourly (up until 19.00) **buses** from Kerman (300,000 rials each way) that take just under 3 hours, but may be longer depending on the time spent at security checkpoints along the way.

WHERE TO STAY AND EAT

Tourist Inn (30 rooms) Imam Khomeini St; \034 44313321; e jahangardibam@yahoo.com. A reliable ITTIC hotel with a good restaurant (**$$**) & pleasant staff. **$$**

Akbar's Tourist Guesthouse (15 rooms) Seyyed Jamal al-Din St; m 0913 2460831. A pleasant guesthouse with an inner courtyard & parking. Popular with travellers coming to Iran with their own vehicles. Accommodation is very simple, but it serves the purpose. **$**

WHAT TO SEE AND DO A walk in the **walled town**, the citadel, known as **Arg-e Bam** (⊕ 09.00–18.00; entry 500,000 rials) before the earthquake was unforgettable. Surrounding an area of approximately 3km diameter, the main defence wall was over 12m high, with ramparts 3m wide, four gates and an external moat. It housed the bazaar, various noble houses and mosques, of which there is little left. Enough remained for the visitor to see the main housing, shops, work units (including a bakery and police station), caravanserai and the main mosque, all located just inside this wall. Above, defended by a further wall, were the barracks, stabling and housing for the bureaucrats and soldiers, while a third enclosing wall protected the inner citadel and the governor's apartments. Right at the top were a **watchtower** and **pavilion** of the four seasons, both offering marvellous panoramic views over the plain, but it was these upper sections that were most severely damaged in 2003. Originally the tower was seven-storeyed but in the 1810 Qajar dismantling, three floors were demolished. Below, on the second level, a massive repair and rebuilding programme had just been completed before the earthquake and, perhaps because of this strengthening work, this area has suffered less. It contains the **officers' quarters**, a series of rooms around courtyards set behind the main street. On the way down to the next gate there are more **barracks** and also a huge water **cistern** to the right. The walkway led down to the second gate, which is now no longer extant. At ground level, the avenue to the left led to a small caravanserai, which had been converted into a restaurant, its two main chambers cooled by multi-vent *badgirs*. This area and beyond, containing a *hosseiniyeh* (with a characteristic 'theatre' stage and 'boxes' for the audience), a school, and a large mosque perhaps founded in the 7th century were largely levelled in the 2003 earthquake. It is unclear whether a large domed building to the left, in the distance, still stands. This was a *zurkhaneh*, possibly the earliest surviving Iranian example, complete with its octagonal wrestling pit (see box, page 172). Walking around the main wall past the ticket kiosk you will eventually arrive at the cupola-shaped **Mirza Ebrahim Tomb**, built for this member of the Bam nobility during the Qajar period. Outside the structure is not that impressive, but it certainly is inside, despite the scaffolding.

The road from Bam towards Zahedan is marked with the remains of a number of historic signal towers, the most important being at **Fahraj**, 100km from Bam. Its signal tower, **Mil-e Naderi**, stands 19m high with a diameter of 13m and was perhaps built on 10th-century foundations, but the brickwork pattern dates from the reign of Nader Shah Afshar (d1747). Beacons would be lit for signalling communication to Kerman and beyond, and they served to guide the trade caravans making their way into and from central Iran; another beacon lies some 15km away to the north near Shurgaz.

Security warning Note that travelling further south beyond Bam may be considered hazardous and inadvisable, and unless you are travelling in a specially organised group or with an Iranian friend, single travellers (especially women) should reconsider their journey plans.

ZAHEDAN زاهدان *Telephone code 054*

Zahedan (population 600,000, but the figure fluctuates depending on the numbers of Afghani refugees in the vicinity) is the capital of Sistan and Baluchestan province, the only Iranian province bordering Pakistan. It is also one of the few cities in Iran with a Sunni (predominantly Hanafi branch) majority. Zahedan is only around 90 years old and lacks historical sites. It is, however, an important transfer point between Iran and Pakistan. Thanks to the surrounding mountains, the climate here is dry. Do, however, avoid visiting the province during the summer months, the windy season, which will hamper your enjoyment.

GETTING THERE AND AWAY From Bam, a road south leads to Minab and Bandar Abbas, but the main Kerman–Bam road continues to the Irano-Pakistani frontier beyond Zahedan; petrol stations are few and far between. Aside from road transport from Bam, there are daily **flights** from Tehran; other cities, namely Esfahan, Kerman, Mashhad and Chabahar (on the coast) are served less frequently. Long-distance **bus** services link Zahedan to all the major centres of Iran. There is a daily train service from Tehran to Zahedan (22hrs; 870,000 rials) and the **railway** has now been extended from Bam to Zahedan, which already has a railway station linked to the network in Pakistan, but at present there is no train service between the two countries. It is also possible to reach the frontier by scheduled bus or by shared or private **taxi**. Zahedan and Quetta used to be on the hippy trail in the early 1970s, but since then services have deteriorated badly. **Enghelab bus terminal** is a 20-minute taxi ride from the city centre.

The whole region has a reputation for drug trafficking, so expect a stringent searching of vehicles and lengthy document checking, both in town and on the road. Also there is large-scale smuggling into Afghanistan and Pakistan of cheap Iranian petrol contained in secret compartments underneath the intercity/frontier buses. There is, however, no official crossing point into Afghanistan here.

So few Westerners now come this way that their presence attracts much interest. Be careful when travelling in this region. Once in Pakistan, however, do not expect a carefree travelling experience; you will most likely be assigned a police escort for the whole duration of your stay in the Pakistani Baluchestan.

WHERE TO STAY AND EAT

Esteghlal Hotel (75 rooms) Azadi Sq; \33238068. Currently the best hotel in town with extensive facilities & a swimming pool. $$$

🏠 **Tourist Inn** (35 rooms) Jam-e Jam St, opposite Khatamolandia Hospital; 📞 33224898, 33220113. Rooms are spacious & bright. There are family rooms as well as separate bungalow-style accommodation. **$$**

🏠 **Sarboog Hostel** (22 dorm beds, 1 private) 20, 27 Alley, Daneshgah Bd; **m** 0903 0902400; **e** sarboog.hostel@gmail.com. First hostel in the province with a wide range of services & WiFi, it is the best budget option in the area. **$**

OTHER PRACTICALITIES Zahedan's central **post office** is behind the museum. On Azadi Street itself and inside the gold shops arcades there are a few **foreign exchange kiosks**. The **Farabi Pharmacy** (📞 33222466) is centrally located a few metres up from Gilan Guesthouse. The **Khatamolandia Hospital** (across the road from the Tourist Inn) is the main hospital in town.

For **shopping** head to Mustafa Khomeini Street and the Bazaar-e Ruz for tailor-made Baluchi clothes (colourful women's dresses cost up to US$50; and men's long two-pieces are tailor-made in a day and cost, depending on the quality of the fabric, around US$10 for a shirt and matching trousers).

Whether you are in Zahedan for a visit, or heading towards the Pakistani border, for any assistance contact **Abdulhamid Hassan** (**m** 0939 3718973; **e** abdulhamid863@yahoo.com), who works for the regional office of the Iranian Cultural Heritage, Handicrafts and Tourism Organisation.

Visa information

🅴 Indian Consulate 8 Kafami St; 📞 33222337; **e** hoc.zahidan@mea.gov.in; ⏲ 09.30–noon Sun–Thu, for visa application submission & 16.30–17.00 for visa collection. Visas issued on approval within 72hrs from the Indian embassy in the country of the applicant. The process is usually hassle-free & consulate personnel are very helpful.

🅴 Pakistani Consulate 134 Razmju Moghaddam St; 📞 33223389; **e** parepzahedans@ yahoo.com; ⏲ 08.30–11.00 Sun–Thu. Pakistani visas are not issued to third country nationals. Personnel are polite, but do not even count on friends in Karachi to help with a formal invitation letter. In short, do not arrive at the Pakistani border (⏲ 07.00–16.00) without a visa. It is highly recommended to obtain a double-entry visa to Pakistan in your home country, if you are returning by this route as well. The Pakistani embassy in New Delhi will not process your application either.

WHAT TO SEE AND DO Zahedan has little to offer other than its **bazaars** and the newly built **Zahedan Museum** (Motahhari St; ⏲ 09.00–18.00 Sat–Thu, 16.00–19.00 Fri; entry 500,000 rials), with a collection of artefacts from the UNESCO World Heritage-listed Shahr-e Sukhteh archaeological site (see below). The surrounding landscape, however, is strewn with the crumbling remains of caravanserais and signal towers.

Approximately 174km north of Zahedan towards **Zabol** (زابل) lies the site of **Shahr-e Sukhteh** (شهرسوخته) (site ⏲ 08.00–19.00; entry 500,000 rials); and museum on the opposite side of the Zahedan–Zabol motorway (⏲ 08.00–noon & 16.00–20.00; entry 300,000 rials), awarded UNESCO status in 2014. The site, whose name means 'Burnt City', was excavated by an Italian archaeological team from the mid 1960s until 1978, but exploration work by the Iranian authorities has been ongoing here since 1997. A series of rectangular buildings was uncovered, some with walls still 3m high, with doorways, windows, staircases and roofing timbers in a fine state of preservation, 'as if kept in a pot of pickles', covered in a thick layer of saline earth. It turned out that what were first identified as floor levels were in fact the roofs of buildings. Four main periods of settlement were identified: Level I (c3100–2900BCE), then Levels II and III, with pottery similar to that found at Bampur from c2500–1900BCE, and Level IV, about 500 years later and characterised by pottery animal figurines. A huge burial site over 42ha, containing about 40,000 graves of nine types, was found with 'literally tens of thousands' of skeletons laid in a horizontal 'kneeling' position facing east, the largest known Bronze-Age cemetery in the Middle East. The rich pottery (often decorated with stylised scorpion motifs), over 40,000 clay figurines, flint tools and beads point to a prosperous community dating back over 5,000 years, but the whole settlement seems to have been destroyed in an intense fire c1250BCE, and abandoned after the river changed course. The finds again prove a strong trading connection both with the northern Indian subcontinent and with Oman. In the vicinity is the excavated and similarly dated *tappeh* of **Rud-e Biyaban**, where the remains of some 50 large kilns were found, dating from the 3rd millennium BCE. Approximately 10km further north, near the village of **Sekuheh** the well-preserved towers and walls of **Qaleh Sam** are visible. Further on there are some 14th-century buildings, but the proximity to the Afghan border means the authorities may wish foreigners to avoid the area; which you will do if following British government advice (page 42). Some 6km southwest from here is **Qaleh Rostam**, locally associated with the Persian warrior-hero in the *Shahnameh* epic (the *Sohrab and Rostam* of Matthew Arnold). Noted as an attractive town in its own right during the mid 1970s, Qaleh Rostam has clearly had a long history of settlement, as over eight prehistoric mounds have been identified and there are signs of an important Sasanid fort.

The road leads on to **Zabol** (زابل), about 55km away, where for many years the Italian archaeological team of Shahr-e Sukhteh had its headquarters. The proximity of the Afghan border means a heavy military and police presence in Zabol and the surrounding region.

The site of **Kuh-e Khajeh**, some 30km southwest of Zabol on Lake Hamun, is visible from a distance. This mound has been revered by both Zoroastrians and Muslims for centuries, and every Nou Rouz pilgrims still come to pay their respects. **Lake Hamun** (دریاچه هامون) (originally known as Kasaoya, and mentioned in the *Avesta*) is where Zoroastrians believe their messiah, Saoshyants, will be conceived. The lake is seasonal with varying water levels, depending on the amount of rainfall and melting snow from the surrounding mountains. While in the past the mound was accessible only by boat, at present the lake has almost entirely dried up and there is a road leading all the way to the bottom. On the site, known as *kohan dezh*, a small fire temple complex could perhaps date from the Achaemenid period but many believe it to be later, pointing out similarities in layout with the Azargoshnasp fire sanctuary at Takht-e Soleyman in the Zagros Mountains (see box, page 232). Extensive Parthian and Sasanid remains were uncovered, with plaster wall frescoes of a king and queen, attendants and a line of deities, which formerly decorated a Parthian palace compound. Unfortunately they are no longer in situ, but two pieces are in the Metropolitan Museum of Art, New York. Archaeological work has been carried out since the mid 1990s and remains of a citadel with a religious precinct including a fire temple have been found, dating from early Sasanid times, 3rd–4th century CE. **Bibi Dust** is situated about 35km from here, where again there are clear signs of historic occupation. Just to the southeast are the ruins of **Deh Zahedan** (also known as Deh Reza), perhaps once the old city of Zaranj, with a citadel, forts and mosque.

Travelling from Zahedan due south towards the Persian Gulf

A series of old forts and caravanserais mark the landscape, but few have been securely identified or dated. One of the sites much further south, excavated in the mid 1960s, is **Bampur** (بمپور), close to **Iranshahr** (ایرانشهر) where you can overnight in the small **Ghasr Hotel**, which has a good restaurant (Intersection Talegnani St & Azad Jonubi (Haji Zadeh) St; ☎ 0543 7224953, 7229933; $$). The dig focused on a site west and northwest of the post-medieval citadel mound; six stratified levels were found, with interesting pottery and other finds proving that as early as c2500–1900BCE there were strong trade links with Afghanistan and Oman. Much of this region was destroyed during Timurid times in revenge attacks by Timur Leng and his son, and it has never recovered. We know that Alexander the Great passed through on his campaigns to India and, as the Persepolis reliefs suggest, earlier there had been close military co-operation between the people of Sistan (or Drangiana as it was then known) and the Achaemenid Empire. The region was considered strategically important during Parthian times, some saying that a local ruler Gondophernes (r20–48CE) was none other than Caspar, one of the Three Wise Men.

CHABAHAR AND BEYOND

The motorway from Iranshahr continues on for 309km south towards **Chabahar** (چابهار), Iran's largest port in the Gulf of Oman. Here the sweet smell of Indian spices and scents becomes more discernible, mosque architecture takes on a distinctive Indian style and increasingly more girls parade their beautiful hennaed hands and feet. The city has had close historical links to India and locals often travel to Pakistan and beyond via the border that otherwise remains closed for ordinary tourists. Planned and established during the last monarchy, Chabahar itself is comparatively unimpressive. It is nonetheless important for its strategic location and direct access to the Indian Ocean. India, the third-largest oil importer in the world, has as a consequence been increasing its presence in the area and in December 2018 Indian Ports Global Ltd (IPGL) took over the operations over the Chabahar Shahid Beheshti port for a period of 18 months with a possibility of extending the lease for ten years. The port deal is part of the extensive Chabahar Agreement aimed to ease trade between Iran, India and Afghanistan. The modest Chabahar Konarak Airport that at present services up to four daily flights to Tehran (2hrs 10mins) will also hopefully see the benefits of the increasing trade. Otherwise peaceful and quiet, in 2018 the city of Chabahar was shaken by a terrorist attack, when a suicide bomber drove a truck with explosives into a police station, killing two and injuring 48 people.

Once here, you can visit the small **Chabahar Museum** (⊕ 09.00–19.00 Sat–Thu; entry 300,000 rials) and do some duty-free **shopping** in the Pardis and Sadaf shopping centres. Thanks to the free trade zone, prices in Chabahar are significantly lower than in the rest of the country and shopping centres are plentiful. Money can be exchanged in Ararat Exchange (Pardis Shopping Centre; ☎ 0543 5313797, 5313798). Outside Chabahar on the way to Konarak, you may also like to visit the scanty remains of a **Portuguese fort** rising on the hill above the village of Tiss. Although not that impressive, it is nonetheless a distraction if staying here a day or two.

WHERE TO STAY AND EAT

Laleh Hotel (38 rooms) Chabahar Port, Imam Khomeini St; ☎ 054 35324850. Not without charm, although in need of some freshening-up, this is nonetheless a pleasant place to stay. Rooms are a little small, but bright & comfortable & some even come with sea views. On a hot summer day, male guests will certainly appreciate the outdoor pool (outdoor pools in Iran are for men only). **$$$$**

Ferdows Hotel (73 rooms) Tejarat St, next to the Ferdows Shopping Centre; ☎ 054 35314670, 35314673; e ferdowsinthotel@yahoo.com.

Opened in early 2016, the hotel is a little flashy, although rooms are somewhat dull in contrast to the lobby & halls. That said, the staff are helpful & the location is conveniently central in the free trade zone near shopping centres. **$$$**

Khalij Restaurant Shilat Sq; m 0911 1281697, 0933 6508063; ⊕ noon–16.00 & 20.00–midnight. Best local fish dishes served with Iranian charm & hospitality. Food is excellent & the terrace overlooking the sea & fishing harbour is most pleasant. Portions are generous. **$$**

EAST OF CHABAHAR The coast of the Gulf of Oman, especially further south towards the border with Pakistan, is scenic and worth a day trip if coming this way. Private taxi is effectively the only form of transport here, as *savari* services are sporadic. The first village along this route, approximately 12km south of Chabahar, the small fishing harbour of **Ramin** (رمین) offers excellent **windsurfing** opportunities. Note, though, that women need to be creative and imaginative to find appropriate wear. Further on in the same direction lie the famous **miniature mountains**, impressive formations stretching for a few kilometres along the coastal road, which continues on to the border with Pakistan. **Beris** (بریس) is a small fishing village further on and the first place with tourist accommodation, if planning to overnight in the area. **Beris Ecolodge** (4 rooms; m 0939 3874122) run by Ehsan Parhizgar was opened in 2018 and offers basic rooms in which to unwind and taste local cuisine. The last stop before Pakistan is **Guatr** (گواتر) famous for its Guatr Bay, home to bottlenose dolphins (*dolfin-e binibotri*) and mangrove forests. Here you can overnight in the very spartan **Azh Ecolodge** (5 rooms, Guatr Village; m 0915 5458087).

If returning to Chabahar and travelling northwards from here, why not take the road via **Konarak** to **Jask** past some of the characteristic landscape of grey-beige mountains. This is not a popular route, but has some attractions along the way as well as the bumpy surface to add thrill to the drive. Make sure not to miss the turn to the beautiful **Darak** (درک) beach where sand dunes disappear into the sea.

12

Mashhad and Khorasan

Ancient or Greater Khorasan once formed an enormous province encompassing Iranian Khorasan, sections of today's Turkmenistan, Uzbekistan, Tajikistan and most of Afghanistan. Its boundaries fluctuated and at different times extended to Rey in the west and all the way to the Pamir Mountains in the east. Famous for its agricultural and fertile land and called the 'granary of Iran', Iranian Khorasan today remains a major producer of rice and saffron, the world's most expensive spice. Khorasan province (in 2004 it was split into North Khorasan, South Khorasan and Razavi Khorasan provinces) was not always under Iranian authority, so its historic monuments record the patronage of such dynasties as the Khwarizm shahs, the Mongol Ilkhanids and the Timurids, as well as the Safavids, the short-lived Afsharid dynasty and the Qajars. Greater Khorasan was also centre stage of the first major military event in the history of Islam, the Abbasid Revolution (746–749), that resulted in the overthrow of the Umayyad dynasty and brought the Abbasids to power.

Known to be warlike and belligerent, the local population was allowed, even after the Arab conquest in 650, to bear arms, which was otherwise contrary to the Arab practice of allowing only Muslims to carry weapons. Khorasanis were also numerous in the newly reformed professional army of the Abbasids (749–1258) and proved to be receptive and welcoming to the spread of Islam, in particular the Shi'a branch.

The cultural, spiritual and religious importance of Khorasan cannot be underestimated. It was here that Zarathustra was born and preached and Ferdowsi composed his masterpiece *Shahnameh*. In Khorasan is the city of Mashhad, the holiest city in Iran and renowned as the burial place of the eighth imam, Reza, the only one of the Twelve Imams who is buried in present-day Iran.

This chapter looks at the region east of Gonbad-e Qabus and Shahrud (page 208), Mashhad and sites close to the Afghan border. The security situation near the Afghan border is presently good but the gendarmerie advises that road journeys should be completed before sunset, as there have been isolated incidents of cross-border robbery and kidnapping. Additionally, the Dogharoon border crossing is open only from 08.00 to 16.00.

RAZAVI AND NORTH KHORASAN PROVINCES

The road east runs for 98km from Gorgan to Gonbad-e Qabus and then for another 485km towards Mashhad, quickly leaving rice fields and sloping farm roofs behind, winding up into wooded hills populated by wild boar and deer. It also passes **Golestan National Park** (formerly Mohammad Reza Shah Park), Iran's oldest national park that has been protected since 1956, at least in theory. At

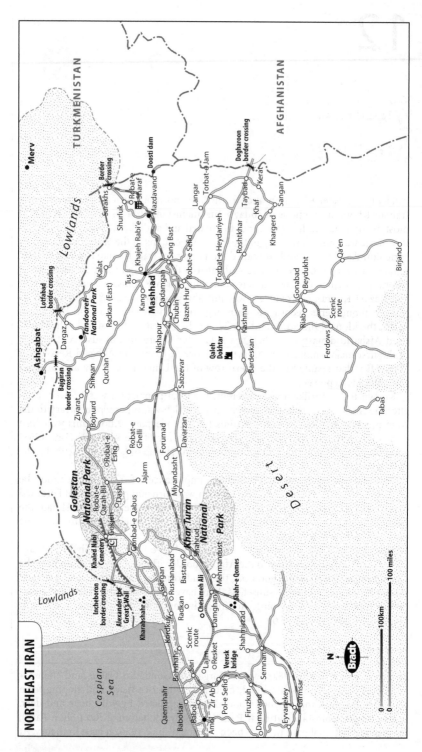

NORTHEAST IRAN

TURKMENISTAN

AFGHANISTAN

Merv

Ashgabat

Caspian Sea

Lowlands

Lowlands

Desert

Golestan National Park

Khar Turan National Park

Bandooreh National Park

Lotfabad border crossing

Bajgiran border crossing

Incheboron border crossing

Alexander the Great's Wall

Khaled Nabi Cemetery

Dogharoon border crossing

Border crossing

Doosti dam

Mashhad

Birjand

N

Bradt

0   100km
0   100 miles

present the motorway effectively runs through the park and the human presence has further damaged the area's flora and fauna. Continue on by cutting through shrubby hillsides that are ideal trekking or riding territory. Close to the road are three known Timurid caravanserais dating from c1487, and probably many more are still to be identified, as the then governor of Astarabad (historic name of Gorgan), Mir Ali Shir, is known to have built 49 altogether in his lifetime to serve this important trade and pilgrimage route. **Robat-e Qarah Bil** is situated 25km east of **Dasht** in the village of the same name, behind the roadside gendarmerie post. (If a ruined caravanserai isn't appealing, the numerous inquisitive *pika* 'gerbils' that inhabit the site are.) Its south entrance once led immediately into the stables along this façade and on both sides. Despite the caravanserai's present state, even a casual inspection will reveal the different phases of construction, with certain chambers built in the late 16th century to provide more stabling. The vestibule led into a four-*ivan* courtyard, 16m², with living quarters on all sides. This essential plan was followed in two other caravanserais, both a day's journey away in pre-motoring times: **Robat-e Eshq**, 23km east off the main road at Chaman Bid, which also included a small mosque on site, and **Robat-e Ghelli**, 30km southeast. From Robat-e Qarah Bil or Robat-e Eshq, **Jajarm** is about 55km due south. Its position on the former main caravan route from Nishapur to Bastam presumably accounted for the need for a protective fortress, whose remains are still visible. This is the masjed-e jame, which is surprisingly small in size, and probably dates from the late 15th century.

The good road skirts the mountainous barrier between Iran and today's Turkmenistan Republic through **Bojnurd** (بجنورد), capital of North Khorasan, and **Shirvan** (شیروان), passing petrochemical and cement works. This area is inhabited by a numerous Kurdish minority (of approximately 2 million people) who, unlike other Kurds in Iran, speak Kurmanji dialect. It is believed that Kurdish tribes came to the region in the late 1500s during the Safavid period to defend the province from invaders. Some 6km west of Shirvan is **Ziyarat**, so called after its Ziyarat-e Timur Leng located in a modern cemetery. It is not the main, centrally placed building with a brick-patterned dome, the interior of which is decorated with a beautiful star-burst ceiling of plaster *muqarnas*, that has interested scholars, but the octagonal tomb behind it. Some think this dates from the 1330s but others, looking at its kite-shaped squinches in the zone of transition and other architectural details, argue that, as its name suggests, it is Timurid, c1430. Local children will happily show you the internal staircase up to the roof. Hardly anything now remains of the painted internal drum inscription and medallions recorded in the mid 1970s.

North of **Quchan** (قوچان) and close to the Turkmenistan border, 3km northwest of Dargaz, the Iranian Archaeological Service has been carrying out excavations at **Bandian** (بندیان) since 1994. From the brief reports published so far, a Sasanid columned hall with a corridor and room with remains of rich plaster decoration, the largest of its kind from the Sasanid period, to a height of 70cm have been unearthed. These depict scenes of hunting, battle and feasting, resembling both in content and composition the (later) painted walls at Penjikent, Tajikistan, southeast of Samarkand in central Asia. Fragmentary Pahlavi inscriptions carved into the plaster refer obliquely to two military commanders controlling this region, one of whom is recorded as serving under the Sasanid shah Bahram V (r420–38CE). The work is lively but atypical and, according to the usual Sasanid scale of proportions, the figures have overlong arms. The archaeologists now think this was a Zoroastrian fire temple complex including a 'tower of silence'. Thus, the name of the site in Persian – Ateshkadeh Bandian.

Well worth a short detour for its early 13th-century tomb tower is **Radkan** (رادکان), known in certain publications as Radkan East (Radkan West tower is south of Kordkuy; page 206). Some 75km before Mashhad, after Quchan and the village of Seid Abad, there is a turn-off for the village. The village roundabout, boasting a modern replica of the tower, soon comes into view, with a signpost to the actual monument, which is on a narrow asphalted road across agricultural land. The tower is said to be 13th century CE and most probably the seemingly unevenly spaced perforations in the walls confirm its supposed astronomical function; there is now a small guidebook (in Farsi) with many illustrative diagrams of these features. Here and there are fragments of turquoise-glazed inserts, also used for the *Kufic* inscription. Only the exterior tent roof survives but inside the octagonal chamber, the brick supports for the internal dome are still visible. Take care where you tread inside as local shepherds keep a few sheep and donkeys in the tower. Looking around, you can see the ruins of a huge four-towered caravanserai, also used for local flocks, and in the village there's an ice house.

Back on the main road, just before hitting the outskirts of Mashhad, is **Tus** (توس) (also called **Ferdowsi**; see page 349 for more information), the birthplace of the famous medieval poet, Ferdowsi (d1020). The confusing road directions indicate

SHAH RUKH

The fourth son of Timur Leng (Tamerlaine, as he is known in the West), Shah Rukh owed his name to the moment of his birth, which coincided with his father taking his opponent's castle (*rukh*) at chess. As Mongol tradition laid down that territorial possessions should be split between the ruler's sons, he was appointed governor of Mazandaran, Khorasan and Sistan in 1397 at the age of 22, but arguments between the brothers continued. He had two wives: Ghawhar Shad and, to keep the bloodline of Genghis Khan in the Timurid house, he married the young Malikat Agha, widow of one of his brothers. On Timur's death in 1405 he made no move to take the throne but bided his time until Timur's successor died two years later. Shah Rukh immediately went into action, installing his son, Ulugh Beg (who gave the mathematical world sine tables) as governor of Samarkand while he remained in Herat. Through his generals, he restored Timurid authority in the steppes of today's Turkmenistan, crushed local warlords and difficult nephews attempting to seize control of the Isfahan region in 1417, and then successfully moved against the Qara Qoyunlu in Azerbaijan.

A ruler who preferred to hunt around Sarakhs and to visit Mashhad than lead his troops on the battlefield, Shah Rukh ordered many gardens to be built in his capital of Herat, but he was also known for his piety, personally accompanying Muslim officials to remove the secret wine stores of his son and grandson. He was heartbroken when his favourite son died, and powerful factions centred around both queens broke out at court. The target of at least one assassination attempt, he was stabbed in the stomach when leaving Friday prayer in 1427 but made a full recovery. The intrigue continued, especially when he fell seriously ill during 1444, and Ghawhar promoted her own candidate as the rightful heir apparent. Many court officials were banished from the Herat palace when Shah Rukh's health improved. He died in 1447 (Ghawhar survived for another ten years) and, within 15 years, the house of Timur Leng had fallen and the empire was in fragments.

only Ferdowsi, but local bus companies refer to 'Tus'. It is probably easier and quicker to continue into Mashhad and then come here by local taxi or bus.

MASHHAD مشهد *Telephone code 051*

It was here, when the town was known as Sanabad, that the famous Abbasid caliph, Harun al-Rashid, died in 809CE; 19th-century Western literature always associated him with the anthology *Tales of 1,001 Nights*, written centuries later. His son, al-Ma'mun, ordered a tomb for his father, and another to commemorate his son-in-law, Reza, in whose death in 817CE he was strongly implicated. This is the Imam Reza, honoured in Shi'a Islam as the eighth in the line of Twelve Imams and to whom today's **huge shrine complex** is dedicated. Almost 200 years later the mausoleum to Imam Reza was destroyed by the local Sunni ruler, who forbade any rebuilding, but Sultan Mahmoud of Ghazni (r998–1030), inspired by a dream – or perhaps the need to win the loyalty of his Shi'a subjects – ordered its reconstruction in 1009. From then on, the town's fortunes were inextricably linked to the shrine.

But the city's vulnerable location offered rich pickings for any marauding force, such as the Turkoman in 1153, or the Mongols in 1221, and the shrine was always hit during such attacks. Piecemeal repairs were undertaken by local Sunni rulers, but major rebuilding was undertaken only by the son of Timur Leng, Shah Rukh (r1405–47; see box, opposite), from 1418 along with the construction of gardens and a royal pavilion to enhance the shrine. His queen, Ghawhar Shad, whose name translates as 'Jewel of Happiness', an active architectural patron in their capital, Herat, Afghanistan, was already having a new madrasa built. A century later it was the Shi'a Safavid regime that promoted the city as a major Iranian pilgrimage centre. The shrine's main dome and minarets were gilded and much of the Timurid eastern section was demolished to cater for the thousands of Iranian pilgrims flocking here, rather than undertaking the long, hazardous hajj to Mecca and Medina, then in Ottoman control. The mausoleum domes were first made golden in 1607 by Shah Abbas I, but a part of the structure was later destroyed in the earthquake. During the rule of the Safavid dynasty a number of prominent clerics (*ulama*) settled here and the city's royal association continued into the 18th century.

Sweeping away the remnants of Safavid power, Nader Shah Afshar (d1747), though a Sunni, had his son marry the daughter of the Safavid shah Tahmasp II here, established his capital in Mashhad, ordered costly and highly visible repairs to the shrine after his successful Indian campaigns, and was buried here. Re-establishing the Ithna 'Ashari Shi'a faith as the state religion, the Qajar shahs then undertook a massive restoration programme in the shrine, extensively covering surfaces with tiles and mirror work and regilding the dome. Official pressure in the 19th and early 20th centuries caused many in the Jewish and Christian communities in Mashhad to move to Afghanistan or central Asia, where their expertise in both manufacture and commerce were fully utilised; but at least one church still survives in Mashhad, close to the hotels Asia and Jam.

Although Qom is acknowledged as Iran's leading theological training centre, Mashhad is the country's holiest city and the second largest after Tehran. Shi'a pilgrims coming on a 'mini-hajj' here are allowed to be called *mashhadi*, attesting to the religious and holy importance of the city. Located at the altitude of 985m, Mashhad has grown significantly since 1979, now having more than 2.7 million residents. Numerous houses and bazaars have been demolished to improve access to the shrine area and give way to newer and more fashionable commercial centres.

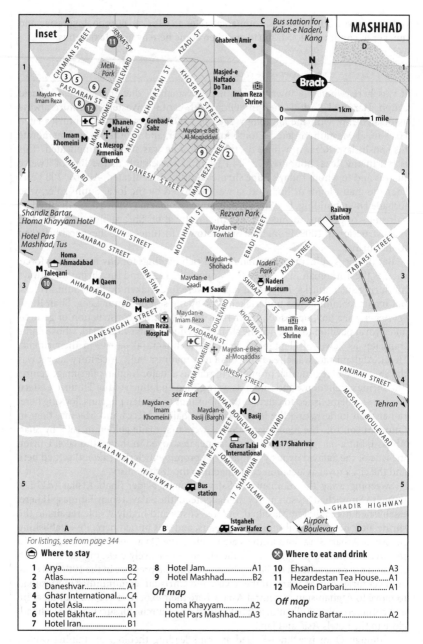

MASHHAD

Inset

Bus station for Kalat-e Naderi, Kang

Ghabreh Amir

Masjed-e Haftado Do Tan

Imam Reza Shrine

Melli Park

Maydan-e Imam Reza

Khaneh Malek

Gonbad-e Sabz

Maydan-e Beit Al-Moqaddasi

Imam Khomeini

St Mesrop Armenian Church

Shandiz Bartar, Homa Khayyam Hotel

Rezvan Park

Maydan-e Towhid

Railway station

Hotel Pars Mashhad, Tus

Homa Ahmadabad

Maydan-e Shohada

Naderi Park

Naderi Museum

Taleqani

Qaem

Maydan-e Saadi

Saadi

page 346

Shariati

Maydan-e Imam Reza

Imam Reza Hospital

Maydan-e Beit al-Moqaddas

Imam Reza Shrine

see inset

PANJRAH STREET

Tehran

Maydan-e Imam Khomeini

Maydan-e Basij (Bargh)

Basij

Ghasr Talai International

17 Shahrivar

Bus station

Istgaheh Savar Hafez

Airport Boulevard

AL-GHADIR HIGHWAY

For listings, see from page 344

Where to stay

1	Arya	B2
2	Atlas	C2
3	Daneshvar	A1
4	Ghasr International	C4
5	Hotel Asia	A1
6	Hotel Bakhtar	A1
7	Hotel Iran	B1
8	Hotel Jam	A1
9	Hotel Mashhad	B2

Off map

| Homa Khayyam | A2 |
| Hotel Pars Mashhad | A3 |

Where to eat and drink

10	Ehsan	A3
11	Hezardestan Tea House	A1
12	Moein Darbari	A1

Off map

| Shandiz Bartar | A2 |

GETTING THERE AND AWAY Be aware that all means of transport, especially trains, are heavily booked at holiday times and peak pilgrimage seasons.

By air Mashhad has an international airport and is served by Iraqi Airways operating direct flights from Najaf, Turkish Airlines and Qatar Airways, as well as all local airlines, including Aseman Airlines, IranAir, Mahan Airlines and Zagros

Airlines. Within Iran there are up to ten daily flights from Tehran (4,000,000–7,000,000 rials) and direct flights from most of the important cities in the country, including from Kish and Qeshm islands.

By train Mashhad is well connected to the rest of the country by the intercity rail network. An overnight train service links Tehran to Mashhad in 12 hours (530,000–2,400,000 rials, depending on service & class). There is also a train from Esfahan (1,300,000 rials) and from Shiraz (1,500,000 rials), but the journey of up to 18 and 24 hours respectively is tedious.

By bus Most buses bound for Mashhad arrive at the central Imam Reza bus terminal and there are numerous bus services from all over the country to this popular pilgrimage centre. From the Tehran direction there are two main roads eastwards: a northern one skirting the Caspian Sea to Gorgan, Shirvan and Quchan to Mashhad, and the more southerly route following the old caravan trade road from Shahrud via Sabzevar and Nishapur.

The best time for travelling in Iran's eastern provinces is in the late spring (April and May) and early autumn (late September and October), as the winters in Khorasan province are long and bitter, with heavy snow- and rainfall – as one 11th-century ruler, Amir Qabus Ibn Wushmagir, found to his cost (page 207). Below there is a bus departure schedule showing selected times from major Iranian cities:

From	Departure	Price (rials)
Esfahan (Kaveh)	14.30; 15.00; 15.30; 16.00; 17.00; 18.00; 19.30	930,000
Esfahan (Sofeh)	13.45; 15.15; 15.30; 16.15; 16.30; 19.00	930,000
Shiraz (Karandish)	14.30; 15.00; 15.30; 16.00	680,000–1,150,000
Tehran (southern)	08.30; 10.30; 14.05; 14.30; 18.45; 19.00; 19.30; 20.30; 21.00	810,000–970,000
Tehran (western)	17.30; 18.00; 20.00; 21.30	810,000–970,000
Tehran (Beyhaghi)	20.00; 21.00; 21.30	810,000–970,000
Tehran (Pars)	18.30; 20.30; 21.45	810,000–970,000

GETTING AROUND The quickest and easiest way to sites in and around Mashhad is undoubtedly by local **taxi**. Be prepared to spend upwards of 100,000 rials for a short taxi ride. For the more intrepid, there is a fairly efficient local **bus** (fare 10,000 rials payable to the driver) network within the city (Imam Reza Street bus line operates 24 hours) and a two-line **metro** system which goes all the way to the airport. Metro tickets also cost 10,000 rials and can be purchased from one of the kiosks or the ticket office at each station. The official Mashhad metro website is alas in Persian only and so is the map online. For the location of metro stations, see the city map, opposite.

There are good road maps (Persian with some English) available for free in hotels, or you can purchase a Persian-language detailed map around Saadi Square or shops at tourist sites, eg: Naderi Museum. Shrine maps in English are available from the small information kiosk opposite the Bab al-Reza entrance to the shrine.

TOUR GUIDE For cultural visits in Mashhad, Nishapur and around, contact local guide **Samira Godakhteh** (m 0935 1193664; e sa.godakhteh@yahoo.com).

WHERE TO STAY As the hotels cater for tens of thousands of pilgrims visiting during Ramadan, Moharram and the following Muslim month of Safar, accommodation is much easier to find outside these times. **Budget** hotels as such have almost disappeared and the quality of rooms and service in **mid-range** hotels is usually quite good. Rooms on average are reasonably large, to accommodate visiting pilgrims and their families and most mid-range hotels have a choice of rooms with squat-style or Western-style toilet facilities. Enquire at reception in case of preference. When looking for addresses vis-à-vis Imam Reza Street, remember that the number refers to a side alley off Imam Reza Street, not a house number.

Above average

Ghasr International Hotel [342 C4] (219 rooms) Imam Reza St; 38090; w hotelghasr. com. Ideally located for the shrine, the hotel has a blindingly shiny lobby with perfectly polished floor tiles. The rooms are a little small & poorly lit, but technically well equipped. The furniture is modern, albeit some appliances are in need of repair. The service overall is excellent. **$$$$**

Homa Khayyam Hotel [342 A2] (210 rooms) Khayyam St; 37611001; w homahotels. com. Swimming pool with separate gender timings & a variety of restaurants. In its own grounds, far from the shrine, but with a lovely garden for a stroll or a cup of tea. Furniture & room décor are a little old-fashioned, but well maintained & some rooms are equipped with a kitchenette. **$$$$**

Hotel Iran [342 B1] (164 rooms) Khosravi St; 32228010; w irhotel.com. In operation for over 40 years, Hotel Iran is comfortable & conveniently located away from the hectic Imam Reza St, but still within walking distance of the shrine. Previously in the mid-range bracket, prices here have almost doubled over the past 3 years. **$$$$**

Hotel Mashhad [342 B2] (137 rooms) Imam Reza St; 32222666; w mashhad-hotel. com. Built in 1975, this central hotel is popular with travellers & often fully booked. Rooms, in particular fitted apts, are spacious & comfortable. **$$$$**

Hotel Pars Mashhad [342 A3] (228 rooms) Vakilabad St; 38689201, 38689250; w pars-hotels.com. Built in 2000 on a 5ha site the hotel offers a wide range of facilities, shopping, tennis courts & a swimming pool with separate gender timings. Some way west of the centre & you would have to get a taxi or a metro ride to the shrine. Has lovely grounds with a garden & some rooms come with a view of a small lake. **$$$$**

Mid-range and lower mid-range

Atlas Hotel [342 C2] (188 rooms) Beit al-Moqaddas (Ab) Sq, look up for the large hotel sign; 38545061, 38545063; e manager@ altasgrandhotel.com. Very central with the façade overlooking the Bab al-Reza of the shrine, which is wonderfully lit at night. **$$$**

Arya Hotel [342 B2] (47 rooms) Imam Reza St, Danesh Crossroads; 38545571, 38549919; e arya.hotel.mashad@gmail.com. Very central with simple décor, but clean rooms & good service. Rooms to the back are quiet, while the main façade is facing the busy Imam Reza St. The staff are accommodating & helpful. **$$**

Hotel Asia [342 A1] (154 rooms) Pasdaran St; 32220071, 32220074; w asiahotel.ir. Has gone up in price significantly, but rooms are bright & the overall atmosphere is hospitable. The staff are helpful & obliging. This hotel administers a number of hotels around Mashhad; enquire about other locations if fully booked. **$$**

* **Hotel Jam** [342 A1] (153 rooms) Pasdaran St; 18590041, 18590045; w jam-hotel. com. The best in the lower mid-range price scale & identical to the hotels above in service. Rooms are large & some come with small balconies. Close to Hotel Asia, with a good travel agent next door. **$$**

Basic

Hotel Bakhtar [342 A1] (38 rooms) Pasdaran St; 32253011, 32253013. Located in a 5-storey building, the Bakhtar was built just over 30 years ago & offers Iranian 3-star quality accommodation, & simple, clean rooms away from the buzz of Imam Reza St. There is no Wi-Fi. **$$**

Daneshvar Hotel [342 A1] (32 rooms) 8th Chamran St; 32282900, 32282905. Offers very clean, standard accommodation. Single rooms are small & windowless with toilet facilities in the hall. Ideal for budget travellers, spending most of their time outdoors. Couples or groups should consider one of the mid-range hotels above. **$**

WHERE TO EAT AND DRINK

✳ ✗ **Shandiz Bartar** [342 A2] Vakil Abad Bd, Danesh Amuz metro station; m 0915 1156644; ⏱ noon–16.00 & 19.30–midnight. Walk with confidence through the ground-floor KFC restaurant towards the lift to take you to the 1st floor, where the actual Shandiz Bartar is. Here awaits a pleasant & airy décor, albeit a little European, although the menu offers excellent Iranian & local specialities. *Shishlik* is succulent, *dough* (yogurt-based drink), *mast* (yogurt) & butter are all homemade & an abundant set menu of starters will not disappoint. $$–$$$

✗ **Ehsan** [338 A3] Ahmadabad St, across the street from Homa Ahmadabad Hotel; ☎ 38402260; ⏱ noon–midnight daily. Not so traditional in décor, but certainly in menu. *Shishlik* is good, but wonderfully greasy *mahicheh* lamb shank cooked with garlic & fried onions is what you would really come here for. $$

✗ **Moein Darbari Restaurant** [342 A1] Pasdaran St, across the road from the Hotel Bakhtar; ☎ 38598898; w moeindarbari.com; ⏱ noon–16.00 & 20.00–23.00. Serves delicious *shishlik* & other classic Iranian dishes. $$

✳ ✗ **Hezardestan Tea House** [342 A1] Jannat St, Jannat Bazaar; ☎ 32254757; ⏱ 11.00–16.00 & 18.00–23.00. A beautiful traditional tea house that functions as a museum as well. Photography is not permitted. Offers excellent *sofreh* & good *dizzi*. $–$$

WHAT TO SEE AND DO

Shrine of Imam Reza ✳ [map, page 346] (⏱ 24hrs; small bags, wallets & mobile phones are allowed, but no cameras; depositories available at the entrance where you will be asked for ID (a copy is sufficient); women must wear a chador, available to rent (100,000 rials) in a nearby shop selling chadors. Ask the man at the depository for directions. When returning the garment, the shop owner will try to sell it to you for 500,000 rials, which you are welcome to decline.) Since the establishment of the Islamic Republic, much more money has been spent on the shrine – known locally as Haram-e Razavi – including the gilding of the main dome and minarets using four times more gold than before, retiling, construction of new courtyards and so on. The main road, which formerly encircled the shrine, now runs underground. The former walled complex of some 30 historic structures, the oldest dating to the 14th century, connected by four huge courtyards, has been transformed with additional courtyards. The result is bewildering and aesthetically unsatisfactory.

Non-Muslims were previously not allowed to enter by the main pilgrims' entrance and could not visit most sections of the shrine, but there are currently no restrictions in place. To avoid being told *mamnua'* (not allowed) too many times, do leave at the hotel or depositories everything except your phone and some cash for the museums. Following a bomb explosion here in the mid 1990s, all belongings (and there are body searches) are very rigorously checked at each entry point. All female visitors in addition to wearing a chador must also ensure their hair is fully covered at all times, otherwise the guardians won't miss an opportunity to point at your hair with their long dust brushes.

'Fluvius' (see box, page 80) has been fortunate in witnessing the blowing of long alpine-like horns, some 2.5m in length, at the shrine's roof levels. This means a miracle has occurred to a supplicant within the complex but, as he warns, 'this cannot be organised to fit into a tourist schedule'. You can, nonetheless, walk around the shrine and its museums while observing the faithful perform their religious duties. It is an active shrine always buzzing with locals and visitors from abroad, in particular from Saudi Arabia and Iraq.

The main **museum** (⏱ 08.00–17.30, holidays 08.00–noon, daily; entry 300,000 rials) with its numerous sections displays selected treasures of the shrine on three floors; some are outstanding, such as two 14th-century *mihrabs* of Kashan

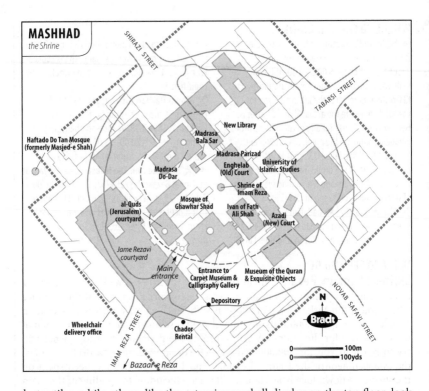

lustre tiles, while others, like the extensive seashell display on the top floor, look decidedly out of place. A number of 19th- and 20th-century paintings are shown, indirectly revealing which styles have 'official approval'. (A small collection of framed photographs on the ground floor record the totally ruinous state of the other Mashhad monuments before 1960; for this reason, no detailed description of the heavily reconstructed buildings has been included in this guide.) Labels are mainly in Farsi but there is also some information in English, and the exhibits are well displayed. A little further on is the **Carpet Museum** (⊕ 08.00–12.30 Sat–Wed, 08.00–11.30 Thu; entry 300,000 rials; if visiting both parts of the museum, in theory 1 ticket should cover both), arranged on two floors, a collection of mainly late 19th- and early 20th-century carpets, including some rare and decidedly beautiful Indian Moghul examples, two fine double-sided pile 'curtain' carpets as well as some bucolic Qajar work. Labelling here is in English and Farsi. The section called the **Museum of the Quran and Exquisite Objects**, with the former on the first floor and the latter on the ground floor, is now fully open; the opening hours are the same as for the main museum, above.

The most sacred place is the **tomb chamber** of Imam Reza, situated within the structures lying southwest of the Old Court. It was laid out in Safavid times along with the sanctuary of Allahverdi Khan, who ordered the construction of the famous Allahverdi Khan Bridge in Esfahan. Some 13th-century ceramic lustre tiles may still remain in situ within the shrine but the tall golden sanctuary portal and its two flanking minarets were constructed in the late 15th century. Restoration work was carried out in the mid 18th century on the order of Nader Shah Afshar, and the mirror work added by the Qajar regime. To the west when walking to the al-Quds (Jerusalem) courtyard built in the 1980s, you'll glimpse the dome of the **Mosque of Ghawhar Shad**, which the Timurid queen had constructed in 1416–18. A masterpiece by the Shirazi architect, Qavam al-Din, thought also to have designed the madrasa at Khargerd (page 357), it was built on the four-*ivan* plan with two minarets, with beautiful proportions and an emphatic rhythm of arcading and galleries. The mirror work was installed in the late 19th century. How much of the original extensive tilework, 'the most beautiful example of colour in architecture ever devised' (Robert Byron), still survives is questionable as the north and south *ivans* were demolished in 1977 and then rebuilt; the southeastern façade is clearly new work. The high portal, taller than usual, necessitated a very tall drum and dome, the latter replaced by a concrete one in the 1960s.

Close to the Mosque of Ghawhar Shad was built the four-*ivan* college, the **Madrasa Parizad**, possibly paid for by Ghawhar Shad or one of her attendants. Both this and the **Madrasa Bala Sar** to the east were extensively repaired in 1680 and restored in the 1970s, as was the adjoining 1439 **Madrasa Do-Dar**, used as a college until 1975. Then it was still possible to see wonderful 15th-century decorative plasterwork, 'more surviving than any other Timurid monument', in the barrel vault of the latter's mosque entrance. The college was donated by a governor of Qom, Yusuf Khafa (d1443), who is interred in the southern dome chamber, where the drum inscription reminded visitors that the only access to paradise is through love of the Prophet.

Many of the great and good have been laid to rest in the shrine and city: **Allahverdi Khan**, the Safavid kingmaker (page 184), whose tomb was constructed

IMAM REZA

The last years of Ali al-Reza, the eighth imam in Shi'ism, encapsulates the tensions at the Baghdad court and throughout the Abbasid Empire in the early 9th century. Exploiting the Shi'a cause, the Abbasid family had overthrown the Umayyad regime in 749CE, but quickly proclaimed its allegiance to Sunni Islam. Before his death in 809CE the Abbasid ruler, Harun al-Rashid, tried to ensure a smooth succession by securing the agreement of all concerned to his two named heirs: al-Amin, and his brother al-Ma'mun, then governor of Khorasan. But within two years al-Amin had reneged on the agreement, and al-Ma'mun in Merv (Turkmenistan) retaliated by proclaiming himself caliph. Al-Amin's action won few friends and he was killed in 813CE. Chaos ensued in the heartlands of Abbasid authority with Shi'a uprisings throughout Iraq, threatening the capital Baghdad. Court officials raced to Merv hoping to persuade al-Ma'mun to leave his stronghold and take charge; they also advised he join forces with the young Ali al-Reza (765CE), living in Medina near Mecca, who was recognised among Ithna 'Ashari Shi'a as the eighth imam. Imam Reza (his title within his community) agreed to go to Merv in 816CE and within a year al-Ma'mun named him as his heir, and marriages between the two families were arranged. Finally yielding to pressure, al-Ma'mun left Merv for Baghdad, but one of the court advisors who had stressed the importance of Imam Reza's support was assassinated. Imam Reza too died unexpectedly on the journey (September 818CE), supposedly after eating grapes sent by al-Ma'mun. Al-Ma'mun continued on to Baghdad and seized control, eventually dying in 833CE, knowing that the Ithna 'Ashari community held him directly responsible for Imam Reza's death.

12

with a soaring 21m-high dome and superb tilework, while another important Safavid vizier was commemorated in the Gonbad-e Khatemkhaneh of 1609. Then, of course, there was Nader Shah, whose tomb was rebuilt in the 1960s complete with a huge sculpture in the 'Soviet Realism' style; the tomb now operates as a small **Naderi Museum** [342 C3] (⊕ 08.00–16.30 daily; entry 300,000 rials) with exhibits dedicated essentially to the military bravura and artefacts of the short-lived Afshar dynasty. Labelling is in Persian only, but the building and the gardens are a pleasant space for a stroll.

Haftado Do Tan Mosque or Mosque of 72 Martyrs [map, page 346] (Formerly Masjed-e Shah) (Exterior visible only; now offices & closed to the public) Leaving the shrine of Imam Reza by the same entrance you entered through, walk a short distance, keeping the shrine's perimeter fence on your right, to see at comparatively close quarters a lovely 1451 building, the former Masjed-e Shah repaired in 1708. To Professor Pope, doyen of Iranian architectural history, its Timurid dome was the perfect form, but his contemporary Robert Byron felt it had 'an uncouthness which has no parallel' in other similarly dated buildings in the region. It was built as a double-domed structure, the exterior shell resting on eight internal brick buttresses. The tilework is still good on the exterior, especially the fine-quality 'mosaic' work by a Tabrizi tile cutter, with a green hexagonal tile dado, once embellished with gold stencilled decoration and a tiled inscription in the portal with a Hafez couplet: 'Written in gold on this emerald arcade / Nothing will remain except the good of the generous.'

Presently, the exterior, with its two corner minarets, retains most of its original tilework and its deep jewel-like colouring, despite a restoration programme completed in 1977.

The shops around here form one of Mashhad's many **bazaars**, selling tourist mementos such as posters and 'instant' prayer sets consisting of a rosary, *mohr* (clay tablet) and cloth, perfume, etc, and green fabric swatches for touching the grilles in the holy sanctuaries. On their return home, pilgrims will cut the swatch up and distribute the pieces among family and friends to share its *barakat* (blessings). **Bazaar-e Reza** in the vicinity of the Shrine is the most popular, but shiny new commercial centres have in recent years sprung up on every corner.

Mashhad is also (perhaps justly) famous for its saffron, as well as for turquoise sold in great chunks (see box, page 354), set in 21-carat gold, and sheepskin waistcoats. There is a noticeable use of the Cyrillic alphabet on shop signs, as in the early 1990s President Rafsanjani worked at revitalising the historic Silk Road routes with the new republics of Tajikistan, Uzbekistan and Turkmenistan, even extending the railway to the Turkmenistan border.

The centre of Mashhad conceals a few more historically interesting buildings. Off Imam Khomeini Street is the small **St Mesrop Armenian Church** [342 A2], built in 1941 by the Armenians living in Mashhad. Its distinctive pointy dome rises modestly from behind a tall wall, gaily painted with flowerpots. The church, alas, remains permanently closed. Just around the corner from it is the historic **Khaneh Malek** [342 A2], a rare example of late Qajar architecture in Mashhad. Currently a handicrafts shop and tourism office, this house belonged to a famous Iranian merchant and philanthropist, Hajji Hossein Malek. On the parallel street, walking back towards the main shrine, you will pass the mausoleum of Sheikh Momen Astarabadi, the **Gonbad-e Sabz** (Green Dome) [342 B2], located in the middle of the small square of the same name. Mir Mohammad Momen Astarabadi, a member of the Safavid court, left Iran for the Indian Deccan to serve as the top advisor at Qutb Shah's court from c1581–1626. An outstanding scholar, Astarabadi played an important role in the planning of the new capital city Hyderabad.

AROUND MASHHAD

Several half- and full-day excursions may be made from Mashhad. East of the city centre lie the popular recreation areas of Chandiz and Chalidarreh, full of restaurants and very busy on weekends. Just a few kilometres further along the road, 30km away from Mashhad, is the small village of **Kang** (کنگ), known as Masouleh of Khorasan for its houses built on the slope of the mountain. Although most buildings here are clearly in need of repair, a day or two could easily be spent hiking around this pleasant rural area. A newly opened **Kang Kohan Ecolodge** (4 rooms; ✆ 051 34363464; m 0915 9790295, 3000543; w kangkohan.com; **$$**) run by the most pleasant Mariya Masoudi, has cosy rooms traditionally furnished with *kursi* heating and a restaurant serving traditional food.

Northwest of Mashhad lies **Tus** or **Ferdowsi** (names are used almost interchangeably), the birthplace of the medieval Persian poet, Ferdowsi (d1020), author of the renowned epic poem, the *Shahnameh*, narrating the exploits and adventures of the legendary kings of Iran (see box, below). Tus was sacked in 1389 by Timur Leng and then largely abandoned a century later as Mashhad assumed

FERDOWSI AND THE *SHAHNAMEH*

As England's national poet is William Shakespeare, so Ferdowsi is seen to embody Iranian history and culture, saving from oblivion the Persian language, legends and history. He started work on composing the 60,000 couplets that were to form his *Shahnameh* ('Book of Kings') when he was 40 years old, c980ce, working from at least three versions. The work was finally completed in 994–95. Despite being the son of a prosperous landowner in Tus, he soon needed to look for financial support and approached Mahmoud of Ghazni (d1030) who, it is said, promised him a gold coin for every couplet written but paid only a silver pittance. Ferdowsi was practically destitute when his great work was completed.

The opening chapters concern the creation of the world and the first rulers who brought civilisation and culture to the people of Iran, whether it was the skill of weaving or the invention of fire. Ferdowsi then saw later developments as a series of cyclic events, in which just rule descended into periods of anarchy and despair redeemed only by the superhuman strength of spirit, courage and family loyalty of the individual. Progress was marked by a constant battle between good and evil, vividly portrayed throughout this epic poem, concluding with the reign of the last Sasanid king and the Arab invasion, c640ce. The couplets relate court intrigue and sibling rivalry, military triumphs and disasters, and immense strength and heroism pitted against supernatural demons and wicked rulers. The imagery remains powerful even after a millennium; no-one in the late 1970s could fail to understand political posters depicting the late shah as Ferdowsi's despotic ruler Zahhak, whose wickedness was manifested by two snakes growing from his shoulders; indeed, this same imagery, with the faces of Hitler, Himmler and Goebbels, was used in World War II British propaganda distributed in the Middle East.

growing importance, but remnants of its citadel walls are still visible from the modern **gardens and tomb** (☉ 08.30–18.00; entry 300,000 rials, plus 300,000 rials for the separate museum) commemorating the poet. In 1908 Englishman Fraiser found Ferdowsi's grave and eventually a memorial of a ponderous stone structure (not at all like his poetry) with architectural details loosely based on Achaemenid work was erected after the tomb of Cyrus the Great in Pasargadae. The tomb was refurbished in 1935 as part of the new nationalism programme initiated by Reza Shah and the project was supervised by a prominent Zoroastrian parliament representative and head of the Tehran Zoroastrian Association – Kay Khosrow Shahrokh. Contemporary limestone panels depicting various characters or episodes linked to the *Shahnameh* decorate the steps down into the cavernous basement, where a similar theme forms the decorative friezes.

About 1km before the Ferdowsi gardens is a much earlier but heavily restored mausoleum, **Haruniyeh**, said to be that of the Abbasid caliph, Harun al-Rashid (d809CE). The mud-brick ruins in the fields behind the tomb are known locally as Harun's Palace, but most scholars think this mausoleum in fact marks the burial place of the Muslim philosopher, al-Ghazali (d1111). Is a taxi drive worth the expense? Yes, definitely, especially if you combine your visit with one to the spectacular tomb tower at Akhangan, nearby off the branch road to Sarakhs, or with a drive to Kalat (see below).

Mil-e Akhangan is an early 15th-century Timurid mausoleum in good condition with an unusual prismatic 'pleated' roof, now banded in turquoise- and cobalt-blue tiles. The cylindrical brick exterior is broken by eight rounded, engaged columns forming frames for (one-time) tiled stars and crosses; those have long since gone but their imprint remains. With such detail it's easy to believe the local tradition that it was constructed to honour the sister of Queen Ghawhar Shad. It is located 22km north of Mashhad in agricultural land some 4km off the main road between Dorqi and Faimad on the road to Kalat.

KALAT كلات ✳

(also known as Kalat-e Naderi) The 145km drive north on the signposted Kalat and Kabud-e Gonbad roads will take a full day but the light industrial buildings on the outskirts of Mashhad are quickly left behind for dramatic but gaunt scenery, with hairpin bends and long curves climbing up into the hills that mark the frontier with today's Turkmenistan. Signposts are few and far between once you reach this region; just a few distance markers. At the bridge over Qara Su (Black Water), the road tunnel will take you directly into the village of Kalat, which occupies a long, fertile east–west valley (altitude 765m) between two hill chains – a superb natural defence. Buses from Terminal-e Kalat in northern Mashhad take up to 3 hours and depart hourly.

As Lord Curzon wrote in the late 19th century: 'If in their war with Olympian Zeus the Titans had ever occasion to build for themselves an unassailable retreat, such might well have been the mountain fortress that they would have reared.' This was the place where Nader Shah Afshar (d1747) returned after his victories in India, with so much booty that his army could stagger back at only four miles a day. He ordered the building of a large octagonal pavilion, the **Kakh-e Khorshid** (☉ 07.30–17.00; entry 300,000 rials) set in a garden, perhaps as his mausoleum, but early 20th-century writers said that the vault was never intended to be a crypt but a secure place for his treasures. Its rose-pink sandstone, the fluted drum-tower and the carved exterior panels depicting flowering plants all speak of Mughal Delhi, but the painted interior recalls Safavid Esfahan. Originally, marble slabs brought from Orumiyeh 1,900km away, embellished the lower internal walls.

Directly opposite the garden entrance is the 18th-century **Blue Dome Mosque** (Kabud-e Gonbad), so called due to the use of blue tiles on its dome. Built on the four-*ivan* plan with enough of the original tiling remaining to show the decorative scheme, its actual chambers – including the large domed chamber – have been completely replastered and/or painted. Approximately 4km along the road past the mosque is the visually impressive 25m-high **Naderi Dam** (Band-e Naderi) constructed on the Jarf River by Nader Shah to ensure a good water supply to the village. The dam has three openings at different levels above the ground for controlling and distributing water.

SARAKHS (سرخس) AND ROBAT-E SHARAF Another day trip (or a long half-day if only the nearer Robat-e Sharaf is visited) lies to the east of Mashhad, leaving by the Hemmat Highway; Sarakhs, some 175km away, is also one of the border crossings with Turkmenistan. The train station is outside the town and there are two daily train departures from Mashhad to Sarakhs at 10.40 and 19.30 and at 05.40 and 14.40 for the return journey. The only place to overnight in Sarakh is the basic **Hotel Dosti** (19 rooms; Gomrok Bd, a few hundred metres from the border crossing; ↖051 34520093, 34520094; **$$**) with a passable restaurant and basic facilities. It is frequently used by locals for wedding banquets and can be very noisy. Sarakhs has little to offer other than the 1356 **Mausoleum of Sheikh Baba Loqman** (Maghbareh Loghman Baba; ⏱ 08.00–15.00; entry free), a famous 10th-century storyteller. Located on its far western outskirts on agricultural land, the mausoleum has a similar plan to the Haruniyeh near the Ferdowsi tomb, but both have been heavily restored. Only a little remains of a shallow plaster inscription set with a tight arabesque scroll over the door, and of the blue glazed inserts in the ruined soffit arch of the entry portal. Inside, two internal staircases (now blocked) led to the upper gallery running between the four deep *muqarnas* alcoves. Before reaching Sharluk, there is a view of Robat-e Mahi, another caravanserai, on the far side of the railway.

Some 65km from Sarakhs (or 125km from Mashhad) is the Seljuk caravanserai, **Robat-e Sharaf** (رباط شرف) ✳ (⏱ 09.00–16.00; entry 80,000 rials); take the minor road (southeast) at the roadside village of **Shurluk**, and the signposted caravanserai is 6km away. Located on what was the old Merv–Nishapur trade route, this historic inn is simply wonderful, although the overall sight is spoilt with the tall wire fence across the entire perimeter. There are two entrance gates to the caravanserai and if the lower one is locked, try the upper gate; the guardian is usually on site. Here there is simple accommodation (500,000 rials) in the form of two double rooms, kitchen and toilet facilities. The person in charge of the site

> **BORDER CROSSING TO TURKMENISTAN**
>
> The main border crossing from Khorasan to Turkmenistan is in Sarakhs (⏱ 07.00–15.00 daily), frequently used by Silk Road route cyclists from Europe. Frontier formalities here involve much time and patience, and extra checks and questioning are to be expected owing to the sensitive nature of the area. The other two border crossings are at Bajgiran only 50km away from Ashgabat, and at Lotfabad.
>
> Please note that visas to Turkmenistan cannot be issued at the border and must be obtained in advance. Please apply in advance to the embassy or if already in Mashhad, to the Turkmenistan Consulate at w mashhad. tmconsulate.gov.tm/en.

and accommodation is Agha Azizi (m 0915 1237481, 9757481) who will kindly explain every detail about the caravanserai itself.

Probably constructed in 1115 with changes made to its layout some 40 years later, it is called a caravanserai but the patterned brickwork and plaster decoration have led scholars to wonder whether it once served as a royal lodge. The exterior looks like a fortress with one main entrance, but inside it is fit for a king. There are two *ivans*, both with courtyards displaying amazing brick patterns, dome supports, carved plaster, decorative brick end-plugs and intricately plaited *Kufic* inscriptions. Inside the caravanserai there is the usual arrangement of stabling and rooms, each decorated in its own particular style. There is a mosque, complete with plaster *mihrab*, in each of the courts, and at the far end of the second *ivan* there are rooms with underground cisterns (*zakhir-e ab*). The second courtyard, known as *shahneshin*, was used exclusively by the sultan and his family and consists of a number of rooms grouped around a central *khowzeh* water basin, the largest of its kind in Iran. Its mosque has a double *mihrab*, one for the men-only section of the mosque and the other at the back for women. As yet a kitchen area or 'refectory' has not been identified, nor is there sign of a bathhouse, but a number of rooms and chambers were blocked off or altered during the mid 12th century. This work is recorded in the beautiful plaster and brick inscription of the portal leading into the second courtyard, giving the date 1154 and mentioning Sultan Sanjar (whose father is commemorated in Esfahan's masjed-e jame). As Sanjar was then a prisoner of the Turkomens in Merv, it is thought his wife ordered this work, possibly to repair damage inflicted by these marauding tribesmen after their sacking of Nishapur.

When the caravanserai was discovered, the lower sections were buried at least 1m deep under the earth and more than 200 trucks were required to clear it all, revealing the beautiful original cobblestones.

KHAJEH RABI'E آرامگاه خواجه ربیع Returning to Mashhad from Robat-e Sharaf, look for road signs on the ring road for this shrine 6km northwest of the centre, now within the city confines. It commemorates Rabi'e Ibn Khuthaym, who led 4,000 men to help Ali, the son-in-law of the Prophet Mohammad, and as such was visited by the eighth imam, Reza. However, the structure today dates from the first quarter of the 17th century, financed by Shah Abbas I in 1618, and its design is said to have influenced the form of the world-famous Taj Mahal in Agra, India. Immediately to the right of the entrance, a small chamber has been made into a memorial to a local theologian, and his two sons killed in 1974. Much of the exterior tilework and painting has been restored but look for two small dragon heads worked in Safavid 'mosaic' tiles around to the far left of the entrance. Inside, a great deal of the Safavid gilded plaster ornament remains, but it is in dire need of cleaning.

NISHAPUR AND AROUND

Easily reachable from Mashhad (hourly buses depart from Imam Reza terminal & take about 2hrs; or by *savari* from Hafez pick-up area (*istgaheh savar hafez*) in southern Mashhad), Nishapur is a cultural and historic jewel. Approaching the city from Mashhad you drive past **Qadamgah** ('Place of the Foot'), which has a small 17th-century octagonal shrine erected by the Safavid shah Soleyman in 1642 and restored by the Qajars, in honour of a large black stone bearing the imprint of two highly arched feet: those, it is believed, of Imam Reza. A conservation team has been working on the painted ceiling and vaults so scaffolding may yet again mar the view. Nearby is a well-preserved Safavid caravanserai called Fakhri-e Da'ud, and another as you near Nishapur.

Just the name 'Nishapur' – like that of Tashkent – conjures up images of medieval buildings, busy bazaars, camel trains and a dramatic landscape. Unfortunately, like today's Uzbek capital, virtually nothing historical is left in **Nishapur** (نیشابور) despite its well-chronicled past. When Omar Khayyam (page 354) lived here, only Constantinople was larger in size. The original settlement was destroyed by an earthquake, so the Sasanid shah Shapur II (r309–79CE) rebuilt the city, recorded in its new name Niv Shapur (Shapur's good deed), and if it was true that one of the four sacred fires of Zoroastrianism, the Adur Burzin Mihr of the agricultural class, was located nearby, this would have had added importance for the Sasanid court. Finally taken by the Arabs in 661CE, it became the administrative centre of Khorasan province (then including Afghanistan) and later of the Seljuk sultan Toghrol Beg (d1063), who established well-stocked libraries and two universities here. However, if Westerners recognise the city's name today, they associate it either with the splendidly decorated slip-painted earthenware ceramics, made in the region during the 10th–11th centuries, or with the poet and mathematician, Omar Khayyam (d1131). A catalogue of disasters – serious earthquakes in 1115 and 1145, followed by Turkoman incursions, then the Mongol conquests of the 1220s and Timur Leng's destructive campaigns c1390 – meant few historic buildings survived. In later centuries, Mashhad's growing importance as a pilgrimage centre and then as Nader Shah Afshar's capital meant Nishapur received little investment. It is now a city with around 270,000 residents and is worth a detour essentially for its historical glory and Omar Khayyam's tomb.

The two-*ivan* **masjed-e jame** was largely rebuilt in 1494 by Ali Kurukhi, a local notable, whose tomb is to the left of the entrance through an office. The foundation inscription in the *qibla ivan* gives him the title of *pahlavan*, which suggests he was a champion warrior or indeed wrestler (see box, page 172). His wish that 'this building remain as a memorial for the town of Nishapur' has been honoured, but only at the expense of extensive reconstruction. The *mihrab* records many early 18th-century repairs to the building, but because its Quranic verses (Q36:55; Q89:27–30) relate more to a mausoleum than a mosque, there is some debate whether this *mihrab* was moved here as part of those repairs. An inscription on the entrance portal tiles speaks of further work undertaken in 1869, and in the courtyard there is much new tiling. In the vicinity of the mosque is the Nishapur **Bazaar** with easily the greatest variety of turquoise jewellery in Iran. Almost every shop here has its own workshop, so you are guaranteed to purchase an item of local craftsmanship.

In the southeastern outskirts, driving past the old city walls and the newly built planetarium (awaiting its telescope, delayed due to the sanctions) the road to the right leads to the **gardens** (☉ 08.00–20.00; entry 300,000 rials) where under a modern, tiled canopy is the grave of the famous Qajar painter Kamal al-Molk, a few metres away from the tomb of poet-scientist Farid al-Din Attar, author of *The Assembly of Birds*, a deeply mystical work. Local tradition has it that his tomb was built by the penitent Hulagu, grandson of Genghis Khan, who had ordered the execution of this renowned mystic in 1221 but, as Farid al-Din died around 1194, this is unlikely. Today's double-domed tomb probably dates from the late Qajar period, as an earlier Safavid building was seen in ruins in 1909. A majestically tall pillar gravestone of 1486, now encased in glass, recalls this saintly man: 'Who was such a fine perfumer (*attar*) that from his breath / The world from one end to another was fragrant.'

In the fields beyond at the *shadyakh* archaeological site you find the remains of old Nishapur, excavated in the 1930s by the Metropolitan Museum, New York,

12

To my unpractised eye there was nothing different in that one hill from any of the others around. It was apparently composed of the same dark-coloured rock that is so common throughout the country ... The only implements used by the miners are short iron jumpers about eighteen inches in length, and a small hammer with which they drive holes into the rock, which is then blasted out with common country gun-powder ... outside a lot of small boys break the rock into little pieces with small hammers and pick out any bits of green or blue they see ...

Turquoises at the mines are divided into three kinds – first, the *Angushtari*, or stones fit for rings; second, the *Barkhana*, or stones fit for trappings, and third, the *Arabi*, or stones fit for Arabia. The first are all carefully cut and polished at Mashhad, and are always sold separately ... The first two [grades of the second category] ... are largely exported to Europe, while the third is sold in Persia for the ornamentation of *qalian* ['hubble-bubble'] pipe-heads, horses' trappings, and small-arms, etc. The third kind are as a rule bad and light-coloured stones, for which there is no sale in Persia. The name arose owing to some of the miners going on pilgrimage to Mecca ... and found a good sale for them in Arabia, which is now the market for them and the origin of the name.

C E Yate, *Khurasan and Sistan*, 1900, pp 400–1, 406

which yielded numerous finds of decorated plaster, glass and slip-painted ceramics, produced before Hulagu's devastation of the region in 1220.

Coming back to the intersection and about 1km further along the tarmac road lies the **Tomb of Omar Khayyam** ✴ (🕑 08.00–20.00; entry 300,000 rials) in the modern canopy honouring one of Iran's greatest poets and scientists. Much liked in the West thanks to Edward Fitzgerald's translation, Khayyam is somewhat neglected in modern Iran due to his rather frequent poetic references to life's pleasures, such as wine. It was Khayyam, nonetheless, who developed Iran's first and still-in-use solar calendar, known as the *Jalali calendar*. He was also an outstanding astronomer, so the nearby planetarium location is no accident.

In the nearby village of **Chubin** (دهکده چوبین), around 10km southeast of Nishapur, lies a unique example of wooden architecture, the famous **Wooden Mosque** (*masjed-e chubi*) (entry 300,000 rials). Part of a large complex comprising a library and museum, it was built from resistant wood that can withstand earthquakes of a magnitude up to 8 on the Richter scale.

The mountains to the northeast of Nishapur are rich in turquoise mines. Here lies **Sabzevar** (سبزوار), some 115km further west of Nishapur, once a small town in the shadow of the more prosperous **Khosrowgerd** (خسروگرد), less than 10km west. Both towns suffered severely from the Mongol invasions and then from the Timurid armies in 1381 but miraculously their **Seljuk minarets** survived. The one at Khosrowgerd was constructed in 1111 and today stands with glorious brick patterning about 18.5m high, whereas the Sabzevar minaret is not quite as tall. To see the latter, ask in Sabzevar for Masjed-e Pa Menar off Maydan 22 Bahman, situated near the gendarmerie. The minaret is small and invisible until close; the best views are from the opposite side of the street or from a nearby courtyard, which has the advantage of clean toilets (serving the mosque, no doubt, but open).

Head some 75km further west to Davarzan, then north up into the hills to the village of **Forumad**, charming in the 1970s and now rapidly being swamped with new buildings. Dating from Seljuk times, its two-*ivan* masjed-e jame was revamped around 1320 when the small town became important to the local Ilkhanid rulers, who built a good hospital and library. The building may have seen better days, but the interlaced terracotta square tiles, the plasterwork and glazed brick inserts are high quality and it is worth a short detour; the guardian lives nearby.

Returning to the main road, another 70km or so brings you to **Miyandasht** (میاندشت). Boasting no fewer than three caravanserais linked together, it gives some indication of the huge numbers of travellers and pilgrims along this road in the 19th century. The smallest, about 50m² and situated to the left of the main entrance, was constructed in the early 17th century. Following the typical Safavid plan, it is octagonal in layout with the main chambers located in the eight corners, and stabling behind protected by the outer wall. It was repaired in Qajar times when two large additions were made to cater for increased traffic: the caravanserai that is now the main central courtyard with accommodation, and another one adjoining immediately to the right. The guardian is delighted to show the various staircases to the roof areas. Two *ab anbar*, or water cisterns, are located in the central court and at least one other is outside.

Another 110km brings you to Shahrud (page 208).

SOUTH OF MASHHAD

Bus services in the southward direction leave from Mashhad's central Imam Reza bus terminal, but departures are irregular, depending on the destination, and do not follow a specific schedule. Travelling by *savari* taxi is easy and paying for two passengers can ensure speedy departure off season or in the evenings, especially on Fridays. It is preferable, although not a must, that female travellers occupy the back seat of the vehicle when in this part of the country. Most residents here are Baluchi and Sunni, often attested by the men's attire and white turban. *Savari* rates vary, but be prepared to pay between 60,000 and 100,000 rials per person for stretches of road 60km to 100km long.

The road south offers some interesting sites, especially if you like Timurid buildings (some interiors are very dark so a torch is useful) or if you are interested in Sufism. Just as you leave the city, after the bus terminal and following signs for Torbat-e Heydariyeh, are two popular shrines. The first commemorates **Khajeh Abbasalt** (*sic*) **Haravi** (dc851CE) who, it was said, witnessed the death of Imam Reza, who died after eating poisoned grapes from his father-in-law, the Abbasid caliph al-Ma'mun. In the 1970s the shrine still retained elements of its Safavid construction. Not today. Words fail us. Less than 5km further south along this main road – look for an avenue of trees from the roadside leading into the hillside – is **Khajeh Murad,** commemorating a famous orator of the Karbala story (d832CE). The gift of such narrators is difficult to communicate, but perhaps you too have stood entranced with other non-Farsi speakers listening as a storyteller speaks to Iranian Shi'a pilgrims in the Great Mosque of Damascus. The shrine building itself is small and unremarkable but it is a pleasant family picnic spot with stalls, an airy cafeteria and even a small photographic studio offering the sitter a backdrop of the Mashhad shrine, Caliph al-Ma'mun handing Imam Reza the lethal grapes, or even Bruce Lee fighting a dragon.

There are richer treasures further south along this road in both the southeast and southwest directions. Travelling southeast towards **Torbat-e Heydariyeh,** do look out for the village of **Bazeh Hur**, some 65km before Mashhad. Its late

15th-century caravanserai **Robat-e Sefid** behind the roadside shops is unloved and rapidly collapsing (there are much better, restored ones, on the road to Mashhad) but it's worth stopping at the lime kilns just before the shops to take a photograph of the restored 3rd-century CE Zoroastrian fire temple set on the hills. Travelling in a southeastern direction instead, to Torbat-e Jam brings you quickly to the Sang Bast junction.

SANG BAST سنگ بست A white building, formerly the caravanserai **Robat-e Sang Bast**, marks the turning leading to the (possibly) 11th-century tomb (locally known as Mil-e Ayaz) built for Arslan Jadhib, former governor of this region for the Ghaznavid dynasty of Afghanistan. The caravanserai's internal location of stabling, staircases in the vestibule area, raised platforms, etc, has suggested to scholars that it was built around 1400, with further stabling facilities added before its use in 1856 as barracks during the Qajar campaigns against Herat. It then served as a gendarmerie and is now a prison, so access is not permitted.

The **Mil-e Ayaz tomb**, important for architectural historians as the only surviving Ghaznavid monument on the Iranian side of the Afghan border, stands now in a deserted area pockmarked with small craters, not the result of mortar shelling but of illicit digging for medieval ceramics and other artefacts. It was Arslan (Lion) who advised Sultan Mahmoud of Ghazni (d1030) to cut off the left thumb of every man taken captive in his military campaigns, thus preventing them using a bow in battle again. Sultan Mahmoud may have concurred but it didn't stop Seljuk tribesmen from later controlling most of Iran and present-day Turkey, following their victories over Mahmoud's successors. Essentially, this tomb follows the Sasanid fire temple plan of a cube broken by four arches (now blocked) surmounted by a dome. Very little of its decoration survives, but in the mid 1970s the external dome inscription consisted of Quranic verses (Q21:35–6 and Q12:101), while on the inside a painted band (Q10:25–6) could be seen alongside a quatrain asking for heavenly rain; there was also some decorative brickwork. Close by is a 20m brick minaret, c1028, with a *Kufic* inscription (Q41:33) naming the builder as coming from Sarakhs, but there is no sign of the mosque it once served.

LANGAR لنگر If Timurid history or Persian poetry is a passion, you'll want to make a short detour to see a small building at Langar, 25km northwest before Torbat-e Jam, just off the asphalt road signposted to Mahmud Abad. This village was the birthplace of the Persian poet al-Jame, but the late 15th-century square building (restored in 1966; ⊕ 09.00–17.00; entry free) with two deep alcoves inside is not a memorial to him. It was dedicated to the mystical poet Qasem-e Anvar, who worked with the great Timurid ruler and scientist Ulugh Beg (d1449) in Samarkand, and it probably functioned as a *khanqah* or Sufi meeting place with a kitchen (or *langar*; thus the village name) to accommodate eager disciples. A short distance away is the water cistern with stepped dome, of the same date.

TORBAT-E JAM تربت جام Some 160km southeast from Mashhad, Torbat-e Jam is known for its striking complex **Aramgah-e Mazar-e Sheikh Ahmad Jam** ✳ (⊕ 08.00–23.00 daily; entry free) honouring the memory of the mystic, noted author and teacher, Sheikh Ahmad Ibn Abdul Hassan (d1141). Make sure to leave your shoes outside at the main entrance with the guardian. The central domed chamber dates to 1236, while the five-bay chamber to the east, with its rich plaster decoration, *muqarnas* vaulting and rib-network is of the mid 14th century. The work in the west chamber of Gonbad-e Sefid is similarly dated, but not as elaborate or exquisite. Nothing remains of a mosque built around 1320 behind the five-bayed hall, nor much from the so-called 'new' mosque erected in 1440–43; only a mass of new brickwork and white plaster is visible. The small high-domed 1441 building to the west was probably conceived as a madrasa and mausoleum for Amir Jalal al-Din Firuzshah, chief commander to Shah Rukh, but never finished before his fall from grace. His 35-year service and status should have ensured him burial in Herat, then the Timurid capital but, inadvisably, when Shah Rukh (see box, page 340) was taken seriously ill, he openly supported the favourite son of Ghawhar Shad instead of the official heir apparent. Shah Rukh recovered and exacted revenge.

TAYBAD AND AROUND From Torbat-e Jam it is 60km to **Taybad** (تایباد), close to the Afghan border (225km southeast of Mashhad), passing villages with small barrel-vaulted houses topped with small windcatchers that resemble miniature periscopes. The reason for coming to Taybad is the 14th-century **Masjed-e Mowlana** ✴ (🕐 07.00–17.00; entry free) honouring an influential Sufi mystic Sheikh Mowlana Zayn al-Din (d1389), whose grave lies in front of the main *ivan* portal surrounded by trees, which are believed by some to symbolise the good nature of the person buried. Timur Leng visited him in 1381 before attacking Herat, and was well pleased to hear that only the Angel of Death would prove his better. Built by a vizier for Shah Rukh, and completed in 1444–45, it is an intimate building although at first the portal looks disproportionately tall. The tile decoration here (including Q18:1–11, the story of the Seven Sleepers) is exquisitely elegant, especially the lyrically flowing calligraphy in clay set on a turquoise tiled ground, and scholars have linked both the building and decoration to Mashhad (Ghawhar Shad's madrasa) and Khargerd (see below), suggesting it is the work of the same architect. The guardian will gladly open the actual prayer chamber and, despite continuing problems with dust and damp, the visual impact of the 'virtuoso complexity' of the *muqarnas* vaults and rib-network is stunningly beautiful.

About 30km further on at **Kerat** there is a beautiful Seljuk minaret (c1106) by the side of the road. Its very location on a slope suggests it served more as a lighthouse for travelling caravans than for a mosque. Here and there a few glazed inserts survive among the complex brick patterns.

SOUTHWEST FROM TAYBAD Here you will find an area rich in historic sites and mosques. In **Sangan** (سنگان), 80km away, there is a historic masjed-e jame. It is used by locals for *namaz* once a week and if coming here without a guide you may be required to locate the key. Its *ivan* portal was damaged in the earthquake, but the skewed leaning is due to a *qanat* running nearby. Approximately 24km northwest from here lies the village of **Nashtifan** (نشتیفان), famous for Sasanid windmills that are still used during windy summer months. There are a few more of such windmills further on in the town of **Khaf**, the terminus of the Tehran-Khaf railway line, which is currently being extended to Herat in Afghanistan. Approximately 3km before Khaf lies the small town of **Khargerd** (خرگرد) notable for its mid-15th-century Timurid **Madrasa Ghiyasiyeh** ✴ (🕐 08.00–18.00 daily; entry 80,000 rials. If closed, you can find the key with Meysam Rezayat from Ghyasyh Ecolodge (page 358)). Over 25 years of restoration work remains unfinished, but at least it hasn't been as heavy-handed as elsewhere. It has the typical four-*ivan* groundplan, with a very symmetrical arrangement of arcades and galleries working to a strict set of proportions. For at least one scholar, the careful arrangement and proportions of windows, niches and arches create a 'visual crescendo' where everything works in harmony. Just enough remains of the original tiling to show the various pattern schemes and, despite the grime, pigeon droppings and repairs, the *muqarnas* decoration of both chambers either side of the entry portal – the small mosque on the right, the main lecture hall on the left – is fine work. But virtually nothing now survives of the painted wall decoration, recorded in the mid 1970s. In the court, staircases in each corner lead to the upper accommodation. Each room comes with a niche for books and belongings, and a chimney. Behind the far *ivan* a *badgir* (wind tower) has been constructed.

If you can't get here, you can see an example of the superb original workmanship by visiting the British Museum and the Victoria and Albert Museum in London or indeed New York's Metropolitan Museum, all of which managed to 'acquire' samples of the tilework, especially the star tiles. The inscriptions record that the patron of this beautiful college, far away from any centre, was not a member of the Timurid house but one of their long-serving viziers, Pir Ahmad Khafi, born in the area and linked with this monument. Whether it was an act of piety or a guarantee against royal confiscation if he fell from power (by consigning his property and land as an endowment) is unclear. Directly in front of Madrasa Ghiyathiyeh is the small and cosy family-run **Ghyasyh Ecolodge** (8 rooms; m 0915 3324956, 0919 3339850; $).

There is alas nothing left of the former remains of the Seljuk **Madrasa Nizamiyeh** (c1154) named after its patron, another famous vizier, Nizam al-Molk, linked with the superb domed chamber in the masjed-e jame in Esfahan.

Another 3km northwest is **Khaf** (خواف). Its masjed-e jame was built about 1503, a date given on the seven-stepped *minbar* (a section is now in the Mashhad Imam Reza Shrine Museum; page 345), but has been much repaired since. It is probable that the domed prayer chamber and its *ivan* are Timurid, if not earlier, but the two winter prayer rooms could well be a product of the extensive repair programme of 1971. **Roshtkhar** is about 55km from **Torbat-e Heydariyeh**; in the mid 1970s its masjed-e jame was collapsing, but something of the Seljuk vaulting remained, with a domed prayer chamber and splendid herringbone brickwork. The painted inscription around the zone of transition consists of Quranic verses (Q48:1–14) with a date of 1455.

You could extend your journey west from Torbat-e Heydariyeh to **Kashmar** (کاشمر), which possesses two *imamzadehs*, one dedicated to Hamza and totally renovated in modern times, and the other at the end of a long avenue of trees, the **Imamzadeh Seyyed Murtadeh**, essentially a Safavid construction but restored in 1975. The road west goes through a lovely landscape of vineyards behind mud walls, each with one or more drying sheds. About 10km before Bardeskan is a minor road north to **Ali Abad Kashmar**, leading to the village *hamam* and then the magnificent **tomb tower**, standing among the houses. Its exterior is basically 12-sided, presumably to remind visitors of the Twelve Imams, but with alternate flanged and rounded engaged columns with moulded turquoise tile inserts highlighting aspects of the brick decoration. It is a masterpiece of 13th-century architecture but very dark inside, so a torch is useful.

Local children will readily fetch the guardian to unlock the door to the octagonal interior and then race up the internal staircases to the upper gallery, to the space between the inner and upper domes, to peer down on you. This region was also Assassin country in the 12th century. One of their strongholds, very effectively dismantled by the Mongols, is at Qaleh Dokhtar, about 6km east of Khoshab village, northeast of Bardeskan.

TOWARDS GONABAD AND TABAS

Travelling south of Torbat-e Heydariyeh at your own speed but without a vehicle is challenging. Public traffic is scarce and the only options are taxi or hitchhiking, but the latter is not recommended for safety reasons.

Approximately 50km before you reach the historic city of Gonabad you will see one of Iran's numerous salt lakes, **Kal-e Shur**. Although it is not as impressive in colour as the salt lake outside Shiraz or in scenery as the Varzaneh salt lake, it is worth making a detour here, time allowing, to see the remains of a Safavid bride. Alternatively, continue on towards **Gonabad** (گناباد), which is famous for its functioning Sufi orders centred in the nearby village of Beydukht (it is, however,

---

SUFISM

Sufism, or Islamic mysticism as it is also known, originated in Iran in the 7th–8th centuries and has since had a great influence on Shi'a Islam, leading some prominent Sufi thinkers to even declare the two as one. An important common trait is the adoration of the figure of the first imam, Imam Ali, considered to be holy by Sufis and Shi'a alike.

At the heart of Sufism is the belief that within everybody is a spark of the Divine, the Creator, and that through dedicated ritual and practice, this spark may be ignited so that the individual becomes one with the Divine, perhaps for a mere split second, perhaps longer. (The word 'Sufi' is traditionally thought to come from the *suf* or woollen robe worn by devotees during their meetings.) This higher state is called *sidq* or pure truth.

There are only four Sufi schools, each taking its origin either from the prophet Mohammad or one of the Twelve Imams. Sufism is taught and practised in Sufi orders or fraternities based around a meeting place called *khanqah*. Presently, the most famous order in the West is the Meylavi, known popularly as the whirling dervishes. Following the ideas of the 13th-century Iranian mystic, Jalal al-Din Rumi, buried in Konya, Turkey, the ritual practised by this Sunni Sufi order is characterised by devotees moving in a large circle around a room while spinning clockwise to music arranged in four musical movements, each representing a season of the year. There is also the Naqshbandi fraternity (which, incidentally, has a keen following in Peckham, south London), again among the Sunni community, which has no esoteric ritual but dedicates all actions and deeds to the Divine. The ritual may be just the rhythmic voicing of the name of Allah, as it is with one order in Deptford, Kent (UK). The aim is the same, the sublimation of the material self and ego, thus freeing the spirit so that the divine spark may ignite.

Historically the government and the established clergy have often expressed hostility towards the Sufi orders because the fraternities were often organised as lodges separate and dissociated from the mosques, and their *sheykh* or *pir* (master) were rarely reticent in pointing out any social injustices, worldliness or sham devotions of the *ulama*. Also, women were often given greater access within these 'unofficial' circles, which could include visiting dervishes who had given up their home and family life to show others the 'way'. One of the greatest mystics was Rabi'a of Basra (d801ce) who caused an outcry among the *ulama* when she announced: 'I have ceased to exist and have passed out of self. I exist in God and am altogether His.'

recommended to refrain from visiting any Sufi sites). The other main reason to come here is to see the **Qasabeh** *qanat* (w qasabehqanat.com), which together with the other ten *qanats* across Iran was in 2016 inscribed on the UNESCO World Heritage List. The significance of the *qanat* system cannot be underestimated and Qasabeh has a number of special and distinctive features. It is the oldest known, the deepest and potentially the most extensive *qanat* in Iran. Only a few sections have been fully studied and just a couple are open to the public.

Around Gonabad, you can overnight in the historic village of **Riab** (ریاب), just 5km away. Here there is the pleasant family-run **Alipour Historic House** (Ghavamiyeh) (6 rooms; ℡57463488; m 0915 7271687, 0935 2201212; $). Opened in 2016 as the first ecolodge in Razavi Khorasan, the original building dates from the Qajar period and has hot and cold baths, fed by underground water channels. These are currently being restored.

Venturing further south, bear in mind that public transport in this part of the country is scarce and buses between Mashhad and Esfahan and Shiraz pass by the town of **Ferdows** only after 19.00 and there is no guarantee there will be free seats available. The road from Gonabad to Ferdows is a scenic mountain route continuing on to the village of **Deyhuk** with its clearly visible remains of an ancient settlement, where it then turns towards Tabas. En route, find time to stop in **Esfahak** (اصفهاک), an oasis with date trees at the foothills of the mountains. Almost entirely destroyed in the earthquake, the village has been carefully and finely restored to its original charm. Here you can overnight in the delightful **Esfahak Ecolodge** (35 rooms; m 0913 2533442; w esfahk.ir; $$), incorporating a number of restored traditional houses.

Esfahak is only 40km away from **Tabas** (طبس), which was alas devastated and mostly destroyed by the 1978 earthquake and uniformly rebuilt in dreary yellow brick; historic it may once have been but all is now obscured. Its **Bagh-e Golshan** public garden is an exception and a pleasant retreat from the summer heat. The water in the garden channels flows all the way from the hot- and cold-water springs in the scenic **Morteza Ali** gorge, famous for its spectacular 60m-high **Abbasi Dam** (طاق شاه عباسی) ✴ built more than 500 years ago. From here you can continue on to Yazd on one of the late evening buses passing through Tabas. This route is essentially used for transporting goods to and from the Pakistani and Afghan border crossings and there is otherwise little non-commercial traffic.

Appendix 1

LANGUAGE

FARSI For background information, see page 31. Pronunciation is fairly straightforward except for the letters 'kh', which have a guttural sound, similar to the 'ch' in the Scottish 'loch'.

Greetings

Hello	*salaam*	سلام
Goodbye	*khodaa-haafez* (pronounced 'ho-da fiz')	خدا حافظ
Good morning	*sobh-bekheyr*	صبح بخیر
Good evening	*shab-bekheyr*	شب بخیر
How are you?	*hal-e shomaa chetoreh* (formal)	حال شما چطوره؟
	khoobeed (informal)	خوبید؟
Fine, thank you	*khoobam, mersee*	خوبم، مرسی
	khoobam, motshakeram	خوبم، متشکرم

Useful words and phrases

It is closed	*bast'ast*	بسته است
It is open	*baazeh*	باز است
Excuse me! Sorry!	*ma'zerat meekhaaham*	معذرت می خواهم
	bebakhsheed (to get attention/apologise)	ببخشید
Help!	*komak*	کمک
A cup of tea, please	*yek chaee, lotfan*	یک چایی لطفا
Thank you	*mersee/motshakeram*	مرسی / متشکرم
You are welcome	*khaahesh meekonam*	خواهش می کنم
yes	*baleh*	بله
no	*nakheyr/na*	نه \ نخیر
I	*man*	من
I am ill	*mareezam*	مریضم
I am English	*man engelisi hastam*	من انگلیسی هستم
(American/Canadian)	*(amrikaa'i/kaanaadaa'i)*	... امریکایی \ کانادایی ...
I don't speak Farsi	*man faarsee nemeedaanam*	من فارسی نمی دانم
I don't understand	*nemeefahmam*	نمی فهمم
you (polite)	*shomaa*	شما
How much is it?	*chand ast*	چند است؟
Please help me	*bema komak koneed*	به من کمک کنید
Where is ... ?	*... kojaast*	کجاست؟
... the toilet	*dastshuee, kojaast*	دستشویی کجاست؟

Appendix 1 LANGUAGE

A1

Please show me the way to the ...	raah raa ta ... beman neshaan bedaheed	راه را تا ... به من نشان بدهید
airport	foroodgaah	فرودگاه
bank	baank	بانک
bus station	eestgaah-e otobus	ایستگاه اتوبوس
church	keleesaa	کلیسا
embassy	sefaarat	سفارت
hospital	beemaarestaan	بیمارستان
hotel/budget hotel	hotel/mehmaankhaaneh	هتل \ مهمانخانه
mosque	masjed	مسجد
museum	moozeh	موزه
police	polees	پلیس
police station	edareh-e polees	اداره پلیس
post office	edareh-e post	اداره پست
railway station	eestgaah-e raah aahan	ایستگاه راه آهن
restaurant	restooraan	رستوران
station	eestgaah	ایستگاه
toilet	dastshuee	دستشویی
I need a ...	man ehtiyaj be ... daaram	من احتیاج به ... دارم
ticket 1st (2nd/3rd) class	beleet-e darajeh yek (dou/se)	بلیط درجه یک \ دو
... for	baraayeh ...	برای ...
doctor	doktor	دکتر
dentist	dandaan pezeshk	داندانپزشک
room for 1/2/3 nights	otaaq baraayeh yek/dou/seh shab	اتاق برای یک \ دو \ سه شب
taxi	taaksee	تاکسی

Numbers

1	yek	۱		8	hasht	۸
2	dou	۲		9	noh	۹
3	se	۳		10	dah	۱۰
4	chahaar	۴		11	yaazdah	۱۱
5	panj	۵		12	davaazdah	۱۲
6	shesh	۶		100	sad	۱۰۰
7	haft	۷		1,000	hezar	۱۰۰۰

Days of the week

Saturday	shanbeh	شنبه
Sunday	yek shanbeh	یکشنبه
Monday	dou shanbeh	دوشنبه
Tuesday	se shanbeh	سه شنبه
Wednesday	chahaar shanbeh	چهارشنبه
Thursday	panj shanbeh	پنجشنبه
Friday	jom'eh	جمعه

Appendix 2

GLOSSARY

ab anbar	'Water storage/reservoir' is a traditional underground drinking water reservoir usually with a cone-shaped dome and *badgir* towers (see below).
'alam	Standard (tool), of the type carried in Moharram ceremonies.
ateshkadeh	Also known as *adrian*, refers to Zoroastrian fire temple.
ayatollah	Literally 'sign of God' (Q41:53); an honorific title for theologians used much more frequently since the 1950s; in the past it was occasionally bestowed by public acclaim on any notable, fully qualified Muslim jurist of superior learning.
badgir	Literally 'windcatcher', meaning tower used for ventilation and air-conditioning purposes in traditional Iranian houses.
baft-e tarilkhi	'historical texture' (literally), refers to historic and old part of town.
bagh	The 'Persian' garden. The original Persian word *pairidaeza* (later *firdaws*) passed into Greek, and later into Middle English as 'paradise'.
barsom	Broom of twigs for tending the sacred fire in the Zoroastrian context.
caravanserai	A pre-car 'inn', often built by rulers and governors to provide accommodation for travellers and their pack animals on the caravan routes, generally sited one day's journey (approximately 35km) apart.
chador	A full-length fabric wrap, roughly semicircular in form and often black in colour, worn by Iranian women. As Ayatollah Khomeini announced that the (black) chador was the 'flag of the Islamic Revolution', it is required dress for women in government service.
chaparkhaneh	From Persian 'house of courier' and refers to Achaemenid-era postal service stations located at various stops along the main road. In modern Persian *edareh-e post* stands for post office.
chehelkhaneh	Room or building where Sufis pass 40 nights in devotions.
dervish	Literally 'door', 'path'. A mendicant Sufi who has removed himself from his family in search of the ultimate truth, largely dependent on the charity of others.
ghelim	Traditional tapestry-woven carpet or rug usually of bright colours and geometric designs. In English often referred to as 'kelim'.
gonbad	Tomb tower constructed to commemorate a deceased individual.
hajj	Annual Muslim pilgrimage to Mecca.
hajji	Title of a person who has at least one in his lifetime undertaken a *hajj*.
hamam	'Turkish bath' developed in the Islamic world from the Roman bathhouse. Consists of three main chambers: the first room, the

	frigidarium, was where you undressed and later relaxed in the company of others; the *tepidarium*; and finally, the hot room, the *caldarium*. Like the 17th-century European coffee house, it was and is a place for gossip, business and meeting friends.
hosseiniyeh	A congregation hall for Shi'a mourning ceremonies during the month of Moharram.
imamzadeh	A tomb or shrine honouring an immediate relative of the Twelve Imams of Ithna 'Ashari Shi'ism in Iran; over time, local shrines without such a proven family association have also been given this title.
ivan	A tall, vaulted portal or doorway, fully developed in Seljuk architecture from the 11th century.
kashkul	A ceremonial metal or wooden bowl, often finely engraved, and used by wandering dervishes or Sufis as a sign of their renouncement of worldly possessions.
khan	The historic equivalent of a bonded warehouse for the storage and transit of a specific kind of goods from wholesalers to retailers.
khanqah	A place for meetings and gatherings of Sufis orders, as well as for teachings and prayer.
Kufic	An Islamic calligraphic script, characterised by a definite horizontal base line and vertical letter strokes, often with angular letter forms.
lahaf toshak	Iranian roll-up mattress used in for sleeping on in traditional houses.
masjed-e jame	Pronounced 'jameh'. Literally 'congregational mosque', often called a Friday mosque. In past centuries only one mosque in any given town or city was licensed to have the imam give a homily at the main prayer time on Fridays.
maydan	An open square in a city or town.
mihrab	A niche or panel, often very decorative, showing the correct direction to align yourself for prayer prostrations (see *qibla* below).
minbar	A stepped construction, often made of wood or stone, situated near the main *mihrab* within a mosque, from which the Friday homily was given.
mohr	Clay tablet used by the devout Shi'a Muslim between his forehead and the prayer mat or other surface during prayer. Also known as *turbah*.
muezzin	The mosque official who calls the faithful to prayer three times a day in some Shi'a communities (five times in the Sunni world and some Shi'a groups).
muqarnas	Architectural detail usually found decorating vaults, domes and door lintels, formed of separate 3D units composed into a 'honeycomb' layout.
nakhl	Literally date palm; palm-shaped wooden structure representing the bier of Hossein which, draped in black cloth, is carried in Moharram processions.
namazkhaneh	Prayer room; from Persian *namaz* meaning 'prayer' and *khaneh* for 'house'. Stranded and tired travellers are always welcome to relax and have a nap in *namazkhaneh*.
Nastaliq	First calligraphic script used exclusively for writing in Persian; appeared in the first half of the 15th century.
padam	A white mask used by Zoroastrians to avoid polluting the sacred fire.
pahlavan	A champion athlete, especially a wrestler.
Pahlavi	The Persian script largely abandoned after the 7th-century Arab conquests; also the dynastic name adopted by Reza Khan (d1941).

qaleh	Persian/Arabic word for fort, fortress or fortification, often translated into English as 'castle'.
qibla	The direction for prayer, eg: towards Mecca, usually marked in a Muslim religious building by a *mihrab* niche.
satrap	Governor of a province (*satrapy*) in ancient Persia.
SAVAK	Acronym for the Organisation of Intelligence and National Security; also known as the shah's secret police, established in 1957.
Shi'a	From Arabic 'followers of Ali', refers to those who favoured the rule of Ali, the Prophet Mohammad's cousin, after the Prophet's death in 632CE. Shi'a Muslims constitute the largest Muslim group after the Sunni.
Sufi	A Muslim, Shi'a or Sunni, seeking an individual spiritual path to achieve mystic union with the Divine, often through initiation and ritual practices. Traditionally associated with wearing a woollen garment (*suf*: wool).
Sunni	From Arabic 'tradition'/'practice' of the Prophet Mohammad and refers to the largest branch in Islam, whose followers believed that Mohammad's companions were to succeed the Prophet after his death in 632CE. This contradicts the bloodline approach adopted by the Shi'a branch (see above).
tabarzin	Dervish or Sufi axe.
talar	Veranda or terrace; in royal pavilions, often used for public audiences.
tappeh	Archaeological mound, alternatively known as *tel*.
taziyeh	Passion play retelling the Karbala story, performed as part of Moharram religious commemorations.
tekiyeh	Historically a place for holding *taziyeh* performances.
timcheh	A small caravanserai or inn within a bazaar, but essentially a space for storing goods of high quality, eg: carpets.
yakhchal	Literally 'ice pit'. A cone-shaped ice cooler used to store ice, water and even food during hot summer months.
ziggurat	Terraced-pyramid-shaped structure originating in Mesopotamia; part of a larger temple complex.
zurkhaneh	Gymnasium where wrestlers practise.

ARCHITECTURAL TERMS

arch-soffit	The underside of an arch, often decorated.
cartouche	Oval-shaped frame taken from the French word for 'cartridge'.
chahar bagh	Traditional Persian garden arrangement, meaning 'fourfold garden'.
chahartaq	Meaning a 'four-way arch' in Persian (*tetrapylon* in Greek), it refers to a fundamental Persian architectural style used in religious and secular buildings, particularly during the Sasanid period.
cuerda seca	A ceramic glaze technique whereby different coloured opaque glazes (eg: on a tile) are kept separate from each other by manganese oxide. (Confusingly, several art historians use this specific technical term when referring to both under- and over-glaze painted decoration on clay.)
gowdal	Also known as *gowdal-e bagcheh*. Sunken inner courtyard in traditional Iranian merchant houses.
groundplan	The disposition of the parts of a building at ground level in diagrammatic form.
howz	A small symmetrical axis pool in the centre of an inner courtyard of a traditional dwelling in Iran.

kashi	Persian word for 'tile', often used as *karikashi* to describe traditional Iranian tile decoration technique.
khesht	Sun-dried bricks historically used for construction of houses in Iran. In combination with mud, the architectural style is known as *kheskt-o-ghel*.
Level I, II, etc	Refers to the strata seen in archaeological excavations and dated usually by means of finds within them.
'mosaic' tilework	Predetermined shapes cut from monochrome glazed tiles, and reassembled as a jigsaw, held in place on a plaster bed.
shahneshin	Central room in traditional houses, reserved for royalty (literally means 'shah sitting down'), usually slightly raised vis-à-vis the other rooms in the house.
sharom	Narrow passageway around the sunken yard (*gowdal-e bagcheh*) in traditional Iranian merchant houses.
shobbaq	Glazed tile windows in traditional houses for looking through from the inside without revealing your identity.
squinch	An architectural load-bearing structure essentially in the form of a hollow half of a hemisphere placed over a corner to support the weight of the dome.
strapwork	Ornament consisting of interlaced bands.
tabestanneshin	(literally sitting down in the summer) Section of the traditional house for spending hot summer days, as it is always cooler than the other rooms in the house.
trilobed	Three lobes or compartments (within a squinch).
zamestanneshin	(literally sitting down in the winter) Section of the traditional house for spending cold winter days, as it is always warmer than the other rooms in the house.

MOST FREQUENTLY USED STREET NAMES

17 Shahrivar (1357)	(corresponding to 08 September 1978) and known as Black Friday, when thousands of people were killed during the anti-Shah demonstration at Jaleh Square in Tehran. Often described as a key moment in the revolutionary movement.
Beheshti	Mohammad Hossein Beheshti (d1981) was a prominent cleric who played a major role in the establishment of the Islamic Republic.
Enghelab	Meaning 'revolution' in Persian, this street/square name commemorates the 1979 Islamic Revolution.
Imam	(also Imam Khomeini) Refers to either the 12th Imam in Shi'a Islam or Imam Khomeini himself, believed by some to have been the actual Imam.
Jomhuri	(also Jomhuri Islami) Persian word for 'republic', given to place names in honour of the Islamic Republic.
Motahhari	Morteza Motahhari (d1979) was a cleric and Islamic theoretician as well as a pupil of Imam Khomeini.
Shariati	Ali Shariati (d1977) was one of the most outspoken critics of the last shah and a brilliant thinker and proponent of Shi'a Islam as a form of social justice.
Shohada	Persian word for 'martyrs', referring to the martyrs of the Iran–Iraq War (1980–88).
Taleqani	(also spelt as Talegnani) Mahmoud Taleqani (d1979) was an important ideologue of the Islamic Revolution.
Valiasr	Reference to the 12th Imam, meaning the 'master of time'.

readable account. The literature in English about **Jews** in Iran is scarce, but in a newly published *Between Iran and Zion* (Stanford University Press, 2019), Lior B Sternfeld looks at various, at times conflicting, narratives of Jewish history in Iran. In *the Lion's Shadow: The Iranian Schindler and His Homeland in the Second World War* (The History Press, 2012) by Fariborz Mokhtari is a gripping biography of Abdol Hossein Sardari and his service in the Iranian embassy in Paris during World War II, when he helped many Jews escape deportation by issuing them with Iranian passports. There is a wealth of sources and books about **Islam** and **Shi'a Islam**. Etan Kohlberg's *Belief and Law in Imami Shi'ism* (Variorum, 1991) is an excellent place to start. This collection of articles by one of the world's leading experts on Shi'a Islam, is informative and wonderfully written. Those interested in Ismaili Islam will certainly enjoy reading Farhad Daftary's *Ismaili History and Intellectual Traditions* (Routledge, 2017). To find out more about the role of the Ismailis and the Assassins during the Crusades, Bernard Lewis's small book *The Assassins: A Radical Sect of Islam* (Phoenix, reprinted 2004) has not yet been bettered. The well-acclaimed novel *Alamut* (North Atlantic Books, 2012) by Slovenian writer Vladimir Bartol, translated into English in 2004, will also be of interest. To learn about **Sufism**, Annemarie Schimmel's *Mystical Dimensions of Islam* (The University of North Carolina Press, 2011) is a good place to start.

Travellers' accounts No-one can argue that most contemporary travel accounts pale in comparison with those of 19th-century Western writers, who indefatigably asked all the right questions, checked the responses and recorded everything in detail. A particular favourite is Isabella L Bird, author of *Journeys in Persia and Kurdistan*, vols I & II (originally printed 1891; reprinted Virago Press, London 1989), and the abridged account of an earlier traveller, Sir John (Jean) Chardin, *Travels in Persia, 1673–77* (Dover, New York 1988) is still available and very, very entertaining. If you can't get hold of it, R W Ferrier produced a commentary of those travels: *A Journey to Persia … Jean Chardin* (I B Tauris, 1996). Robert Byron's waspish wit comes through in his *The Road to Oxiana* (Picador, London, reprinted 2000); his comments on architecture force you to look again. For climbers and anyone with a soft spot for mountains, *The Face of Iran. Selected Climbs* by Christiane Hupe, Gerald Krug, Kristina Friedrichs and Nasrin Nikbaksh (Halle, 2017) is highly recommended.

Archaeology Anything by Alireza Shapour Shahbazi, one of the world's most outstanding Persian archaeologists, is highly recommended. John Curtis of the British Museum has written an informative introduction to pre-Islamic archaeology in Iran, *Ancient Persia* (British Museum Press, London, reprinted 2000), while D T Potts examines in detail the Elamite region and civilisation up to the 4th century CE in *The Archaeology of Elam* (Cambridge University Press, 1999). Time-Life's publication *The Persians: Masters of Empire* (Lost Civilizations series, 1995) is a clear, readable account aimed at the general reader with good maps and an interesting selection of images. It is both entertaining and intriguing to read Herodotus (490–480BCE) for his views on Achaemenid history, the court intrigues and the military campaigns (*The Histories*, Penguin Classics). Josef Wiesehöfer's book *Ancient Persia from 550BCE to AD650* (I B Tauris, London reprinted 2004) has a strong academic flavour but does provide interesting information. For Dutch readers, the 1993 Brussels exhibition catalogue *Hofkunst van de Sassanieden* (KMvKG) has both an informative text and superb photographs of Sasanid pieces; available in the UK on inter-library loan. *Forgotten Empire: The World of Ancient Persia*, edited by John Curtis and Nigel Tallis (British Museum Press, 2005), is a catalogue to accompany a major exhibition of the same name at the British Museum. A recently published Italian title *Iran: Cities, Routes, Caravanserais* by Alessandra De Cesaris, Laura Valeria Ferretti and Hassan Osanloo (EDILSTAMPA, 2014) offers a detailed glimpse into Silk Road inns. *On the High Road. The*

History of Godin Tepe, Iran by Hilary Gopnik and Mitchell S Rothman (Mazda Publishers, Inc, 2011) is a hefty and technical, but very informative account for those with interest in ancient *tappehs* of Iranian Azerbaijan. *The Royal City of Susa. Ancient Near Eastern Treasures in the Louvre*, eds Prudence O Harper, J Aruz and F Tallon (The Metropolitan Museum of Art, New York, 1992) is an exceptionally interesting and well-structured book about archaeological findings at Susa.

Islamic art and architecture One of the best introductions to Islamic art and architecture is Barbara Brend's *Islamic Art* (British Museum Press, London 1991), while Patricia L Baker's book *Islam and the Religious Arts* (Continuum, 2004) approaches the subject from a different angle. The *Arts of Persia* (Yale University Press, 1989) under the editorship of R W Ferrier examines certain art forms in more detail. Lisa Golombek and Donald Wilber's *Timurid Architecture in Iran and Turan* (1988) has already been mentioned in the introduction to this guide, along with the work of Bernard O'Kane on 14th–15th-century Timurid architecture, essential for any serious in-depth research: *Timurid Architecture in Khurasan* (1987). Similarly, the studies of Sheila Blair on historic inscriptions are seminal: see, for example, *Islamic Inscriptions* (Edinburgh University Press, 1998). Any keen student of Islamic architecture should aim to acquire Robert Hillenbrand's *Islamic Architecture: Form and Function* (Edinburgh University Press, 1994), which contains a wealth of material.

Sheila Canby's book *The Golden Age of Persian Art, 1501–1722* (British Museum Press, 1999), which gives a good overview of the arts in the Safavid period, is still available. On contemporary Iranian art with a strong political content, the paperback *Picturing Iran: Art, Society and Revolution,* edited by Shiya Balaghi and Lynn Gumpert (I B Tauris, 2002), is highly recommended. To these may be added *Peerless Images: Persian Painting and its Sources*, Eleanor Sims (Yale University Press, 2002) and Sheila Canby, *Shah 'Abbas: The Remaking of Iran* (British Museum Press, 2009) to accompany the first major exhibition dedicated to Shah Abbas I.

Crafts Hans E Wulff's *Traditional Crafts of Persia* (MIT), published in the 1960s has not been matched since. He traces the history and technology of the major crafts including agricultural implements and building skills, as well as ceramics and breadmaking. There are numerous publications about carpets, often not worth the paper they are printed on, but if you can find a copy of A C Edwards's *The Persian Carpet* (Duckworth, 1953, reprinted 1983), it records the state of carpet weaving in Iran in the 1950s; his concept of a 'carpet aesthetic' and regional identification has, rightly or wrongly, proved to be very influential. See also Patricia L Baker's *Islamic Textiles* (British Museum Press, London 1995).

Literature, biography and fiction *Shahnameh: The Persion Book of Kings* by Abolqasem Ferdowsi, translated by Dick Davis (2006) and *Persian Love Poetry*, edited by Vesta Curtis and Sheila Canby (2005). We simply could not put down Sattareh Farman Farmaian's *Daughter of Persia* (Bantam, London/New York reprinted 2000), a critical but affectionate account of her family and Iranian society from the 1920s until the first years of the revolution. A tender and often humorous book in strip-cartoon format is Marjane Satrapi's *Persepolis: A Story of a Childhood* (Jonathan Cape, London 2003), first published in France; the title and format do not prepare the reader for its political content. This has since been made into an animated film, *Persepolis* (2007). *In the Rose Garden of the Martyrs* by Christopher de Bellaigue (HarperCollins, 2004) compares and contrasts his memories of Iran in the late 1970s with today's actualities, and has been critically acclaimed. *The Saffron Kitchen* by Yasmin Crowther (Little, Brown, 2006) is a haunting story taking place both in the UK and in eastern Iran.

The satirical and political novel *My Uncle Napoleon*, by Iraj Pezeshkzad, translated by Dick Davis, offers insight into Iranian perceptions of the West. It is also highly recommended to read classic pre-revolutionary writers, such as Sadeq Hedayat (author of *The Blind Owl*), Simin Daneshvar and Dowlat Abadi, and these are relatively easy to find in English. Modern Iranian literature is rich and flourishing, although translations are not always readily available and the quality of the translated text does not always reflect the original. Zoya Pirzad, in particular in her *Things We Left Unsaid,* wonderfully describes the life and habits of the Armenian community in Iran before and after the revolution. *Symphony of the Dead* (1989) by Abbas Maroufi is a beautifully written drama about a family from Ardabil, which some argue is the best Persian-language book of the past few decades. A few novels by Fariba Vafi, writing about female identity and the role of women in Iran, have been translated into English and German. *Persian Literature*, edited by Ehsan Yarshater (Columbia University Press, 1988), is a useful academic survey of classical and contemporary literature.

Other relevant guides For a full list of Bradt's Middle Eastern destination guides, see w bradtguides.com/shop.

Doyle, Paul *Lebanon*, 2nd edn, Bradt, 2016
Hann, Geoff and Dabrowska, Karen *Iraq*, 2nd edn, Bradt, 2015
Walsh, Tony and Darke, Diana *Oman*, 4th edn, Bradt, 2016
Wilson, Samantha and Oleynik, Maria *Israel*, 3rd edn, Bradt, 2018

ASSOCIATIONS AND INSTITUTES

The British Institute of Persian Studies (c/o British Academy, 10 Carlton Hse Terrace, London SW1Y 5AH; ✆ 020 7969 5203; w bips.ac.uk) Publishes an annual academic journal, *Iran*, which contains recent research on the art, archaeology and history of pre-Islamic and Islamic Iran, and organises a number of public lectures. The Tehran office is again open after 30 years of closure and there is a hostel in Iran for members undertaking research. For details contact the secretary.

The Institute of Ismaili Studies (210 Euston Rd, London NW1 2DA; ✆ 020 7756 2700; w iis.ac.uk) Publishes teaching materials and organises a graduate teaching programme.

The Iran Society (25 Eccleston Pl, London SW1W 9NF; ✆ 020 7235 5122; w iransociety. org) Has a programme of lectures and meetings; membership subscription. For details contact the secretary.

The Iran Heritage Foundation (63 New Cavendish St, London W1G 7LP; ✆ 020 7493 4766; w iranheritage.org) A non-governmental organisation, sponsors various activities in the UK, including exhibitions, occasional lectures, conferences, concerts, poetry readings, and film showings concerning the cultural heritage of Iran, past and present. For details contact the secretary.

Zoroastrian Centre (440 Alexandra Av, Harrow, Middx HA2 9TL; ✆ 020 8866 0765; w ztfe.com) A friendly organisation running a series of classes and lectures examining the beliefs, civilisation and history of Iranian Zoroastrians and the Parsi communities. Part of the world Zoroastrian organisation.

Bahai Faith National Centre (27 Rutland Gate, London SW7 1PD; ✆ 020 7584 2566; w bahai.org.uk) For information about the Bahai community.

Bahai Institute for Higher Education (BIHE; w bihe.org) Also known as the Bahai Open University, founded in 1987, BIHE offers university education and training courses to members of the Bahai community in Iran.

FILM Over the last few decades Iranian film directors have produced some of the world's finest cinema, acknowledged at film festivals abroad as well as in Iran itself. Modern Iranian cinema addresses some of the most poignant issues in Iranian society, namely traditions, family and the role of women in society and numerous films can be interpreted as having strong feminist undertones. Niki Karimi is both an outstanding actress and a prominent film director. Asghar Farhadi is well known in the West for his numerous prize-winning films while Jafar Panahi is that little bit more political, which has earned him house arrest. Here are some of the recommended titles: *The White Balloon* by Abbas Kiarostami, 1995; *Taste of Cherry* by Abbas Kiarostami, 1997; *The Willow Tree* by Majid Majidi, 2005; *About Elly* by Asghar Farhadi, 2009; *A Separation* by Asghar Farhadi, 2011; *Here without Me* by Bahram Tavakoli, 2011; *What is the time in your world?* by Safi Yazdanian, 2014; *Taxi Tehran* by Jafar Panahi, 2014; *Inversion* by Behnam Behzadi, 2016; *Orange Days* by Arash Lahooti, 2018.

WEBSITES There are thousands of websites on Iran: some are markedly partisan, others less so; some informative but most with outdated telephone regional codes and numbers for hotels, etc. More and more Iranian companies involved in tourism operate websites but these can vary greatly in quality, from the informative to the 'useless'.

w **bbc.co.uk/news/world-middle-east-14541327** The BBC has a reliable country profile and timeline.

w **cais-soas.com** The Circle of Ancient Iranian Studies at SOAS, the School of Oriental and African Studies, University of London, is excellent for information on ancient Iranian sites.

w **cultureofiran.com** Collection of articles and information about Iran, compiled by social anthropologist Massoumeh Price.

w **en.mehrnews.com** Iran's Mehr News Agency's informative English-language website offering an Iranian point of view on national and international events.

w **gov.uk/foreign-travel-advice/iran** To check the latest advice on visiting conditions and requirements.

w **iran-daily.com** and w **tehrantimes.com** If you wish to keep up with the news as published in Iran, two of the Tehran English-language papers are available on the internet: *Iran Daily* and *Tehran Times*.

IRAN ONLINE

For additional online content, articles, photos and more on Iran, why not visit w bradtguides.com/iran?

Index

Page numbers in **bold** indicate major entries; those in *italics* indicate maps

377

INDEX OF ADVERTISERS